MCSE Study Guide

Windows 95 and Networking Essentials

Joe Casad
Leigh Anne Chisholm
Drew Heywood
Tim McLaren
Mike Wolfe

New Riders

MCSE Study Guide: Windows 95 and Networking Essentials

By Joe Casad, Leigh Anne Chisholm, Drew Heywood, Tim McLaren, and Mike Wolfe

Published by:
New Riders Publishing
201 West 103rd Street
Indianapolis, IN 46290 USA

Printed in the United States of America 5 6 7 8 9 0

Library of Congress Cataloging-in-Publication Data

MCSE study guide : Windows 95 and networking essentials / Joe Casad ... [et al.].
p. cm.
Includes index.
ISBN 1-56205-568-2
1. Microsoft Windows (Computer file)--Examinations--Study guides. 2. Operating Systems (Computers)--Examinations--Study guides. 3. Computer networks--Examinations--Study guides. 4. Electronic data processing personnel--Certification. I. Casad, Joe, 1958- .
QA76.76.063M42 1996
005.4'469--dc20 96-244896
CIP

Warning and Disclaimer

This book is designed to provide information about the Microsoft MCSE certification requirements. Every effort has been made to make this book as complete and as accurate as possible, but no warranty or fitness is implied.

The information is provided on an "as is" basis. The author(s) and New Riders Publishing shall have neither liability nor responsibility to any person or entity with respect to any loss or damages arising from the information contained in this book or from the use of the disks or programs that may accompany it.

Publisher *Don Fowley*
Publishing Manager *Emmett Dulaney*
Marketing Manager *Mary Foote*
Managing Editor *Carla Hall*

Acquisitions Editor
Stacia Mellinger

Development Editor
Joe Casad

Project Editor
Lillian Duggan

Copy Editors
Amy Bezek
Susan Christopherson
Christopher Cleveland
Jeff Durham
Laura Frey
Chuck Gose
Dayna Isley
Sarah Kearns
Nanci Sears Perry

Technical Editor
Jeff Bumgardner

Associate Marketing Manager
Tamara Apple

Administrative Coordinator
Karen Opal

Cover Designer
Karen Ruggles

Cover Production
Aren Howell

Book Designer
Sandra Schroeder

Production Manager
Kelly Dobbs

Production Team Supervisor
Laurie Casey

Graphics Image Specialists
Stephen Adams, Debra Bolhuis
Daniel Harris, Clint Lahnen
Ryan Oldfather, Casey Price
Laura Robbins, Jeff Yesh

Production Analysts
Jason Hand
Bobbi Satterfield

Production Team
Daniel Caparo, Krena Lanham,
Erich J. Richter, Scott Tullis,
Christine Tyner, Karen Walsh

Indexer
Brad Herriman

About the Authors

Joe Casad is a freelance writer and editor who specializes in programming and networking topics. He was the managing editor of the short-lived but well-received *Network Administrator Magazine,* a journal of practical solutions for network professionals. Mr. Casad received a B.S. in engineering from the University of Kansas in 1980 and, before becoming a full-time writer and editor, spent ten years in the computer-intensive areas of the structural engineering profession. He now lives in Lawrence, Kansas with wife Barb Dinneen and a pair of pint-sized hackers named Xander and Mattie.

Leigh Anne Chisholm is a network consultant and trainer in Edmonton, Alberta, Canada. She is a Microsoft Certified System Engineer specializing in Windows NT 3.51, TCP/IP, System Management Server 1.1, and Microsoft Exchange. She also is a Certified NetWare Engineer.

Drew Heywood has been involved in the microcomputer industry since he purchased an Apple IIe in 1979. For the past nine years, he has focused on networking. From 1991 through February 1995, Drew was a product line manager at New Riders, where he launched New Riders' networking book line and expanded the line to include some of the most successful book titles in the industry. For over fifteen years, Mr. Heywood has been involved with personal computers as an educator, an application programmer, and a system manager of local area networks and minicomputers. Drew Heywood is currently vice president of InfoWorks, Inc., a company that specializes in technical communication and computer consulting. Drew is a busy author who has authored or coauthored eight books in the last three years. His most recent book is *Networking with Microsoft TCP/IP* from New Riders. Drew also is the author of the popular *Inside Windows NT Server* and *Inside NetWare 3.12,* both from New Riders, and has contributed to several volumes in New Riders' NetWare Training Guide series of CNE certification books.

Tim McLaren is a Microsoft Certified Systems Engineer who provides technical support on a variety of Microsoft products to networking professionals across Canada.

Mike Wolfe currently works for Chevron Information Technology Company as a member of the Common Operating Environment (COE) Team at the company campus in San Ramon, California. He provides top-level network software support, project management, and internal company consulting in an interesting and challenging workplace. Mike holds certifications as both a Novell Master CNE and a Microsoft MCSE. He is heavily involved in the corporate-wide deployment of Windows 95 and the eventual migration of network operating systems at Chevron from Novell NetWare to Windows NT Server. He was a mainframe applications developer for many years before switching to PCs and network computing. Mike lives in San Ramon, California, with his wife, Maggie. You can contact Mike at the address 73464,22@compuserve.com.

Trademark Acknowledgments

Acknowledgments

All thanks begin with Barbie. I would also like to thank Mr. Emmett Dulaney for his trust and support, and I would like to thank Amy Bezek, Stacia Mellinger, Tad Ringo, and all the other experts at New Riders who helped make this book happen. Thanks also to ace freelancer Lillian Duggan, an inspiring lead editor who sees deeper than words.

—Joe Casad

I would like to thank Dean Iacovelli for his significant contributions to the Windows 95 material. Dean has generously shared his Windows 95 expertise with many people, and a significant portion of this study guide is the direct result of his expertise and input.

In addition, kudos go to the team at New Riders for crafting the work (of art?) you are holding. In particular, Joe Casad, Lillian Duggan, and Stacia Mellinger have provided many thoughtful insights.

Finally, I wish to thank Sarah Gibson for all the support and encouragement she provided throughout the project.

—Tim McLaren

Many fine books have already been published about Windows 95. However, it is my sincere hope that this book will help you become certified. It is also my firm belief that we all need goals that measure how well we have done and that keep us constantly challenged. Certification on any of the Microsoft software products, such as Windows 95, helps to provide that measurement. For myself, I wish to acknowledge the encouragement and support of several key people in this fine effort.

First, to my wife, who put up with all the study time after work and on the weekends so that I could become certified. When at long last she thought that all that effort was finished, she helped me find the extra time to write for this book. Second, to several of my coworkers, who helped make my job easier: Mike DeVito, Jim Lisiak, Kiran Movva, Mike Becher, and Mark Butler. Third, to two of my managers, Dick Schmitt at Exxon and Joe Fielding at Chevron, for the wonderful leadership and direction they both have provided. Finally, to my grandfather, Melvin Wolfe, for teaching me how to work hard, not to take life too seriously, and to have fun. He always found time to stop and smell the roses.

—Mike Wolfe

Contents at a Glance

Table of Contents

Part II: Networking Essentials

14 The OSI Model 553

15 Transmission Media 613

Introduction

The *MCSE Study Guide: Windows 95 and Networking Essentials* is designed for advanced end-users, service technicians, and network administrators who are considering certification as a Microsoft Certified Systems Engineer (MCSE) or as a Microsoft Certified Product (MCP) Specialist. The Windows 95 exam tests your ability to implement, administer, and troubleshoot systems as well as your ability to provide technical support to users of the Microsoft Windows 95 operating system. The Networking Essentials exam tests your ability to implement, administer, and troubleshoot the basic networking components of both Windows 95 and Windows NT.

Although this book is designed to prepare you to take and pass these Microsoft certifications exams, there are no guarantees. Read this book, work through the exercises, and take the practice assessment exams.

When taking the real certification exams, make sure you answer all the questions before your time limit expires. Do not spend too much time on any one question. If you are unsure about an answer, answer the question as best you can, and mark it for later review when you have finished with all the questions. It has been said, whether correctly or not, that any questions left unanswered will automatically cause you to fail. Good luck.

Who Should Read This Book

This book is designed to help advanced users, service technicians, and network administrators who are working for MCSE certification prepare for the MCSE Windows 95 exam (#70-63) and the MCSE Networking Essentials exam (#71-58).

This book also can help advanced users and administrators who are not studying for the MCSE exam but are looking for a single-volume reference on Windows 95 and general networking technology.

How This Book Helps You

This book takes you on a self-guided tour of all the areas covered by the MCSE Windows 95 and Networking Essentials exams and teaches you the specific skills you need to achieve your MCSE certification. You'll also find helpful hints, tips, real-world examples, exercises, and references to additional study materials.

You'll get a chance to practice for the certification exams using sample questions in the "Review Questions" section at the end of each chapter and additional questions on the accompanying CD-ROM. The review questions test your knowledge of the subjects covered in the chapter. The questions on the CD-ROM provide a more thorough and comprehensive look at what your certification exams really are like. The CD-ROM includes the Microsoft Education and Certification Roadmap—a publication from Microsoft that provides a thorough outline of the certification process. The Roadmap Assessment Exam includes the best available examples of the kinds of questions you'll find on the certification exam. The Roadmap also includes the Planning Wizard, an online tool that helps you quickly map out a plan for achieving your certification goals.

Most Roadmap Assessment Exams are based on specific product versions, and new elective exams are available on an ongoing basis. The Microsoft Education and Certification Roadmap is a quarterly publication. You can obtain updates of the Roadmap at any of the following locations:

Microsoft Education: Call (800) 636-7544

Internet: ftp://ftp.microsoft.com/Services/MSEdCert

CompuServe Forum: GO MSEDCERT

The enclosed CD-ROM also includes MCP Endeavor, an interactive practice test application designed exclusively for Macmillan Publishing that will help you prepare for the MCSE exams.

In addition to MCP Endeavor and The Microsoft Education and Certification Roadmap, the CD-ROM includes demos for the following CD-ROM technical references:

- Microsoft TechNet
- Micro House Technical Library

You learn more about Microsoft TechNet and the Micro House Technical Library in Chapter 23, "Network Troubleshooting Techniques."

The CD-ROM also includes a white paper from Microsoft entitled "Comparing Windows 95 and Windows NT Workstation."

This book also can help you by serving as a desktop reference for information on Windows 95 and other PC networking topics, such as cabling, data transmission, protocols, and network technologies.

Microsoft Certification Process

To become a Microsoft Certified Professional, candidates must pass rigorous certification exams that provide a valid and reliable measure of their technical proficiency and expertise. These closed-book exams have on-the-job relevance because they are developed with the input of professionals in the computer industry and reflect how Microsoft products are actually used in the workplace. The exams are conducted by an independent organization—Drake Prometric—at more than 700 Drake Authorized Testing Centers around the world.

Currently Microsoft offers four types of certification, based on specific areas of expertise:

- **Microsoft Certified Product (MCP) Specialists.** Qualified to provide installation, configuration, and support for users of at least one Microsoft desktop operating system, such as Windows 95. In addition, candidates may also take additional elective exams to add areas of specialization. MCP Specialist is the first level of expertise.
- **Microsoft Certified Systems Engineers (MCSE).** Qualified to effectively plan, implement, maintain, and support information systems with Microsoft Windows NT and other Microsoft advanced systems and workgroup products, such as Microsoft Office and BackOffice. The Windows 95 exam can be used as one of the four core operating systems exams. MCSE is the second level of expertise.
- **Microsoft Certified Solution Developers (MCSD).** Qualified to design and develop custom business solutions using Microsoft development tools, technologies, and platforms, including Microsoft Office and Microsoft BackOffice. MCSD also is a second level of expertise, but in the area of software development.

- **Microsoft Certified Trainers.** Instructionally and technically qualified by Microsoft to deliver Microsoft Education Courses at Microsoft authorized sites. Microsoft Certified Trainers must be employed by a Microsoft Solution Provider Authorized Technical Education Center or a Microsoft Authorized Academic Training site.

You can find complete descriptions of all Microsoft Certifications in the Microsoft Education and Certification Roadmap on the CD-ROM that comes with this book.

Microsoft Implementing and Supporting Windows 95 Exam

The Windows 95 exam (#70-63) covers 12 main topic areas. On the CD-ROM that comes with this book, you'll find document lpr70-63.doc, which is the exam preparation guide prepared by Microsoft. lpr70-63.doc describes what you will be tested on and suggests ways to prepare for the exam. The exam objectives, listed by topic area, are as follows:

Planning and Installation

- Identify appropriate hardware requirements for Microsoft Windows 95 installation
- Maintain program groups and user preferences when upgrading from Windows 3.1
- Determine when to use Windows 95 and when to use Microsoft Windows NT Workstation
- Configure a Windows 95 computer on a network using the appropriate protocol
- Select the appropriate security to meet various needs
- Determine the appropriate installation method for various situations
- Install the Windows 95 operating system

- Troubleshoot setup and system startup
- Set up files for network installation and for shared use
- Recognize files used in troubleshooting the installation process

Architecture and Memory

- Compare and contrast the memory usage of a Microsoft MS-DOS–based application, a 16-bit Windows-based application, and a 32-bit Windows-based application operating in Windows 95

Customizing and Configuring Windows 95

- Identify and explain the differences between the Windows 3.1 interface and the Windows 95 interface
- Set up a dual-boot system for Windows 95
- Install new hardware devices on various systems that support Plug and Play
- Given a specific bus configuration, identify areas of limitation for full Plug and Play
- Configure the Taskbar
- Configure shortcuts
- Add items to the Start menu
- Choose an appropriate method to accomplish a specified task using the user interface
- Customize the desktop for a specified set of criteria
- Use the Windows 95 interface to create, print, and store a file
- Configure and use Windows Explorer
- Access the network through Network Neighborhood

- Configure the property sheet for an object
- Define the purpose of the Windows 95 Registry
- Classify types of information in the Registry
- Determine where the Registry is stored
- Identify situations in which it is appropriate to modify the Registry
- Modify the contents of the Registry
- Choose the appropriate course of action when OLE information in the Registry becomes corrupted

Editing User and System Profiles

- Modify a user workstation to meet specified criteria
- Grant remote administration privileges on your computer
- Modify user profiles
- Set up user profiles
- Set up computer policies
- Define the System Policy Editor, and describe how it is used
- Create, share, and monitor a remote resource
- Administer a remote computer

Networking and Interoperability

- Configure a Windows 95 computer to access the Internet
- Configure a Windows 95 computer to use NetWare user-level security
- Configure a Windows 95 computer as a client or server in a NetWare network

- Identify the limitations of a Windows 95 NetWare server
- Configure a Windows 95 computer to use Windows NT Server user-level security
- Configure a Windows 95 computer as a client in a Windows NT Server domain
- Configure a Windows 95 computer as a client in a NetWare network
- Recognize how the UNC is used
- Configure Browse Master for Microsoft networks
- Configure Browse Master for NetWare
- Identify advantages and disadvantages of user-level and share-level security
- Identify elements of the Windows 95 operating system network architecture
- Install and configure TCP/IP for use with Windows 95

Managing Disk Resources and Utilities

- Manage long and short filenames in a mixed environment
- Troubleshoot problems and perform disk compression
- Select the appropriate disk-management tool for a given situation
- Use Disk Defragmenter to optimize for speed
- Use ScanDisk in appropriate situations
- Use Backup in appropriate situations

Managing Printers

- Implement printers for Windows 95
- Identify situations in which metafile spooling is appropriate

- Set up Point and Print printing
- Access a printer through a NetWare network
- Create, reorder, and delete a Windows 95 print queue
- Set up and remove printer drivers in Windows 95
- Use Windows 95 to share a printer on the network

Running Applications

- Configure Windows 95 to run MS-DOS–based applications
- Predict potential problems when configuring 16-bit Windows-based applications
- Distinguish between MS-DOS Mode and the standard method for running MS-DOS–based applications
- Determine when an application should be run in MS-DOS Mode
- Resolve general protection faults
- Determine the appropriate course of action when the application stops responding to the system

Mobile Services

- Implement the appropriate level of security for use with Dial-Up Networking
- Choose applications that would be appropriate to run over Dial-Up Networking
- Configure Dial-Up Networking to be a client
- Configure Dial-Up Networking on a server
- Configure a modem to meet a specific set of user requirements

- Implement the various telephony options to meet a specific set of user requirements
- Use a Briefcase to transfer and synchronize data between two computers

Microsoft Exchange

- Share a fax
- Configure a fax for both stand-alone and shared situations
- Configure Microsoft Exchange to access the Internet
- Configure a Windows 95 computer to send and receive mail
- Configure a Windows 95 computer to access CompuServe mail

Plug and Play

- Explain how Windows 95 handles components that are not compatible with Plug and Play
- Explain hot docking and the potential consequences of the dynamic device changes
- Given a specific configuration, use Device Manager to manually reconfigure a Plug and Play device

Troubleshooting

- Resolve problems using appropriate resources
- Select appropriate tools for troubleshooting
- Monitor Windows 95 performance, and resolve performance problems
- Audit access to a Windows 95 local resource
- Optimize the system to use the Windows 95 drivers
- Optimize a computer for desktop performance

- Optimize a computer for network performance
- Optimize printing
- Discriminate between preemptive and cooperative multitasking
- Explain Windows 95 multitasking of 16-bit Windows-based applications and 32-bit Windows-based applications
- Discriminate between a process and a thread
- Discriminate between resource usage in Windows 3.1, Windows 95, and Windows NT
- Explain how Windows 95 performs memory paging as compared to Windows 3.*x*
- Choose the appropriate course of action when the installation process fails
- Use the startup disk to repair a faulty network setup
- Choose the appropriate course of action when an application fails
- Choose the appropriate course of action when a print job fails
- Choose the appropriate course of action when the boot process fails
- Choose the appropriate course of action when file system problems occur
- Choose the appropriate course of action when Dial-Up Networking problems occur
- Predict the consequences to the operating system when MS-DOS–based applications, 16-bit Windows-based applications, and 32-bit Windows-based applications fail to respond to the system while running under Windows 95

Microsoft Networking Essentials Exam

This certification examination measures your ability to implement, administer, and troubleshoot local and wide area networks with emphasis on the Microsoft BackOffice network. Successful completion of this exam may be applied as core credit for the Microsoft Certified Systems Engineer certification.

You should have a comprehensive understanding of Microsoft Windows NT version 3.51 concepts and procedures, which include configuration, optimization, and troubleshooting solutions.

Networking Essentials for Microsoft BackOffice Examination Objectives

Microsoft lists the following exam objectives for the Networking Essentials exam:

Standards and Terminology

- Define common networking terms for LANs and WANs
- Compare a file-and-print server with an application server
- Compare share-level security with user-level security
- Compare the implications of using connection-oriented communications with connectionless communications
- Distinguish whether SLIP or PPP is used as the communications protocol for various situations
- Define the communication devices that communicate at each level of the Open Systems Interconnection (OSI) model
- Describe characteristics and purpose of the media used in IEEE 802.3 and IEEE 802.5 standards
- Explain the purpose of NDIS and Novell ODI network standards

Planning

- Select the appropriate media for various situations. Media choices include twisted-pair cable, coaxial cable, fiber-optic cable, and wireless. Situational elements include cost, distance limitations, and number of nodes.
- Select the appropriate topology for various Token Ring and Ethernet networks
- Select the appropriate network and transport protocol or protocols for various Token Ring and Ethernet networks. Protocol choices include DLC, AppleTalk, IPX, TCP/IP, NFS, and SMB.
- Select the appropriate connectivity devices for various Token Ring and Ethernet networks. Connectivity devices include repeaters, bridges, routers, brouters, and gateways.
- List the characteristics, requirements, and appropriate situations for WAN connection services. WAN connection services include X.25, ISDN, frame relay, and ATM.

Implementation

- Choose an administrative plan to meet specified needs, including performance management, account management, and security
- Choose a disaster recovery plan for various situations
- Given the manufacturer's documentation for the network adapter, install, configure, and resolve hardware conflicts for multiple network adapters in a Token Ring or Ethernet network
- Implement a NetBIOS naming scheme for all computers on a given network
- Select the appropriate hardware and software tools to monitor trends in the network

Troubleshooting

- Identify common errors associated with components required for communications
- Diagnose and resolve common connectivity problems with cards, cables, and related hardware
- Resolve broadcast storms
- Identify and resolve network performance problems

Hardware and Software Needed

As a self-paced study guide, much of the book expects you to use Windows 95 and follow along through the exercises while you learn. Microsoft designed Windows 95 to operate in a wide range of actual situations, and the exercises in this book encompass that range. Some of the exercises require only a single stand-alone PC running Windows 95. Others (those that explore some of the Windows 95 networking options) require a small Microsoft network. Some exercises refer to a pair of computers (one running Windows 95, and one running Windows 95 and Windows NT Server) configured as follows:

Computer 1

- Computer on the Microsoft Hardware Compatibility List
- 486DX 33-Mhz (or better) processor for Windows 95
- 8 MB of RAM (16 MB recommended) for Windows 95
- 200-MB (or larger) hard disk for Windows 95
- 3.5-inch 1.44-MB floppy drive
- VGA (or Super VGA) video adapter
- VGA (or Super VGA) monitor
- Mouse or equivalent pointing device

- Two-speed (or faster) CD-ROM drive
- Network Interface Card (NIC)
- Presence on an existing network, or use of a 2-port (or more) mini-port hub to create a test network
- MS-DOS 5.0 or 6.*x* and Microsoft Windows for Workgroups 3.*x* pre-installed
- Microsoft Windows 95 (CD-ROM version)

Computer 2

- Computer on the Microsoft Hardware Compatibility List
- 486DX2 66-Mhz (or better) processor for Windows NT Server
- 16 MB of RAM (minimum) for Windows NT Server
- 340-MB (or larger) hard disk for Windows NT Server
- 3.5-inch 1.44-MB floppy drive
- VGA (or Super VGA) video adapter
- VGA (or Super VGA) monitor
- Mouse or equivalent pointing device
- Two-speed (or faster) CD-ROM drive (optional)
- Network Interface Card (NIC)
- Presence on an existing network, or use of a 2-port (or more) mini-port hub to create a test network
- MS-DOS 5.0 or 6.*x* and Microsoft Windows for Workgroups 3.*x* pre-installed
- Microsoft Windows 95 (floppy version)
- Microsoft Windows NT Server (CD-ROM version)

Computers 1 and 2 should be running at least MS-DOS 5.0 and Windows for Workgroups 3.11 at the start. In fact, it is best if the computers have only MS-DOS 5.0 and Windows for Workgroups 3.11 at the beginning. Otherwise, you may be tempted to use a computer that contains real work and files that cannot be replaced easily. These computers should be test computers. You should not be afraid to format the hard drive and start over should it be necessary.

It is somewhat easier to get access to the necessary computer hardware and software in a corporate business environment. It is harder to allocate enough time within the busy workday to complete a self-study program. Most of your study time may occur after normal working hours, away from the everyday interruptions and pressures of your regular job. If you have access to a only single, non-networked computer, you will not be able to complete all of the networking exercises.

Tips for the Exam

Remember the following tips as you prepare for the MCSE certification exams:

- **Read all the material.** Microsoft has been known to include material not specified in the objectives. This course has included additional information not required by the objectives in an effort to give you the best possible preparation for the examination, and for the real-world network experiences to come.

- **Complete the exercises in each chapter.** They will help you gain experience using the Microsoft product. All Microsoft exams are experienced-based, and require you to have used the Microsoft product in a real networking environment.

- **Complete all the questions in the "Review Questions" sections.** Complete the questions at the end of each chapter—they will help you remember key points. The questions are fairly simple, but be warned, some questions may have more than one answer.

- **Review the exam objectives in the Microsoft Education and Certification Roadmap.** Develop your own questions for each topic listed. If you can make and answer several questions for each topic, you should pass.
- **Complete the Roadmap Assessment Exam and visit the relevant topics in the MCP Endeavor application.** Do not make the mistake of trusting all the answers in the Assessment Exams—they're not always correct. Look at this not as a bug, but as a feature to test your knowledge; not only do you have to know you are right, you have to be sure about it, and you have to know why each of the answers is wrong.

Remember, the object is not to pass the exam, it is to understand the material. Once you understand the material, passing is simple. Knowledge is a pyramid; to build upward, you need a solid foundation. The Microsoft Certified System Engineer program is designed to ensure that you have that solid foundation.

Good luck!

New Riders Publishing

The staff of New Riders Publishing is committed to bringing you the very best in computer reference material. Each New Riders book is the result of months of work by authors and staff who research and refine the information contained within its covers.

As part of this commitment to you, the NRP reader, New Riders invites your input. Please let us know if you enjoy this book, if you have trouble with the information and examples presented, or if you have a suggestion for the next edition.

Please note, though: New Riders staff cannot serve as a technical resource during your preparation for the Microsoft MCSE certification exams or for questions about software- or hardware-related problems. Please refer to the documentation that accompanies Windows 95 or to the applications' Help systems.

If you have a question or comment about any New Riders book, there are several ways to contact New Riders Publishing. We will respond to as many readers as we can. Your name, address, or phone number will never become part of a mailing list or be used for any purpose other than to help us continue to bring you the best books possible. You can write us at the following address:

New Riders Publishing
Attn: Publisher
201 W. 103rd Street
Indianapolis, IN 46290

If you prefer, you can fax New Riders Publishing at (317) 581-4670.

You can also send electronic mail to New Riders at the following Internet address:

`edulaney@newriders.mcp.com`

NRP is an imprint of Macmillan Computer Publishing. To obtain a catalog or information, or to purchase any Macmillan Computer Publishing book, call (800) 428-5331.

Thank you for selecting *MCSE Study Guide: Windows 95 and Networking Essentials*!

Part 1

Windows 95

Chapter 1

Planning and Installation

Installation of Windows 95 requires careful planning, an understanding of the hardware and software requirements, an appreciation for the steps in the installation process, and the ability to troubleshoot any problems that arise. Although the Windows 95 Setup program is designed to handle most types of hardware configurations, you might be called upon to respond to many of the common problems. Experience in performing the Windows 95 installation is the best teacher.

This chapter is your guide to understanding the Windows 95 installation. In this chapter, you will learn about the following:

- Windows 95 installation media options
- Preparing for Windows 95 installation
- Windows 95 hardware and software requirements
- Installation decisions
- The four phases of the Windows 95 installation process
- Troubleshooting the Windows 95 installation
- Installing either locally or from the network

Windows 95 is positioned as the successor to Microsoft's *Disk Operating System* (DOS), Windows 3.*x*, and Windows for Workgroups 3.*x* products. It is part of the Microsoft Windows operating system family, which also includes Microsoft Windows NT. However, Windows 95 is intended to be the standard operating system for the general-purpose user, and runs only on an Intel-based PC. Windows NT is designed for leading-edge systems, running on Intel-based as well as RISC-based architectures. The key differences between Windows 95 and Windows NT are covered later in this chapter in the section "Making Installation Decisions." In that section, you learn when to use Windows 95, and when to use Windows NT Workstation.

If you are new to Windows 95, two other books from New Riders Publishing, *Inside Windows 95* and *Windows 95 for Network Administrators*, offer greater detail about Windows 95 than this book, which primarily focuses on the certification process. If you do not already own a copy of the *Windows 95 Resource Kit* from Microsoft Press, you should purchase one.

Microsoft Windows 95 Key Features

Within Windows 95, there are significant improvements. It is now a true operating system, by combining elements of DOS and Windows 3.*x*. Designed to become the desktop standard, Windows 95 is tuned to deliver the best performance from personal and business applications in either stand-alone computers or networked workstations. With millions of previously installed MS-DOS and Windows 3.*x* platforms existing today, Windows 95 is ideally suited as an upgrade product. The following sections describe key features of Windows 95 that explain why someone should upgrade.

A Better, More Intuitive User Interface

Microsoft conducted usability studies to improve the ease-of-use aspects of Windows 95. The *user interface* (UI) in Windows 95 had to meet certain requirements: it should be easy to set up, intuitively simple to learn, quick to use through the start button, and much better to manage and support. This simplicity should exist for both the novice or experienced user alike. Not only are the interface icons different, but the layout of the desktop makes it easy to find and use resources.

32-Bit Operating System Architecture

The 32-bit architecture and superior resource handling within Windows 95 produce a more stable operating system environment. The 32-bit, protected-mode subsystems built into Windows 95 are more crash-resistant. A bad application, whether 16-bit or 32-bit, is less likely to stop the operating system. Even though the architecture is 32-bit, Windows 95 uses a combination of 32-bit and 16-bit code. The 32-bit code maximizes the performance of the system. The 16-bit code helps maintain compatibility with existing applications and drivers.

Preemptive Multitasking

The previous versions of Windows 3.*x* use *cooperative multitasking*, whereas Windows 95 uses *preemptive multitasking*. To the end user, the difference is subtle. Preemptive multitasking means that the Windows 95 operating system is tracking and preemptively allocating system resources. Cooperative multitasking means the operating system is relying on each application under Windows 3.*x* to cooperate in giving up control and system resources while running. This feature allows Windows 95 users to carry on several simultaneous computing tasks more smoothly than ever before.

Plug and Play Technology

Windows 95 is compatible with the *Plug and Play* (PnP) technology specification. Hardware devices written to this specification can identify themselves and their settings to Windows 95. When these hardware devices are added or re-configured, Windows 95 can adjust the computer's hardware configuration automatically to operate with those hardware device changes. It is a design philosophy that allows for automatic installation and configuration of new devices without any intervention by the user.

Built-In, Integrated Networking Support

For the network administrator, Windows 95 is the perfect client workstation. Windows 95 comes with 32-bit networking components that allow it to work with all major networks, including Microsoft, Novell, and Banyan. These networking components include the redirector, the protocol, the network adapter and various network services such as file and print sharing. They are written for the multitasking environment, take up no real-mode memory, and offer fast, stable networking support.

Centralized Security and System Policies

Windows 95 supports "pass-through," server-based security for both Microsoft Windows NT and Novell NetWare networks. Users can be required to *log on* (Windows NT) or *log in* (NetWare) before they can use Windows 95 in a networked environment. This allows increased system security and control, which enables the network administrator to use existing user-based security rules to manage access rights. The use of system policies allows further control over user access to the network. System policies also can be used to restrict a user's Windows 95 desktop functionality.

Support Built-In for Mail, Fax, and Telecommunications Functions

Mail, fax, and telecommunications functions are now part of the Windows 95 operating system. A universal in-box is provided for all messaging services that support the Messaging Application Programming Interface (MAPI). Users need only go to one location to retrieve electronic mail and fax information. The Microsoft Network and Internet Explorer allow users easy access to online services and the Internet.

Support for Mobile Services and Remote Access

Windows 95 supports the use of *PCMCIA* adapters as well as "hot" docking and undocking. Users can add or remove a device such as a PCMCIA card while the computer is running. The computer automatically detects the change and adjusts the system settings accordingly. Windows 95 helps mobile computing by supporting dial-up network remote access and file synchronization.

Compatibility for Devices and Applications

Windows 95 was designed with *backward compatibility* in mind. Much of the existing hardware and software in use today will work with the new operating system. Windows 95 supports 32-bit applications and remains backward-compatible with existing DOS-based and 16-bit Windows-based applications.

Multimedia Capability

Windows 95 expanded the existing Windows multimedia capabilities. No additional software is required to use most business and entertainment multimedia programs.

The video playback engine (Video for Windows) and CD-ROM file system (CDFS) are new 32-bit components of Windows 95 that deliver smoother video and sound reproduction.

Long Filenames

A Windows 95 filename can be a total of 255 characters long. Windows 95 uses a new *Virtual File Allocation Table* (VFAT) system that allows filenames with up to 255 mixed-case characters and spaces. Completely compatible with MS-DOS and Windows 3.1, VFAT writes two filenames to disk for each file saved on a VFAT volume: one is an 8.3 short filename, also referred to as an alias, and the other a long filename. By creating two filenames, the VFAT system allows users to create files with long filenames using 32-bit Windows applications. Windows 95 opens files using the 8.3 filename in 16-bit Windows and DOS applications.

New Tutorial and Help Files

Windows 95 includes a new tutorial called the "Windows Tour" as well as a new task-based help file. Very little actual written documentation comes with Windows 95. The hope is that using Windows 95 is very easy. So easy that between the new tutorial and the help file, little actual training will be required for new users.

Microsoft Windows 95 Installation Options

Two versions of Windows 95 are available; a full version and an upgrade version. The upgrade version is used when the PC already contains a copy of DOS in combination with Windows 3.*x* or Windows for Workgroups 3.*x*, or the PC contains a copy of OS/2. The full version is intended for new PCs that do not already have an operating system or for installing Windows 95 on a new, unpartitioned, unformatted hard drive. Except for new computer vendors and suppliers, often called *Original Equipment Manufacturers* or OEMs, most Windows 95 installations will be upgrades. The cost of a full version is roughly twice the cost of an upgrade.

The upgrade version is checking for the existence of specific files in order to validate the installation. If you get stuck with a newly formatted hard drive on a system that had both MS-DOS and Windows 3.*x* on it, follow these steps:

1. Format the drive with an MS-DOS 5.0 or better bootable disk using the FORMAT command.
2. Make the drive bootable by using the FORMAT /S command-line option to copy the system files after the format is completed.
3. Run the floppy disk upgrade version of the Windows 95 Setup program from MS-DOS to begin the restoration of the hard drive.

   If the computer has a CD-ROM, load enough of MS-DOS to get access to the CD-ROM drive. Then run the CD-ROM version of the Windows 95 Setup program from MS-DOS to begin the restoration of the hard drive.

Windows 95 checks a valid setup disk from any upgrade-qualifying product listed on the Windows 95 box, which is either MS-DOS 3.31 or later in combination with Windows 3.0 or later, or OS/2 2.0 or later. This can be confusing. Just remember MS-DOS AND Windows, OR only OS/2. An MS-DOS setup disk will fail the upgrade check. Instead, use a valid Windows 3.0 or later setup disk or an OS/2 2.0 or later installation disk.

> If the hard drive has an existing Windows installation, the Windows 95 Setup program checks for the following files to determine whether the current installation is an upgrade to Windows 3.*x*: WINVER.EXE, USER.EXE, WIN.COM, SYSTEM.INI, and WIN.INI, plus PROTOCOL.INI in Windows for Workgroups 3.*x*. Version information is part of this check; false files with the same names will not work. The first three files are the key files being checked. Keep your upgrades legal.

You can choose either the floppy disk or CD-ROM media for Windows 95. But, after learning to do the "floppy shuffle" with 13 to 14 floppy disks, you quickly begin to appreciate the value of a CD-ROM version. In addition, the floppy disk version leaves some minor things out such as the Online Help Documentation (7.8 MB) and the Windows 95 Tour (2.5 MB). The CD-ROM version includes many useful administration extras that can help you become certified.

Windows 95 installation is done through a program called *Setup*, which is a Windows 3.1-based application. Setup is usually run from within Windows, though it can be launched from MS-DOS. When you start from MS-DOS, a stripped-down Windows 3.1 environment is loaded, with just enough functionality to activate the Windows portion of the installation, beginning in real-mode then switching to protected mode. The entire installation process is covered in greater detail later in the section "Installation Process" later in this chapter.

Using Floppy Disks

Windows 95 can be installed from floppy disks. The first disk (Disk 1—Setup) is used to start the installation. Be aware that Disk 2 and those following are formatted with the new Microsoft *Distribution Media Format* (DMF), which allows more data to be stored on one disk. This format means that MS-DOS disk commands such as COPY and DISKCOPY will not work. For the average user, there was no way to make backup copies of these disks needed.

While Microsoft hasn't released a disk-formatting utility to duplicate the 1.68-MB DMF disks, some shareware utilities are now available that can. One such utility, Win Image, is available from CompuServe. Use it to make backup copies of your Windows 95 floppy disks.

Using CD-ROM

When using the CD-ROM to install Windows 95, the "floppy shuffle" goes away. It is the same procedure as the floppy disk installation, but easier. As mentioned before, the CD-ROM also contains additional components, including administration tools, that are not included with the floppy disk version. It would be worthwhile to browse the CD-ROM after your first installation to see exactly what it contains. One hidden jewel found on the CD-ROM is the *Windows 95 Resource Kit* help file.

While storing the Windows 95 installation files on the local hard drive is not one of the official installation methods, it might be the safest one, should the installation fail and either the CD-ROM or the network become unavailable. The Windows 95 installation files take up over 33 MB of space on the hard drive. The Hard Drive Usage Maxim states that "the amount of free space available is inversely proportional to the length of time the hard drive has been in service." For you as an installer, there might not even be enough hard drive space for Windows 95, let alone a copy of the installation files. Table 1.4 shows the approximate disk space requirements for Windows 95.

This method of storing the Windows 95 installation files locally is very sound for laptop users, who are often disconnected from the network and cannot afford to carry extra media around with them as they travel.

Using the Network

Windows 95 can be installed across a network. It can be installed from either a file server, such as Microsoft's Windows NT Server, Novell's NetWare Server, or from another network shared resource.

The initial Windows 95 administrative setup option is done with a program called *NETSETUP*. This option is used to place the Windows 95 files on a network server. Do not try using the regular program used in the floppy disk or CD-ROM with the earlier administrative options of "/a" or "/n" because they are not available with Windows 95.

You must run NETSETUP from a Windows 95 workstation. The files can be written only to a mapped network drive on which you have full security rights. During a network setup, which must be done from a CD-ROM media version of Windows 95, all the necessary files are transferred to the mapped network drive (do not try to use \\UNC mappings), which configures these files as a server-based Setup copy.

Depending on the Windows 95 installation policy option selected while running NETSETUP, you can allow users to (a) install to the local hard drive from the network, (b) install a "shared copy" networked Windows version, or (c) choose between the two. After completing the network setup, users can install Windows 95 from the server-based copy to either a stand-alone computer or as a shared Windows 95 copy that runs from the server, depending on the policy option.

In a networked environment, this installation offers the best performance overall. Storing 87 MB of the Windows 95 installation files on a network drive, and then making that drive readily available to all of the installers, gives you the most flexibility. However, do not neglect to have some backup media ready in case you get stuck and lose network connectivity

continues

on the Windows 95 computer near the end of the Windows 95 installation. The Windows 95 Setup program reboots your computer under Windows 95 and uses network (or CD-ROM) drivers to complete the installation. If Windows 95 is unable to make a connection to the network (or to your local CD-ROM), it cannot continue and complete the installation.

If needed, you can point to alternative sources for the installation files, so keep a copy of the floppy disks handy, just in case. The Iomega ZIP drive, which can attach to the parallel port of the computer as a guest drive and provide 100 MB of disk storage, provides another alternative source. All the Windows 95 installation files fit on a single Iomega ZIP disk.

Networked Windows

Microsoft refers to networked Windows as running a "shared copy" from a server. During this Windows 95 installation, the user simply connects to the server-based copy the network administrator has previously created and shared. In this installation option, the network administrator may have restricted the user to install only a shared copy of Windows 95. This restriction is set by selecting the Server radio button during the administrative setup. As an exercise in Windows 95 installation, you will do an administrative setup later in this chapter.

The networked Windows 95 option installs the minimal files required into a temporary directory on the computer and starts Setup from that temporary directory. Therefore, most of the actual code remains on the server, not on the local computer. The advantages of this option include less disk space required on the local computer and better administrative control. The disadvantages are increased network traffic, shared space (approximately 87 MB) on the server, and slower load times for both Windows 95 and any shared applications.

The networking world is split between those who believe Windows should be run locally on the stand-alone computer and those who believe it should be run as a shared, networked copy. There are many valid arguments, and both viewpoints have merit. The author firmly believes that network bandwidth is a critical resource. With both Windows and other applications getting larger and more complex, the extra network traffic generated by running a shared, network copy of Windows 95 is not worth the trouble. Save that bandwidth for multimedia and video, because those applications are going to need it in the near future.

Batch File Automation

The previous installation options dealt with where the Windows 95 installation files were loaded from to begin the actual installation. Batch file automation offers the capability to use a batch script file to automate much, if not all, of the installation of Windows 95. A batch script file is used in either a CD-ROM, local hard drive, or a network setup.

The administrator can predetermine most of the settings required for Windows 95 installation. In an extreme case, depending upon your configuration and degree of standardization, installation could be wholly automated from start to finish. These batch script files (*.INF) can be called from Setup using the filename as a command switch, without the slash (/) leading character. It is best to leave the autodetect feature on during automated installations, so Windows 95 can detect the hardware devices installed on a computer.

In the case of network drivers, especially Novell NetWare, Setup keeps any 16-bit real-mode network drivers such as NETX or VLMs instead of installing the 32-bit protected-mode clients. A batch file can be used to force the installation of a new device driver, regardless of what was previously installed. Network drivers are covered in greater detail in Chapter 5, "Networking and Interoperability."

Preparing for Installation

Some activities can be done ahead of time to ensure the Windows 95 installation goes smoothly. The end-user of the computer can perform most of them, with some guidance from you. The following sections present questions that constitute a preparation checklist. Such a checklist produces several benefits. First, it forces careful consideration and planning. Second, it involves the end-user in the process. Third, it improves the chances of a trouble-free installation. Finally, it allows for easier troubleshooting and recovery in the event installation should fail.

Is the Hardware Supported?

The Microsoft Hardware Compatibility List (HCL) details whether or not your computer hardware is supported. Newer computer hardware might not appear on the list. If in doubt, check with the manufacturer. These Hardware Compatibility Lists are periodically updated, so contact Microsoft to obtain the latest list. Read the Windows 95 README file and SETUP.TXT file on the installation disks; these are valuable sources of information. If you don't see the hardware component listed in the Add New Hardware wizard list, either select a close, emulated component or seek installation disks (*.INF) from the manufacturer directly.

Does the Computer Meet the Minimum Requirements?

Check table 1.1 (later in this chapter) for the minimum hardware requirements to run Windows 95. One design goal for Windows 95 is to have it run on computers capable of running Windows 3.*x*, but in reality, the minimum hardware requirement is much higher. Whereas Windows 3.1 will run on a Intel 286 computer, with 2 MB of RAM and an EGA monitor, Windows 95 needs more. The real published minimum hardware requirements for Windows 95 are an Intel 386DX computer, 20 Mhz (or higher) with 4 MB of RAM, and a VGA monitor.

Now the question becomes one of economics. Is it cheaper to upgrade older computers or simply replace them with new computers? Anything less than an Intel 486DX computer, 33 Mhz should be replaced. Non-standard hardware components might also need to be replaced to get away from having to run real-mode drivers within the CONFIG.SYS file.

There are useful utility programs that can test a computer to see if it will run Windows 95. A simple one, supplied by Microsoft, is called W95CHECK. It is available on CompuServe. This program scans a single machine for the following: Processor, Memory (RAM), Disk Space, and Applications. It does a basic test and is not intended to serve as an all-inclusive diagnostic check for every known hardware and software compatibility issue with Windows 95. If something more complex is needed, the author recommends Touchstone Software's WIN'95 Advisor.

Backup Completed for Important User Document Files?

Always backup your files. Network Administrators harp on this theme, though most end-users do not listen. At a bare minimum, backup your key document files. The applications can always be re-installed, but the document files are difficult, if not impossible to replace. The single question you can use that drives home the point is as follows: "If your hard drive were to crash tomorrow, what key files would you save today?"

Have TSRs and Virus Checking Been Disabled?

Terminate and Stay Resident (TSR) programs and Anti-Virus programs get loaded in the CONFIG.SYS and AUTOEXEC.BAT files, loaded and run from the WIN.INI file, and found in the Startup Group within Windows itself. These programs should all be disabled. Those that should not be disabled include the following:

any required for partition or hard drive management, network drivers, video drivers, or devices like CD-ROMs and Sound Cards. The safest method, if possible, is to move both the CONFIG.SYS and AUTOEXEC.BAT aside by renaming them, and entering Windows without any other programs running.

Some motherboards also support BIOS anti-virus checking upon boot-up, which needs to be disabled. See the Windows 95 README file and SETUP.TXT on the installation disks. These files are valuable sources of information on specific software products.

Can Any Unused Programs Be Removed or Uninstalled?

Hard drives tend to collect programs, applications, and data like home owners store things in the garage. Soon there is barely enough room to park a car inside. Old, forgotten applications sit idle on the hard drive, taking up valuable space. Do some spring cleaning by removing anything that is no longer needed. Most Uninstall programs will help you in this effort by tracking down all the various pieces of an application. Newer programs often include an uninstall program, while many older programs do not. Reclaim some of that space on the hard drive.

Is the Hard Drive Scanned and Defragmented?

Windows 95 will do a ScanDisk during the installation. What ScanDisk does is a quick check of the integrity of the hard drive where Windows 95 will be installed. Users might want to run earlier versions of this program that shipped with version 6.2*x* of MS-DOS, before the Windows 95 installation.

In addition, the Defrag utility is useful to defragment the hard drive. Over time, the performance of a hard drive can deteriorate as the files stored on the hard drive become fragmented and written to different portions of the hard drive.

Are All the Key System Files Backed Up?

There are key system files that should be backed up, as a precaution. These are as follows:

- All initialization (*.INI) files in the Windows directory
- All Program Manager Group (*.GRP) files in the Windows directory
- The Registry (*.DAT) files in the Windows directory
- All password (*.PWL) files in the Windows directory
- The CONFIG.SYS and AUTOEXEC.BAT files in the root directory
- Any critical hardware drivers and support programs listed in either the CONFIG.SYS or the AUTOEXEC.BAT files
- Any batch files called from the AUTOEXEC.BAT
- All network configuration (NET.CFG) files (programs to connect with the network)

Is the Network Software Working Correctly?

Make sure the network connectivity is working properly before installing Windows 95. During setup, Windows 95 uses the settings to help configure itself. If there are problems with the network drop, the network interface card, the network configuration, access rights and privileges, and so on, they need to be resolved before the Windows 95 installation.

Understanding Hardware and Software Requirements

The hardware and software requirements for Windows 95 need to be clearly understood. These requirements are confusing, especially with older hardware and software combinations. If you have an Intel 386 computer with 4 MB of RAM and at least 50 MB of hard drive space, and the only change being made to the computer is the installation of Windows 95, then the following applies: the performance should be the same, or even better, than Windows 3.*x* with the same hardware. This hardware configuration is what Microsoft labels a "minimal" computer for Windows 95. What is not said is that the performance of Windows 3.*x* on that minimal computer is poor in comparison to the standard Pentium computer in wide use today.

Identifying Appropriate Hardware Requirements for Installation

The minimum hardware requirements for running Windows 95 from the hard disk are detailed in table 1.1. Remember that Windows 95 is designed only to run on Intel-based 386DX or higher processors such as Intel's 386, 486, Pentium, or Pentium Pro processors. For backward compatibility, this minimum hardware requirement is exactly the same as that recommended for Microsoft Windows for Workgroups 3.*x*. In reality, however, it should be considered the bare minimum. A mouse or similar pointing device is listed as optional, however, you also should consider this a requirement due to the graphical nature of the Windows 95 user interface.

Table 1.1

Hardware Requirements

Component	Minimum for Windows 95
Computer	386DX, 20-Mhz (or higher) processor. See the following warning about the B-step 386 processor.
Memory	4 MB (or more)of RAM, 420 KB of conventional memory within Windows or 470 KB conventional memory from MS-DOS (600 KB total below 1 MB)
Floppy and Hard Drive	A high-density (HD) floppy-disk drive and a hard drive if installing locally to the computer

Component	Minimum for Windows 95
Disk Space	Approximately 10 to 87 MB of hard drive space, depending upon the installation options chosen; plus space for a swap file whose size is at least 14 MB (minus the RAM size installed on the computer)
Video Display	VGA (or better)
Optional	A mouse or similar pointing device CD-ROM drive Modem Sound Card Network Interface Card (NIC)

These minimum hardware requirements reflect computers that have been in broad scale use since the late 1980s. If you purchase a new computer, you will see that the Pentium processor has become the standard, with the computer having 8–16 MB of RAM and a hard drive of 1 GB or more. A basic rule of thumb when purchasing a new computer is to purchase the best computer you can afford, since the average corporate life-cycle before obsolescence is now only two to three years.

Windows 95 should not be loaded on a machine with a B1 (stepping) chip, which is the designator for Intel 386 microprocessors dated before April 1987. These chips introduce random math errors when performing 32-bit operations, making them incompatible with Windows 95.

If your 386 chip was manufactured before April 1987, or has a label on it that reads "For 16-bit operations only," contact your hardware manufacturer about a microprocessor upgrade. There exist several third-party companies offering 486 chip, Mhz clock-doubling upgrade processors that plug into the processor socket of a 386 motherboard. Rather than replacing the entire system, just upgrade the processor.

Before you purchase that Pentium Pro computer, be aware that its processor has been optimized for 32-bit operating systems such as Windows NT. The Pentium Pro, often referred to as either the New Pentium or P6, is the latest processor from Intel. Windows 95 still contains 16-bit code and is not the ideal operating system for this processor. The performance difference between a Pentium and a Pentium Pro, both running at the same megahertz (Mhz) speed, is minimal when running Windows 95. The extra cost of a Pentium Pro computer over a Pentium computer is not worth the gain.

These minimum hardware requirements often show up as a test question, if nothing other than to drive home the point that Windows 95 will actually run on an Intel 386 with 4 MB of RAM. The author loaded it on an IBM Thinkpad 701C laptop 486 processor that came standard with only 4 MB of RAM. After a few minor changes, including setting up a new 10+ MB swap file within Windows 3.1, it installed properly and worked surprisingly well.

Identifying Appropriate Software Requirements for Installation

You can install the retail version of Windows 95 as either a new install or as an upgrade over an existing operating system. You can also install Windows 95 over a number of different Microsoft operating systems, including MS-DOS, Windows 3.*x*, and Windows for Workgroups 3.*x*. It can also be installed over Novell DR DOS (or Novell DOS), IBM's PC-DOS, and as a dual-boot operating system with either IBM's OS/2 or Microsoft Windows NT.

The following lists the minimum operating system software required to install an upgrade version of Windows 95:

- MS-DOS version 3.2 or higher, or an equivalent version from the hardware manufacturer (such as Compaq version 3.31) that supports partitions greater than 32 MB; MS-DOS version 5.0 or better is recommended.

- Windows 3.*x* (in combination with MS-DOS).
- Windows for Workgroups 3.*x* (in combination with MS-DOS).
- OS/2 2.*x*.
- Dual-boot with OS/2 (with MS-DOS installed).
- Dual-boot with Windows NT (with MS-DOS installed).

You do not need to meet all these software requirements, merely a combination of either MS-DOS and Windows, or OS/2. The ability to dual-boot Windows 95 with either OS/2 or Windows NT requires you to install over a previously installed version of MS-DOS. Dual-boot with both OS/2 and Windows NT is discussed in greater detail in Chapter 3, "Customizing and Configuring Windows 95."

Windows 95 Setup checks the version of DOS as well as whether or not there is enough disk space to complete the installation. This space requirement is based on which Windows 95 components are selected for installation. If you are installing on a computer with partitions of 32 MB or less in size, you are better off using FDISK to delete the partitions. From that point, format the hard drive using the FORMAT command and install a new copy of MS-DOS. Use Microsoft DOS version 5.0 or better, because that will make the upgrade to Windows 95 run more smoothly and allow you to enable a PF8 menu choice to boot into the older version of DOS if necessary.

To check the DOS version installed on the computer, enter **ver** (version) at the command prompt.

To check the Windows version installed on the computer, enter **winver** (windows version) at the command prompt. From within Windows, pull down the Help, About Program Manager dialog box to check the version.

After you install Windows 95 on a machine, try these two commands, ver and winver, again. Compare and contrast the difference in the results. The ver command under MS-DOS gives its version; under Windows 95, it lists Windows 95. The winver command under the older versions of Windows gave an MS-DOS reply of the Windows version; while under Windows 95, it opens a dialog window. These differences highlight the fact that the new version of MS-DOS (version 7.0) has been incorporated directly into the Windows 95 operating system.

Many early versions of DOS were heavily modified by the Original Equipment Manufacturer (OEM) to meet their specific hardware and tuning requirements. Even now, special utilities appear in the DOS directory of some laptops for such things like power management and hardware configuration. There are very subtle differences between the different companies' versions of DOS. Be aware that there might be problems with the installation because of these differences. Chapter 6 in the *Windows 95 Resource Kit* contains a Setup Technical Discussion that covers the installation of Windows 95 over different versions of DOS.

Setup Type and Hard Drive Space Requirements

Within the Windows 95 Setup, you can choose from several types of installation options. To a large degree, the choice you make will dictate the size of the Windows 95 installation on the computer. It also dictates the number of optional components installed, and the amount of control you will have in customizing the installation. Table 1.2 lists the setup types.

Table 1.2

Setup Types

Setup Type	Description
Typical	The default option, which Microsoft recommends for most users with desktop computers. This option performs most installation steps automatically for a standard Windows 95 installation with minimal user action. You need to confirm only the directory where Windows 95 files are to be installed, provide user and computer identification information, and specify whether to create a startup disk.
Portable	The recommended option for mobile users with portable computers. Installs the appropriate set of files for a portable computer. This includes installing Briefcase for file synchronization and the supporting software for direct cable connections to exchange files.
Compact	The option for users who have extremely limited disk space. Installs only the minimum files required to run Windows 95.
Custom	The option for users who want to select application and network components to be installed, and confirm the configuration settings for devices. Installs the appropriate files based on user selections. This type of Setup is recommended for advanced users who want to control all the various elements of Windows 95 Setup.

Table 1.3 compares many of the differences in the optional components installed for all four types of installation. The X means the component is pre-selected, and the O indicates that it is not pre-selected, but may be optionally selected. Notice that for Custom Setup, the options pre-selected by default are the same as for a Typical installation. For the Portable Setup, the options pre-selected are designed to assist mobile users. For Compact Setup, no optional components are pre-selected, except for two disk utilities. Regardless of which setup type is initially selected, you have the choice to see the list of components and can then choose which to install.

Table 1.3

Optional Components Installed During Installation

Optional Component	Typical	Portable	Compact	Custom	MB Size
Accessibility Options	X	X	O	X	0.3
Audio Compression	X	X	O	X	0.2
Backup	O	O	O	O	1.0
Briefcase	O	X	O	O	0.0
Calculator	O	O	O	O	0.1
CD Player	O	O	O	O	0.2
Character Map	O	O	O	O	0.1
Defrag	X	X	X	X	0.3
Desktop Wallpaper	O	O	O	O	0.6
Dial-Up Networking	O	X	O	O	0.4
Direct Cable Connection	O	X	O	O	0.5
Disk Compression Tools	X	X	X	X	1.0
Document Templates	X	O	O	X	0.1
Games	O	O	O	O	0.6
HyperTerminal	X	X	O	X	0.4
Media Player	X	X	O	X	0.2
Microsoft Exchange	O	O	O	O	3.6
Microsoft Fax Services	O	O	O	O	1.7
Microsoft Fax Viewer	O	O	O	O	0.3
Microsoft Mail Services	O	O	O	O	0.6
Mouse Pointers	O	O	O	O	0.2
Net Watcher	O	O	O	O	0.1
Online User's Guide	O	O	O	O	7.7

Optional Component	Typical	Portable	Compact	Custom	MB Size
Paint	X	O	O	X	1.2
Phone Dialer	X	X	O	X	0.1
Quick View	X	X	O	X	1.4
Screen Savers	X	X	O	X	0.1–0.2
Sound and Video Clips	O	O	O	O	0.4–6.5
Sound Recorder	X	X	O	X	0.2
System Monitor	O	O	O	O	0.1
The Microsoft Network	O	O	O	O	2.0
Video Compression	X	X	O	X	0.4
Volume Control	X	X	O	X	0.1
Windows 95 Tour	O	O	O	O	2.4
WordPad	X	O	O	X	1.2

Note: X = installed by default; O = optional

For information about how Windows 95 Setup treats disk partitions created under other operating systems, see the *Windows 95 Resource Kit.* Table 1.4 discusses the approximate hard disk space requirements for Windows 95. This table does not indicate the maximum requirements, just the average requirements based on the default components installed. The actual space required depends on which options you choose to add during the Windows 95 installation. The bottom line, however, is Windows 95 requires more space than previous versions of both MS-DOS and Windows. The operating system and all of its programs are getting increasingly larger. If your hard drive is getting cluttered with unused programs and files, it might need cleaning up before the installation.

Table 1.4

Approximate Disk Space Requirements for Windows 95

Installation Base	Typical	Portable	Compact	Custom
New installation	47 MB	47 MB	44 MB	48 MB
DOS upgrade	55 MB	55 MB	45 MB	55 MB
Windows 3.*x* upgrade	40 MB	40 MB	38 MB	40 MB
WFWG 3.*x* upgrade	40 MB	40 MB	38 MB	40 MB

Setup Switches

Windows 95 Setup provides standard command-line options to control the installation process. These options, or switches, are specified on the command line as arguments for the setup command (such as setup /?). Similar to MS-DOS command arguments, the specific option is preceded by a forward slash (/) character, not the backslash character used to specify directory mappings.

Windows 95 Setup can be run with the setup command with the switches shown in table 1.5.

Table 1.5

Setup Switches

Switch	When Used
/?	Provides help for syntax and use of setup command-line switches. Available from both MS-DOS and Windows.
Troubleshooting Switches	
/C	Instructs Windows 95 MS-DOS Setup not to load the SmartDrive disk cache.
/d	Instructs Windows 95 Setup not to use the existing version of Windows for the early phases of Setup. Use this switch if you have problems starting Setup that might be due to missing or damaged supporting DLL files within the existing version of Windows.
/in	Instructs Windows 95 MS-DOS Setup not to run the Network Setup module when installing Windows 95.

Switch	When Used
/im	Instructs Windows 95 Setup not to check for the minimum conventional memory required to install Windows 95.
/id	Instructs Windows 95 Setup not to check for the minimum disk space required to install Windows 95.
/iq	Instructs Windows 95 Setup not to perform the ScanDisk quick check when running Setup from MS-DOS. You probably want to use this switch if you use compression software other than DriveSpace or DoubleSpace. Also used from Windows in conjunction with /is not to perform the cross-linked hard disk check.
/is	Instructs Windows 95 Setup not to run the ScanDisk quick check. You probably want to use this switch if you use compression software other than DriveSpace or DoubleSpace.
/ih	Runs ScanDisk in the foreground so that you can see the results. Use this switch if the system stalls during the ScanDisk check or if an error results.
/iL	Loads the Logitech mouse driver. Use this option if you have a Logitech Series C mouse.
/nostart	Instructs Windows 95 Setup to install the required, minimal Windows 3.*x* DLLs used by the Windows 95 Setup, and then to exit to MS-DOS without installing Windows 95. These files are copied in a :\WININST0.400 directory.
Administrative Switches	
File.inf	Instructs Windows 95 Setup to use settings in the specified script file to install Windows 95 automatically; for example, executing **setup mybatch.inf** specifies that the Setup program should use the settings in the MYBATCH.INF script file.
/IW	This new switch enables you to bypass the license agreement screen. It is very useful when creating an automated script file that will run without stopping. The switch must be entered in capital letters.
/t:tempdir	Specifies the directory where Setup is to copy its temporary files. If the directory does not exist, it will be created. Be aware that any existing files in this directory will be deleted.

In a large corporate environment, if you can automate the Windows 95 installation by using script files, you will save yourself and your installers a lot of work. Murphy's Law states "what can go wrong, will." This exception processing approach to installing Windows 95 automatically enables you to focus on the real problem installations. Expect installation problems so you are not surprised when they occur.

> Hopefully, you will never need to use the Troubleshooting Switches for Setup, but it is important to know they are available and when to use them. Remember that /a and /n are no longer valid, use the NETSETUP program instead.

Making Installation Decisions

Some installation pre-planning is needed before starting the installation of Windows 95. There is plenty of material to help guide you in these efforts. The *Windows 95 Resource Kit* includes a Deployment Planning Guide that lays out a pretty detailed project plan for Windows 95. As a certified MCSE or MCP, you need to be knowledgeable about where to find the answers. This section of the chapter is devoted to helping you make some of these installation decisions.

What Setup Information Is Needed?

At a minimum, three pieces of information are needed for a successful Windows 95 installation. Most everything else can be automatically detected by the Windows 95 Setup program, including the current computer's hardware configuration. The following three pieces of information are unique to each Windows 95 installation:

- **Default User Name.** The initial user defined to the Windows 95 computer. User names are limited to 15 characters with no embedded spaces and can contain any of the following special characters including the period:

  ! @ # $ % ^ & ( ) - _ ' { } ~ .

This name should be unique and correspond to your rules for user names in either the Windows NT domain environment or the Novell NetWare bindery/NDS environment, especially when using user-level access control. Although Windows NT and Novell NetWare allow longer names, most user names get no longer than eight characters. This is to allow mapping to the user's home directory on a file server.

- **Computer Name.** The Windows 95 computer name that is known on the network. The computer names are also limited to 15 characters, with no embedded spaces, and can contain any of the following special characters including the period:

  ! @ # $ % ^ & ( ) - _ ' { } ~ .

  This name should be unique and correspond to your rules for computer names for either the Windows NT domain environment or the Novell NetWare bindery/NDS environment. When you share computer resources on the network, other users reference that shared resource by using a combination of the computer name and the share name. For example, if your computer was named JACK-PC1 and the Windows 95 install directory was shared using the name of WIN95-INSTALL, then users would connect to \\JACK-PC1\WIN95-INSTALL.

  Along with the computer name, you can have an optional *computer description.* This description can be up to 48 characters in length, and allows other information to be shared about the Windows 95 computer. Information such as the owner's full name, telephone number, building or room, and type of computer can be included. This description can contain embedded spaces but no commas. When browsing the Microsoft Network, both the computer name as well as the computer description are available. Using a good description makes the browsing easier.

- **Workgroup Name.** The logical grouping of computers with which the Windows 95 computer most often connects to share resources or data, or exchange e-mail. The workgroup names are also limited to 15 characters, with no embedded spaces, and can contain any of the following special characters including the period:

! @ # $ % ^ & ( ) - _ ' { } ~ .

The workgroup name should be unique. A Windows 95 computer can freely join any peer-to-peer workgroup by simply changing the name. Instead of a workgroup name, you might need to specify a Windows NT *domain name* and/or a Novell NetWare *preferred server*. These last two names would be used to connect to either a Windows NT domain or to a Novell NetWare server/directory services network.

These three pieces of information, the user name, the computer name, and the workgroup name, are unique to each computer installation. Duplicate computer names can prevent the Windows 95 computer from joining the Microsoft Network. Wrong workgroup names affect the browse list generated when you open your Network Neighborhood. Incorrect or missing computer descriptions cause confusion to users wanting to share resources or data. In a corporate environment, it is important to agree on some standard naming convention that everyone adheres to and supports. It can make administration of the Windows 95 network much easier for all concerned.

The requirement for unique names stems from the way information is shared on a Microsoft Network. Try bringing up a second computer onto a Microsoft Network when the computer name is not unique. The second computer will not be allowed to join the Microsoft Network. No big deal, you might say, until it causes problems.

Suppose you are doing Windows 95 installations from the network, and the new Windows 95 computer will not connect to the Microsoft Network. If one of the network shares is the actual Windows 95 installation files from which you are installing, they will not be available because you are an isolated computer. Duplicate computer names can be very troublesome to track down and resolve. A short-term fix is to use a temporary computer name, complete the Windows 95 installation, and then sort out the computer names later.

Standard naming conventions and naming provisions for multiple computers under each user's name should allow you to keep things unique and minimize this problem from happening. Good computer descriptions with accurate location information will help track down duplicate computer names.

How to Maintain Program Groups and User Preferences When Upgrading from Windows 3.1

Setup will detect whether Windows 3.1*x* or Windows for Workgroups 3.*x* is installed on the computer. Should it find one of them, it will offer to install Windows 95 in the same directory in order to upgrade the existing installation.

If you choose to install into the same directory, the Windows 95 Setup program takes the Windows 3.*x* or Windows for Workgroups 3.*x* Program Manager groups and converts them into folders in the Programs directory. This is so they can be displayed from the Windows 95 Start menu, under Programs. These folders can be opened or explored to find shortcuts to the applications previously contained within each Program Manager group. The Windows 3.*x* application icon converts into a Windows 95 shortcut. The Windows 95 Setup program also moves the configuration settings in SYSTEM.INI, WIN.INI, and PROTOCOL.INI, plus file associations from the Windows 3.*x* Registry, into the Windows 95 Registry. This enables all applications and networking settings to work automatically in the new Windows 95 environment.

If you don't want to re-install all your applications, just upgrading the existing Windows environment to Windows 95 will save you a lot of work. This is a key exam question. Just remember, if you want to keep your old configuration, upgrade to Windows 95 on top of it.

There are several questions about this in the Microsoft Self-Assessment Windows 95 exam, so be open to other possible means of getting access to your Windows 3.1 environment.

You must choose to install Windows 95 in a new directory if you want to preserve the existing MS-DOS or Windows installation. When you do install into a new directory, you might have to reinstall most Windows-based applications before they can function properly in the new environment. If you are serious about setting up dual-boot capability, Chapter 3 will provide you with some experience.

Determine When to Use Windows 95 and When to Use Microsoft Windows NT Workstation

When should you use Windows 95 over Windows NT Workstation? The best answer at this time is "It depends on what you are trying to do with the computer." Microsoft has published a white paper on the subject. A copy of that document is included on the CD-ROM. But the criteria for determining when to use one instead of other can be simplified into several key differences:

Windows 95

- Windows 95 is focused on making computing easier for anyone using a wide range of personal and business applications on desktop and portable computers. To protect their current investment, these Windows 95 users require the highest level of backward compatibility with today's applications and device drivers (32-bit, 16-bit Windows, and MS-DOS).

- Windows 95 runs only on an Intel 386 and better platform, 4 MB or more RAM, 40 MB or more hard drive space.
- Windows 95 uses a new Windows (Next Generation) user interface.
- Windows 95 provides Plug and Play technology support.

Windows NT Workstation

- Windows NT Workstation is focused on providing the most powerful desktop operating system for solving complex business needs. It delivers the highest level of performance to support the most demanding business applications for developers, technical, engineering, and financial users, and for critical line-of-business applications.
- NT Workstation will run some MS-DOS applications, 16-bit and 32-bit Windows applications, plus POSIX, and OS/2 1.*x* applications, but supports only 32-bit Windows device drivers.
- It will run on Intel 386 and better platforms, as well as PowerPC, MIPS, and DEC Alpha-based RISC systems with 12–16 MB RAM, 90–110 MB hard drive space.
- Windows NT Workstation supports symmetric multiprocessor (SMP) configurations for scaleable performance without changing the operating system or applications.
- Windows NT Workstation offers C-2 certifiable user-level security access to a stand-alone workstation. Files, folders, and applications on both the desktop and the server can be restricted to specific users.
- Windows NT Workstation has a Windows 3.1 (Previous Generation) user interface, which will be upgraded in a future release.
- Windows NT Workstation has limited Plug and Play technology Support, which will be upgraded in a future release.

Exercise 1.1 will help you make the choice between a Windows 95 or Windows NT operating system.

Exercise 1.1: Choosing between Windows 95 and Windows NT

In each of the following cases, indicate which Windows operating system should be used, either Windows 95 or Windows NT:

1. Office environment with general tasks such as word processing, spreadsheet analysis, electronic mail running on an installed base of Intel-based personal computers, where management wants to maximize their existing investment.

2. Engineers, scientific researchers, statisticians, and other technical users who often use processing-intensive applications for data analysis and design activities.

3. Employees who spend a lot of their working hours away from their office (at a customer site, in a hotel, or out in the field) and rely on personal laptop computers to help them perform their jobs.

4. Banking and defense workers who need to protect sensitive data or application files with high levels of security.

5. Home-based users who find computers challenging and unfriendly. They want to be able to take advantage of new capabilities such as multimedia and easily access online information services.

6. Experienced computer users who require very high levels of availability and performance, and cannot afford downtime, regardless of the application that they are running.

You should understand the fundamental differences between Windows 95 and Windows NT Workstation. Although Microsoft will endeavor to bring them closer in synchronization with each other, such as the release of Windows NT Workstation Version 4.0, they are targeted to separate groups of users. Check the wording in each test question for clues as to which product would be best suited. If both seem likely, choose Windows 95, since the test you are taking covers Windows 95 certification.

New Microsoft joint licensing rules in 1996 for both Windows 95 and Windows NT Workstation in the corporate environment will blur these key differences even more. Users will be able to switch from one to the other, and back again, depending on their requirements.

Configure a Windows 95 Computer on a Network Using the Appropriate Protocol

Whenever someone mentions protocols, think of the language used for transporting data across the network. Often called either *transport protocols* or simply *networking protocols*, the word *protocol*, when used without an adjective, can be a bit confusing. The OSI model associates the networking protocol as a protocol driver, which is responsible for the routing of data and application messages in the Transport (Layer 4) and Network (Layer 3) layers. For the purposes here in Windows 95, the protocol is the language a computer uses to communicate. Different computers must use the same protocol, otherwise they will not be able to communicate. A Windows 95 computer can support multiple protocols running at the same time.

Protocols shipped with Windows 95 are implemented as 32-bit, protected-mode components. These protocols can be shared among the installed network clients. For example, a single TCP/IP protocol stack can be bound to both the Microsoft Client for Microsoft Networks as well as the Microsoft Client for NetWare Networks.

By default, Windows 95 installs both the Microsoft NetBEUI and IPX/SPX-compatible protocols.

Three of the protocols included with Windows 95 (NetBEUI, IPX/SPX, and TCP/IP) are Plug and Play enabled. These protocols can sense when the network is not available and unload themselves after sending notification to any dependent applications. The following protocols are the most commonly used:

- **NetBEUI (NetBIOS Extended User Interface) Protocol.** A very fast protocol intended for small networks. It is not routable, which means it cannot pass through a larger network that uses routers to segment the network. The NetBEUI protocol stack included with Windows 95 is compatible with existing networks using NetBEUI. Windows for Workgroups, Windows NT Workstation and Server, LAN Manager, and the Workgroup Add-On for MS-DOS are some examples. NetBEUI's speed and ease of administration make it ideal for small local area networks.

- **IPX/SPX-Compatible (Internetwork Packet Exchange/ Sequence Packet Exchange) Protocol.** The standard protocol used in the Novell NetWare environment. Microsoft has written its own implementation of this protocol stack, which is compatible with the Novell NetWare IPX/SPX implementation. This protocol is routable, and will run on most larger networks that are designed for IPX/SPX routing. It also includes support for "packet burst," which offers improved network performance by reducing the number of packets required to send data. As a routable protocol, most users in medium- to large-sized networks prefer it over NetBEUI.

  A big enhancement to Microsoft's implementation of the IPX/SPX-compatible protocol was Windows Sockets (WinSock) programming interface support. Because of this enhancement, any WinSock 32-bit applications can run on top of the IPX/SPX-compatible protocol using Windows 95. NetBIOS support also enables you to run NetBIOS applications.

- **TCP/IP (Transmission Control Protocol/Internet Protocol).** A standard protocol for connecting to the Internet and Unix environments. This protocol stack is fully routable, offers standard connectivity to most networks, and is rapidly becoming the industry standard for many corporate wide-area networks. Within Windows 95, the TCP/IP protocol stack is implemented as a 32-bit, high-performance VxD. It includes most of the standard utilities such as ftp, telnet, arp, ping, route, netstat, and ipconfig. The TCP/IP protocol stack includes DHCP support for the automatic assignment of IP addresses. It also includes WINS support for IP address to NetBIOS name resolution and DNS support.

The TCP/IP protocol implementation includes Windows Sockets (WinSock) programming interface support and a WinSock DLL for both 16-bit and 32-bit applications. NetBIOS support also enables you to run NetBIOS applications.

In Exercise 1.2, you select the protocol that is most appropriate for a variety of situations. See Part II, "Networking Essentials," for more detailed information about protocols.

Exercise 1.2: Choosing a Protocol

In each of the following cases, determine which protocol should be used—either NetBEUI, IPX/SPX, or TCP/IP:

1. A local area network, running against both a Novell NetWare Server and a Windows NT Server
2. A small office network with only Windows 95 computers, plus some Windows for Workgroup computers that have not been upgraded yet
3. A wide area network, connecting to Unix Servers and the Internet.

There will be several test questions about the use of protocols within Windows 95. Remember that by default, Windows 95 installs both Microsoft NetBEUI and IPX/SPX-compatible protocols. You might be tempted to choose the TCP/IP protocol stack for Microsoft Networking, but the new Microsoft defaults for both Windows 95 and Windows NT are the IPX/SPX-compatible protocols (called NWLINK in Windows NT). These three protocols are not the only ones supported under Windows 95. Shipped with Windows 95 is support for the following: Banyan VINES, DEC Pathworks, IBM DLC, Microsoft DLC, Novell IPX ODI, and SunSoft PC-NFS. Other protocols can be added.

Select the Appropriate Level of Security to Meet Various Needs

Multiple levels of security are built into Windows 95. These levels include the security of the Windows 95 computer itself, the resources (folders, drives, printers, CD-ROMs) that are shared on the network in a peer-to-peer manner, and the file server security. While Windows 95 does not have the C2 level of security found in Windows NT, there are actions that can be done to keep your Windows 95 computer secure. Chapter 19 of the *Windows 95 Resource Kit* does a good job of explaining the security features of Windows 95. The following are some basic security procedures to understand:

- Unified logon process is where users on a Windows 95 computer can log on to all configured network clients and Windows 95 with a single prompt, providing they use the same user name and password. The initial logon prompt seen by the users when logging on to Windows 95 depends on the selection as the Primary Network Logon on the Network properties sheet. The same user name and password is sent to all configured network clients and Windows 95. If the user name or the password is different, the user will see additional prompts to log on.

- Windows 95 logon security is possible with the use of a system policy that prevents the user from easily logging on to Windows 95 if their Windows NT logon or Novell NetWare login is not validated. The user could still break in by either (1) doing a re-boot and then PF8 to get to the Windows 95 boot menu, (2) using a Windows 95 startup disk, or (3) bypassing the logon prompt by using the Cancel button to get a default Windows environment. This is not as secure an operating system logon as the one used by Windows NT. To use this Windows 95 logon security feature you must enable the "Require Validation By Network For Windows Access" policy. See Chapter 4, "Editing User and System Profiles," for more information on the use of system policies.

- Share-level security is an access control level security that allows the user to assign passwords to shared resources on the Windows 95 computer. The computer running Windows 95 can allow both read-only or full access to a resource, with different passwords for each. Share-level security is normally used in small peer-to-peer networks, and is the default security access control when Windows 95 is installed. Share-level security is only available if you are running file and printer sharing for Microsoft with the Microsoft Client for Microsoft Networks. It is not available if you are running file and printer sharing for NetWare with the Microsoft Client for NetWare Networks.

- User-level security is an access control level security. It allows the user to base the access to shared resources on the Windows 95 computer on a user accounts list stored on one of the following: a Windows NT Workstation, a Windows NT Server, a Windows NT Domain Controller, or a Novell NetWare Server. What makes this work is the use of *pass-through security*, which passes the authentication requests to either Windows NT or Novell NetWare, so that the Windows 95 computer need not implement its own unique user-level security scheme. Instead, Windows 95 leverages off the network as a central security provider. This is normally used in larger networking environments that have some form of centralized security administration. The users attempting to access the resource are validated by the central security provider. The user's rights, once validated, remain defined on the Windows 95 computer.

- Password caching is the mechanism for saving the passwords when connecting to a password-protected resource. It is enabled by default when you install Windows 95. As you access a password-protected resource for the first time, you will be given the option to check a box to "save this password in your password list." The password list file (*.PWL) is encrypted and stored in the Windows directory on the Windows 95 computer. The Windows 95 logon opens this file, enabling the saved passwords to be given when connecting to the corresponding password-protected resource.

There are many levels of security within Windows 95. The unified logon process allows the user to log on once and use that same user name and password for all the configured networks. Share-level security requires that users themselves administer shared resources. User-level security makes use of user accounts already defined on another computer or file server to grant access to shared resources. This other computer or file server is responsible for administering user accounts and validating the passwords. Windows 95 logon security forces the user to be validated against the computer or file server providing user-level security. Finally, password caching allows the Windows 95 user's password to be used to save other passwords and to use those saved passwords when connecting to networked resources.

The password list file (*.PWL) is secured by each user's Windows 95 password. To cut down the number of different passwords a user must track and maintain, some network administrators advocate the use of a blank Windows 95 password. However, the use of a blank Windows 95 password along with password caching can expose your user's network resources to unauthorized use. This author recommends not using a blank Windows 95 password.

The Password List Editor, PWLEDIT is used to edit a user's password list file. Use it to view the entries and remove specific password entries if problems are encountered using a cached password.

To install this tool on your local hard disk, use the following procedure:

1. Choose the Add/Remove Programs option in the Control Panel.
2. Select the Windows Setup tab.
3. Click the Have Disk button.
4. Install the ADMIN\APPTOOLS\PWLEDIT directory from a Windows 95 CD-ROM.

In Exercise 1.3, you choose the optimal level of security for a variety of situations.

Exercise 1.3: Selecting a Security Level

In each of the following cases, select the appropriate level of security: user-level, share-level, or no (no file and printer sharing) security:

1. A local area network, running against both a Novell NetWare Server and a Windows NT Server
2. A small office network, only Windows 95 computers, plus some Windows for Workgroup computers that have not been upgraded.
3. A wide area network, connecting to Unix Servers and the Internet.

Security and how to properly set it up under Windows 95 can be tricky. Using system policies is one way to keep your computer secure. The key point here is to understand the differences between user-level and share-level security, and how it relates to the sharing of a Windows 95 computer's resources.

Security is a very important issue, especially in a corporate environment. Windows 95 is leading the trend toward closer integration with Internet access. The Microsoft Network (MSN) optional component that comes with Windows 95 has easy links into the World Wide Web (WWW). Microsoft Plus! includes the Microsoft Internet Explorer (MSIE), which can be downloaded for free by any user. The Service Pack upgrades to Windows 95 in 1996 will further blur the boundary between applications and the Internet, with an updated Windows 95 user interface. Peer-to-peer networking across this corporate environment opens many challenges for a network administrator.

A potential security problem exists with users running either Microsoft or NetWare file and print services with remote administration enabled. Microsoft has released updated drivers for both of these services to close any possible security breach. These security update files, Vservupd.exe and Nwservupd.exe, are available on CompuServe.

Determine the Appropriate Installation Method (or Options)

As an advanced user or a network administrator, you can select among various installation options for Windows 95. These options can be thought of as a series of choices that help determine the method you use for Windows 95 installations. The decision of which choice to use is yours. Chapter 3 of the *Windows 95 Resource Kit* covers this in greater detail.

The following sections discuss the options you should consider.

Run Setup from MS-DOS or Windows?

The Windows 95 Setup program can be run from either an MS-DOS command prompt or from within Windows 3.1 or Windows for Workgroups 3.1*x*. The preferred method is to run from within Windows. Run from the MS-DOS command prompt when neither Windows 3.1 nor Windows for Workgroups 3.1*x* is installed on the computer, but MS-DOS, Windows 3.0, OS/2, or Windows NT is installed.

If either Windows 3.1 or Windows for Workgroups 3.1*x* is on the computer, the Windows 95 Setup program offers to install itself into the same directory to upgrade the existing Windows installation. If you choose to install into the same directory, the configuration settings in SYSTEM.INI and WIN.INI (and PROTOCOL.INI for Windows for Workgroups), plus any file associations from the Windows 3.*x* Registry, are moved into the Windows 95 Registry. In addition, the Windows 3.*x* Program Manager groups are converted into folders off the Start Menu's Program selection. This upgrade allows programs and network settings to work automatically in the Windows 95 environment.

Whenever possible, run the Windows 95 Setup program from within Windows 3.1 or Windows for Workgroups 3.1*x* and install into the existing Windows directory. This minimizes any extra setup work needed to get all your applications to run properly under Windows 95. You will soon realize that the easy part was doing the Windows 95 installation—the hard part is getting all the various applications to function properly. You might have to reinstall each application again if you chose to install Windows 95 into a new directory.

Which Installation Type?

Within the Windows 95 Setup program, you can choose from four types of installation options. The choice you select affects the size of the Windows 95 installation, the computer, the components pre-selected for installation, and the amount of control you have in customizing the installation. You can install a typical compact or custom option for a desktop computer, or a portable option for a laptop computer.

The custom type of installation offers the most flexibility. Regardless of which type of installation you select, however, you can add any missing components later through the Add/Remove Programs icon in the Control Panel folder.

Local or Shared Windows?

You can choose to run Windows 95 from the local hard disk of the computer or as a shared copy from a network file server.

The Windows 95 installation files are available through the retail channels in three basic media versions:

- CD-ROM upgrade version
- 3.5-inch floppy disk upgrade version
- 3.5-inch floppy disk full version

All the upgrade versions check for valid upgrade files on the computer or qualifying setup disks and prompt for a serial number key. The full version allows for a formatted hard drive before starting the installation, and then prompts for a serial number key.

You can copy the Windows 95 source files (33 MB) to a shared network directory. Depending on your license agreement, such as Microsoft Select Licensing, any authorized licensed users can connect to this directory and run the installation from there. If you do a server-based setup to a network directory, the complete set of Windows 95 source code (87 MB) can be used to install either a local copy or a shared copy of Windows 95 to the computer.

If you choose to support installing and running a shared copy of Windows 95 from a file server, you can configure it in one of three ways:

- On a computer with a local hard drive, with system files stored on and running from the file server.
- On a computer with only a floppy disk drive, booting from the floppy disk, with system files stored on and running from the file server.
- From a Novell NetWare File Server that supports diskless workstations and an RIPL boot to a startup disk image stored on the file server, then using system files stored on and running from the file server.

For a shared copy of Windows 95, the system files reside on the file server and not on the local hard drive of the computer. The instructions for running a shared copy of Windows 95 can be found in Chapter 4 of the *Windows 95 Resource Kit.*

If possible, choose to run a local copy of Windows 95. The overall performance is better, and your users will thank you for it.

Manual, Customized, or Automated Setup?

You can choose to run the Windows 95 Setup program manually from each computer, configure a customized setup script, or automate the entire installation process to run remotely for many computers.

The manual method involves sitting down at each computer and running the Windows 95 Setup program. Depending on which setup type of installation you do, the installer might have to respond to only a few questions (Typical) or many questions (Custom). This manual method can take between 30 to 60 minutes for each installation.

To speed up this process of installing Windows 95, a custom setup script can be created. This script answers most, if not all, of the Windows 95 Setup program questions. These custom scripts are based on the MSBATCH.INF file format. Custom scripts can contain pre-defined options for all the Setup options and can be extended to contain instructions for installing additional software. A network administrator can use a customized setup script to standardize Windows 95 installations and reduce the support requirements. This method can significantly reduce installation time because few, if any, interruptions occur.

The automated method involves using both a customized setup script and an automated mandatory installation process for installing Windows 95 on multiple computers with the Windows 95 source code on a file server. Several different approaches can be used to automate installation:

- Use a login script to run Setup with a custom setup script, which is installed when each user logs onto the file server.
- Use the System Management Server (SMS) to distribute a mandatory Windows 95 Installation Package that runs Setup using a custom setup script.
- Use a network management software distribution package, such as Norton Administrator for Networks (NAN), to install Windows 95, automatically running Setup using a custom setup script.

An automated installation of Windows 95 saves a great deal of time when deploying Windows 95 within a large company, allowing the network administrator to focus on the few Windows 95 installations that might run into problems.

Repair Setup or Perform Maintenance?

Problems will arise during either the Windows 95 installation, normal operations, or the configuration of any hardware or software upgrades. You can choose among several troubleshooting methods to fix those problems. The Windows 95 Setup program or the maintenance applications in the Control Panel folder are available for your use.

The Windows 95 Setup program can be used to provide safe recovery during a failed installation or to repair a computer that has a damaged or corrupted installation. In addition, if after Windows 95 has been installed, you encounter missing, incorrect version, or damaged files within the operating system, the Windows 95 Setup program can replace, verify, or repair the files.

During the course of a Windows 95 installation, you have the option to create an emergency startup disk, which can be used to start the computer in case of configuration problems. You can also create an emergency startup disk from the Add/Remove Programs Properties sheet within the Control Panel folder. You should create at least one Windows 95 emergency startup disk for troubleshooting purposes.

Instead of running the Windows 95 Setup program, you can choose to run one of the various maintenance applications located within the Control Panel folder. The maintenance applications allow you to install and configure applications, hardware devices, the display monitor, printers, modems, and network services.

The System application within the Control Panel folder allows you to examine and repair your computer system configuration, and should be the first place you examine when hardware problems occur.

The best way to address this exam objective is by example. Exercise 1.4 is aimed at helping you determine the appropriate installation method to use for some given installations.

Exercise 1.4: Choosing an Installation Method

For each of the cases listed, choose from the following list the letter that corresponds to the correct response:

a. Setup from MS-DOS

b. Setup from Windows 3.*x*

c. Typical, compact, or custom setup type

d. Portable setup type

e. Local Windows

f. Shared Windows

g. Manual install

h. Customized Setup Script install

i. Automated install

j. Repair install

k. Maintenance applications

1. A key Windows 95 system file has become corrupted, how would you fix it?
2. A computer with MS-DOS 5.0 and Windows 3.0 needs to be updated to Windows 95, where would you start setup?
3. If the computer is running Windows 95 from the local hard drive of the computer, it is said to be running what kind of Windows?
4. What Setup type of Windows 95 installation should you use to heavily customize both components and settings during installation?

5. An installation of a home computer without a CD-ROM drive that needs to be updated with Windows 95 is an example of which kind of installation?

6. If a computer with MS-DOS 6.22 and Windows for Workgroups 3.11 needs to be updated to Windows 95, where do you start setup?

7. What setup type of Windows 95 installation should you use for a laptop computer on which you want to run Windows 95 mobile computing components?

8. A computer running Windows 95 from a file server rather than its local hard drive is running which kind of Windows?

9. A batch file, like MSBATCH.INF, that is used to pre-select Windows 95 installation settings is an example of which kind of installation?

10. If a Windows 95 component is not installed during the Windows 95 installation, how might you add it later?

11. A Windows 95 installation program that can be set for a mandatory start during the network logon is an example of which kind of installation?

The correct responses are as follows:

1. j
2. a
3. e
4. c
5. g
6. b
7. d
8. f

9. h
10. i
11. k

Make a list of the questions you would ask in order to determine the best method of installing Windows 95 at your location, then flowchart the process. Keep these queries in mind when you take the exam. Using CD-ROM is the best stand-alone method available. Using the network, along with a standard customized Setup script and a fully automated installation is the optimum method for doing whole-scale corporate-wide Windows 95 installations.

Installation Process

The Windows 95 Setup program is a Windows 3.1-based program. It will not run under Windows 3.0, but rather needs to be run under either Windows 3.1x or Windows for Workgroups 3.*x*. The Windows 95 Setup program can be started from DOS, if you have only Windows 3.0 or no version of Windows installed on your computer. The preferred method is to run the installation from within Windows.

If you start the Windows 95 Setup program from DOS, a minimal version of Windows 3.*x*, approximately 1 MB, will be copied to the hard drive into a temporary C:\WININST0.400 directory. This version requires about 600 KB of RAM (470 KB conventional memory) to launch the complete Windows 95 Setup program. It is often called *Minimal Windows* because it has only enough functionality to bring up the Windows portion of the Windows 95 installation. It starts in real mode and then switches to protected mode before beginning the hardware detection phase.

Microsoft realizes that the key ingredient to the successful installation of Windows 95 is the Windows 95 Setup program. It needs to handle the millions of different hardware and software combinations. It only needs to look easy to those users installing Windows 95 for the first time. It needs to be able to safely recover from most of the problems encountered during the installation. The Windows 95 Setup program uses a wonderfully complex installation process. As part of the certification process, you need to understand what is happening behind the scenes, and be able to troubleshoot any Windows 95 installation problems.

The Windows 95 installation process is extremely modular. The Windows 95 Setup program steps through this process, only running the modules either requested or needed. For example, the hardware detection phase will identify specific components on the computer, and the Windows 95 Setup program will run only those installation modules that match. Some of the modules used by the Windows 95 Setup program are standard wizards, such as the setup for network components, modems, printers, and display monitors.

There are four logical phases to Windows 95 installation:

- Startup and information gathering
- Hardware detection
- File copy
- Final system configuration

The next few sections explore the Windows 95 installation process in greater detail.

From the Workstation Perspective

From the workstation perspective, the Windows 95 Setup program performs a series of steps when installing Windows 95. The first few steps depend upon from where the Windows 95 Setup program was started. At one point in the middle of the Windows 95 installation process, both the Windows 95 Setup program started from MS-DOS and the same Windows 95 Setup program started from within Windows 3.*x* end up running Windows in protected mode. This merge in the Windows 95 installation process occurs just before starting the hardware detection phase as illustrated in figure 1.1.

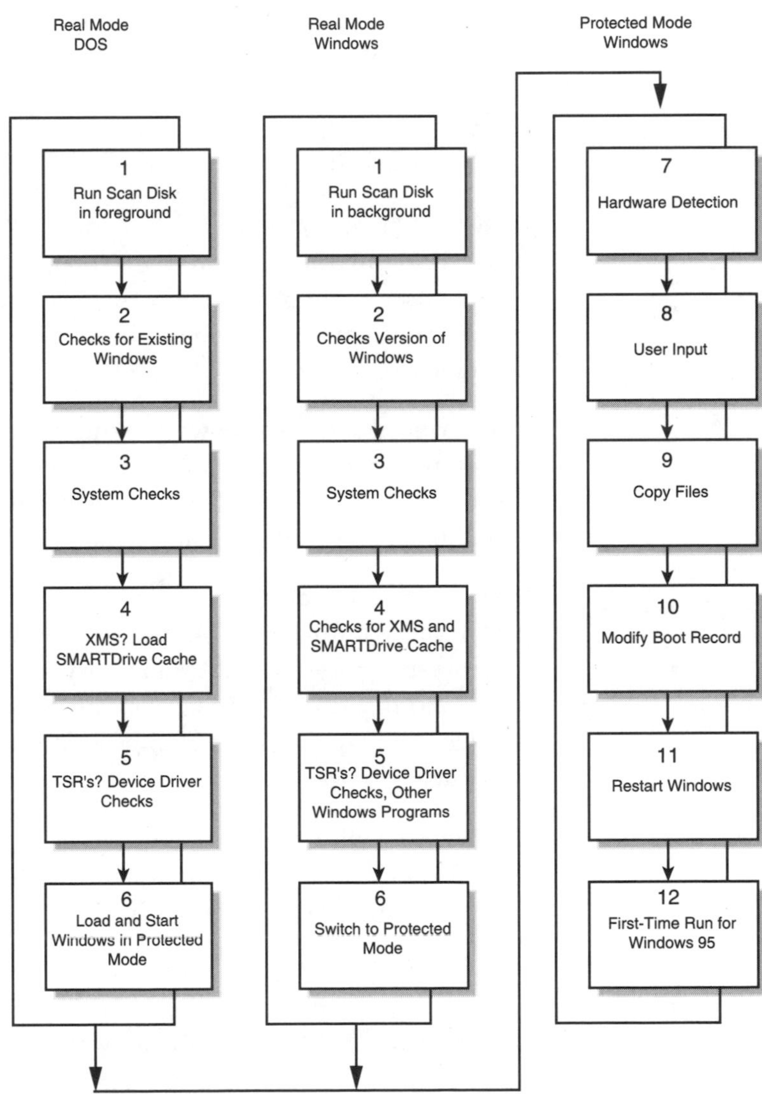

Figure 1.1

The workstation perspective on the Windows 95 installation process.

The Windows 95 Setup program automatically takes 12 steps during installation. You will not be aware that these steps are being performed; however, you should understand what is happening to the computer during installation. The 12 steps are as follows:

1. From DOS, the Windows 95 Setup program runs the ScanDisk version 7.0 program in the foreground.

   From Windows, the Windows 95 Setup program runs the ScanDisk 7.0 in the background, after displaying a message box about how long the process will take and asking the user to click on Continue to perform a routine check on the computer.

2. From DOS, the Windows 95 Setup program searches the local hard drives for a previous version of Windows 3.1 or better. If found, the Windows 95 Setup program suggests that the user start the existing version of Windows and then run the Setup program. You can bypass this suggestion and continue to run from DOS.

   From Windows, the Windows 95 Setup program checks the version number because it needs Windows 3.1 or better in order to run successfully. If you are trying to run from Windows 3.0, an error message should appear.

3. System checks are done to confirm the computer is capable of running Windows 95. These checks provide information on processor, amount of RAM memory, amount of disk space, and the MS-DOS version on the computer. If there is a problem, the Windows 95 Setup program will halt and inform the user.

4. The Windows 95 Setup program checks for extended memory (XMS) and installs an XMS provider if none is present. If there is not any existing disk caching loaded, the Windows 95 Setup program automatically loads SmartDrive.

5. Certain Terminate-and-Stay-Resident (TSR) programs and Device Drivers can cause problems with the Windows 95 installation. Those known to cause problems are tested for and either closed or unloaded. If unable to close or unload them, the Windows 95 Setup program halts and asks the user to disable or close them before re-starting.

From Windows, the program checks for any other processes running and asks the user to close those processes before continuing.

6. From DOS, the Windows 95 Setup program installs a minimal Windows 3.*x* environment and starts it with a shell=setup.exe command, running in protected mode.

   From Windows, the Windows 95 Setup program switches to protected mode. At this point, a Windows graphical user interface is shown to the user.

7. From this step onwards, the Windows 95 Setup program runs the same, whether started from DOS or Windows. Certain user information gets gathered, such as where to install Windows 95, what setup option to use (typical, portable, compact, or custom), user name and company, and other related information.

   Hardware detection is accomplished, as the Windows 95 Setup program examines the computer for all installed hardware devices. The Registry gets created to contain the hardware configuration information for the computer.

8. The Windows 95 Setup program asks for user input on what components to install, how to configure the network, identification information, and whether to create a Windows 95 startup disk. If the Windows 95 Setup program cannot determine the hardware or configuration settings, the user is prompted to provide the information.

9. The required files are copied onto the computer's hard drive, according to where the Windows 95 Setup program was instructed to install them.

10. After all files have been copied, then the Boot Records are modified. This is where the computer is changed from its previous operating system to Windows 95.

11. The computer gets restarted with Windows 95.

12. There are some first-time run programs that run when Windows 95 is installed. These include the Plug and Play hardware configuration (if any of these hardware devices exist), plus any final system configuration: setting up the control panel, migrating existing program group settings, adding programs in the Start Menu, creating Windows Help, MS-DOS program settings, and setting the time zone. A final reboot might be required to finalize any newly installed Plug and Play hardware devices.

From the User's Perspective

From a user's perspective, much of the Windows 95 installation process is automatic. Microsoft uses a Setup Wizard to guide you through the installation, prompting for information and requesting some decisions throughout the entire process. A lot of effort was expended in making the installation easy for the user. This section covers the typical interaction that you as a normal user will see during the Windows 95 installation.

As soon as you start the Windows 95 Setup program, a dialog box indicates that a routine check is being run on the system. During this earliest phase, several files needed to run Setup are copied to the local computer, and Setup runs ScanDisk to check the integrity of the hard disk. If successful, another dialog box appears as the Setup Wizard is being initialized.

The license agreement is shown. To continue with the installation, you must respond and agree to the licensing terms. If the licensing terms are declined, the Windows 95 Setup program terminates.

If the hard drive does not contain a copy of the software to be upgraded, you will be prompted to insert a disk to verify qualification for the upgrade. Usually this does not happen, because a previous, qualifying version of software is already installed on the hard drive.

The Setup Wizard, once loaded, divides the remaining activity in the Windows 95 installation into the following three parts:

- **Gathering User and Computer Information.** You are prompted for information that the Windows 95 Setup program needs to complete the setup. This part includes the hardware detection done when analyzing your computer.
- **Copying Windows 95 Files.** The Windows 95 Setup program copies those files to your computer that are required based on your hardware configuration and the components you have chosen to install.
- **Restarting the Computer and Finishing Setup.** Windows 95 starts up and completes the final settings needed to run properly.

The Setup Wizard initial screen (see fig. 1.2) and the steps it follows to complete the Windows 95 installation reinforce this user perspective. This initial screen appears again at each of the three parts of the process, with the current part highlighted in bold type, and with a small triangular arrow pointing to it on the screen. This allows you to follow along in the Windows 95 installation process.

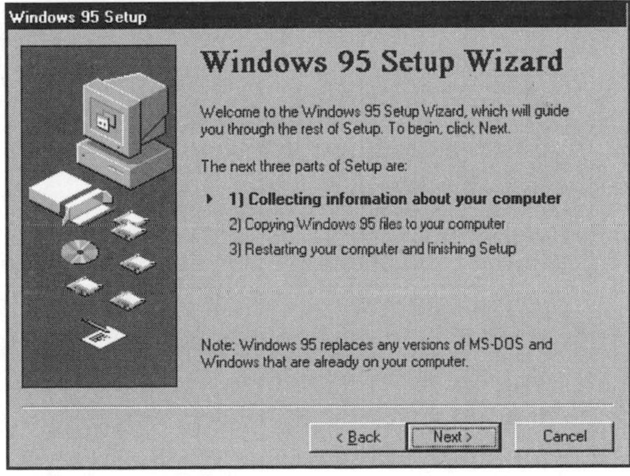

Figure 1.2

The user's perspective on the Windows 95 installation process.

Gathering Information

The first part of the Windows 95 installation process gathers information about the computer.

This only begins after the following has been done:

- The startup process has been completed.
- A routine check has been run on the system.
- The Windows 95 Setup Wizard has loaded.
- You have approved the Microsoft Windows 95 license agreement by entering OK.

> To navigate through the Windows 95 Setup program, click the Next or **B**ack buttons. Either click on the Next button or press Enter to accept the choices you have made on the current screen and to continue forward to the next screen. Click on the **B**ack button to return to the previous screen to review or make changes.

Choosing the Windows Directory

Should a previous installation of Windows 3.1*x* or Windows for Workgroups 3.*x* exist, the Windows 95 Setup program asks you to confirm the directory where Windows 95 is to be installed. The directory containing the existing Windows installation is selected, by default (see fig. 1.3).

Should you choose to install Windows 95 in a new directory, you might need to re-install all the Windows-based applications. This is because Windows 95 uses the Registry rather than initialization (*.INI) files in Windows 3.*x* for storing configuration information. It is also because application support (*.DLL) files normally found in the Windows 3.*x* System directory will be missing from the new Windows 95 directory.

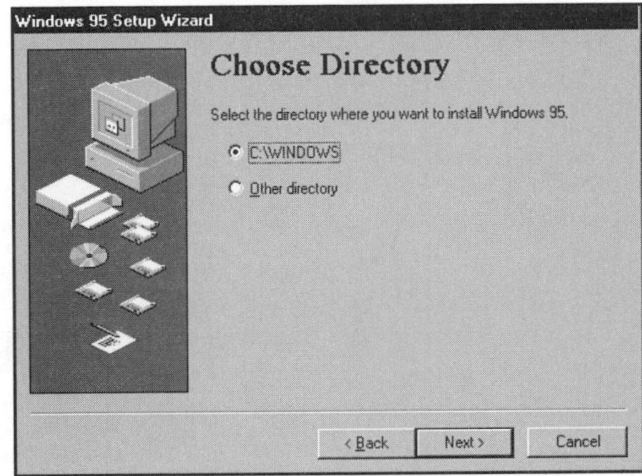

Figure 1.3

Choose the directory in which to install Windows 95.

The Windows 95 Setup program checks next for previously installed components and whether or not there is sufficient disk space on the computer. If the Windows 95 Setup program thinks there is not enough disk space, you will get a warning. As a general rule, pay close attention to any warnings while running the Windows 95 installation.

Selecting the Type of Setup

The Windows 95 Setup program asks you to select the type of setup you want. For a description of these options, refer to table 1.2 in the "Setup Type and Hard Drive Space Requirements" section. By default, the Typical Setup Option is selected.

Figure 1.4 shows the Setup Options dialog box where you choose the type of setup you want to install.

Although the Typical Setup Option is the default, it is usually the easiest, fastest, and safest way to install Windows 95. The detection process is much simpler, as most hardware gets automatically detected and configured with default settings.

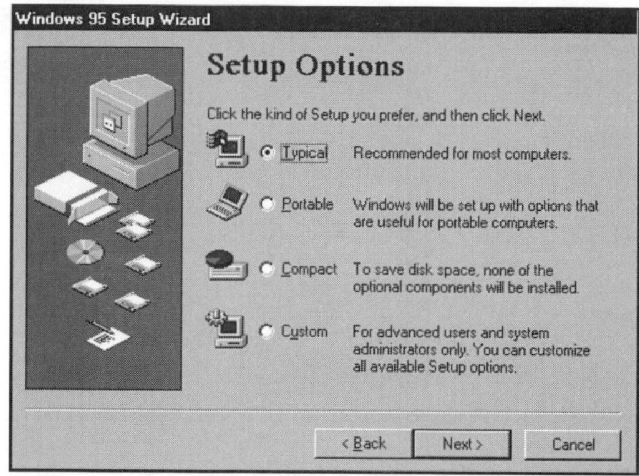

Figure 1.4

Choosing the type of setup option.

However, for network administrators and service technicians, the Custom Setup Option offers the most flexibility and control over the detection process and the configuration settings. This option is used when the computer's hardware components are not using the normal default settings. It also is used when the Windows 95 Setup program needs to be told about hardware it will not automatically recognize during hardware detection.

Providing User Information

Whatever setup option is selected, you will be asked to supply user information (see fig. 1.5). Windows 95 uses this information to identify both the user's name and company. This information will show up in the Windows 95 Help About dialog boxes and the FAX configuration dialog box. The user name also gets truncated and is used to populate the Computer Name and Description fields on the Computer Identification Screen later in the Setup process.

You must type and verify a response for Setup to continue.

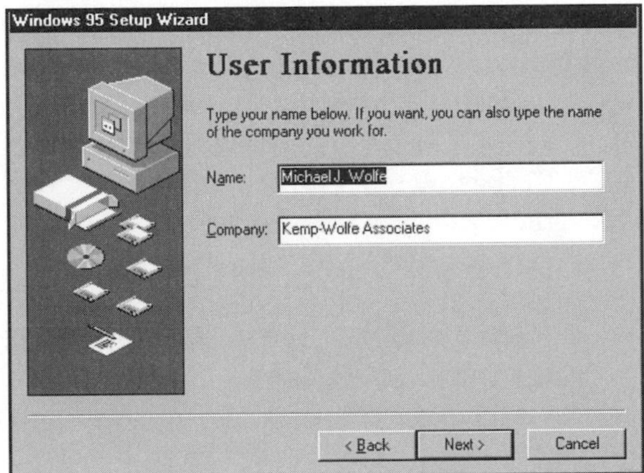

Figure 1.5

Entering user information.

Windows 95 Setup next requests a product identification number. You must type and verify a response for Setup to continue, or just choose **N**ext to continue. If no product identification number is entered, a warning message appears; choose **I**gnore to continue. The Product ID dialog box might not appear if you are installing Windows 95 from the network, depending on the license agreement at your site. The product ID number can be found on your Windows 95 floppy disks, CD-ROM jacket, or on your Certificate of Authenticity.

Analyzing Your Computer

After you enter the user information, the Windows 95 Setup program prepares to analyze your computer. This is the hardware detection phase. Setup will search automatically for the all basic system components such as disk drives and controllers, display devices, pointing devices, and keyboards. The detection process involves a series of approaches to detect these hardware devices.

The first approach determines whether the computer is already running Windows 95. If so, any Plug and Play components are identified and noted.

The second approach is called *safe detection.* This involves methodically searching the computer for software clues that can indicate the presence of certain devices. The CONFIG.SYS, AUTOEXEC.BAT, and all Initialization (*.INI) files are checked. Certain memory locations are checked for installed drivers. If these safe methods suggest the presence of a device, then it gets configured.

If some devices cannot be identified during this safe detection, you will be prompted for the existence of certain classes of devices (see fig. 1.6). These classes of devices are the following:

- CD-ROM drives (Proprietary Cards)
- Sound, MIDI, or Video Capture Cards
- Network adapters
- SCSI devices

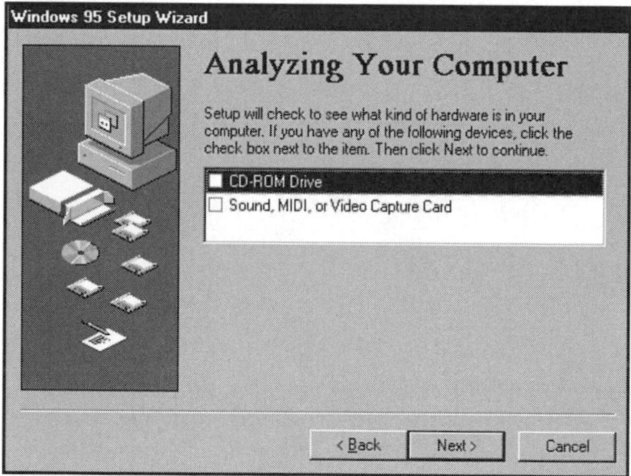

Figure 1.6

Analyzing your computer.

The third approach involves interactive query routines to spot any additional devices. This process of examining specific memory locations, testing values and return codes, and actively probing for devices can cause the computer to lockup during hardware detection. If the computer should fail during this detection process, you will need to re-boot, and restart the Windows 95 Setup program once again. The Setup Failure and Recovery process will avoid the trouble area, and continue from that point. Troubleshooting is discussed later in this chapter in the section "Troubleshooting Setup and System Startup."

For information about specific device types supported in Windows 95, see the Manufacturers and Models lists in the Add New Hardware wizard, as well as the Windows 95 README and SETUP.TXT files.

Hardware Detection

The hardware detection process can take several minutes. The progress indicator shows what portion of hardware detection has been completed. Notice that this is also the point at which Windows 95 Setup can stall if hardware detection fails for a particular system component, see figure 1.7.

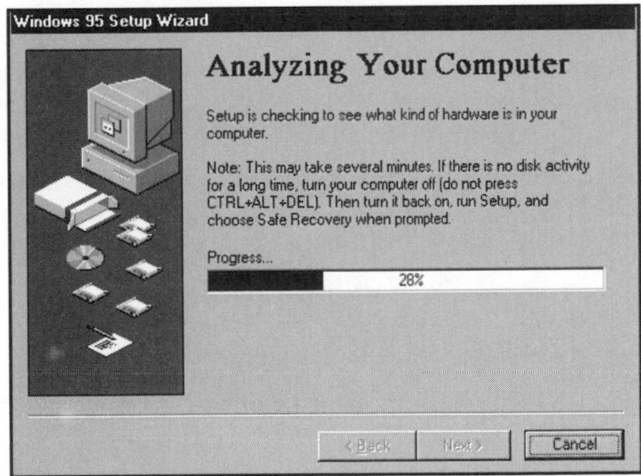

Figure 1.7

The hardware detection phase.

Getting Connected

After the hardware detection completes, the Windows 95 Setup program asks whether or not you want to install a variety of tools that allow you to access various services. The three choices included in the Windows 95 installation are the following:

- **The Microsoft Network.** Installs files required to access the Microsoft Network (MSN). MSN is an online server run by Microsoft that enables electronic mail, bulletin board access, chat sessions online, file library information, and Internet connectivity. When you select this, you do not automatically sign-up, that must be done later. In order to have access, you must have a modem.
- **Microsoft Mail.** Installs files that enable connectivity to a Microsoft Mail Post Office running on a local area network file server. This component is only the service provider portion, which is to distinguish it from the Microsoft Exchange client application, which enables it.
- **Microsoft FAX.** Installs files that enable you to use your computer to send and receive faxes from the computer. In order to use this, you must have a fax modem.

If any of these three choices are selected by you, the Microsoft Exchange client application is installed as well (see fig. 1.8). This extra component requires another 4.6 MB of hard disk space, plus a minimum of 8 MB of RAM to operate properly.

Windows Components

The Windows Components screen is a key screen. The Windows 95 Setup program asks you whether or not you want to install the common components. This is based upon the setup option (Typical, Portable, Compact or Custom) that was selected previously. As stated before, the Custom Setup Option gives you the most control over the Windows 95 installation process. Under the Custom Setup Option you will not even see this screen. However, whatever the Setup Option selected, you will get a chance to select amongst the various components (see fig. 1.9).

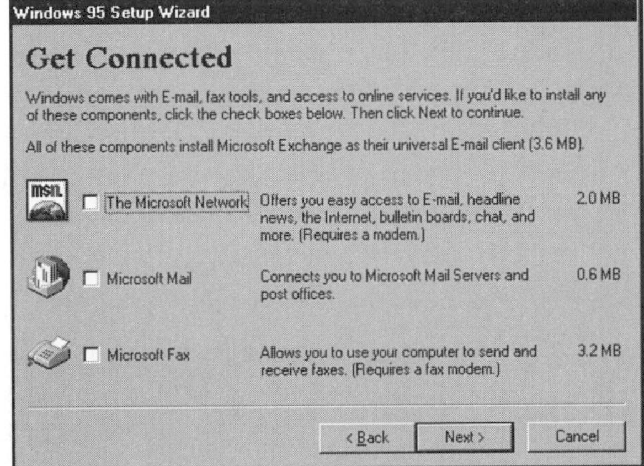

Figure 1.8

Getting connected components.

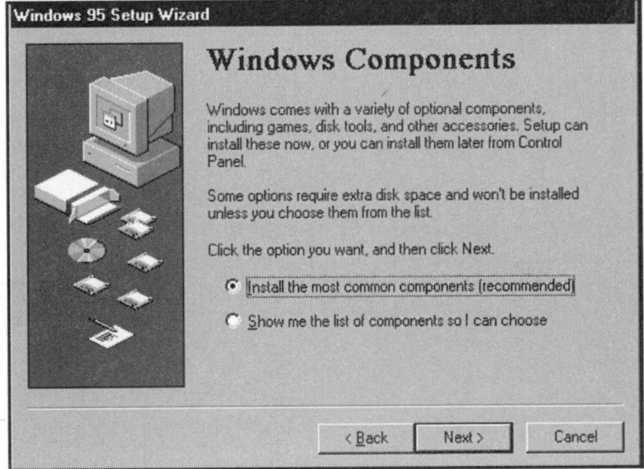

Figure 1.9

Windows components decision.

If you trust the components that Microsoft has recommended for installation under each of these Setup Options, then accept the default selection and Continue. If you know, however, that there are some components you want to add during installation that are optional (refer to table 1.3 in the earlier "Setup Type and Hard Drive Space Requirements" section), select the radio button that states "Show me the list of components so I can choose."

Should you choose the option for customizing the list of components to be installed, or selected the Custom Setup Type of installation, the Windows 95 Setup program shows you the Select Components dialog box (see fig. 1.10). This is the one place where you will see actual information about the amount of cumulative disk space required for the Windows 95 installation. As each component is either selected or deselected, the space needed by the Windows 95 Setup program will change.

Figure 1.10

Selecting Windows components.

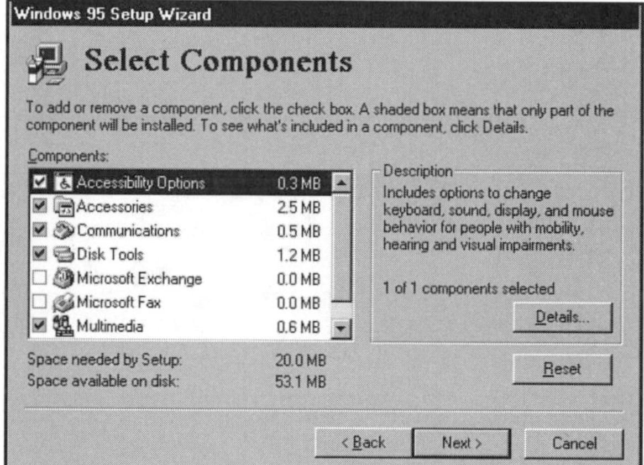

Within the Select Components dialog box, use the following instructions to select or deselect components:

- From the **C**omponents list, select a component category, and then click the **D**etails button. A dialog box appears, listing the components in the category.
- Select the component you want to install, and then click OK. To add a component, make sure the component is checked.
- To prevent a component from being installed, make sure the component is not checked.

You can install or remove any of these components after Windows 95 is installed. You can achieve this by using the Add/Remove Programs option in Control Panel, which will be discussed in Chapter 4.

In Exercise 1.5, you calculate the disk space required to install every optional hardware component.

Exercise 1.5: Determining Hard Disk Space Required for Installing All Optional Components

While doing an actual Windows 95 installation (see Exercise 1.6 later in this chapter), determine how many MBs of additional hard disk space are required to install every component listed above and beyond the hard disk space required for the base Windows 95 operating system. Use the **R**eset button to return to the original pre-selected components.

If you add up all the greatest numbers in the size column of table 1.3, the total for all the components listed is approximately 36 MB.

Network Connection

The Windows 95 Setup program allows you to specify network components and settings. With a Typical Setup Option installation, this will be done for you if you have a network adapter or choose to install Dial-Up Networking. The Network Wizard will allow you to configure these settings. Because this is covered in greater detail in Chapter 5, "Networking and Interoperability," this discussion is bypassed for the moment.

The Windows 95 Setup program provides appropriate settings based on the hardware and software detection for the network components running when you start Setup. You should accept the default settings unless you know that particular settings need to be changed. Those settings can always be changed later.

Identification

The Windows 95 Setup program, after configuring network components and settings, will prompt for a unique identifier for your computer. The rules for naming were covered earlier in the section "What Setup Information Is Needed?" In the Identification screen, you are asked for a computer name, a workgroup if you plan to use Microsoft Networks, and an optional computer description (see fig. 1.11).

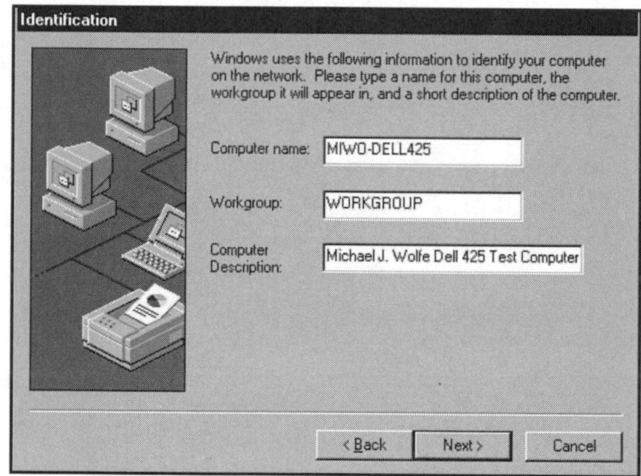

Figure 1.11

Identification for Microsoft networking.

Creating the Startup Disk

A startup disk is a Windows 95 bootable floppy disk that contains utilities you can use to troubleshoot a malfunctioning system. The startup disk loads the operating system and presents an MS-DOS command line. It is strongly recommended that you create a startup disk for Windows 95. You can create a Windows 95 startup disk during the file copy phase of Windows 95 Setup (see fig. 1.12). You can also create or update a disk after the Windows 95 installation by using the Add/Remove Programs option in Control Panel.

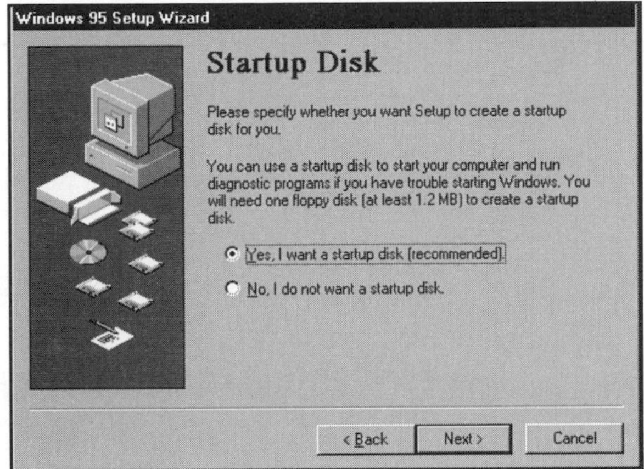

Figure 1.12

Creating a Windows 95 startup disk.

To create a startup disk, Windows 95 formats the floppy disk in drive A, and then copies files to the disk in drive A. These 16 files take up 948 KB of space on a 1.44-MB floppy disk. Table 1.6 describes the files that are copied. Other programs and files need to be added to support access to CD-ROM drives, the network, or any other special requirements.

Table 1.6

Files Found on the Startup Disk

File	Description
attrib.exe	File attribute utility
chkdsk.exe	Disk check utility
command.com	Core operating system file
debug.exe	Debug utility
drvspace.bin	Disk compression utility
ebd.sys	Utility for the startup disk
edit.com	Text editor
fdisk.exe	Disk partition utility

continues

Table 1.6 Continued

File	Description
format.com	Disk format utility
io.sys	Core operating system file
msdos.sys	Core operating system file
regedit.exe	Real-mode Registry Editor
scandisk.exe	Disk status and repair utility
scandisk.ini	Disk status utility configuration file
sys.com	System transfer utility
uninstal.exe	Uninstall utility

For recovery purposes, you might also want to copy the following files into a subdirectory on the startup disk: SYSTEM.DAT, CONFIG.SYS, AUTOEXEC.BAT, WIN.INI, and SYSTEM.INI, plus any CD-ROM or other device drivers. If you do not place these files into a subdirectory, you'll have to rename them to prevent problems with the startup disk.

It is strongly recommended that you create at least one startup disk during a Windows 95 Setup. If you want to create a startup disk after Windows 95 has been installed, you can use the Add/Remove Programs option in Control Panel to create one. Because there is nothing special about a Windows 95 Startup Disk, you can save some time during Windows 95 installations by not creating extras.

After hardware detection is complete and Windows 95 Setup has obtained all required information, the next phase of Windows 95 Setup begins. During this phase, the Windows 95 files are copied to the destination drive and directory.

Copying Windows 95 Files

This second part of the Windows 95 installation process uses the information gathered in the first part to start copying all the files it needs. The source for these files are the Windows 95 Cabinet (*.CAB) files. If you are installing from floppy disks, here comes the floppy shuffle. Installing from CD-ROM or from the network is a lot faster. Depending upon the speed of your computer and where the Windows 95 installation files are coming from, this part can take anywhere from 20 minutes to an hour (see fig. 1.13).

Figure 1.13

Copying Windows 95 files.

The first group of files copied are those used to create a startup disk. At about the 20 percent stage, if you had chosen to have the Windows 95 Setup program create a startup disk, Setup asks you to insert a floppy disk into drive A. The disk does not need to be formatted or empty, but any information you have stored on the disk will be permanently deleted. After you insert the disk, click OK to create the startup disk. The Windows 95 Setup program formats the disk and copies the appropriate files (see table 1.6). This disk will be useful when troubleshooting problems with Windows 95.

When the copying of Windows 95 files is completed, the Windows 95 Setup program updates the configuration files. This process can take a couple of minutes. Finally, the Windows 95 Setup program asks you to remove any disks from the floppy disk drives (see fig. 1.14). After you click on Finish the computer is restarted and the third and final part of the installation process begins.

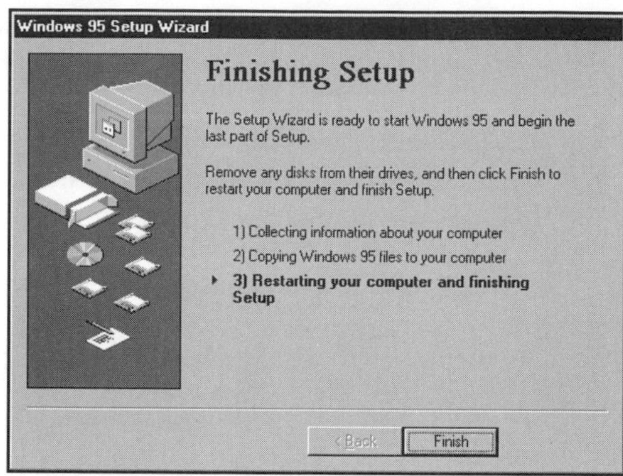

Figure 1.14

Restarting for final Windows 95 installation.

Preparing the Computer to Restart

Just before actually restarting the computer, the Windows 95 Setup program renames existing MS-DOS boot files, copies a new IO.SYS and MSDOS.SYS, and modifies the boot records and the boot track to point to the new IO.SYS file.

Up to this point in the Windows 95 installation, your old operating system was still available should the Windows 95 installation fail. The Safe Recovery feature of Windows 95 would allow you to simply restart the Windows 95 Setup program in your old operating system. Now you are running Windows 95. Beyond this point, if the Windows 95 Setup program should fail, you'll need to restart in Windows 95 to complete the installation. For most cases, the remainder of the Windows 95 installation goes easily.

Restarting Your Computer and Completing Setup

This initial boot-up of Windows 95 is called *First-Time Run,* because it is the first time that Windows 95 has been started on this computer. The standard Windows 95 bitmap is displayed, with the lower banner indicating that this the first time startup. This is the third and final part of the Windows 95 installation.

Windows 95 might prompt you to log on to the computer. The user ID and password entered can optionally be saved into a Password List (*.PWL) file.

Windows 95 sets up the hardware configurations and recognizes any Plug and Play devices.

Finally, Windows 95 asks you to complete several configuration options. These are the run-once options that Windows 95 starts the first time it is run. These run-once options are the following:

- **Control Panel configuration.** Sets up the control panel icons and programs.
- **Programs on the Start Menu configuration.** Builds the Start Menu shortcut, converts old Program Manager Groups into folders and menu selections.
- **Windows Help File configuration.** Builds the Help File index for search capability.
- **MS-DOS Program Settings.** Creates the default MS-DOS shortcut.
- **Time Zone configuration.** You are asked to select the time zone appropriate to your location, and whether or not the clock should automatically adjust to Daylight Savings changes. This is a nice graphic map representation where you can click on a location on the map and it selects the appropriate time zone for you. You can adjust both date and time later from either the Control Panel or from the Task Bar.
- **Printer configuration.** You can use the Printer Wizard to define either a local or network printer. You can add printers later using the Printers folder located in My Computer. This configuration option might not always appear. If printers were set up under an earlier version of Windows that was updated to Windows 95, the previous printer configuration is used.

Completing Windows 95 Setup

Depending on which options you selected during Setup, the hardware devices you have, or the computer you have, additional Run-Once options might need to be completed. One example is the wizard for configuring MIDI devices. After all the Run-Once options are completed, all of the files are installed, and the computer is ready to run Windows 95. Some hardware devices, including Plug-and-Play-enabled hardware devices, might require yet another reboot of the computer before they are fully configured.

Setup Failure Detection and Recovery

Windows 95 has been designed to install without problems. However, Murphy's Law states that "whatever can go wrong, will." Hardware and software can cause problems during a Windows 95 installation. So Microsoft has wisely built in mechanisms for the Windows 95 Setup program to detect failure and to recover automatically. It might not be a very sophisticated process, but it does ensure a high percentage of successful Windows 95 installations.

The Windows 95 Setup program maintains a setup log (SETUPLOG.TXT) during the installation and can determine where failures have occurred. The most likely place for failure is during hardware detection. A detection log (DETLOG.TXT) keeps track of what the Windows 95 Setup program discovers during the hardware detection phase. These files will be covered in the next section.

If any previous attempt to install Windows 95 has failed, Windows 95 Setup provides you with an option to use the Safe Recovery feature or to simply run a full new Setup process (see fig. 1.15). If the Safe Recovery dialog box appears when you start the Windows 95 Setup program, you should always select the Use Safe Recovery option. When you select this option, Windows 95 Setup can use various built-in methods to avoid the problems that occurred previously.

The following are basic Safe Recovery rules for you to know in case a failure happens:

- Before hardware detection begins, the Windows 95 Setup program uses SETUPLOG.TXT to determine the point of failure when you restart. The Windows 95 Setup program then knows what to redo and what it can skip.

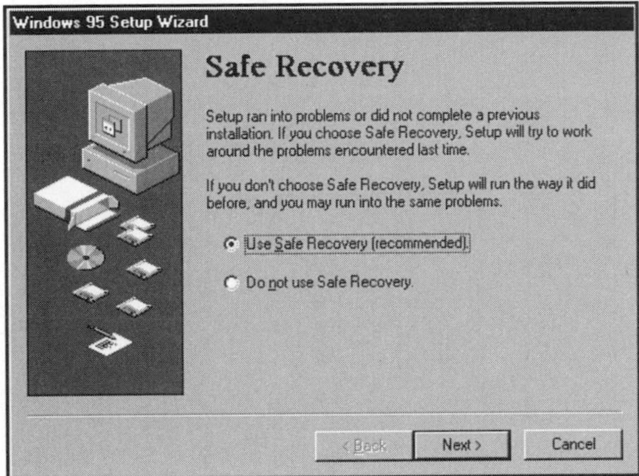

Figure 1.15

Using Safe Recovery.

- During hardware detection a DETCRASH.LOG is created. When the Windows 95 Setup program is restarted, it finds this file and uses it to determine which detection module was running at the point of failure. In a Safe Recovery mode, the Windows 95 Setup program reads the Registry to verify all the devices detected already, and skips any detection modules up to the point of failure. It also skips any detection modules that caused the failure, or any previously logged failure. Safe Recovery then proceeds to the next detection module. When the hardware detection phase finishes, the DETCRASH.LOG is deleted.
- After hardware detection phase finishes, the Windows 95 Setup program recognizes that the hardware detection is successfully completed, and will skip past this point. It assumes that all the necessary hardware information is stored in the Registry.

The Safe Recovery process depends on where in the Windows 95 installation process the Windows 95 Setup program reached before encountering problems. It continues from that point onward, attempting to bypass the problems. Although this approach enables the Windows 95 Setup program to complete the Windows 95 installation, it might leave these problems for you to resolve later.

To continue if Windows 95 Setup stops during hardware detection, do the following:

1. Press F3, or click the Cancel button to quit Setup.

   If the computer does not respond to the Cancel button, restart the computer by turning it off and then back on again. Do not just warm boot or hit the reset button.

2. Run Setup again. The Windows 95 Setup program prompts you to use Safe Recovery to recover the failed Windows 95 installation.
3. Choose Use Safe Recovery (should be the default), and then click on the Next button.
4. Repeat your installation choices. Hardware detection then runs again, but the Windows 95 Setup program skips the portion that caused the initial failure.
5. If the computer stops again during the hardware detection process, repeat this procedure until the hardware detection portion of Setup completes successfully.

Your most likely point of failure will occur during the hardware detection phase. With the millions of Intel computers in use today, the countless number of hardware configurations, old legacy hardware, and the new Plug and Play hardware available, this is where you are going to see most of the problems. Only a limited number of Interrupts (IRQs), DMA channels, I/O address assignments, and upper memory space allocations are available. There might be conflicts—especially if you add multimedia capability, CD-ROMs, Network Interface Cards, SCSI adapters, and other hardware devices to your computer.

These resource conflicts might already be resolved before you begin the installation of Windows 95. If your computer is running successfully, and no hardware changes are made, you can reasonably expect that simply upgrading to Windows 95 will not create any problems. If the computer is being upgraded with new hardware devices at the same time as the upgrade to Windows 95, however, conflicts might occur. It is much easier to resolve these conflicts if the new hardware devices are added after Windows 95 is installed.

Safe Recovery helps you blow safely past the hardware detection conflicts. It does not solve them. You'll need to be knowledgeable about the computer configuration in order to uncover the conflicts and fix them. As you install Windows 95 across a variety of computers, you will very likely get this opportunity.

If the Windows 95 Setup program fails after the boot records have been modified, you would simply restart Windows 95 to complete the installation. There is no need to start the Windows 95 Setup program from the beginning.

Recognize Files Used in Troubleshooting the Installation Process

The Windows 95 Setup program creates several log files—SETUPLOG.TXT, DETLOG.TXT, DETCRASH.LOG—during hardware detection failure, and others—NETLOG.TXT and BOOTLOG.TXT—as Windows 95 starts up the first time. Some of these have been mentioned previously, but several are new. The following list looks at these files in detail:

- **SETUPLOG.TXT.** This is an ASCII text file that contains the Windows 95 Setup information created during installation. As Windows 95 is being installed, entries are written into this text file for each step in sequence. This file will show any error conditions encountered. It is used by the Windows 95 Setup program in case of setup failure, and you can also use it to troubleshoot errors during the installation process.

  The Windows 95 Setup program uses the information contained within SETUPLOG.TXT to ensure that the Windows 95 installation program does not fail twice on the same problem. When you restart the Windows 95 Setup program after a failure, the contents are reviewed to see which process started, but did not complete successfully. These processes are skipped, and the next process in sequence is run. The DETLOG.TXT and DETCRASH.LOG files, which are discussed next, are used to skip any hardware detection modules that failed.

Buried on the CD-ROM version of Windows 95 is a helpful program called LOGVIEW.EXE, which enables you to examine all the text files mentioned in this list in a manner similar to the SYSEDIT.EXE program found in earlier versions of Windows. To find this program, look in the OTHER\MISC\LOGVIEW directory.

SETUPLOG.TXT is stored as a hidden file on the computer's root directory. Information is added to this file in the same order as the installation process. If you need to determine what caused the Windows 95 Setup program to fail, look at the entries at the bottom of this file before restarting again.

- **DETLOG.TXT.** This is an ASCII text file that contains a record of all devices found during the hardware detection phase of installation. If a device is found, the detected parameters are identified and recorded.

  If the hardware detection phase should cause the computer to stall or lock up, a binary file named DETCRASH.LOG is created. While DETLOG.TXT is an ASCII file for you to read, the Windows 95 Setup program reads the binary information in DETCRASH.LOG to determine what steps successfully completed.

  DETLOG.TXT is stored as a hidden file on the computer's root directory. Information is added to this file in the same order as the hardware detection phase. If you need to determine what caused the Windows 95 Setup program to fail or lockup, look at the entries at the bottom of this file before restarting again.

- **DETCRASH.LOG.** This is a binary file that only exists during the hardware detection phase. It tracks the entire process in case of errors for the Windows 95 Setup program. You need to be aware of its existence, but you would use the DETLOG.TXT ASCII file to do any troubleshooting.

- **NETLOG.TXT.** This is an ASCII text file that contains a record of all detected network components found during installation. There are four parts to the network detection phase. These correspond with the four class types of network configuration: network clients; network protocols; network adapters; and network services, such as file and print sharing.

  This file is stored as a non-hidden file on the computer's root directory. Information is added to this file in the same order as the network detection phase. If you need to determine what caused the Windows 95 Setup program to not communicate across the network, look at the entries in this file.

- **BOOTLOG.TXT.** This is an ASCII text file that contains a record of the current startup process when starting Windows 95. As Windows 95 is started for the first time, this file gets created automatically. This file records the Windows 95 components and drivers as they are loaded and initialized, and also records the status of each step.

  The information in BOOTLOG.TXT is written in sequence during startup. You might need to examine it closely to determine which error occurred. The *Windows 95 Resource Kit* has a good description of the sections within this file. You can also create this file by pressing F8 during the "Starting Windows 95" startup and selecting menu option 2—normal with a boot log.

  This file is stored as a hidden file on the computer's root directory. Information is added to this file during the Windows 95 startup process. If you need to determine what caused the Windows 95 to fail or lockup, look at the entries within this file before restarting again.

The three key files used to troubleshoot the Windows 95 installation process are the SETUPLOG.TXT, DETLOG.TXT, and BOOTLOG.TXT ASCII text files. The *Windows 95 Resource Kit* provides code for a batch file you can create that looks at these key files and extracts the information.

Troubleshooting Setup and System Startup

The Windows 95 installation is usually successful. But on occasion there can be problems. These problems are usually due to hardware configuration and software difficulties. This section is directed toward helping you troubleshoot both the Windows 95 installation and normal system startup. Some basic troubleshooting techniques are also discussed in much finer detail in the *Windows 95 Resource Kit*'s chapter on general troubleshooting. You should review it.

The author uses a simple approach to problem solving, which you can adopt (or adapt) for your own use as well. This simple approach can be characterized as making the solution "FIT" the problem. The following details how this particular problem-solving approach works:

- **F**ind the problem by drawing a box around it. Collect the symptoms of the problem, under what conditions it occurs, and when it happens. Draw a box around the problem to determine and narrow the scope. Consult any technical resources to see if it is a known problem. If the problem is a known problem, it might already have a known solution or work-around.
- **I**solate and diagnose the problem. Make an assumption about what is causing the problem. Don't overlook the obvious. Ask what has recently changed, and why.

- Test the solution to the problem. By eliminating recent changes or controlling the number of variables, you can methodically test each modification to see if it solves the problem. Return the computer to the original state after each test. If you change three things and this somehow fixes the problem, which change was the effective one? Document your solution for the next time, or for the next person.

Troubleshooting Aids for Setup and Startup

Windows 95 has many troubleshooting aids to assist you in fixing problems that occur during either the setup or the startup process. The following troubleshooting aids are available:

- Safe Recovery during Windows 95 Setup
- Windows 95 Startup Disk
- Installed Components Verification
- Startup Menu Options and Safe Mode
- WIN.COM switches

Because both Safe Recovery and the Windows 95 Startup Disk have been discussed previously, please review those earlier sections of this chapter. The remaining three troubleshooting aids are covered in this section.

Installed Components Verification

Windows 95, like the previous versions of Windows and DOS, is comprised of many system programs and files. The loss, data corruption, or incorrect replacement of a single system program or file could result in problems when running Windows 95. The system program or file might have been inadvertently deleted, become corrupted because of an errant application, been infected by a virus, or been updated to a different version that will not work with all applications or devices. There can be many likely causes.

Windows 95 provides a setup option for verification of installed components when the Windows 95 Setup program detects an existing Windows 95 installation. Figure 1.16 illustrates the screen that is displayed when running the Windows 95 Setup program on a computer that has Windows 95 already installed.

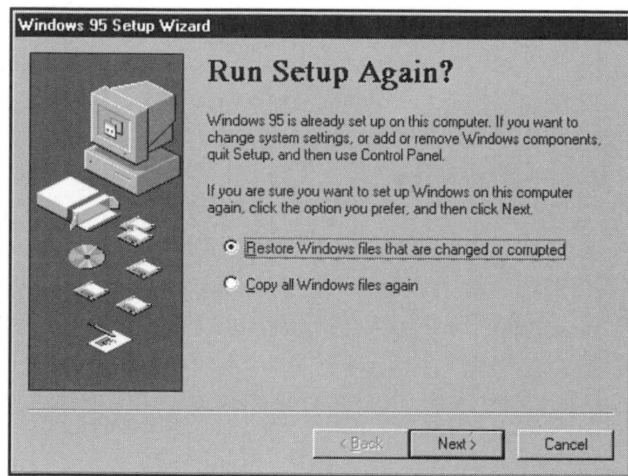

Figure 1.16

Verifying Windows 95 installation.

When you run the verify option, the Windows 95 Setup program reads SETUPLOG.TXT for the installed components and then reruns the Setup process to verify all system components. If verify finds a missing or damaged file, the Windows 95 Setup program reinstalls that file. As part of the verification, VMM32.VXD also gets rebuilt.

Startup Menu Options and Safe Mode

Should the system fail to start and need to be re-booted, Windows 95 will display a startup menu. Table 1.7 outlines the menu items on the startup menu. You can also invoke this startup menu yourself if you immediately press the F8 key when you see the message at boot-up saying "Starting Windows 95."

Table 1.7

Microsoft Windows 95 Startup Menu

Menu Item	Description
Normal	Start Windows, loading all normal startup files and Registry values.
Logged	Runs system startup, creating a startup (\BOOTLOG.TXT) log file named BOOTLOG.TXT on the boot directory.
Safe Mode	Start Windows, bypassing startup files and using only basic system drivers. You can also start this option by pressing F5 or typing **win /d:m** at the command prompt.
Safe Mode with network support	Start Windows, bypassing startup files and using only basic system drivers, including basic networking. You can also start this option by pressing F6 or typing **win /d:n** at the command prompt.
Step-By-Step Confirmation	Start Windows, confirming startup files line by line. You can also start this option by pressing **F8** when the Startup menu is displayed.
Command Prompt Only	Starts the operating system with startup files and Registry, displaying only the command prompt.
Safe Mode Command Prompt Only	Starts the operating system in Safe Mode and displays only the command prompt, bypassing startup files. You can also start this option by pressing SHIFT+F5.
Previous version of MS-DOS	Starts the version of MS-DOS previously in stalled on this computer. You can also start this option by pressing F4. This option is only available if BootMulti=1 is in the MSDOS.SYS file.

Safe Mode

Sometimes Windows 95 does not start properly in the normal way. The opening graphical screen freezes, and the computer does not respond. The Windows 95 Registry might even be corrupted.

Whatever the reason, Windows 95 automatically selects Safe Mode when the computer is re-booted because it detects that system startup has failed. The Windows 95 Startup Menu is displayed, and Safe Mode is the default selection.

Select Safe Mode from the Startup Menu to conduct troubleshooting. Safe Mode bypasses all the startup files, including the Registry, CONFIG.SYS, AUTOEXEC.BAT, and both the [Boot] and [386Enh] sections of the SYSTEM.INI file. It does provide you access to the Windows 95 configuration files, where you can make some corrective changes and then restart Windows 95.

When you start Windows 95 in the Safe Mode, only the mouse, keyboard, and VGA device drivers are loaded. Little Safe Mode messages are posted on each corner of the Windows 95 Desktop as reminders that you are running in Safe Mode. Not all the System Properties information will be available when running in Safe Mode, but at least you have access to make some changes.

Often the best course of action when forced to troubleshoot your computer in Safe Mode is to remove the suspected problem hardware device using the System Properties, Device Manager tab within the Control Panel folder. Although the Registry information is not available to resolve conflicts, removing the hardware device might enable you to restart Windows 95. Then the hardware device can be added back again through the Add New Hardware application in the Control Panel folder. Be sure to let Windows 95 perform a complete hardware detection.

Using incorrect display drivers can also force you into starting Windows 95 in Safe Mode, which loads only a default VGA driver. This is similar to starting Windows NT in VGA Mode, since both startup methods allow you to make corrections to the display drivers.

WIN.COM Switches

When you start the computer at the command prompt, you can use switches with the win command to control the Windows 95 startup for troubleshooting purposes (see table 1.8).

Table 1.8

WIN.COM Command Switches

Switch	Description
/d:f	Turns off 32-bit disk access. This is equivalent to 32BitDiskAccess=False in the SYSTEM.INI file
/d:m	Starts Windows 95 in Safe Mode
/d:n	Starts Windows 95 in Safe Mode with networking support
/d:s	Tells Windows 95 not to use the ROM space between F000 and 1 MB for a break point. This is equivalent to SystemROMBreakPoint=False in the SYSTEM.INI file.
/d:v	Tells Windows 95 to use the ROM routine to handle interrupts from the hard disk controller. This is equivalent to VirtualHDIRQ=False in the SYSTEM.INI file.
/d:x	Excludes all the upper memory area (UMA) from being used by Windows 95. This is equivalent to EMMExclude=A000-FFFF in the SYSTEM.INI file.

Windows 95 System Startup Files

See table 1.9 for a description of the old files used in pre-Windows 95 DOS and the new files used in Windows 95 for system startup. There are not many obvious differences; however, now under Windows 95 the two older MS-DOS system files (IO.SYS and MSDOS.SYS) are replaced by a new IO.SYS. IO.SYS is a real-mode operating system file containing the information needed to start the computer. The new MSDOS.SYS is a text file containing special information for Windows 95. It was kept around for backward compatibility because certain applications require this file to be present before they will install successfully. The CONFIG.SYS and

AUTOEXEC.BAT are mostly optional files under Windows 95, because certain settings are incorporated directly into either the IO.SYS or the MSDOS.SYS files (see table 1.10).

Table 1.9

System Startup Files

Pre-Windows 95 DOS	Windows 95
IO.SYS	IO.SYS
MSDOS.SYS	MSDOS.SYS {text file}
COMMAND.COM	COMMAND.COM
CONFIG.SYS	CONFIG.SYS {optional}
AUTOEXEC.BAT	AUTOEXEC.BAT {optional}

Table 1.10

Default Settings for Windows 95

Setting	Description
HIMEM.SYS	Enables access to High Memory Area(HMA). Loads and runs the real-mode Memory Manager.
DOS=HIGH	Specifies MS-DOS should be loaded into the HMA.
DOS=UMB	If EMM386.EXE is loaded in CONFIG.SYS, the Upper Memory Blocks (UMB) are set to allow both DeviceHigh and LoadHigh settings in the CONFIG.SYS and AUTOEXEC.BAT.
SETVER.EXE	Included for compatibility reasons. Some MS-DOS applications require specific versions of MS-DOS to be running. This TSR-type device responds to those applications that query for version number by responding directly from an internal table.
IFSHLP.SYS	Installable File System (IFS) Helper, which loads device drivers that allow Windows 95 to make calls to the file system.

Setting	Description
FILES=60	Specifies number of file handle buffers to create for files opened by MS-DOS calls. Not required by Windows 95. Included for backward compatibility. Default value is 60.
BUFFERS=30	Specifies number of file buffers to create. Used by applications using IO.SYS calls. Not required by Windows 95. Default value is 30.
LASTDRIVE=Z	Specifies the last drive letter available for assignment. Not required by Windows 95, but included for backward compatibility. If the Windows 95 Setup program finds this value, it is moved into the Registry. Default value is z.
FCBS=4	Specifies the number of file control blocks that can be open at the same time. Older programs might require such a setting in the CONFIG.SYS file. Default value is 4.
STACKS=9,256	Specifies the number and size of stack frames. Not required by Windows 95, but included for backward compatibility. Default value is 9,256.
SHELL= COMMAND.COM	Indicates what command process to use. Adds the /p switch by default to make the command process permanent.
PATH=<*windir*>; <*windir*>\command	Default path statement points to the Windows 95 directory and the Windows 95 command directory.
TMP=<*windir*>\TEMP	Temporary working directory default.
TEMP=<*windir*>\TEMP	Temporary working directory default.
PROMPT=pg	Default MS-DOS prompt option shows current drive and path followed by the greater-than character (>).
COMSPEC=<*windir*> \command\command .com	Another default reference to the command process.

These Windows 95 default settings make it possible to not have either a CONFIG.SYS or an AUTOEXEC.BAT file. In fact, one good method of improving your Windows 95 installation success ratio is renaming both these files just before running the Windows 95 Setup program.

Chapter 35 on general troubleshooting in the *Windows 95 Resource Kit* is a good source of information. As part of your preparation in this exam area, study it carefully.

Troubleshooting Scenarios

The *Windows 95 Resource Kit* lists many of the errors you might encounter with Windows 95. Here are some of the more common ones:

- **The Windows 95 Setup program fails to start.** Check if there is enough free RAM; conventional memory, upper memory, and expanded (XMS) memory—use **mem /c/p** at the DOS command prompt. Check for viruses. Check and disable extra lines in both the CONFIG.SYS and the AUTOEXEC.BAT files.

- **The Windows 95 Setup program starts but reports an error.** These errors usually have an error message, which describes what caused the error. Check for viruses. See the SETUPLOG.TXT and DETLOG.TXT files.

- **The Windows 95 Setup program reports a B1 error.** The older Intel 386 processors are not supported. Upgrade the processor and re-install.

- **The Windows 95 Setup program has problems during the file copy phase.** There could be problems with virus detection software or virus protection BIOS setups. Either unload or disable BIOS virus protection and re-install.

- **The Windows 95 Setup program cannot find a valid boot partition.** A valid MS-DOS partition must exist. Either there is an actual partition error, or disk compression software or network components are mapping over the boot drive. Use FDISK to verify that a valid, active MS-DOS partition exists.

- **The Windows 95 Setup program stalls during the first restart of Windows 95.** Legacy hardware might be incorrectly configured before the Windows 95 installation. Remove settings in the CONFIG.SYS and AUTOEXEC.BAT files. Ensure all SCSI devices are properly terminated. The ISA enumerator (device=ISAPNP.386) in the [386Enh] section of the SYSTEM.INI might need to be commented out by adding a semi-colon in front of the line.

- **At Windows 95 Startup, bad or missing filename.** Where the filename is the actual file causing the problem, check the existence, location, version number, and integrity of the file named. You might need to restart the Windows 95 Setup program with the Verify option to replace missing or damaged files.

- **At Windows 95 Startup, the System Registry File is missing.** The Windows 95 System Registry file is actually two files, SYSTEM.DAT and USER.DAT, which are backed up after each successful startup of Windows 95. These copies are called SYSTEM.DA0 and USER.DA0, and will be used to attempt a recovery. This is very similar to the "Last Known Good Boot" process of Windows NT. See Chapter 4 for more information about troubleshooting the System Registry.

- **At Windows 95 Startup, the wrong programs are running.** The WIN.INI is still processed, as well as the converted Startup Group, which is now the Start Menu Startup folder. You might also have previously designated an alternate Startup Group in the PROGMAN.INI file. Check all these locations and modify as needed. To correct this last item, you will need to alter the Registry, see the *Windows 95 Resource Kit* for details.

- **At Windows 95 Startup, not all devices are available.** The hardware detection phase and subsequent first run configuration of Plug and Play devices might still leave some hardware devices not working correctly. See Chapter 12, "Troubleshooting," for further information about troubleshooting your hardware configuration.

Because the Windows 95 Registry plays such an important role in the operation of Windows 95, it is a good idea to always make backup copies of your Registry files (SYSTEM.DAT and USER.DAT) before making any modifications.

If you create a Windows 95 Startup disk, verify it works before you have to use it. Always add backup copies of the Windows 95 configuration files, including the Registry. A good time for backing up these files and updating the Windows 95 Startup disk is after you have installed new hardware devices or applications, and you have a good working computer configuration.

Another recent book from New Riders Publishing is *Windows 95 Registry Troubleshooting.* You might want to add that to your Windows 95 library.

Installation Exercises

The following section is designed to run you through the process of installing Windows 95 on your computer using a variety of methods. You should have access to at least two computers, one for Windows 95 and the other for Windows NT Server. (You can get by with only a single computer, but the networking exercises will not be possible).

Install the Windows 95 Operating System

Exercise 1.6 should be treated as a normal installation, so run this from the CD-ROM on Computer 1. The end result will be to have Computer 1 running Windows 95.

Exercise 1.6: Windows 95 CD-ROM Setup

Install Windows 95 on Computer 1 using a CD-ROM drive. This is a hands-on exercise that requires about 60 minutes. Walk through the following steps:

1. Reboot Computer 1, loading MS-DOS and Windows for Workgroups. Access the Windows 95 CD-ROM from the File, Run option in Program Manager and start the Windows 95 setup.exe program.

   A routine check of the system is done, followed by the preparation of the Setup Wizard.

2. The software license appears. After reading it, tab or click on the Yes button to continue.

3. The Setup Wizard appears to start collecting information about your computer. Click Next to continue.

4. When prompted for a location to install Windows 95, take the default, which is C:\WINDOWS. Click Next to continue.

5. Windows 95 will prepare the directory, check for installed components and check for available disk space.

6. Because you upgraded from Windows for Workgroups, you will be prompted whether or not to Save System Files. With these files saved, you could easily uninstall Windows 95, if desired. These files take up approximately 6 MB of disk space. If you want to be able to cleanly uninstall Windows 95, as if it were another software application, click on the Yes button and then click Next to continue.

7. Choose the type of installation, the default is Typical. Click Next to continue.

8. For User Information, enter your full name and the name of your organization or company. Click Next to continue.

9. For Product Identification, enter the product key code from the CD-ROM cover.

Setup will analyze your computer, searching for all hardware devices available.

10. If asked to check for specific hardware such as CD-ROM drive or Sound Cards, check the appropriate boxes, then click Next to continue.
11. After hardware detection, a Getting Connected dialog box will appear. Do not select any of these components.
12. You will be prompted to install the default components, as determined by your setup option. Accept the defaults, and click Next to continue.
13. Verify your network configuration, if prompted. For a stand-alone installation, you will not see these screens.
14. If asked to identify your computer and workgroup, enter the appropriate information. Ensure that computer name is unique. Click Next to continue.
15. When asked whether you want to create a Startup Disk, accept the default. Choose Yes, I want a startup disk. Click Next to continue.
16. The Setup Wizard begins copying files to your computer. Click Next to continue.
17. The copy process might take a while, enter a Startup Disk floppy, when prompted.
18. The Setup Wizard reappears to finish the Windows 95 installation on your computer. Click Finish to continue.
19. Windows 95 starts and prompts you for your name and password. The Control Panel, Start Menu, and Help system will be configured.
20. When prompted for Time Zone, click on your approximate location on the world map, which helps select the correct time zone. Click Close when done to continue.
21. If you have a printer, ignore this setting and continue. You will install printers in Chapter 7, "Managing Printers."

22. The Welcome to Windows 95 screen appears. Click on the buttons to take both the Windows 95 Tour and to see What's New in Windows 95.

The Windows 95 Setup program is very automated and modular. In most cases, very little information is required in order to install Windows 95.

Set Up Files for Network Installation and Shared Use

Exercise 1.7 should be treated as a network (or server-based) installation. Run this from the CD-ROM on Computer 1. This requires access to either a mapped, shared drive on Computer 2 or a new separate directory on Computer 1 if using only one computer. Warning: This installation requires up to 87 MB of hard disk storage.

Ensure Computer 2 is running Microsoft Networking under Windows for Workgroups and that both computers are in the same workgroup name. Each computer should be able to see the other before proceeding.

Use Netsetup.exe to install Windows 95 source files on a network server, and to prepare for either network installations or shared installations of Windows 95. (This tool replaces SETUP /A used in earlier versions of Windows.)

It is recommended that you run NETSETUP from the CD-ROM.

For more information about server-based setup, see Chapter 4 of the *Windows 95 Resource Kit.*

Exercise 1.7: Windows 95 Server-Based Setup

1. From Computer 1, with CD-ROM drive, start Windows 95. On Computer 2, install both DOS and WFWG. In this case, the server-based install can be to either Computer 2, as a network shared drive, or to a Windows NT Server or a Novell NetWare Server.

For the purposes of this exercise, use Computer 2. If you only have one computer, install to a new directory.

2. Establish an Install directory share with full rights on Computer 2. If using a Windows NT Server or a NetWare Server, be sure to grant sufficient privileges or rights if required.

3. Run NETSETUP from the ADMIN\NETTOOLS\NETSETUP directory on Computer 1 from the Windows 95 CD-ROM. The server-based setup program can only be run from a computer that is already running Windows 95.

4. The Server Based Setup dialog box, as seen in figure 1.17, will be displayed. Click on the Set **P**ath button to specify the server path where the Windows 95 installation files will be installed. Click OK when done. If the server path was previously defined, the button name is Change **P**ath.

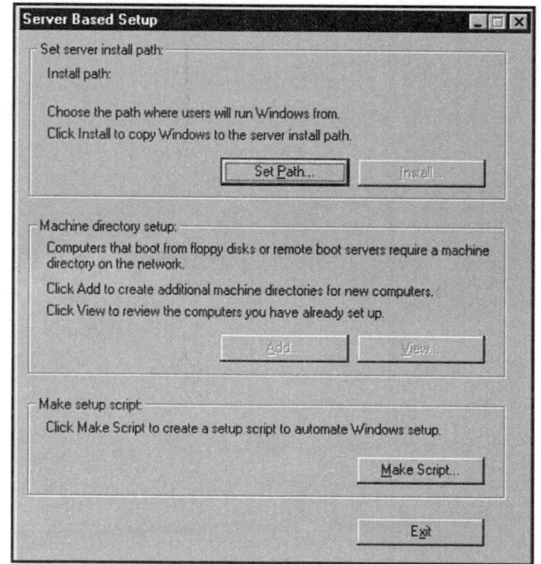

Figure 1.17

Server-based setup.

5. Click on the **I**nstall button to start the installation.

6. You will be presented with a series of dialog boxes. These boxes will confirm the paths to install from and to. The dialog boxes will also specify how the users can install Windows 95 from the server to a local hard drive as a shared copy or

user's choice. Make it user's choice for the purposes of this exercise. Click on OK to continue.

7. Click on **D**on't create setup batch scripts because you will be doing this in the next exercise.
8. Enter the Product Identification number when prompted. Click on OK to continue with the server-based setup.
9. You will receive a dialog box when the server-based setup is complete. Click on OK, but do not close the Window. You want to examine a batch file script in the next exercise.

The Windows 95 server-based setup program is simple, and makes it easy to install Windows 95 on a server. With the Windows 95 installation files on a server, installations are much faster.

Automated Setup Using Batch Files

One of the command-line switches for the Setup program allows the reference to a batch script file that contains the setup options. There are several ways to create this text file. You will use one in Exercise 1.8.

Exercise 1.8: Windows 95 Batch File Creation

1. From Computer 1, with CD-ROM drive, start Windows 95.
2. If you left the server-based Setup program running at the end of Exercise 1.7, then go to step 2. If, however, you are beginning anew, run NETSETUP from the ADMIN\NETTOOLS\NETSETUP directory on Computer 1, from the Windows 95 CD-ROM. The server-based setup program can only be run from a computer already running Windows 95.
3. The Server Based Setup dialog box (refer to figure 1.17) will be displayed. Click on the Make Script button to specify that you want to create a batch script.
4. Select the MSBATCH.INF file from the server-based setup directory. A Properties sheet (see fig. 1.18) will be displayed

that enables you to graphically create a batch script file for use in automating your Windows 95 installations.

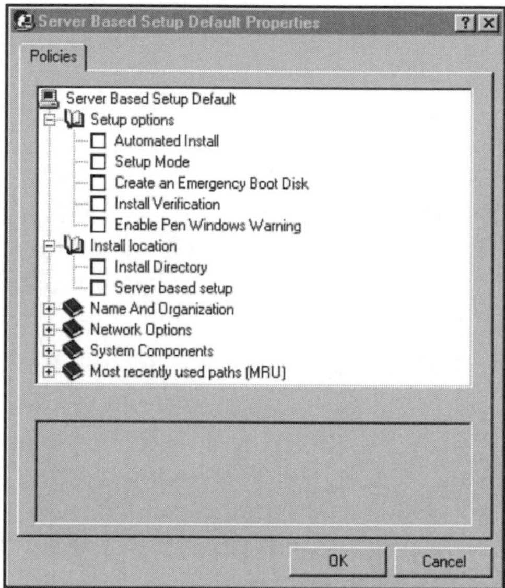

Figure 1.18

Batch file server-based setup.

5. See the *Windows 95 Resource Kit* for full explanation behind each field and check mark. Set a few values, save by clicking on OK, then Exit.

6. Start the Notepad application by choosing Start, **P**rograms, Accessories, Notepad and open the text file MSBATCH.INF in your server-based setup directory. You will see how the information gathered in the previous step is translated into options, fields, and values that the Windows 95 Setup program can read and understand.

Many ways are available to create a custom script file for a Windows 95 installation. As you did in Exercise 1.8, you can use the server-based setup (Netsetup.exe) program. This program also enables you to install source files and create machine directories for a shared network installation. There is another Windows-based program called Batch Setup (Batch.exe) that makes it easy to create custom scripts. Finally, you can use a text editor, such as Notepad (Notepad.exe) to directly edit the custom script file.

See Chapter 5 on custom, automated, and push installations in the *Windows 95 Resource Kit* for further reference material. It is a good idea to read and understand all the basics surrounding automated installation of Windows 95.

Removing Windows 95 from a Computer

If you upgraded from Windows 3.1*x* or Windows for Workgroups 3.*x*, then you will be presented with an option to Save System Files. This saves the existing MS-DOS–based and Windows-based system files and enables you to easily uninstall Windows 95 from the computer if required. These files require about 6 MB of hard disk space. To remove Windows 95, use the Windows 95 Startup Disk's Uninstall (Uninstal.exe) program.

The following exercise works properly only if you selected the Save System Files during the Windows 95 installation. Otherwise, you need to follow a longer series of steps, as described in Chapter 6 of the *Windows 95 Resource Kit* under "Removing Windows 95 with Your Previous Operating System."

Exercise 1.9: Removing Windows 95

1. From Computer 1, place your Windows 95 Startup disk in the floppy drive.
2. From the Start Menu, choose Run. Type **a:\uninstal.exe** and press Enter.
3. From the Windows 95 Uninstall dialog box, click Yes to begin the uninstall process.

   Windows 95 will then shut down, and the uninstall will continue automatically.

Your previous configuration will be restored. When finally prompted, remove the Windows 95 startup disk from the floppy drive, and press Enter to re-boot your computer.

Exercise 1.9 will remove Windows 95 from the computer. To continue with the remaining exercises in this study guide, please either do a standard Windows 95 install to Computer 1, as previously outlined in Exercise 1.6, or a clean Windows 95 install to Computer 1, as outlined in the next exercise, Exercise 1.10.

Clean Windows 95 Installation

How do I load Windows 95 on the hard drive of a computer after formatting the hard disk? This is the key question that many network administrators would like to know the answer to.

Currently, there is no easy way to format a computer's hard drive and copy down an "image" of another standard Windows 95 computer. When used in this context, the word *image* refers to a backup copy of an entire computer's hard drive that is stored on a network file server.

Under MS-DOS and Windows 3.*x*, it is possible to take a standard computer and create an image that could be downloaded on top of a newly formatted hard drive on one or more computers. As long as the computers were roughly identical, this strategy could save you a significant amount of time conducting many installations. Otherwise, you could easily take a day per computer to reinstall and test, on a clean hard drive, the operating system, Windows, and all the applications. This time estimate also assumes you have easy access to all the license software setup disks, and backups of key data files.

This same strategy of creating a Windows 95 image is not very practical. The Registry plays a much more important role under Windows 95. The Registry entries of each machine are different. This makes creating a usable image extremely difficult. What can be done is to format the hard drive and then install Windows 95. After Windows 95 is installed, there are automated processes that you can use to load the rest of the applications.

There are several workable approaches to this clean Windows 95 installation process that work, and they all follow a set pattern:

1. Use a Windows 95 Startup disk to boot the computer to a Windows 95 command prompt:
   - If installing from floppy disk, continue.
   - If installing from CD-ROM, ensure that the CD-ROM is accessible to the system by adding references to both the CONFIG.SYS and AUTOEXEC.BAT files.
   - If installing from the network, load network drivers and map the Windows 95 installation drive.
2. Fdisk and format the hard drive(s), adding Windows 95 system files to the C:\ drive.
3. Access the Windows 95 Setup program and run. If installing from the network, ensure that the network configuration is setup correctly.

The floppy version of Windows 95 that is for computers without Windows already includes a Boot Disk. This version runs an OEMSETUP.EXE program to accomplish the task. Upgrade versions of Windows 95 will prompt you for setup of disk 1 of Windows 3.*x* or Windows for Workgroups 3.*x*, or an OS/2 2.*x* installation disk in order to verify that you qualify for running the upgrade.

While the procedure in Exercise 1.10 installs a clean copy of Windows 95 on the computer, it still leaves the network administrator with the arduous task of re-installing all the applications. A better approach might be to create a clean MS-DOS and Windows 3.*x* image with all the applications already installed, download that image, and then upgrade the computer to Windows 95.

Exercise 1.10: Windows 95 Clean Install

This exercise uses either the floppy disk or CD-ROM version of Windows 95 to do a clean installation. Here are the steps for doing an installation with the floppy disk version. If you have removed Windows 95 in the previous exercise, please complete this exercise as well.

1. From Computer 1, boot with the Windows 95 Startup Disk, format the hard drive, and add the Windows 95 system files to the boot drive (Format c: /s).
2. Insert disk 1 of the floppy version of the Windows 95 installation disks into the floppy drive and run Setup.exe from the command prompt.
3. Complete the Windows 95 installation (see Exercise 1.6).

If you have only the CD-ROM version of Windows 95, you have to boot the computer with an earlier version of MS-DOS that has all the files required to access the CD-ROM drive, or create a modified Windows 95 Startup disk that adds the equivalent files to allow access to the CD-ROM drive. Here are the steps for doing an installation with the CD-ROM version:

1. From Computer 1, boot with either the Windows 95 Startup disk or an equivalent MS-DOS boot disk. The boot files on the disk, CONFIG.SYS and AUTOEXEC.BAT, must be able to allow access to the CD-ROM drive. Format the hard drive and add the Windows 95 system files to the boot drive (Format c: /s).
2. Insert the CD-ROM version of the Windows 95 installation disks into the CD-ROM drive and run Setup.exe from the command prompt.
3. Complete the Windows 95 installation (see Exercise 1.6).

Review Questions

The following questions will test your knowledge of the information in this chapter. For additional questions, see MCP Endeavor and the Microsoft Roadmap/Assessment exam on the CD-ROM that accompanies this book.

1. The lowest Intel processor recommended to run Windows 95 is ______.

   A. 80286

   B. 80386SX

   C. 80386DX

   D. 80486

   E. Pentium

2. The minimum amount of RAM that Windows 95 requires is ______.

   A. 2 MB

   B. 4 MB

   C. 8 MB

   D. 14 MB

   E. 16 MB

3. Which three of the following installation options are available for Windows 95?

   A. From 5.25-inch floppy

   B. From 3.5-inch floppy

   C. From CD-ROM

   D. From the network

   E. From optical disk

4. On the "minimal" computer, as defined by Microsoft, the performance of Windows 95 should be ______ and ______ using Windows 3.1 with the same hardware (Choose two):

   A. worse than

   B. about the same as

   C. possibly improve over

   D. much faster than

   E. twice as fast as

5. Windows 95 will not run on which two of the following types of Intel 386 processors?

   A. 386SX (with 16-bit I/O buffers)

   B. 386DX B-Step Processor

   C. 386DX Non-B-Step Processor

   D. 386DX with ID 0303

   E. 386DX with ID other than 0303

6. The minimum amount of RAM recommended for running either Microsoft Exchange Inbox, Microsoft Network, or multiple 32-bit Windows-based applications is ______.

   A. 2 MB

   B. 4 MB

   C. 8 MB

   D. 14 MB

   E. 16 MB

7. As a rule of thumb, the amount of RAM on a Windows 95 computer, and the amount of free space needed for a swap file, should total at least ______.

   A. 2 MB

   B. 4 MB

   C. 8 MB

   D. 14 MB

   E. 16 MB

8. When installing over an MS-DOS–based operating system, Windows 95 will only install on a computer with an operating system equivalent to ______ or later.

   A. MS-DOS 3.2

   B. MS-DOS 3.3

   C. MS-DOS 4.0

   D. MS-DOS 5.0

   E. MS-DOS 6.0

9. Windows 95 installs into which of the following two types of partitions?

   A. HPFS

   B. NTFS

   C. CDFS

   D. FAT

   E. Unformatted

10. Which one of the following is not a Windows 95 Setup Type of Installation?

    A. Custom

    B. Compact

    C. Express

    D. Typical

    E. Portable

11. The Windows 95 Setup program can be run from which two of the following places?

    A. Within OS/2

    B. Within Windows NT

    C. From within Windows

    D. From a Windows DOS box

    E. From DOS

12. The preferred method for running the Windows 95 Setup program is from within ______ and ______.

    A. MS-DOS

    B. MS Windows 3.1*x*

    C. an MS-DOS window inside Windows

    D. MS Windows for Workgroups 3.*x*

    E. a bootable floppy

13. Windows 95 uses ______ multitasking.

    A. cooperative

    B. cohabitive

    C. preemptive

    D. presumptive

    E. shared

14. Long Filename (LFN) support on a Windows 95 computer works because it uses the ______ file system.

    A. FAT

    B. HPFS

    C. NTFS

    D. CDFS

    E. VFAT

15. What are the three differences in the Windows 95 upgrade between the floppy version of Windows 95 and the CD-ROM version?

    A. Windows Tour

    B. What's New

    C. Full online help

    D. Accessibility options

    E. Administrative extras

16. Most of the Windows 95 installation disks are formatted in the ______ format.

    A. FAT

    B. VFAT

    C. DMF

    D. CDFS

    E. NTFS

17. The Windows 95 Administrative Setup is done by running the ______ program (and parameters).

    A. Setup /a

    B. Setup /n

    C. Setup /as

    D. Netsetup

    E. Batch

18. A batch script file can be used in which three of the following Windows 95 installations?

    A. From 3.5-inch floppy disk
    B. From CD-ROM
    C. From the network
    D. From the local hard drive
    E. From 5.25-inch floppy disk

19. The minimum hardware requirements for Windows 95 are ______ the minimum needed for Windows 3.1.

    A. lower than
    B. the same as
    C. higher than
    D. no different than
    E. approximately the same as

20. Windows 95 will run on the ______ processor.

    A. Intel 286
    B. Intel 386 and higher
    C. DEC Alpha
    D. PowerPC
    E. MIPS

21. The B1 error that can happen on a Windows 95 installation is the result of ______.

    A. step B1, hardware detection, generating an error on the second floppy drive
    B. the processor being an SX type, without a math coprocessor

C. the processor being a 386 B1 stepping chip, which can generate random math errors, making it incompatible with Windows 95

D. failure of the network configuration having failed

E. corruption of the boot sector

22. The Windows 95 option to boot into the previous version of DOS is only available if upgrading from which version of DOS or better?

    A. MS-DOS 3.2

    B. MS-DOS 3.3

    C. MS-DOS 4.0

    D. MS-DOS 5.0

    E. MS-DOS 6.0

23. To check the version of DOS on the computer that you want to upgrade to Windows 95, use the ______ command.

    A. Setver

    B. Winver

    C. Dosver

    D. Ver

    E. Getver

24. The approximate disk requirements for Windows 95 in a typical setup upgrade of Windows is ______.

    A. 20 MB

    B. 30 MB

    C. 40 MB

    D. 47 MB

    E. 55 MB

25. What three of the following command switches can be used with the Windows 95 Setup program?

    A. /?
    B. /B
    C. /ID
    D. /D
    E. /IS

26. The naming standards for ______ are all the same: limited to 15 characters, no embedded spaces, and can contain these special characters:

    ! @ # $ % ^ & ( ) - _ ' { } ~ .

    A. user's full name
    B. default user's name
    C. computer name
    D. workgroup name
    E. computer description

27. To migrate program groups and system settings when upgrading from Windows 3.*x* to Windows 95, do which of the following?

    A. Upgrade into a new Windows 95 directory.
    B. Upgrade into an existing Windows directory.
    C. Copy group and initialization files into a new Windows 95 directory.
    D. Copy older DLL files into the new Windows 95 directory.
    E. Run GRPCONV to convert older program groups into folders.

28. The Windows 95 Setup program will not run from Windows 3.0, but instead wants to run from MS-DOS. How much conventional memory is required to run from MS-DOS?

    A. 370 KB

    B. 420 KB

    C. 470 KB

    D. 512 KB

    E. 640 KB

29. Which one of the following is not a logical phase in the Windows 95 installation?

    A. Startup and information gathering

    B. Hardware detection

    C. Software detection

    D. File copy

    E. Final system configuration

30. Which three of the following are differences between starting the Windows 95 Setup program in MS-DOS versus starting it in Windows?

    A. ScanDisk running in the foreground rather than the background

    B. Searching for Windows version versus checking Windows version 3.1 or better

    C. Checking for TSRs versus checking for TSRs and other Windows programs running

    D. System checks done in DOS versus Windows

    E. DOS graphical interface versus Windows graphical interface after starting protected mode

31. You are prompted for user name and company during the ______ part of running the Windows 95 Setup program.

    A. initial startup and Setup Wizard load
    B. gathering user and computer information
    C. copying Windows 95 files
    D. restarting the computer and finishing setup
    E. after Windows 95 is completely installed

32. You are asked to remove the newly created Startup disk during the ______ part of running the Windows 95 Setup program.

    A. initial startup and Setup Wizard load
    B. gathering user and computer information
    C. copying Windows 95 files
    D. restarting the computer and finishing setup
    E. after Windows 95 is completely installed

33. You are asked to unload any detected TSRs during the ______ part of running the Windows 95 Setup program.

    A. initial startup and Setup Wizard load
    B. gathering user and computer information
    C. copying Windows 95 files
    D. restarting the computer and finishing setup
    E. after Windows 95 is completely installed

34. You are asked to enter a time zone for the computer during the ______ part of running the Windows 95 Setup program.

    A. initial startup and Setup Wizard load
    B. gathering user and computer information
    C. copying Windows 95 files
    D. restarting the computer and finishing setup
    E. after Windows 95 is completely installed

35. You can ask to run the verify option for the computer during the ______ part of running the Windows 95 Setup program.

    A. initial startup and Setup Wizard load
    B. gathering user and computer information
    C. copying Windows 95 files
    D. restarting the computer and finishing setup
    E. after Windows 95 is completely installed

36. Which one of the following is the default Windows 95 setup type of installation?

    A. Custom
    B. Compact
    C. Express
    D. Typical
    E. Portable

37. The Startup Disk contains all the following files except ______.

    A. IO.SYS
    B. MSDOS.SYS
    C. COMMAND.COM
    D. CONFIG.SYS
    E. REGEDIT.EXE

38. The Startup disk, when created by the Windows 95 Setup program, contains 16 files and uses ______ of disk space?

    A. 640 KB
    B. 948 KB
    C. 1.0 MB
    D. 1.20 MB
    E. 1.44 MB

39. Which two of the following statements are true about the Windows 95 Startup Disk?

    A. It can only be created during a Windows 95 installation.

    B. It needs a pre-formatted floppy disk at the start.

    C. It enables you to boot to the Windows 95 command prompt.

    D. It includes CD-ROM drivers, if needed.

    E. It enables you to troubleshoot your Registry Files.

40. Which three of the following networking protocols included with Windows 95 are Plug and Play enabled?

    A. Ethernet

    B. TCP/IP

    C. NetBEUI

    D. Token Ring

    E. IPX/SPX

41. Which level of security would be used for a stand-alone computer with multiple users, each of whom has different Windows 95 preferences and desktops?

    A. Windows 95 access control

    B. Unified logon process

    C. Windows 95 logon security

    D. Share-level security

    E. User-level security

42. Which level of security would be used to base the access rights to shared resources on the Windows 95 computer using a user accounts list stored on a Novell NetWare Server?

    A. Windows 95 access control
    B. Unified logon process
    C. Windows 95 logon security
    D. Share-level security
    E. User-level security

43. Which level of security would be used to base the access rights to shared resources on the Windows 95 computer on a password-assigned basis?

    A. Windows 95 access control
    B. Unified logon process
    C. Windows 95 logon security
    D. Share-level security
    E. User-level security

44. If the hardware detection fails at a certain point in the process, what can you do?

    A. You cannot do anything.
    B. Restart the Windows 95 Setup program in Safe Recovery.
    C. Restart the Windows 95 Setup program and run the entire hardware detection repeatedly until it clears up.
    D. Call technical support to test your computer.
    E. If you are technical support, call Microsoft.

45. If you do not install a Windows component during the Windows 95 installation, you will have to ______.

    A. restart the Windows 95 Setup program again to add a component
    B. restart the Windows 95 Setup program in verify mode and then add the component
    C. use the Add/Remove Programs option in Control Panel
    D. use the Install Components Wizard from My Computer
    E. restart the Windows 95 Setup program from scratch and reinstall Windows 95

46. Which one of the following log files is not used during the Windows 95 installation?

    A. SETUPLOG.TXT
    B. HARDWARE.TXT
    C. DETLOG.TXT
    D. NETLOG.TXT
    E. BOOTLOG.TXT

47. Which three of the following are the key files used to troubleshoot the Windows 95 installation process?

    A. SETUPLOG.TXT
    B. HARDWARE.TXT
    C. DETLOG.TXT
    D. NETLOG.TXT
    E. BOOTLOG.TXT

48. Which Function Key allows you to see the Windows 95 Start-up Menu when Windows 95 is first booting?

    A. F1

    B. F4

    C. F5

    D. F6

    E. F8

49. In safe mode, Windows 95 only loads which three of the following device drivers?

    A. CD-ROM

    B. Mouse

    C. Keyboard

    D. Sound

    E. VGA

50. At Windows 95 Startup, you receive an error message saying there is a bad or missing file, and gives you the file's name. Which three of the following can you do to track down this error?

    A. Check for the existence and location of the file.

    B. Check for the version and integrity of the file.

    C. See if the applications all still running.

    D. Restart the Windows 95 Setup program with the Verify option to replace missing or damaged files.

    E. Call Microsoft technical support.

Review Answers

1. C
2. B
3. B C D
4. B C
5. B D
6. C
7. D
8. A
9. D E
10. C
11. C E
12. B D
13. C
14. E
15. A C E
16. C
17. D
18. B C D
19. C
20. B
21. C
22. D

23. D
24. C
25. A C E
26. B C D
27. B
28. C
29. C
30. A B C
31. B
32. C
33. A
34. D
35. E
36. D
37. D
38. B
39. C E
40. B C E
41. A
42. E
43. D
44. B
45. C

46. B
47. A C E
48. E
49. B C E
50. A B D

Chapter 2

Architecture and Memory

Windows 95 was designed to run on Intel 386 or better processors. The design allows Windows 95 to take advantage of the system protection built into the Intel 386 or better processors, access more memory using a flat memory model, and run multiple applications in a virtual memory mode. Windows 95 is now a true operating system. Earlier versions of Windows 3.*x* were just a graphical user interface (GUI) running on top of DOS.

You might recall the old wife's tale about the bride wearing "something old, something new, something borrowed, something blue..." to ensure a happy marriage. Windows 95 is similar to that bride's wedding apparel. It has features and capabilities of the older versions of both DOS and Windows. Windows 95 includes many great new features that were not present in previous versions of either DOS or Windows. Windows 95 borrows heavily from the 32-bit architecture of Windows NT. Finally, Windows 95 will not make you blue when you're trying to run most of your older DOS and 16-bit Windows applications.

This chapter gives you an overview of the architecture of Windows 95, and how Windows 95 manages memory. In this chapter, you will learn about the following:

- Windows 95 System Services
- Windows 95 virtual machines
- Windows 95 virtual memory
- Windows 95 task scheduling and multitasking
- Windows 95 internal messaging
- Application memory usage comparison

Ring 0 versus Ring 3

Windows 95 uses an Intel 386 or better processor to support multiple privilege levels for executable code. Of the four levels, or "rings" in the Intel 386 protection model, Windows 95 uses Rings 0 and 3. These rings provide different levels of protection and privileges. The lower the ring number, the higher the levels of protection and privileges.

Figure 2.1 illustrates the layout of the ring architecture for Windows 95. Components of Windows 95 are divided between Ring 0 and Ring 3 code. Each ring offers a different level of system protection. The Ring 0 code is protected by the Intel processor architecture and consists of all the low-level operating System Services, such as the File Management subsystem and the Virtual Machine Manager subsystem. The Ring 3 code is protected from other running processes by protection services provided in the operating system. The Ring 3 code runs the System Virtual Machine and any Virtual DOS Machines.

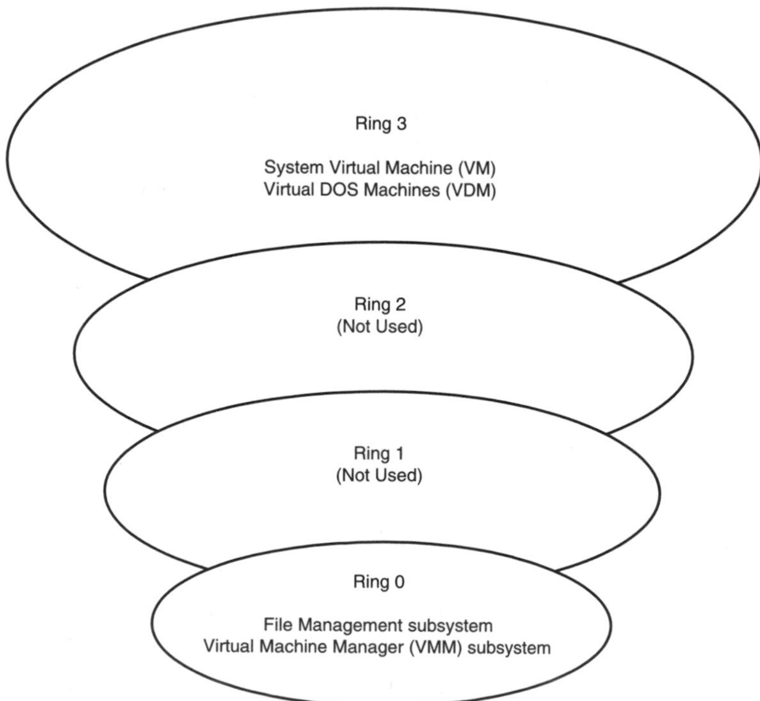

Figure 2.1

The ring architecture of Intel 386 or better processors.

Ring 0 components are protected by the processor architecture. The processor prevents the component code from writing over another existing component's code. These Ring 0 components are the core elements of Windows 95. They can run all privileged operations, including direct communication with the hardware components. They have access to the entire computer system. A bad component in Ring 0 can bring down the computer system, therefore every component running in Ring 0 needs to be extremely reliable. All the low-level Windows 95 core components run in Ring 0.

Ring 3 components have no processor protection. The operating system must provide protection for Ring 3 components. Ring 3 components cannot write to the hardware components. They must communicate to a Ring 0 process to write to a hardware component. A bad application component in Ring 3 does not necessarily bring down the computer system. Usually you can recover from any problems associated with a Ring 3 component by simply closing down that component. Applications and non-critical System Services of Windows 95 components run on Ring 3.

Windows 95 Components

Understanding how the various components of an operating system such as Windows 95 fit together can be difficult. The *Windows 95 Resource Kit* and the New Riders book *Inside Windows 95* provide better reference material on this subject. This section provides some perspective on Windows 95 components.

Figure 2.2 contains a diagram of the Windows 95 components that run in both Ring 0 and Ring 3 of the Intel 386 protection model.

Ring 3 hosts the virtual machines (VMs) in which MS-DOS, Windows 16-bit, and Windows 32-bit applications execute. The MS-DOS applications all run in separate VMs, known *as Virtual DOS Machines* (VDMs). All Windows applications, whether Windows 16-bit or 32-bit, execute in the System VM. The System VM allow multiple concurrent applications to run. Whereas all Windows 32-bit applications are isolated in private address spaces, all the active

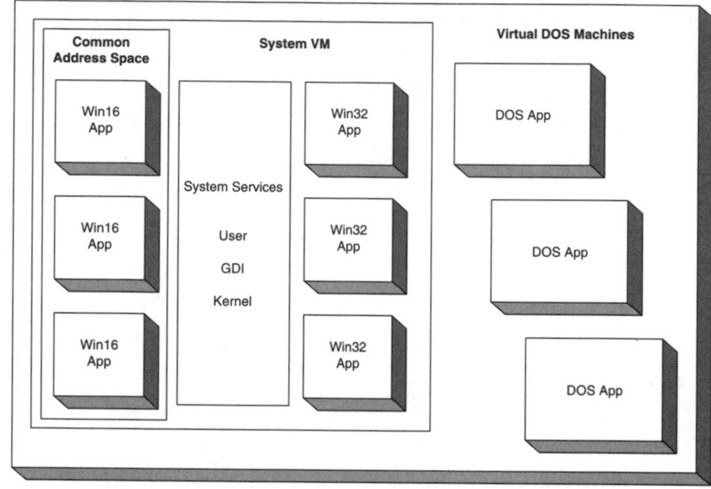

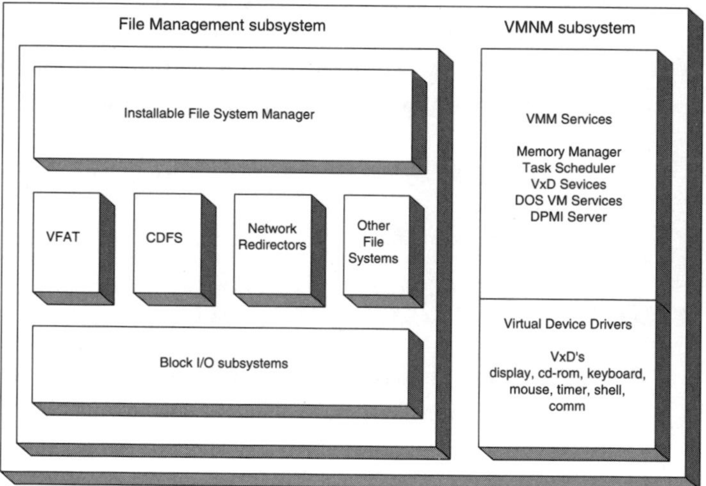

Figure 2.2

Windows 95 system architecture.

Windows 16-bit applications share a single, common address space. These applications are managed by the VMM Memory Manager in Ring 0. As a result, the Windows 16-bit applications operate much as they did under Windows 3.1, where they are cooperatively multitasked. Windows 32-bit and MS-DOS applications are preemptively multitasked. (See Chapter 1, "Planning and Installation," for a discussion of cooperative and preemptive multitasking.) The central components of the Windows graphical environment also run as System Services. These include Kernel, GDI, and User. The next section looks at these System Services in greater detail.

Ring 0 hosts both the Virtual Machine Manager (VMM) subsystem and the File Management subsystem. The VMM subsystem provides the resources needed for each application and system process running on the computer, including memory management and task scheduling. Virtual Device Drivers (VxDs) are 32-bit, protected-mode drivers that manage a system resource, such as a hardware device or installed software. They allow more than one application to use the resource at the same time. The File Management subsystem features an Installable File System Manager, which supports multiple file systems such as VFAT, CDFS, and Network redirectors. This Installable File System Manager also supports an open file system architecture, so future file systems can be added later. The Block I/O subsystems are responsible for the interaction with the physical storage devices.

Windows 95 System Services

Much of the code within Windows 95 is either new 32-bit code or older Windows 3.*x* code rewritten as 32-bit code, rather than 16-bit code. Windows 95, however, is not completely a 32-bit operating system. Windows 95 strikes a balance between three requirements: delivering compatibility with existing applications and drivers, decreasing the size of the operating system to run on 4 MB of RAM, and offering improved system performance. To provide this balance, Windows 95 uses a combination of both 32-bit and 16-bit code.

Windows 95 employs 32-bit code wherever 32-bit code significantly improves performance without sacrificing application compatibility. Existing 16-bit code is retained where it is required to maintain compatibility, or where 32-bit code would increase memory requirements without significantly improving performance. All the I/O subsystems and device drivers in Windows 95, such as networking and file systems, are fully 32 bit. All memory management and scheduling components, such as Kernel and Virtual Memory Manager, are 32 bit as well. Figure 2.3 depicts the relative distribution of 32-bit code versus 16-bit code present in each of the Windows 95 System Services. The sizes of the boxes in the figure illustrate the number of lines of code for each 16-bit and 32-bit version of the three System Services files.

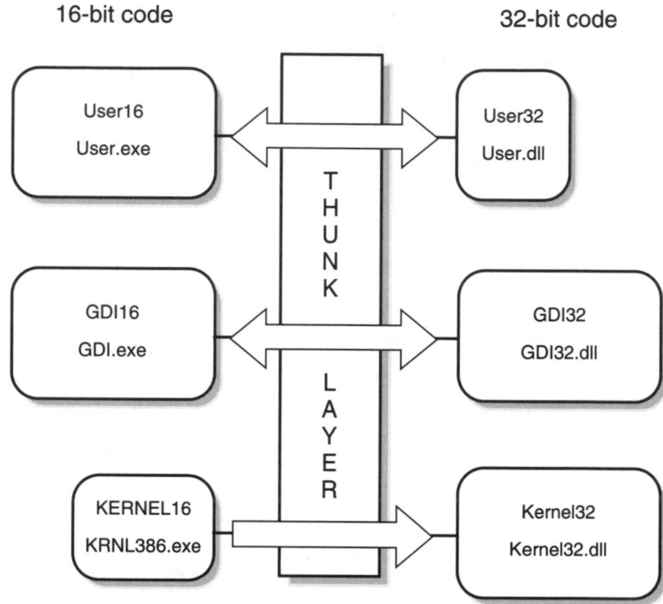

Figure 2.3

Ring 3 System Services.

Three sets of files constitute the Windows 95 System Services: Kernel, Graphics Device Interface (GDI), and User:

- The Kernel (KRNL386.EXE and KERNEL32.DLL) provides base operating system functions, including file I/O services, virtual memory management, application management, and task scheduling.
- The GDI (GDI.EXE and GDI32.DLL) controls the graphics operations that create images on the system display and other devices such as printers.
- The User (USER.EXE and USER32.DLL) creates and maintains windows on-screen and carries out all requests to create, move, size, or remove a window. The User also handles requests regarding the icons and other components of the user interface. It also directs input to the appropriate application from the keyboard, mouse, and other input sources.

As illustrated, most of the System Services provided by the operating system Kernel are provided as 32-bit code. The remaining 16-bit code consists of hand-tuned assembly language, delivering performance that rivals the 32-bit code. Many functions provided by the GDI have been moved to 32-bit code, including the spooler and printing subsystem, the font rasterizer, and the drawing operations performed by the graphics DIB engine. Roughly half of all GDI calls are handled in the 32-bit code. The 16-bit code for GDI contains most of the drawing routines. Much of the window management User code still remains 16-bit to maintain Windows 16-bit application compatibility.

The *Thunk Layer*, shown in figure 2.2, makes reference to the term *thunking*. This special term describes how 16-bit code components communicate with their 32-bit code component counterparts. The thunking process translates memory addresses between 32-bit calls and 16-bit calls. A slight performance degradation occurs in the translation, however it is hardly noticeable.

In general, the 32-bit code is provided in Windows 95 to maximize the performance and reliability of the system. The 16-bit code balances the requirements for reducing the size of the operating system while maintaining compatibility with existing applications and drivers.

Windows 95 Virtual Machines

All applications and dynamic link library (DLL) programs run in Ring 3. They execute in a *virtual machine* (VM), which from the application's perspective, looks like a separate computer. A VM is an environment created by Windows 95 to simulate a complete computer, with all the resources available to a physical computer, such as hard disk controllers and a timer. The Virtual Machine Manager (VMM) creates and maintains the virtual machine environments and provides each application the system resources needed to run the system.

The System VM runs the System Services as well as all Windows 32-bit and 16-bit applications. The 16-bit Windows applications all run in a shared, common address space. The 32-bit Windows applications each run in their own private address space. Each MS-DOS application runs in its own separate Virtual DOS Machine

(VDM). The Virtual Machine Manager, in addition to creating and maintaining all these virtual machines, provides several key services:

- **Memory Management.** Controls the 4 GB of addressable virtual memory, paging from RAM to the hard disk, and performs memory address translation. This is discussed in the following section, "Windows 95 Virtual Memory."
- **Task Scheduling and Multitasking.** Allocates system resources and time to the applications and other processes running on the computer. These are discussed in the section "Windows 95 Task Scheduling and Multitasking" later in this chapter.
- **MS-DOS Mode support.** For MS-DOS applications that need exclusive access to system resources. This special mode of Windows 95 operations should not be confused with the Virtual DOS Machine, or VDM. It is a separate and exclusive MS-DOS operating environment, and is discussed further in Chapter 8, "Running Applications."

To illustrate the point about how Windows 95 manages virtual machines, follow Exercise 3.1 to count the number of virtual machines running on your Windows 95 computer.

Exercise 2.1: Counting Virtual Machines

1. From your computer, start Windows 95.
2. If you installed Windows 95 on your computer with the Typical Setup option, the System Monitor program might not be installed, because it is an optional component.

   To determine whether the System Monitor utility program is installed, from the Start menu, choose Programs, Accessories, System Tools, then System Monitor. If System Monitor is not available, you must add it to your computer by following these steps:

a. From the Start menu, go to **S**ettings and choose **C**ontrol Panel. From the Control Panel program group, choose the Add/Remove Programs icon.

b. Click on the Windows Setup tab, double-click on Accessories, and add a check mark to the System Monitor checkbox. Press Enter or choose OK. Press Enter or choose OK again to install the System Monitor.

3. From the Start menu, go to **P**rograms, Accessories, System Tools, then System Monitor. The System Monitor utility program displays key system information in either a Line Chart, Bar Chart, or Numeric Chart format.

4. Any items previously selected are displayed when the System Monitor utility program starts. When the System Monitor utility program is run for the first time, the Kernel Processor Usage (%) appears in a Line Chart.

5. All current items need to be removed to run this exercise. Highlight any items you want to remove, then from the **E**dit menu, choose **R**emove Item.

6. From the Edit menu, choose **A**dd Item to open the Add Item dialog box. From the Category list, click on Kernel to display the list of Kernel items.

7. Choose Virtual Machines from the Item list. If you need an explanation of each item, choose E**x**plain to see that this shows the number of virtual machines present in the system. Press Enter or choose OK to add the item Virtual Machines as a selection.

8. From the View menu, choose **N**umeric Charts to obtain the number of virtual machines that currently are active. Normally this value is 1, because the Windows 95 computer has just been started. It could be higher.

9. Open some Windows program applications or the Windows Explorer. Has the number of virtual machines changed? The number of active virtual machines should not change when Windows programs are started.

10. Start an MS-DOS command prompt by choosing Start, **R**un to open the Run dialog box, or choose Start, **P**rograms, then MS-DOS Prompt. Has the number of virtual machines changed? It should change, because each MS-DOS application will start another virtual machine.

11. Start another MS-DOS command prompt, and then a third. What happens to the count of virtual machines after you start each new MS-DOS command prompt? Each time another MS-DOS command prompt is started, the number of virtual machines should increase by a count of 1. If the initial count was 1, then starting three MS-DOS command prompts increases the number to 4.

12. Close down all three MS-DOS command prompts. How many virtual machines are currently active? The count of virtual machines should be back down to 1, or the starting number in step 8.

    Based on what you know about virtual machines, explain why the count changes during the exercise.

    All the Windows 16-bit and 32-bit applications run in a single system virtual machine. But each MS-DOS application runs in its own Virtual DOS Machine. Opening a new MS-DOS command prompt causes the virtual machine count to increase by 1.

13. When you finish viewing the System Monitor utility information, close the System Monitor.

Windows 95 Virtual Memory

Windows 95 uses two types of memory: physical and virtual memory. Most users are familiar with the amount of RAM, or physical memory, on the computer itself. As mentioned previously in Chapter 1, the minimum requirement for RAM on a computer running Windows 95 is 4 MB. The recommended amount of RAM is at least 8 MB. The author even suggests 16 MB of RAM for Windows 95. With Windows 95, all the available physical memory on the computer is used by the operating system. Hardware memory limitations can be overcome through the use of virtual memory.

The Windows 95 operating system uses a *flat memory model*, which leverages off the Intel 386 or greater processor's capability to handle 32-bit addresses. This flat memory model provides a logical address space range of up to 4 GB. Although current computer hardware does not yet handle up to 4 GB of physical memory, some file servers can now run with up to 1 GB of RAM. Virtual memory bridges the gap between physical memory and logical memory.

The 4 GB of addressable space used as virtual memory under the flat memory model is implemented through the use of both RAM and a swap file. The Windows 95 operating system performs memory management, called *demand paging*, whereby code and data are moved in 4-KB pages between physical memory and the temporary Windows 95 swap file on the hard drive. The Virtual Memory Manager controls paging and maintains a page table. The page table tells which pages are swapped to the hard drive, and which remain in RAM, and to which system process or application they belong.

Application programs are allocated a virtual memory address space, which is the set of addresses available for use by that program. Both 32-bit Windows and MS-DOS based programs are allocated private virtual memory address space. All 16-bit Windows-based programs share a single, common virtual memory address space. Figure 2.4 shows how Windows 95 allocates the 4 Gb of virtual memory to each address space. Each process is allocated a unique virtual address space of 4 Gb. The upper 2 Gb is shared with the system, whereas the lower 2 Gb is private to the application.

Figure 2.4

Virtual memory address space allocation.

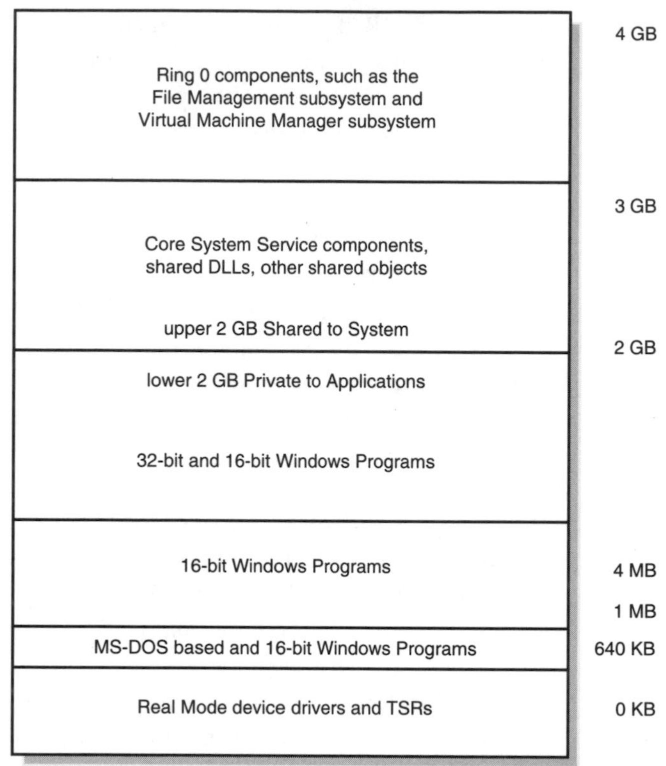

The virtual memory is allocated as follows:

- **0–640 KB.** If not used for a Virtual DOS Machine (VDM), this memory is made available for any Real-Mode device drivers and terminate-and-stay-resident (TSR) programs.
- **0–1 MB.** In a VDM, this memory is used to execute MS-DOS programs. If a shared, common, 16-bit Windows virtual machine is used, then 16-bit Windows applications operate much as they do under Windows 3.1.
- **1–4 MB.** Normally this memory is unused. Windows 95 does not use this space, nor do Windows 32-bit applications. If this memory is needed by 16-bit Windows applications, it is available.

- **2 MB–2 GB.** This memory is used by 32-bit Windows applications and some 16-bit Windows applications. Each Windows 32-bit application has its own address space, whereas Windows 16-bit applications all share a common address space.
- **2 GB–3 GB.** This memory is used to run all Core System Service components, shared DLLs, and other shared objects. Those components are available to all applications.
- **3–4 GB.** This memory is reserved for all Ring 0 components, such as the File Management subsystem and the VMM subsystem. Any VxDs are loaded in this address space.

Virtual memory and virtual addresses enable you to have more memory available to programs than actually exists on the computer in physical RAM. The Windows 95 swap file implementation is much improved over that from Windows 3.1.

With Windows 3.1, you can have either a temporary or permanent swap file. Windows 3.1 recommends how much hard disk memory to allocate to the swap file. If the hard-disk controller is compatible with 32-bit disk access, running 32-bit disk access will improve performance. A temporary swap file that does not need to be on contiguous hard disk space is created when Windows 3.1 starts. This same temporary swap file is released when the user exits Windows. Although a permanent, contiguous swap file provides better performance than a temporary swap file, because it is a static file, hard disk space is not freed up when the user exits Windows.

In Windows 95, the swap file configuration is much easier. The best features of temporary and permanent swap files are combined through improved virtual memory algorithms and 32-bit access methods. By default, Windows 95 uses a dynamic swap file, which shrinks and grows based on the needs of the operating system and the available hard disk space. A permanent swap file has little benefit in Windows 95.

The best way to ensure swap file performance is to put the swap file on a hard disk that has ample free space so that the swap file can shrink or grow as required. If you have multiple hard drives, select the one with the fastest access time as well as the most free space.

Windows 95 Task Scheduling and Multitasking

Windows 95 uses a task scheduler to determine the order and priority of processes running on the computer. These processes run as threads. A *thread* is a unit of executable code. Each thread has a base priority, which is the priority the thread normally wants to run.

MS-DOS applications and 16-bit Windows applications usually have a single thread. Newer 32-bit Windows applications can take advantage of running multiple threads to improve performance. Some tasks within the 32-bit Windows application can be spun off as separate threads that run concurrently.

Windows 95, like Windows NT, uses priority levels to help schedule processes. There are 32 priority levels, ranging from the lowest priority level of 0 to the highest of 31. A thread may have its base priority altered by as much as two levels higher or lower than the original priority level. Applications have low priority, and critical system tasks have high priority.

Figure 2.5 illustrates how the two parts of the scheduler process, the primary and secondary scheduler, work. The primary scheduler evaluates all thread priorities and gives the thread with the highest priority a time slice of execution time. If two or more threads have the same priority, they are stacked. Each stacked thread is then granted a time slice of execution in sequence until no threads have the same priority. The actual length of a time slice depends on the configuration of the computer.

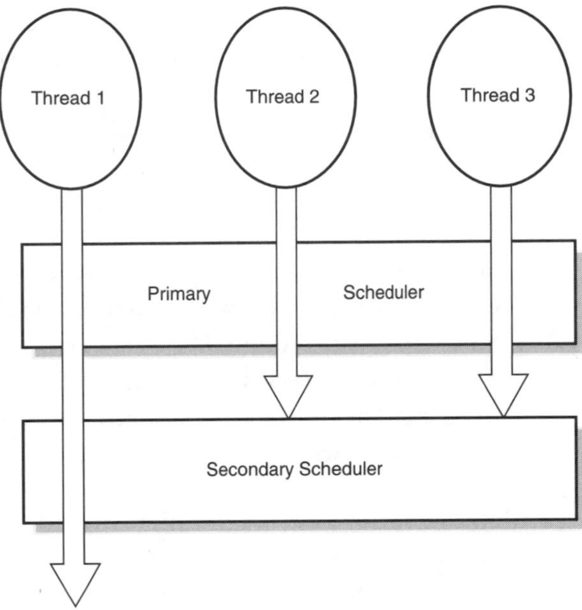

Figure 2.5

Scheduling threads to run.

The secondary scheduler can boost the priority of non-executing threads. This priority boost helps prevent threads that have a lower base priority from being blocked from receiving execution time. The secondary scheduler also adjusts the priority of threads over time to smooth the execution of programs. Windows 95 adjusts threads as follows:

- Threads waiting for user input (in the foreground) get a priority boost, making the system more responsive.
- Threads completing a voluntary wait get a priority boost.
- All threads periodically receive a priority boost to prevent them from locking shared resources needed by higher priority threads.
- Compute-bound threads get a priority decrease, so that I/O operations are not blocked.

The task scheduler is the Windows 95 component responsible for providing system resources to the applications and other processes.

It also schedules processes in a way that enables multiple applications to run concurrently. This method of concurrent process scheduling is called *multitasking*. Windows 95 uses cooperative multitasking as well as preemptive multitasking.

With Windows 3.1, applications run concurrently using cooperative multitasking. Cooperative multitasking requires the application to periodically check the message queue and cooperatively release control of the system to other applications that are running. Applications that do not check the message queue regularly can "hog" CPU cycles and prevent other applications from running. For backwards compatibility, Windows 95 cooperatively multitasks Windows 16-bit applications.

For Windows 32-bit applications, Windows 95 uses preemptive multitasking, which allows the operating system to take control of which processes are running at any time. Preemptive multitasking is a more efficient means of multitasking. The task scheduler decides which processes acquire control of the system, preemptively allocating system resources. The priority of the process itself is used to help the scheduler allocate time to processes to execute.

Windows 95 Internal Messaging

Windows applications use a *message-passing* model to help control programs. An event such as a keyboard entry, mouse movement or click, the receipt of data by a hardware buffer, and so on generates an interrupt. These events are converted by the interrupt handler into messages. Windows applications generate messages to request the operating system to perform a function or to pass data to another Windows application.

One bottleneck for Windows 3.1 is that it uses only a single message queue for all applications. If only one application fails to retrieve its messages, then the system becomes unstable and hangs because the other applications are blocked from retrieving their messages. As a result, the computer locks up, and you have to reboot your system.

This bottleneck does not exist in Windows 95. Although a single message queue exists for all Windows 16-bit applications for backwards compatibility, each Windows 32-bit application thread has its own private message queue. Figure 2.6 illustrates this new internal messaging structure. The Windows 95 operating system takes messages from the raw input queue and passes them to the appropriate Windows 32-bit application thread or, if the message is for a Windows 16-bit application, to the Windows 16-bit subsystem. Therefore, if one of these processes or applications hangs and no longer receives its incoming messages, the other processes are unaffected.

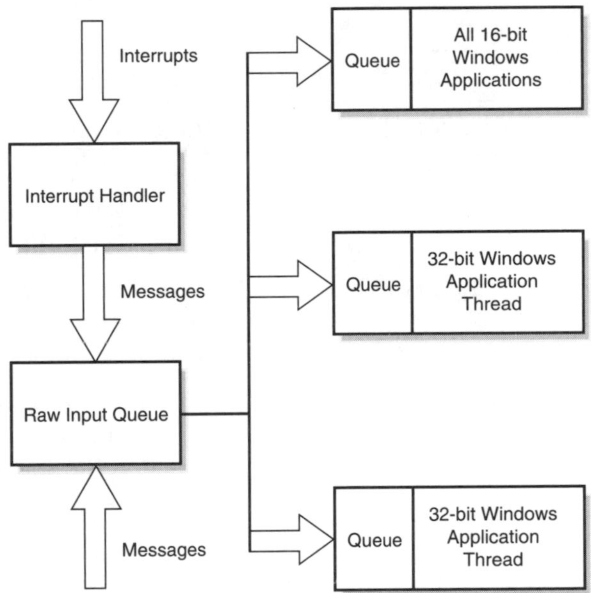

Figure 2.6

Windows 95's message-passing queue structure.

For study purposes, remember the following:

- Windows 32-bit applications have a message queue for each thread.
- Windows 16-bit applications share a common message queue. If a Windows 16-bit application fails, messages are blocked for all running Windows 16-bit applications until the failed program is cleared.
- MS-DOS applications do not use the message-passing design and do not have a message queue.

Architectural Evaluation

This topic area has only a single exam objective. To properly address it, however, you need a clear understanding of the Windows 95 system architecture. Chapter 8 discusses the details of running applications under Windows 95.

Table 2.1 compares and contrasts the memory usage of a Microsoft MS-DOS based application, a 16-bit Windows-based application, and a 32-bit Windows-based application operating in Windows 95.

Table 2.1

Comparing Memory Usage

Application	Memory Usage
MS-DOS	Each runs in a private Virtual DOS Machine (VDM). No message queue. Loaded in the lower 1 MB of virtual memory.
Windows 16-bit	All run in a common address space and share a single message queue. Loaded in the lower 2 GB of virtual memory.
Windows 32-bit	Each runs in a private address space, and each thread has its own message queue. Loaded in the 4 MB to 2 GB range of virtual memory.

Review Questions

The following questions will test your knowledge of the information in this chapter. For additional questions, see MCP Endeavor and the Microsoft Roadmap/Assessment Exam on the CD-ROM that accompanies this book.

1. Windows 95 executes in which two of the following Rings of the Intel 386 protection model? Select the two best answers:

    A. Ring 0

    B. Ring 1

C. Ring 2

D. Ring 3

E. Ring 4

2. Which of the following Rings of the Intel 386 protection model offers the most privileges?

   A. Ring 0

   B. Ring 1

   C. Ring 2

   D. Ring 3

   E. Ring 4

3. Which of the following Rings of the Intel 386 protection model offers no processor protection, but instead needs the operating system to provide processor protection?

   A. Ring 0

   B. Ring 1

   C. Ring 2

   D. Ring 3

   E. Ring 4

4. In which of the following Rings of the Intel 386 protection model do the MS-DOS, Windows 16-bit, and Windows 32-bit applications run?

   A. Ring 0

   B. Ring 1

   C. Ring 2

   D. Ring 3

   E. Ring 4

5. In which of the following Rings of the Intel 386 protection model do the System Services run?

   A. Ring 0

   B. Ring 1

   C. Ring 2

   D. Ring 3

   E. Ring 4

6. In which of the following four Rings of the Intel 386 protection model does the Virtual Machine Manager run?

   A. Ring 0

   B. Ring 1

   C. Ring 2

   D. Ring 3

   E. Ring 4

7. Which of the following components make up System Services? Select the three best answers:

   A. User

   B. Thunk

   C. GDI

   D. GUI

   E. Kernel

8. Which of the following applications do not run in separate, private virtual machines?

   A. Windows 32-bit

   B. Windows 16-bit

   C. MS-DOS

   D. All of the above

   E. None of the above

9. Every time you open an MS-DOS application, the count of the number of virtual machines running under Windows 95 ______.

    A. decreases by two
    B. decreases by one
    C. stays the same
    D. increases by one
    E. increases by two

10. Virtual memory is comprised of which two of the following components? Select the two best answers:

    A. ROM
    B. RAM
    C. VMM
    D. A swap file
    E. A page table

Review Answers

1. A D
2. A
3. D
4. D
5. D
6. A
7. A C E
8. B
9. D
10. B D

Chapter 3

Customizing and Configuring Windows 95

Making Windows 95 work the way you want it to work involves knowing how to customize and configure Windows 95. This requires you to be very knowledgeable about how the Windows 95 user interface can be adjusted to suit your style, improved to offer better ease of use, and protected against configuration errors. Experience in making these type of changes is the best teacher. This chapter is your guide to understanding how to customize and configure Windows 95. In this chapter, you will learn how to do the following:

- Configure dual-boot computers
- Customize the Windows 95 Desktop
- Configure the Taskbar
- Configure shortcuts
- Configure and use the Windows Explorer
- Get your work done using Windows 95
- Understand what makes up the Windows 95 Registry
- Fix errors in the Windows 95 Registry

For many Windows 3.*x* users, Windows 95 represents a big change. The new Windows 95 graphical user interface (GUI) has significantly changed over the user interface within the Windows 3.*x* or Windows NT 3.*x* versions. Windows 95 also features improvements in ease of use, performance, compatibility, and built-in support for networking and communications. These same improvements have contributed to making Windows 95 the new choice as the standard desktop operating system for upgrading either Windows 3.*x* or Windows for Workgroups 3.*x* running on top of MS-DOS.

This chapter looks at ways to customize and configure Windows 95 to work the way you want it to work. You should expect a lot of questions on the test in this topic area. To help you better understand how to make Windows 95 work for you, most of the exam objectives covered in this chapter contain hands-on exercises.

Making Windows 95 Work for You

The Windows 95 Project Team worked hard to ensure that Windows 95 was easy to use for both novices and experienced users. Novice users are people who have never used a computer before, or who have used one infrequently. Novices have trouble navigating the user interface and need more information or coaching, so an online help system is provided. Experienced users make more use of the operating system than novice users, and they want it to easily allow them to configure and customize the computer to meet their requirements. The goal for Windows 95 is to make it easy to work the way you want to work.

The Windows 95 user interface design centers around answering one basic question: How can the user interface in Windows 3.1 be improved? Through usability tests, focus groups, educator feedback, and a suggestion database, the Windows 95 Project Team gathered input. The end result was an operating system with a user interface that incorporates the following:

- **Ease of use.** Most of the common and essential features of Windows 95, such as launching an application, task switching, and finding a file, are easily discoverable through the Taskbar, with its Start menu and push-button task switching.
- **Speed and power.** Windows 95 promotes efficiency, control, and easy customization via the use of shortcuts, secondary mouse clicks, properties sheets, and the new Windows Explorer.
- **Compatibility.** The user interface has features and online help files that make Windows 95 easy to learn, especially for those already familiar with previous versions of Windows 3.*x*.

Windows 95 employs an object model as a mechanism to define and use hardware devices, programs, and other resources. Although Windows 95 is not a true object-oriented operating system, users have a better grasp of how Windows 95 works if everything is represented as an object.

Working with Windows 95 Objects

An object has a form (icon) and attributes (properties) that the user can easily understand. In general, objects can be opened or explored by clicking an icon, and objects have properties that can be viewed. These properties define what the object can do, or what can be done to the object. Object behavior is consistent—once you know how to work with one object, other similar objects work the same way.

The properties of an object, its settings and parameters, are found on the object's properties sheet. These properties can be changed or adjusted as required. The properties sheet provides a consistent and convenient way to view an object's properties. To view the properties sheet for an object, highlight the object with a single click of the right mouse button. A context menu is displayed from which Properties can be selected. Again, the specific properties shown on an object's properties sheet depend on the type of object itself.

An optional mouse or similar pointing device becomes almost a requirement to use the Windows 95 user interface effectively. Which button becomes the left mouse button and which becomes the right mouse button depends on how you have configured the mouse. If you are right-handed, the left mouse button is usually the left mouse button, making the right mouse button the right mouse button. If you are left-handed, you want to configure the mouse buttons in the opposite way.

To configure the Windows 95 mouse buttons, use the Mouse icon in the Control Panel. Be sure to keep in mind the differences in primary versus right mouse button assignments when preparing for the exam—the left versus the right.

Improving the Windows 95 User Interface

In trying to make Windows 95 a more intuitive operating system, the Windows 95 Project Team put extra effort into several user interface design areas that seemed to cause Windows 3.*x* users the most problems. These areas include the following:

- **Windows management.** The desktop was confusing. Open Windows overlapped each other, or were minimized out of sight on the desktop. Some users would open numerous windows and then become overwhelmed or lose track of running programs. Windows 95 provides the Taskbar, which enables quick access to all active programs by maintaining a title button for each open program on the Taskbar itself.
- **Hierarchical Views.** File Manager hierarchies of storage were confusing. The concept of storing one object in another, in yet another, caused users problems in knowing where to look to find their favorite programs or utilities. Files were lost in the catacombs of subdirectories. Information in Windows 95 is stored in folders (directories) and files. The Windows 95 Explorer lets users view a hard disk in a consistent manner, whether the local hard drive or a mapped network drive.
- **Double-clicking.** The action of double-clicking to launch an application was not discoverable. Single-clicking would not always open programs nor produce the desired results within the confines of an active window. Most actions in Windows 95 can now be accomplished with a single click. Double-clicking still exists, but it is used to start or open from a shortcut, plus a few odd backward-compatible events, such as closing a window using the icon in the upper right corner.
- **Task switching.** The way to switch from one active task to another was not discoverable. Many users never ran multiple applications because they did not know how to task switch. The Windows 95 Taskbar now makes it easy to switch between open programs or start new ones.
- **Overlapping functionality.** There was too much overlap among the Windows middle-management functions of

Program Manager, File Manager, Print Manager, Windows Setup, and Control Panel under Windows 3.*x*. This is streamlined in Windows 95.

- **Short 8.3 filenames restrictive.** The MS-DOS 8.3 file and directory naming limitation often led to cryptic and easily forgettable names. Windows 95 supports the use of Long File Names (LFNs) that can be up to 255 characters long. The length of a filename might be less, because the maximum length for both the path and filename cannot exceed 258 characters. The longer the path, the shorter the filename allowed.

- **User interface not customizable.** This limitation created an active market for third-party software companies to improve the look and feel of and ability to customize the Windows 3.*x* desktop. The Windows 95 Desktop is neat, clean, and logical. Users start with a default desktop, but are not restricted in how to customize their Windows 95 Desktop.

- **Network and connectivity integration.** This integration was poor under Windows 3.*x*, depending on which network operating system was in use. Windows 95 has been called the perfect network client because of its great network integration features. Remote access is also built-in to the Windows 95 operating system.

Customizing and Configuring Windows 95

Windows 95 is extremely easy to customize and configure. This is great for the end-user; however, this same strength can cause serious headaches for support staff, who need to respond to any end-user problems. The following are three basic rules for the customization and configuration of Windows 95:

- Use properties sheets to configure objects. From the context menu for an object, select Properties.

- If you need help, ask for it. From the Start menu, select Help. Always install the full Online Help file, and add the *Windows 95 Resource Kit* Help file for good measure.

- Never play with the Windows 95 Registry. It's like running through the house with open scissors—very dangerous. Use Control Panel functions to safely change the Windows 95 Registry values.

Two excellent books for your Windows 95 bookshelf are the Que book, *Windows 95 Installation and Configuration Handbook*, and New Riders' *Inside Windows 95*.

Customizing Windows 95

When Windows 95 first installs, the default Windows 95 Desktop is presented. The Windows 95 Desktop is the most significant change as well as the most significant advancement. The Windows 95 Desktop can be used to launch applications, store files and folders, maintain shortcuts to files or programs, and provide easy access to your Windows 95 configuration settings.

Windows 95 can be easily customized to make it your own in terms of ease of use, flexibility, and desktop appearance. This section covers setting up a dual-boot system, the fundamentals of Plug and Play, adding items to the Start menu, and customizing your Windows 95 Desktop.

Setting Up a Dual-Boot System

Many users are hesitant to jump into Windows 95 without a safety net that permits them to continue to get work done using their previous operating system while they adjust to the new operating system. Larger corporate sites will experience a long transition to either Windows 95 or Windows NT Workstation and might need to operate in multiple, mixed environments. One way to accomplish both these objectives is to enable dual-booting.

Dual-boot is a generic term for having multiple operating systems on the computer at the same time and using a menu-system front-end to select the operating systems with which to boot the computer.

It is possible to operate Windows 95 in a dual-boot mode. Table 3.1 outlines useful information about installing Windows 95 as an upgrade to other pre-existing operating systems, and which of the operating systems combinations can support dual-boot with Windows 95.

Table 3.1

Installing Windows 95 with Pre-Existing Operating Systems

Operating System	Upgrade to Windows 95?	Dual-boot?
MS-DOS 3.2 versions or greater	Yes, if Windows 3.1*x* or Windows for Workgroups 3.*x* is on the PC, it is recommended to install from within Windows.	Yes (with MS-DOS 5.*x* or 6.*x*)
Novell(DR)DOS	Yes	No
PC-DOS versions	Yes	Yes (with PC-DOS versions 5.*x* or 6.*x*)
Windows 3.0	Yes, must install from MS-DOS	Yes, by installing to a different directory with version 5.*x* or 6.*x* of MS-DOS or PC-DOS.
Windows 3.1*x*	Yes	Yes, by installing to a different directory with version 5.*x* or 6.*x* of MS-DOS or PC-DOS.
Windows for Workgroups 3.*x*	Yes	Yes, by installing to a different directory with version 5.*x* or 6.*x* of MS-DOS or PC-DOS.
Windows NT	No	Yes, with MS-DOS already installed. Must

continues

Table 3.1 Continued

Operating System	Upgrade to Windows 95?	Dual-boot?
		install Windows 95 to a different directory, FAT partition.
OS/2 2.*x* or greater	Yes, install from MS-DOS	Yes, with MS-DOS already installed. Must install Windows 95 to a different directory, FATpartition.

Upgrading to Windows 95 over Existing Operating Systems

You can install Windows 95 as the only operating system on the computer. This represents a clean install. More likely, however, you will install Windows 95 as an upgrade. As previously discussed in Chapter 1, "Planning and Installation," Windows 95 is primarily designed to be an upgrade to either Windows 3.1*x* or Windows for Workgroups 3.*x* in combination with MS-DOS. Windows 95 can be installed over other operating systems (refer to table 3.1). This section explains your upgrade options.

You can install Windows 95 over most versions of DOS, which might have an existing Windows 3.*x* or Windows for Workgroups 3.*x* installation. During installation, the Windows 95 Setup program detects whether Windows 3.1*x* or Windows for Workgroups 3.*x* is already installed on the computer. If found, the Windows 95 Setup program offers to install Windows 95 into the same directory in order to upgrade the existing Windows installation.

Installing into the Existing Windows Directory

If you choose to install into the existing Windows directory, the Windows 95 Setup program uses any existing configuration settings to configure Windows 95. This includes configuration settings in SYSTEM.INI, WIN.INI, and PROTOCOL.INI, plus file associations from the Windows 3.*x* Registry. These configuration settings are moved into the Windows 95 Registry so applications and networking settings automatically work in Windows 95.

Windows 3.*x* Program Manager groups are also converted into folders in the Programs folder (directory), which enables them to be displayed from the Windows 95 Start menu, under Programs.

The Windows 95 Setup program deletes some of the old DOS files, replaces the compression programs such as DBLSPACE or DRVSPACE with Windows 95 versions, and renames the boot files. For the best detailed reference on these changes to both DOS and Windows, see Chapter 6, "Setup Technical Discussion," of the *Windows 95 Resource Kit.* Please note that some of the old DOS files are deleted only if you install Windows 95 into the existing Windows directory.

Installing into a New Windows 95 Directory

If you choose to install Windows 95 into a new directory, or to not upgrade an existing Windows installation, you can dual-boot to your previous version of DOS and Windows if you are running version 5.*x* or 6.*x* of either MS-DOS or PC-DOS. The Windows 95 MSDOS.SYS file is automatically updated to include the entry BootMulti=1, which enables dual-boot capabilities with your previous version of DOS.

Windows NT cannot be upgraded to Windows 95; you must install Windows 95 to a new directory. The Windows NT computer must already be configured to dual-boot between Windows NT and MS-DOS before you install Windows 95. The Windows NT installation documentation outlines the details of how to configure the dual-boot between Windows NT and MS-DOS. Windows 95 needs to be installed from an MS-DOS prompt, so start the Windows NT computer using MS-DOS, then run the Windows 95 Setup program.

Depending how Windows NT was initially installed, if you try to install Windows 95 into the same directory as Windows NT there might be some problems. Both Windows 95 and Windows NT have DLL names in common between the two operating systems, and both store these DLLs in the SYSTEM directory. Thus, if Windows 95 were installed to the same directory, one or both of the operating systems will not run properly. Windows 95 needs to be installed in a FAT partition, which has enough room for Windows

95 and its swap file. NTFS, or even HPFS, partitions are not available from within Windows 95.

Although OS/2 3.*x* qualifies as an operating system that can be upgraded to Windows 95, you must install Windows 95 in a new directory. The Windows 95 Setup program cannot migrate any of the desktop or other configuration settings from OS/3. Any Windows-based applications have to be re-installed to run under Windows 95. The OS/2 computer must already be configured to dual-boot between OS/2 and MS-DOS before you install Windows 95. The OS/2 installation documentation outlines the details of how to configure the dual-boot between OS/2 and MS-DOS. Windows 95 needs to be installed from an MS-DOS prompt, so start the OS/2 computer using MS-DOS, then run the Windows 95 Setup program.

The OS/2 operating system supports either dual-boot or an OS/2 Boot Manager. If your computer has the OS/2 Boot Manager, the Boot Manager will be disabled by the Windows 95 Setup program in order to complete the Windows 95 installation. All the OS/2 files are kept intact. To restore the OS/2 Boot Manager, make the OS/2 Boot Manager partition active again by using OS/2 Boot disks, and then running the OS/2 version of the FDISK utility. Windows 95 needs to be installed in a FAT partition, which has enough room for Windows 95 and its swap file. HPFS partitions are not available from within Windows 95.

Dual-Booting Windows 95 with Existing Operating Systems

You can install Windows 95 with existing operating systems on the computer. This type of installation typically represents an upgrade install. If you choose to install Windows 95 into a different directory, most Windows applications need to be reinstalled to update the WIN.INI, SYSTEM.INI, and the Registry, as well as reload any application files (DLLs) into the Windows 95 WINDOWS/SYSTEM and WINDOWS directories. Table 3.1 lists the dual-boot options for Windows 95 and existing operating systems. This section explains your dual-boot options.

Dual-Boot with DOS and Windows 3.x

The versions of MS-DOS supported for upgrading Windows 95 are versions 3.2 or higher, or an equivalent version from a hardware manufacturer (such as Compaq version DOS 3.31) with partitions greater than 32 MB. Other versions of DOS include IBM's PC-DOS and Novell's DR-DOS. However, due to conflicts with DOS naming standards in Windows 95, Novell's DR-DOS cannot be dual-booted with Windows 95. You would need to first update Novell's DR-DOS to MS-DOS 6.*x*, and then upgrade to Windows 95 in order to dual-boot.

To install dual-boot capabilities for DOS, the computer must be running version 5.*x* or 6.*x* of MS-DOS or PC-DOS. Previous versions of DOS often were heavily modified by manufacturers, so the Windows 95 Setup program checks both the type and version number. The controlling factor in configuring dual-boot is the pre-existing operating system. If Windows 3.1*x* or Windows for Workgroups 3.*x* is detected on the computer, you must choose to install Windows 95 in a different directory to enable dual-boot.

Dual-boot needs the Windows 95 install to be made into a new directory that does not contain a version of Windows 3.*x*. The Windows 95 Setup program makes all the changes needed to preserve your existing version of DOS, Windows 3.1*x*, or Windows for Workgroups 3.*x*, and your current CONFIG.SYS and AUTOEXEC.BAT files. The older DOS files are not deleted, enabling you to dual-boot and start the computer using the older version of DOS.

Several original MS-DOS boot files are renamed for future use. These are shown in table 3.2, and have DOS extensions. When you press F8 at the Windows 95 Startup and choose the option to start the previous version of MS-DOS, or press F4 at Windows 95 Startup, the Windows 95 versions of these same files are renamed with W40 extensions (except for IO.SYS), and the DOS files are renamed with their original extensions. In dual-boot mode, regardless of the previous choice at boot-up, Windows 95 starts each time.

Table 3.2

MS-DOS or Windows 95 Files Renamed During Dual-Boot

Boot Files	MS-DOS Versions	Windows 95 Versions
IO.SYS	IO.DOS	WINBOOT.SYS
MSDOS.SYS	MSDOS.DOS	MSDOS.W40
COMMAND.COM	COMMAND.DOS	COMMAND.W40
CONFIG.SYS	CONFIG.DOS	CONFIG.W40
AUTOEXEC.BAT	AUTOEXEC.DOS	AUTOEXEC.W40

To illustrate how dual-booting between MS-DOS and Windows 95 works, during the Windows 95 installation the Windows 95 Setup program renames existing MS-DOS boot files and creates a new set of Windows 95 boot files. All the old MS-DOS boot files are given a file extension of DOS. While the computer boots into Windows 95, there are only two sets of boot files: the Windows 95 boot files and the renamed MS-DOS version. When you choose to start the previous version of DOS, the Windows 95 boot files are renamed with the file extension W40, though IO.SYS is renamed WINBOOT.SYS. The old MS-DOS boot files are renamed to their original names, and then the computer is rebooted. While the computer boots into the old version of DOS there are still only two sets of boot files: the older MS-DOS boot files and the renamed Windows 95 boot files. These sets of boot files are renamed back and forth, depending on which of the two operating systems is actually booting the computer.

To set up dual-boot capabilities after Windows 95 is installed, follow the directions in the section "Installing Windows 95 for Dual-booting with Windows 3.*x*" in Chapter 6, "Setup Technical Discussion," of the *Windows 95 Resource Kit*.

To take advantage of Windows 95 dual-boot capabilities with versions 5.*x* or 6.*x* of MS-DOS or PC-DOS, the entry `Boot-Multi=1` must be set in the Windows 95 MSDOS.SYS file in the root directory. If you are installing Windows 95 to a different directory that does not contain a copy of Windows 3.*x*, dual-boot is automatically enabled.

Dual-booting to a down-level operating system (for example, MS-DOS 6.22 or earlier) can cause long filename problems when certain commands such as MOVE, COPY, REN, MD, RD, DEFRAG, and ScanDisk are used. Furthermore, almost any third-party or shareware file-maintenance utility that uses the same APIs as these commands likely causes long file-name errors when the utility is used under the down-level operating system. Be aware of this problem. Long file names are discussed in Chapter 6 of this book, "Managing Disk Resources and Utilities."

DriveSpace (disk compression) drives are accessible under Windows 95. However, if you're using MS-DOS 5.*x*, and you decide to compress your drive in Windows 95 with DriveSpace, you will not be able to dual-boot because both DriveSpace (DRVSPACE) and DoubleSpace (DBLSPACE) file-compression utilities are specific to MS-DOS version 6.*x*.

If you choose to install Windows 95 to a non-boot hard drive, approximately 8 MB of space is required on the root of the host boot drive.

Exercise 3.1 leads you through the process of dual-booting with DOS and Windows 3.1.

Exercise 3.1: Dual-Boot with DOS and Windows 3.1

Treat this dual-boot exercise as a custom installation to Computer 2; run this from the shared CD-ROM on Computer 1 or from a CD-ROM drive on Computer 2. If Computer 2 still has the network-based Windows 95 directory from Exercise 1.7, the Windows 95 installation also can be run from there.

Computer 2 should still be running both MS-DOS and Windows for Workgroups. The end result will have Computer 2 running Windows 95 in a dual-boot configuration. This is a hands-on exercise, with a 60-minute duration. Walk through the following steps:

1. Reboot Computer 2, loading MS-DOS and Windows for Workgroups. From a Windows 95 installation directory, start the Windows 95 SETUP.EXE program by one of the following means:
   - Shared CD-ROM on Computer 1
   - CD-ROM on Computer 2 itself
   - Server-based Setup of the Windows 95
   - A routine check of the system, followed by the preparation of the setup wizard
2. The software license appears. Read it, then choose Yes to continue.
3. The Setup Wizard appears to start collecting information about your computer. Choose Next to continue.
4. When prompted for a location to install Windows 95, do not take the default, C:\WINDOWS. Instead, select to install to an Other directory. Then choose Next to continue.
5. Install into a new Windows 95 directory, C:\WIN95. Choose Next to continue.
6. A Setup warning message appears, which tells you that installing Windows 95 to a new directory requires the reinstallation of all your Windows-based programs to make them work properly under Windows 95. Choose Yes to continue.
7. Windows 95 prepares the directory. Check for installed components and available disk space.
8. Choose the type of installation—the default is Typical. Choose Custom. Choose Next to continue.
9. For User Information, enter your full name and the name of your organization or company. Choose Next to continue.
10. For Product Identification, enter the product key code from the CD-ROM cover.

Setup analyzes your computer, searching for all hardware devices available.

11. If asked to check for specific hardware such as a CD-ROM drive or Sound Card, check the appropriate boxes, then choose Next to continue.

12. After hardware detection, a Getting Connected dialog box appears. Do not select any of these components.

13. You are prompted to install the default components, as determined by your setup option. Choose the options you will most likely use, then choose Next to continue.

14. Verify your network configuration, if prompted by the Windows 95 Setup program. With a Windows for Workgroups connected computer you might not see these prompts.

15. If asked to identify your computer and workgroup, enter the appropriate information. Make sure the computer name is unique. Choose Next to continue.

16. The Computer Settings screen is displayed. Verify all your computer settings, then choose Next to continue.

17. When asked whether you want to create a startup disk, accept the default; that sets the radio button to Yes, I want a startup disk. Choose Next to continue.

18. The Setup Wizard begins to copy files to your computer. Choose Next to continue.

19. The copy process might take a while; enter a Startup Disk floppy when prompted.

20. The Setup Wizard reappears to finish the Windows 95 installation on your computer. Choose Finish to continue.

21. Windows 95 starts and prompts you for your user name and password. The Control Panel, Start Menu, and Help system are configured.

22. When prompted for the time zone, choose your approximate location on the world map to help select the correct time zone. Choose Close to continue.

23. If you have a printer, ignore the printer wizard and continue. Chapter 7, "Managing Printers," discusses printer installation.

24. The Welcome to Windows 95 screen appears. From the Start Menu, run Notepad.exe and open the MSDOS.SYS file on the root of drive C. Verify MSDOS.SYS contains the entry for enabling dual-boot, `BootMulti=1`. Close the application.

25. Be aware that network Plug and Play adapters might not always configure themselves properly, so network browsing might be impacted. Check Hardware Configuration if any errors are encountered.

The Windows 95 Setup program should automatically enable dual-boot because Windows 95 is installed into a new directory, and the version 5.*x* or 6.*x* of MS-DOS was installed on the computer.

Dual-Boot with Windows NT

Windows NT has a built-in multi-boot capability called the *Windows NT Boot Loader* (NTLDR). When you first boot your computer, if MS-DOS was loaded when you initially installed Windows NT, the Windows NT Boot Loader appears and lets you choose between Windows NT and MS-DOS. Windows 95 must be installed to a FAT partition big enough to hold Windows 95 and its swap file. NTFS, as well as HPFS, partitions are not available for Windows 95 to install into.

To install Windows NT on a computer on which Windows 95 is already installed, switch to the directory containing the Windows NT installation files and type **winnt /w**. This starts the MS-DOS–based Windows NT setup, but allows the Windows NT Setup program to run under Windows. Otherwise, you are forced to exit to an MS-DOS 7.0 prompt and start from there. The 32-bit Windows version of the Windows NT Setup program, WINNT32.EXE, does not run under Windows 95. In Exercise 3.2, you install Windows NT in a dual-boot configuration.

Exercise 3.2: Dual-Boot with Windows NT

Treat this exercise as a routine installation of Windows NT 3.51 Server to Computer 2. Run the exercise from the shared CD-ROM on Computer 1 or from a CD-ROM drive on Computer 2. Computer 2 must meet the hardware requirements for a Windows NT Server. If you are new to Windows NT Server, two other good books from New Riders Publishing are recommended: *Inside Windows NT Server* and *Windows NT Server Professional Reference.* MCSE candidates must master Windows NT Server as part of the core operating system requirements.

The installation process for Windows NT Server 4.0 is more Windows 95-like. The new user interface update is the most significant improvement in the new version of Windows NT. If you are installing Windows NT Server 4.0, rather than the older Windows NT Server 3.51, review this exercise for the appropriate settings only. Be aware that the Microsoft certification exam objectives and test questions usually reflect the newer versions of software after four to six months.

Computer 2 should still be dual-booting both MS-DOS/Windows for Workgroups and Windows 95 (following Exercise 2.1). The end result has Computer 2 running Windows 95 in a multiple, dual-boot configuration. This is a hands-on exercise with a 60-minute duration. Walk through the following steps:

1. Reboot Computer 2, loading Windows 95. From a Windows NT Server installation directory—either on a shared CD-ROM on Computer 1 or a CD-ROM on Computer 2; start the Windows NT Server Installation (WINNT.EXE) program. Please have four pre-formatted, 1.44-MB HD 3.5-inch floppies handy to create the Windows NT boot disks and an emergency repair disk.

2. Use the winnt /w option from either within Windows 95 after it has finished rebooting or during reboot, press F8 at Windows 95 Startup, choose the option to start the command prompt only, and then run winnt.

3. Confirm when you are prompted that the current directory is the one on which the Windows NT Server installation files reside.

4. Insert disk 3 into the floppy drive and follow the Windows NT Server Setup program instructions.

   The three bootable Windows NT disks are created in reverse order, and the files are copied.

5. Restart the computer with disk 1, the Windows NT Boot Disk in drive A.

6. Choose where to install Windows NT, select a hard drive, as suggested by the Windows NT Server Setup program. All hard drives are displayed, showing available free space.

7. Leave the current file system intact (no changes). Do not convert to NTFS.

8. Choose the directory name for the Windows NT Server install. Accept the suggested default.

9. The Windows NT Server files are copied, and the computer is restarted with zero time at the Windows NT Boot Loader in order to complete the installation. Enter name and company information.

10. Make this computer a Primary Domain Controller. You have to re-install Windows NT Server to change this selection.

11. Enter a computer name, following the same naming rules as for Windows 95 computer names (see Chapter 1).

12. Accept the language default—English.

13. Skip the Printer setup.

14. For the network card, accept the default protocols, NWLINK (IPX/SPX compatible) and NetBEUI.

15. Assign the Primary Domain Controller a domain name, which you can use later. Keep the name simple.

16. For the default user-id-named administrator, press OK to use a blank password.

17. Select the appropriate time zone for the computer.

18. Test the screen display, then choose OK.

19. Restart Windows NT Server.

20. Create an emergency repair disk when prompted.

21. Modify the Windows NT Boot Loader menu selection. Go to Control Panel, System, and choose MS-DOS as the default startup, rather than Windows NT Server Version 3.5*x*, which is the original default. Choose OK to save your changes.

22. Using Windows NT File Manager, change the properties of the BOOT.INI file on the root to remove the Read-Only property so the file can be edited. Using Notepad, change MS-DOS line to read "Windows 95" rather than "MS-DOS" and then save the file. Change the properties of the BOOT.INI file back to Read-Only.

23. Shut down and then restart the computer.

To install Windows 95 on a computer already configured to use the Windows NT Boot Loader for Windows NT (as well as MS-DOS), you need to start the computer using the MS-DOS operating system. The FAT partition must be large enough to accommodate both Windows 95 and the swap file. Where you install Windows 95 depends on where Windows NT was installed, and whether or not there was a copy of Windows 3.*x* on the computer. Your options are as follows:

- **Windows NT only, no MS-DOS.** Boot MS-DOS from a floppy disk to install Windows 95. Install Windows 95 to a different directory than Windows NT. The Windows NT Boot Loader will be disabled, so restore it using the Windows NT emergency repair disk and select the Repair option. You will need to manually add the Windows 95 option to the BOOT.INI file if the Repair option does not recognize Windows 95 as another Windows NT boot option.

- **Windows NT and only MS-DOS.** Run the Windows 95 Setup program from an MS-DOS prompt. Install Windows 95 to a different directory than Windows NT. The Windows NT Boot Loader still might reference MS-DOS, so modify the BOOT.INI file as described in Exercise 3.2, so it reads Windows 95 rather than MS-DOS.

- **Windows NT and Windows 3.*x* sharing a directory.** If both Windows NT and Windows 3.*x* are installed in the same directory, you cannot update the existing copy of Windows 3.*x* to Windows 95. Install Windows 95 to a different directory. You need to re-install each of your Windows applications to run them under Windows 95.

- **Windows NT and Windows 3.*x* in different directories.** If Windows NT is installed in a different directory than the existing copy of Windows 3.*x*, you have the option of updating Windows 3.*x* to Windows 95. However, you can choose to install Windows 95 into a third directory, which requires you to re-install each of your Windows applications to run them under Windows 95.

To complete the Windows 95 installation, the computer might need to reboot once or twice, depending on the presence of Plug and Play devices. If the Windows NT Boot Loader is still working, select the MS-DOS option each time the computer is rebooted until the Windows 95 installation is successfully completed.

As a general rule, do not install Windows NT and Windows 95 into the same directory. They share common DLLs, which are stored in the same location in the directory. The last install over-writes the former and causes serious problems for one, if not both, of the operating systems. For example, Windows 95 replaces the Windows 3.*x* DLLs in the Windows System subdirectory to support both 16-bit and 32-bit Windows applications. Windows NT depends on the old Windows 3.*x* DLLs to run 16-bit Windows applications.

Dual-Boot with OS/2

OS/2 has several built-in multi-boot options, one called *dual-boot* and the other the *OS/2 Boot Manager*. The dual-boot option uses a BOOT.COM program to switch between the key boot files of either OS/2 or MS-DOS and then reboot the computer. The last boot selection is the one that runs when you start the computer. The OS/2 Boot Manager is like the Windows NT Boot Loader in that a menu front-end is displayed at system startup and the user selects which partition on the computer to make active at the startup. See your OS/2 documentation for details. New Riders Publishing's *OS/2 Certification Handbook* outlines both of these multi-boot options.

Remember that Windows 95 must be installed to a FAT partition that is big enough to hold the Windows 95 and the swap file. HPFS partitions are not available for Windows 95 to install into.

If installing OS/2 after Windows 95, follow the standard OS/2 installation instructions. If installing OS/2 with Windows support built-in, you should not impact the Windows 95 setup. If, however, you have the version of OS/2 that needs an existing copy of Windows 3.*x*, you should have both Windows 3.*x* and Windows 95 installed into separate directories. OS/2 then uses the existing Windows 3.*x* programs to run 16-bit Windows applications.

To install Windows 95 on a computer in which OS/2 has already been installed, switch to DOS before beginning the installation. The Windows 95 Setup program warns you that the OS/2 Boot Manager is disabled. After Windows 95 is installed, run the OS/2 Fdisk utility from the OS/2 boot disk to reactivate the OS/2 Boot Manager.

Dual-boot is a very useful feature that allows you to run multiple operating systems on the same computer. As a support person, you might be asked to help set up dual-boot capability. Expect some questions, especially about running either previous versions of DOS/Windows or in conjunction with running Windows NT. The exercises enable you to run through all the steps.

Limitations for Full Plug and Play

Plug and Play (PnP) is discussed in much greater detail in Chapter 11. The goal of Plug and Play is to enable changes to be made to the computer's configuration without requiring any active intervention by the user. You simply plug in the hardware device, and it works. Plug and Play is a standard set of industry specifications, developed by a group of hardware and software companies, for new computer hardware devices. With all the legacy hardware and software in existence, however, full Plug and Play implementation is limited in some computers in use today. The goal of this exam objective is that you understand the various computer bus configurations and the limitations these bus configurations have under the Plug and Play specification.

A bus configuration refers to the types of bus architecture used on the computer. The bus configurations in the following list have been improved and have matured over time as the Intel-based personal computer has evolved. (These bus configurations are not limited to only Intel-based PCs, but because Intel is the predominant PC architecture, the two are often linked.) The standard bus configurations are as follows:

- **Industry Standard Architecture (ISA).** The bus design of the 1984 IBM PC/AT computer. The bus supports the original 8-bit or 16-bit edge adapter cards, configured through the use of jumper pins and dip switches. These adapter cards are often called legacy adapter cards, because of the their age and the appearance of newer hardware bus designs. New generation ISA adapters now fully support Plug and Play. The ISA bus design can be found along with either the VL local bus or PCI local bus configurations on many newer computers.
- **Micro-Channel Architecture (MCA).** A bus design created by IBM in 1987. MCA improved on the ISA bus, but was too closely associated with the IBM PS/2 line of computers. The bus supports 32-bit edge adapter cards, which were configured through software. Stiff royalties and licensing rules by IBM discouraged wide-scale use by IBM clone manufacturers.

- **Enhanced Industry Standard Architecture (EISA).** A bus design by non-IBM companies in late the 1980s that competed with MCA. It offers the same features as MCA. The bus supports 32-bit edge adapter cards, which are configured through software. EISA often is found in high-end Intel computers used as network servers. For the individual computer user, EISA offered few advantages over ISA and did not justify the increased cost.
- **Video Electronic Standards Association or VESA Local bus (VL).** A bus design produced in 1992 by a standards group responsible for creating display and monitor specifications. The original goal was to improve the video throughput, achieve higher display resolutions, and faster display refresh scan rates (kilohertz). This local bus enables high-speed connections to peripheral hardware devices, not just video adapters, and is used with the ISA bus configuration.
- **Peripheral Component Interconnect bus (PCI).** A bus design produced by Intel in 1993 that competes with VL. PCI is a local bus design being promoted as the logical successor to VL. It enables high-speed connections to peripheral hardware devices. The PCI bus design can be found with ISA bus configurations on many Pentium computers.
- **Small Computer Standard Interface (SCSI).** A bus design that supports chaining multiple hardware devices together. Usually a SCSI bus can support up to seven hardware devices, such as hard disk drives and CD-ROM drives. Each hardware device is assigned a number from zero to seven for communication with the SCSI controller, and is often configured through software. This specification has been improved to support faster speeds across the bus, and even double the number of hardware devices.
- **Personal Computer Memory Card International Association or the new name, PC Card (PCMCIA).** A bus design standard originally developed to support adding memory expansion cards to portable computers. This specification has expanded to include a wide range of credit-card-sized interface cards for portables, docking stations, and regular desktop computers.

Table 3.3 outlines the bus configurations in the preceding list and identifies their key Plug and Play limitations:

Table 3.3
Bus Configuration Plug and Play Limitations

Bus	Plug and Play Limitation
ISA	Legacy cards. You can mix and match Plug and Play ISA and standard ISA adapter cards. Windows 95 polls the card or asks the user to supply values. Static data is stored in the Registry. Hardware resources are assigned before other Plug and Play hardware devices, and have priority.
EISA	Meets most Plug and Play requirements. Bus enumerator used to query nonvolatile RAM on adapter card for resource requirements. Cannot be reconfigured by Windows 95.
MCA	Meets most Plug and Play requirements, like EISA, but OEM (IBM) must provide the bus enumerator used to query nonvolatile RAM on card for resource requirements. Cannot be reconfigured by Windows 95.
SCSI	Multiple-device chained interface, which does not currently support Plug and Play. Like ISA in some regards. Difficult to configure due to both host adapter configuration and the SCSI bus termination, in addition to other issues.
VL\PCI	Secondary bus, used for high-speed video or other devices. Plug and Play compatible, but dependent on primary bus architecture. VL bus enumerators provided by OEM. PCI can also share IRQs, whereas ISA devices cannot. BIOS must be set to prevent IRQ overlaps.
PCMCIA	PC Card standard. Card and socket services allow dynamic configuration. Supports all the Plug and Play functionality, plus hot docking, which allows PC Card insertion with the power on.

Many of these bus configurations are compatible with the Plug and Play specifications. Windows 95 groups hardware devices and the various bus configurations into classes for purposes of installing and managing device drivers as well as allocating the computer's resources. Not every bus configuration is 100 percent compliant with Plug and Play. Windows 95 deals with each differently, gathering as much needed information as possible before prompting the user to supply additional information.

The Windows 95 hardware tree is a record of the current system configuration, based on the configuration information for all classes in the Hardware Branch of the Registry. The hardware tree is created in RAM each time the computer is started and can be dynamically modified. Some changes require a reboot of the computer before they become effective.

Although Plug and Play solves many of the hardware configuration issues, you occasionally need to manually change device settings. For example, in the dual-boot setup of Windows for Workgroups 3.*x* and Windows 95, or Windows 95 and Windows NT, the network interface card settings might prevent you from connecting to the network. Non-Plug and Play operating systems have default settings for the cards, whereas Windows 95 allows a Plug and Play adapter to select its own settings. In these cases, you might need to disable the Plug and Play features of the network interface card and manually set them.

In the following exercise you identify which devices are present on your Windows 95 computer. You use the Device Manager to view the computer's hardware tree. If some hardware device on your computer is not working correctly, the Device Manager tab on the System property sheet will display either a yellow or red icon on top of the hardware device icon. Keep in mind, however, that the Device Manager is only the second step in your hardware troubleshooting. The first step to any type of computer hardware troubleshooting can be summarized by three Cs—connection, current, and configuration.

Connection refers to ensuring that the hardware device is properly connected to the computer. The simple act of re-seating an adapter card can often restore a connection that has worked itself loose through constant use. *Current* refers to verifying that the hardware device has power. Make sure the power is turned on at the power strip, check that the power cable is properly inserted, or plug in the secondary power converter to a socket for a device that needs power. *Configuration* refers to reading the device manual and using any utilities or vendor-supplied INF files to ensure the hardware is properly configured. Make sure you take note of any special resource requirements, such as I/O ports, Interrupts, or DMA channels. You may need to use these resource values to configure the hardware device.

If you eliminate the obvious sources of your hardware problems, and the problem still exists, the Device Manager is the next best place to look. In Exercise 3.3 you examine the hardware configuration of your computer.

Exercise 3.3: Viewing the Hardware Tree

1. From a Windows 95 computer, select Start, **S**ettings, **C**ontrol Panel, and double-click on the System icon. The System Properties sheet appears (see fig. 3.1).

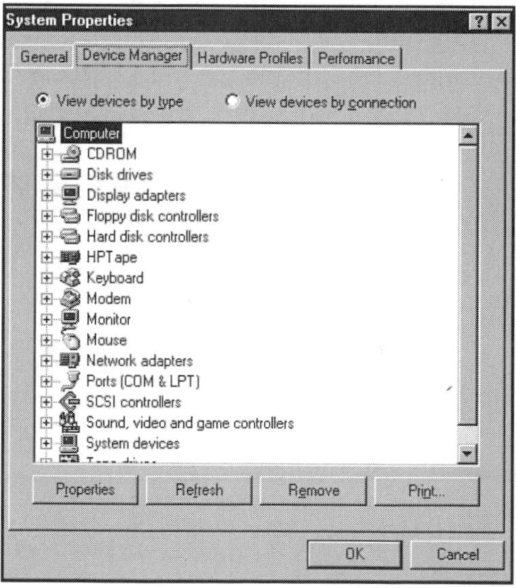

Figure 3.1

The Device Manager tab of the System Properties sheet.

2. Select the Device Manager tab on the System Properties sheet to view the hardware configuration.

Which of the bus configurations listed in table 3.3 can be found on your computer? The most common workstation bus configuration is an ISA bus, followed by a combination of either ISA and VL, or ISA and PCI.

The Device Manager allows you to change the configuration of most devices located on the computer. You can view devices by type or connection. Problems with the hardware configuration on the computer show up in the Device Manager tab of the System Properties sheet. Refer to figure 3.1 to see a sample hardware configuration.

Adding Items to the Start Menu

On the Windows 95 Taskbar, the Start button is used to initiate most of your computer activity. The Start button is the main starting point for running applications. Choose Start to see a list of key menu features and functions:

- **Programs.** Menu selection that corresponds to the Windows 3.*x* concept of program groups within Program Manager. If you install Windows 95 in an existing Windows 3.*x* directory, all your groups are converted into folders, and those application shortcuts are displayed with this menu selection.

- **Documents.** Menu selection that displays a list of the most recently edited or saved files. This list is kept in a hidden folder called Recent, which stores shortcuts to the actual documents themselves.

- **Settings.** Menu selection that allows you to open the Control Panel, the Printers folder, and the Taskbar Properties sheet.

- **Find.** Menu selection that locates a folder or a file on your computer, a shared resource on the network, or a location on The Microsoft Network.

- **Help.** Menu selection that provides information from the extensive Windows 95 Help System. Installing the optional Online User's Guide component makes this menu selection the best method for users to get information, especially with the new help index and find features. You can also use the F1 key to open the Windows 95 Help System.

- **Run.** Menu selection that allows you to launch applications directly from the Start menu. You can specify the name of an executable file, folder, document, or shared folder from the command line. A list of previously used commands are cached and can be retrieved from a drop-down list.
- **Shut Down.** Menu selection that offers you the choice to shut down, restart, restart in MS-DOS Mode, close all programs and, if you are on a network, to log on as a different user. You should always use the Shut Down option before turning off your computer. Following this practice ensures that all programs and files are closed properly before you actually turn off the power.
- **Suspend.** This optional menu selection (for laptops with advanced power management) can be added to the Start menu by selecting a check box on the Taskbar Properties sheet. Suspend puts the computer in suspended or sleep mode. This choice is available only on computers that support this feature.
- **Eject PC.** This optional menu selection allows a controlled undocking of laptops from a docking station that supports hot docking. This choice is present only on computers that support this feature.

To add items to the Start menu you can either (1) drag and drop the item onto the Start button, or (2) open the Taskbar Properties sheet. To open the Taskbar Properties sheet, either a) right-click on a open area of the Taskbar and select Properties, or b) choose Start, Settings, Taskbar.

In Exercise 3.4, you add one of your favorite programs to the Start menu. If you do not have a program in mind, add the program WORDPAD.EXE, which, if installed, can be found in the Accessories folder of the Program Files subdirectory. The quotes around the path to a particular program are required if the path includes a long filename with embedded spaces.

Exercise 3.4: Adding a Program to the Start Menu

1. From Computer 1, open the Start menu. Choose Settings, Taskbar to open the Taskbar Properties sheet.

2. Select the Start Menu Programs tab on the Taskbar Properties sheet (see fig. 3.2).

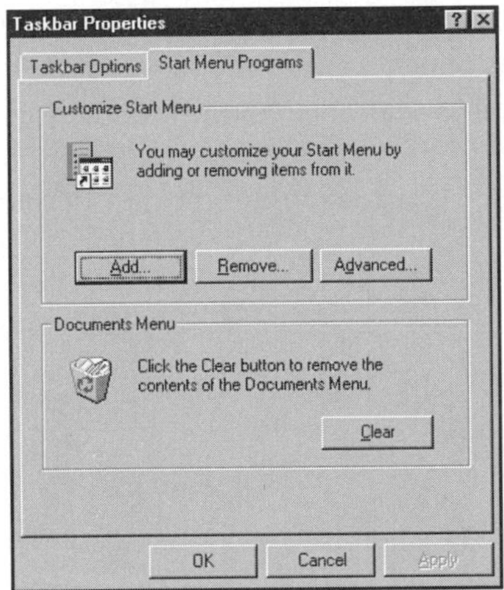

Figure 3.2

The Start Menu Programs tab of the Taskbar Properties sheet.

3. Click on the Add button, and a create shortcut wizard dialog window appears. In the command-line box, enter "**C:\Program Files\Accessories\Wordpad.exe**" or click on the Browse button to find a different program. The double quotes are necessary for the Wordpad.exe program because the Program Files folder includes a space in its name between the words "Program" and "Files."

4. Choose a location in the Start menu to place the new shortcut. Choose to put the shortcut into the Start menu folder. Give the shortcut an appropriate long filename, such as "Wordpad Program." Select Finish when done. Choose OK to close the Taskbar Properties sheet.

5. Open the Start menu to display all the key menu features and functions. Where in the Start menu does the program appear? Usually you will see the new program at the top of the Start menu. Be aware there is a limit on the number of

items in the Start menu, depending on whether you are using large or small icons.

There is a limit to the number of programs that can be placed on the first level of the Start menu. Depending on the icon size used to display the Start menu and your display resolution, you can have approximately 13 to 17 menu selections available. More than that will not be displayed. The Advanced button on the Taskbar Properties sheet allows you to view all the various Start menu levels at one time. You can then drag and drop, or copy between the folders, which can be found within the Start menu folder under the Windows folder on the computer.

> You can use your keyboard and cursor keys to access the Start menu. Press Ctrl+Esc to bring up the Start menu and show the Taskbar (if it is hidden). The Microsoft Natural keyboard, as well as some of the newer Windows 95-ready keyboards, include special Windows keys that enable single keystroke access to the Start menu.

Customizing the Desktop

The Windows 95 Desktop consists of several different components with a much different user interface than previous versions of Windows. For most users, the Windows 95 Desktop represents their first view of the new operating system.

Users initiate most actions from the Windows 95 Desktop, and they may organize the objects on the Desktop to suit their needs. The Windows 95 Desktop can contain icons, shortcuts, folders, files, windows, and the Taskbar. These are all objects and they can be manipulated as objects. Favorite folders and files can be left on the Windows 95 Desktop, where they are easily accessed. Several objects common to most Windows 95 Desktops include the following:

- **My Computer.** Represents the computer object, and loosely corresponds to the File Manager in previous versions of

Windows. My Computer is a folder that gives you quick access to your entire computer, as well as to the Control Panel folder, Printers folder, and Dial-Up Networking folder. All objects stored on your computer can be accessed through the My Computer folder.

- **Network Neighborhood.** Represents the network object; it exists only if the computer is on a network. Network Neighborhood is a folder that gives you access to computer icons that represent members of your workgroup and an icon that represents the entire Network. Chapter 5, "Networking and Interoperability," discusses the Network Neighborhood in greater detail.

- **Inbox.** Represents a built-in universal inbox for Windows 95, which is used to send, receive, and organize e-mail, faxes, items from online services, and other information. Although it refers to Microsoft Exchange when started, it is not the full client that comes with Microsoft's Exchange server. See Chapter 10, "Microsoft Exchange," for more information.

- **Recycle Bin.** Represents a trash-bin object. Any folders and files you delete are automatically moved to this folder. Recycle Bin provides you with an opportunity to recover deleted files by opening the Recycle Bin icon, selecting the files you want to recover, and then choosing File, Restore. You can purge any deleted files by selecting File, Empty Recycle Bin.

- **My Briefcase.** Represents a briefcase object that contains files and folders you want to keep current. The Briefcase is very useful for working with files off-site, perhaps on a portable computer. It is a special folder that you can use to synchronize files between two computers, or between your computer and a network file server to help ensure that the files are up-to-date. See Chapter 9, "Mobile Services," for more information.

- **Microsoft Network.** Represents the Microsoft Online Service object, which is used to connect to the Microsoft Network (MSN) service. You can use the Microsoft Network to exchange messages; read the latest news, sports, weather, and financial information; download programs; and connect to the Internet. It is similar to CompuServe, America Online, and Prodigy.

- **The Taskbar.** Represents a list of all active programs by maintaining a title button for each active program. The Taskbar allows you to quickly switch between programs. At the far right of the Taskbar is the notification area, which is used for status information. By default, the notification area contains the clock, but it can also show battery status on your portable computer, print job status, modem status, speaker volume status, and so on. At the far left of the Taskbar is the Start button.

- **The Start button.** Represents the Start program menu. Most computer activities can be initiated from the Start menu. You can also use the Start button to start any application.

To customize the Windows 95 Desktop, start with the Display Properties sheet. To open the Display Properties sheet, either right-click in an open area of the Windows 95 Desktop and select Properties from the pop-up menu; or choose Start, Settings, and Control Panel, then choose the Display icon. Figure 3.3 shows the Display Properties sheet.

Figure 3.3

The Display Properties sheet.

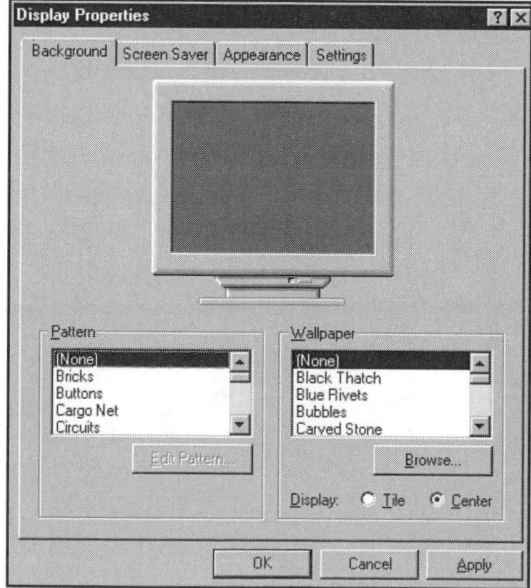

The Windows 95 display parameters are divided into four tabs if Microsoft Plus! is not installed, and five tabs if it is installed. The following tabs are available:

- **Background.** Use the Background tab to establish settings for the background pattern and wallpaper. Both are mutually exclusive, with wallpaper taking precedence over the background pattern. You can select your own bitmap (BMP) file to use as the wallpaper by using the Browse button. Depending on the size of the bitmap, you can tile or center it.

- **Screen Saver.** Use the Screen Saver tab to add a Windows 95 screen saver. The default screen saver is Flying Windows. Other Windows 95 screen savers are included, and you also can add additional ones with Microsoft Plus!. Each installed screen saver has settings that control its appearance. You can also password-protect your computer, and the screen saver password can be different from your other passwords. You change the screen-saver password through the Screen Saver tab on the Display Properties sheet.

- **Appearance.** Use the Appearance tab to configure the look of all the various components of your windows and desktop. You can choose from pre-defined color schemes or create one of your own.

- **(Microsoft) Plus!.** The Plus! tab is an optional fifth tab on the Display Properties sheet. You can use it to change the standard icons, mouse pointer, folder icons, and so on using Desktop Themes. Several new features can dramatically improve the look and feel of your Windows 95 desktop, all of which come with the Microsoft Plus! package. One option allows you to stretch the desktop wallpaper to fit the screen resolution.

- **Settings.** The Settings tab contains configuration options for the monitor. You can make changes to the color palette, desktop area resolution (if supported by your display driver), font size and type, and specification of both the display driver and monitor type.

One of the Display settings you most likely will want to change is font size, especially when running at higher resolutions for the display. At 800x600 or higher display resolutions, you can change the font size. Larger fonts can make text easier to read as your display resolution increases. Windows 95 enables you to dynamically change the display resolution by adjusting the slider bar (which appears only if your adapter and monitor can support the higher resolutions).

tip

> The higher the display resolution, the slower the display refreshes. If you dynamically change your resolution setting using the Display Properties sheet, Windows 95 gives you the following warning message:
>
> `Windows will resize your desktop. This could take a few minutes, during which your screen might flicker. If Windows does not reappear correctly, wait 15 seconds, and your original settings will be restored.`
>
> If your screen changes to the newer resolution without problems, you receive a second message, as follows:
>
> `You resized your desktop. Do you want to keep this setting?`
>
> You can either choose **Y**es to accept the change, or **N**o (default) to return to the previous setting. However, if your screen does not change properly, or turns black, you need to reboot into Safe Mode, which loads a standard VGA driver, then shut down again and restart Windows 95 to restore your earlier settings. Make sure you choose an adapter and monitor type for the display that matches the equipment installed on your computer.

In Exercise 3.5, you experiment with the look and feel of your desktop by making changes to the Display Properties sheet.

Exercise 3.5: Customizing Your Windows 95 Desktop

1. From your computer, choose Start, Settings, and Control Panel, then choose the Display icon. The Display Properties sheet opens (refer to figure 3.3).

2. Select the Background tab. Click on the scroll box in the Wallpaper field to select a bitmap (BMP) file, or choose Browse to select your own file.
3. Explore the various tabs on the Display Properties sheet and change your display settings as desired.
4. When you finish, choose OK to close the Display Properties sheet.

What happens when you make changes to the Desktop settings? The changes are shown first to the Display Properties sheet's display monitor, and are applied only when you click on the Apply button or choose OK to close.

The Windows 95 Desktop is yours to customize to the way you work. Learn how the objects on the Windows 95 Desktop function and what changes can be made to the various properties sheets.

Configuring Windows 95

One of the first impressions you will form about Windows 95 is that it is significantly different than Windows 3.*x* in both look and behavior. You can configure Windows 95 to suit your own needs. This tweaking (making minor adjustments) to the standard Windows 95 setup is often needed.

No two computer systems are entirely the same. Each is unique. Each has its own setup and configuration. Even if two computers are the same make and model, they may start out alike, but that rapidly changes as hardware and software changes are made to the computers. Windows 95 must be both flexible enough to handle these differences and still be simple enough to configure.

Windows 95 can be easily configured to make it your own in terms of how it operates, shortcuts, and the settings and attributes of objects. This section covers the key differences between Windows 3.*x* and Windows 95, installing Plug and Play hardware devices, and configuring the various components of the Windows 95 user interface. How to configure a printer is covered in Chapter 7.

Identify and Explain the Differences between the Windows 3.1 and Windows 95 Interfaces

What are the differences between the Windows 3.*x* interface and the Windows 95 interface? If you think about the interface of Windows 3.*x* and then try to draw comparisons to the interface of Windows 95, you are well on the way to understanding this exam objective—there is no single correct answer. Many of the key concepts found in the interface for Windows 95 have historical connections to the previous versions of Windows, like Windows for Workgroups 3.*x* and Windows NT. Table 3.4 compares the two interfaces to highlight the key differences.

Table 3.4

Interface Differences between Windows 3.x and Windows 95

Windows 3.*x*	Windows 95
Program Manager	Explorer runs the Desktop, and the Start menu launches programs. Program Manager (PROGMAN.EXE) is still included as an optional interface at installation time.
Program Groups (grp); no nested groups allowed.	Converted into Start menu folders; nested folders allowed.
Minimized programs show as the icons on desktop, or might be hidden behind open windows. Some active programs might be hidden.	All active programs appear on Taskbar, which itself can be hid den to the edge of the screen using the Auto Hide feature.
Close programs through the menu or by double-clicking on the command bar on the upper left side of the screen.	Close programs through the menu, by double-clicking on the program icon, or by clicking on the Close button on the upper right side of the screen.
Maximize, Minimize buttons; up and down arrow heads.	Maximize, Minimize buttons; full windows and Taskbar line.

Windows 3.*x*	Windows 95
Icons in Program Manager	Shortcuts
File Manager	Explorer and My Computer programs; File Manager (WINFILE.EXE) is still included, if needed.
Directories, subdirectories	Folders
File extensions shown	Known file extensions not shown. Use the View menu options on the View tab to see all file extensions.
Short 8.3 filenames	Long File Names, up to 255 characters; maximum 258 characters for both path and filename.
Connect network drives through File Manager	Use Network Neighborhood to see available network resources; or Explorer to connect network drives.
DOS delete/undelete	Recycle Bin
Control Panel	Control Panel folder opened by choosing Start, Settings, Control Panel; or from My Computer folder.
Print Manager	Printer Folder and Printer Wizard, opened by choosing Start, Settings, Printers; or from My Computer folder.
Task list (CTRL-ESC)	Taskbar; Task Manager (TASKMAN.EXE) is still included, if needed.
Clock must be started.	Clock part of Notification Area. Can turn off display of clock from the Taskbar Properties sheet.
MS-DOS Prompt	Start menu, Programs, MS-DOS Prompt; or Run command program.
Run command in File Manager	Start menu, Run command

Exercise 3.6 makes use of two computers to compare and contrast the differences between Windows 3.*x* and Windows 95. It will be helpful to you in this exam objective area to visually compare the two versions of Windows. If you only have a single dual-boot computer, run down each column before dual-booting between the two versions of Windows.

Exercise 3.6: Explain Windows 3.1 and Windows 95 Differences

Dual-boot Computer 1 to Windows for Workgroups, and leave Computer 2 running Windows 95. Go through each entry in Table 3.4 and compare the user interfaces between the two computers. How do you start an application program in Windows 3.1 versus Windows 95?

Other sources of information about the differences between Windows 3.*x* and Windows 95 can be found in the Windows 95 Help File Contents, "If you've used Windows before" section. Also, in the small manual that comes with the Windows 95 operating system, called *Introducing Windows 95*, look in the Welcome section, "If you've used Windows before."

Installing New Hardware Devices

One of the toughest areas for you to configure in Windows 95 is hardware. Computer owners are finding that new applications are demanding more—more RAM memory, more hard disk space, more speed in quicker video refresh rates, more display size and better resolution, more modem speed, and so on. Although Windows 95 does not require you to make any system changes and hardware upgrades, it does encourage you to seriously consider them.

Any user who has previously chosen to add hardware devices to his or her computer knows how difficult it can be to reconfigure the operating system and get all the software to work correctly with the new hardware. A new operating system upgrade might also force you to spend a considerable amount of valuable time getting all the hardware devices to work correctly. It makes you wonder if all the pain is worth the gain. Windows 95 hopes to change this through support for the Plug and Play (PnP) specification.

Chapter 11 covers Plug and Play in greater detail. However, for the purpose of addressing this exam objective, this section looks at the many ways to configure Windows 95 using Plug and Play hardware devices.

In order to fully support the Plug and Play specification, a computer system needs three major components:

- Plug and Play hardware devices capable of identifying themselves and declaring their resource requirements. For ISA bus hardware, this capability requires a new generation of modified hardware devices, since the current generation is not capable of communicating this information.
- A Plug and Play computer BIOS that can accept and respond to the resource requirements communicated from Plug and Play hardware devices.
- A Plug and Play operating system that orchestrates all hardware components in the system by loading and configuring Plug and Play device drivers, and by responding to hardware changes and automatically reconfiguring the system without any user intervention.

Not all three major components are necessary to enjoy some of the benefits of Plug and Play. The Windows 95 operating system supports Plug and Play hardware devices. Older computers usually have a BIOS version that does not support Plug and Play, as well as older installed hardware devices that are not Plug and Play capable. So the only component that does support Plug and Play may be the Windows 95 operating system itself. Older computers and hardware devices that do not support Plug and Play are called *legacy hardware.* The Windows 95 operating system autodetects many of your hardware devices and automatically sets them up properly. But beware, sometimes Plug and Play performs more like Plug and Pray. Chapter 11 covers this in much greater detail.

Many newer hardware devices that might be used to upgrade the hardware on older computers support Plug and Play. You can configure Plug and Play hardware devices in one of the four following ways:

- **Use the Windows 95 Setup program.** Plug and Play hardware devices are automatically detected (default) during the hardware detection phase of the Windows 95 installation.
- **Add new Hardware Wizard.** The Windows 95 Control Panel can run through the same automatic detection of Plug and Play hardware devices (default) as is done during Windows 95 installation.
- **During the normal boot process.** Windows 95 loads the Registry Databases according to the user information (USER.DAT) and system information (SYSTEM.DAT) on your computer. If a new Plug and Play hardware device is discovered, it is set up automatically.
- **During warm- or hot-docking situations.** Windows 95 tests for Plug and Play hardware devices, such as a docking station or even PC Cards in laptop computers. *Warm-docking* refers to docking or undocking a laptop computer in suspended mode (minimum power); whereas *hot-docking* refers to docking a laptop computer running at full power. PC Cards can be detected at boot or when inserted into the computer.

Depending on the hardware configurations of your computers, you might have several new hardware devices that now support Plug and Play. The newer Network Interface Cards (NICs) from companies like 3Com, which makes the 3C509B Ethernet Adapter, all support Plug and Play. Check the hardware device specifications or talk to the manufacturer's technical support staff to be sure.

Updating to the Windows 95 operating system may provide you with your first encounter with Plug and Play hardware devices. Newer computers are fully Plug and Play compatible. You may have seen this Plug and Play configuration occur during the installation exercises in Chapter 1, or again earlier in this chapter in the dual-boot installation exercises. In Exercise 3.7, you add a Plug and Play hardware device. You can either re-install a Plug and Play hardware device already on your computer (if one exists) or add a new Plug and Play hardware device.

Exercise 3.7: Configuring a Plug and Play Hardware Device

1. If adding a new Plug and Play hardware device, shut down the computer and install the device, then go to step 5.
2. If reinstalling an existing Plug and Play hardware device, choose Start, Settings, and Control Panel, and double-click the System icon. The System Properties sheet appears (refer to figure 3.1).
3. Select the Device Manager tab on the System Properties sheet to view the hardware configuration.
4. Find a Plug and Play hardware device, highlight the device, and click on the Remove button to remove the Plug and Play hardware device, which you want the system to automatically detect in the next step. Shut down the computer.
5. Restart the computer. The normal Windows 95 boot process should recognize the Plug and Play hardware device and add it to the system configuration.
6. If the Plug and Play hardware device is not automatically added, you must choose Start, Settings, Control Panel, and double-click on the Add New Hardware icon to run the hardware detection process.

What happens during the automatic detection of Plug and Play hardware devices? The hardware devices should be automatically recognized by Windows 95. Are you prompted for any configuration information? If the hardware device has Plug and Play enabled, you should not be prompted for any configuration information.

What separates promise from reality is the experience you must acquire to properly configure hardware devices under Windows 95. Plug and Play promises installations that are simple and fail-safe. For hardware devices, the installation would be automatic: plug in the device, turn on the computer, and it just works. The reality of the situation is you need to be aware of IRQs, I/O port addresses, DMA channels, and memory ranges assigned to the various hardware components of your computer. The Device Manager tab on the System Properties sheet can help you ferret out the problems; however, experience is the greatest teacher.

Configuring the Taskbar

The Windows 95 Taskbar is new in the Windows interface. It provides quick access to all your active programs by maintaining a set of buttons that represent the programs' title boxes. The Taskbar is always available to easily let you switch between active programs by clicking the programs' buttons. Or you can use the Start button to open programs. A notification area displays the clock and status information. Figure 3.4 shows the Windows 95 Taskbar.

Figure 3.4

The Windows 95 Taskbar.

The Windows 95 Taskbar is comprised of three sections, shown in figure 3.4 from left to right: the Start button, Taskbar active program buttons, and the Notification Area. The Notification Area is used for the clock, and a space exists for status information. The status information displays small icons for programs running in the background. The background programs can be printers, modems, and sound cards. The Microsoft Plus! package includes a System Agent that also displays a small icon if any scheduled events are pending. Many Windows 95 applications also use this notification area.

By default, the Taskbar sits at the bottom of the screen. You can reposition the Taskbar by dragging it to either side or to the top of the screen. Just grab the Taskbar with your mouse pointer and drag it to another location on-screen. The Taskbar sits only on the four edges of the display: left or right side, top or bottom. You can resize the Taskbar to take up more or less room on-screen. Move the mouse pointer over the inner edge of the Taskbar. When the mouse pointer changes to a double-sided arrow, press and hold your left mouse button and drag the Taskbar to size it as you like.

You can use the Taskbar Properties sheet to adjust several options for the Taskbar. To open the Taskbar Properties sheet, right-click on a clear section of the Taskbar and select Properties, or choose Start, Settings, Taskbar. Figure 3.5 shows the Taskbar Properties sheet.

Figure 3.5

The Taskbar Properties sheet.

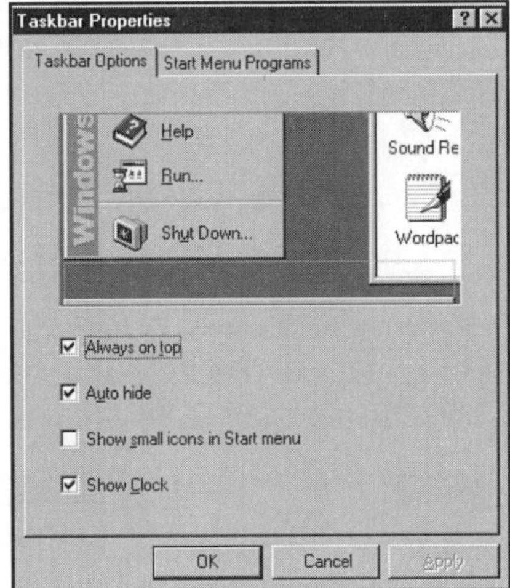

Taskbar options include the following:

- **Always on top.** This option keeps the Taskbar visible, even when using a full-screen program. When Always on top is used with Auto Hide, the Taskbar reappears over any full-screen program when activated.
- **Auto hide.** This option leaves the screen vacant by automatically hiding the Taskbar to the side of the screen where it is placed. It reappears when the cursor is moved to that edge of the screen.

- **Show small icons in Start menu.** This option changes the default large icons used in the Start menu to smaller icon versions. This option also reduces the size of the Start menu when you click the Start button.

- **Show Clock.** This option displays a digital clock with the computer's time in the notification area. Not displaying the clock does not remove the entire notification area. Having the cursor pointer positioned over the clock displays the date. Double-clicking the clock opens the Date/Time Properties sheet of the Control Panel.

In Exercise 3.8 you configure the Windows 95 Taskbar. It is important for the exam objective to know the various options available to you and what each option enables you to do when you configure the Windows 95 Taskbar.

Exercise 3.8: Configuring the Taskbar

1. On your computer, run Windows 95.

   Drag the Taskbar to each of the four sides of the screen display. Leave the Taskbar on the side that makes the most sense to you; the default is the bottom edge of the screen.

2. Resize the Taskbar by placing the tip of the mouse pointer on the inner edge of the Taskbar until a double-sided arrow appears. With the left mouse button depressed, drag the inner edge to resize the Taskbar. Leave the Taskbar at a comfortable size for your needs.

3. Go to the Start menu. Choose Settings, Taskbar to open the Taskbar Properties sheet (refer to figure 3.5).

4. Select Auto hide and choose OK. The Taskbar all but disappears. It is still there, but the only visible sign is a thin line of pixels on the side of the screen. Move the mouse pointer to the very edge of the screen where the Taskbar currently resides. The Taskbar will reappear.

5. Move the mouse pointer away from the edge of the screen where the Taskbar currently resides. You will see the Taskbar automatically hide again.

6. Experiment with various combinations of Taskbar options and select one that works best for you.

If you have a lot of active programs or open windows the Taskbar can become busy, and the size of each button can be reduced to the point that it is difficult to determine what is what. The best solution is to position the Taskbar on one side of the screen, resize the width to a usable size to read each button, and use the Auto Hide feature to have the Taskbar appear only when you need it. The Auto Hide feature is less useful if you make use of the Taskbar to quickly switch from one active program to another. Plus, if you use a full-screen application with scroll bars near the edge of the screen, you occasionally activate the Taskbar, which gets in your way and covers the scroll bar until it finally disappears once again after a few seconds of inactivity.

Configuring Shortcuts

Windows 95 introduces the concept of shortcuts. A *shortcut* is a connection or pointer between an icon and the physical location of an object. It is a virtual mapping. The shortcut itself is an object that points to the original object. The shortcut object has an LNK extension, or link extension, and this object's file type appears as shortcut in file folder details.

Shortcuts give you an easy way to make commonly used programs, folders, or files readily available. It does not matter where the original object is actually located, the shortcut makes it appear to exist where the shortcut object is located. To start or open a shortcut, simply double-click on the shortcut.

You can distinguish between the original object and the shortcut to that object by the small arcing arrow box in the lower left-hand corner of the icon. You can add shortcuts directly onto your Windows 95 Desktop, place them inside a folder, or add to the Start menu.

To create a shortcut, you can use any one of several methods:

- Secondary mouse-click from an open spot on the Windows 95 Desktop and choose New, Shortcut. Type the path and filename in the command line, or browse to find the object. You can change the name of the shortcut before you finish.
- Drag and drop from Windows Explorer to the Windows 95 Desktop. If you use the primary mouse button, the object is moved. However, if the object is an application, dragging and dropping will create a shortcut. If you use the secondary mouse button to drag and drop the object, a context-sensitive menu opens, giving you the option to move, copy, or create a shortcut.
- Secondary mouse-click on the object to open a pop-up context-sensitive menu, then choose Create Shortcut to directly create a shortcut. A new shortcut then is created in the same folder. You will be repositioned on the newly created shortcut, and you can then drag and drop the new shortcut where you like.

Creating a shortcut is different than just copying or moving an object. If you need to make changes to the properties of the original object, go to the object rather than the shortcut. The best analogy is an icon in a Windows 3.1 Program Manager group that points to the file. Shortcuts are just pointers to the original object. Changing or deleting the shortcut does not affect the original object. A copy command creates two separate objects, and a move command relocates the object.

A shortcut object has properties that include the location of the original object. To view a shortcut's properties sheet, click the shortcut with the right mouse button. From the pop-up menu, select Properties. In Exercise 3.9, you create a shortcut that you will use later in the chapter.

Exercise 3.9: Configuring a Shortcut

1. From your computer, choose Start, Programs, Windows Explorer, to open the Windows Explorer program.

2. Explore the Windows 95 directory and locate the Registry Editor (REGEDIT.EXE) application.

3. Highlight the REGEDIT object using the primary mouse button. With the button held down, drag and drop a shortcut onto the Windows 95 Desktop.

4. Exit Windows Explorer.

5. Click on the shortcut's name field below the icon titled "Shortcut to Regedit.exe" and change it to read "Registry Editor."

6. Right-click on the newly created shortcut and select Properties from the pop-up menu to display the Registry Editor Properties sheet. Assign the shortcut a hot key combination of Ctrl+Alt+R. The shortcut opens when you enter those keys (see fig. 3.6). Choose OK to save the change.

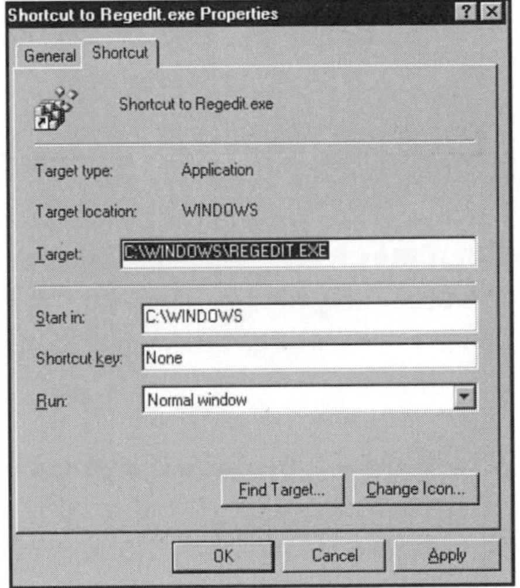

Figure 3.6

A Windows 95 Shortcut Properties sheet.

What happens to the original object when you make changes to the shortcut's settings? Nothing, since the shortcut's properties apply only to the shortcut itself.

A shortcut points to the original object through a one-way pointer link. This link can break if the original object is moved or deleted. Windows 95 attempts to automatically update a shortcut if the original object has been moved, but if Windows 95 is unsuccessful, this might cause an orphaned shortcut. If this occurs, you need to find the moved file and re-enter the full path name to the file in the target text box, or delete the shortcut object.

Shortcuts can make your Windows 95 Desktop much easier to use. A shortcut icon usually has a small arcing arrow box in the lower left-hand corner of the icon, except when the shortcut is added to the Start menu. If you look closely at the Start menu folder under Windows 95, you will notice that all the programs listed are actually shortcuts.

Configuring and Using Windows Explorer

Whereas the Start menu presents an easy way to launch applications, the Windows Explorer offers you a hierarchical view of folders and files shown in the context of the entire computer system. The Windows Explorer provides a structured path to your computer, where you can view and manage your files, plus other objects. Although similar to the Windows 3.*x* File Manager, the Windows Explorer gives you much greater functionality and flexibility.

The Windows Explorer is tightly integrated into the Windows 95 user interface. The Windows 95 Desktop itself is managed by the Windows Explorer. If you examine in detail the workings of the Windows Explorer, you will discover that the Windows 95 Desktop is nothing more than an expanded Windows Explorer contents pane view using large icons. The Windows Explorer is always running in the background, helping to manage your Windows 95 Desktop.

To illustrate the point that the Windows Explorer is always running in Windows 95, secondary mouse-click on the My Computer icon to open a context menu. Select Explore to open the

Windows Explorer program (see fig. 3.7). From the left side tree pane, click on the Desktop folder. The right side contents pane displays the contents of the Desktop folder. The contents of the top-level Desktop folder are the same as the objects located on your Windows 95 Desktop.

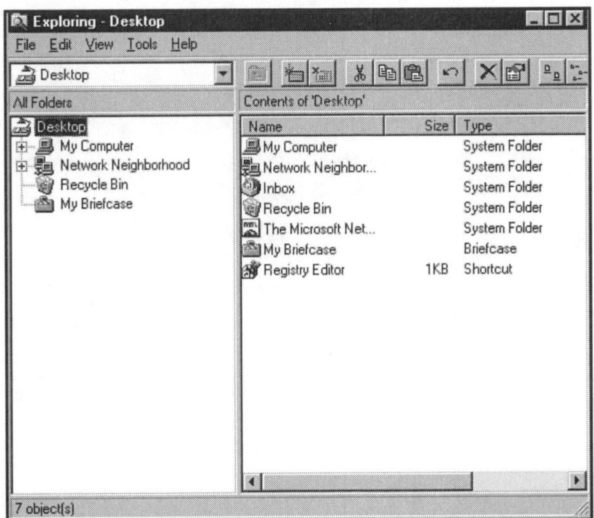

Figure 3.7

The Windows Explorer.

Opening versus Exploring

In Windows 95, objects allow you to either open them or explore them. The difference between opening and exploring is subtle, but the results of each action are much different. Knowing about these differences will help you understand the results of both opening and exploring.

You open an object by either double-clicking the object with the left mouse button, or single-clicking the object with the right mouse button and selecting Open from the context menu. The results of opening an object depend on what the object does. Opening a program starts the program. Opening a folder or a system folder, such as My Computer, provides a window with a single-pane view of the objects contained inside the folder. By default, opening an object produces a new window, either starting the program or showing the object's contents.

Every successive new window opened on-screen can cause confusion, especially if the title bar on the window is truncated due to the size of the window. Some objects, like My Computer or Network Neighborhood, allow you to specify view options that close the previous window when a new window is opened. To set this view option, select **View**, **Options** and select the option Browse folders by using a single window that changes as you open each folder. This view option greatly reduces the number of open windows. To move up through the hierarchy of folders, use the backspace key.

You explore an object by right-clicking on the object and selecting Explore from the context menu to open a Windows Explorer double-pane window. The left pane contains the object's files and folders displayed in a hierarchical tree that includes all the objects in the system. The right pane displays the object's contents, the same view produced if the object were opened.

Every time you select another object within Windows Explorer, the double-pane window displays the new object's contents. As you transverse the hierarchical structure during a search, the left pane shows your last-opened level, and the right pane displays the contents. This makes it easy to keep track of where you are without cluttering your screen with open windows.

Unlike the Windows 3.*x* File Manager, the Windows Explorer allows access to both local and network resources from the same system view. You can scroll directly to the appropriate resource and view its contents without having to open another window. Objects in the Windows Explorer tree contain a small plus sign [+] in front of them if they contain additional folders. To expand a folder to show the next level of subfolders, either click on the plus sign, or double-click on the object. The small plus sign changes to a small minus sign [–] as you expand the folder. Collapsing folders can simplify the tree view and speed up your search.

Configuring Windows Explorer

The Windows Explorer can be used with most objects and configured by the user. You can use the View menu to customize Windows Explorer. The View menu contains the following options:

- **Toolbar.** Adds a toolbar to the top of the Windows Explorer. The toolbar contains a series of buttons that duplicate menu selections and make using the Windows Explorer even easier.
- **Status Bar.** Adds a message bar at the bottom of the Windows Explorer. This message bar displays information about the various parts and functions of a Windows Explorer session.
- **Large Icons.** Shows the contents of the folder as large icons with a description under each icon.
- **Small Icons.** Shows the contents of the folder as small icons with a description to the right of each icon.
- **List.** Shows the contents of the folder as a list. This view is very similar to the Small Icons view except that the scroll bar appears below the list rather than to the right of it.
- **Details.** Shows the contents of the folder as a detailed list. The detailed list contains the name, size, type, and date of most recent modification.
- **Arrange Icons.** Leads to another menu that allows the contents to be sorted alphabetically by name, by size, by type, or by modification date. If either Large Icons or Small Icons is selected, then the contents can be set by default to be automatically arranged.
- **Line up Icons.** If either Large Icons or Small Icons is selected, this option is used to arrange the icons. The Line up Icons option is unnecessary if the Auto Arrange option is set.
- **Refresh.** Refreshes the contents of the folder. The Refresh option can be helpful if you are exploring a series of floppy disks or removable media drives.

- **Options.** Leads to a dialog property box that can set what types of files are displayed, whether certain file extensions are visible, and what extensions are associated with certain programs.

Other options might be available in Windows Explorer, depending on the type of object. For example, the Windows 95 Fonts folder replaces the Small Icons option with a List Fonts by Similarity option.

Of all the Windows Explorer view options, the Toolbar option is the most powerful. It contains a number of tools you can use to select a new current folder, move to the current folder's parent folder, connect or disconnect a network drive, manipulate the contents of the folder, or change the contents pane view. The Toolbar option is not selected as a default. If selected, you can quickly determine a toolbar button's function by holding the cursor over the toolbar button briefly and reading the tooltip description.

Windows Explorer Command-Line Switches

The Windows Explorer, EXPLORER.EXE, has several command-line switches you can use to add flexibility to how a window or folder is viewed. These command-line switches are not available when you open the Windows Explorer by choosing Start, Programs, Windows Explorer. Instead, you add these command-line switches by choosing Run from the Start menu to open the Run dialog box, then entering **explorer.exe**. The syntax for the Windows Explorer command line is as follows:

explorer [/n] [/e][,/*root,object*][[,/*select*],*subobject*]

Each of the command-line switches is explained in table 3.5. Experiment with the various combinations to properly use the Windows Explorer.

Table 3.5

Windows Explorer Command-Line Switches

Switch	Function
/n	Opens a new window. Opens a single pane view for each item selected, even if doing so duplicates an already open window.
/e	Opens a new Windows Explorer double-pane view for each item selected. This is the default view.
/root,object	Specifies the object to use as the root in the tree view. The default is the normal name space root (the Desktop). Whatever object is specified for the root is where the window begins the display. If a subobject is also specified (optional) without the use of /select, that subobject is opened in the contents view.
/select	Specifies the folder or object to receive the initial focus.
subobject	Specifies the object to open in the contents pane. If used with /select, the parent folder is opened and the specified subobject is only selected or highlighted, rather than opened.

Exercise 3.10 will help you understand the impact of using the various command-line switches with the Windows Explorer. A shortcut can be created on the Windows 95 Desktop to the Windows Explorer using these command switches. This enables you to quickly open an Explorer window.

Exercise 3.10: Running Explorer from the Command Line

1. From your computer, choose Start, Run. In the Run dialog box enter the following series of Windows Explorer commands, as detailed in steps 2 through 7. Each command opens a new Windows Explorer instance.

2. Run Explorer with the /n option by entering **explorer /n**

3. Run Explorer with the /e option by entering **explorer /e**

4. Run Explorer with the /root option by entering **explorer /root,c:\windows**

5. Run Explorer with the /e and /root options by entering **explorer /e,/root,c:\windows**

6. Run Explorer with the /e, /root, and subobject options by entering **explorer /e,/root,c:\windows,system**

7. Run Explorer with the /e, /root, /select and subobject options by entering **explorer /e,/root,c:\windows,/select,system**

8. Exit by closing the various Explorer windows.

The exercise helps you understand the use of the various command-line switches with the Windows Explorer. You can expect at least one question about the Windows Explorer on the exam.

If you use the Windows Explorer often, you might want to either create a shortcut on the Windows 95 Desktop or move the Windows Explorer to the top level of the Start menu. This will be easier than always running Explorer by choosing Start, Programs, Windows Explorer. The Windows Explorer always appears last in the Programs list, and depending how crowded your menu selections are, might be cascaded to a second column and therefore be difficult to locate and run quickly.

Configuring the Mouse

The Windows 95 user interface is designed to be used with a mouse or a similar pointing device. With Windows 95, both the left and right mouse buttons provide expanded features and capabilities. You can use the Mouse Properties sheet to configure the mouse buttons, customize the mouse cursor appearance, set the mouse speed, and so on (see fig. 3.8). Different functions might be available, depending on the pointing device being used with your computer.

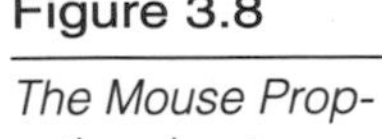

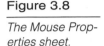

Figure 3.8

The Mouse Properties sheet.

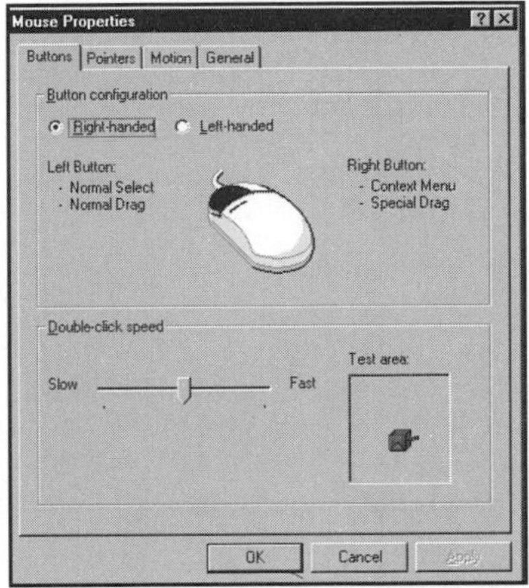

It is important for you to understand the differences between the primary (left) and secondary (right) mouse buttons, and how you can use the mouse to manipulate multiple objects in the same manner as a single object.

Primary Mouse Button

The primary mouse button, usually the left button for right-hand users and the right button for left-hand users, is used in the traditional mouse activities of selecting, pointing at, or dragging an object. The usual functionality associated with selecting and dragging a file is to move a file on a single drive, create a copy of a file on another drive, or create a shortcut to an executable file. Most drag-and-drop functions default to the left mouse button.

Secondary Mouse Button

The secondary mouse button, usually the right button for right-hand users and the left button for left-hand users, is now used as an object menu button. Clicking on an object with the right mouse button presents a context menu, offering choices of actions you can take with the object. Depending on the object, these choices commonly include the following:

- Open
- Explore

- New
- Send To
- Create Shortcut
- Print
- Quick View
- Cut
- Copy
- Delete
- Rename
- Properties

When you use the right mouse button to drag and drop an object, a menu of options appears. The following options are the most common:

- Move Here
- Copy Here
- Create Shortcut(s) Here
- Cancel

Manipulating Multiple Objects

You can also use the mouse to manipulate multiple objects at one time. You may select a series of objects by drawing a box around them or use the left mouse button to click a series of objects while holding down the Ctrl key. Once selected, you can manipulate all the objects as if they were a single object.

Exercise 3.11 will help you configure the mouse under Windows 95. Your Mouse Properties sheet might vary, depending on the type of pointing device installed on your computer.

Exercise 3.11: Configuring the Mouse

1. From your computer, choose Start, **S**ettings, **C**ontrol Panel, and double-click on the Mouse icon to open the Mouse Properties sheet.

2. Alter the button configuration by switching the left mouse button from one side of the mouse to the other. Notice how the highlighted mouse changes to match the selection. The text that describes what each button does also changes to match the configuration. Set the mouse button configuration to match your preference.

3. Slide the double-click speed to match your style. Try it all the way to the fast end. The test area allows you to check the setting. This author could never activate jack-in-the-box using a double-click at the fast setting, can you? Adjust to match your preference.

4. From the Pointers tab, review the various bitmaps for the mouse pointer. Select a scheme that appeals to you. Keep in mind that animated cursors require more overhead to run.

5. Close the Mouse Properties sheet.

Configuring the Properties Sheet for an Object

Throughout the earlier exercises in this chapter, you had the opportunity to configure several properties sheets for objects within Windows 95. An object's properties, the settings and parameters, are found on the object's properties sheet. These properties might be different from one object to another object, depending on the type of object. The properties sheet provides a standard way to view an object's properties. When you want to view the properties sheet for an object, highlight the object with a single click of the right mouse button. A context menu is displayed, from which P**r**operties can be selected. For a selected file or a folder, the File menu also has an option named Properties.

These properties can be configured as required by using the object's properties sheet. The use of a properties sheet is a convenient and consistent way to review, change, or adjust the settings and parameters of an object. Figure 3.9 shows a sample file properties sheet, which shows when the file was first created, last modified, and last accessed.

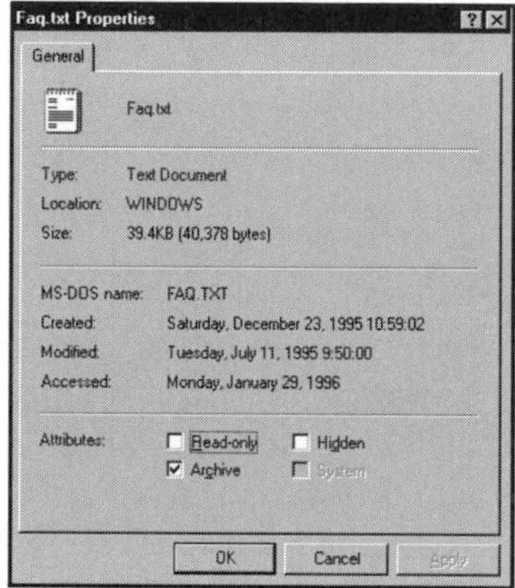

Figure 3.9

A file properties sheet.

Exercise 3.12 will help you find and configure different properties sheets under Windows 95.

Exercise 3.12: Configuring a Properties Sheet

1. From your computer, choose Start, Find, and select Files or Folders. The Find: All Files dialog box appears.

2. Enter the following filenames. As each one is located, use the right mouse button to examine the properties sheet of each selected file:

    a. Find "*.txt" (all text files) within the Windows 95 directory. Both faq.txt and tips.txt are good files for you to review. Open and examine their properties sheets (refer to figure 3.9).

    b. Find "*.dll" (all dynamic link library files) within the boot drive, usually c:\. Open and examine several of the DLL files' properties sheets. A second tab on the properties sheet called Version details useful information about the DLL file, including the file version. This information is useful when resolving DLL version problems.

   c. Find "xcopy*.exe" (all xcopy executable files) in the Windows 95 directory. One, xcopy.exe, is a DOS-based application, and the other, xcopy32.exe, is a Windows 95 application. Open and examine both of the properties sheets. You will see the differences between the properties sheets, depending on the type of application program.

   d. Find the Windows folder in the boot drive, usually drive C. Open and examine the folder's properties sheet. This is a quick way to determine a folder's size. If the folder is shared on the network, the Sharing tab contains information on the shared folder's properties.

3. Exit by closing the Find: All Files dialog box and any open file properties sheets.

While this exercise did not have you make any changes in the properties sheet settings and parameters, you did examine several different kinds of properties sheets. It is important for you to understand the use of properties sheet information, and how this information might be different between one object type and another. As with the properties sheets for DLL and EXE programs, useful information can be gained by viewing the properties sheet for the object.

Using the Windows 95 User Interface

Using the Windows 95 user interface to get your work accomplished is the whole purpose behind your customization and configuration efforts. The following sections cover different ways of using the Windows 95 user interface; creating, printing, and storing documents; and accessing your Network Neighborhood.

Using the User Interface

The Windows 95 graphical user interface (GUI) is significantly different from the Windows 3.*x* interface. Accomplishing tasks is easier in Windows 95. This exam objective is targeted toward your understanding and familiarity with using the Windows 95 user interface. Common questions judge your experience in getting your work done in Windows 95.

When you open the Windows 95 software box, you will find a slim, paperback manual from Microsoft entitled *Introducing Microsoft Windows 95*. Read through this 80-odd page manual in detail. Focus on how you would accomplish the following tasks:

- Work with the Windows Explorer
- Find something on your computer
- Get help
- Change system settings
- Organize files and folders
- Install software
- Install hardware
- Set up your computer to use a network
- Optimize your computer

This chapter covers how you might customize and configure Windows 95 to get your work done. However, working with Windows 95 is by far the best way to prepare for the Windows 95 exam. One of the best references on Windows 95 is the New Riders Publishing book *Inside Windows 95*. In Exercise 3.13 you accomplish some tasks in Windows 95 that might appear on the exam.

Exercise 3.13: Using the Windows 95 Interface

1. From your computer, find the Windows 95 SCANDISK.EXE program by using three different methods: (1) My Computer, (2) the Windows Explorer, and (3) the Find option on the Start menu.

2. Create a shortcut on the Desktop for the SCANDISK.EXE program and start the program from the shortcut.

3. Find all the TXT files in the Windows subdirectory.

4. Run Help from the Start menu, and examine each of the How to items in the Contents tab.

5. Open the System Tools folder by choosing Start, Programs, Accessories, System Tools. Check if the Windows 95 System Monitor is installed in the System Tools folder. If not, use the Add/Remove Programs option in Control Panel to install it. Run System Monitor.

6. Select multiple files and use the Send To option on the secondary mouse context menu to send multiple files to a floppy disk.

7. Shut down and restart your computer.

Another set of exercises you might find useful can be found on the Microsoft TechNet CD-ROM, under Personal Systems, Windows 95, Training Materials, Labs 1 and 2.

Using the Windows 95 Interface to Create, Print, and Store a File

This exam objective covers fundamental tasks of creating a file, printing its contents, and saving the file. The file can be either textual, graphical, or both. Windows 95 comes with several applications for working with both text files and graphics files. These applications are listed in table 3.6.

Table 3.6

Windows 95 Applications

Application	Description
Notepad	Automatically installed. Notepad is limited in the size of text file that it can open. Will open a file in WordPad if it is too large.
WordPad	A mini-version of the Microsoft Word program. Replaces both Windows 3.*x* Write and Notepad.

continues

Table 3.6 Continued

Application	Description
	A 32-bit text editor that supports OLE and MAPI. An optional Windows 95 component.
Paint	A mini-version graphics program, replaces Windows 3.*x* Paintbrush. A 32-bit graphical editor that supports OLE and MAPI. An optional Windows 95 component.

In an earlier exercise to configure the Start menu, WordPad (or your own favorite application) might have been added as an option to your Start menu. In Exercise 3.14, you use the WordPad application to create a document, print it, and save the file when you are done.

Exercise 3.14: Using WordPad

1. From your computer, open the WordPad application. If WordPad is not available, use Add/Remove Programs in Control Panel to install it.
2. Edit a new document, using the features of WordPad to change text font and color. Be creative; add a bitmap, change the text boldness and underline and so on.
3. If a printer is installed, print the document. (See Chapter 7 for steps on how to configure a printer.)
4. Save the document to your My Documents folder.
5. Exit WordPad.

Accessing the Network through Network Neighborhood

The Network Neighborhood is a new concept in Windows 95. Chapter 5 discusses networking and interoperability in greater detail. This exam objective, however, covers using the Network Neighborhood to access network resources.

If your computer is set up to use a network, the Network Neighborhood icon appears on your Windows 95 Desktop. When you double-click on the Network Neighborhood icon, you see the computers in your workgroup or any NetWare servers to which you are connected. If your workgroup name happens to match a Microsoft domain name, then your Microsoft network browsing capability is enhanced. You can see other computers on the network, those not in your workgroup, by double-clicking the Entire Network icon, which appears in the Network Neighborhood.

Windows 95 is a good networking client. Network configuration is simple and straightforward. Setting up your computer to use a network requires two major steps: setting up hardware and setting up software. First, your computer hardware needs to be correctly installed, which includes the network interface card (NIC), cabling, and hubs. Second, the network configuration of network clients, adapters, protocols, and services needs to be performed. For Microsoft networking, several key pieces of information need to be supplied—default user name, the computer name, and workgroup name. The access control security level needs to be established, whether share-level (default) or user-level security. You might also need to install or configure some other supporting networking components, such as pass-through file server security, mobile dial-up networking, agents for backup and remote administration, and support for system policies and user profiles.

Chapter 5 discusses setting up your computer on the network. Another good reference book from New Riders Publishing is *Windows 95 for Network Administrators.* If you are a network administrator, your Windows 95 library should include a copy.

To quickly display the Network Properties sheet in the Control Panel, right-click on the Network Neighborhood icon on the Windows 95 Desktop, and select Properties. If you have trouble seeing other computers in your browse list, check the workgroup name on the Identification tab of the Network Properties sheet.

Using the Registry

The key to Windows 95 is the Windows 95 Registry. First, a word of caution is in order. If you can avoid making Windows 95 Registry changes using the Windows 95 Registry Editor, do. If you must make Windows 95 Registry changes using the Windows 95 Registry Editor, be careful. The Windows 95 Registry contains all your Windows 95 configuration information. If it gets corrupted, your Windows 95 computer will not run properly.

The nearest analogy is working with electricity. Precautions should always be taken. Never deal with it lightly. Be careful. Know what you are doing because this is one area where you can seriously mess up. You might have a margin for error, but it is a slim one.

This section covers the Windows 95 Registry. There are many other good references available, including the Microsoft *Windows 95 Resource Kit* and the New Riders Publishing book, *Windows 95 Registry Troubleshooting.*

Defining the Purpose of the Registry

In Windows 3.*x*, the Registry Database is a single file, named REG.DAT, that contains only file associations and Object Linking and Embedding (OLE) registration information. The remainder of the system information for Windows 3.*x* was scattered in various INI files. This caused problems for configuration management due to the following:

- Information was stored in several different locations, including CONFIG.SYS, AUTOEXEC.BAT, WIN.INI, SYSTEM.INI, PROTOCOL.INI, and other INI and GRP files.
- The INI files were text-based, limited to 64 KB in size, and used APIs that allowed only simple get/write operations.
- The INI file information was non-hierarchical (flat) and supported only two levels of information: key names by section. It did not support multiple configurations for a specific key value.

- Configuring the INI files properly was complicated, they stored little or no user information, and they could not be administrated remotely with ease.

To solve these problems, the Windows 95 Registry was designed with the following purposes in mind:

- To centralize all the configuration information
- To utilize a tree-structured, hierarchical database structure, rather than text-based, limited capability INI files
- To provide a means to store user, application, and computer-specific information
- To simplify the support burden and allow both local and remote access to configuration information

Rather than a single file, the Windows 95 Registry is stored in two files. The SYSTEM.DAT file contains the computer hardware configurations, and the USER.DAT file contains user-specific settings. Together these two files are the central repository of information for the Windows 95 operating system. Windows 95 needs a clean Registry to boot properly. After each successful boot of Windows 95, copies of both files are saved as SYSTEM.DA0 and USER.DA0 (The "T" in the file extension is replaced with a zero "0"). This is very much like Windows NT's "last-known good configuration," though not as simple to recover from if a problem occurs.

Some Windows 95 references include a third file, CONFIG.POL, that stores administrative policies that are setup on a network server. CONFIG.POL is not a required component of the Windows 95 Setup, and when implemented, it is stored on the network server rather than the local computer.

Microsoft provides the REGEDIT utility to view and change the contents of the Windows 95 Registry. Before you make changes to the Windows 95 Registry, first make a backup copy of the two Registry files—SYSTEM.DAT and USER.DAT. Both of these files are hidden in the Windows folder.

For backward compatibility, the older Windows 3.*x* configuration files, such as CONFIG.SYS, AUTOEXEC.BAT, WIN.INI, SYSTEM.INI, PROGMAN.INI, CONTROL.INI, and PROTOCOL.INI, still exist. The 16-bit Windows APIs used to update the INI files also still exist; however, developers of 32-bit Windows-based applications are encouraged to use the Registry APIs to load application-specific information into the Registry.

Classifying Types of Information in the Registry

The Windows 95 Registry is a database created during Windows 95 startup. It is a front-end for all your Windows 95 configuration information, including system configuration, hardware configuration, the setup information for 32-bit Windows-based applications, and user preferences. The actual files in which this configuration information is stored are called USER.DAT, SYSTEM.DAT, and, optionally, CONFIG.POL. These files are not in readable format. To view and change your current user and system configurations, you need to run REGEDIT.EXE, the Windows 95 Registry Editor. Figure 3.10 shows the hierarchical tree-like structure of the Windows 95 Registry database.

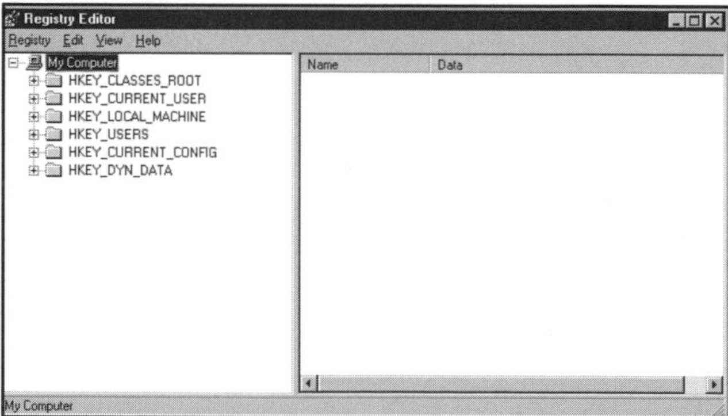

Figure 3.10

The Windows 95 Registry Editor.

The Windows 95 Registry is made up of six root keys. Although more complex than the simple registry in Windows 3.*x*, the Windows 95 Registry is not as comprehensive as the Windows NT registry. The following sections describe the six root keys:

HKEY_CLASSES_ROOT

This key contains the same type of data as the simple REG.DAT registry file in Windows 3.*x* and provides backward compatibility for OLE and DDE support. It also contains OLE and association mapping information to support drag-and-drop operations, Windows 95 shortcuts (that are, in fact, OLE links), and core aspects of the Windows 95 user interface. The association mappings allow Windows 95 to run or print from an application when a specific file type is selected.

This key merely points to the Registry branch within another root key, HKEY_LOCAL_MACHINE\SOFTWARE\Classes. The three basic key types within HKEY_CLASSES_ROOT are file extensions, file associations, and OLE2 objects.

HKEY_CURRENT_USER

This key contains user-specific settings for applications, desktop configurations, and user preferences, in much the same way that WIN.INI does under Windows 3.*x*. This key is created at run time (when the user logs on to Windows 95) from information stored in the user's entry under HKEY_USERS. If the user does not already exist, the .DEFAULT information is used.

These user-specific settings are copied back into the HKEY_USERS branch when you shut down Windows 95. There are several different key types: events, schemes, user-specific Control Panel settings, most recently used (MRU) location of installation files, keyboard layout, network, dial-up networking settings, and software settings.

HKEY_LOCAL_MACHINE

This key contains computer-specific information about the type of hardware installed, drivers, and other system settings. This information used for all users that log on to the computer. It is the same information stored within the SYSTEM.DAT configuration file and is required to properly run the hardware.

Multiple hardware configurations are listed under the Config key, in the case of a laptop computer with a docking station and both docked and undocked configurations. Much of the device manager information can be found under the Enum key, though this information is easier to view through the System icon in the Control Panel. There are several different key types: hardware configurations (usually only one), device manager information, network-specific security information, installed software information, and system settings.

HKEY_USERS

This key contains information about all users who log on to the computer, including the .DEFAULT generic user settings. The generic program and system settings act as a template for any new users on the computer. See the earlier section "HKEY_CURRENT_USER" for the list of user information stored under this key. It is the same information stored within the USER.DAT configuration file and is required to properly run the system.

HKEY_CURRENT_CONFIG

This key contains information about the current running hardware configuration. It is used when multiple hardware configurations are available to the computer. The prime example of multiple hardware configurations is a laptop computer that can be either docked or undocked in a docking station. The information for this key is directly copied from the various configuration information contained in the HKEY_LOCAL_MACHINE key.

HKEY_DYN_DATA

This key contains the dynamic status information for various devices as part of the Plug and Play configuration. It is regenerated every time the system starts up. This information can change as hardware devices are added to or removed from the computer. The information kept for each hardware device includes the associated hardware key, any problems, and current status. This key also contains information on system monitoring being performed using the System Monitor tool. This key is not part of either registry file and is always dynamically created.

The Windows 95 Registry Editor program is not available from the Start menu for a very good reason. The Registry is self-maintaining and should only be modified in extreme cases. Any modifications to the system are best done through the appropriate user interface, such as the System icon, Device Manager tab, or with the other Control Panel icons.

If you need to change the Registry, make a backup copy first.

In Exercise 3.15, you explore your computer's Registry using a shortcut created in Exercise 3.9.

Exercise 3.15: Examining Your Registry

1. From your computer, start the Windows 95 Registry Editor program. The shortcut created on your Windows 95 Desktop uses a hot key combination of Ctrl+Alt+R. Either use the hot key combination or double-click on the shortcut.

2. Examine all six keys of the Windows 95 Registry. Do not make any changes to the information, just view the settings.

3. Exit the Windows 95 Registry Editor program.

Determining Where the Registry Is Stored

The Windows 95 Registry contains all the Windows 95 system and user information. It is an ASCII database that pulls information from the three files listed in table 3.7. These files are not in readable form, so you can view or change their contents only by using a Windows application, such as the Windows 95 Registry Editor program, the Control Panel icons, or the System Policies Editor (for the optional CONFIG.POL file).

Table 3.7

Files in the Windows 95 Registry

Registry File	Description
SYSTEM.DAT	Contains hardware-related and computer specific settings.

continues

Table 3.7 Continued

Registry File	Description
USER.DAT	Contains user-specific information found in user profiles, such as user rights, desktop settings, and so on.
CONFIG.POL (Optional)	Contains policy information related to the system and user settings. The information in the system policies file can override information in both SYSTEM.DAT and USER.DAT files. This is an optional file.

Always make backup copies of your Windows 95 Registry files before you make any changes. Use the Windows 95 Registry Editor program, **R**egistry menu, **E**xport Registry file option to create a REG file. This exported REG file represents the contents of the DAT files at a given point in time. The Windows 95 CD-ROM includes two other useful utilities. They can be found in the Other\Misc subdirectory. The first is an Emergency Recovery Utility (ERU.EXE) that saves key Windows 95 files to either a floppy drive, a local drive, or a network drive. The second is a Configuration Backup (CFGBACK.EXE) utility that can save and restore up to nine configurations of your Windows 95 Registry. Periodically, you can also run a simple batch file to save copies of both the SYSTEM.DAT and USER.DAT files.

Deciding When It Is Appropriate to Modify the Registry

In general, the Windows 95 Registry is not where you should make your changes. Most of the configuration information you can modify in the Windows 95 Registry can be changed using a GUI front-end; however, some configuration information cannot. Only in these situations is it appropriate to modify the Registry using the Registry Editor program.

Modifying the Contents of the Registry

The only modification to the Windows 95 Registry that this author has seen that might be of worth is tweaking the 8.3 naming conventions when using long filenames in Windows 95. The tilde character (~) and a number are tacked onto the short version of your long filenames. This can differ from the default long file naming that Novell NetWare servers follow when using OS/2 Name Space to support long filenames.

In Exercise 3.16, you make a very minor modification to the Windows 95 Registry. This modification changes the naming behavior so that unique, auto-generated, DOS 8.3 names do not use tilde-type tails (see fig. 3.11). Remember to make a backup first. See the earlier section, "Determining Where the Registry Is Stored," for instructions on how to make a backup copy of your Registry.

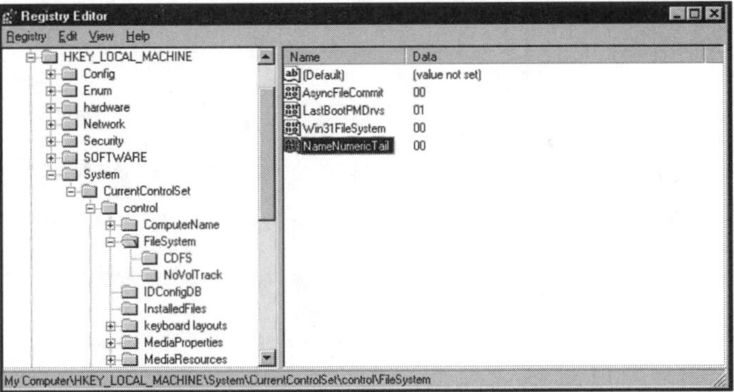

Figure 3.11

Add Registry Entry.

Exercise 3.16: Modifying Your Registry

1. If you have not backed up your Registry files on your computer already, please do so now.

2. From your computer, start the Windows 95 Registry Editor program. The shortcut created on your Windows 95 Desktop uses a hot key combination of Ctrl+Alt+R. Use the hot key combination or double-click the shortcut itself.

3. Locate the following Windows 95 Registry entry:

   HKEY_LOCAL_MACHINE\System\CurrentControlSet \control\FileSystem

4. Add a binary value with the name NameNumericTail and value 00 by selecting **E**dit, **N**ew, **B**inary Value.
5. Exit for the Windows 95 Registry Editor.

If you get into trouble changing the Registry, restore by following these steps:

1. Choose Start, Sh**u**t Down.
2. Choose Restart the computer in **M**S-DOS mode, and then choose **Y**es.
3. Change to your Windows directory. For example, if your Windows directory is C:\Windows, type the following:

   cd c:\windows

4. Type the following commands, pressing Enter after each one (note that System.da0 and User.da0 contain the number zero):

   attrib –h –r –s system.dat

   attrib –h –r –s system.da0

   copy system.da0 system.dat

   attrib –h –r –s user.dat

   attrib –h –r –s user.da0

   copy user.da0 user.dat

5. Restart your computer.

Following this procedure restores your registry to the state in was in when you last successfully started your computer.

When OLE Information in the Registry Becomes Corrupted

In the previous section in this chapter, “Classifying Types of Information in the Registry,” you learned that all the OLE information is stored in HKEY_LOCAL_MACHINE\SOFTWARE\Classes. This includes both OLE1 and OLE2 support. The *Windows 95 Resource Kit*, Chapter 22, "Application Support," discusses using OLE to share data between applications. When this data becomes corrupted, your OLE operations no longer function. You have several courses of action to fix the corruption:

- Restore the Registry files from a backup copy. This action assumes that the previous versions have non-corrupted OLE information.
- Import into the Registry from a REG ASCII file containing the entries to correct the corrupted OLE information. This action assumes that correct information was exported previously.
- Reinstall the application whose OLE information was corrupted. This action assumes that the reinstall updates the corrupted OLE information.
- Compare Registry OLE information between the corrupted computer and one in which the OLE operation is working. This task is laborious, and it might or might not fix the problem. Keep in mind that every problem you discover might hide several more problems.

Whatever course of action you take, talking with a Microsoft help desk representative will improve your chances of finding and fixing the problem. Remember that the rules for working with the Windows 95 Registry are like the rules for working with electricity. Precautions should always be taken.

Review Questions

The following questions will test your knowledge of the information in this chapter. For additional questions, see MCP Endeavor and the Microsoft Roadmap/Assessment Exam on the CD-ROM that accompanies this book.

1. With Windows 95, the Windows 95 Project Team tried to answer one basic question, "How can the user interface in

Windows 3.1 be improved?" The end result was an operating system with a user interface that incorporates the following (choose the three best answers):

A. Ease of use

B. Better Windows 3.1 applications

C. Speed and power

D. Compatibility

E. C2-level security

2. An object has which of the following two characteristics, as defined under Windows 95?

   A. Behavior

   B. Polymorphism

   C. Form (icon)

   D. Inheritance

   E. Attributes (properties)

3. Which one of the following operating systems cannot be dual-booted with Windows 95?

   A. MS-DOS 5.*x* or greater

   B. Novell (DR) DOS

   C. IBM PC-DOS 5.*x* or greater

   D. Windows NT

   E. OS/2 2.*x* or greater

4. If you upgrade an existing version of Windows, which three of the following occurs?

   A. Dual-boot with your previous version of DOS is automatically set up.

   B. Your older versions of some DOS files are deleted—those that do not support long filenames or conflict with Windows 95.

C. Configuration settings in SYSTEM.INI, WIN.INI, and PROTOCOL.INI are used to configure Windows 95.

D. The information in the Windows 3.*x* Registry, such as file associations and OLE, is added into the Windows 95 Registry.

E. All your Windows applications have to be re-installed in order to work properly under Windows 95.

5. Which one of the following operating systems cannot be upgraded to Windows 95?

   A. MS-DOS 5.*x* or greater

   B. Novell (DR) DOS

   C. IBM PC-DOS 5.*x* or greater

   D. Windows NT

   E. OS/2 2.*x* or greater

6. In a dual-boot setup with a previous version of DOS, the older DOS boot files have which of the following extensions when running Windows 95?

   A. SAV

   B. W40

   C. DOS

   D. OLD

   E. BAK

7. The Windows NT Boot Loader program uses which of the following files to list the boot options?

   A. MSDOS.SYS

   B. CONFIG.SYS

   C. NTBOOT.INI

   D. BOOT.INI

   E. WIN.INI

8. Which one of the following statements is true?

    A. Windows 95 can be installed into a FAT partition.
    B. Windows 95 can be installed into an NTFS partition.
    C. Windows 95 can be safely installed into the same directory as Windows NT.
    D. Windows 95 can be installed into an HPFS partition.
    E. Windows 95 can be installed into the same directory as OS/2.

9. Which one of the following bus architectures fully supports the Plug and Play specification?

    A. ISA
    B. EISA
    C. MCA
    D. SCSI
    E. PC Card

10. Application programs dragged and dropped onto the Start menu appear where?

    A. Under Programs
    B. Under Settings
    C. Under Run
    D. In the Start menu itself
    E. They cannot be placed in the Start menu.

11. Which of the following objects does not appear on the Windows 95 Desktop when first installed?

    A. My Computer
    B. Recycle Bin
    C. Taskbar

D. Control Panel

E. Start button

12. If you want to change your display settings, what would you do? Choose the two best answers:

A. Run the Display program.

B. Right-click the Windows 95 Desktop and select Properties.

C. Open the Control Panel and select the Display icon.

D. Reinstall Windows 95.

E. Boot into safe mode.

13. Which three major components comprise the Plug and Play specification?

A. Plug and Play application software

B. Plug and Play hardware devices

C. Plug and Play BIOS

D. Plug and Play connections

E. Plug and Play operating system

14. Which of the following is not a way to configure a Plug and Play hardware device?

A. Windows 95 Setup program

B. Add New Hardware icon in the Control Panel

C. Flip a dip switch on the hardware device

D. During the normal boot process

E. During warm- or hot-docking situations

15. What are the three sections that comprise the Windows 95 Taskbar?

    A. Launch button

    B. Start button

    C. Active program buttons

    D. Notification area

    E. Clock

16. Which of the following is not an option on the Taskbar Properties sheet?

    A. Always on top

    B. Auto Hide

    C. Show small icons in Start menu

    D. Show Date

    E. Show Clock

17. To create a shortcut, you can use which three of the following actions?

    A. Select Ne**w**, then **S**hortcut using the right mouse button context menu on an open spot of the Windows 95 Desktop.

    B. Use **P**rograms, Create shortcut from the Start menu.

    C. Drag and drop an application from the Explorer to the Windows 95 Desktop.

    D. From an object itself, right-click to open the context menu, create the shortcut.

    E. Copy a file from one folder on the C drive to another folder also on the C drive.

18. Which of the following is not a view option when exploring a folder?

    A. Large Icons
    B. Small Icons
    C. List
    D. Group
    E. Details

19. An object's settings and properties can be found where?

    A. Registry
    B. Control Panel
    C. INI file
    D. Properties sheet
    E. Readme file

20. The Windows 95 Registry is comprised of which three of the following files?

    A. CONFIG.SYS
    B. SYSTEM.DAT
    C. WINSYS.DAT
    D. USER.DAT
    E. CONFIG.POL

Review Answers

1. A C D
2. C E
3. B
4. B C D

5. D
6. C
7. D
8. A
9. E
10. D
11. D
12. B C
13. B C E
14. C
15. B C D
16. D
17. A C D
18. D
19. D
20. B D E

Chapter 4

Editing User and System Profiles

Windows 95 contains a number of features that can be used by an administrator to control computer-specific and user-specific settings on a Windows 95 computer. Some of these features include:

- The ability to modify a computer's settings through the Properties sheet, Control Panel, and Registry settings to modify many Windows 95 variables
- The use of hardware profiles
- The use of user profiles, which allow different user-specific settings on the same Windows 95 computer
- The ability to remotely administer another computer from the administrator's computer
- System and User policies, which allow the administrator to control various settings and restrict what a user can change
- The Net Watcher tool, which can be used to control and monitor shared folders remotely

In this chapter, the following Windows 95 administration topics are discussed:

- Using the Control Panel, Properties sheets, and the Registry to configure and administer a Windows 95 computer
- Using Hardware Profiles to maintain different hardware configurations for a Windows 95 computer
- Using User Profiles to maintain different software configurations for multiple users on a single Windows 95 computer

- Implementing User and System policies to enforce specific controls in a Windows 95 environment
- Using the Windows 95 Remote Administration tools

Administration

The configurable settings of the Windows 95 operating system, the computer hardware, and Windows 95-compatible applications are stored in a database on the Windows 95 computer known as the *Registry*. The Registry entries can be set automatically by Windows 95 or a compatible application, or they can be modified manually. To display or modify specific Registry entries, the following items can often be used:

- The Control Panel
- The Properties sheet of an object
- The Registry Editor

Many objects can be configured from any of these locations.

Control Panel

The Control Panel contains numerous applets for graphically configuring various components of the Windows 95 operating system. Exactly which configuration applets are present in a Windows 95 Control Panel depends on which Windows 95 components or compatible applications have been installed. For example, the Control Panel shown in figure 4.1 contains some standard Windows 95 Control Panel applets, in addition to the 32-bit ODBC configuration applet that was installed during a Microsoft Access 95 installation.

Figure 4.1

A typical Control Panel window.

Some of the Control Panel applets are described in table 4.1, although additional applets may be present. Online help is available for most of the Control Panel applets by choosing the question mark button in the upper right corner of a dialog box and selecting a field.

Table 4.1

Some Common Control Panel Applets

Applet	Description
Accessibility Options	Options to make Windows 95 easier to use for individuals with disabilities
Add New Hardware	Used to configure new hardware
Add/Remove Programs	Used to install or remove Windows components and other applications
Display	Used to change the display driver video monitor information, colors, screen savers, and the appearance of the Desktop
Fonts	Used to view installed fonts or install new fonts
Keyboard	Used to change the type of keyboard used, the language of the keyboard, or options such as the rate of display of typed characters

continues

Table 4.1 Continued

Applet	Description
Modems	Used to configure a modem
Mouse	Used to change mouse or pointer options
Multimedia	Used to change options and drivers for audio/video devices such as MIDI devices, sound cards, or video boards
Printers	Used to add or configure printers
Sound	Used to modify sound schemes if a sound card or speaker driver is installed
System	Used to display and modify various settings related to the operating system and hardware properties

Properties Sheets

Many objects in Windows 95 have a Properties sheet that can be used to configure that object. The Properties sheets are often displayed by right-clicking on the object and selecting Properties from the context-sensitive menu that appears. For example, if you right-click on a blank space on the Desktop and select Properties, the Display Properties sheet appears enabling you to change such things as the wallpaper and screensaver used. Similarly, the Properties sheet for a file in Explorer reveals the file properties such as time last modified and attributes such as Hidden or Read-Only.

Registry Editor

Information pertaining to a Windows 95 client's hardware devices, operating system settings, and application configurations is stored in the Windows 95 Registry on the local computer. Applications that are designed for Windows 95 can add additional information to the Registry and can also query the Registry for existing information. To display a document as it would print out, for example, word-processing applications can query the Registry to find out what driver is currently set as the default printer.

As discussed in Chapter 3, "Customizing and Configuring Windows 95," the Registry information is stored in two files on the hard drive of the local computer:

- **SYSTEM.DAT.** Contains computer-specific information such as the devices present and their configured settings.
- **USER.DAT.** Contains user-specific settings and preferences such as the shortcuts displayed on the Desktop and the applications installed in the Start menu programs.

The hierarchical, tree-like structure of the Registry enables configuration information to be logically grouped together in branches of the tree called *keys*. Information about installed Microsoft applications, for example, may be found under the HKEY_LOCAL_MACHINE\SOFTWARE\Microsoft key.

The Registry can be viewed and modified using the Registry Editor. To start the Registry Editor, enter **regedit** from the Run dialog box opened from the Start menu.

Any changes made to the Registry can prevent the operating system from functioning properly and can prevent the system from initializing. You should make a backup copy of the SYSTEM.DAT and USER.DAT files before using the Registry Editor in case you need to revert to the previous settings. Any settings in the Registry normally can be modified safely through the Control Panel or through the application involved.

In Exercise 4.1, you change a value in the Network Control Panel Applet, the Network Neighborhood Properties sheet, and the Registry, and see how the change is reflected in the other locations. To perform this exercise, you must have a network adapter installed in the Network Control Panel Applet. If you do not already have one installed, install the Microsoft Dial-Up Adapter driver by opening the Network Control Panel Applet and adding Microsoft's Dial-Up Adapter driver from the list of adapters.

Exercise 4.1: Changing a Configurable Setting

1. Select Settings from the Start menu, then Control Panel. The Control Panel opens.
2. Double-click on the Network icon. The Network dialog box is displayed.
3. Record the computer name on a piece of paper.
4. Select the Identification tab, type **CONTROLPANEL** for the computer name, and choose OK. The Network Control Panel Applet is closed.
5. When you are prompted to restart the computer, choose No.
6. Right-click on the Network Neighborhood icon on the Desktop. The context-sensitive menu is displayed.
7. Select Properties. The Network dialog box is again displayed.
8. Select the Identification tab. The Computer Name now is listed as CONTROLPANEL, the name that was entered through the Network Control Panel Applet.
9. Change the computer name to PROPERTIES and choose OK. The Network Control Panel Applet is closed.
10. If you are prompted to restart the computer, choose No.
11. Select Run from the Start menu. The Run dialog box opens.
12. Type **regedit** and choose OK. The Registry Editor is displayed.
13. Click on the plus sign next to HKEY_LOCAL_MACHINE. The HKEY_LOCAL_MACHINE key is expanded.
14. Click on the plus sign next to System. The CurrentControlSet key is displayed.
15. Click on the plus sign next to CurrentControlSet and then expand the Control subkey. The ComputerName subkey is displayed.

16. Click on the plus sign next to ComputerName to display the subkey that also is named ComputerName. Figure 4.2 shows an example of the ComputerName subkey.

Figure 4.2

Registry Editor subkeys.

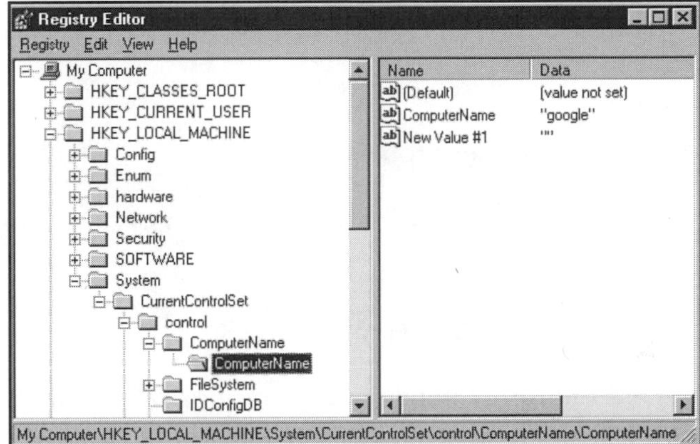

17. Select the ComputerName subkey. The Values named [Default] and ComputerName are displayed on the right half of the Registry Editor.

    Notice that the ComputerName value is PROPERTIES as set from the Network Neighborhood Properties sheet.

18. Double-click the ComputerName value to edit it. The Edit String dialog box is displayed.

19. In the Value data field, enter the original computer name you wrote down at the start of this exercise and choose OK. The ComputerName value displays the original computer name.

20. Exit the Registry Editor.

Profiles

Windows 95 uses profiles to customize the configurable settings for different circumstances. A profile enables the Registry to contain different configurations used for different scenarios. Completely different Desktop configurations, for example, may be maintained for different users who will access the Windows 95 computer. When one of the users logs on, Windows 95 can use the Registry settings specific to that user.

The following are the two types of profiles:

- Hardware profiles
- User profiles

Both of these profile types are described in the following sections.

Hardware Profiles

For non-mobile configurations, Windows 95 usually uses a single hardware profile that contains all the computer-specific, hardware-related configuration information. Additional hardware profiles can be created, however, that use different configuration information. A mobile computer, for example, may have one hardware profile that is used when it is attached to a network and a different profile used when it is away from the network. The non-networked profile would not include a network adapter in the configuration settings, and therefore the computer would not waste time attempting to connect to the network at startup.

The hardware profiles affect the HKEY_LOCAL_MACHINE keys in the Registry, which are stored in the SYSTEM.DAT file. For more information on the use of hardware profiles, refer to the Chapter 3, "Customizing and Configuring Window 95," and to the section "Hardware Profiles" in Chapter 11, "Plug and Play."

User Profiles

If multiple users use the same Windows 95 computer, each user can have his or her own user-specific configuration information stored in a different user profile. Some of the information that can be contained in a user profile includes:

- Shortcut icons on the desktop
- Applications contained in the Start menu

- Customized Desktop settings such as colors, backgrounds, fonts, and more
- Persistent network connections
- Recently used documents under the Start menu Documents list

By default, all users use the same profile. Exercise 4.2 demonstrates how to enable individual users to maintain user profiles.

Exercise 4.2: Creating User Profiles

1. Select Settings from the Start menu, then Control Panel. The Control Panel opens.
2. Double-click on the Passwords icon. The Passwords Properties dialog box is displayed.
3. Select the User Profiles tab. By default, the All users of this PC use the same preferences and desktop settings option is selected.
4. Select the following options:

   Users can customize their preferences and desktop settings.

   Include desktop icons and Network Neighborhood contents in user settings.

   Include Start Menu and Program groups in user settings.

   Choose OK. You are prompted to restart the computer.
5. Choose OK to restart the computer.
6. Log on with the user name TESTPROFILE and type **password** for the password. You will be prompted to verify the password by typing it again.

Do not press Enter after typing the user name without first typing a password. If you do, the password will be blank, and you will not see the user logon screen again when you next log on. If a blank password is used with a user name, that user is automatically logged on, and a different user name cannot be used. To fix this situation, change the password to something other than blank using the Passwords Control Panel Applet.

7. Confirm the password by typing it again. A message appears asking if you want to save the settings for the user in a user profile.
8. Choose Yes to save the sessions settings in a user profile. The default Desktop is displayed.
9. Right-click on the Desktop and select Properties from the context-sensitive menu. The Display Properties sheet appears.
10. Select a different wallpaper for the Desktop and choose OK. The new wallpaper is displayed.
11. Select Shut Down from the Start menu. The Shut Down Windows dialog box opens.
12. Select Close all programs and log on as a different user?, then choose Yes. All programs close, and the Enter Windows Password logon screen is displayed.
13. Log on with a different user name. The original default wallpaper or pattern appears on the Desktop.
14. Log off and log back on with the TESTPROFILE user name. The wallpaper that was selected for that profile appears on the Desktop.
15. Log off and then log on with your normal user name. The original settings are displayed.

16. Start the Explorer and open the Windows 95 folder and the Profiles subfolder. The Profiles folder contains a subfolder for each of the profiles that have been created on the computer.

17. Examine the contents of each folder in the Profiles folder. You will notice a user.dat file that was created for each profile. In addition, there may be Start Menu, NetHood, Desktop, and Recent folders for each profile, depending on which options were chosen in the User Profiles tab of the Passwords Control Panel Applet.

When a user profile is created, the user-specific information is stored in a subdirectory of the \<*systemroot*>\Profiles directory (where <*systemroot*> is WINDOWS, for example). The subdirectory has the same name as the user name and contains a USER.DAT file with the user-specific Registry entries. The user profiles are stored in the HKEY_USERS keys in the Registry. When a user is logged on, the USER.DAT file is accessed, and the entries for that user are copied to the HKEY_CURRENT_USER keys in the Registry. When a user logs off, the changes are saved to the USER.DAT file.

User profiles also can be configured so that a network user can use the same user profile no matter which Windows 95 computer he or she logs on to. Thus, the user has the same settings, preferences, and shortcuts available on any Windows 95 computer. To use the same profile on another Windows 95 computer, that computer must have user profiles enabled. Next, a copy of the users USER.DAT should be copied to the user's home directory on a Windows NT or NetWare server. When the user logs on, his USER.DAT file is copied from the server to the Windows 95 computer. Those settings are then used for the session. When the user logs off, any further changes to the USER.DAT are copied back to the USER.DAT file on the server.

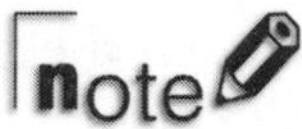

For information on creating a home directory on a Windows NT or NetWare server, refer to the Windows NT or Novell NetWare documentation.

If you do not want to allow a user to customize her user profile settings, you can use a mandatory user profile. To do this, copy the user's USER.DAT file to her home directory on the server. Next, rename the USER.DAT file to USER.MAN and change the file properties to Hidden and Read-Only. When the user logs on, the USER.MAN file is copied to the USER.DAT file on the local computer. When the user logs off, however, the changes are not copied to the server, so the original USER.MAN user profile settings are used the next time the user logs on. If you have a guest account available for a Windows 95 computer, however, you might want all guests to use the same user profile settings, and thus not be able to save changes to the guest account user profile.

For even more control over what settings users can and cannot modify, you may define policies for the Windows 95 users and computers.

User and System Policies

Windows 95 policies enable an administrator to set various Registry entries and control whether a user can change such settings. Computer-specific (HKEY_LOCAL_COMPUTER) Registry entries can be enforced through a Computer policy. User-specific Registry entries can be enforced through User policies. In addition, Group policies can be created to enforce user-specific settings for groups of user accounts defined on a Windows NT or NetWare server.

System Policy Editor

Computer, User, and Group System policies are created using the System Policy Editor, POLEDIT.EXE. The System Policy Editor is located on the Windows 95 CD-ROM in the \ADMIN\APPTOOLS\POLEDIT directory. Exercise 4.3 demonstrates how to install the System Policy Editor.

Exercise 4.3: Installing the System Policy Editor

1. Select Settings from the Start menu, then Control Panel. The Control Panel opens.
2. Double-click on the Add/Remove Programs icon. The Add/Remove Programs Properties dialog box is displayed.
3. Select the Windows Setup tab and choose Have Disk. The Install from Disk dialog box appears.
4. Choose Browse and locate the \ADMIN\APPTOOLS\POLEDIT directory on the Windows 95 CD-ROM. The grouppol.inf and poledit.inf files are displayed.
5. Choose OK twice, select Group Policies and System Policy Editor, and choose Install. The files are copied to the hard drive, and the Start menu is updated.
6. From the Start menu, select Programs, Accessories, System Tools, System Policy Editor. The System Policy Editor is displayed, and you are prompted for the template file to be used.
7. Select ADMIN.ADM as the template to use for creating policies. The System Policy Editor displays a blank window.
8. Close the System Policy Editor.

The System Policy Editor uses a template that defines which keys in the Registry can be affected by the System policy. The template ADMIN.ADM, which is included with the System Policy Editor, allows many standard policies to be enforced, such as the following:

- Restricting access to various Control Panel applets
- Disabling the Registry Editor
- Requiring a user to be validated by a Windows NT or NetWare server
- Specifying certain applications to run at startup

In addition to creating System policies, the System Policy Editor can be used to perform the following functions:

- Access the local Registry settings defined in the System policy template being used
- Access the Registry settings on a remote Windows 95 computer to change the settings defined in the template

Remote Administration must be enabled on a computer to allow another computer to access the Registry over a network. See the following section "Remote Administration" to learn how to enable Remote Administration.

Policies created with the System Policy Editor are saved with the file-name extension POL. The System policy to be used should be given the name CONFIG.POL and must be placed in the default location. For computers using share-level security, CONFIG.POL should be placed in the *<systemroot>* directory—for example, c:\WINDOWS. For computers using user-level security, CONFIG.POL should be placed in the user's home directory on the Windows NT or NetWare server. The default location for the CONFIG.POL file can later be changed using a specific policy setting.

Registry information in the CONFIG.POL file can overwrite any existing information in the computer's Registry. The policy setting also can be configured so that it will not change the Registry setting if it already exists. Therefore, even if a Registry on a computer has a certain setting, that setting can be changed to the setting in the CONFIG.POL policy file.

In Exercise 4.4, you create a simple System policy and set up a system so that the policy overwrites the previous Registry setting.

Exercise 4.4: Creating a System Policy

1. Start the System Policy Editor. The System Policy Editor is displayed, and you are prompted for the name of the template file to be used.

2. Locate the \<*systemroot*>\INF\ADMIN.ADM file and choose OK. The ADMIN.ADM template is loaded, and a blank System Policy window is displayed as shown in figure 4.3.

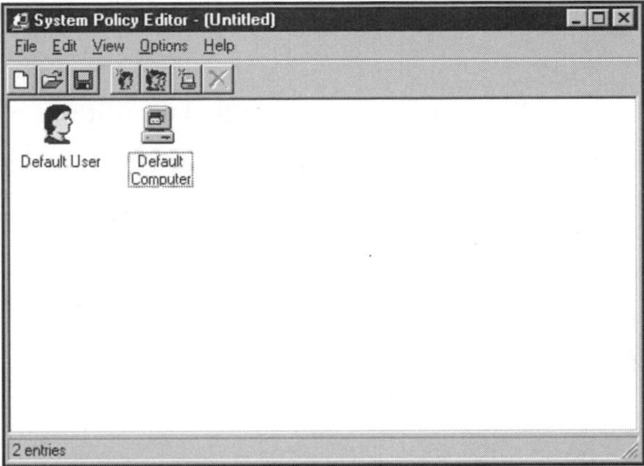

Figure 4.3

The System Policy Editor.

3. Select **N**ew File from the **F**ile menu. The Default User and Default Computer icons are displayed.

4. Double-click on the Default Computer icon. The Default Computer Properties sheet is displayed (see fig. 4.4).

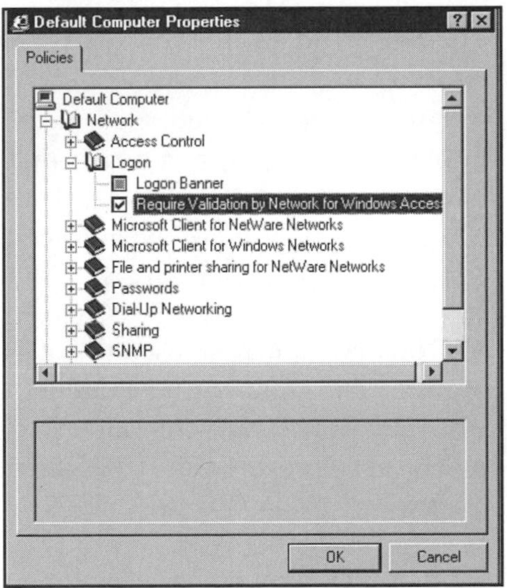

Figure 4.4

The System Policy Default Computer Properties sheet.

5. Click on the plus sign next to Network. The Network policy sybkeys are displayed as shown in figure 4.4.

6. Click on the plus sign next to Logon. The Network logon policy settings are displayed.
7. Click on the box next to Logon Banner until a checkmark appears in the box. The Caption and Text fields are displayed.
8. Type **System Policies Test** in the Caption field and **Welcome** in the Text field and choose OK. The Default User and Default Computer icons are again displayed.
9. Select Save As from the File menu and save the filename as CONFIG.POL in the <*systemroot*> directory.
10. If user-level security is used, move the CONFIG.POL file to the home directory for your user on the server.
11. Shut down and restart the computer. All applications will close.
12. Log on to the computer. The Logon Banner specified in CONFIG.POL is displayed during logon.
13. Delete the CONFIG.POL file to disable the policy.

The System policy check boxes will be in one of three states: cleared, checked, or gray. A clear or blank box means the policy will not be implemented. A checked box means the policy will be implemented. A gray box means the previous policy will be maintained if one previously existed. The gray boxes are used when two or more policies will be enforced one after another, such as when Group policies are used.

A Group policy may be used to enforce a User policy for a group of users. The group must be defined on the Windows NT or NetWare server, and each computer in the group using the Group policy must have the GROUPPOL.DLL copied to their <*systemroot*>\system directory.

To create a Group policy, select Add Group from the Edit menu of the System Policy Editor and enter the name of the group.

A User policy is processed after a Group policy, and therefore overrides any policies set by the Group policy, unless the policy setting check box is gray. If multiple Group policies are defined, and a user belongs to more than one group, the order in which the Group policies are processed can be defined in the Group Priorities menu item of the Options menu. Group policies with a higher precedence override the policies set by the lower precedence policies.

Other Registry keys can be set using System policies by using a different template. The template can be selected from the Options menu of the System Policy Editor. The templates are specially designed text files that define what policy options are available. For sample templates and information on creating a custom policy template, refer to the *Windows 95 Resource Kit*.

Remote Administration

Windows 95 includes several tools to enable you to administer Windows 95 computers from a remote location on the network. These Remote Administration tools include the following:

- Remote Registry Administration
- Net Watcher
- System Monitor
- Remote File System Administration

These tools are described in the following sections.

Remote Registry Administration

If a Windows 95 computer has Remote Administration enabled, other computers that are granted permission to do so can remotely manipulate that computer's Registry. This service is available only if user-level security is being used. Once permission has been granted to remotely administer a computer, the administrator can open the Registry of the remote client using either the Registry Editor or the System Policy Editor.

Exercise 4.5 demonstrates how to remotely administer another computer using the Registry Editor.

Exercise 4.5: Remote Administration Using the Registry Editor

1. Select Settings from the Start menu, then choose Control Panel. The Control Panel opens.
2. Double-click on the Passwords icon. The Passwords Properties dialog box is displayed.
3. Select the Remote Administration tab, then select the Enable Remote Administration of this server check box. The administrator accounts are displayed in the Administrators field as appropriate.
4. Add or remove administrator accounts to or from the Administrators field as required and choose OK. The dialog box closes.
5. From another Windows 95 computer, log on with one of the administrator's accounts from the previous step and enter **regedit** from a command prompt. The Registry Editor is displayed.
6. From the Registry menu, select Connect Network Registry. The Connect Network Registry dialog box is displayed.
7. Type the computer name of the first Windows 95 computer and choose OK. The Registry settings from the other Windows 95 computer are displayed.
8. Close the Registry Editor.

Net Watcher

The Net Watcher is included in the Accessories group and can be used to view connections to the local computer or to remote computers if Remote Administration is enabled on the remote computer. Net Watcher is primarily used to display the status of connections to shared folders. The features of Net Watcher enable an administrator to remotely perform the following tasks:

- Create a new shared folder
- List the shared folders on a server
- Stop the sharing of a folder
- Show which users are connected to a shared folder
- Show how long a user has been connected to a shared folder and how long the user has been idle
- Disconnect users or close files opened by a user

Figure 4.5 shows an example of a Net Watcher display.

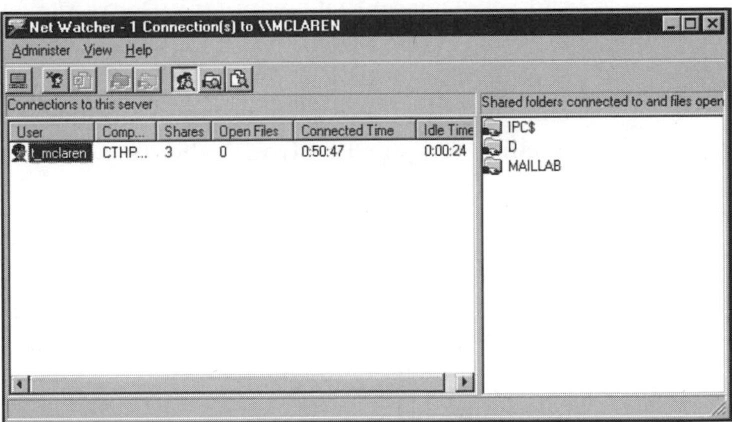

Figure 4.5

A Typical Net Watcher screen.

Net Watcher also can be accessed through the Network Neighborhood by right-clicking on a computer and selecting Properties from the context-sensitive menu. Choose Net Watcher from the Tools tab to view the shared folders and the users accessing those folders on the selected computer.

System Monitor

The System Monitor is a Windows 95 accessory used to display data on various performance counters in Windows 95. With System Monitor and Remote Administration enabled, you can connect to remote computers to view their system performance through the System Monitor as shown in figure 4.6.

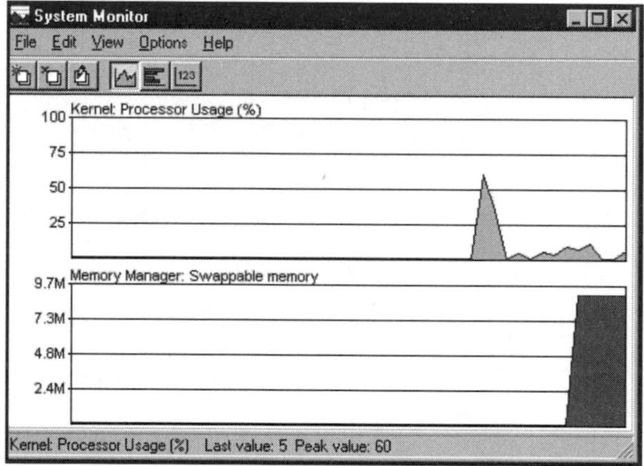

Figure 4.6

A typical System Monitor screen.

You also can quickly enable monitoring of a remote computer by right-clicking on that computer in Network Neighborhood and selecting Properties from the context-sensitive menu. Choose System **Monitor** to start the applet and connect to the selected computer. The Windows 95 System Monitor is discussed in further detail in Chapter 12, "Troubleshooting."

Remote File System Administration

Remote File System Administration enables an administrator to manipulate and control the sharing of files and printers on a remote system. This tool, along with Net Watcher and System Monitor, can be accessed through the Tools tab on the Properties sheet of a computer displayed in the Network Neighborhood.

Review Questions

The following questions will test your knowledge of the information in this chapter. For additional questions, see MCP Endeavor and the Microsoft Roadmap/Assessment Exam on the CD-ROM that accompanies this book.

1. Which three of the following are locations in which Windows 95 settings can be viewed and configured?

   A. The Control Panel

   B. The Properties sheet for the object

   C. The System Monitor

   D. The Windows 95 Registry

2. Which three of the following are common Control Panel applets?

   A. System

   B. Display

   C. Accessibility Options

   D. Drivers

3. The Windows 95 Registry consists of which pair of files?

   A. USER.DAT and USER.REG

   B. USER.REG and SYSTEM.REG

   C. SYSTEM.DAT and CONFIG.POL

   D. USER.DAT and SYSTEM.DAT

4. A Windows 95 System policy ______.

   A. assigns priorities to applications accessing memory

   B. assigns priorities to users

   C. enables an administrator to set various Registry entries

   D. is a summary of configuration details

5. The primary purpose of a Windows 95 System policy is to ______.

   A. limit the ability of users to customize their environment

   B. increase the ability of users to customize their environment

   C. make the system run more efficiently

   D. make the system more adaptable

6. Which three of the following can be used as Windows 95 Remote Administration tools?

   A. Registry Editor

   B. Net Watcher

   C. Remote Access Manager

   D. System Monitor

7. To edit a Windows 95 Registry from another computer on the same network, you must enable Remote Administration from the ______ Control Panel Applet.

   A. System

   B. Passwords

   C. Modems

   D. Network

Review Answers

1. A B D
2. A B C
3. D
4. C
5. A
6. A B D
7. B

Chapter 5

Networking and Interoperability

Windows 95 includes many enhancements to the networking subsystem used in other Windows-based operating systems. This chapter explores the following Windows 95 networking topics:

- The new features of the Windows 95 networking subsystem
- The Windows 95 networking architecture
- How to share and manage files and printers over a network
- How to install and configure support for various network operating systems, including Microsoft and Novell NetWare networks
- The different Microsoft transport protocols available in Windows 95
- How to install and configure the Microsoft TCP/IP protocol with Windows 95

Windows 95 Networking Features

Windows 95 includes many new interesting networking features, including support for the following:

- File and printer sharing as a peer-to-peer server
- Windows 95 as a multi-protocol universal client
- Universal Naming Convention (UNC)
- Plug and Play network cards

- Unified logon and browsing
- Remote access

These features are discussed in the following sections.

Windows 95 as a Peer-to-Peer Server

A Windows 95 computer can act as a server for a peer-to-peer network, sharing its files and printers with other computers. In a peer-to-peer network, also known as a *workgroup*, there is no central user accounts database, unlike a Windows NT domain. Therefore, security in a workgroup is achieved by requiring passwords to connect to a peer server's directory and printer shares. This security model is known as *share-level security*.

Share as a verb means to allow others to access a resource. As a noun it is a directory or print queue that others can access.

The other security model that a Windows 95 server can use is known as *user-level security*. With user-level security enabled, a Windows 95 server requires that peers accessing its resources are validated by a security provider such as a Windows NT Server, Windows NT Workstation, or NetWare bindery server. This process, known as pass-through authentication, is used when a client attempts to access a share on a Windows 95 server using user-level security.

A Windows 95 server is simply any Windows 95 computer with the File and Printer Sharing Service enabled.

Windows 95 as a Universal Client

The networking functionality built into Windows 95 allows a Windows 95 computer to be a client on a wide variety of the most common networks. A Windows 95 client may run multiple network protocols, services, and clients at the same time and thus can be a client on many different networks at the same time.

Windows 95 includes software to support the following networks:

- Microsoft Windows NT
- Microsoft Windows 95
- Microsoft Windows for Workgroups 3.*x*
- Microsoft LAN Manager
- Novell NetWare version 2.15 and later
- Banyan VINES version 5.52 and later
- DEC Pathworks version 4.1 and later
- SunSoft PC—NFS version 5.0 and later

Windows 95 can have only one 16-bit network client installed at a time, but can run multiple 32-bit clients. The 32-bit clients that come with Windows 95 are the Microsoft Client for Windows Networks and Microsoft Client for NetWare Networks.

In addition, the modular architecture of Windows 95 allows Windows 95 components written by other network vendors to be installed.

The following sections look at some specific requirements for operating Windows 95 on a particular network.

Microsoft Networks

A Microsoft Network may include Windows NT, Windows 95, Windows for Workgroups, and LAN Manager Server computers. To communicate with another computer, both computers must run the same network protocol.

A *network protocol* is a set of rules and conventions used by computers to exchange messages on a network. It is analogous to a language by which two computers communicate. The terms *network protocol*, *transport protocol*, or *protocol* are often used interchangeably. For a more detailed description, refer to the section "Transport Protocols" later in this chapter.

Microsoft Network computers can communicate using any one or more of the following protocols:

- Microsoft NetBEUI
- Microsoft TCP/IP
- Microsoft NWLINK (IPX/SPX-compatible)

For detailed information on each of these protocols refer to the section titled "Configuring Network Protocols" later in this chapter.

For a Windows 95 computer to communicate with another computer on a network, both computers must have the same protocol installed. In addition, the appropriate client software and a network adapter card driver must be installed. Exercise 5.1 demonstrates the installation of these three components by installing the NetBEUI protocol, Client for Microsoft Networks, and an appropriate network adapter card driver.

Exercise 5.1: Configuring Windows 95 for a Microsoft Network

1. From the Start menu, select Settings and Control Panel. The Control Panel is displayed.
2. Double-click on the Network icon. The Network dialog box is displayed as shown in figure 5.1.
3. Before removing all components, except the network adapter, write down the name of each component and any additional configuration information from the properties sheet(s) for each component. Double-click on an item to display its properties sheet.

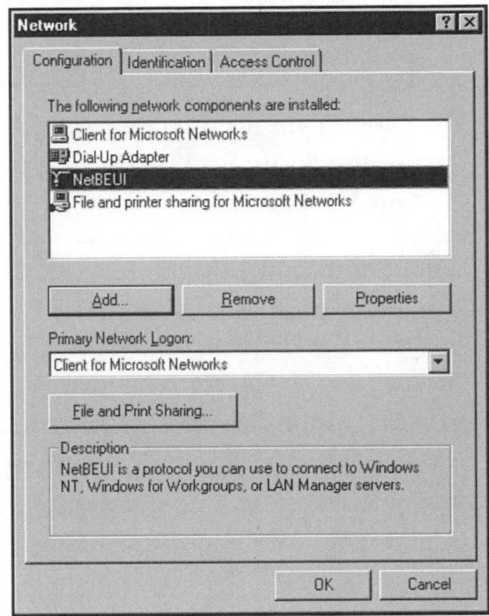

Figure 5.1

A typical Network Control Panel Applet screen.

4. Remove all components except the adapter card by selecting the item and choosing **R**emove. The adapter is displayed.

5. Choose **A**dd, select Client, and choose **A**dd. The manufacturers list is displayed.

6. Select Microsoft and Client for Microsoft Networks and choose OK. The Client for Microsoft Networks is added, along with the NetBEUI and IPX/SPX-compatible protocols.

7. Select IPX/SPX-compatible protocol and choose **R**emove. The client, adapter, and NetBEUI protocol remains.

8. Choose OK and restart the computer.

NetWare Networks

Windows 95 integrates well with NetWare networks running Novell NetWare version 3.11 or higher. Windows 95 includes the 32-bit Client for NetWare Networks, or a 16-bit NETX (NetWare 3.*x*) or VLM (NetWare 4.*x*) Novell NetWare client can be used.

The advantages of using the 32-bit Microsoft Client for NetWare Networks include the following:

- It runs in protected-mode memory and thus does not use any conventional memory.
- The 32-bit architecture offers a 50–200 percent increase in network file I/O operations over the 16-bit versions running on Windows 3.*x*.
- It allows additional network clients to be used at the same time, such as the Microsoft Client for Microsoft Networks.

The Client for NetWare Networks can be used to access NetWare servers running NetWare 2.15 and above and NetWare 4.*x* servers using bindery emulation. The Client for NetWare Networks runs only with the IPX/SPX-compatible protocol, which is installed by default when the client is installed.

Although the 16-bit Novell NetWare clients do not provide all of the advantages of the 32-bit client, a 16-bit NETX or VLM client is required if any of the following are used:

- NCP packet signature security
- NetWare IP protocol
- Helper Terminate-and-Stay-Resident (TSR) applications loaded from DOS (such as 3270 emulators)
- Custom Virtual Loadable Modules (VLMs) with functionality not provided by the Windows 95 components such as Personal NetWare (PNW.VLM)
- Novell utilities such as NWADMIN or NETADMIN
- NetWare Directory Services (NDS)
- IPX ODI protocol
- Monolithic IPX (IPX.COM) or ARCnet protocols

Banyan VINES

Banyan VINES version 5.52 and later may be used with Windows 95. However, computers running only Banyan VINES cannot use the browser services. For example, Banyan VINES computers are not visible in the Network Neighborhood.

Windows 95 Banyan VINES computers must use NDIS network card drivers rather than monolithic network drivers.

DEC Pathworks

Digital Equipment Corporation (DEC) Pathworks is a LAN Manager-compatible protocol. The Pathworks 4.1 and 5.0 and above protocols are included with Windows 95 for use with the Client for Microsoft Networks. Pathworks uses a STARTNET.BAT file called from AUTOEXEC.BAT to load the Pathworks drivers.

Windows 95 Pathworks computers can use the Microsoft NetBEUI, Microsoft TCP/IP, or DEC DECnet protocols. DECnet is not included with Windows 95.

PC-NFS

The SunSoft PC-NFS client and protocol support is included with Windows 95 for use on PC-NFS networks running version 5.0 or later. Computers running only PC-NFS cannot use the browser service, nor are they visible when browsed from other computers.

Universal Naming Convention (UNC)

The *Universal Naming Convention* (UNC) is a standardized nomenclature for specifying a share name on a particular computer. The computer name is limited to 15 characters, and the share name is usually limited to 15 characters, depending on the network. Share names can be given to a print queue or a directory of files, WINAPPS or HP4 for example.

The UNC uniquely specifies the path to the share name on a network. The UNC path takes the form of *computername**sharename* [*optional path*]. For example, the UNC path of the printer share LPS20 created on the server ALPHA would be \\ALPHA\LPS20.

A UNC name does not require a drive-letter assignment. Windows 95 takes full advantage of network connectivity using UNC names so that you can connect to a remote directory or printer share without having to map a drive letter to it. However, for DOS-based applications that require a drive letter or port to be used, you can map a drive-letter to a shared directory or a port to a shared printer.

The UNC also can specify the full path to a file in a subdirectory of a file share. For example, to share the entire C drive on the computer BIGBEN, the share name CDRIVE could be created for the root directory c:\. To specify the directory c:\windows\system using a UNC path with these share names, use \\BIGBEN\CDRIVE\windows\system.

Add a dollar sign ($) to the end of the share name to prevent a share name from being visible to another computer through a browser such as Network Neighborhood. The share name TOPSECRET$, for example, would not be visible to other computers browsing the computer.

Exercise 5.2 illustrates the use of a UNC name. For this exercise, you must be connected to a network and be able to browse file shares on other computers on the network.

Exercise 5.2: Using UNC Names

1. Open Network Neighborhood from the Desktop. The other computers in your workgroup or domain are displayed.
2. Double-click on another computer that contains a share to which you have access. The shares on that computer are displayed.
3. Note the computer name and share name on a piece of paper.
4. Select Programs, MS-DOS Prompt from the Start menu. A command prompt window is opened.

5. Enter **DIR** ***computername\sharename***, using the computer name and share name you recorded. The directory listing from the remote network share is displayed.

Plug and Play Network Cards

If a network interface card is Plug and Play compliant, it can be automatically detected and configured with Windows 95. Simply plug the network card into the appropriate expansion slot and start Windows 95. The model of the card will be detected, and the appropriate Windows 95 driver will be installed. Windows 95 then assigns an available interrupt (IRQ) and memory address range to the network card as appropriate and configures the card to use these settings. All the administrator needs to do is install the client and protocol software to be used with the network card.

For more information on Plug and Play hardware, refer to Chapter 11, "Plug and Play."

Unified Logon and Browsing

As mentioned previously, a Windows 95 computer can have more than one network client installed at a time. A single network wire may have multiple network protocols running on it. For example, if a network contains both Windows NT and Novell NetWare servers, the Windows 95 computer can run both the Client for Microsoft Networks and the Client for NetWare Networks. If the passwords are the same for the two networks, then the unified logon feature of Windows 95 requires that the password be entered only once for both networks. Similarly, if the Windows password is the same as the network password, the password needs to be entered only once. If the passwords are not the same, they need to be entered individually.

Windows 95 also features unified browsing—all computers that can be browsed by Windows 95 are displayed together in the Network Neighborhood. For example, NetWare servers appear along with Windows-based computers in the Network Neighborhood if both the Client for Microsoft Networks and Client for NetWare Networks are installed.

Remote Access

Windows 95 enables network connections to be made via a modem or null-modem cable. For more information on remote access, refer to Chapter 9, "Mobile Services."

Networking Architecture

Windows 95 has a modular, layered architecture. Each layer needs to communicate directly only with the layers above and below it. Therefore a component of the architecture, such as a network adapter driver, needs to be compatible only with the layer adjacent to it, which is the device driver interface in this case. Thus, only one version of the network adapter driver needs to be created as the driver will work with any of the Windows 95-compatible transport protocols.

The modularity of the Windows 95 networking architecture means that components can be interchanged and new components easily added, as long as the component can communicate properly with the adjacent layers. The interoperability is made easier by the use of programming interfaces that are written by Microsoft and contain a standardized set of commands and procedures that the adjacent layers can use to intercommunicate.

The layers of the Windows 95 networking architecture are as follows:

- Application Interface
- Network Providers
- Installable File System (IFS) Manager
- Redirectors and Services
- Transport Programming Interface
- Transport Protocols
- Device Driver Interface

Application Interface

The Application Interface layer contains two interfaces that allow an application to access the Windows 95 networking services. The application interfaces contain a standardized set of commands and procedures that an application can use to communicate with the network provider. This allows a developer to create an application that works with any Windows 95 network protocol, since the application only needs to be able to communicate directly to the application interfaces.

The two interfaces functioning at this layer are the Win32 Print Applicator Programming Interface (API) and the Win32 WinNet Interface.

The Win32 Print API handles network printing-related functions. For more information on the Print API, see the architecture section of Chapter 7, "Managing Printers."

The Win32 WinNet Interface handles all other networking functions not performed by the Win32 Print API.

Network Providers

The network providers provide a more network-specific programming interface for access to networking services. Windows 95 ships with three network providers, but other third-party network providers written for Windows 95 can be incorporated into a third-party network protocol.

The network providers allow access to shared files and printers and provide browsing services. The network providers included with Windows 95 are as follows:

- Windows Network Provider/Print Provider
- NetWare Network Provider/Print Provider
- WinNet16

The Windows Network Provider/Print Provider is a 32-bit provider that supports networking products that use the Server Message Block (SMB) file-sharing protocol. It may be used by both 16-bit and 32-bit Windows-based applications.

The NetWare Provider/Print Provider is a 32-bit provider for use with NetWare networks that use the NetWare Core Protocol (NCP) file sharing service. The NetWare Provider/Print Provider can be accessed by both 16-bit and 32-bit applications on a NetWare network.

The WinNet16 network provider can be used for backwards-compatibility with older network applications that require it.

Installable File System (IFS) Manager

Installable File Systems (IFSs) can be dynamically loaded into memory to handle files in Windows 95. Examples of Installable File Systems are the Compact Disk File System (CDFS) and the virtual file allocation table (VFAT).

The IFS Manager handles the communication between the various Installable File Systems, the Network Provider, and the network redirectors and services.

Redirectors and Services

At this layer, information passing between the application and transport protocol layers is processed and converted to the proper data format for the next layer. The redirectors and services residing at this layer each perform a specific function on the information.

Redirectors

The redirector maps network names used by an application to network device names to which the transport can send the information.

Windows 95 includes the following two redirectors:

- Microsoft Networking Redirector used with SMB-based networks
- NetWare Networking Redirector used with NCP-based networks

Services

Networking services are individual dynamic-link libraries (DLLs) or virtual device drivers (VxDs) that can be loaded into memory to provide certain networking services. The networking services are installed using the Add button from the Network Control Panel Applet (NCPA).

The networking services included with Windows 95 are shown in table 5.1. Additional services not included with Windows 95 can also be added through the NCPA.

Table 5.1

Networking Services Included with Windows 95

Service	Description
Arcadia Backup Exec Agent	Network file backup service
Cheyenne ARCserve Agent	Network file backup service
Hewlett-Packard JetAdmin	Remote Administration for HP JetDirect Network Interface Printers
HP JetAdmin for NetWare	Remote Administration for HP JetDirect Network Interface Printers on NetWare networks
Microsoft File and Print Sharing for Microsoft Networks	Printer and file sharing on a Microsoft network
Microsoft File and Print Sharing for NetWare Networks	Printer and file sharing on a NetWare network

continues

Table 5.1 Continued

Service	Description
Microsoft Network Monitor	Reports information to a Remote Network Agent Monitoring Utility (for example System Management Server (SMS)
Microsoft Remote Registry Agent	Allows the Registry to be administered by another computer
Simple Network Management (SNMP) Protocol Agent	Reports information to a third-party SNMP Manager

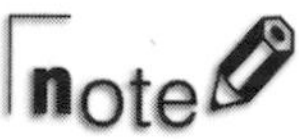

Only one file and print sharing service may be installed on a computer at a time. The Network Monitor Agent, Remote Registry Service, and SNMP Agent are found on the Windows 95 CD-ROM in the \admin\nettools directory.

Transport Programming Interface

The Transport Programming Interface provides a standardized set of commands to allow the network redirector and services to send information to the underlying transport protocols.

The Transport Programming Interface allows the services of the upper layers of the networking architecture to communicate with any of the Windows 95-compatible transport protocols such as NetBEUI, TCP/IP, or IPX/SPX.

Windows 95 has two Transport Programming Interfaces: the NetBIOS Interface and the Windows Sockets Interface.

The Network Basic Input/Output System (NetBIOS) interface allows NetBIOS names and commands to be passed to the Transport protocol layer. Examples of NetBIOS names are computer names, share names, and workgroup names. Thus, when a Windows 95 computer connects to a computer named SERVER01 using the NetBEUI protocol, the NetBIOS interface passes instructions from the redirector to the NetBEUI protocol to start a connection with the NetBIOS computer named SERVER01.

The Windows Sockets Interface allows sockets-based applications to pass instructions back and forth to the transport protocols. *Sockets* are two-way communication paths between two computers. Sockets have traditionally been used with TCP/IP applications such as File Transfer Protocol (FTP), but can be used with any Windows 95 protocol.

Transport Protocols

The transport protocol is responsible for putting the information in the correct format so that it can be understood by the network device to which the message is being sent.

A *transport protocol* is essentially a language that network devices use to communicate. In order for one network device such as a computer to communicate with another, both devices need to use the same transport protocol. In other words, they both need to "speak the same language."

The following protocols are included with Windows 95:

- Microsoft NetBEUI
- Microsoft TCP/IP
- Microsoft IPX/SPX-compatible (NWLINK)
- Microsoft DLC

In addition, several protocols written by third-party vendors are included with Windows 95:

- Banyan VINES
- DEC Pathworks versions 4.1 and 5.0
- IBM DLC
- Novell IPX ODI
- SunSoft PC-NFS

These protocols and additional Windows 95-compatible transport protocols can be installed using the Network Control Panel Applet.

For more information on choosing the protocol to use on a network, refer to the "Configuring Network Protocols" section later in this chapter.

Device Driver Interface

The Device Driver Interface handles communication between the transport protocol and the network card driver. This interface contains a standardized set of commands and procedures that the protocol and network card driver can use to communicate with each other. Since the protocol directly communicates with only the Device Driver Interface, it doesn't matter which network card driver is used as long as it can understand the Device Driver Interface specifications. Therefore, a hardware vendor needs to develop only a single device driver that can be used with any Windows 95-compatible protocol.

The transport protocol and the device driver must be written to one of the three specifications supported by Windows 95:

- **NDIS 3.1.** A specification that supports NDIS 3.*x* protected-mode drivers in addition to Plug and Play. Protected-mode drivers do not use conventional memory. An NDIS 3.*x* driver usually has a VXD extension.
- **NDIS 2.** A specification for real-mode drivers, which use conventional memory. The NDIS 2 drivers usually have a SYS or DOS extension.
- **Open Datalink Interface (ODI).** Designed by Novell, ODI is similar to the NDIS 2 specification.

Security

If a Windows 95 computer has file- and print-sharing service enabled, the print queues and directory on that computer can be shared with others on the network.

> To ensure a computer can share its printers and files, select both check boxes of the File and Printer Sharing option in the Network Control Panel Applet. These check boxes are "I want to be able to give others access to my files." and "I want to be able to allow others to print to my printer(s)."

After file or print sharing has been enabled, a user must share the file or printer with others and decide whether, and how, they will prevent unauthorized access to these resources.

Windows 95 has two different methods for determining who can access a share Windows 95 resource. The user must decide which of these two security models to implement on the Windows 95 computer. The security models are share-level and user-level.

Share-Level Security

Share-level security is used by default when File and Printer Sharing for Microsoft Networks is installed.

> File and Printer Sharing for NetWare Networks must use user-level security. The share-level security option is unavailable if File and Printer Sharing for NetWare Networks is installed.

With share-level security, passwords are assigned to permit access to a directory or printer share. In order to access the share, a user must supply the correct password.

When creating a shared directory using share-level security, one of three types of access can be granted:

- **Read-only.** If the correct password is entered, a remote user can access a directory, its subdirectories, and its files, but the user cannot delete files or write files to that directory.
- **Full.** A remote user who supplies the correct password has read and write privileges to that directory and all its files and subdirectories.

- **Depends on password.** Two different passwords can be created—one allowing Read-only access, and one allowing Full access. The type of access granted to a user will depend on the password that that user has supplied.

If no password is used, any users will have Full or Read-only access to the directory, depending on which option was specified when the shared directory was created.

In Exercise 5.3, you create a directory share using share-level security.

Exercise 5.3: Sharing a Directory Using Share-Level Security

1. From the Start menu, select Settings and then Control Panel. The Control Panel is displayed.
2. Double-click on the Network icon. The Network dialog box is displayed.
3. Select the Access Control tab and select Share-level access control.
4. Select the Configuration tab and choose File and Print Sharing. The File and Print Sharing dialog box is displayed.
5. Select both the "I want to be able to give others access to my files" and the "I want to be able to allow others to print to my printer(s)" check boxes to allow others to access your printers and files and choose OK. File and Printer Sharing for Microsoft Networks is automatically installed.
6. Choose OK and restart the computer.
7. Start Explorer and select a directory on your hard drive.
8. Right-click on the selected directory. The context-sensitive menu is displayed.
9. Select Sharing from the context-sensitive menu. The Sharing dialog box opens as shown in figure 5.2.

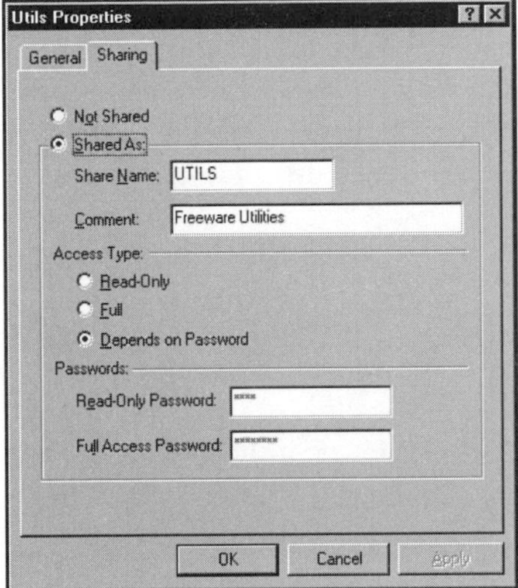

Figure 5.2

The Properties sheet for a shared directory using share-level security.

10. Type **TEST** for the share name and select Access Type: **R**ead-Only. Enter a password for Read-only access and choose OK. The sharing hand symbol replaces the folder symbol for the shared directory.

11. If you have another computer on the network, browse the first computer in Network Neighborhood to display the share name. The share name TEST is displayed under the appropriate computer name.

12. Double-click on the share name TEST. You are prompted for the password.

13. Enter the password and choose OK. The directory contents are displayed.

14. Try to copy a file to the local hard drive. The file read will be successful.

15. Try to delete a file in the shared directory. The file delete will not be allowed.

Print queues can also be shared with other network users using share-level security. If a password is specified for the share, a network user has to enter that password to access the print queue and connect to that printer. If a printer is shared with a blank password, any users can connect to and print to that printer. For more information on sharing a printer, see Chapter 7.

Since share-level security relies on access passwords, this form of security has the following disadvantages:

- To access different shares, a network user has to know numerous passwords.
- Passwords can easily be forgotten. Windows 95 can cache passwords so that a user does need to enter them each time. However, if the creator of the share forgets the password, then the password has to be changed to allow another user to access the share.
- There is nothing preventing a user from disclosing the password to an unauthorized user.

User-Level Security

User-level security can be used to overcome the shortcomings of share-level security. With user-level security, specific user accounts or group accounts can be granted access to a shared directory or printer. Instead of relying on a password that could be used by anyone, the user account accessing a shared resource must be authenticated to ensure that that account has been granted access.

Windows 95 does not manage user accounts by itself. It must use pass-through authentication to have a Windows NT or NetWare server authenticate the user who is trying to access the resource.

In order to use user-level security, the Windows 95 computer must obtain a copy of the accounts list from one of the following sources:

- Windows NT Server 3.5 (or later) computer
- Windows NT Workstation 3.5 (or later) computer

- NetWare 3.*x* server running SYSCON
- NetWare 4.*x* server running NETADMIN and bindery emulation

With user-level security, when a directory is shared, the users or groups to have access to the share are assigned privileges. Each user or group can be given one of the following privileges:

- **Read-only.** Users can access files and subdirectories in a directory, but cannot delete or save files to that share.
- **Full access.** Users can read, write, and delete files in the directory.
- **Custom.** Any number of the following privileges can be granted:

  Read Files

  Write to Files

  Create Files

  List Files

  Delete Files

  Change File Attributes

  Change Permissions

When sharing a printer, users or groups can be added to a list of users with access to that printer. For more information on sharing printers, refer to Chapter 7.

Exercise 5.4 demonstrates how to give a network user access to a directory share. For this exercise, you must be part of a domain that contains a server with a user accounts database. If the user accounts are on a NetWare server, then you should install the Client for NetWare Networks, the IPX/SPX-compatible protocol, and File and Printer Sharing for NetWare Networks.

Exercise 5.4: Sharing a Directory Using User-Level Security

1. From the Start menu, select **S**ettings, then **C**ontrol Panel. The Control Panel is displayed.
2. Double-click on the Network icon. The Network dialog box is displayed.
3. Select the Access Control tab and select **U**ser-level access control as shown in figure 5.3.

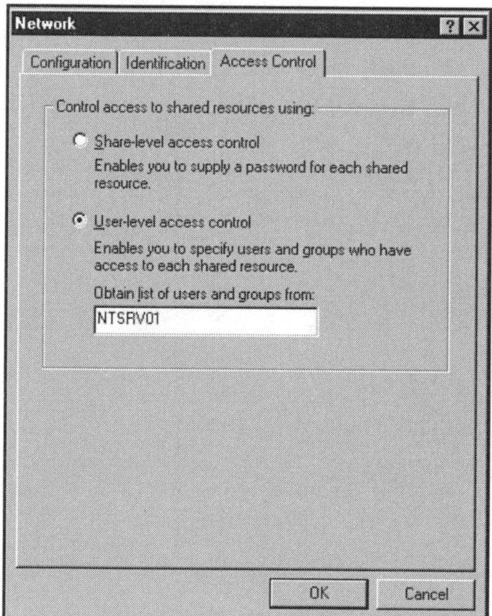

Figure 5.3

Enabling user-level security.

4. Type the name of the server with the user accounts database on it. Windows 95 attempts to access the Windows NT or NetWare server to obtain the users list.
5. Select the Configuration tab and choose **F**ile and Print Sharing. The File and Print Sharing dialog box is displayed.
6. Select both the "I want to be able to give others access to my **f**iles" and the "I want to be able to allow others to **p**rint to my printer(s)" check boxes to allow others to access your printers and files and choose OK. File and Printer Sharing for Microsoft Networks is automatically installed.
7. Choose OK and restart the computer.

8. Start Explorer and select another directory on your hard drive. The new directory is highlighted in Explorer, but the directory from the previous exercise is no longer shared due to the changed security model.

9. Right-click on the selected directory. The context-sensitive menu is displayed.

10. Select Sharing from the context-sensitive menu. The Sharing dialog box is displayed as shown in figure 5.4.

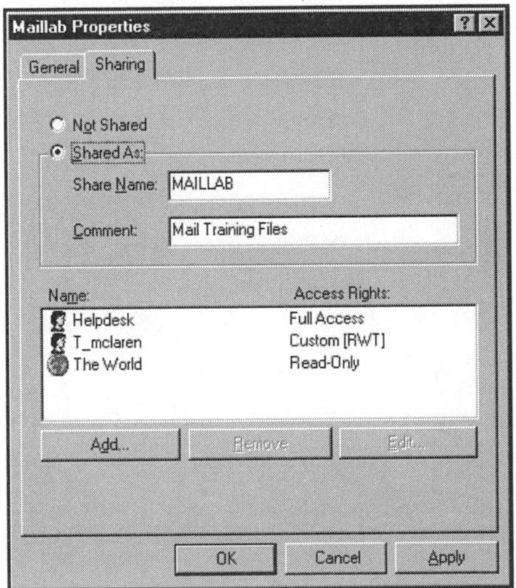

Figure 5.4

The Properties Sheet for a shared directory using user-level security.

11. Type **TEST2** for the share name and give a user Full access privileges by selecting the user and choosing Full Access. Choose OK. The folder symbol for the shared directory is replaced with a folder being held by a hand.

12. Log on to another computer on the network using the user name to which you gave Full access permissions. Locate the share name TEST2 in the Explorer by browsing the entire network. The share name TEST2 is displayed under the appropriate computer name.

13. Double-click on the share name TEST2. The directory contents is displayed.

14. Try to copy a file to the shared directory. The file write is allowed.

Networking Configuration

The flexible networking architecture of Windows 95 allows many interchangeable networking components to be installed and configured to meet the requirements of a network. The configurable networking components of Windows 95 include the following:

- Client software
- Adapter drivers
- Transport protocols
- Network services

Most of these components are interchangeable, allowing a Windows 95 computer to be configured to support many network environments. For example, multiple 32-bit clients, network adapters, protocols, and services can be installed to allow a Windows 95 computer to perform many different tasks in a heterogeneous networking environment.

Only one 16-bit client may be installed at a time. Similarly, only one file and print sharing service may be installed on a Windows 95 computer.

The following sections look at how to install and configure the various Windows 95 networking components.

Configuring Network Clients

The Windows 95 networking clients provide a user interface for the networking software. Each type of network requires the proper client to be used to interact with the rest of network. The following client software is included with Windows 95:

- The 32-bit Client for Microsoft Networks
- The 32-bit Client for NetWare Networks
- Various 16-bit clients for other networks

Microsoft Networks

The 32-bit Client for Microsoft Networks is recommended for all SMB-based networks. The configuration of the Client for Microsoft Networks is different depending on whether the Windows 95 computer is part of a Windows NT domain or part of a peer-to-peer workgroup without a domain controller or centralized accounts database.

Windows NT Server Domain

A Windows NT domain contains at least one Windows NT Server that acts as the domain controller and maintains a user accounts database. When a Windows 95 computer participates in a domain, it can use user-level security to share and access resources on a per user account basis. Furthermore, Windows 95 can process Windows NT logon scripts during logon.

There are many other benefits to participating in a Windows NT domain discussed in the Windows NT documentation.

In Exercise 5.5, you configure a Windows 95 computer to participate in a Windows NT domain. If the Client for Microsoft Networks is not already installed, perform Exercise 5.1 before proceeding.

Exercise 5.5: Configuring Windows 95 for Use in a Windows NT Domain

1. From the Start menu, select Settings then Control Panel. The Control Panel is displayed.

2. Double-click on the Network icon. The Network dialog box is displayed.

3. Select Client for Microsoft Networks and choose Properties. The Client for Microsoft Networks Properties sheet is displayed.

4. Select Log on to Windows NT domain, enter the Windows NT domain name, and choose OK. The Client for Microsoft Networks Properties sheet is again displayed.

5. Select the Identification tab and type the Windows NT domain name in the Workgroup field.

6. Enter a computer name and optional description in the other fields and choose OK. You are prompted to restart the computer.

7. Restart the computer and log on to Windows 95 using your Windows NT domain account. If your domain password is the same as your Windows password, enter the password once.

Peer Workgroup

A peer workgroup consists of Windows-based computers that are not part of a Windows NT domain. Workgroups must use share-level security since the clients do not access a central Windows NT or NetWare accounts database.

To configure a Windows 95 computer to participate in a peer-to-peer workgroup you need only to specify the computer name and workgroup name in the Identification tab of the Network Control Panel Applet.

File and Printer Sharing for Microsoft Networks

To allow other computers on a Microsoft Network to access a Windows 95 computer's print queues or files, you need to configure the following:

- Enable the appropriate sharing option(s) in the File and Print Sharing dialog box of the Network Control Panel Applet.

- If user-level security is to be used, configure that option in the Access Control tab of the Network Control Panel Applet.

- The specific directory or printer queue must be shared and the appropriate access permissions must be granted.

NetWare Networks

Windows 95 clients can easily join existing Novell NetWare networks and share many of the benefits of other NetWare clients. For interoperability with NetWare networks, Windows 95 includes the following components and features:

- The 32-bit Client for NetWare Networks
- Support for 16-bit Novell NetWare clients
- A NetWare logon script processor
- The IPX/SPX-compatible protocol
- The IPX ODI protocol for compatibility with older NetWare networks
- The File and Printer Sharing for NetWare Networks service

16-Bit and 32-Bit NetWare Clients

Where possible, the 32-bit Client for NetWare Networks is recommended for interoperability with NetWare networks. The 32-bit client does not use any conventional memory and provides other benefits such as unified logon and unified browsing services, which have been discussed previously.

When the Client for NetWare Networks is installed, the IPX/SPX-compatible protocol automatically installs as well. This protocol must be used with the Client for NetWare Networks, although additional protocols also can be installed.

In Exercise 5.6, you install and configure the Client for NetWare Networks. You must have a network adapter driver already installed in the Network Control Panel Applet.

Exercise 5.6: Configuring the Client for NetWare Networks

1. From the Start menu, select Settings then Control Panel. The Control Panel is displayed.
2. Double-click on the Network icon. The Network dialog box is displayed.

3. Choose **A**dd, select Client, and choose **A**dd. The Manufacturers list is displayed.

4. Select Microsoft and Client for NetWare Networks and choose OK. The Client for NetWare Networks and the IPX/SPX-compatible protocol are installed.

5. Select the Client for NetWare Networks and choose **P**roperties. The Client for NetWare Networks Properties sheet is displayed.

6. Select the General tab and type in the Preferred server field the name of the NetWare server that should process the logon.

7. In the **F**irst network drive field, select the first drive letter to be available to be mapped by a NetWare login script and choose OK twice. You are prompted to restart the computer.

8. Restart the computer and enter your NetWare user name at the unified logon screen. If your NetWare password is the same as your Windows password, you have to enter the password only once.

   If your NetWare password is different from your Windows password, change your NetWare password to your Windows password by entering the SETPASS command from the SYS/PUBLIC directory on the NetWare server.

File and Printer Sharing for NetWare Networks

To enable directories and print queues to be shared with other NetWare users, add the File and Printer Sharing for NetWare Networks service in the Network Control Panel. If the File and Printer Sharing for Microsoft Networks service is already installed, remove that service first.

After File and Printer Sharing for NetWare Networks is installed, enable sharing by choosing the appropriate File and Print Sharing options from the Network Control Panel Applet.

File and Printer Sharing for NetWare Networks must use the user-level security model.

The computer name of the NetWare server that maintains the list of user accounts must be specified in the Access Control tab of the Network Control Panel Applet.

Other Networks

To install network clients for other networks, refer to the documentation provided by the third-party network vendor.

Configuring Network Adapter Drivers

Windows 95 includes drivers for many of the most popular network adapter drivers. Additional network adapter drivers may be supplied by the network adapter vendor for use with Windows 95. Before you can install any other Windows 95 networking components, you must first install a network adapter driver through the Network Control Panel Applet. If you do not have an actual network card in the computer, you can use the Microsoft Dial-Up Adapter driver along with a compatible modem for network connectivity.

Network adapter card drivers are configured by selecting the adapter in the Network Control Panel Applet and choosing **P**roperties. If the network card supports the Plug and Play standard, Windows 95 can automatically configure the driver according to information the card provides to the Windows 95 operating system. Otherwise, the card should be configured according to the manufacturer's documentation.

The Windows 95 exam does not cover configuration of network adapter drivers. For more information on this topic, refer to Part II of this book, "Networking Essentials."

Configuring Network Protocols

A network transport protocol is similar to a language that the network computers use to communicate among themselves. For two computers to communicate, they both must speak the same language—they must both use the same network transport protocol. The following transport protocols are included with Windows 95:

- Microsoft NetBEUI
- Microsoft IPX/SPX-compatible (NWLINK)
- Microsoft TCP/IP
- Microsoft DLC
- Other third-party vendor transport protocols

The NetBEUI and IPX/SPX-compatible protocols are installed by default when a network adapter driver is installed.

If the Windows 95 computer needs to communicate with other computers, it must have the same protocol installed as the other computers. For example, if the other computers on the network are running DEC Pathworks 4.1, install that protocol on the Windows 95 computer. If a common protocol on the network has not yet been established, refer to the following sections for information on each of the protocols.

Unless you are required to use a third-party protocol to communicate with other computers, use one of the Microsoft protocols to take full advantage of the Windows 95 networking features. Furthermore, the third-party protocols provided often require extra components, licenses, and configuration.

NetBEUI

The NetBIOS Extended User Interface (NetBEUI) protocol is relatively easy to implement because it does not require that additional network addresses be configured for each computer other than the computer name and domain or workgroup name.

The advantages of the NetBEUI protocol include the following:

- Communication is fast.
- Performance is dynamically self-tuned.
- The only configuration required is a NetBIOS computer name and workgroup or domain name.

IPX/SPX

The IPX/SPX protocol is a routable protocol that is commonly used with NetWare networks. IPX/SPX must be installed if the Client for NetWare Networks is used, although other protocols can be installed as well.

TCP/IP

Windows 95 comes with the Microsoft 32-bit TCP/IP protocol, related connectivity utilities, and an SNMP client.

To install the TCP/IP protocol on a Windows 95 computer, follow these steps:

1. Select Settings then Control Panel from the Start menu.
2. Double-click on the Network icon and select the Configuration tab.
3. Choose Add to open the Select Network Component Type dialog box.
4. Select Protocol and choose Add to open the Select Network Protocol dialog box.

5. Select Microsoft from the Manufacturers list and TCP/IP from the Network Protocols list.

6. Choose OK to return to the Network dialog box.

After installing TCP/IP on a Windows 95 computer, the tabbed TCP/IP Properties dialog box appears from which you configure the appropriate values. To reconfigure TCP/IP, choose the Network icon from the Control Panel to open the Network dialog box again.

To configure TCP/IP for Windows 95, follow these steps:

1. From the Network dialog box Configuration tab, select TCP/IP and choose Properties.

2. From the TCP/IP Properties dialog box, select the IP Address tab shown in figure 5.5. Select Obtain an IP address automatically if there is a Dynamic Host Configuration Protocol (DHCP) server on the network configured to supply this machine with an IP address. Otherwise, type the IP address and subnet mask in the spaces provided.

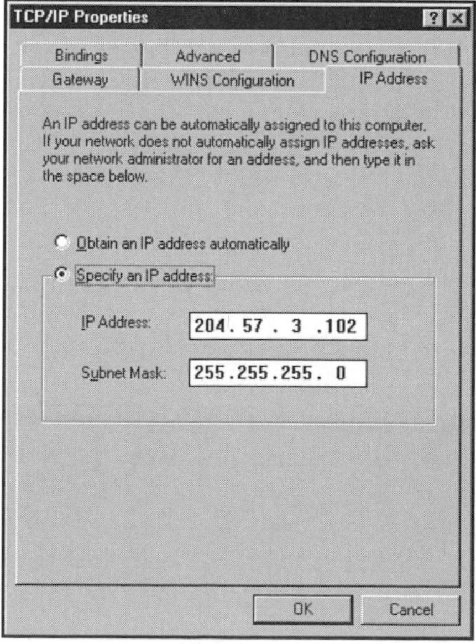

Figure 5.5

The IP Address tab of the TCP/IP Properties sheet.

An incorrect IP Address or Subnet Mask can cause communication problems with other TCP/IP nodes on the network. If an IP Address is the same as another already on the network, it can also cause either machine to hang. DHCP can help prevent duplicate addresses by automatically configuring TCP/IP on the client using parameters set on the DHCP server. The DHCP server will keep track of IP addresses it has assigned to clients, and will not assign the same IP address to two different DHCP clients.

3. Each of the other tabs in the TCP/IP Properties dialog box contain optional configuration information. For each of these tabbed properties sheets, type the appropriate values as required. Choose OK when done to restart the computer and initialize TCP/IP.

The following TCP/IP Properties sheet tabs contain optional TCP/IP configuration parameters:

- Gateway
- WINS Configuration
- DNS Configuration
- Bindings
- Advanced

It is highly recommended that a default gateway be configured for the Windows 95 client using the Gateway tab. The default gateway can help route TCP/IP messages to remote destinations.

Gateway

When the route needed for an IP message to reach a destination is not known, the message is forwarded to the default gateway. The *default gateway* is a router connected to other TCP/IP network segments to which messages are initially sent when it is not known on which segment the destination is. The Gateway tab sheet contains the IP addresses of default gateways that may be used in the order they appear on the list.

> Only one gateway is used to route messages. If a gateway is unavailable (due to hardware problems, for example), then the next gateway on the list is used. If that gateway does not respond, the next gateway is used. A second gateway never is used if the first one is available, even if the destination computer is unavailable, or the message is undeliverable.

WINS Configuration

A Windows Internet Name Service (WINS) server can be used to register and resolve NetBIOS names to IP addresses. For example, if the Windows 95 computer wants to map a drive to the computer name SERVER3 on a remote TCP/IP network, it can query the WINS server to find out the IP address of SERVER3.

Communication using TCP/IP must always use IP addresses; therefore a WINS server or some other form of NetBIOS name-to-IP-address-resolution must be used if communication using NetBIOS names is required. The alternatives to using a WINS server include using a static LMHOSTS file in the <*systemroot*> directory, which contains NetBIOS name-to-IP-address mappings. However, a WINS server is preferred because NetBIOS names can be automatically and dynamically registered with the WINS server, which is much more flexible and accurate than an LMHOSTS file or other method.

The three choices of WINS configuration for a Windows 95 TCP/IP client are as follows:

- Enable WINS Resolution
- Disable WINS Resolution
- Use DHCP for WINS Resolution

If WINS resolution is enabled, then you must enter the IP address of one or two WINS servers in the appropriate fields. If the primary WINS server is unavailable for some reason, TCP/IP accesses the secondary WINS server if one is configured.

If WINS is disabled, then an alternate form of NetBIOS name resolution is required to resolve NetBIOS names to computer names for destinations on remote networks.

If DHCP has been enabled in the IP address tab, you can select the Use DHCP for WINS Resolution option to use the WINS servers specified by the DHCP Server options.

This last option does not mean that a DHCP server provides name resolution. The option is used when a DHCP server has been configured to advise the DHCP clients of the IP address(es) of the WINS server(s).

DNS Configuration

The Domain Name Service (DNS) provides address resolution for DNS host and domain names. Host names are used with Windows Sockets applications. The host name for a Windows-based computer is often the same as the computer name, but the domain name is usually something like domain.company.com. World Wide Web addresses often consist of DNS host names appended to the DNS domain name to form a Fully Qualified Domain Name such as `www.microsoft.com`, where `www` is the host (computer) name, and `microsoft.com` is the domain name.

To access a computer using a DNS name over TCP/IP, the DNS name must be resolved to an IP address. This can be done using a static HOSTS file in the <*systemroot*> directory, or by accessing a DNS server. The DNS server contains a database that is distributed over an internetwork. If a DNS server cannot fully resolve a domain name to an IP address, it can pass the request on to another DNS server until the name is found and resolved.

The DNS Server Search Order list in the TCP/IP Properties sheet shown in figure 5.6 lists the order in which DNS servers will be queried for DNS name resolution. The Domain Suffix Search Order list lists the order in which domain names can be appended to a host name to try to resolve the resulting Fully Qualified Domain Name. For example, if the Domain Suffix Search Order list contains `microsoft.com`, and if the host name `fred` cannot be resolved, DNS then attempts to resolve the name `fred.microsoft.com`.

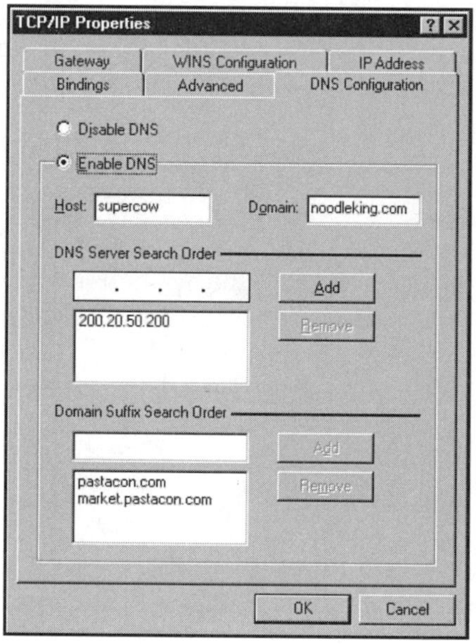

Figure 5.6

The DNS Configuration tab of the TCP/IP Properties sheet.

Bindings

The Bindings tab shows network components that can use the TCP/IP protocol. If a component has a check mark next to it, it will bind to TCP/IP and can then use the TCP/IP protocol for communication. To improve performance, remove the check marks from any components that do not require TCP/IP.

Advanced

The Advanced tab can be used to specify whether you want the TCP/IP protocol to be the default or preferred protocol. By default, the NetBEUI protocol is the default protocol if it is installed.

Microsoft DLC

The other Microsoft-written network protocol included with Windows 95 is Microsoft DLC. However, this protocol is used only for communicating with certain network interface printers and mainframe systems. DLC is not used for peer-to-peer networking of Windows 95 computers.

Other Protocols

The other third-party vendor protocols may be installed to support preexisting third-party networks. For information on each, refer to the vendor documentation.

Configuring Network Services

The network services included with Windows 95 include third-party network backup software, Hewlett-Packard network printing software, and the Microsoft File and Printer Sharing services. For information on the network backup software, contact the appropriate vendor. The Hewlett-Packard network printer support services are discussed in Chapter 7. The File and Printer Sharing services are discussed throughout this chapter and in the following section, "Browsing."

Browsing

When users access the Network Neighborhood, they are viewing a list of computers on the network known as a *browse list.*

Microsoft and NetWare networks can use NetBIOS to distribute browse lists throughout a domain. The browse list contains all NetBIOS computers and shared resources in the domain. The browse list is compiled by the master browser of the domain.

When the master browser has compiled the browse list, it distributes the list to the backup browsers. When a client requires access to the browse list, it obtains it from a backup browser so that the master browser does not become overloaded with requests from all the computers.

The decision of which computers are master and backup browsers is determined through browse elections. If a primary domain controller is present, that controller will always be the master browser. Each type of operating system in the network has a different potential to be a browser. Windows NT computers are more favored to be browsers than Windows 95 computers. If a computer is a preferred browser, it can be elected to be a browser depending on the operating system it is running and whether or not it has been manually configured to be a preferred browser.

When a network client needs to consult a browse list to browse the network, it contacts one of the backup browsers for a copy of the current browse list. The backup browsers periodically receive updated browse lists from the master browser to make sure the browse lists remain current.

Normally, the browse lists are maintained and exchanged using local broadcasts. If the domain spans routers, however, extra steps are required to ensure the browse lists are passed across the routers. Refer to your network protocol documentation if this is the case.

A Windows 95 computer can be configured to maintain or to not maintain browse lists by configuring the File and Printer Sharing service with one of the following options:

- Automatically decide if the Windows 95 computer is needed to be a browser by participating in the browser elections
- Disable browse list maintenance so that the Windows 95 computer does not compile browse lists
- Be a preferred browser for the browser elections

Normally, you let the browser elections automatically determine who are the browsers. However, if you do not want the potential performance load on the Windows 95 computer that can result from browsing, you can configure the computer to never be a browser. In addition, you can set a particular computer, on which an extra network load would have little effect, to be a preferred browser.

The browser configuration is performed using the properties for the File and Printer Sharing for Microsoft Networks service or the File and Printer Sharing for NetWare Networks service.

Browsing on Microsoft Networks

To access the browser configuration options for a computer running File and Printer Sharing for Microsoft Networks, perform the following steps:

1. Start the Network Control Panel Applet and select the File and Printer Sharing for Microsoft Networks service.
2. Choose **P**roperties and select the Browse Master property as shown in figure 5.7.

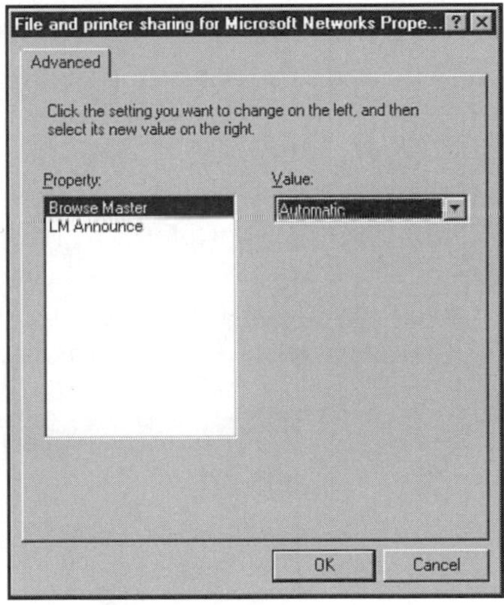

Figure 5.7

Configuring browse list maintenance for Microsoft Networks.

3. Select Automatic as the value to have Windows 95 automatically determine if the computer is needed as a browse server.
4. Select Disabled as the value to prevent the computer from maintaining browse lists for the network.

> Selecting the Disabled option does not prevent the computer from browsing the network resources. It prevents the computer from maintaining a browse list for itself and other computers. As long as at least one computer on the network is a browser, other computers can use the browsing service.

5. To give the computer a higher weighting for the browse elections, select Enable for the value. This computer will then be preferred over other Windows 95 computers that have automatic set for the Browse Master value for the browse elections.

6. Choose OK twice and restart the computer.

Browsing on NetWare Networks

To access the browser configuration options for a computer running File and Printer Sharing for NetWare Networks, perform the following steps:

1. Start the Network Control Panel Applet and select the File and Printer Sharing for NetWare Networks service.

2. Choose **P**roperties and select the Workgroup Advertising property as shown in figure 5.8.

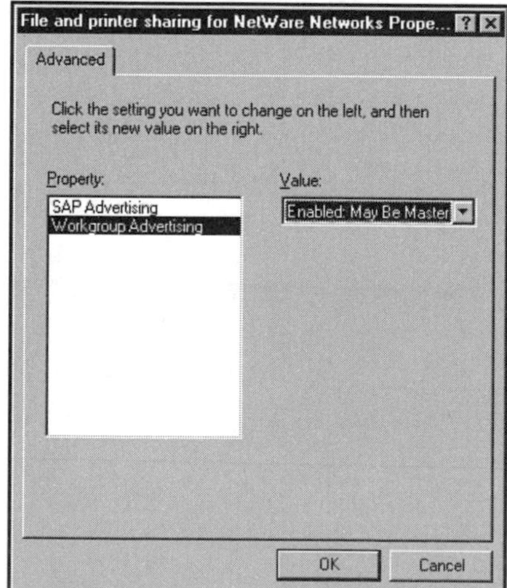

Figure 5.8

Configuring browse list maintenance for NetWare Networks.

3. To have Windows 95 automatically determine if the computer is needed as a browse server, select Enabled: Maybe Master for the value.

4. To prevent the computer from maintaining browse lists for the network, select Enabled: May not be Master for the value.

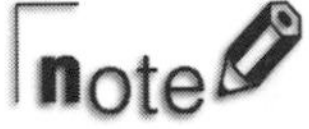

The Enabled: May not be Master option does not prevent the computer from browsing the network resources. It prevents the computer from maintaining a browse list for itself and other computers. Select the Disabled option to prevent the computer from using the browse service.

5. To give the computer a higher weighting for the browse elections, select Enabled: Preferred Master for the value. This computer will then be preferred over other Windows 95 computers that have automatic set for the Browse Master value for the browse elections.

6. To prevent the computer from using the browser service to browse network resources, select Disabled for the value.

7. To allow the computer to send SAP broadcasts announcing its presence to real-mode NetWare clients, select the SAP Advertising property and change the value to Enabled.

8. Choose OK twice and restart the computer.

Remote Access

Windows 95 computers can be configured to use dial-up access to access a network over a modem line. This allows users to connect to a remote network, including the Internet, from any location with a telephone connection. For more information on remote network access, see Chapter 9, "Mobile Services."

Review Questions

The following questions test your knowledge of the information in this chapter. For additional questions, see MCP Endeavor and the Microsoft Roadmap/Assessment Exam on the CD-ROM that accompanies this book.

1. Windows 95 includes software to support which three of the following networks?

   A. Banyan VINES

   B. DEC Pathworks

   C. Novell NetWare

   D. Apple AppleShare

2. Which two protocols are installed by default when the first network adapter driver is installed?

   A. AppleTalk

   B. NetBEUI

   C. TCP/IP

   D. IPX/SPX-compatible

3. Which two of the following are advantages of Microsoft Client for NetWare Networks as opposed to Novell's NETX workstation software?

   A. Microsoft Client for NetWare Networks allows you to use TSR applications loaded from DOS.

   B. Microsoft Client for NetWare Networks runs in protected mode and thus does not use any conventional memory.

   C. Microsoft Client for NetWare Networks allows additional network clients to be used at the same time.

   D. Microsoft Client for NetWare Networks supports the ArcNet protocols.

4. What is the full UNC path for a file named test.bat in a directory named BATCH located in a share named PUBLIC on a server named FREDSPC?

   A. \\PUBLIC\BATCH\test.bat

   B. \\FREDSPC\BATCH\test.bat

   C. \\FREDSPC\PUBLIC\BATCH\test.bat

   D. None of the above

5. In order to use Unified Logon, the ______ for all networks must be the same.

   A. network operating systems

   B. topologies

   C. network protocols

   D. passwords

6. Which two of the following are interfaces functioning at the Windows 95 Application Interface layer?

   A. Win32 WinNet Interface

   B. WinNet 16

   C. HP JetAdmin

   D. Win32 Print Applicator Programming Interface

7. A ______ maps network names used by an application to a physical network device name.

   A. device driver

   B. redirector

   C. requestor

   D. transport interface

8. Which three of the following are layers in the Windows 95 networking architecture?

   A. Transport Programming Interface

   B. Internal File System Manager

   C. Device Driver Interface

   D. Network Providers

9. DNS stands for ______.

   A. Downloadable Network Share

   B. DOS-Node Server

   C. Domain Name Service

   D. Domain Network Server

10. The ______ registers and resolves NetBIOS names to IP addresses.

    A. DNS Server

    B. IFS Manager

    C. Network Adapter Card

    D. WINS Server

Review Answers

1. A B C	6. A D
2. B D	7. B
3. B C	8. A C D
4. C	9. C
5. D	10. D

Chapter 6

Managing Disk Resources and Utilities

One of the key functions of any operating system is its capability to manage the storage and retrieval of information. The software processes and drivers that enable writing to storage devices and reading from them are known collectively as the *file system.* Previous to Windows 95, MS-DOS-based computers used a *FAT-based* file system. FAT stands for *File Allocation Table,* which is the storage area on any hard disk or floppy disk that tracks the used/unused space on that medium. Windows 95 also implements a FAT-based file system, but the Windows 95 FAT-based file system includes numerous enhancements intended to maximize performance and usability.

In addition to providing an enhanced file system, Windows 95 also includes utilities that enable users to perform various maintenance tasks, as well as safeguard their data against corruption or destruction.

This chapter examines the structure and features of the Windows 95 file system and disk utilities. The major topics of discussion include the following:

- Installable file system architecture
- File system caching
- Long filename support
- Troubleshooting the file system
- Disk utilities

Installable File System Architecture

A key feature of Windows 95 that allows it to adapt to developing technologies is its modular design. With Windows 95's modular design, generic features of Windows 95 subsystems, such as networking, printing, and communications, are implemented into a universal component (for example, the Universal Printer Driver), whereas functions specific to a type or brand of hardware/software are implemented in a type-specific driver (for example, the printer mini-driver for a Hewlett-Packard LaserJet). In this way, if a generic printing function is called by the operating system, it is handled by the Universal Printer Driver, and functions specific to an HP LaserJet are handled by the mini-driver.

Microsoft uses a modular architecture for the Windows 95 file systems; all I/O requests are first handled by a universal file system manager. Thus, instead of reengineering the operating system to implement compatibility with other existing or future file system structures, all that is needed to accommodate a new type of file system is to develop a file system driver that can communicate with the universal file system driver and that handles the unique functions of that file system. Figure 6.1 illustrates the file system architecture of Windows 95.

The Windows 95 file systems are known as *installable* file systems because they can be loaded into and removed from the system memory as needed; another indication of the modularity of the Windows 95 file system components.

File operations are handled by the Installable File System (IFS) components of Windows 95. These components include the following:

- IFS Manager
- File System Drivers
- I/O Supervisor

- Volume Tracker
- Type Specific Drivers
- Port Drivers

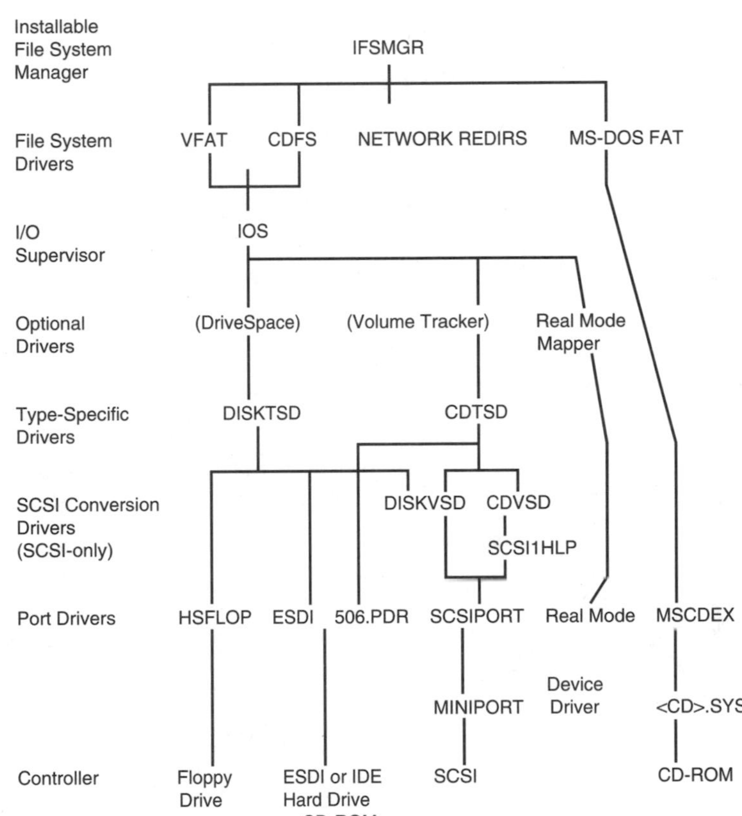

Figure 6.1

File system components.

IFS Manager

The *IFS Manager* is responsible for analyzing incoming I/O requests from applications and other processes and determining which file system driver is able to fulfill requests most effectively. When a new file system driver is installed, it registers itself with the IFS manager, notifying the IFS Manager of what types of I/O requests it is able to process. The important thing to note is that the file system driver does not need to know how to communicate with applications or other processes directly; it only needs to know how to communicate with the IFS Manager.

File System Drivers

The file system drivers allow I/O requests to be sent to and from the installed file systems. Windows 95 includes support for the following file systems (although others can be added using third-party drivers):

- 32-bit Virtual-FAT (VFAT)
- 32-bit CD-ROM file system (CDFS)
- 32-bit network redirectors
- 16-bit FAT

VFAT File System Driver

The *VFAT file system driver* (FSD) is the primary FSD for the system and cannot be disabled. It is responsible for all local hard disk I/O requests (including SCSI). This FSD gives Windows 95 a fully 32-bit virtualized MS-DOS FAT file system. Like all FSDs, VFAT supports long filenames (which are discussed in more detail later in the "Long Filename (LFN) Support" section of this chapter).

VFAT is used only for hard drives that have the 32-bit disk access components installed. If a drive is accessed through real-mode drivers (for example, an Ontrack Disk Manager driver in the CONFIG.SYS), the drive is accessed through MS-DOS Compatibility Mode and will not take advantage of the 32-bit VFAT.

In the case of SCSI drives, once the TSD for hard drives determines that a given I/O request is intended for a SCSI drive, a number of sublayers come into play. The TSD passes the request to one of two SCSI translators: for hard drives or for CD-ROM drives. The translator is responsible for translating generic I/O commands into commands the SCSI bus can understand—these are known as *SCSI Command Descriptor Blocks.*

The SCSI Manager then takes control and acts as the intermediary between the SCSI Translator and the lowest layer—the miniport drivers, which are responsible for communicating with specific brands of SCSI adapters (for example, there might be a specific miniport driver for all Adaptec SCSI controllers or for one particular product line).

CDFS File System Driver

Because data on a CD-ROM is stored and accessed in a different fashion than data on a hard drive, a separate FSD for CD-ROM file access is required. CDFS passes on the CD-ROM I/O request to a specific device driver based on one of four possible CD-ROM configurations:

- IDE CD-ROM
- SCSI CD-ROM
- Proprietary CD-ROM controller
- Real-mode CD-ROM drivers specified in CONFIG.SYS or AUTOEXEC.BAT

IDE CD-ROM

With this configuration, the CD-ROM is typically attached to the IDE hard drive controller of the PC and the I/O request is passed on to the ESDI_506.PDR port driver, which is the same driver used to communicate with IDE hard drives.

SCSI CD-ROM

This type of CD-ROM is connected on the SCSI bus of the PC, along with any SCSI hard drives or other SCSI devices. It is supported through the various SCSI driver layers mentioned earlier.

Proprietary CD-ROM Controller

This type of CD-ROM controller is often integrated on a sound card. Currently, Windows 95 ships with protected-mode drivers for proprietary controllers from Sony, Panasonic, and Mitsumi. Any other type of proprietary CD-ROM controller must be supported through protected-mode drivers from the OEM or through real-mode CD-ROM drivers until protected-mode drivers become available (see the following section "Real-Mode Drivers").

Real-Mode Drivers

All CD-ROM drives that do not fall under the preceding categories are supported using MS-DOS-based drivers specified in CONFIG.SYS or AUTOEXEC.BAT. The CD-ROM drive is said to be operating in MS-DOS compatibility mode.

Any hard drive or CD-ROM drive running in MS-DOS compatibility mode cannot take advantage of protected-mode caching. Smartdrive must be used instead.

Network Redirector File System Drivers

If the IFS Manager determines that an I/O request cannot be satisfied locally and is likely intended for a remote device, it attempts to pass the request to one of the 32-bit network file system drivers (if any Windows 95 networking components have been installed). The network redirectors are examined in more detail in Chapter 5, "Networking and Interoperability."

I/O Supervisor

The *I/O Supervisor* is responsible for overseeing all local I/O requests (as opposed to network-based requests). When the IFS Manager has determined that a given I/O request can be fulfilled on the local computer, it passes the request on to the I/O Supervisor. The I/O Supervisor's other duties include registering port and mini-drivers when a new device is installed and sending dynamic messages to drivers as needed (for example, in the case of a Plug and Play event).

Volume Tracker

The *Volume Tracker* component is responsible for identifying and monitoring removable media such as CD-ROMs, floppies, and removable hard drives. It must ensure that the correct type of media is present and that the media is not removed or inserted at the wrong time. It is this component, for example, that allows CD-ROMs to auto-execute when inserted. This is possible because the Volume Tracker polls the CD-ROM drive constantly for new insertions. When it detects such an event, it scans the CD for a file called AUTORUN.INF. If it finds this file, it executes the commands in the file. The Volume Tracker also identifies disk geometry, noting, for example, when a 1.44 MB floppy is removed, and a 720 KB floppy is inserted.

Type Specific Drivers

Type Specific Drivers (TSD) are drivers intermediate to the I/O Supervisor and the physical device drivers (port drivers) that actually communicate with the hardware. They are responsible for all functions associated with a particular type of hardware, such as CD-ROMs, floppy drives, or hard disks. Thus, a TSD for CD-ROM drives handles functions specific to CD-ROMs, but not those specific to SCSI CD-ROMs.

Port Drivers

Port drivers, the last in the chain of command, are responsible for translating logical I/O requests (for example, "put this data on the CD") into physical requests ("put these bytes on track 9, section 5 of the CD").

File System Caching

One of the main performance issues associated with hard drive or CD-ROM access is repetitive requests for information. A cache enables your PC to store recently used (or frequently used) information in RAM so that when you need it again, you can access it quickly. Because hard disk access speeds are much slower than memory access speeds (milliseconds versus nanoseconds), it is much faster to read the discarded data from the cache than to access it from the hard disk. This process is known as *read-ahead* caching and is implemented for hard drives using VCACHE, and for CD-ROM drives using CDFS caching.

VCACHE Hard Drive Caching

VCACHE is the Windows 95 successor to Windows 3.1's Smartdrive. It is a 32-bit protected-mode cache subsystem used by all FSDs except CDFS. Two types of caching are implemented by VCACHE: *read-ahead* caching (described in the preceding paragraph) for read operations, and *lazy-write* or *write-behind* caching for write operations.

Because the number of requests to write data to a hard disk tends to fluctuate a great deal from moment to moment, another way to increase the efficiency of the file system is to stagger those requests by a matter of seconds in order to create a more constant level of activity and prevent bottlenecks. These staggered writes are termed "lazy" writes because they do not happen immediately when requested.

CDFS Caching

The CDFS maintains its own cache separate from the VCACHE because the nature of CD-ROM data and the way it is accessed is fundamentally different from that of hard drive data.

First, the CDFS cache uses only read-ahead caching, since you cannot write to a conventional CD-ROM drive.

Furthermore, CD-ROMs typically contain large amounts of multimedia information such as video clips or sound recordings. Data of this type does not usually benefit from an MRU (most recently used) approach to keeping data in a cache. For example, if you have just finished playing a video clip, under the standard read-ahead cache system, the cache currently holds data pertaining to the end of the video clip. If you want to replay the video clip, there are no performance benefits to having the last part of it cached because you will likely want faster access to the beginning of the clip.

In addition, due to the sheer volume of data that can be accessed from a CD-ROM, sharing a cache with the rest of the operating system quickly results in the cache being overrun with multimedia data that likely will not be reused.

A unique feature of the CDFS cache is that it is swappable, which means it can be written to disk if the operating system needs to maximize available memory. Because CD-ROM drives are much slower than hard drives, it remains more efficient to read the data from the hard drive than reread it from the CD-ROM drive.

Long Filename (LFN) Support

Windows 95 has built-in support for descriptive filenames up to 256 characters, including blank spaces. In order to remain backward-compatible with Windows 3.1 and DOS applications, however, Windows 95 also automatically generates an 8.3 format short filename (known as the *alias*) for each LFN. The algorithm for the auto-generation of this short filename is as follows:

1. Remove any characters illegal in an MS-DOS filename, such as spaces and so on.
2. For the eight-character name, take the first six remaining characters of the LFN and add a tilde character (~) and an incremental number beginning with 1.

The number is added to ensure unique short filenames. It is possible, for example, that two files named "November Sales Forecast" and "November Marketing Report" would both auto-generate the character name "Novemb~". In order to differentiate them, one would be named "Novemb~1", and the other named "Novemb~2". If more than nine similar files exist, the first five characters are used, plus a tilde (~) and a two-digit number.

3. To create the three-character extension, take the first three remaining characters after the last period. If the long filename contains no period, the extension is omitted.

Long filenames preserve the case of characters, but are not case-sensitive.

Rules for the Construction of Long and Short Filenames

The following rules are applied when creating a long filename and when generating a short filename alias:

- The symbols \ / : *? " < > | are illegal in both long and short filenames.
- The symbols + , ; = [ ] are permitted in a long filename, but not in a short filename alias.
- Lowercase characters in a long filename are converted to uppercase in a short filename alias.

Long Filename Data Structure

In a standard FAT-based operating system, the root directory of a hard disk can contain a maximum of 512 directory entries. Under MS-DOS, each file or subdirectory typically takes up an entry. In the case of long filenames, however, each requires a minimum of two directory entries: one for the alias, and one for every 13 characters of the long filename. Thus, a long filename that consists of 79 characters would require 7 entries (78/13=6, plus 1 for the alias).

This requirement for additional directory entries is especially important to remember when dealing with LFNs in the root directory because the MS-DOS limit of 512 entries in the root directory still applies. Those entries are used up much more quickly with LFNs.

Exercise 6.1 illustrates the creation and use of LFNs in Windows 95.

Exercise 6.1: Creating and Using Long Filenames

1. Choose Start, Programs, and MS-DOS Prompt. A DOS window appears.
2. Type **MD\LFNTEMP** and press Enter. A directory called LFNTEMP is created.
3. Type **CD\LFNTEMP** and press Enter. The current directory changes to LFNTEMP.
4. Type **DIR > "Directory Listing"** and press Enter to save the directory listing to a file. You are returned to a command prompt (note the quotations around the filename).
5. Type **DIR** and press Enter. Note that the alias for the file that was created is listed on the left, whereas the LFN is on the right.
6. Type **DIR > "Directory Listing 2"** and press Enter. You are returned to a command prompt.
7. Type **DIR** and press Enter. Note how the alias has been autonumbered sequentially, and yet the full name is preserved on the right.
8. Type **DIR >*DIRLIST** and press Enter. You receive a `File creation error` error message because the * is illegal.
9. Shut down Windows 95. You are in MS-DOS mode (no LFN support).
10. Type **CD\LFNTEMP** and press Enter. The current directory changes to LFNTEMP.
11. Type **DIR** and press Enter. Note that LFNs no longer are displayed in the directory.
12. Type **COPY DIRECT~1 C:** and press Enter. The file that was created earlier is copied to the root of C.

13. Restart Windows 95 by typing **EXIT** and pressing Enter.

14. When Windows 95 is open, open a DOS window and type **CD** and press Enter, then type **DIR** and press Enter. Note that the file that was copied to the root no longer has an LFN associated with it (only the alias remains).

Issues with Long Filenames

When working in an environment where both long and short filenames may be in use, you should be aware of a number of issues. These issues include the following:

- LFNs are active only when Windows 95 is running. Because they are integrated with the 32-bit file system native to Windows 95, LFNs are not visible, for example, when Command Prompt Only is selected from the Boot Menu when the system is booted (however, LFNs are visible from a DOS prompt inside Windows 95).

- When specifying LFNs with imbedded spaces, it is necessary to enclose the name in double quotes.

- Even if you do not add an extension to a file when you create it, the application you are using may automatically add an extension to the file (for example, Wordpad would, by default, add the extension DOC to any saved file).

- Using file utilities that are not long-filename-aware (such as those in MS-DOS 6.*x* and earlier) to copy or rename a long filename destroys the long filename, leaving only the alias.

- If you are using a Windows 3.1 application and choose Save As (effectively renaming the file), the long filename is lost, but if you choose Save, the long filename is preserved because the existing name is reused.

- Using a disk-repair utility that is not long-filename-aware, such as MS-DOS 6.*x* Scandisk or Norton Disk Doctor, on a volume that contains LFNs might destroy the LFNs. The utility interprets the new long filename data structure as errors in the file system that must be corrected.

- Windows 95 can read LFNs from an NTFS volume, but only at a remote location (across a network). For security reasons pertaining to Windows NT, Windows 95 does not read local NTFS volumes at all.
- If you perform a search on a group of files, Windows 95 searches both the long filename and the alias for occurrences of the given search criteria.
- It is possible to disable long-filename support by altering the Registry as illustrated in figure 6.2.

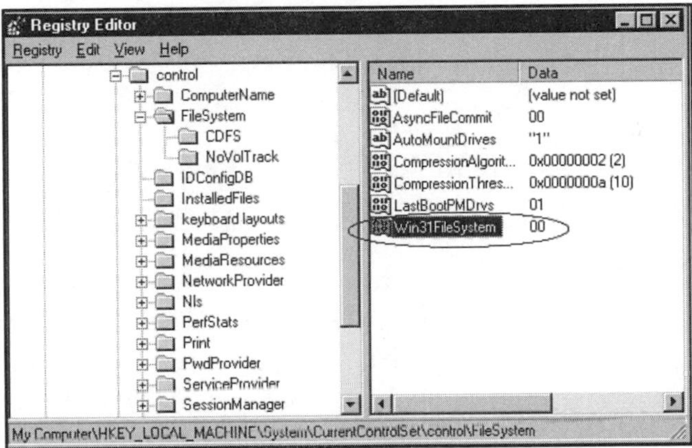

Figure 6.2

Disabling long filename support using the Registry.

Troubleshooting the File System

If you encounter difficulty with any applications and you suspect the file system might be involved, you can disable a number of file system features using the Performance tab of the My Computer Properties sheet in order to isolate the problem. The features that can be disabled include the following:

- File sharing
- Long filename preservation for old programs
- Protected-mode hard disk interrupt handling
- 32-bit protected-mode disk drivers
- Write-behind caching

Disabling File Sharing

File sharing can be disabled for applications that are incompatible with the way Windows 95 typically implements file sharing (SHARE.EXE can be used until the application is updated to support Windows 95 file sharing).

Disabling Long-Filename Preservation for Old Programs

If an application requires the directory space used by LFNs in Windows 95, you might have to disable this support for older applications.

Disabling Protected-Mode Hard Disk Interrupt Handling

The Disable protected-mode hard disk interrupt handling option disables Windows 95's normal practice of intercepting all MS-DOS-level disk I/O requests and handling them with a 32-bit protected-mode driver. Disk performance is degraded, but compatibility with older applications is enhanced.

Disabling All 32-Bit Protected-Mode Disk Drivers

If a hard drive is experiencing problems reading or writing information while Windows 95 is running, you can disable all 32-bit disk drivers in order to enhance compatibility with older applications. Once again, disk performance is degraded.

Disabling Write-Behind Caching

The Disable write-behind caching for all drives option is useful when data integrity is crucial and you cannot risk losing data due to it being in the write-behind cache when a power failure occurs. When write-behind is disabled, all write operations are performed immediately. Yet again, performance likely will be degraded.

Exercise 6.2 illustrates how to access the troubleshooting switches for the file system.

Exercise 6.2: Using File System Troubleshooting Switches

1. Right-click on the My Computer icon and choose Properties. The System Properties window appears.
2. Choose the Performance tab. Various statistics regarding the performance status of the operating system are displayed.
3. Click on the File System button at the bottom of the window. The File System Properties window appears.
4. Click on the Troubleshooting tab. The list of troubleshooting switches appears.
5. Place a check in the Disable all 32 bit protect-mode disk drivers box and choose OK to close the File System Properties window and the System Properties window. You are prompted to restart your system.
6. Choose Yes to restart.
7. When Windows 95 has rebooted, go back to System Properties, choose Performance and note that all drives are listed as being in MS-DOS compatibility mode. Notice that the system performance has been degraded.
8. Choose File System Properties again from the System Properties Performance tab and select the Troubleshooting tab.
9. Remove the check from the Disable all 32 bit protect-mode disk drivers check box, and choose OK twice to close the File System Properties window and the System Properties window. You are prompted to restart your system.
10. Choose Yes to restart. The system restarts, and the 32-bit drivers are loaded once again.

Disk Utilities

There are five key disk-management utilities included with Windows 95. Each is intended to address particular file system issues or problems. A summary of the disk-management utilities and the issues they address is provided in table 6.1.

Table 6.1

Windows 95 Utilities for Various File System Issues

Utility	Issue
Disk Defragmenter	Preventing file system performance degradation due to inefficient hard disk access
Scandisk	Correction of cross-linked files, lost clusters, and other hard disk errors
Backup	Prevention of data loss due to power failures, corruption, hard disk failures
Disk Compression	Maximizing available hard disk space
Recycle Bin	Recovery of deleted files

Disk Defragmenter

One of the most common performance issues related to the FAT file system, which is native to both MS-DOS and Windows 95, is disk fragmentation. When a hard drive is new and contains no information, it is possible for the file system to write all the data for a new file to a contiguous area of the hard drive. As the hard drive fills up and files are deleted and recopied numerous times, the space available to new files no longer is contiguous. The file system is forced to put part of the new file in one location, part at another location, and so on. When a request is made to read the file, the hard disk must access all these different locations to reconstitute the file. This takes longer than reading the whole file from one location on the hard disk.

Windows 95 includes a utility called *Disk Defragmenter* that is designed to address this issue. It does so by rewriting all the files on the hard drive to contiguous locations, thus enhancing file system performance for that drive. This procedure can be time-consuming because, as the drive becomes full, there is less room to temporarily store the various parts of a file before it is rewritten to a new location.

Although the Disk Defragmenter existed in MS-DOS 6.2 and is still a 16-bit application, the Windows 95 Disk Defragmenter utility has the following enhancements:

- It is much faster at optimizing DoubleSpaced and DriveSpaced drives from MS-DOS 6.x.
- The utility no longer requires any INI files as all settings are stored in the Registry.
- The utility now has a Windows 95 GUI interface.
- The Windows 95 Disk Defragmenter is capable of running as a background application, freeing the user to perform other tasks.

It is important to remember that, although the Defragmenter can run in the background, if another application is writing to disk (and consequently changing the locations of files), the Defragmenter may be forced to restart the defragmentation process from the beginning. If the process reaches 50 percent, and disk writes occur, the process will restart at 50 percent rather than zero.

Exercise 6.3 demonstrates how to initiate the defragmentation process.

Exercise 6.3: Using the Disk Defragmenter

1. Right-click on the My Computer icon and choose Explore. The Exploring window appears.

2. From the list of drives, right click on C: and choose Properties. The Properties sheet for drive C appears.

3. Select the Tools tab. From this tab, you can run Scandisk, Backup, or the Disk Defragmenter.

4. Click on the **D**efragment Now button. A Disk Defragmenter window appears, telling you what percentage of drive C is fragmented.

5. Choose the **A**dvanced button, make certain that the **F**ull defragmentation and Check drive for errors check boxes are selected, and choose OK. You are returned to the previous screen.

The Full Defragmentation option places all files in contiguous order and at the start of the hard drive's allocable space, whereas Defragment Files Only places the files in contiguous order, but does not move them to the start of the hard drive. Consolidate Free Space simply moves files to the start of the hard disk.

6. Choose the **S**tart button and then the Show **D**etails button. You are presented with a screen showing all the clusters on drive C as they are reorganized.

7. Choose the **L**egend button. You are shown a list of the different color codes for clusters and what each color code signifies.

8. At this point, you can allow the defragmentation to complete (which might take some time), or you can choose **S**top and then Exit to halt the procedure. If you choose to stop, you are returned to the hard drive Properties sheet. If you choose to follow through, you are notified when the procedure is complete.

Certain types of files are not handled by Disk Defragmenter in the normal fashion:

- Files with Hidden and System attributes are not moved.
- Files with Hidden or System attributes are moved.
- Mounted DriveSpace or DoubleSpace volumes are not moved.

The following points should also be noted when using the Disk Defragmenter:

- If Disk Defragmenter reports errors (usually at the beginning of the process), Scandisk should be run (including a surface scan).
- This utility should not be run on Stacker drives, as the compression scheme on such drives is different than that of DriveSpace and DoubleSpace.

Scandisk

Another file system issue that pertains to both performance and data integrity is the issue of cross-linked files and lost clusters. If either of these problems is suspected or the user wants to ensure they do not impact the integrity or performance of the PC's drives, Scandisk should be used regularly.

Under a FAT file system like that of MS-DOS and Windows 95, data is stored on a hard drive in such a way that the clusters (an allocation) containing data pertaining to a certain file are not necessarily stored contiguously on the drive. More often, the clusters for a specific file are scattered throughout the drive. Each cluster for the file contains both data and a pointer to the location of the next cluster in the chain. When a file is requested, the file system looks up the name of the file in the directory tree (which tells where the first cluster for the file is located) and then begins to read through the various clusters, collecting the file's data.

Problems can occur when the pointer to the next cluster becomes corrupted. If, for example, file A has a cluster with some data and a pointer to cluster 12, and file B has a cluster that also points to cluster 12, these files are said to be cross-linked. The data at cluster 12 cannot belong to both files; therefore, there is a logical inconsistency in the file structure of the drive. Scandisk is able to detect such inconsistencies, but it is unable to determine to which file the cluster truly belongs. Scandisk defaults to making a copy of the cluster so that each file can make use of the information in the cluster. This increases the chance that at least one of the two files in question can be salvaged.

Another associated problem is that the clusters that should have been in the chain after the corrupted cluster are now not referenced by any file, and are thus "orphaned" or lost. These clusters may still contain valid data, but they no longer are part of any file on the drive. Scandisk is able to find these clusters and either save them as files to be examined later, or mark the clusters as available to the file system, thus freeing up space on the drive.

Operation Modes

Scandisk can perform two levels of testing on hard drives: standard and thorough. Standard mode is best used on a daily basis, whereas thorough mode is best used when you suspect a problem with the hard drive.

In *standard* mode, Scandisk performs logical tests against the File Allocation Table (FAT) of the file system, checking for the logical inconsistencies outlined earlier. In addition, the standard scan checks for various other potential problems, such as invalid filenames and invalid date and time stamps.

In *thorough* mode, Scandisk performs all the tests included in Standard mode, but also performs a surface scan. Each cluster on the drive is checked for physical defects that would make the cluster in question unsafe for data storage. A surface scan is performed by reading the information from the cluster and then rewriting it back to the same cluster. If the information matches what Scandisk read the first time, the cluster is likely to be safe. If the data is different, a media problem might exist, in which case Scandisk marks the cluster as bad.

Scandisk does not test clusters that have been marked as bad in the FAT by other programs.

Exercise 6.4 demonstrates how you can use Scandisk to correct various drive problems.

Exercise 6.4: Using Scandisk to Correct Drive Problems

1. Right-click on the My Computer icon and choose **E**xplore. The Exploring window appears.
2. From the list of drives, right-click on C: and choose P**r**operties. The Properties sheet for drive C appears.
3. Click on the Tools tab. From this tab, you can run Scandisk, Backup, or the Disk Defragmenter.
4. Click on **C**heck Now to start Scandisk. The Scandisk window appears.
5. Choose the **A**dvanced button, verify that Make **c**opies is selected under Cross-linked files and that Con**v**ert to files is selected under Lost file fragments, and then choose OK. You are returned to the main Scandisk window.
6. Verify that Stan**d**ard testing is selected and choose the **S**tart button. The status bar shows the progress of the tests.
7. When the tests are complete, choose Close to clear the Scandisk Results window. You are returned to the main Scandisk window.
8. Optionally, you may run the Thorough test, although it is very time-consuming.

Other Features of Scandisk

Scandisk contains a number of additional features, such as the following:

- Scandisk can be run from the command line (SCANDSKW.EXE), with parameters to specify how it will run, or from the Windows 95 graphical interface.

An MS-DOS version of Scandisk also is included with Windows 95 (SCANDISK.EXE).

- Scandisk can fix problems on hard drives, floppy disk drives, RAM drives, and removable media such as PCMCIA hard cards and Bernoulli drives.
- Scandisk can detect and repair errors in LFNs (the MS-DOS version can only detect them).
- Scandisk can be used to test and maintain the integrity of DoubleSpace and DriveSpace volumes (if the volumes are mounted; if not, the volumes can be tested from the command-line version of Scandisk).
- It is possible to have Scandisk log activities (the results of the scan are stored in the file SCANDISK.LOG in the root of the drive that has been examined).

Further Notes on Scandisk

Additional information that the user should note when using the Scandisk utility includes the following:

- Scandisk cannot fix errors on CD-ROMs, network drives, drives created by Interlnk, or drives referenced via MS-DOS commands such as ASSIGN, JOIN, or SUBST.
- As with the Disk Defragmenter, it is possible to multitask with Scandisk, but if any disk write activity occurs, Scandisk may be forced to restart the testing process.

Backup

In order to ensure that data on the system is not lost due to power failures or other forms of corruption, Windows 95 includes a Backup utility that enables users to make a copy of the data on their hard drives and store it on alternate media.

Backup Destinations

When making a backup copy of important data, a number of media types can be used to store the copy. The Windows 95 Backup program supports backup to three storage media types:

- Backup to a tape drive
- Backup to floppies
- Backup to a network location

Backup to Tape

The capability to backup to a tape drive is new to the Windows 95 version of Backup (previous MS-DOS versions supported only floppy backups). The type of tape media that is supported is called *Quarter-Inch Cartridge* (QIC) and it comes in various specifications. The supported tape drive specifications are as follows:

- QIC 40, QIC 80, and QIC 3010 tape drives connected through the primary floppy disk controller (various manufacturers)
- QIC 40, QIC 80, and QIC 3010 tape drives connected to a parallel port (Colorado Memory Systems only)

SCSI tape backup units are not supported by Windows 95 Backup.

Windows 95 should be able to detect any supported tape drives automatically. If it cannot detect the tape drive, a message to that effect appears upon starting Backup, and a number of troubleshooting suggestions are listed.

Backup to Floppies

Floppies are the standard backup destination for both the MS-DOS and Windows 3.1 versions of Backup. Files are transferred from the local hard drive to a number of floppies.

Backup to a Network Location

This backup destination enables the user to back up files to a remote location on the network. Backing up to a remote network location can be useful if, for example, a network administrator wants all users to back up their files to one central location on the network to simplify the administrator's management tasks.

Backup Types

Files can be backed up in two ways: by a full backup and by an incremental backup. In a *full backup* scenario, all selected files are backed up. An *incremental backup* copies only those files that have changed since the last full backup. Such files are determined by the time/date stamp on the file. Typically, incremental backups are used to maintain archives without unnecessarily backing up files that have not changed since the last full backup, thus conserving disk space at the backup destination.

Backup Sets and File Sets

A *backup set* is a collection of files that have been backed up. A backup set is created during each backup procedure and contains not only the actual files, but also the parameters that were set for the backup (for example, which file types to include in the backup). A *file set* is a list of files you want to backup. You can save file sets so that you do not have to reselect the files for backup every time you perform the backup.

Using Backup

Exercise 6.5 demonstrates the use of the Windows 95 Backup utility. Please ensure that you have at least 6 MB of free space on drive C in order to complete this exercise.

Exercise 6.5: Using the Windows 95 Backup Utility

1. Right-click on the My Computer icon and choose Explore. The Exploring window appears.

2. From the list of drives, right-click on C: and choose Properties. The Properties sheet for drive C appears.

3. Click the Tools tab. From this tab, you can run Scandisk, Backup, or the Disk Defragmenter.
4. Click on the Backup Now button. The Microsoft Backup screen appears.
5. Click on the plus sign (+) next to the C drive. The tree expands to show the subdirectories of C.
6. Click on the + next to the Windows subdirectory. The tree expands to show the subdirectories of Windows.
7. Click on the + next to the Media subdirectory. The tree expands to show the files in the Media subdirectory.
8. Click on the box next to Media. Note that all the files in the Media subdirectory now are checkmarked for backup.
9. Having selected the files for backup, choose the Next Step button. You are prompted for a backup destination.
10. Click on the A drive icon. This selects the root of A as the destination directory.
11. Click on the Start Backup button. You are prompted for a backup set name.
12. Type **TEST** and press Enter. A status screen appears, showing the progress of the backup.
13. Choose OK when the backup is complete. You are returned to the main Backup window.
14. Click on the Restore tab. You are prompted to select a backup set to restore.
15. Click on the icon for the A drive. The TEST backup set is displayed in the root of A.
16. Double-click on the TEST backup set. You are prompted to select the files you want to restore.
17. Click three times in the check box next to TEST to select all files in the backup set.

18. From the **S**ettings menu, choose **O**ptions. The Settings - Options dialog box appears.

19. Click on the Restore tab, verify that Overwrite **f**iles is selected under Advanced options, and choose OK. You are returned to the main Backup window.

20. Click on the Start Restore button. A status screen shows the progress of the restore procedure.

21. When the restore is complete, choose OK twice to return to the main Backup window.

Other Features of Windows 95 Backup

Windows 95 contains a number of additional features, including the following:

- It is possible to perform a compare between a backup set and the directories from which it was backed up in order to determine any differences between the two.
- LFNs are fully supported.
- It is possible to drag and drop backup sets onto a Backup icon to restore the set.
- During a full system backup, Windows 95 also backs up the Registry by copying it to a temporary file. When the backup set is restored, the Registry files are merged back into the existing Registry.
- Backup allows the filtering of file types for inclusion or exclusion from a file set.

MS-DOS 6.2 and Windows 3.1 backup sets cannot be restored using the Windows 95 Backup utility due to incompatibility issues with LFNs in MS-DOS 6.2 and earlier.

Disk Compression

Windows 95; implements a form of disk compression known as *on-the-fly* compression. On-the-fly compression is so named because the compression/decompression process occurs automatically in the background and is transparent to the user. On-the-fly disk compression is the process of intercepting normal MS-DOS read/write calls and compressing the data before writing it to the hard disk, thus allowing the data to consume less space. Similarly, when the data is read back, it is automatically uncompressed before being transferred to the application or process that requested it.

Disk compression, as implemented in Windows 95 (and in the versions released with MS-DOS 6.x), consists of two processes. The first, called *token conversion*, replaces with a token, which takes up less space, repetitive patterns that occur in a given piece of data.

The second, called *sector allocation granularity*, involves changing the way data is stored on a hard drive, circumventing the often large amounts of wasted space created under a normal FAT file system. Any FAT file system operates based on a cluster being the smallest traceable unit of measure. Therefore, if the cluster size is 4 KB, for example, and a 2 KB file is stored in that cluster, 2 KB can be wasted. If 1000 such files exist on a hard drive, 1000×2 KB would be wasted. With disk compression in place, the smallest allocation unit shrinks to one sector, or 512 bytes, which can greatly reduce the amount of wasted space on a drive.

DoubleSpace and DriveSpace Structure

Disk compression (called DoubleSpace) was first introduced in version 6.0 of MS-DOS. It was later re-released as DriveSpace in version 6.2, with some changes to the compression routines and with a new feature: the ability to uncompress a drive. The structure of the compression structure has remained fairly consistent.

As illustrated in figure 6.3, once disk compression is installed and the files initially compressed, the files are stored in the *Compressed Volume File* (CVF), which is actually a large hidden file that sits on the physical drive C. When the system boots up, however, the CVF is assigned the drive letter C. The physical C drive, which now contains only a few files since everything else is in a compressed state inside the CVF, is assigned a higher drive letter, typically H. The process of switching the drive letters and making the CVF available for viewing in MS-DOS and Windows is called *mounting*. From this point on, any file operation is handled through the disk compression routines, which are responsible for compressing and uncompressing files as disk I/O requests are made by the operating system.

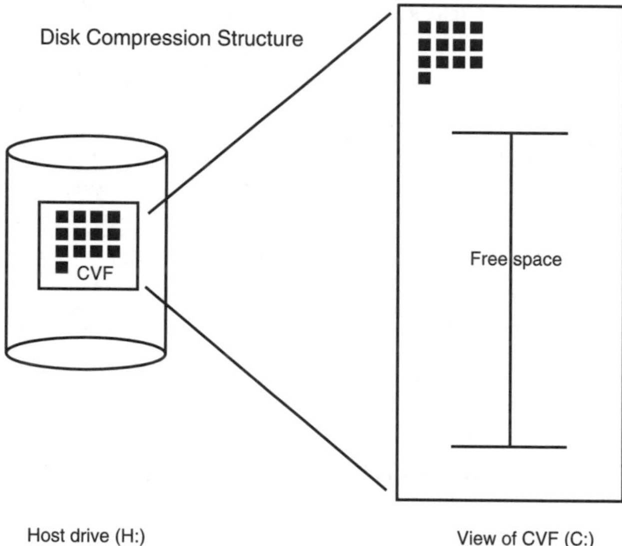

Figure 6.3

Compression structure under MS-DOS and Windows 95.

Advantages of Windows 95 Disk Compression

Windows 95 disk compression contains many features that have been specifically optimized. The main advantages to using Windows 95 disk compression are as follows:

- Disk compression is implemented with 32-bit code for better performance.
- It does not use any conventional memory.
- It is integrated with the operating system for ease of use and better performance.

Using Disk Compression

Exercise 6.6 illustrates how disk compression can be used in Windows 95. Please note that due to the considerable amount of time involved in compressing an entire hard drive, the exercise focuses on compressing a floppy disk. The exercise requires a formatted floppy with at least 512 KB of free space.

Exercise 6.6: Using Windows 95 Disk Compression

1. Choose Start, Programs, Accessories, System Tools, and then click on DriveSpace. The DriveSpace menu appears.
2. Select the A drive and choose Compress from the Drive menu. A window appears, showing the free/used space before and after compression (estimated).
3. Choose the Start button. The drive is checked for errors, and a status bar shows the progress of the compression procedure.
4. When the procedure is complete, choose Close. You are returned to the main DriveSpace window. (Note that drive A now shows as compressed, and there is now a host drive H for drive A.)

When a floppy is compressed, the DriveSpace drivers load only when the floppy is in the drive. In general, the DriveSpace drivers load only when compressed media (hard drive or floppy) is detected.

Further Notes on Windows 95 Disk Compression

The following information should be noted whenever a user is considering Windows 95 disk compression:

- Windows 95 is compatible with third-party compression software such as Stacker versions 2.x, 3.x, and 4.x, and with all versions of SuperStor, but these use real-mode compression and thus take up conventional memory and are usually slower.
- The maximum size of a compressed volume is 512 MB.

Recycle Bin

To minimize the consequences associated with the accidental deletion of files, Windows 95 includes a utility known as the *Recycle Bin.* The Recycle Bin reduces the chance of losing deleted data by storing the data for a time before it is actually deleted. When a file is deleted using the Explorer, for example, rather than being erased from the hard drive, it is copied to a hidden directory on the drive called \RECYCLED. The file is kept in \RECYCLED until the maximum amount of space allocated to the \RECYCLED directory is reached (expressed as a percentage of total space on the drive—the default is 10 percent). At this point, the file is actually deleted to make room for more recently deleted files. Thus, on a 100 MB drive, 10 MB is allocated by default for recycled items.

At any point before the file is actually deleted, the user can open the Recycle Bin on the desktop (which is a specialized view of the \RECYCLED directory) and restore the file to its original location.

Exercise 6.7 illustrates how to restore files from the Recycle Bin.

Exercise 6.7: Restoring Files from the Recycle Bin

1. Right-click on the My Computer icon and select **E**xplore. The Exploring window appears.

2. Click on the plus sign (+) next to the C drive. Subdirectories of the C drive are displayed.

3. Click on the + next to the Windows subdirectory. The tree expands to show the subdirectories of Windows.

4. Click on the Command folder. The files in the Command folder are displayed on the right side of the Explorer window.

5. Click on the Attrib file on the right side of the Explorer window and press Del. You are prompted to verify whether you want to move this item to the Recycle Bin.

6. Choose **Y**es. The item is removed from the directory.

7. From the Desktop, right-click on the Recycle Bin icon and choose Open. The Recycle Bin window appears, showing the ATTRIB file.

8. Right-click on the ATTRIB file and select Restore from the File menu. The file is restored to its original location.

Review Questions

The following questions will test your knowledge of the information in this chapter. For additional questions, see MCP Endeavor and the Microsoft Roadmap/Assessment Exam on the CD-ROM that accompanies this book.

1. A key feature of Windows 95 that will allow it to adapt easily to future technological developments is its ______.

   A. preemptive multitasking

   B. VCACHE cache subsystem

   C. modular design

   D. peer-to-peer networking support

2. Which three of the following are components of the Installable File system (IFS)?

   A. I/O Supervisor

   B. VFAT file system driver

   C. TSD Supervisor

   D. CDFS file system driver

3. The ______ is responsible for the insertion and removal of media.

   A. Drive Controller

   B. IFS Manager

C. System Driver Supervisor

D. Volume Tracker

4. A drive that is accessed through ______ cannot take advantage of the 32-bit VFAT.

   A. protected-mode drivers

   B. real-mode drivers

   C. virtual device drivers

   D. network redirector file system drivers

5. VCACHE is used by all Windows 95 file system drivers except ______ file system drivers.

   A. CDFS

   B. VFAT

   C. network redirector

   D. SCSI

6. The auto-generated alias for the long filename *The Departmental Budget.wks* is ______.

   A. THEDEPAR.~1

   B. THEDEP~1.WKS

   C. THEDEP~1

   D. BUDGET~1.WKS

7. What Windows 95 disk utility would you use to locate and free lost clusters?

   A. DoubleSpace

   B. DriveSpace

   C. Disk Defragmenter

   D. Scandisk

8. What Windows 95 disk utility would you use to compress the data on your hard drive?

   A. DoubleSpace

   B. DriveSpace

   C. Disk Defragmenter

   D. Scandisk

9. If clusters from two files have pointers to the same cluster, the two files are said to be ______.

   A. cluster-crossed

   B. cross-referenced

   C. linked

   D. cross-linked

10. Disk Defragmenter will not move files that have both of which two of the following attributes?

    A. System

    B. Read-only

    C. Hidden

    D. Archived

11. Scandisk cannot fix problems on ______.

    A. compressed hard drives

    B. defragmented hard drives

    C. high-density floppy disks

    D. CD-ROMs.

12. Which of the following tape backup systems is not supported by Windows 95?

    A. QIC 3010 through parallel port

    B. QIC 3010 through floppy disk controller

C. QIC 3010 through SCSI port

D. QIC 80 through floppy disk controller

13. Which two of the following are ways in which disk compression maximizes disk space?

A. Cluster conversion

B. Token conversion

C. ASCII collapse

D. Sector allocation conversion

Review Answers

1. C
2. A B D
3. D
4. B
5. A
6. B
7. D
8. B
9. D
10. A C
11. D
12. C
13. B D

Chapter 7

Managing Printers

Windows 95 includes many improvements to the printing process for both local and network printers. This chapter looks at the following aspects of printing under Windows 95:

- The new features of the Windows 95 printing subsystem
- How Windows 95 handles print jobs using different printer driver models
- How to install a local printer and create a printer queue
- Configurable settings for a print queue
- The Windows 95 network printing architecture
- Creating a shared network print queue on various types of operating systems
- How Windows 95 can ease the configuration process for connecting to shared network print queues
- The Registry keys associated with network printing support
- How to manage documents in a print queue
- How to configure third-party network printing providers

Windows 95 Printing Features

Windows 95 includes many new printing features, including support for the following:

- Plug and Play (PnP) Printers
- Extended Capabilities Ports (ECPs)
- Image Color Matching (ICM)
- A unidriver/mini-driver Printer Driver model
- Point and Print Setup
- Drag and Drop Printing
- Enhanced Metafile (EMF) Spooling
- Improved Conflict Resolution
- Deferred Printing

Plug and Play (PnP) Printers

Windows 95 can take full advantage of the automatic configuration features of Plug and Play (PnP) Printers. Devices complying with the PnP standards are automatically detected and configured by Windows 95 each time that the operating system is initialized. Thus, when a PnP-compliant printer is plugged into a port on the computer, and Windows 95 is started, the operating system can detect the model of printer and set up the printer in the Printers folder.

The PnP setup uses bidirectional communication through the printer cable to obtain information on the printer, including the following:

- Manufacturer and model
- Memory installed
- Font cartridges installed

The printer model is reported as a device ID defined in the IEEE1284 Plug and Play standards. If Windows 95 has a printer driver for that specific device ID, then it installs the driver and creates a print queue for that printer in the Printers Folder.

If Windows 95 does not have the exact driver for that device ID, a dialog box appears, giving the following options:

- The user can insert a floppy disk with a Windows 95 driver for the printer.
- The user can select a driver for a printer that Windows 95 has determined to be compatible.
- The user can choose not to install the printer.

The bidirectional printer communication capability of Windows 95 also enables printers to send unsolicited messages to the operating system, such as being out of paper, low on toner, or other messages that the printer can report.

To enable the bidirectional printing features of Windows 95 including PnP configuration, you must have the following:

- A printer that supports bidirectional communication
- A printer with a PnP BIOS (if PnP is to be used)
- An IEEE 1284-compliant printer cable (this has "1284" stamped on the cable)
- A port configured for two-way communication in the Windows 95 Device Manager. For example, if the port is in AT-compatible mode, it should be changed to PS/2-compatible mode.

For more information on the PnP features of Windows 95, see Chapter 11, "Plug and Play."

Extended Capabilities Port (ECP)

An Extended Capabilities Port (ECP) allows Windows 95 to use data compression to speed the data transfer to an attached printer. The improvements in printing speed are even faster if the printer is also ECP-compliant.

By default, the ECP features are not enabled, even though the ECP Port may have been detected by Windows 95. To enable ECP support, you must follow these steps:

You must have an ECP printer port installed to perform the following steps.

1. Determine the IRQ and DMA settings required for the ports according to the documentation for the computer or ECP card.

2. Double-click on the System icon in Control Panel and select the Device Manager tab.

3. Click on the plus sign next to Ports to display the installed ports. Select the ECP port and choose Properties.

4. Select the Resources tab to display the I/O address range that has been automatically detected for the ECP.

5. Select Basic Configuration 2 in the Settings based on field.

6. In the Resource settings list box, select Interrupt Request and choose Change setting.

7. Type the IRQ value you noted in Step 1 in the Edit Interrupt Request dialog box and choose OK. The Conflict information field should report "No devices are conflicting." If not, you must change the IRQ setting for the conflicting device.

8. In the Resource settings list box, select Direct Memory Access and choose Change setting.

9. Type the IRQ value you noted in Step 1 in the Edit Direct Memory Access dialog box and choose OK. The Conflict information field should report "No devices are conflicting." If not, you must change the DMA setting for the conflicting device.

10. Shut down and restart the computer so the changes can take effect. After restarting, you can take advantage of fast I/O capabilities offered by the ECP.

Image Color Matching (ICM)

A problem that has always been associated with color printing is that you can never be too sure what a color will look like when it is printed, and how closely it will match what you see on-screen. A traditional solution was to use hard copy color samples, printed on the color printer so that you could see exactly what shade the red would be, or how blue the blue really was. Unfortunately, this required a hard copy for each printer to be used, which could be cumbersome, especially if you were working with 64 million colors.

To solve this problem, a group of industry hardware vendors (chiefly Kodak, Microsoft, Apple Computer, Sun Microsystems, and Silicon Graphics) created a color matching specification (known as InterColor 3.0). Windows 95 implements Kodak's Image Color Matching (ICM) technology, which conforms to the InterColor 3.0 specification to ensure that the colors displayed on a monitor closely match colors printed from any ICM supporting printer.

Each color monitor, printer, and scanner supporting ICM has a color-matching profile stored in the <*systemroot*>\SYSTEM\COLOR directory (where <*systemroot*> is WINDOWS, for example). The profile takes into account how closely the device matches various colors to the international (CIE) color reference standards. The Windows 95 operating system then takes these color-matching capabilities into account and makes any modifications necessary when displaying that color on the monitor, so what you see is as close as possible to the color that is printed out.

For example, if printer A generally prints a darker red than printer B, the ICM profile for printer A tells Windows 95 to display a darker red on the screen when the driver for printer A is selected. In addition, if that document is open at another computer whose monitor displays the colors slightly differently, then the ICM profile for the monitor causes Windows 95 to adjust the on-screen colors so that they look the same as in the original document.

In summary, the benefits of ICM are as follows:

- The color on-screen closely matches the color of the printout if ICM devices and applications are used.
- The colors used are consistent on any ICM-compliant devices, ensuring colors that match the international standards regardless of which ICM device they are printed to or displayed on.

Printer Drivers

The Windows 95 printer driver architecture is similar to that used with Windows NT. Printing is controlled through a Microsoft-written universal driver along with a small machine-specific minidriver supplied by the printer manufacturer. Thus, a printer manufacturer needs to write only a small amount of code to customize the driver to the particular requirements and features of that printer.

The HP Color Inkjet requires a monolithic driver.

Unidrivers

Windows 95 uses two universal drivers: one for PostScript printers and one for non-PostScript printers.

Non-PostScript

The non-PostScript universal driver (unidriver) has built-in support for almost all the existing printer control languages, such as the following:

- HP PCL
- Epson ESC P/2
- Canon CaPSL
- Lexmark PPDS
- Monochrome HP-GL/2
- Most dot-matrix technologies

The non-PostScript driver also supports device-resident Intellifont and TrueType scalable fonts, as well as downloading TrueType fonts for rasterizing by the processor of a PCL printer.

PostScript Universal Driver

Unlike the Windows 3.*x* PostScript driver, the Windows 95 PostScript universal driver supports PostScript Level 2 commands for advanced PostScript printing support. In addition, Adobe PostScript Printer Description files (PPDs) are supported for version 4.2 and older PPDs. Another new feature of the Windows 95 PostScript universal driver is the off-loading of ICM processing to the printer's PostScript processor. This reduces the processor load on the computer, which improves system performance.

Minidrivers

Windows 95 includes a large number of minidrivers for the most common printers. In addition, because of the Windows 95 driver architecture, a manufacturer can create a minidriver for its printer much more quickly and easily. Furthermore, since most of the driver code is in the universal driver, the possibility of the minidrivers needing to be updated to fix programming bugs is decreased.

Point and Print Setup

A network printer serving as a Windows 95, Windows NT, or NetWare print server can be configured as a Point and Print printer. When a Windows 95 client on the network first attempts to print to the network printer, or "points" to the printer by opening the print queue in Network Neighborhood, the printer driver files can be automatically copied to and installed on the Windows 95 client. In addition, if the print queue is on a Windows 95 server, settings such as printer memory, paper size, and so on can be automatically configured on the client.

With a print queue configured for Point and Print setup, a Windows 95 user can have the printer drivers automatically installed on the Windows 95 client, without having to worry about what the printer model is, what driver to use, and so on.

For information on how to configure and use a printer for Point and Print setup, refer to the section "Point and Print Installation" later in this chapter.

Drag and Drop Printing

Do you have a document that you want to quickly send to a printer without having to manually open the document in an application? Simply click on the document, keep the mouse button held down, and drag the document until it is over the printer icon. When you release the mouse button, the application associated with the document opens, the document is sent to the print queue, and the application then automatically closes.

Most applications support this feature. If an application does not support this feature, you have to open the file in the application and then print the file.

If you right-click on a document and select Print from the context-sensitive menu, the same process occurs, except that the document is sent to the default printer. If you want to print to a different print queue, you can use the drag and drop method if the application supports printing to a non-default printer.

Enhanced Metafile (EMF) Spooling

For non-PostScript printing, Windows 95 generates an Enhanced Metafile (EMF) instead of sending the raw data directly to the printer. Spooling to an EMF allows control to be returned to an application approximately two times faster than if the data is sent directly to the printer. Thus, you can continue working in an application much sooner under Windows 95 than under Windows 3.1.

With Windows 3.1, raw printer data (such as HPPCL commands or escape codes) is sent directly to the printer driver for rendering and submission to the Print Manager queue. The application is busy until all the data has been rendered and sent to the Print Manager queue. During this time, the user is unable to do anything else in that application, such as work on another document.

With Windows 95, the Graphical Device Interface (GDI) generates an EMF using the document information generated by the application. The EMF is a collection of Windows 95 commands for creating an image, such as commands to draw a rectangle and put some text underneath it. The EMF can be created in about half the time it would take to send the raw data directly to the printer. After the EMF is created, the application no longer is busy, and the user can continue to work in it.

The EMF is then interpreted in the background by the 32-bit printing subsystem, which translates the EMF into raw printer data that can be sent to the printer. EMF spooling adds an intermediate step in the print process, but returns control to an application much more quickly.

Figure 7.1 illustrates the differences between the Windows 3.1 and Windows 95 print processes.

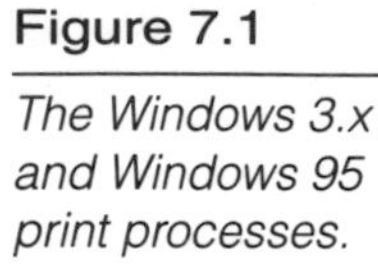

Figure 7.1

The Windows 3.x and Windows 95 print processes.

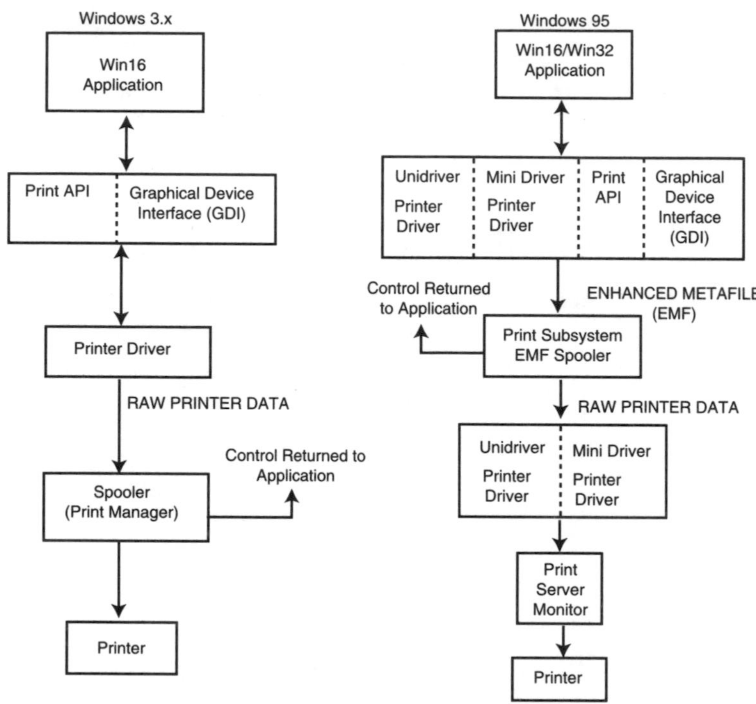

EMF spooling works with most Windows applications; some applications, however, may be capable of printing to a driver using only raw printer data. For these applications, you might need to bypass the EMF spooling. Exercise 7.1 illustrates how to disable EMF spooling.

Exercise 7.1: Disabling EMF Spooling

1. Right-click on the Printer icon and select Properties. The Properties sheet for the printer is displayed.
2. Select the Details tab and choose Spool Settings. The Spool Settings dialog box is displayed.
3. In the Spool data format list box of the Spool Settings dialog box, select RAW and choose OK. Data sent to this printer no longer will be spooled to an EMF file.

Conflict Resolution

The Windows 95 printing subsystem handles conflicts between different MS-DOS and Windows applications trying to print to a printer port simultaneously. This functionality is an improvement over the Windows 3.1 printing subsystem.

Deferred Printing

The spooling capabilities of Windows 95 allow a job to be spooled to a print queue, even if the printer is currently unavailable. For a remote user, Windows 95 automatically detects that the laptop is not connected to a local or network printer and sets the print queue to Work Offline mode. The job still is sent to the print queue but does not print until a connection to that printer is detected. For example, when the user returns to the office, attaches to the printer or the network, and starts Windows 95, the jobs can be sent to the printer as a background process.

You can also manually set a print queue to hold print jobs by right-clicking on the Printer icon and selecting Pause Printing. This may be useful if you want to hold the jobs until later in the day, for example. To resume sending jobs to the printer, right-click on the printer icon and deselect Pause Printing.

Windows 95 Printing Process

The printing model for Windows 95 is made up of modular components, which enable a great deal of flexibility because individual components can be substituted. For example, if a PostScript printer driver is used, the EMF component of the printing model is not used.

To illustrate the Windows 95 printing model, the following list contains the three different printing processes that can occur:

- Printing from a non-Windows application

- Printing from a Windows application to a non-PostScript printer
- Printing from a Windows application to a PostScript printer

Regardless of which print process is used, the print job eventually is formatted into raw printer data that is sent to the local print spooler on the Windows 95 computer.

Print Spooler

A *print spooler* essentially is an internal print queue where the print job data is written while the print job is being processed. Any printing done in Windows 95 uses the local print spooler on the Windows 95 client. In addition, if a Windows application prints to a non-PostScript printer, an additional spooler known as the *EMF sprint spooler* may be used. If the network printer is used, the local print spooler passes the print job to the spooler on the network print server.

As the print jobs are spooled, they are written to a temporary file on the hard disk. For Windows 95 computers, the print jobs are queued in <*systemroot*>\SPOOL\PRINTERS; for example, C:\WINDOWS\SPOOL\PRINTERS.

When a job begins to spool, it is the responsibility of the Print Monitor to decide when to send the information to the printer. Using the default settings, and assuming that the printer is available to accept a new print job, the Print Monitor starts sending the job to the printer after the first page has spooled. To change this, choose Spool Settings from the Details tab of the properties sheet for the printer. The print monitor writes the spooled data either to a port (if the printer is locally connected) or to a print spooler on a network print server.

After the job has printed, the print monitor can display a pop-up message informing the user that the job has printed.

Printing from a Non-Windows Application

For non-Windows (that is, DOS) applications, the application sends information to the printer driver, which converts the information into raw printer data using a printer control language that the printer understands. For example, to print a circle, an HP LaserJet driver would send an HPPCL command to the printer specifying the size of the circle and the location on the page. The raw data is then sent to the print spooler, and control is returned to the application after all the raw data has been submitted to the print spooler.

Printing from a Windows 95 Application to a Non-PostScript Printer

When you select a network printer in a Windows application, Windows 95 can copy the printer driver to the local directory <*systemroot*>\SYSTEM (for example, C:\WINDOWS\SYSTEM). If the file has already been copied, then the print server driver is not copied to the local computer unless the local driver is an older version than the driver on the print server. Similarly, if a local printer is selected, then the driver already is on the local computer.

When the client has the correct printer driver on the hard drive, the driver is loaded into RAM. The Windows application can then query the printer driver for the current print settings (such as page orientation) to produce a What-You-See-Is-What-You-Get (WYSIWYG) image on the screen.

To print the document, the Windows 95 GDI (which is responsible for displaying how the screen looks—for example, drawing the test in a certain font) sends a series of commands to the Windows 95 graphics engine. The Windows 95 graphics engine then translates the GDI commands into an EMF, using the EMF spooler. After the EMF has been created, control is returned to the application. The EMF spooler then processes the EMF information in the background using the printer minidriver. The minidriver converts the EMF to raw printer data, which is then spooled to the print spooler.

Printing from a Windows Application to a PostScript Printer

This process is the same as for non-PostScript printers, except the GDI does not generate commands for an EMF file. Instead, to print a document, the PostScript driver generates a series of raw printer commands to tell the printer how to print the specified pages. The raw printer data (in the PostScript language) is then sent to the print spooler.

Installing a Local Printer in Windows 95

A local printer can be installed in Windows 95 using either Plug and Play hardware detection or the Add Printer Wizard, if the printer is not Plug and Play compliant.

Installing a Plug and Play Printer

If a Plug and Play-compliant printer is connected to the Windows 95 computer at start up, the printer is detected, and the appropriate printer driver is automatically installed. If Windows 95 cannot determine the proper driver to be used, it prompts the user to specify the correct driver.

Installing a Printer Using the Add Printer Wizard

The Add Printer Wizard is used to install a printer driver in Windows 95. The Add Printer wizard can be accessed from the Printers folder. To access the Printers folder, select it from the Start menu Settings option or open it after opening My Computer.

The Printers folder can be used to perform the following functions:

- Install a printer
- Share a printer on a network
- Set permissions for accessing a printer
- Connect to a network printer
- Manage printers
- Change printer properties, such as page size

Exercise 7.2 demonstrates how to use the Add Printer Wizard to install a locally attached printer.

If you do not have an actual printer attached to your computer, you can still perform this exercise and select FILE: as the port to print to. When you print to FILE:, you are prompted for a filename and path to which to save the output. Printing to FILE: is usually used with the Generic / Text Only printer driver to create text output in a file.

Exercise 7.2: Adding a Local Printer with the Add Printer Wizard

1. Open the Printers folder.
2. Double-click on the Add Printer wizard and choose Next. You are asked whether the printer is attached directly to the computer or is accessed from the network.
3. Select Local Printer and choose Next.
4. Select the printer manufacturer from the Manufacturers list.
5. Select the printer model from the Printers list. If you do not have an actual local printer, you may select the Generic / Text Only driver after selecting Generic as the manufacturer.

6. From the list of Available ports, select the port to which the printer is connected. For example, for a parallel port, you may need to select LPT1:. If you do not have a local printer attached, select FILE:.

7. Choose Next and assign the printer a printer name. You can accept the default name, or you can use a more descriptive name, such as LaserJet II in Room 312.

8. If you want print jobs to be sent to this printer by default, choose Yes and then choose Next. Otherwise, choose No and then Next.

9. The Add Printer wizard then asks you whether you want to print a test page, and then copies the files from the Windows 95 distribution media. If Windows 95 cannot find these files, you are prompted for the path.

10. An icon for the printer is created in the Printers folder. To configure the printer, see the following section.

Configuring a Printer in Windows 95

The settings on a printer are controlled through the Properties sheet for that printer. To access the Properties sheet, right-click on the printer icon and select Properties.

The Properties sheet contains the following tabs:

- General
- Details
- Paper
- Graphics
- Fonts
- Device Options
- PostScript

These tabs are described in the following sections.

General

The General tab specifies the printer name and any additional descriptive comments that the user enters. In addition, if the user wants to print a separator page between print jobs, this instruction can be specified here.

Details

The Details tab specifies the printer driver to be used, as well as various port settings. For example, the Transmission retry setting specifies the number of seconds Windows 95 will wait before reporting a timeout error if the printer is not responding. In addition, the Spool Settings dialog box is accessed from the Details tab.

Paper

The type of information in this tab varies depending on the printer driver used. The Paper tab may contain configuration settings for some of the following items:

- Default paper size
- Default orientation (for example, landscape or portrait)
- Paper source (for example, tractor feed or upper paper tray)
- The number of copies to print for each print job

Graphics

The configurable information in this tab varies depending on the printer driver used. It may contain settings such as the following:

- **Resolution.** Specifies the number of dots per inch (dpi) used for printing graphics or scaleable fonts.
- **Dithering.** Specifies how the colors are blended together for a color printer.
- **Intensity.** Specifies the degree of lightness or darkness of the print job.

Figure 7.2 shows an example of a typical Graphics tab from the Properties sheet of a printer.

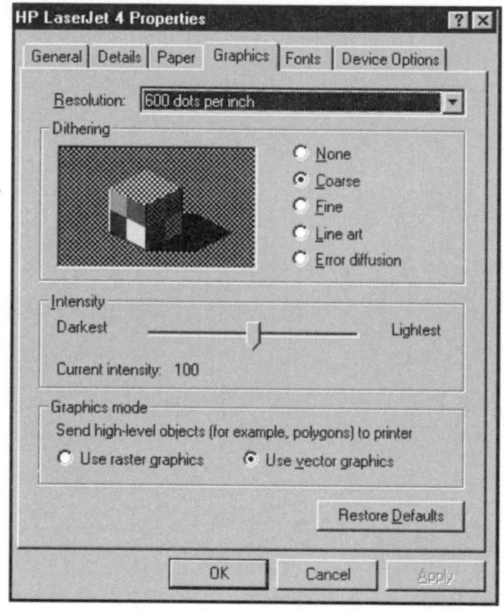

Figure 7.2

A typical Graphics tab from a printer Properties sheet.

Fonts

The Fonts tab is usually available for laser printers. If cartridges are installed on the printer, they can be specified here. In addition, you can specify whether to use TrueType fonts or built-in printer fonts. In general, the fonts built into the printer can be rendered more quickly. For PostScript printers, a font substitution table can be configured to substitute TrueType fonts with PostScript fonts.

Device Options

If this tab is available, it can be used to configure information specific to the printer. For example, the printer manufacturer may include options to specify the amount of memory installed or other printer-specific features. An example of the Device Options tab is shown in figure 7.3

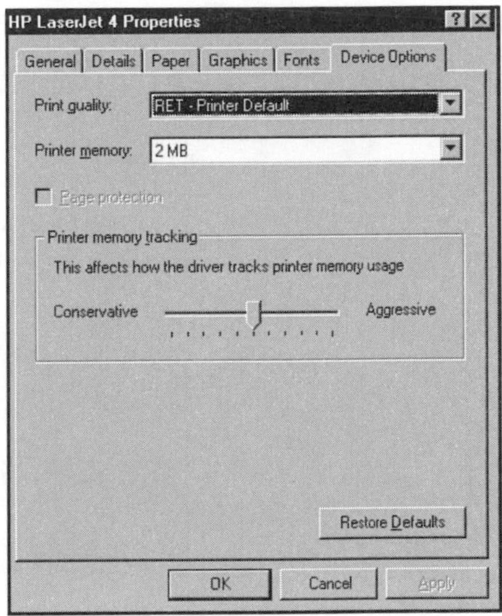

Figure 7.3

A typical printer Properties Device Options tab.

PostScript

This tab is available on PostScript printers and can be used to configure the PostScript options, such as the following:

- **Output Format.** Used for file compatibility.
- **Header.** By default, a PostScript header is sent with each print job containing printer-specific configuration information. If the printer is accessed only locally, you may want to change this setting so that a header need not be sent with each print job.
- **Error Information.** Allows error messages to be printed out by the printer.
- **Advanced.** Additional information such as the PostScript language level and data format can be specified. Windows 95 supports PostScript Levels 1 and 2.

An example of the PostScript tab for a PostScript printer is shown in figure 7.4.

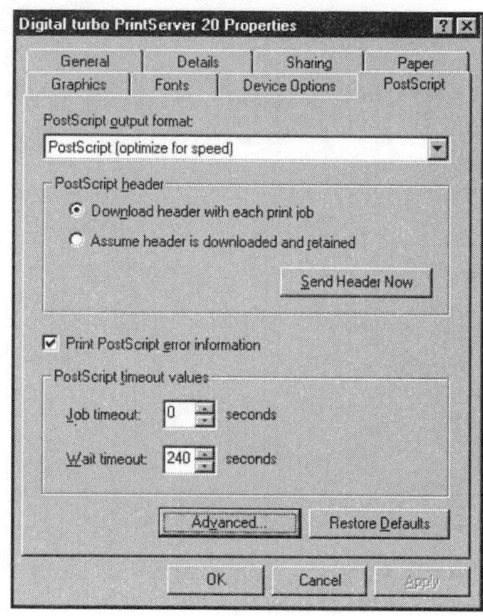

Figure 7.4

The PostScript tab for a PostScript printer.

Windows 95 Network Printing

Windows 95 network printing support includes a number of new features:

- A modular architecture, which allows for different print providers for different types of networks
- Point and Print installation, which allows printer drivers to be automatically installed over the network
- The capability to assign network permissions to print queues, which can prevent unauthorized changes to the print queues or print jobs
- Support for different network print servers, including HP JetDirect printers and DEC PrintServer printers

Architecture

The modular format of the Windows 95 printing subsystem uses a layered model. The four layers are the following:

- Print Application Programming Interfaces (APIs)
- Print Router
- Print Provider Interface
- Print Providers

Print Application Programming Interfaces (APIs)

The *Print Application Programming Interfaces* (APIs) are used to pass information to and from the Windows application and the print router. Windows 95 includes the 16-bit Win16 API for use with 16-bit Windows applications, as well as the 32-bit Win32 API for use with Win32 applications. The Print APIs provide functions such as opening, writing, and closing print jobs. The Print APIs also are used for print queue management.

Print Router

The *Print Router* passes printing requests from the Print APIs to the proper Print Provider Interface (PPI). The PPI in turn passes on this information to the correct print provider. For example, if the printing request is for a local printer, the Print Router sends the information through the PPI to the Windows 95 Local Printing Print Provider.

Print Providers

A *Print Provider* is a 32-bit dynamic-link library (DLL) that contains code for printing and network support, as appropriate. The print providers translate requests from the PPI into the appropriate network or local printer requests.

The following print providers are included with Windows 95:

- Local Printing Print Provider
- Microsoft 32-bit Network Print Provider
- Microsoft 16-bit Network Print Provider
- NetWare Network Print Provider

In addition, third-party network vendors can supply their own print providers, which can be designed to fit in with the modular Windows 95 printing subsystem.

Local Printing Print Provider

The Local Printing Print Provider is found in the SPOOLSS.DLL file along with the Print Router. This print provider handles the local print queue and manages print jobs that are sent to local printers (a printer directly connected to a port on the Windows 95 client).

Microsoft Network Print Provider

Two print providers for Microsoft Network printing support exist. The 32-bit print provider, known as WinNet32 Network Print Provider, is contained in the file MSPP32.DLL. The 16-bit print provider, WinNet16 Network Print Provider, is actually a part of MSPP32.DLL, which translates PPI requests into 16-bit WinNet16 requests for backward compatibility with 16-bit Microsoft Network drivers.

When a print job is submitted to a Microsoft Network printer, the PPI interacts with the Microsoft Network Print Provider (MSPP32.DLL) and the Microsoft Network support library (MSNET32.DLL if a 32-bit network client is used; MSNET16.DLL if a 16-bit network client is used) and sends the print job to the network printer using the Installable File System Manager (IFSMGR.VXD). The IFS Manager then interacts with the network redirector (VREDIR.VXD) to send the job over the network.

For print queue management (for example, viewing a print queue), the print provider and network support library send requests directly to the network redirector.

NetWare Network Print Provider

Similar to the Microsoft Network Print Provider, the NetWare Network Print Provider uses the IFS Manager to submit jobs to the network redirector. For a NetWare network, the network redirector is NWREDIR.VXD.

> Windows 95 currently supports bindery-based NetWare print queues, but not NetWare Directory Services (NDS)-based print queues common with NetWare 4.*x* servers.

As well, the NetWare Network Print Provider can translate print requests into 16-bit calls if a real-mode (16-bit) NetWare client is used.

Third-Party Network Print Providers

Third-party network vendors can write their own print provider and print provider interface that communicates with their own network redirector software. A third-party network print provider can be installed using the Control Panel Network applet.

Printing to a Network Printer

To connect to a network printer, you must first install, configure, and share the printer on the network server. For information on installing and configuring the driver on the network server, refer to the preceding sections on local printer installation and configuration.

After the Windows 95 printer driver has been configured on the network print server attached to the printer, the printer must be shared to allow other users to access it. To share a printer in Windows 95, the network print server must be running a 32-bit, protected-mode client, and a file and printer sharing service must be enabled. (Refer to Chapter 5, "Networking and Interoperability," for information on enabling file and printer sharing.) Exercise 7.3 demonstrates how to share a network printer.

Exercise 7.3: Sharing a Network Printer

1. Right-click on the Printer icon and select Properties to display the Properties sheet.
2. Select the Sharing tab to display the Sharing configuration settings as shown in figure 7.5.

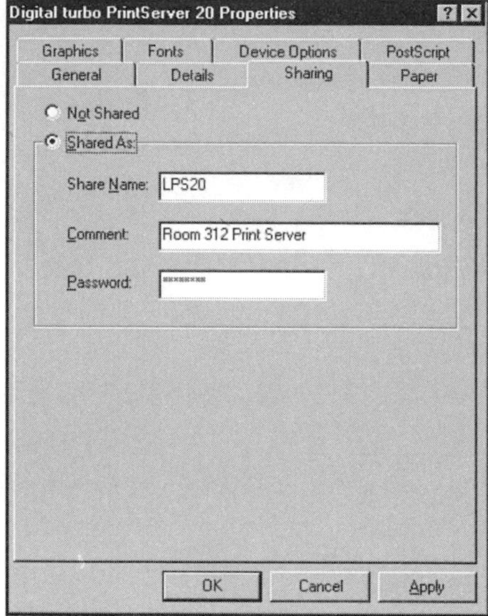

Figure 7.5

The printer Sharing tab.

3. Select **S**hared As and enter a share name and an optional descriptive comment for the printer. Windows 95 does not allow a share name to contain invalid characters including spaces. The share name also must not exceed 12 characters.

4. You also must grant permissions to access this printer. If share-level permissions are used, you must assign a password to the printer. To access the print queue, users must supply the correct password. If user-level permissions are used, you must add the users who will be granted access to this print queue. For example, to allow everyone to print to the print queue, you would add the Everyone group and give it the print access right.

5. Choose OK to share the printer. The printer icon now appears as a hand holding or sharing the printer with others. Remote users with the correct permissions can now access the print queue after setting up the correct printer driver on their computers.

When the printer has been configured and shared on the network print server, a Windows 95 client can be configured to connect to the print server and print to the printer over the network. This configuration can be done either manually with the Add Printer Wizard or by configuring the network printer for Point and Print setup.

Connecting to a Network Printer Using the Add Printer Wizard

To manually configure a Windows 95 client to print to the network printer using the Add Printer Wizard, perform the steps shown in Exercise 7.4.

Exercise 7.4: Using the Add Printer Wizard to Connect to a Network Printer

1. Start the Add Printer wizard from the Printers folder.
2. In the Printer Type field, select Network Printer and choose Next.
3. Enter the Universal Naming Convention (UNC) path of the network printer; for example, \\SARAH\HP4.
4. If you will not be using MS-DOS applications to print to this printer, you may select No under Do you print from MS-DOS-based programs?. In order to have the printer associated with a printer port such as LPT1:, you should select Yes for this option. Choose Next.
5. If you have specified that you will print to this printer using MS-DOS-based applications, you are prompted to select the desired port from the Capture Printer Port dialog box. Choose OK to continue.
6. Choose Next and select the printer manufacturer and model from the Manufacturers and Printers lists.
7. Enter a name for the printer; for example, HP4 in Room 11.
8. If you want to test that you can print properly to the network printer, select Send Test Page. Choose Finish to have Windows 95 begin copying the printer driver files to the hard

drive if the latest drivers are not already on the hard drive. If Windows 95 cannot find the files, you are prompted to enter the path to the Windows 95 distribution files.

9. An icon for the network printer is created in the Printers folder. If desired, you may drag a copy of this icon to the desktop to create a shortcut.

Connecting to a Network Printer Using Point and Print Setup

To connect to a network printer that is *not* configured for Point and Print setup, a client must know the correct printer driver to be used. In addition, the client must know other information such as the share name and network server name. However, after a network printer has been configured to enable Point and Print setup, the printer driver installation on the client is greatly simplified. The Point and Print printer supplies the client with information such as the UNC path, the printer driver to be used, and other information.

To install the printer drivers for the Point and Print printer on a Windows 95 client, locate the icon for the printer in the Network Neighborhood. Next, drag the printer icon onto the Desktop. Alternatively, you can right-click on the network Printer icon and select Install.

In addition, if you try to drag and drop a document onto the network printer icon, the printer driver will be installed on the Windows 95 client, if it has not already been installed. If the driver version on the network printer is more recent than the version on the client, the later printer driver version will be copied to the client.

A Point and Print printer can be configured on any of the following servers:

- Windows 95 server
- Windows NT server (including both Windows NT Server and Windows NT Workstation servers)
- NetWare bindery-based server

Windows 95 Server

A Windows 95 server is simply a computer running Windows 95 that has a file and printer Sharing service enabled. Any printers directly connected to the Windows 95 server are automatically enabled for Point and Print setup. No further configuration is required.

Windows 95 copies to the client the printer driver that is in use on the Windows 95 server. Thus, any settings that have been configured for the server printer (such as memory) also are copied to the Windows 95 client.

Windows NT Server

Point and Print setup is also automatically enabled for a printer queue on a Windows NT server running Windows NT (Server or Workstation) version 3.1 or greater. Because Windows 95 uses a slightly different printer driver than that on the Windows NT server, however, the driver is not actually copied to the Windows 95 client. Instead, Windows 95 attempts to install a printer driver with the same name from the Windows 95 distribution files. If no Windows 95 printer driver bears the same name as the Windows NT printer driver, the user is prompted to select the proper driver to be installed.

Because the Windows NT printer driver is not copied to the client, any settings required for this driver must be manually configured on the Windows 95 client. Only Windows 95 servers have the capability to pass on their configuration settings to the Windows 95 client.

NetWare Bindery-Based Server

Since the NetWare server software does not know about Windows 95 Point and Print setup, some Point and Print configuration information must be written to the NetWare server's bindery to provide Point and Print services. To write this information, you must log onto the NetWare server with Supervisor or equivalent privileges from a Windows 95 client.

To enable Point and Print setup for a NetWare bindery-based print server, perform the following steps:

1. Log into the NetWare server from a Windows 95 client using an account with Supervisor or equivalent privileges. For more information on performing this step, refer to Chapter 5.

2. Select a NetWare print queue from the Network Neighborhood and click the right mouse button to display the context-sensitive menu. Selecting **P**oint and Print Setup from the menu will display the Set Printer **M**odel and Set Driver **P**ath options.

3. Select Set Printer **M**odel and select the printer model from the list. Choose OK to continue.

4. Select Set Driver **P**ath and enter the UNC path where the printer driver files for this printer are located. For example, enter **\\NW312\SYS\PUBLIC**.

5. Copy the required Windows 95 printer drivers from the Windows 95 distribution files to the directory specified in the preceding step.

6. To use Point and Print setup, a user must have at least Read and File Scan privileges to the directory specified in step 4. If the SYS\PUBLIC directory is used, all users have these privileges by default.

7. The printer queue, driver, and privileges information is written to the NetWare Bindery. Users then can automatically install the printer driver on the Windows 95 client after dragging the printer icon from the Network Neighborhood onto the Desktop. The printer driver also is installed on the Windows 95 client if a document is dragged and dropped onto the NetWare printer icon.

Registry Keys

Windows 95 stores configuration information in the Registry. Printers that have been set up in the Printers folder have entries found under the HKEY_LOCAL_MACHINE\System\CurrentControlSet\Control\Print key. To view the subkeys, open the Registry by running the REGEDIT application from a command prompt.

> Any changes made to the Registry can severely affect the operating system. You should make a backup copy of the Registry files to prevent accidental changes. See the section "Registry Editor" in Chapter 4, "Editing User and System Profiles," for more information.

Managing a Print Queue

Double-clicking on a printer icon displays the print queue for that printer. The print queue shows the status of any jobs that are printing or waiting to print on that printer. The print jobs are sent to the printer in the order in which they appear.

Settings for the print queue can be changed from the Printer menu when the print queue is displayed or from the context-sensitive menu displayed after right-clicking on the printer icon. These settings include the following:

- Using a separator page between print jobs—this can be set in the General tab of the printer's properties sheet
- Setting the printer to be the default printer for the Windows 95 client
- Setting the printer offline so that jobs will queue but not be printed until otherwise specified

In addition to being used to change print queue settings, a Windows 95 print queue window also can be used to manage print jobs.

Managing Print Jobs

Any user can display a print queue that he or she has permission to access. Users can also manage the print queue if the printer is attached locally. If the print queue is on a network printer, users can manage the print queue if they have the proper permissions, and if user-level security is used. If a user does not have permission to manage the print queue, that user can still manage print jobs that he or she has submitted. The following functions can be performed on a print job:

- Canceling a print job
- Pausing a print job
- Resuming a print job
- Changing the order of print jobs

Figure 7.6 shows an example of a Windows 95 print queue. In this example, the first job sent to the queue has been paused, the second job is being deleted, and therefore the third job will be printed next.

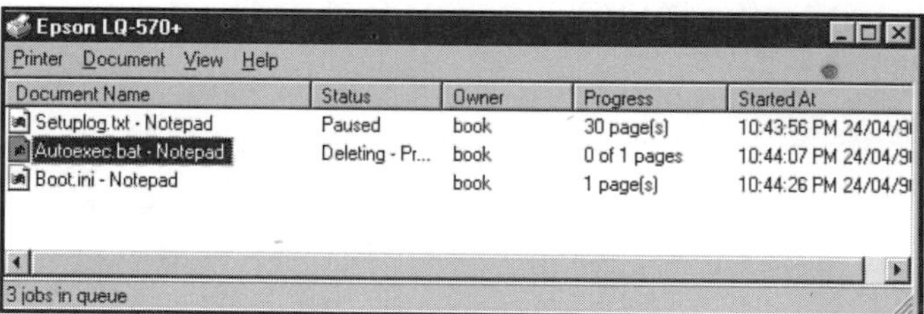

Figure 7.6

A Windows 95 print queue.

Canceling a Print Job

If a print job has not already started printing, you can delete it from the print queue by selecting the print job from the print queue and pressing the Delete key. Alternatively, you may select Cancel Printing from the Document menu of the print queue after selecting the print job.

For a network print queue, users can delete only their own print jobs. For a local printer, users can delete any print jobs in the print queue.

If a document is already printing, then you cannot cancel the print job. If for some reason the job hangs in the print queue, you might have to manually delete the spooled file from the print spool directory. For a Windows 95 print queue, this usually is C:\WINDOWS\SPOOL\PRINTERS.

Pausing a Print Job

If a print job has not yet started printing, you may pause the job, which allows other print jobs to print ahead of it. To pause a print job, select the print job and select Pause Printing from the Document menu of the print queue. The print job remains in the queue until the user selects the paused print job and deselects Pause Printing from the Document menu.

For a network print queue, users can normally pause only their own print jobs. A user with administrator privileges may be able to pause any print jobs, if the network software supports that action.

Any user with access to a local print queue may pause any or all of the print jobs.

You also can pause the entire print queue by selecting Pause Printing from the context-sensitive menu or from the Printer menu of the print queue. You also can pause a network print queue if you have the proper permissions.

Resuming a Print Job

To allow a print job to be sent to the printer, select the paused job and deselect Pause Printing from the Document menu of the print queue. To resume a paused print queue, remove the check mark from Pause Printing on the Printer menu or from the context-sensitive menu. Again, you must have the proper permissions to resume printing on a network print queue.

Changing the Order of Print Jobs

If more than one print job is waiting in the print queue, you can change the order in which these jobs print by dragging one of the documents and placing it in front of another. For a network print queue, user-level security must be used, you must have administrator permissions, and the network software must support this operation.

Print Servers

A benefit of the modular architecture of the Windows 95 printing subsystem is that several different types of print servers can be used depending on the network requirements. The print servers that ship with Windows 95 include the following:

- Microsoft Network Print Server
- Microsoft Print Agent for NetWare Networks
- HP JetAdmin Print Server
- Digital (DEC) PrintServer

Microsoft Network

The Microsoft Network Print Server is the default print server used for Windows 95 printing. This print server is used even if File and Printer Sharing for NetWare Networks is installed. No additional configuration is required beyond installing the appropriate printer and network drivers.

Microsoft Print Agent for NetWare Networks

The Microsoft Print Agent for NetWare Networks service can be used to despool print jobs from a NetWare or a Windows 95 print queue. If the computer running the Microsoft Print Agent for NetWare Networks service is attached to a printer, jobs originating from Windows 95 or NetWare print queues can be printed.

Whereas a NetWare PSERVER print server must be running on a dedicated MS-DOS computer, a Windows 95 print server running Microsoft Print Agent for NetWare Networks also can run numerous other applications at the same time.

When you start the Microsoft Print Agent for NetWare Networks, the service logs on to the NetWare print server and obtains information on how to configure the print jobs. For example, the NetWare print server may specify the banner to be used preceding each print job. The Microsoft Print Agent for NetWare Networks then can obtain jobs from the NetWare print queue, print them, and send a message to the NetWare print queue saying that the job has been printed. The NetWare print queue then removes the job and informs the user that the job has been printed.

The Microsoft Print Agent for NetWare Networks service must be installed on a Windows 95 computer running the Microsoft Client for NetWare Networks. The Windows 95 computer need not be running File and Printer Sharing for NetWare Networks, however.

Exercise 7.5 demonstrates how to install and enable Microsoft Print Agent for NetWare Networks.

For this exercise, the Windows 95 computer must be able to access a NetWare print server and a MS-DOS computer running the PSERVER utility. Furthermore, the Microsoft Client for NetWare Networks must be installed prior to starting this exercise. Attempting to install both the client and the service at the same time will cause the installation to fail.

Exercise 7.5: Installing and Enabling Print Services for NetWare

1. From the Start menu, select Settings, then Control Panel, and then double-click on the Network icon. The Network Control Panel Applet is displayed.
2. Choose Add and select Service from the Select Network Component Type dialog box.

3. Choose **A**dd and then choose **H**ave Disk.
4. Type the path to the \ADMIN\NETTOOLS\PRTAGENT directory and choose OK.
5. Select Microsoft print agent for NetWare networks and choose OK.
6. Ensure that the NetWare print server and the MS-DOS computer running PSERVER are functioning correctly.
7. From the Printers folder, select the printer on the Windows 95 client to which you will direct the NetWare print queue jobs.
8. Right-click on the Printer icon and select P**r**operties from the context-sensitive menu to display the Properties sheet for the printer.
9. From the Print Server tab, select **E**nable Microsoft Print Server for NetWare.
10. From the **N**etWare Servers drop-down list, select the NetWare Server that contains the NetWare print queue.

You must be logged into the NetWare server with an account that has access to the NetWare print queue in order for the previous step to succeed.

11. After a NetWare server is selected, the available print servers appear in the **P**rint Server list. Select the MS-DOS PSERVER from this list.
12. Under P**o**lling, specify the time interval between attempts to obtain print jobs from the NetWare print queue. The default is 30 seconds.
13. Choose OK to start the Microsoft Print Agent for NetWare Networks service.

HP JetAdmin

The HP JetAdmin Print Server is used to send and administer print jobs to a Hewlett-Packard printer connected directly to the network using an HP JetDirect network interface card. The HP JetAdmin utility can be used to perform the following functions:

- Configure an HP JetDirect network interface card
- Configure printer settings
- Filter and sort HP JetDirect network printers in the list
- Add or remove print queues
- Select printer drivers to install
- Select the printer operating mode
- Set a description for the printer

To install the HP JetAdmin utility, follow these steps:

1. From the Start menu, select Settings, then Control Panel, and then double-click on the Network icon. The Network Control Panel Applet is displayed.
2. Choose Add and select Service from the Select Network Component Type dialog box.
3. Choose Add and select HP JetAdmin from the list of Network Services.
4. Choose OK to install the HP JetAdmin utility.
5. If you will be using HP JetAdmin with NetWare, you must supply the following files:
    - NWCALLS.DLL
    - NWIPXSPX.DLL
    - NWLOCALE.DLL

- NWNET.DLL
- NWPSRV.DLL

The preceding files are provided with the Novell NetWare VLM client and by Microsoft with Windows 3.11.

6. After all the files have been copied, restart Windows 95 for the changes to take effect.

   The HP JetAdmin icon is then to be added to the Control Panel.

Digital (DEC) Print Server

Like HP JetDirect printers, Digital (DEC) PrintServer printers can be connected directly to a network using a network interface card. For any network interface printer, the benefit of a direct connection is that computer resources are not needed to spool the print jobs. The results are a much quicker printing completion time and less network traffic. In addition, multiple print spool files are not required for printers connected directly to the network.

To install the Digital Print Server and Digital Print Monitor, the network must be running TCP/IP. In addition, the printer must be configured as a Digital Print Server.

To install the Digital Print Server on a Windows 95 client, perform the following steps:

1. Ensure that both the Digital PrintServer printer and the Windows 95 computer are properly configured to use TCP/IP.
2. From the Printers folder, start the Add Printer Wizard, choose Next, and select Local Printer.

3. Choose Next and select Digital from the list of printer manufacturers. Select the specific model of PrintServer from the list and choose Next. The printer files are copied from the Windows 95 distribution media.

The driver used should have "/Net" at the end of the driver name. This will allow you to add a port during installation and assign it a network address. Alternatively, you can install any printer driver, choose Add Port from the Details tab of the Properties sheet, select Other, and then select Digital Network Port.

4. Choose Add Port to display the Digital Network Port configuration dialog box as shown in figure 7.7.

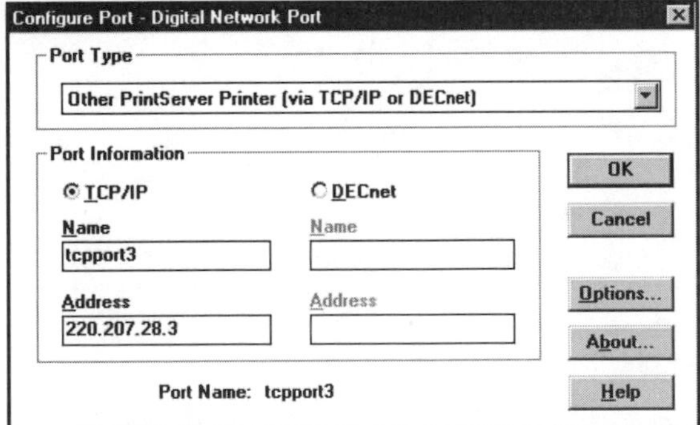

Figure 7.7

Configuring a Digital network printer port.

5. Select TCP/IP and type the host name and IP address of the printer's network interface card in the Name and Address fields, respectively.

6. Type a name to use to refer to the port in the Port Name field and choose OK.

7. Enter a name for the printer, choose Next, and then choose Finish. You can now print to the Digital PrintServer printer located at the specified IP address.

Review Questions

The following questions will test your knowledge of the information in this chapter. For additional questions, see MCP Endeavor and the Microsoft Roadmap/Assessment Exam on the CD-ROM that accompanies this book.

1. ICM stands for ______.

   A. Integrated Circuit Mesh

   B. Image Color Monitor

   C. Image Color Matching

   D. Independent Color Matching

2. The Windows 95 printer driver architecture calls for a ______ (supplied by Microsoft) that interfaces with machine-specific software.

   A. minidriver

   B. unidriver

   C. Print Manager

   D. Print Spooler

3. The major benefit of Enhanced Metafile Spooling is ______.

   A. faster return-to-application time

   B. better control of print queues

   C. better support for color printing

   D. shorter time in the print queue

4. ______ allows a job to be spooled to the print queue even if the printer is currently unavailable.

   A. Print pending

   B. Print holding

   C. Print waiting

   D. Deferred printing

5. The ______ is essentially an internal print queue where the print job data is written while the print job is being processed.

    A. Print Manager

    B. Print Monitor

    C. Print Spooler

    D. Print Cache

6. Which three of the following are Windows 95 print subsystem layers?

    A. Print Transport Interface

    B. Print Router

    C. Print Provider Interface

    D. Print Providers

7. Which of the following procedures can be used to enable a Windows 95 client to submit print jobs to a network printer? Assume the proper permissions have been granted.

    A. Use the Add Printer Wizard to connect to a shared printer on a Windows NT Workstation. The printer share name is NT351WS_2.

    B. Use the Add Printer Wizard to connect to a shared printer on a NetWare print server running the PSERVER utility.

    C. Use Network Neighborhood to view a printer attached to another Windows 95 computer and drag the printer icon to the Windows 95 Desktop.

    D. Select Install from the context-sensitive menu for a printer configured for Point and Print Setup.

8. Windows 95 currently supports ______.

   A. bindery-based NetWare print queues

   B. NDS-based NetWare print queues

   C. both bindery-based and NDS-based NetWare print queues

   D. only Microsoft Network print queues

Review Answers

1. C
2. B
3. A
4. D
5. C
6. B C D
7. A C D
8. A

Chapter

8 Running Applications

The key function of any operating system is to provide the framework within which applications can be run to perform specific tasks. The measure of an operating system is the speed and efficiency with which it performs the tasks that are required of it by an application. Windows 95 provides significant increases in performance over Windows 3.*x* for most application types, due to the 32-bit Windows 95 architecture and the use of preemptive multitasking.

This chapter discusses the issues relating to the use of applications under Windows 95. The topics include the following:

- Windows 95 application support architecture
- 16-Bit Windows applications
- MS-DOS applications
- 32-bit Windows applications
- Application properties and interaction
- Troubleshooting problems with applications

Windows 95 Application Support Architecture

Windows 95 is capable of running three types of applications:

- MS-DOS 16-bit applications
- Windows 3.1 16-bit applications (also known as WIN16 applications)

- 32-bit Windows applications (also known as WIN32 applications; includes most Windows NT software)

Windows 95 can run these varying applications because of a number of architectural design factors, the most important being the idea of virtual machines. In a single-tasking, single-threaded environment like MS-DOS, in which only one application at a time is requesting the operating system's resources, managing those resources is much easier. In an environment such as Windows 95, which is intended to manage multiple applications that might be operating simultaneously, a much greater need for careful management of the system's resources exists, since the PC remains primarily a single-task machine (one processor equals one task at a time, no matter how fast it performs those tasks). In this single-task environment, two processes requesting the use of a device at the exact same moment would be very problematic. Clearly, a procedure in place to arbitrate such requests is necessary.

Windows 95 implements this procedure through virtual machines (VMs). A virtual machine is designed so that every application executed in the Windows 95 environment is executed from within a specialized container created especially for that application (or type of application). This container is intended as much as possible to keep applications separate from each other, thus minimizing the chance that they might not work together. Because some applications (MS-DOS applications) were not designed to function in a multitasking environment, the operating system must deceive them into thinking that they are the only process running on the PC (or they would fail to operate properly).

This deception requires the operating system to simulate all devices and resources that would be present if the system were running under MS-DOS only. This process is called the *virtualization* of hardware devices. Thus, what looks to an MS-DOS application like exclusive access to the PC's devices is in fact hardware access that is being shared with all other running processes of the operating system—but in a way that a legacy application can understand. To varying degrees, this is done for all types of applications.

A number of components in Windows 95 are responsible for managing the elements needed to create virtual machines. They include the following:

- Memory
- Processor modes
- Multitasking
- Multithreading
- Hardware virtualization
- Internal messaging

Chapters 2, "Architecture and Memory," and 3, "Customizing and Configuring Windows 95," introduced you to some of these elements. The following sections describe how Windows 95 uses these elements to run DOS and Windows applications.

Memory

One of the key elements to successfully creating virtual machines lies in creating virtualized memory areas where given applications can function as they expect to under their own environment (if Windows 95 is not their native environment). A space within the total memory available to Windows 95 (which includes both RAM and the paging file) is created and reserved for the operations of that application. One of the main challenges to operating in such a way is ensuring that other applications do not attempt to write or read data from another application's memory space inappropriately, since this can cause serious integrity problems that are detailed in the "Troubleshooting Problems with Applications" section of this chapter.

Processor Modes

Beginning with the Intel 386 processor, processors have been designed with a number of features to meet the needs of multitasking environments. The most important of these is the capability to switch between real mode (the mode in which MS-DOS operates) and protected mode. Protected mode has the capability to regulate the behavior of multitasking processes in two ways: through memory address protection and through graduated levels of processor privilege.

Memory address protection allows the processor to track which memory areas have been allocated to which processes. If an application attempts to access memory other than that allocated to it, the processor interprets this as an error and traps it (see the section "General Protection Faults" later in this chapter).

The second protection scheme consists of having four different levels of privilege or rings at which applications can operate. Each ring, numbered from 3 to 0, has a higher level of privilege with the operating system and so can access a broader set of processor functions. Ring 0 privilege allows complete control of the processor. To simplify operation, Windows 95 uses only Ring 3 and Ring 0. Typically, applications run at Ring 3, and operating system components run at Ring 0. This is done to limit the damage a misbehaving application can do to the operating system (and other applications) since, at Ring 3, applications have very little access to critical system functions.

Multitasking

Another important aspect of creating virtualized machines is the creation of virtualized access to the processor. Because the processor can process only one request at a time, no matter how fast it is, in a multi-application environment the processor must switch back and forth between requests from different processes. If this switching is done quickly enough, it creates the illusion that these processes are occurring simultaneously. The operating system queues all requests from running processes and issues them a priority, which can be reevaluated as time passes and other events occur in the PC. The processor always takes the highest-priority request first.

Two types of multitasking are used in Windows 95, depending on the type of application involved: preemptive multitasking and cooperative multitasking. *Preemptive multitasking* involves dividing the processor's capacity into time slices that are allocated equally among processes requiring them. Thus, one application processes for x number of milliseconds, then it is suspended, and another application processes for the same amount of time, and so on.

Cooperative multitasking is different in that it allows a given process to engage the processor until it voluntarily cedes its control to another process. The disadvantage of this type of multitasking is that a misbehaving application can monopolize the processor's time and effectively stop other processes from executing.

Multithreading

Windows 95 is a operating system. That is, an application designed to take advantage of multithreading is able to submit multiple independent requests to the processor simultaneously. Thus the application can have two separate execution processes multitasked by the processor, creating the impression that the application is itself performing two tasks simultaneously. For example, Word can repaginate a document and allow the user to type at the same time. All multitasking is done at a thread level, with applications submitting either single or multiple threads, depending on the application type.

Hardware Virtualization

Another important component in the creation of virtual machines is hardware virtualization. Especially in the case of legacy MS-DOS and (to a lesser extent) Windows 3.1 applications, simulating the hardware environment in which the application is accustomed to running is necessary. It must seem that all devices are available when needed. This is implemented through software drivers called *Virtual Device Drivers* (VxDs), which are responsible for arbitrating requests (often simultaneous) from running processes and queuing them so that they do not conflict with each other or cause the device in question to fail because it is trying to do two things at once.

Internal Messaging

A message is generated each time a key is pressed or the mouse is clicked, effectively asking an application to do something. In a single-tasking environment, there is no question which application the keyboard or mouse input is intended for. In a multitasking environment, a more complex system of determination and delivery is required. Because you can have multiple applications on-screen simultaneously, where the mouse is clicked or what window is active when a key is pressed determines which application the message is intended for. After the intended application is targeted, the message is placed in the appropriate message queue to be processed.

16-Bit Windows Applications

16-bit Windows applications generally are those created for Windows 3.1. You need to remember the following when dealing with WIN16 applications:

- Windows applications (including WIN32 applications) exist in the *System Virtual Machine*, which is a special VM designed to provide one hardware virtualization layer for all Windows software.
- Within this VM, WIN16 applications share a common address space (this is necessary to maintain backwards compatibility with the way Windows 3.1 applications are designed to interact).

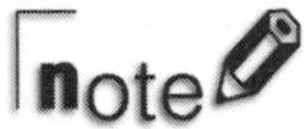

The fact that all WIN16 applications share the same address space makes protecting a WIN16 application from an application that is misbehaving—for example, an application that is attempting to write over data that does not belong to it—more difficult.

- WIN16 applications operate on a cooperative multitasking basis (this is also due to the way applications were designed for Windows 3.1, which did not support preemptive multitasking).
- A single message queue is used for all WIN16 applications.

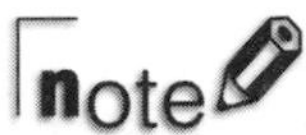

Having a single message queue can become an issue if one application stops responding and thus is not checking the message queue. Because, under a cooperative multitasking scenario, all applications cede control voluntarily, an application that has stopped responding will not relinquish control and therefore will not allow other WIN16 applications to check the message queue and respond to those messages. All WIN16 applications then appear to be hung.

- All WIN16 applications are single-threaded, because Windows 3.1 does not support multithreading.
- WIN16 applications generally load themselves into the virtualized space between 3 GB and 4 GB, and some also use a space between 0 and 4 MB to be able to share data with other WIN16 applications.
- WIN16 applications do not access the Registry because they are designed to use INI files for their stored settings. However, Windows 95 can migrate certain settings from the INI files into the Registry. The WIN16 applications can still continue to access and modify the INI files, and these modifications can then be migrated to the Registry.

- 16-bit applications are not designed to recognize or use LFNs since LFNs are not implemented in Windows 3.1.
- Whereas under Windows 3.1 system resource stacks are 64 KB, these have been converted to 32-bit stacks in Windows 95, dramatically decreasing the likelihood of running out of system resources.

Configuring 16-Bit Applications

When Windows 95 is installed, it automatically migrates the settings for existing WIN16 applications from their native INI files into the Registry. In the event that an application subsequently modifies the INI file again (since a Windows 3.1 application does not know how to write the Registry directly), Windows 95 scans these files at every boot and migrates changes into the Registry as well. In the case of proprietary INI files, these files generally are left untouched, because Windows 95 likely will not recognize the settings they contain.

Typically, Windows 3.1 applications will run under Windows 95 without any modification. Certain software, however, is known to need specific configuration parameters to run under Windows 95. These software packages (and the correct parameters) are listed in the APPS.INF file in the \WINDOWS\INF directory (which is hidden by default).

MS-DOS Applications

MS-DOS applications are 16-bit applications designed to work with MS-DOS version 6.*x* or earlier. As stated previously, because these applications have no understanding of multitasking environments, simulating an MS-DOS environment is necessary for them to function properly. Windows 95 includes a number of improvements in handling MS-DOS applications:

- The capability to run in a window in most cases
- Better access to system resources due to the new 32-bit structure of the system resource stacks

- Improved support for sound devices
- Improved memory protection schemes that allow you to isolate the MS-DOS system area to prevent its corruption by misbehaving MS-DOS programs
- Support for scaleable True Type fonts in MS-DOS windows
- The capability to customize individual MS-DOS VMs with environment variables run from a batch file

The following additional information should be noted when using MS-DOS applications in Windows 95:

- Each MS-DOS application that is executed is assigned its own virtual machine, with separate virtualized device access and addressable memory space.
- The memory space created for an MS-DOS application mirrors that of a stand-alone DOS environment, with 640 KB of conventional memory, 384 KB of upper memory, and whatever extended or expanded memory is specified in the configuration settings of the MS-DOS session.
- Each MS-DOS application run under Windows 95 can execute only one thread at a time because MS-DOS does not support multithreading.

> MS-DOS applications cannot actually create threads of execution themselves. They generate MS-DOS hardware interrupts, which are intercepted by Windows 95 and translated into logical requests for executing a particular function.

- Each MS-DOS application has its own separate message queue to receive keyboard and mouse input.
- The APPS.INF file also contains configuration parameters for MS-DOS applications that are known to require them.

MS-DOS applications can be run in one of three modes:

- In an MS-DOS virtual machine
- In MS-DOS mode after shutting down the Windows 95 Graphical User Interface
- In MS-DOS mode outside of Windows 95 using parameters that have been customized for the application

By default, if Windows 95 detects that the application should be run in MS-DOS mode, it shuts down the Windows 95 graphical user interface and runs the application in an environment similar to that if Command Prompt Only were selected from the Boot Menu. However, the options on the shortcut Properties sheet for the MS-DOS application can be set to force the application to always run in MS-DOS mode or in a customized MS-DOS mode, if required.

If the application does not require or is not configured to use MS-DOS mode, then it will run in an MS-DOS virtual machine.

There are several parameters that can be configured to determine how an application runs in each of the preceding modes. These parameters are set through the Properties sheet of the shortcut for the application and are described in the following sections.

MS-DOS Virtual Machine

MS-DOS virtual machine mode should be used whenever possible because the application can then take advantage of 32-bit protected-mode driver support, preemptive multitasking, increased conventional memory, and other Windows 95 enhancements. By default, all MS-DOS applications are set to run in an MS-DOS virtual machine, whether they are executed by double-clicking on the application from the Explorer or by typing the name of the file from a DOS prompt within Windows 95. However, if Windows 95 detects that the application must have exclusive use of the system resources and must run in MS-DOS mode, you are prompted to have Windows 95 automatically shut down the system and run the application in MS-DOS mode. Most applications should be able to function without incident in a virtual machine. If an application functions, but not as well as it should, you can alter the configuration of the MS-DOS environment for that application.

Numerous settings can be modified to facilitate the operation of MS-DOS programs. These settings are grouped into the following tabs on the Properties sheet for the MS-DOS application:

- Program tab
- Font tab
- Memory tab
- Screen tab
- Misc tab

Program Tab

The Program tab includes settings defining the location of files used to run the application as well as some other settings. The Advanced button of the Program tab is used to force the application to run in MS-DOS mode, as is explained in the later section "MS-DOS Mode."

Figure 8.1 displays the various parameters of the Program tab.

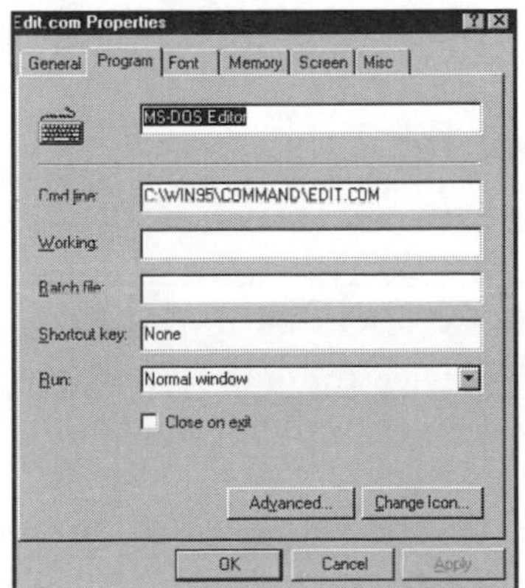

Figure 8.1

The Program tab of the MS-DOS Properties sheet.

The following list describes the parameters of the Program tab:

- **Cmd line.** The path and filename of the MS-DOS program in question. Including command-line parameters is permitted.
- **Working.** Indicates where data files should be stored if they are not in the directory in which the program resides.
- **Batch file.** The name of a batch file that runs and loads any TSRs or specific environment variables that the program needs. For example, you can specify DOSKEY to run before opening up a command prompt.
- **Shortcut key.** The key combination that can be used to run the program .

Verify that the key combination you select is not in use by any other application, since that application will no longer be able to respond to that combination of keys after it is specified.

- **Run.** Indicates whether to run the program in a normal window, minimized, or maximized.
- **Close on exit.** If checked, the virtual DOS machine window closes automatically when the application finishes processing.

Font Tab

The parameters on this tab allow you to specify whether you want to use True Type fonts, bitmap fonts, or both to display characters in the MS-DOS session. You can also select from various font sizes and preview them before making a final selection. Figure 8.2 shows an example of the Font tab.

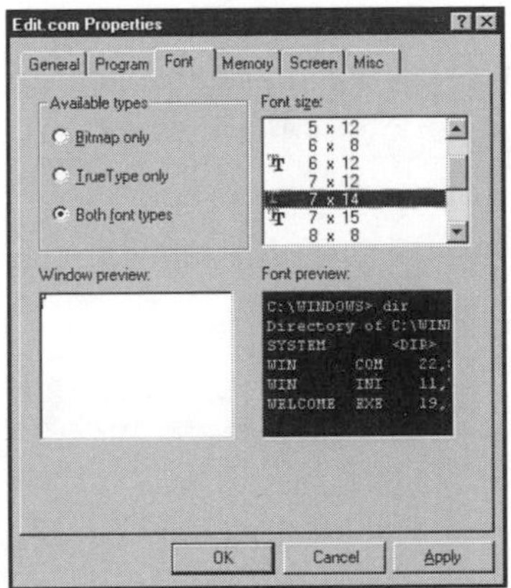

Figure 8.2

The Font tab of the MS-DOS Properties sheet.

Memory Tab

The Memory tab is used to specify what type and quantity of memory the program needs access to in order to function. The four supported types are as follows:

- Conventional
- Expanded (EMS)
- Extended (XMS)
- DOS protected mode (DPMI)

By default, Windows 95 automatically allocates the memory the application needs when the application first requests it during operation, but some applications function better if a fixed amount is allocated to them from the beginning.

The Initial environment setting is used to specify additional environment memory for variables and other MS-DOS settings.

As stated previously, you can use the Protected checkbox to provide a higher level of security for the MS-DOS memory of this program by preventing it from being paged to disk.

Using the Protected checkbox to provide greater security can have a detrimental effect on overall system performance.

Figure 8.3 shows an example of the memory tab for an MS-DOS application.

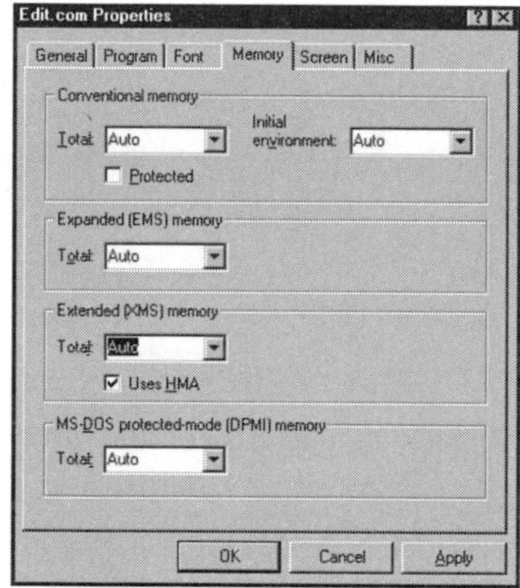

Figure 8.3

The Memory tab of the MS-DOS Properties sheet.

Screen Tab

The Screen tab contains settings to control how the application is displayed and how it uses video memory. Figure 8.4 shows an example of the Screen tab.

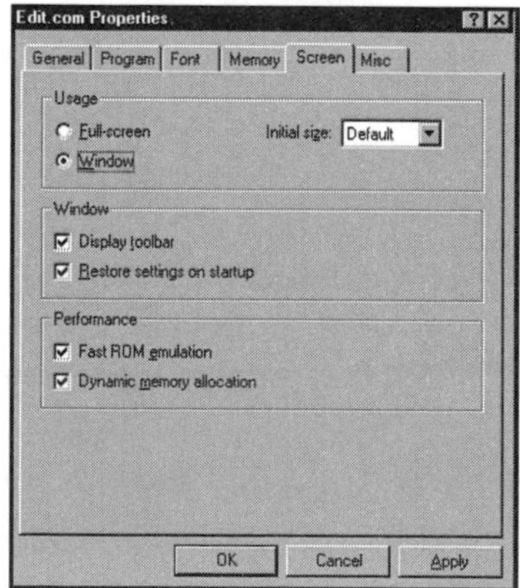

Figure 8.4

The Screen tab of the MS-DOS Properties sheet.

The settings of the Screen tab include the following:

- **Usage.** Specifies in which video mode the program initially appears. The choices are Full-screen (equivalent to what the program would look like in MS-DOS) or Window (a graphical mode simulation), which coexists with other windowed applications. The initial width and height (in characters) can also be specified using the Initial size field.
- **Display toolbar.** Used to specify whether Windows 95 will display a toolbar at the top of a windowed MS-DOS session. The toolbar contains Cut, Paste, and Full Screen buttons, among others.
- **Restore settings on startup.** When checked, restores all window settings (such as size, position, on so on) to what they were when the MS-DOS program was exited after the last time it was run. If this checkbox is not checked, the window uses the default MS-DOS window positioning settings.
- **Fast ROM emulation.** Allows screen updates to be accelerated by simulating video ROM drivers in protected mode. If display problems occur, this option should be disabled.
- **Dynamic memory allocation.** Involves reserving video memory for the application when it switches between video and text mode, in order to speed up this operation.

Misc Tab

The Misc tab contains other miscellaneous uncategorized settings for the application. Figure 8.5 shows a sample Misc tab for an MS-DOS application shortcut.

The following list describes the parameters of the Misc tab:

- **Allow screen saver box.** If checked, prevents any system screen saver from executing while the application is in the foreground. This is useful for applications that are easily disrupted or have a known problem with screen saver activity.

Figure 8.5

The Misc tab of the MS-DOS Properties sheet.

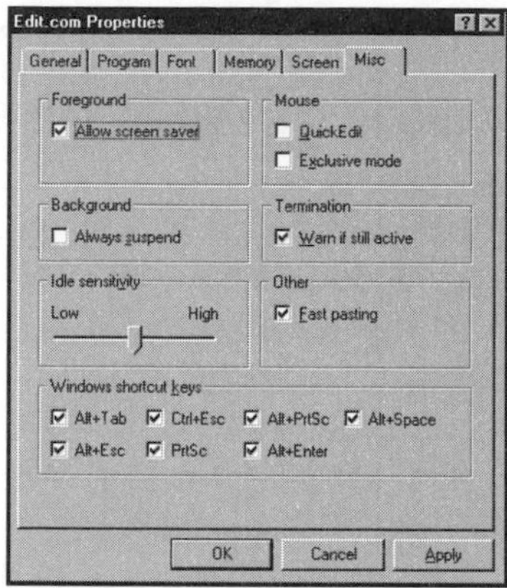

- **Always suspend.** If checked, the application ceases execution when not in the foreground.
- **Idle sensitivity.** This slide bar allows control of the amount of time the operating system waits before declaring the program to be inactive and suspending it.
- **Quick edit.** If checked, enables the user to highlight text in an MS-DOS window with the mouse. This feature should be disabled for applications that have their own DOS-based mouse support.
- **Exclusive mode.** If checked, contains the mouse within the borders of the MS-DOS window, to enforce compatibility with programs that cannot track the mouse properly when the mouse leaves the MS-DOS window.
- **Warn if still active.** If checked, warns users of potential data loss when they attempt to close an MS-DOS window without exiting the application.
- **Fast pasting.** Should be disabled if the application in question does not handle pasting from the Windows 95 Clipboard.
- **Windows shortcut keys.** Each checkbox allows or disallows use of a Windows shortcut key combination within an application. This is useful if an application has a number of shortcut keys that overlap with those of Windows 95.

MS-DOS Mode

Some MS-DOS applications are unable to run in an MS-DOS VM for one of several reasons:

- The application requires direct access to the hardware, which is not permitted in a multitasking environment because of potential device conflicts (this is the most common reason).
- The application has incompatible memory requirements.
- The application's install program, for compatibility reasons, checks to see whether Windows is running and will not continue if Windows is detected.
- The application has video problems (usually with MS-DOS games).

If any of these situations applies to the application in question, you may have to run the application in MS-DOS mode.

In MS-DOS mode, Windows 95 unloads itself from memory, leaving the PC in a single-tasking MS-DOS type of environment. All protected-mode support and drivers are removed, permitting the application to use only the CONFIG.SYS and AUTOEXEC.BAT parameters that were in effect at boot time before Windows 95 loaded. If the application needs a more particular configuration than that provided by default in the normal CONFIG.SYS and AUTOEXEC.BAT, you can create a customized MS-DOS environment for each application.

Customized MS-DOS Mode

If the application in question requires specific configuration parameters that differ significantly from those needed by most MS-DOS applications, you can create a customized CONFIG.SYS and AUTOEXEC.BAT that will be swapped with the standard versions of these files when you double-click on the application. For the settings in these customized files to take effect, Windows 95 must reboot the PC.

When Windows 95 restarts the PC, it uses the customized configuration files and inserts a special command into the CONFIG.SYS. The command reads `DOS=SINGLE` and indicates that this CONFIG.SYS and AUTOEXEC.BAT are to be used only once and that the system should return to the normal versions of these files when this application terminates.

> You need to remember that for Windows 95 to remove this parameter from the CONFIG.SYS and to allow Windows 95 to reboot properly, the application must be exited in the normal fashion. If the application hangs, or the computer is turned off without exiting, the parameter will not be removed, and the system will boot back into the MS-DOS application directly. To remedy this problem, restart the application and exit properly, or press F8 during the boot process and choose to go to a command prompt only, and then manually edit the CONFIG.SYS to remove the DOS=SINGLE parameter.

Exercise 8.1 demonstrates how to configure the various MS-DOS modes for a given application.

Exercise 8.1: Configuring MS-DOS Applications

1. Right-click on the My Computer icon and choose Explore. The Exploring window appears.
2. Click on the plus sign (+) next to the C drive. Subdirectories of the C drive are displayed.
3. Click on the + next to the Windows subdirectory. The tree expands to show the subdirectories of Windows.
4. Right-click on the COMMAND file in the right panel and choose Properties. The Properties COMMAND appears.
5. Click on the Memory tab. The list of configurable memory settings appears.
6. Set the EMS memory parameter to 4096 and choose OK. You are returned to the Explorer window.

7. Double-click on the COMMAND file. An MS-DOS window appears.

8. Type **MEM** and press Enter from the command prompt. Note that the free EMS reads as 4096 KB.

9. Type **EXIT** and press Enter. You are returned to the Explorer window.

10. Go back to the Properties sheet of the COMMAND file and change the EMS memory parameter to 16384 KB, choose OK, and double-click on the COMMAND file again. An MS-DOS window appears.

11. Type **MEM** and press Enter. Note that the free EMS memory now reads 16384 KB.

Even if the amount of memory you assign exceeds the physical RAM of the PC, the parameter will be accepted. The additional memory comes from the paging file system.

12. Type **EXIT** and press Enter. You are returned to the Explorer window.

13. Reset the EMS memory parameter to its original setting of Auto and choose OK. You are returned to the Explorer window.

14. Click on the Command folder. The files in the Command folder are displayed in the right panel of the Explorer window.

15. Right-click on the EDIT file and choose Properties. The Properties sheet for the EDIT file appears.

16. Click on the Program tab and then click on the Advanced button. The Advanced Program Settings window appears.

17. Click in the MS-DOS mode checkbox to enable use of standard MS-DOS mode support for this program. Some of the options below MS-DOS mode parameter become available.

18. Verify that Use current MS-DOS configuration is selected and choose OK. You are returned to the Properties window, and all other settings are disabled, since this file will now inherit all default MS-DOS settings.

19. Double-click on the EDIT file and click on Yes to continue. Windows 95 is unloaded, and the EDIT file is executed.

20. From the File menu, choose Open (or press Alt+F, O) to open a file for editing, type **\CONFIG.SYS** as the filename, and press Enter. The CONFIG.SYS file appears.

21. Note the contents of the file and press Alt+F, X to exit the program. Windows 95 restarts automatically.

22. When Windows 95 has restarted, go back to the Advanced Settings tab and choose to Specify a new MS-DOS configuration. The CONFIG.SYS and AUTOEXEC.BAT for MS-DOS mode are now available and have default settings already in place.

23. Click on the Configuration button. A Wizard appears that helps you select which options you would like to be active in your MS-DOS environment.

24. Verify that Expanded Memory is unchecked and that Disk Cache is checked; choose OK three times to close all Properties windows. You are returned to the Explorer window.

25. Double-click on the EDIT file again and choose Yes to continue. The system restarts, and the EDIT program is executed.

26. Choose File, Open to open a file for editing, type **\CONFIG.SYS** as the filename, and press Enter. The CONFIG.SYS file appears for editing (note that DOS=SINGLE has been added to the file).

27. Choose File, Open to open a file for editing, type **\AUTOEXEC.BAT** as the filename, and press Enter. The AUTOEXEC.BAT file appears for editing (note that a SmartDrive command has been added).

28. Choose File, Exit (or press Alt+F, X) to exit the program and then press any key. The system restarts, and Windows 95 loads normally.

29. Go back to the Properties sheet of the EDIT file and disable MS-DOS mode.

32-Bit Windows Applications

Windows 95 is designed to support and best interact with 32-bit applications specifically designed for Windows 95 or for Windows NT. These applications are best suited to take advantage of the new architectural design features of Windows 95. These design features include the following:

- The capability to take advantage of Windows 95's flat 32-bit, 4-GB memory address space (WIN32 applications typically load into the 4-MB to 2-GB range of memory)
- The capability to pass more information in a single 32-bit programming call than is possible with a single 16-bit programming call, thus increasing processing performance
- The capability to submit multiple simultaneous threads for processing, allowing greater user productivity within the 32-bit application since the user does not need to wait for one task to finish in order to start another
- The capability to take advantage of Windows 95's preemptive multitasking, which is more efficient and runs more smoothly than Windows 3.1's cooperative multitasking
- More comprehensive protection from other applications because each WIN32 application is assigned its own separate address space that is not visible to other applications

- A separate message queue for each thread in a WIN32 application, which prevents other applications from interfering with the receipt or processing of system messages
- The capability to use the Registry to store all application settings on a generic or per-user basis
- The capability of the application to uninstall itself more easily than previous application types, because all changes to the Registry can be tracked and rolled back in the case of uninstallation

WIN32 API Set in Windows 95 versus Windows NT

An *Application Programming Interface* (API) is a library of preprogrammed functions upon which application developers can call when they require an operation to be performed and do not want to develop the programming code for the operation from scratch (for example, drawing a box on the screen with a message in it). To speed up development and enhance the consistency of the Windows 95 look and feel by having developers use the same programming routines to do the same things, Microsoft provides various API sets. Many of the 32-bit functions that are used both internally by the Windows 95 operating system and by third-party developers are contained in an API set called the WIN32 API.

Although a form of this WIN32 API set is available for Windows 3.1 (called WIN32s), the version standard to Windows 95 has these additional features:

- Multithreading
- The capability to create Bezier curves mathematically
- The use of paths to create outlines, shapes, and filled areas
- The capability to generate Enhanced Metafiles, a new page description format used primarily for printing

Windows NT also uses a WIN32 API set, but one that is slightly different from that of Windows 95 in that it supports NT-specific features such as the following:

- Security functions
- Logging system events
- Unicode (multilanguage support)
- Functions specific to the Windows NT Registry

Finally, some features are new to Windows 95 and thus are supported in the Windows 95 WIN32 API but not in that of Windows NT (although they are expected to be implemented in the next release of Windows NT). These features are discussed elsewhere in this book. Briefly, they are as follows:

- Image Color Matching support
- Enhanced modem support features (primarily TAPI)
- User interface-related functions (right-clicking, the Task Bar, and so on)
- Plug and Play support
- Video for Windows support

Configuring 32-Bit Applications

Almost any configuration that needs to be done on 32-bit applications can be done from within the application or from its Properties sheet. As stated previously, all settings for WIN32 applications are stored in the Registry, usually under the key HKEY_LOCAL_MACHINE\SOFTWARE.

In rare instances, these settings can become corrupted due to the following circumstances:

- Corruption of the actual Registry file SYSTEM.DAT
- Aborted application installations, which only partially create the requisite Registry entries

- Repeated installation/uninstallation

In these instances, editing the settings manually in the Registry may be necessary.

Attempt to edit the Registry only if you know exactly which setting to modify in the SOFTWARE subkey. Improper modification of parameters in the Registry can seriously damage the operating system.

Application Properties and Interaction

Exercise 8.2 shows how the properties of different types of applications are reflected in the operating system's behavior. Please verify that the System Monitor component is installed for the purposes of the exercise. As well, make certain no applications other than the System Monitor are running, unless otherwise directed during the exercise. Results during this exercise may vary based on timing, especially where threads are concerned.

Exercise 8.2: Configuring Application Properties

1. Click on the Start button and then choose **P**rograms, Accessories, System Tools and click on System Monitor. The System Monitor window appears, typically showing Processor usage by default.

2. From the View menu, choose Numeric Charts. The display changes from graphical to numeric.

3. From the **E**dit menu, choose **R**emove Item. A list of all currently tracked system items is displayed.

4. Select all items in the list and choose OK to remove them. The items are removed, and you are returned to a blank System Monitor window.

5. From the **E**dit menu, choose **A**dd Item box. The Add Item dialog box appears.

6. From the Kernel category, hold down the Ctrl key and select Threads and Virtual machines as the items to be tracked. Choose OK. You are returned to the System Monitor window, showing the number of currently active threads and virtual machines (note these numbers—they include threads and VMs run by the operating system itself).

7. From the Start menu, select **R**un and open the 16-bit Notepad.exe program. A notepad window appears (the number of threads should increase by 1, and the number of VMs should stay constant).

8. Minimize Notepad and, from the Start menu, open an Explorer window (32-bit program). An Explorer window appears (note that the number of threads jumps by 2 or 3, and the number of VMs again remains the same).

9. From the Start menu, choose **P**rograms, MS-DOS Prompt. An MS-DOS window appears (note that the number of threads jumps by 2, and the number of VMs jumps by 1).

10. Minimize the MS-DOS window and open another MS-DOS Prompt. A second MS-DOS window appears (note that the number of threads again jumps by 2, and the number of VMs jumps by 1).

11. Close all applications except System Monitor. Eventually, the number of threads and VMs should return to their original values.

The important points to note about the preceding exercise are the following:

- All WIN16 and WIN32 applications reside in the System VM, which is always active from the time Windows 95 boots (that is why the VM count started at 1), but each MS-DOS session requires its own VM (thus, as you opened MS-DOS sessions, the VM count increased).

- When a WIN16 application (Notepad) is started, it creates a single thread, whereas a WIN32 application (Explorer in our example) can create several threads.
- MS-DOS sessions generate only one thread.

Although the exercise shows that opening an MS-DOS session actually creates two threads, remember that the application itself uses only one, whereas the other thread is used by associated processes.

Thunking

Windows 95 is divided into two types of core components: those implemented with 16-bit code, and those implemented with 32-bit code. The decision of how to implement each core component was based on issues of performance and compatibility. In other words, if the component's main function was to support backward compatibility with WIN16 applications (the user interface, for example), the component was implemented with 16-bit code. If the main function or objective of the component was to enhance performance (the file system), the component was implemented in 32-bit code.

This creates the problem of communication between the different components, however, because 16-bit applications understand only 16-bit code, and 32-bit applications understand only 32-bit code. To facilitate communication between 16-bit applications that need access to 32-bit components and vice versa, thunking was developed. *Thunking* is the process of translating a 16-bit API call into a 32-bit API call (called *thunking up*) or vice versa (called *thunking down*).

Troubleshooting Problems with Applications

Although applications should normally run without interruption, situations do arise where, due to either programming errors or incompatibilities, applications cease to function properly. The two main problems that occur with applications are General Protection Faults (GPFs) and application hangs.

General Protection Faults

A *General Protection Fault* (GPF) typically is caused by an application that attempts to violate system integrity in one of a number of ways:

- By making a request to read or write to a memory address space owned by another application
- By attempting to access the system hardware directly
- By attempting to interact with a failing hardware driver (drivers operate at Ring 0 and so can seriously impact the operating system)

The GPF is generated when the operating system shuts down an offending application to prevent a system integrity violation. How the offending application is specifically handled is dependent on its application type.

Because MS-DOS applications reside in their own VM and have their own message queue, if they cause a GPF, a message is displayed, and the application is simply terminated without impacting the rest of the operating system.

In the case of WIN16 applications, the procedure is somewhat more complex. Because WIN16 applications share both a common address space and a common message queue, when one application creates a GPF, all others are suspended until the offending application is terminated. After this is done, the remaining applications resume processing.

Finally, with 32-bit applications, the procedure is quite straightforward. Because 32-bit applications exist in their own separate address space, and each has a separate message queue, a GPF in one 32-bit application in no way impacts any other 16- or 32-bit programs. The offending program is simply terminated.

Application Hangs

An application is said to be "hung" when it is running but is not responding to messages from the operating system. Much improved support exists in Windows 95 for a local reboot of the application in question, which permits the application to be terminated without impacting other currently running processes. A local reboot is performed by pressing Ctrl+Alt+Del once, which brings up a Close Program dialog box. Listed in this box are all currently running tasks (including system processes not otherwise listed on the Task Bar). You must then select a process (next to the process name, "Not Responding" usually is indicated in brackets) and click on the End Task button. The operating system then attempts to terminate the process (which might take several seconds). Depending on the reason that the application is hung, you also might be presented with the option to wait a few seconds for the application to respond, and then to terminate the application if no response is received.

The following sections describe some considerations you should make when an application hangs, based on the application type:

- MS-DOS
- Windows 16-bit Subsystem (Win16)
- Windows 32-bit Subsystem (Win32)

MS-DOS Application

A normal local reboot as described previously should work on an MS-DOS session because the MS-DOS application exists in its own VM and has its own message queue—a hung MS-DOS session does not impact the operation of any other process.

An MS-DOS session also can be terminated from the Properties sheet of the session if the session is in a window.

16-Bit Windows Application

As stated earlier, because WIN16 applications share a common memory address space and a common message queue, if a WIN16 process hangs while in the foreground, all other WIN16 processes cease to receive messages from the operating system and also appear hung.

This is due to a flag that is set for WIN16 processes, known as the *WIN16 Mutex* (Mutually Exclusive). Because 16-bit code is considered non-reentrant (it cannot be used by more than one process at a time), a system must be in place to ensure that no two processes attempt to use the same piece of 16-bit code simultaneously. Under Windows 95, this is done by enforcing the rule that only the process that currently owns the rights to the WIN16 Mutex is able to make requests to 16-bit API functions. When the given process is finished using the 16-bit code, it hands the Mutex to the next process.

If an application hangs while it owns the WIN16 Mutex, no other application can access 16-bit API functions. Thus, all 16-bit applications appear to be hung. In addition, any 32-bit application that requires the use, through thunking, of a 16-bit API function (such as writing to the screen) also appears to be hung. The application is still running but cannot make any updates to the screen, and thus appears to be inactive or unresponsive.

To remedy this situation, the 16-bit application that currently holds thc Mutcx must be locally rebooted through the means described previously. After this is done, the Mutex should be reset and available for use by other processes.

32-Bit Windows Application

Just testing to see whether you have been paying attention! A 32-bit application will not hang the system, since it will be preemptively multitasked. In other words, control will be taken away from a misbehaving Win32 application even if does not want to relinquish control.

Review Questions

The following questions will test your knowledge of the information in this chapter. For additional questions, see MCP Endeavor and the Microsoft Roadmap/Assessment Exam on the CD-ROM that accompanies this book.

1. Every Windows 95 application is executed from within a specialized container called ______.

   A. an application box

   B. a virtual partition

   C. a task space

   D. a virtual machine

2. Which two of the following are operating modes for Intel processors?

   A. Enhanced mode

   B. protected mode

   C. Fault mode

   D. Real mode

3. In the Intel ring protection scheme, Ring ______ allows complete control of the processor.

   A. 1

   B. 0

   C. 3

   D. 4

4. Which of the following is true?

   A. Most Windows 95 applications run in Ring 3.

   B. Most operating system components run in Ring 3.

   C. Windows 95 uses all Intel rings.

   D. Windows 95 uses only Rings 1, 2, and 3.

5. WIN16 applications use ______ multitasking.

   A. fault-tolerant

   B. preemptive

   C. cooperative

   D. real-mode

6. Which of the following is true?

   A. WIN16 applications do not access the Registry.

   B. WIN16 applications do not use the System VM.

   C. WIN16 applications support multithreading.

   D. Each WIN16 application has its own message queue.

7. If possible, it is best to run MS-DOS applications in ______.

   A. MS-DOS mode

   B. customized MS-DOS mode

   C. a WIN16 virtual machine

   D. an MS-DOS virtual machine

8. In MS-DOS mode, Windows 95 ______.

   A. unloads itself from memory

   B. remains in memory

   C. runs the application in protected mode

   D. can multithread multiple DOS sessions

9. What command is added to the CONFIG.SYS when you run a customized MS-DOS-mode application?

   A. DOS=Custom

   B. MODE=DOSCUST

   C. DOS=CMODE

   D. DOS=SINGLE

10. Settings for WIN32 applications are stored primarily in the Registry under the key ______.

    A. HKEY_CURRENT_CONFIG\SOFT,WARE

    B. HKEY_LOCAL_MACHINE\SOFTWARE

    C. HKEY_LOCAL_MACHINE\APPLICATIONS\WIN32

    D. HKEY_CLASSES_ROOT\WIN32

11. The process of translating a 16-bit API call to a 32-bit API call is called ______.

    A. bumping

    B. trans-interfacing

    C. retooling

    D. thunking up

12. Which three of the following are common causes for General Protection Faults?

    A. An attempt to access system hardware directly

    B. Failure of a hardware driver

    C. A request to read or write to a memory address space owned by another application

    D. An attempt to access an unTimized protection ring

13. In Windows 95, pressing Ctrl+Alt+Del once produces ______.

    A. a reboot of the system
    B. a local reboot of the application
    C. a system shutdown
    D. a dialog box that lets you shift control to another current application

Review Answers

1. D
2. B D
3. B
4. A
5. C
6. A
7. D
8. A
9. D
10. B
11. D
12. A B C
13. B

Chapter 9

Mobile Services

Windows 95 Mobile Services are a collection of services designed to enhance the connectivity and productivity of remote users. A remote user can be a traveler with a laptop or a desktop user who needs to access a network from a remote location.

In this chapter, the following components of the Windows 95 Mobile Services are discussed:

- Dial-Up Networking architecture
- Configuring a Dial-Up Networking client
- Using applications with a Dial-Up Networking connection
- Using the Microsoft Plus Pack Dial-Up Networking Server
- Optimizing Dial-Up Networking performance
- Using the Briefcase

With the exception of the Briefcase, most of the Windows 95 Mobile Services features are accessed through the Dial-Up Networking tools. Dial-Up Networking typically is used to connect to an Internet service provider or to connect a corporate network from a remote location. For example, Dial-Up Networking can be used to access an Internet e-mail account, or to dial into the company network from home.

Windows 95 offers numerous enhancements to the remote connectivity features of Windows for Workgroups 3.11 as shown in table 9.1. Windows 3.1 does not include any integrated remote networking features, and therefore is not listed.

Table 9.1

Mobile Services Features of Windows 95 and Windows for Workgroups

Windows for Workgroups	Windows 95
As a client, can only use Remote Access Service (RAS)	Can be a RAS, SLIP, PPP, or Novell NetWare Connect client
With a Windows for Workgroups RAS server, a RAS client cannot access the rest of the network	Can function as a RAS or PPP server and act as a gateway to the rest of the network
One phone book for all users using the client computer	Allows user-specific connection settings and phone books
Log file for troubleshooting is MODEMLOG.TXT, which logs only modem commands	PPPLOG.TXT and MODEMLOG.TXT can be used to log connection-specific information and PPP information
Direct cable connections difficult to establish and supported only over serial links	Direct cable connections are wizard-driven supported over serial and parallel links

Additional features of Dial-Up Networking with Windows 95 include the following:

- Support for most LAN topologies such as Ethernet, FDDI (fiber optic), Token Ring, and ARCnet
- The capability to connect to Windows NT, LAN Manager, Windows for Workgroups, IBM LAN Server, Shiva LAN Rover, and other remote access systems using any number of supported protocols
- Advanced security features such as password encryption
- Support for all modems recognized by Windows 95
- The capability to use link compression to increase data throughput

Dial-Up Networking Architecture

The architectural reference model for Dial-Up Networking is shown in figure 9.1. Data from an application is passed down through the layers, across the phone line, and up through the layers to the receiving application. In this respect, the Dial-Up Networking architecture is similar to the OSI Reference Model discussed in Part II of this book, "Networking Essentials." The top layer of the Dial-Up Networking reference model represents the network-aware applications, whereas the bottom layer represents the modem and phone line over which the network protocol frames are sent. The intermediate layers translate and package the application requests into a particular network protocol (TCP/IP, NetBEUI, or IPX/SPX-compatible), and then into a particular line protocol (SLIP, PPP, or RAS). Once the data is in a line protocol format, it can be sent over the line (phone, serial cable, or other) to be received by another computer on the other end of the line.

Figure 9.1

The Dial-Up Networking architecture model.

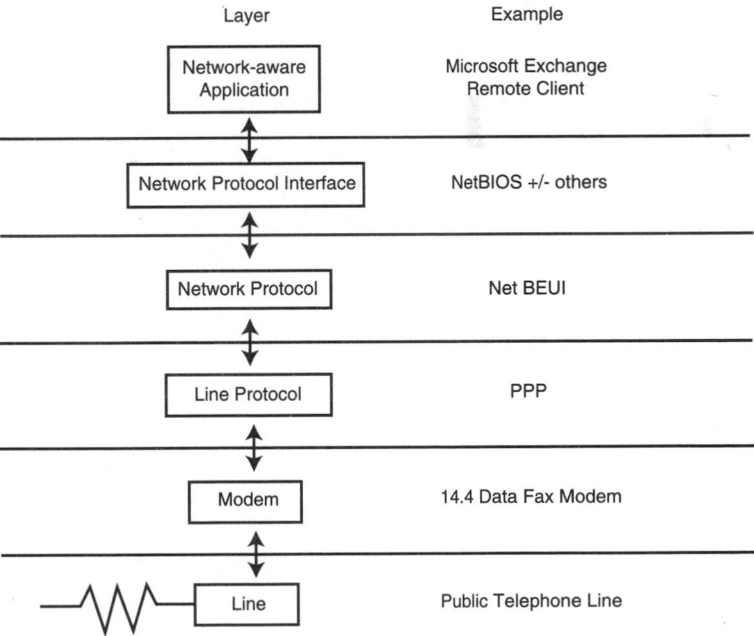

Dial-Up Networking Architecture Model

Network Interfaces

Dial-Up Networking supports any of the following network interface standards:

- NetBIOS
- Mailslots
- Named pipes
- Remote procedure calls
- LAN Manager function calls
- TCP/IP utilities
- Windows sockets

These interfaces are described in more detail in Part II of this book.

Network Protocols

Dial-Up Networking supports the following network protocols:

- NetBEUI (primarily used by Microsoft network LANs and other NetBIOS-compatible networks)
- IPX/SPX-compatible (primarily used by Novell NetWare)
- TCP/IP (used by Unix hosts, the Internet, and most large networks)

These listed protocols are supported only in their 32-bit protected-mode implementations as provided with Windows 95. You cannot use Dial-Up Networking with a real-mode IPX protocol such as that provided by Novell and installed through the AUTOEXEC.BAT, for example.

The listed protocols are discussed in more detail in Chapter 18, "Protocol Suites."

Line Protocols

Line protocols are the means by which network protocols are transported over communication media types for which they were not originally intended. In this way, for example, TCP/IP can be supported over a phone line even if it was actually designed to be transported over network cable. Windows 95 supports four line protocols:

- Point-to-Point Protocol (PPP)
- Serial Line Interface Protocol (SLIP)
- Remote Access Service (RAS)
- NetWare Remote Networking (NRN)

Point-to-Point Protocol (PPP)

The Point-to-Point Protocol is the default when you install Dial-Up Networking. It was originally developed for the TCP/IP environment but has replaced the less flexible RAS as the line protocol of choice.

PPP was designed for the capacity to transport a wide variety of networking protocols across serial links. It has the following additional features:

- Allows multiplexing of sessions across a single serial link, enabling multiple network applications to appear to communicate simultaneously
- Allows multiple network protocols to be transported simultaneously over a single link
- Supports software compression to increase throughput

- Supports automatic negotiation of addressing, thus allowing a dynamic IP address to be assigned to the dial-up client

> To use software compression over PPP, software compression must be supported by both the client and the server portion of the link. Typically only Microsoft applications support both client and server software compression over PPP, so you are likely required to connect to a Microsoft-based server product (such as Windows NT) to take advantage of compression.

- Supports error detection

The following network protocols are supported for use over a PPP line connection:

- TCP/IP
- IPX/SPX-compatible
- NetBEUI

Because PPP supports multiple network protocols, you can connect to many different types of remote systems, including these:

- Windows 95 Dial-Up Networking servers
- Windows NT 3.5 RAS servers
- Shiva LANRover
- Internet dial-up service providers

The resources that can be accessed after you are connected to any of these systems depends entirely on how the remote system is configured (what protocols are being supported, whether the system is connected to a network and acting as a gateway, and so on).

Windows 95 Dial-Up Networking Servers

Connecting to a Windows 95 Dial-Up Networking server gives a PPP client potential access to the following:

- NetWare servers, if the server is attached to a Novell network and is using IPX/SPX as one if its protocols
- Microsoft-based servers such as Windows NT, Windows for Workgroups, and LAN Manager, if the Windows 95 Dial-Up Networking server has NetBEUI installed (or another protocol common to all connected systems) and is connected to a network

Windows NT 3.5 RAS Servers

If you dial in to a Windows NT 3.5 server, you can access the following:

- NetWare servers, if the server is attached to an Novell network and is using IPX/SPX as one if its protocols
- Microsoft-based servers such as Windows NT, Windows for Workgroups, and LAN Manager, if the Windows 95 Dial-Up Networking server has NetBEUI installed (or another protocol common to all connected systems) and is connected to a network
- The Internet, if the NT server is set to act as an Internet gateway and is connected to the Internet

Shiva LANRover

Windows 95 Dial-Up Networking clients can access a Shiva LANRover remote access server to connect to NetWare servers. For information on configuring the Shiva LANRover remote access server refer to documentation for that product.

Internet Dial-Up Service Providers

By dialing into an Internet service provider and using TCP/IP, you can access resources connected to the Internet. For example, many Internet service providers include Internet mail services that you can connect to using PPP.

Serial Line Interface Protocol (SLIP)

SLIP is an older line protocol specification that was popular before the development of PPP. Although SLIP, like PPP, was developed primarily for the TCP/IP environment, it has the following limitations:

- It does not support addressing information, thus both client and server must have preconfigured IP addresses or the user is prompted at logon for the client IP address.
- It does not support multiple protocols, therefore only a single protocol can be transported over the line.
- It has no error detection or correction.
- It has no data compression support (although you can compress the IP header information).

TCP/IP is the only supported network protocol for use with a SLIP line connection.

SLIP can be used to connect to resources such as the following:

- The Internet
- Private TCP/IP networks

Microsoft does not provide any products capable of being a SLIP server. The dial-in SLIP server must be an Internet service provider or other third-party server product.

Remote Access Service (RAS)

Originally introduced in Microsoft LAN Manager 2.1, RAS is a proprietary protocol developed by Microsoft. Although it is a relatively fast and efficient line protocol, it does not support multiple network protocols. It should be used strictly for backward compatibility with older Microsoft products.

The network protocol that RAS supports is NetBEUI. Using RAS, Windows 95 can connect to the following:

- Windows 95 Dial-Up Networking servers
- Windows NT 3.1 and 3.5*x*
- Windows for Workgroups 3.11
- LAN Manager 2.1 and above

The resources that are available when you are connected depend on the configuration of the dial-up server. Generally, the following conditions hold true:

- If connected to Windows for Workgroups, only the shared resources of the dial-up server are available.
- If connected to a Windows 95 Dial-Up Networking server or any Windows NT server, all NetBIOS-compatible resources on the local network are available.
- If connected to a LAN Manager server, all shared NetBEUI resources on the local network are available.

NetWare Remote Networking (NRN)

The NRN line protocol is used exclusively to connect to Novell NetWare Connect servers using the IPX/SPX-compatible network protocol. When you are connected, all NetWare servers that share the network with the NetWare Connect server should be accessible.

NetWare Connect servers also provide the capability to create modem-sharing pools and to remotely control other workstations. These capabilities are not supported using Dial-Up Networking.

Whereas Windows 95 Dial-Up Networking clients can dial into NetWare Connect servers, native Novell workstations cannot dial into Windows 95 Dial-Up Networking servers because they do not support the Microsoft NetBIOS-compatible implementation of the Microsoft IPX/SPX-compatible protocol.

WAN Support

In addition to traditional modem-based Dial-Up Networking support, Windows 95 also supports the following communication media:

- X.25
- Integrated Services Digital Network (ISDN)

X.25

X.25 is a networking communication standard that uses a packet-switching protocol to carry data over a worldwide network, often using public carriers (for example, Datapac).

Integrated Services Digital Network (ISDN)

ISDN is a relatively new standard for digital telephone communication. This standard offers much higher and more reliable transfer rates than analog phone lines (usually 64 Kbps to 128 Kbps) but requires a proprietary ISDN modem type.

Although modems are treated as analog communication media, X.25 and ISDN hardware are treated as network cards, and provide a direct data feed across the network.

Log Files

To diagnose connection problems when using Dial-Up Networking, Windows 95 provides two log files:

- PPPLOG.TXT
- MODEMLOG.TXT

PPPLOG.TXT

The PPPLOG.TXT file contains information on how the software layers of PPP have processed a Dial-Up Networking call. This logging feature is disabled by default. To enable PPP logging, select the Dial-Up Adapter in the Network Control Panel Applet, select the Advanced tab of the Properties sheet, and change the value for "Record a log file" to Yes.

The following is a sample PPPLOG.TXT file:

```
04-29-1996 22:19:40.52 - Remote access driver log opened.
04-29-1996 22:19:40.52 - Installable CP VxD SPAP     is loaded
04-29-1996 22:19:40.52 - Server type is  PPP (Point to Point
➥Protocol).
04-29-1996 22:19:40.52 - FSA : Adding Control Protocol 80fd (CCP)
➥to control protocol chain.
04-29-1996 22:19:40.52 - FSA : Adding Control Protocol 803f
➥(NBFCP) to control protocol chain.
04-29-1996 22:19:40.52 - FSA : Protocol not bound - skipping
➥control protocol 8021 (IPCP).
04-29-1996 22:19:40.53 - FSA : Protocol not bound - skipping
➥control protocol 802b (IPXCP).
04-29-1996 22:19:40.53 - FSA : Adding Control Protocol c029
➥(CallbackCP) to control protocol chain.
04-29-1996 22:19:40.53 - FSA : Adding Control Protocol c027 (no
➥description) to control protocol chain.
04-29-1996 22:19:40.53 - FSA : Adding Control Protocol c023 (PAP)
➥to control protocol chain.
04-29-1996 22:19:40.53 - FSA : Adding Control Protocol c223
➥(CHAP) to control protocol chain.
04-29-1996 22:19:40.53 - FSA : Adding Control Protocol c021 (LCP)
➥to control protocol chain.
04-29-1996 22:19:40.53 - LCP : Callback negotiation enabled.
```

```
04-29-1996 22:19:40.54 - LCP : Layer started.
04-29-1996 22:19:51.38 - Remote access driver is shutting down.
04-29-1996 22:19:51.38 - CRC Errors              0
04-29-1996 22:19:51.38 - Timeout Errors          0
04-29-1996 22:19:51.38 - Alignment Errors        0
04-29-1996 22:19:51.38 - Overrun Errors          0
04-29-1996 22:19:51.38 - Framing Errors          0
04-29-1996 22:19:51.38 - Buffer Overrun Errors   0
04-29-1996 22:19:51.38 - Incomplete Packets      0
04-29-1996 22:19:51.38 - Bytes Received          1
04-29-1996 22:19:51.38 - Bytes Transmitted     213
04-29-1996 22:19:51.38 - Frames Received         0
04-29-1996 22:19:51.38 - Frames Transmitted      4
04-29-1996 22:19:51.38 - Remote access driver log closed.
```

The PPP log file shows the date and time for each entry to the log file as well as a description of the entry. In the preceding log file, the PPP protocols were successfully bound to the Remote Access driver, except that the IPX and IP protocols were not bound, because they were not installed on the client. The log file then shows only a brief callback negotiation period, followed by the Remote Access driver shutting down. This is probably because the client was unable to make a successful connection to the dial-up server. The latter part of the log file shows the transmission and error statistics.

MODEMLOG.TXT

Although the MODEMLOG.TXT log file is not specific to Dial-Up Networking, it is nonetheless very useful in troubleshooting connection difficulties. It records all AT-type commands sent to the modem, and also logs responses from the modem. This logging feature is disabled by default.

> Modem command logging is available only when you use Windows 95 TAPI-compliant communication software. Because Windows 3.1 communication software does not use the same software layers to communicate with the modem, Windows 95 cannot trap the AT commands that these applications send to the modem.

To enable modem command logging, select the modem in the Modems Control Panel Applet, select the Connection tab of the Properties sheet, choose Ad<u>v</u>anced, and then choose Rec<u>o</u>rd a log file.

The following is a sample MODEMLOG.TXT file:

```
04-29-1996 22:14:14.75 - 14.4 Data FAX Modem in use.
04-29-1996 22:14:14.78 - Modem type: 14.4 Data FAX Modem
04-29-1996 22:14:14.78 - Modem inf path: MDMCPI.INF
04-29-1996 22:14:14.78 - Modem inf section: Modem20
04-29-1996 22:14:15.05 - 57600,N,8,1
04-29-1996 22:14:15.36 - 57600,N,8,1
04-29-1996 22:14:15.38 - Initializing modem.
04-29-1996 22:14:15.38 - Send: AT<cr>
04-29-1996 22:14:15.38 - Recv: AT<cr>
04-29-1996 22:14:15.52 - Recv: <cr><lf>OK<cr><lf>
04-29-1996 22:14:15.52 - Interpreted response: Ok
04-29-1996 22:14:15.52 - Send: AT &F E0 V1 &D2 &C1 S95=47 W1
➥S0=0<cr>
04-29-1996 22:14:15.54 - Recv: AT &F E0 V1 &D2 &C1 S95=47 W1
➥S0=0<cr>
04-29-1996 22:14:15.67 - Recv: <cr><lf>OK<cr><lf>
04-29-1996 22:14:15.67 - Interpreted response: Ok
04-29-1996 22:14:15.67 - Send: ATS7=60S30=0L1M1&K3B0N1X4<cr>
04-29-1996 22:14:15.82 - Recv: <cr><lf>OK<cr><lf>
04-29-1996 22:14:15.82 - Interpreted response: Ok
04-29-1996 22:14:15.82 - Dialing.
04-29-1996 22:14:15.82 - Send: ATDT;<cr>
04-29-1996 22:14:17.09 - Recv: <cr><lf>OK<cr><lf>
04-29-1996 22:14:17.09 - Interpreted response: Ok
04-29-1996 22:14:17.09 - Dialing.
04-29-1996 22:14:17.09 - Send: ATDT#######<cr>
04-29-1996 22:14:43.63 - Recv: <cr>
04-29-1996 22:14:43.63 - Interpreted response: Informative
04-29-1996 22:14:43.63 - Recv: <lf>
04-29-1996 22:14:43.63 - Interpreted response: Informative
04-29-1996 22:14:43.63 - Recv: CARRIER 2400
04-29-1996 22:14:43.63 - Interpreted response: Informative
04-29-1996 22:14:43.63 - Recv: <cr>
04-29-1996 22:14:43.63 - Interpreted response: Informative
04-29-1996 22:14:43.63 - Recv: <lf>
04-29-1996 22:14:43.63 - Interpreted response: Informative
04-29-1996 22:14:43.63 - Recv: <cr>
```

```
04-29-1996 22:14:43.63 - Interpreted response: Informative
04-29-1996 22:14:43.63 - Recv: <lf>
04-29-1996 22:14:43.63 - Interpreted response: Informative
04-29-1996 22:14:43.63 - Recv: PROTOCOL: NONE
04-29-1996 22:14:43.63 - Interpreted response: Informative
04-29-1996 22:14:43.64 - Recv: <cr>
04-29-1996 22:14:43.64 - Interpreted response: Informative
04-29-1996 22:14:43.64 - Recv: <lf>
04-29-1996 22:14:43.64 - Interpreted response: Informative
04-29-1996 22:14:43.64 - Recv: <cr>
04-29-1996 22:14:43.64 - Interpreted response: Informative
04-29-1996 22:14:43.64 - Recv: <lf>
04-29-1996 22:14:43.64 - Interpreted response: Informative
04-29-1996 22:14:43.64 - Recv: CONNECT 2400
04-29-1996 22:14:43.64 - Interpreted response: Connect
04-29-1996 22:14:43.64 - Connection established at 2400bps.
04-29-1996 22:14:43.64 - Error-control off or unknown.
04-29-1996 22:14:43.64 - Data compression off or unknown.
04-29-1996 22:14:43.64 - Recv: <cr>
04-29-1996 22:14:44.04 - 57600,N,8,1
04-29-1996 22:14:57.18 - Remote modem hung up.
04-29-1996 22:14:59.20 - Recv: <no response>
04-29-1996 22:14:59.20 - WARNING: Unrecognized response.
➥Retrying...
04-29-1996 22:15:00.46 - Session Statistics:
04-29-1996 22:15:00.46 -                Reads : 344 bytes
04-29-1996 22:15:00.46 -                Writes: 98 bytes
04-29-1996 22:15:00.46 - 14.4 Data FAX Modem closed.
```

In the preceding log file, the following information might be useful for troubleshooting:

```
57600,N,8,1
```

(The maximum transmission rate, parity, data-bits, and stop-bits that have been configured)

```
Send: ATS7=60S30=0L1M1&K3B0N1X4<cr> ... Interpreted response: Ok
```

(A successful modem initialization string)

```
Connection established at 2400bps
```

(Might explain why the connection was so slow. The server modem was likely 2400 bps.)

```
Remote modem hung up.
```

(Could be due either to the client having logged off, or to the server having terminated the connection.)

Configuring a Dial-Up Networking Client

To install Dial-Up Networking (client or server components), the following requirements must be met:

- One or more modems must be installed and configured.
- 2 MB of free disk space for client and server software must be available.
- Optionally, hardware for X.25 or ISDN connections must be installed.

Exercise 9.1 demonstrates the configuration of Dial-Up Networking for the Internet. This exercise assumes you have not yet configured a modem for Windows 95, but that one is physically installed in your computer and has a port associated with it in the Device Manager (for example, an internal modem configured to use COM3 should show up in Device Manager as a COM3 port). If not, you may have to use the Add New Hardware icon to allow Windows 95 to detect the port before proceeding with this exercise. The Dial-Up Networking components should already have been installed through Add/Remove Programs in the Control Panel. The TCP/IP protocol also should have been installed through the Network option in Control Panel. Finally, since this is an Internet-related exercise, if you do not have Internet access, you can substitute another connection type, but your results might vary with those of the exercise.

Exercise 9.1: Installing Dial-Up Networking and Configuring for the Internet

1. Click on the Start button and select Settings, then Control Panel. Control Panel icons are displayed.
2. Double-click on the Modems icon. The Install New Modem wizard appears.
3. Choose the Next button. Windows 95 searches existing modem ports to find an attached modem, and should return with the correct modem type. An example is shown in figure 9.2.

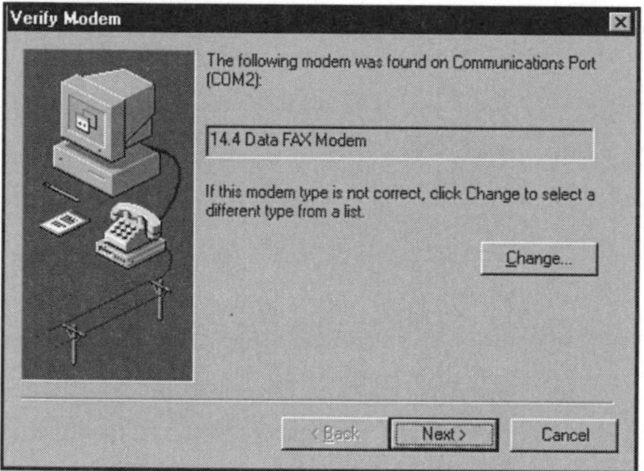

Figure 9.2

Detecting a modem.

If your modem is not auto-detected, you may need to manually specify it, based on the supported modem types with which it is compatible. Contact your modem manufacturer or consult your documentation for this information.

4. Choose the Next button. Windows 95 installs the modem driver.
5. Choose the Finish button. The Modems Properties sheet is displayed.
6. Choose Dialing Properties to display the Dialing Properties sheet.

7. Select your country, area code, and dialing method, and choose OK twice to close the Modems Properties sheet.

8. From the Control Panel, double-click on the Add/Remove Programs icon and select the Windows Setup tab to display the optional Windows 95 components.

9. Double-click on Communications and select Dial-Up Networking. Choose OK twice to close the Add/Remove Programs applet and start the copying of files from the distribution media.

10. Restart the computer when prompted to initialize the Dial-Up Networking components.

11. Choose the Start button and select Programs, Accessories, and then Dial-Up Networking. The Dial-Up Networking folder appears, and the Make New Connection Wizard is launched. Choose Next.

12. Select the modem to be used and type a name to use for the connection settings. Choose Next.

13. Type the phone number and country for the connection you want to make (you may need to get this information from your Internet provider). Choose Next.

14. Choose Finish to exit. The Dial-Up Networking folder will now show the new connection settings you created as an icon.

15. To verify the network-related settings for the new connection, right-click on the icon you created and choose Properties. The main properties sheet for the new connection is displayed.

16. Choose Server Type to view the network settings. The Server Types Properties sheet is displayed as shown in figure 9.3.

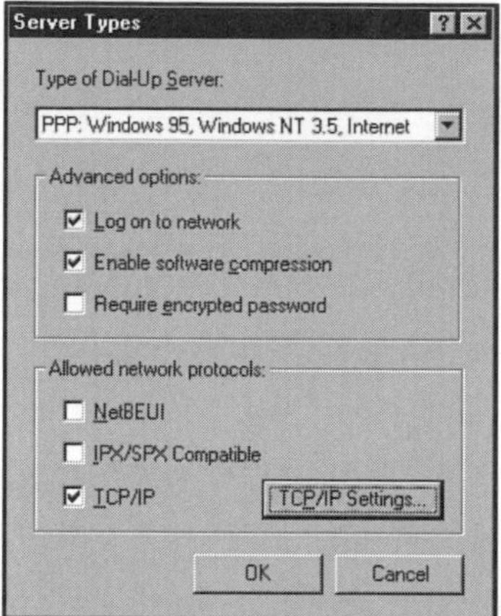

Figure 9.3

Configuring a dial-up connection.

By default, Dial-Up Networking is configured for a PPP connection using the TCP/IP, IPX/SPX-compatible, and NetBEUI protocols. You should uncheck a protocol if it is not needed for better performance.

17. Uncheck the NetBEUI and IPX/SPX Compatible protocols and click on the TCP/IP Settings button. The current settings for TCP/IP are displayed.

18. Enter the appropriate settings for your Internet provider (you need to obtain these from your provider) and click on OK three times until all property sheets are closed. You are returned to the Dial-Up Networking folder.

19. Double-click on the connection icon you created. You are prompted for a user name and password.

20. Type your user name and password for your Internet account, and choose the Connect button. A connection is attempted. If successful, the connection window displays the connection baud rate and active protocols (if Details is selected). You may now use your Internet tools to access Internet resources.

If the logon process for your Internet provider requires more information than just the user name and password, you might have to use the Dial-Up Scripting tool to provide this information at logon time. Consult your documentation for details.

Using Applications with a Dial-Up Networking Connection

You should note that, when you consider applications for use over a dial-up connection, focusing on those applications that are already installed at the server-side is best, because having to download and run the application at the client greatly reduces performance over the link. Ideal candidates for dial-up networking applications would be, for example, client/server products, which send only high-level commands over the link, reducing network traffic.

Using the Microsoft Plus Pack Dial-Up Networking Server

Besides functioning as a client, Windows 95 is capable of acting as a dial-up server to other clients. The Windows 95 Dial-Up Server is included with the Microsoft Plus Pack, which must be purchased separately from the Windows 95 operating system software.

In addition to providing remote users with access to the resources of the dial-up server itself, the Windows 95 Dial-Up Server also can provide remote clients with access to the NetBEUI or IPX/SPX-based resources of any network to which it is connected, effectively acting as a gateway to those resources.

Unlike Windows NT 3.5, Windows 95 cannot act as a gateway to TCP/IP resources or the Internet.

The Windows 95 Dial-Up Server can be configured as a PPP server or as a RAS server. RAS must be used by the older Microsoft operating systems as they do not support PPP. The clients that the Windows 95 Dial-Up Server supports are as follows:

- Windows 95 dial-up client
- Windows for Workgroups or Windows 3.1 (using RAS only)
- Windows NT 3.1 (using RAS only)
- Any client using PPP

Security Considerations

A number of issues must be considered before configuring Windows 95 as a Dial-Up Networking server. These include:

- File and Printer Sharing for either Microsoft or NetWare networks must be enabled on the server.
- User-level security should be enabled on the server to provide the highest level of protection from unauthorized access to shared resources.
- You can use hardware security tools and specific authentication protocols such as Challenge-Handshake Authentication Protocol (CHAP) or Shiva Password Authentication Protocol (SPAP) for additional security.
- You can specify a list of those users who can and cannot connect remotely, even if they are valid users when connected directly to the network.
- Encrypted passwords should be used.

Exercise 9.2 illustrates how the dial-up server can be configured to allow dial-up access to remote users. Please note that the exercise assumes the server components already have been installed from the Microsoft Plus Pack, and that File and Printer Sharing for Microsoft Networks and user-level security have been enabled. If all these conditions cannot be met (for example, if you are not on a Windows NT or Novell NetWare network and therefore cannot enable user-level security), you may use share-level security, but results may vary.

Exercise 9.2: Configuring the Dial-Up Networking Server

1. Click on the Start button, select **P**rograms, Accessories, and then Dial-Up Networking. The Dial-Up Networking folder is displayed.
2. From the **C**onnections menu, choose **D**ial-Up Server. The Dial-Up Server dialog box appears (see fig. 9.4).

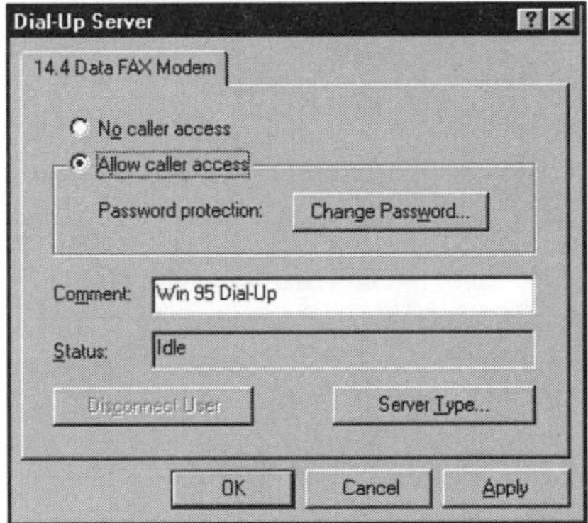

Figure 9.4

Configuring dial-up server security.

3. Select the A**l**low Caller Access radio button, and then choose the A**d**d button. A dialog appears that allows you to specify users who will have dial-up access.
4. Select users as desired, and click on OK. You are returned to the Dial-Up Server dialog box.
5. Choose the Server **T**ype button, verify that Default is selected, and choose OK twice to close all open windows. You are returned to the Desktop and are now ready to receive incoming calls.

If you select Default, Windows 95 automatically switches to a RAS line protocol if a PPP connection fails.

Optimizing Dial-Up Networking Performance

One way in which performance over dial-up connections can be improved is by using either hardware or software compression to reduce the amount of data that must be carried over the link. The distinction between the two types of compression lies in the fact that software compression is performed by the client and server applications, whereas hardware compression is performed by the modems involved in connecting the two systems. In the case of both software and hardware compression, the client and server must be able to support the same type of compression in order for it to function properly. Under Windows 95, only PPP supports software compression. The setting is ignored for other line protocols.

Software compression is generally preferred, if available, because it reduces the net amount of information to be transmitted over the link.

Using the Briefcase

Another tool in Windows 95 that can be used to increase the efficiency of mobile computing is the Briefcase. One of the many difficulties of mobile computing is transporting and maintaining files that, for example, are used both at a central location (an office) and with a laptop computer while traveling. The difficulty lies in ensuring that the user is always working with the latest revision of the file and is not duplicating or negating previous work.

The Briefcase addresses this problem by tracking document revisions and comparing them based on their time and date stamps. If the user chooses to synchronize objects that have been placed in the Briefcase, the Briefcase replaces unmodified revisions with modified ones. If more than one revision has been modified, Windows 95 launches the associated application for that file type so that the changes in both can be merged.

The Briefcase also can track documents used by multiple users on the same network, using the same algorithms to compare changes made by different users.

Exercise 9.3 demonstrates the configuration and use of the Briefcase. The exercise assumes that the Briefcase component has already been installed and a Briefcase icon exists on the Desktop. If this is not the case, you might need to install the Briefcase component through Add/Remove Programs in the Control Panel. You also need a blank formatted floppy for this exercise.

If the Briefcase component does not appear in the list of installable components, the component probably is already installed, but the icon on the Desktop has been deleted. To recreate this icon, simply right-click on the Desktop, choose Ne**w**, and click on Briefcase.

Exercise 9.3: Configuring and Using the Briefcase

1. Right-click on an empty area on the Desktop, choose Ne**w**, and then choose Text Document. You are prompted for a name for the new text document.
2. Double-click on the document. Notepad is launched and the empty document is displayed.
3. Type **REV1** on the first line, from the **F**ile menu choose E**x**it, and then choose **Y**es to save the file. You are returned to the Desktop.
4. Double-click on the Briefcase icon on the Desktop. A Welcome screen briefly describes the use of the Briefcase.
5. Click on the Finish button. The Briefcase file list (currently empty) is displayed.
6. Using the right mouse button, drag the TEST.TXT file from the Desktop to the Briefcase window and, when prompted, choose Make Sync **C**opy. The file is linked to the Briefcase.

7. Close the Briefcase window. You are returned to the Desktop.

8. Insert a blank formatted floppy disk in drive A, right-click on New Briefcase, and from the Se**n**d To menu, choose the A drive. The Briefcase is moved to the floppy.

9. Double-click on the TEST.TXT file on the Desktop. Notepad is launched, displaying the file.

10. Type **REV2** on the second line and from the **F**ile menu, choose E**x**it and then choose **Y**es to save the file. You are returned to the Desktop.

11. Right-click on the My Computer icon and choose **E**xplore. The Exploring window appears.

12. From the **V**iew menu, select **D**etails. Full file details are displayed.

13. Click on the icon for the A drive in the left panel of the Explorer window. The contents of drive A are displayed.

14. Double-click on the New Briefcase icon in the right panel of the Explorer window. The contents of the Briefcase are displayed and should be similar to figure 9.5 (note that the status of the file is Needs updating).

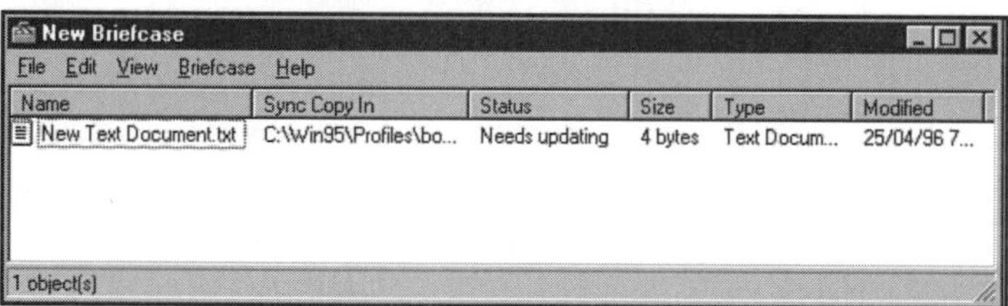

Figure 9.5

A Briefcase after a file modification has been made.

15. Double-click on the TEST.TXT file. Notepad is launched, showing that the file consists of only the line REV1.

16. Close the Notepad window. From the **B**riefcase menu of the Explorer, choose Update **A**ll to display the Update Briefcase dialog box (see fig. 9.6). You are prompted to confirm the update .

Figure 9.6

Synchronizing the Briefcase contents.

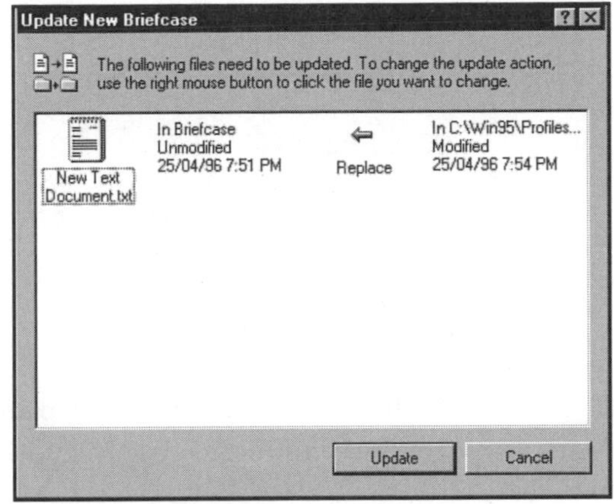

17. Choose Update. The briefcase file is replaced with the more recent file from the Desktop. When the update is complete, double-click on the TEST.TXT file inside the Briefcase. The file now contains the lines REV1 and REV2.

18. Close the Explorer window. You are returned to the Desktop.

Briefcase synchronization works equally well between multiple computers attached by a network or a direct cable connection.

Review Questions

The following questions will test your knowledge of the information in this chapter. For additional questions, see MCP Endeavor and the Microsoft Roadmap/Assessment Exam on the CD-ROM that accompanies this book.

1. The default line protocol for Windows 95 Dial-Up Networking is ______.

   A. SLIP

   B. NRN

   C. RAS

   D. PPP

2. Which two of the following are log files provided by Windows 95 Dial-Up Networking?

   A. PPP.LOG

   B. PPPMODEM.TXT

   C. MODEMLOG.TXT

   D. PPPLOG.TXT

3. Which three of the following protocols are supported over a Windows 95 PPP line connection?

   A. TCP/IP

   B. RAS

   C. IPX/SPX-compatible

   D. NetBEUI

4. ______ is the only line protocol that can transport multiple network protocols over a single link.

   A. NRN

   B. RAS

   C. PPP

   D. SLIP

5. Windows 95 treats which two of the following as it would treat a network card?

   A. A modem

   B. ISDN

   C. A router

   D. X.25

6. To install Dial-Up Networking, you must have ______ free disk space for client and server software.

   A. 1 MB

   B. 2 MB

   C. 5 MB

   D. 10 MB

7. Which of the following statements is true?

   A. The basic Windows 95 package includes Dial-Up Networking server capability.

   B. Windows 95 is able to act as a gateway to TCP/IP resources on the Internet.

   C. The basic Windows 95 package includes a Dial-Up Networking client that supports IPX/SPX.

   D. Windows 95 Dial-Up Networking supports real-mode protocols.

8. A SLIP connection supports which of the following protocols?

   A. NetBEUI

   B. TCP/IP

   C. IPX/SPX

   D. Both A and B

Review Answers

1. D	5. B D
2. C D	6. B
3. A C D	7. C
4. C	8. B

Chapter 10

Microsoft Exchange

This chapter looks at the Microsoft Exchange client that ships with Windows 95. Specifically, it discusses the following topics:

- Exchange client architecture
- Installing the Exchange client
- Configuring the Exchange client
- Sending and receiving messages
- Using Microsoft Fax with the Exchange client

Microsoft Exchange is a client/server messaging platform. Although the Exchange client can be used to send and receive electronic mail, its usefulness extends far beyond that. The Exchange client is built around the *Messaging Application Programming Interface* (MAPI), which is a set of standard procedures used to exchange messages between Windows-based computers.

Because of its use of MAPI (pronounced "mappy") and its modular, extensible architecture, the Exchange client can function as a universal inbox to receive messages from a number of services including Microsoft Fax, The Microsoft Network Online Service (MSN), and any other MAPI-compliant services.

The Exchange client offers a wide range of features, including the following:

- Sending and receiving mail from other MAPI message stores, such as a Windows 95 Workgroup Postoffice, Microsoft Mail Server, Microsoft Exchange Server, or many others

- Sending and receiving secure faxes using the Microsoft Fax service
- The capability to attach electronic files or Object Linking and Embedding (OLE) objects to messages
- The capability to use Rich Text Formatting (RTF) to format messages with numerous fonts, colors, and other effects
- Personal address books that can contain the mail and fax addresses of frequently contacted recipients
- A hierarchical system of folders to easily keep track of your messages

Installing the Microsoft Exchange Client

Depending on the options that were chosen during the installation of Windows 95, the Windows 95 Exchange client may or may not have already been installed. If the Windows 95 Desktop contains an icon titled "Inbox," then double-clicking on this icon starts the Microsoft Exchange client. If the Inbox is not already on the Windows 95 Desktop, then the Exchange client likely has not yet been installed from the Windows 95 distribution files.

To install the Windows 95 Exchange client from the Windows 95 distribution files, perform the steps shown in Exercise 10.1.

Exercise 10.1: Installing the Exchange Client

1. From the Start menu, select Settings and then Control Panel. The Control Panel is displayed.
2. Double-click on the Add/Remove Programs icon. The Add/Remove Programs Properties sheet is displayed.
3. Select the Windows Setup tab, place a checkmark next to Microsoft Exchange, and choose OK. The check box should not be gray since you will be installing all the Exchange client components. The files are installed. You are prompted for the path to the Windows 95 distribution files if they cannot be found.

4. Verify that there is now an Inbox icon on the Desktop and a Microsoft Exchange entry in the Start menu Programs.

Microsoft Exchange Client Architecture

Like many Windows 95 components, the Microsoft Exchange client has a modular architecture. The two main components to the Microsoft Exchange client are as follows:

- Messaging Application Programming Interface (MAPI)
- Services

MAPI enables multiple services to be installed that interact with the Exchange client. Windows 95 includes a number of these services, and additional third-party services can be added as well.

Messaging Application Programming Interface (MAPI)

MAPI is a set of standard commands that can be used by messaging applications to communicate with other MAPI-compliant applications and services. For example, the Exchange client uses MAPI to send mail messages to a Microsoft Exchange Server. In addition, the Exchange client also can communicate with other MAPI-compliant services such as a Microsoft Mail or the CompuServe Mail service.

The messaging architecture of Windows 95 uses a front-end client and a back-end service to send electronic messages. The MAPI specification enables electronic messages to be sent using any MAPI-aware application as a front-end and any MAPI-compliant service as the back-end portion, which is responsible for receiving and exchanging the messages. An example of a MAPI-aware application is Microsoft Word. After a MAPI service has been configured properly, Microsoft Word can be used to send documents directly to the MAPI service using the Mail command under the File menu. Thus, a MAPI-enabled application can send messages without requiring a full messaging client, such as Exchange client.

Services

The Microsoft Exchange client is sometimes referred to as a universal inbox because it can send and receive messages to and from any MAPI-compliant service. For example, the Exchange client can receive electronic faxes or messages from Microsoft Mail, Microsoft Exchange Server, and Internet mail postoffices.

The Microsoft Exchange client uses MAPI-compliant services to communicate with other MAPI-compliant applications such as postoffices, fax services, and messaging applications. Windows 95 includes the following MAPI services that can be used by the Exchange client:

- Exchange Server
- Microsoft Mail (including Workgroup Postoffices)
- Microsoft Fax
- CompuServe Mail
- The Microsoft Network Online Service (MSN)
- Personal Address Book
- Personal Information Store

The first time you start the Exchange client, the Microsoft Exchange Setup Wizard prompts you for the services you want to use with the Exchange client. You also can add and configure services at any later time by selecting Services from the Tools menu in the Exchange client. Services can also be installed or configured using the Mail and Fax icon of the Control Panel.

Exchange Server

The Microsoft Exchange Server service enables a client to send and receive messages to and from a Microsoft Exchange Server. Microsoft Exchange Server is a client/server messaging system that runs on Windows NT Server. An Exchange Server contains features such as the following:

- The use of public folders where users can post messages and use MAPI-aware applications
- Recipient address list replication among Microsoft Exchange Server and Microsoft Mail Server postoffices
- The capability to send and receive mail messages using the security features of a Windows NT domain

After installing the Exchange Server service, the Exchange client will have the following functions enabled:

- **Inbox Assistant.** Enables an Exchange client user to set up rules that apply to new messages in the client's Exchange Server mailbox. For example, Inbox Assistant can be set to forward automatically all high-priority messages to a folder titled "Urgent Mail."
- **Out of Office Assistant.** Enables an Exchange user to set up rules for receiving and automatically replying to new messages. For example, an automatic response to any new messages can be sent saying that the user is out of the office until next week. In addition, new messages also can be forwarded to another mailbox depending on their urgency or on who sent the messages, or even on their content, such as phrases like "you're fired."

The Microsoft Exchange Server CD-ROM contains an updated Exchange client that should be used with an Exchange Server rather than the client that comes with Windows 95. The Exchange client that shipped with Windows 95 does not have all the functionality of the version on the Exchange Server CD-ROM. For example, the client does not have the capability to post messages to public folders.

Microsoft Mail Server

If you have a mailbox on a Microsoft Mail Server, you can access the mailbox using the Microsoft Exchange client configured to use the Microsoft Mail service. Using the Exchange client instead of the Microsoft Mail client allows you to benefit from all the features of the Microsoft Exchange client. As well, unlike the Microsoft Mail client, the Exchange client is a "universal inbox," enabling you to access multiple MAPI services, such as Exchange Server and Internet mail.

To allow the Exchange client to access a mailbox on a Microsoft Mail Server, the Microsoft Mail service is configured with the Universal Naming Convention (UNC) path of the Microsoft Mail Server postoffice. The UNC share name of a Microsoft Mail Server postoffice is commonly something like *SERVER*\MAILDATA.

The Microsoft Exchange client may be preferable to the Microsoft Mail client because the Exchange client can be used with many MAPI services and is truly a universal inbox.

Workgroup Postoffice

If you do not have a Microsoft Mail Server postoffice on your network, you may use or create a Workgroup Postoffice, which is an optional component of Windows 95. The Workgroup Postoffice is similar to a Microsoft Mail Server postoffice except that it cannot be used to exchange mail with recipients on other postoffices. To connect to an existing Workgroup Postoffice, enter the UNC path of that postoffice in the Microsoft Mail service setup dialog box. The UNC share name of a Workgroup Postoffice commonly takes the form *SERVER*\WGPO*????*, where *????* is an incremental number such as 0000.

A Windows 95 computer also can be used to create a Workgroup Postoffice. Exercise 10.2 illustrates the necessary steps for creating a new Workgroup Postoffice on a Windows 95 computer.

Exercise 10.2: Creating a Workgroup Postoffice

1. From the Start menu, select **S**ettings and then **C**ontrol Panel. The Control Panel is displayed.
2. Double-click on the Microsoft Mail Postoffice icon. The Microsoft Workgroup Postoffice Admin dialog box is displayed.
3. Select **C**reate A new Workgroup Postoffice and choose Next. You are prompted for the location of the postoffice.
4. Specify the path to the location where the Workgroup Postoffice should be created, and choose Next. For example, type **C:**. The postoffice files are created in a directory named WGPO0000 in the location specified, and the Enter Your Administrator Account Details dialog box is displayed.
5. You must enter name of the user, the mailbox name, and a password for the administrator account. In the **N**ame and **M**ailbox fields, enter **ADMIN**, for the **P**assword field, enter **PASSWORD**, and then choose OK. A message reminds you that you must share the WGPO0000 directory with all the other users who will be using the postoffice.
6. If WGPO0000 is on the Windows 95 computer, start Explorer and select the WGPO0000 directory. The WGPO0000 directory is highlighted.
7. Click on the right mouse button and select S**h**aring from the context-sensitive menu. The Sharing tab of the WGPO0000 Properties sheet is displayed.
8. Give all postoffice members full control access to the WGPO0000 directory. If share-level security is used, assign a Full Control password to the directory and provide all postoffice members with this password. If user-level sharing is used, give all the postoffice members Full Control permissions by choosing the Permissions button and adding the user accounts to the Full Control list box.
9. Choose OK to share the WGPO0000 directory. The WGPO0000 directory folder symbol is replaced with a sharing hand symbol.

You also need to create a mailbox for each member of the Workgroup Postoffice, as shown in Exercise 10.3.

Exercise 10.3: Creating Workgroup Postoffice Mailboxes

1. From the Control Panel, double-click on the Microsoft Mail Postoffice icon. The Microsoft Workgroup Postoffice Admin dialog box is displayed.
2. Select Administer an existing Workgroup Postoffice and choose Next. You are prompted for the postoffice location.
3. Type the path to the Workgroup Postoffice files, such as **C:\WGPO0000** and choose Next.
4. Enter the administrator mailbox name and password, and choose Next. The Postoffice Manager dialog box is displayed.
5. Choose Add User. The Add User dialog box opens.
6. Enter the name of the user, the mailbox name, the mailbox password, and any additional information for the new user and choose OK. The mailbox is added to the list of users with mailboxes on the postoffice.
7. Add other users if needed and choose Close to close the Postoffice Manager.

You may also use the Manage Postoffice dialog box to delete users, reset a user's password if the user forgets it, and compress mailbox folders to reclaim space from deleted messages.

Microsoft Fax

The Microsoft Fax service can be used to send electronic faxes through a fax modem on the local computer or through a fax modem shared on the network. In addition, the Microsoft Exchange client Inbox can receive electronic faxes sent to the fax modem on the computer. Using the Exchange client, the same address book can be used to address messages to mail or fax recipients. Configuring the Microsoft fax service to be used in the Exchange client enables electronic documents and messages to be sent to fax machines in the same manner as if the destination were a mailbox. The destination for the Microsoft fax can be either a fax machine or a fax modem. To receive an electronic document attachment, the recipient must have a Class 2 fax modem.

For information on how to install and configure the Microsoft Fax service, see the section "Microsoft Fax" later in this chapter.

CompuServe Mail

The CompuServe Mail service enables the Exchange client to send and receive mail directly to and from the CompuServe online service. If you have a CompuServe account, the Exchange client can be configured to dial up the CompuServe online service through a modem and exchange mail with the CompuServe service. To install and configure the CompuServe Mail service, see Exercise 10.5 later in this chapter.

Microsoft Network Online Service Mail

The Microsoft Network (MSN) is an online service similar to CompuServe. The MSN Mail service enables the Exchange client to send and receive mail to and from MSN through a modem connection. If you have an MSN account, the Exchange client can be configured to dial up MSN and send and receive mail to and from MSN.

Exercise 10.6 later in this chapter demonstrates how to install the MSN Mail service.

Personal Address Book

The Personal Address Book service is installed by default with the Microsoft Exchange client. The Personal Address Book can contain the names and addresses of recipients to which a Exchange user commonly sends messages. For example, rather than type the recipient's name and fax phone number manually, you can select them from the Personal Address Book after you add the recipient to your Personal Address Book. Similarly, a frequently contacted recipient can be selected from the Personal Address Book instead of by a search through a large address list of mailboxes on a Microsoft Mail Server or Exchange Server postoffice. Furthermore, the Personal Address Book can be used to create personal distribution lists for messages sent to multiple recipient names.

A Personal Address Book, which has the extension PAB, is stored in a file specified by the user. Thus, multiple PAB files can be created for use by different users using the same Exchange client. In addition, this allows the Personal Address Book to be located on the hard drive of the Exchange client so that the Personal Address Book can be accessible even when the client is not attached to the network or the Exchange or Mail Server.

Personal Information Store

An *information store* is a repository for electronic messages and attachments. When a message is sent to the Exchange client, it is received into the Personal Information Store, which is installed by default with the Exchange client. The Personal Information Store is contained in a file with the extension PST and with a name specified by the user. This feature allows a Personal Information Store to be created for each user using the Exchange client, and for the Personal Information Store to be located on the hard drive of the Exchange client.

The Personal Information Store can contain a number of personal folders that can be defined by a user. By default, the Personal Information Store contains the following folders, as shown in figure 10.1:

- Deleted Items
- Inbox
- Outbox
- Sent Items

Figure 10.1

The Exchange Client showing a Personal Information Store.

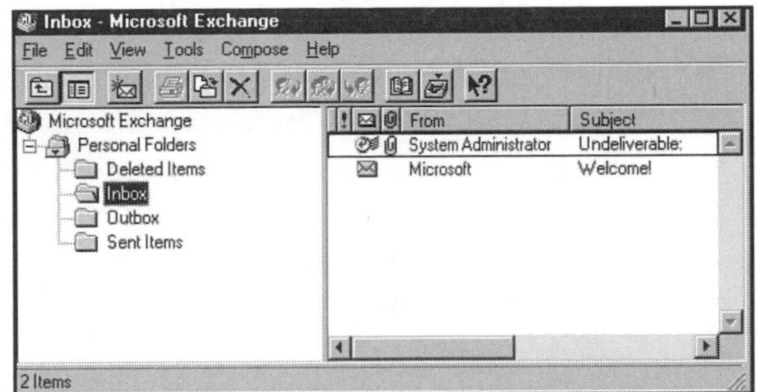

When a message is deleted from a folder, it is moved to the Deleted Items folder so that it can be recovered if the message is later needed. When a user exits the Exchange client, all messages are removed from the Deleted Items folder and are no longer available.

The Inbox contains messages that have been sent to the user. These messages can be from any of the services that have been configured for the Exchange client, including Microsoft Mail, Fax, or Exchange Server.

The Outbox contains messages that have been created by the client but have not yet been sent. When a user sends the message, it is sent using the specified service and is moved to the Sent Items folder.

A user also can create a Personal Folder for organizing messages. For example, a user may want to move all messages pertaining to Top Secret Project X to a folder named "Top Secret Project X Messages."

Configuring a Microsoft Exchange Client

The Microsoft Exchange client contains many configurable features that are explained in the online help files. For the Windows 95 certification exam, you should, at a minimum, know how to configure the Microsoft Exchange client to use the information services mentioned previously that can be installed with Windows 95.

The first time the Microsoft Exchange client is started, by double-clicking on the Inbox on the Desktop or by double-clicking on Mail and Fax in the Control Panel, the Exchange Setup Wizard is displayed. This Setup Wizard allows services to be configured for Microsoft Exchange and allows these settings to be saved in a profile. Any number of profiles may be created on the Exchange client to support multiple configurations. For example, one profile can be created that automatically connects the Exchange client to a Microsoft Mail postoffice on the network, and another profile can be created that prompts you to make a remote dial-up connection to the Microsoft Mail postoffice, using a modem. Additionally, individual profiles can be created for different users who will be using the Exchange client at different times. In short, a profile contains all the information necessary to connect to the appropriate services required.

The profile that the Exchange client uses when the Inbox is opened can be selected through the Mail and Fax icon in Control Panel, or through the Inbox icon Properties sheet.

When the Exchange client is first started, the Setup Wizard asks whether Exchange has been used before or, in other words, whether you already have a profile configured for yourself. If the correct profile has already been created for you, you may select **Y**es and choose the profile to start Microsoft Exchange. To create a new profile, select **N**o when prompted whether you have used Microsoft Exchange before, and choose Next. Modifications to the profile can also be made at a later time by selecting the profile, starting the Exchange client, and making the desired changes. Additional profiles can also be created by choosing **S**how Profiles and then A**d**d from the Mail and Fax applet in Control Panel.

If you want to be prompted about which profile to use when starting the Exchange client, select **O**ptions from the **T**ools menu of the Exchange client and select **P**rompt for a profile to be used when starting Microsoft Exchange.

After a profile is created, the Microsoft Exchange Setup Wizard displays a dialog box enabling you to choose the information services to be used with the profile. For the Windows 95 certification exam, you should know how to add and configure the appropriate service to perform the following exam tasks:

- Configure Exchange to send and receive mail
- Configure Exchange to access CompuServe mail
- Configure Exchange to access The Microsoft Network Online Service (MSN)
- Configure Exchange to send and receive Internet mail
- Configure Exchange to send and receive electronic faxes

Configuring Exchange to Send and Receive Mail

To configure the Exchange client to send and receive mail, at least one mail service must be installed and configured to connect to an electronic mail postoffice. In Exercise 10.4, you configure Exchange to access a mailbox on a Microsoft Mail postoffice. For more information on addressing messages, attaching documents, and sending mail, see the section "Sending Messages Using Microsoft Exchange Client" later in this chapter.

Exercise 10.4: Accessing a Microsoft Mail Server Mailbox

1. From the Control Panel, double-click on the Mail and Fax icon. The MS Exchange Settings Properties sheet is displayed (see fig. 10.2).
2. Choose Add to display the Add Service to Profile dialog box.
3. Select the Microsoft Mail service and choose OK. The Microsoft Mail service Properties sheet is displayed.

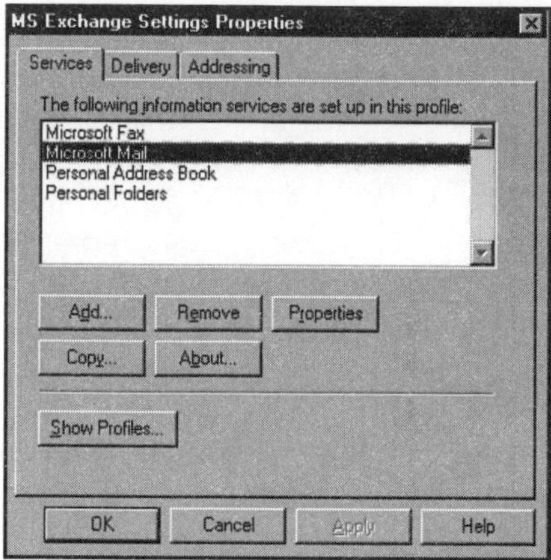

Figure 10.2

Exchange Client services.

4. Type the path to the Microsoft Mail Server postoffice or Workgroup Postoffice and select Automatically sense LAN or Remote. The Exchange client is configured for remote access if a network connection is not detected.

5. Select the Logon tab, enter your mailbox name and password, and choose OK. The MS Exchange Settings Properties sheet is displayed again.

6. Choose OK to save the changes to your Exchange client profile.

7. Double-click on the Desktop Inbox icon to start Exchange. The mailbox is displayed along with some test messages.

Configuring Exchange to Access CompuServe Mail

In Exercise 10.5, you configure the Exchange client to access a mailbox located on the CompuServe online service. To perform this exercise, you must have an existing CompuServe account and a modem on the Windows 95 client.

Exercise 10.5: Configuring CompuServe Mail Service

1. Start the Exchange client, select Services from the Tools menu, and choose Add. The Add Service to Profile dialog box is displayed.
2. Choose Have Disk and enter the path to the \DRIVERS\OTHER\EXCHANGE\COMPUSRV directory on the Windows 95 CD-ROM.
3. Choose OK. The CompuServe Mail Settings Properties sheets are displayed.
4. Type your CompuServe account name, ID, and password in the Name, CompuServe Id, and Password fields in the General tab.
5. Select the Connection tab and type the phone number used to connect to CompuServe in the Phone number field.
6. Select the Advanced tab and choose the Change CompuServe Dir button. Select the path to your CompuServe software directory; for example, select C:\CSERVE. Choose to close the services Properties sheets.

Configuring Exchange to Access MSN Mail

In Exercise 10.6, you configure the Exchange client to access your MSN mailbox. To perform this exercise, the MSN software must be installed, you must have an existing MSN account, and a modem must be installed on the Windows 95 client.

Exercise 10.6: Installing the MSN Mail Service

1. Select Services from the Tools menu of the Exchange client and choose Add. The Add Service to Profile dialog box is displayed.

2. If MSN has been installed on the Desktop, The Microsoft Network Online Service appears in the list of available services to add. If not, install MSN from the Windows Setup tab of the Add/Remove Programs Control Panel applet.

3. Select The Microsoft Network Online Service from the list and choose OK. The MSN service is added to list of services.

4. Select The Microsoft Network Online Service from the list and choose Properties. The Microsoft Network properties sheet is displayed.

5. Inspect the options that are available and choose OK twice to close the properties sheets. The MSN mail service becomes available in the Exchange client.

Using Exchange to Send and Receive Internet Mail

Microsoft Exchange can be used to send and receive mail to and from other clients on the Internet that are using the Simple Mail Transfer Protocol (SMTP).

Almost all mail sent across the Internet uses the SMTP format. SMTP messages are text-only ASCII messages but can include support for binary attachments using protocols such as MIME or UUENCODE.

To exchange mail over the Internet, you must have a service configured that has a gateway to the Internet. Examples of such services include the following:

- Microsoft Mail Server with an SMTP Gateway installed
- Netscape Mail
- Microsoft Plus Pack Internet Mail

Configuring Exchange to Use the Microsoft Fax Service

The Microsoft Fax service can be configured to access a fax modem on the local Windows 95 client or a fax modem that is shared from another location on the network. Fax messages can be sent from an Exchange client to a local fax modem on the same computer or to a shared fax modem on the network. Fax messages can also be directly received in the Microsoft Exchange client Inbox if that computer has a fax modem installed and configured.

> Incoming fax messages are received in the Inbox of the computer that is directly connected to the fax modem. If the fax message is intended for another user on the network, the message must be manually forwarded to the proper recipient by a user on the computer connected to the fax modem.

The following exercises demonstrate using the Microsoft Fax service with a Microsoft Exchange client. In Exercise 10.7, you configure Microsoft Exchange client to send and receive faxes using a local fax modem installed on the Windows 95 client.

Exercise 10.7: Configuring Exchange to Use a Local Fax Modem

1. Select Services from the **T**ools menu of the Exchange client and choose A**d**d. The Add Service to Profile dialog box is displayed.
2. Select Microsoft Fax from the list of services and choose OK. If this option is not available, install Microsoft Fax from the Windows Setup tab of the Add/Remove Programs Control Panel applet. You are prompted as to whether you want to configure your name, fax number, and fax modem in order to send faxes.
3. Choose **Y**es. The Microsoft Fax Properties sheet is displayed.
4. Enter your name and return fax number and any optional information in the User tab.

5. Select the Modem tab, select the modem to use for the fax service, and choose Set as Active **F**ax Modem. The Active Fax Modem field displays the modem you selected; an example is shown in figure 10.3.

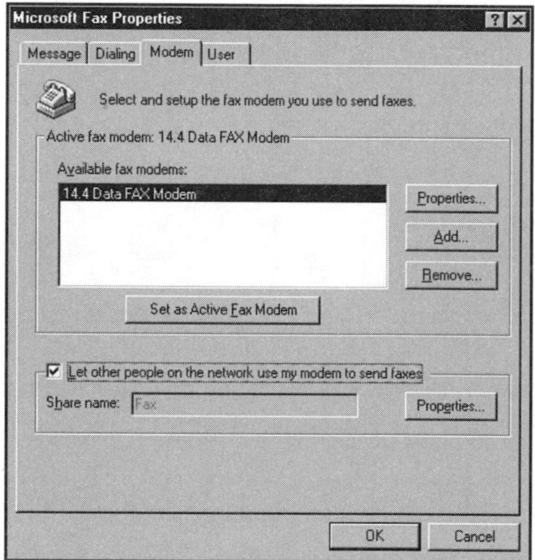

Figure 10.3

The Microsoft Fax Service Properties sheet.

6. If no modems are available, a modem has not been set up in the Control Panel. Choose **A**dd, select Fax modem, and choose OK to detect or install a new fax modem.

7. From the Microsoft Fax Properties sheet Modem tab, choose **P**roperties to configure any additional settings for the fax modem, and choose OK three times. Exit and restart Exchange client to initialize the fax service. Microsoft Exchange is ready to send and receive faxes.

In Exercise 10.8, you configure the Microsoft Exchange client to share a fax modem with others on the network. Then, using another networked computer, you see how you can access a shared network fax modem to send electronic fax messages created with the Microsoft Exchange client.

Exercise 10.8: Sending Faxes Using a Shared-Network Fax Modem

1. Select Services from the Tools menu of the Exchange client. The Services dialog box is displayed.
2. Select Microsoft Fax from the list of services and choose Properties. The Microsoft Fax Properties sheet is displayed.
3. Select the Modem tab (refer to figure 10.3).
4. Place a checkmark in the Let other people on the network use by modem to send faxes check box and choose OK.
5. Choose the Properties button next to the share name to display the shared fax directory dialog box. By default, the directory is `C:\NetFax`, the share name is `FAX`, and all users have full control permissions to the `C:\NetFax` directory. If desired, you can change the share name or the permissions to the shared directory.
6. Choose OK. By default, the local fax modem is shared on the network with the share name FAX under the current computer name.
7. From another computer on the network, start the Exchange client and add the Microsoft Fax service. The Microsoft Fax service appears in the list of services under the Services option of the Tools menu.
8. Select Microsoft Fax from the list of services and choose Properties. You are prompted as to whether you want to configure your name, fax number, and fax modem to use.
9. Choose Yes. The Microsoft Fax Properties sheet is displayed.
10. Enter your name and return fax number and any optional information in the User tab.
11. Select the Modem tab and choose Add. The Add a Fax Modem dialog box is displayed.

12. Select Network fax server and choose OK. The Connect to Network Fax Server dialog box appears.

13. Enter the UNC path to the FAX share you created on the other computer. For example, enter **TESTPC\FAX**. The fax server appears in the list of available fax modems.

14. Select the network fax and choose Set as Active Fax Modem. The fax server is set to the active fax modem.

15. Configure any additional properties you desire, choose OK twice, and exit and restart Microsoft Exchange client. The Microsoft Exchange client is ready to send faxes to the fax server.

16. Select New Fax from the Compose menu. The Compose New Fax Wizard is displayed.

17. Specify Default Location in the I'm Dialing From field. The addressing dialog box appears.

18. Type the name and fax number of the recipient and choose the Add to List button. The recipient name appears in the Recipient list.

19. Choose Next, specify whether you want a cover sheet, choose Next, specify a subject or note for the fax if desired, and choose Next again. The Add File option appears.

20. If you are sending the message to another fax modem, you can attach an electronic document in binary format, which can be unattached by the recipient if the receiving fax modem and software support binary attachments. Choose Next when done, and choose Finish to send the fax. The fax is generated and sent.

Sending Messages Using Microsoft Exchange Client

The online help in the Microsoft Exchange client contains a great deal of information on how to use all the features of the Exchange client. The following sections discuss the basics of sending electronic messages using the Exchange client, including the following topics:

- Addressing
- Rich-Text Formatting
- Attachments
- Delivery

To create a message, select New Message from the Compose menu of the Exchange client. Click on the To: button to display the address book for addressing messages, or type the address directly if you know the exact address format.

Addressing

Select a mailbox recipient from one of the address lists in the Address book to address the message. The address lists includes your personal address book and any address lists for services you have configured, such as the recipients list for a Microsoft Exchange Server. Selecting a mailbox name and choosing the To button adds the user to the list of recipients for that message. Choose OK when done.

Rich-Text Formatting

The body or text of the electronic message can contain ASCII text or Rich-Text Formatting (RTF). RTF can include multiple colors, fonts, and other attributes to spice up the display of the text. The recipient mail client must also support RTF for these attributes to be displayed correctly. If the recipient mail client does not support RTF, the text usually is displayed as unformatted ASCII text.

Attachments

In addition to text, Exchange messages also can include binary file attachments. To add an attachment to a created message, select the Insert menu in the New Message composition window. You may insert either a file or an OLE object at the location of the cursor in the body of the created message. An OLE object appears as an icon that can then open the proper application to view or edit the attachment.

To send attachments over TCP/IP (such as over the Internet), your TCP/IP gateway (called an *SMTP gateway*) must support either the UUENCODE or MIME format. Both of these formats encode the binary attachment as a series of ASCII characters. MIME-formatted messages can be automatically decoded by a MIME-enabled recipient.

Delivery

After creating a message, you can deliver it by choosing Send from the File menu of the New Message composition window. The message is moved to your Outbox and is delivered after a periodic interval specified for the delivery service. To deliver a message immediately, select the message in the Outbox and select Deliver Now from the Tools menu. If you have more than one service installed that can deliver messages, you can select one or all of the services to be used to deliver the message.

Review Questions

The following questions will test your knowledge of the information in this chapter. For additional questions, see MCP Endeavor and the Microsoft Roadmap/Assessment Exam on the CD-ROM that accompanies this book.

1. Which three of the following are MAPI-compliant services included with Microsoft Exchange?

    A. Microsoft Fax

    B. CompuServe Mail

C. America Online Mail

D. Personal Address Book

2. A(n) ______ is a collection of the settings used to connect to a service.

A. information store

B. configuration folder

C. profile

D. MAPI tag

3. Which of the following statements is true of Microsoft Exchange?

A. All electronic messages must be in ASCII format.

B. The Personal Address Book is stored in a file with a PAB extension.

C. The Personal Information Store is stored in a file with a PIS extension.

D. You must request delivery from each mail service separately.

4. Which two of the following statements are true of MAPI?

A. MAPI allows ASCII text-only mail to be sent to and received from any mail system.

B. MAPI helps to ensure that different mail systems can communicate.

C. A MAPI-enabled application such as Microsoft Word can be used to exchange documents with other users without having to use a mail application, such as Microsoft Mail.

D. A MAPI-compatible messaging client can deliver messages using more than one service at a time.

5. Which of the following statements is not a benefit of using a Microsoft Exchange client rather than a Microsoft Mail client?

   A. An Exchange client can connect to mailboxes on multiple Microsoft Mail Servers at the same time.

   B. The Exchange client uses 32-bit code.

   C. The Exchange client enables multiple users sharing the same computer to connect to different mailboxes.

   D. The Exchange client can be configured to send and receive Internet mail, CompuServe mail, or MSN mail.

Review Answers

1. A B D
2. C
3. B
4. B D
5. A

Chapter 11

Plug and Play

Plug and Play technology allows the Windows 95 operating system to automatically detect and configure the devices in the Windows 95 computer. A user is usually not required to know which resource settings to assign to a particular Plug and Play device, or even the model of the Plug and Play device being used. For example, to add a Plug and Play network card in a system that fully supports Plug and Play, you insert the card in the proper adapter slot and start Windows 95. The operating system determines the model of the network card, installs the appropriate driver, and configures the driver with the appropriate resources, such as an interrupt and memory region to use.

In this chapter, the following Plug and Play topics are discussed:

- Resource types
- Viewing resource utilization
- Plug and Play core components
- Four scenarios using Plug and Play
- The hardware tree
- The Plug and Play process
- Using Plug and Play with a laptop computer
- Notes on Plug and Play for various device types
- Modifying Plug and Play device configurations using Device Manager

What Is Plug and Play?

Plug and Play, a set of hardware and software design standards, has been developed as a response to concern among PC users regarding the amount of time and technical knowledge required to properly configure a given set of hardware devices in a PC. All PCs have a finite number of resources; the most common type of resources being memory regions, I/O addresses, and Interrupt Request lines (IRQs). Allocating these resources to the hardware devices that need them is a daunting task, especially since you need to avoid hardware conflicts where two devices try to use the same resource.

The objective of Plug and Play technology is to simplify the initial configuration of a PC and also to simplify adding hardware devices after initial configuration. Ideally, a user should be able to buy a Plug and Play PC fully configured from the factory and, as users add or remove hardware devices (for example, a new modem) from their PC, these changes should be automatically noted by the system and reflected in the PC's configuration parameters immediately, or at the next system restart, depending on the device. It therefore becomes the computer's (and not the user's) responsibility to reallocate resources to meet the needs of the currently installed devices.

The four main characteristics of a Plug and Play system are the following:

- Device identification and specification
- Dynamic configuration changes
- Backwards compatibility with legacy components
- Operating system and hardware independence

These topics are discussed in the following sections.

Device Identification and Specification

Each hardware device that meets the Plug and Play specification must be able to identify both its device type and its manufacturer, as well as what types and number of resources it needs; for example, a modem might need access to one of the PC's IRQs and one of its I/O addresses to function properly. After the system gathers the resource requirements from all installed Plug and Play devices, it can properly allocate the PC's resources as needed.

Dynamic Configuration Changes

A Plug and Play system must be able to detect and compensate for dynamic insertion of new Plug and Play devices. When a new device is inserted, the system is immediately notified of the device's type and resource requirements. The system dynamically reallocates the resources of the PC to accommodate the new device. Applications, if they are Plug and Play-aware, are also notified about the new device. At no point in this process is the user required to intervene, unless the system runs out of resources to allocate.

Backwards Compatibility with Legacy Components

Legacy components include all non-Plug and Play devices. This usually refers to devices designed to existing hardware standards such as ISA, VESA, and EISA. Each of these deals with hardware in its own way, but none of them has the Plug and Play capabilities described here and so cannot be dynamically configured. Thus, a Plug and Play system, after it has identified legacy devices, gives them first priority in resource allocation.

Operating System and Hardware Independence

Plug and Play is an open architecture and is not proprietary to any one company. Thus, any hardware or software manufacturer can develop Plug and Play-compatible products, as long as their products meet the published specifications.

Resource Types

To better understand the details of the rest of this chapter, this section examines the four major resource types used in a standard PC:

- Interrupt Request Lines (IRQ)
- Direct Memory Access (DMA) channels
- Input/output (I/O) ports
- Memory regions

Interrupt Request Line (IRQ)

A standard PC is designed with a certain number of communication lines that are used by peripherals when they need to contact a software process to notify it that a hardware event has occurred. These communication lines are managed by a Programmable Interrupt Controller (PIC) built onto the motherboard. The PIC can typically handle up to 16 IRQ lines, but you need to remember that many of these are reserved for use by devices on the motherboard or standard devices such as keyboard, video, and so on. Thus, many IRQ lines are not available for use by newly introduced peripherals. For example, if you add a network card to the system, the card has to be assigned an available IRQ, such as IRQ 5 or IRQ 10, to communicate with the system.

Direct Memory Access (DMA) Channels

PC systems typically come with eight DMA channels. These are designed to permit peripherals to access portions of the computer's RAM directly, without using the system processor (CPU). DMA speeds up the operation of a periperal by creating buffers to accelerate redundant read/write operations involved between the peripheral and the system memory. As with IRQs, some of the channels are reserved for onboard or standard peripheral use and are not available to new devices. For example, when adding a sound card to a system, the card must be assigned one or more available DMA channels, such as DMA 1 and DMA 5.

Input/Output (I/O) Ports

Input/output ports are small areas of the PC's memory that are reserved for use by peripherals in order for them to execute input/output functions. Peripherals such as a keyboard, mouse, modem, or network card typically use I/O ports.

Memory Regions

Many peripherals, to accelerate their processing of information, reserve a portion of the computer's memory for their own use. Generally, this memory is between 640 KB and 1 MB, although some can use the memory above 1 MB. For example, many network cards require the use of a memory region such as D0000-DFFFF; therefore, the required region must be set aside for the exclusive use of that device. If the region is not reserved for the device that requires it, another device or application may attempt to use that memory region, which can cause the operating system to crash.

Viewing Resource Utilization

Windows provides a number of ways to view resource usage. Although viewing resource usage can be done directly in the Registry, doing so through the Device Manager is much easier (and safer). To help you conceptualize how resources are used, Exercise 11.1 demonstrates how to view which resources have been assigned to which device. The exercise also demonstrates how to reserve a resource so that it is not used by the Plug and Play system.

Exercise 11.1: Viewing Resource Utilization

1. From the Control Panel, double-click on the System icon (alternatively, right-click on the My Computer icon and choose Properties). The System Properties sheet is displayed.
2. Select the Device Manager tab. A list of all hardware devices currently installed appears.

3. Double-click on Computer from the list of hardware devices. The Computer Properties sheet appears, showing the PC's resource usage viewable by IRQ, DMA, I/O, or memory.
4. Select the **D**irect memory access (DMA) radio button. You can see that DMA 2 and DMA 4 are used by the floppy controller and the DMA controller, respectively. Additional DMA resources may be used by other devices, if present.
5. Write down the number of a DMA channel that is not being used. The number will be used later in the exercise.
6. Click on the other resource types to see what IRQs, I/O addresses, and memory ranges are in use. The usage map for each resource type appears.
7. Click on the Reserve Resources tab. The list of reserved resources appears; it is blank.
8. Click on the **D**irect memory access (DMA) radio button. The list of reserved DMA channels appears; it is blank.
9. Choose the **A**dd button. The Edit Resource Setting dialog box appears.
10. Use the arrows to increment the DMA to the value you wrote down earlier. Choose OK twice to close the Properties sheets. You are prompted to restart your PC.
11. Choose **Y**es. Your PC restarts.
12. When Windows 95 has booted, go back to Device Manager and view the DMA channel usage. The DMA channel you noted earlier now lists as "System Reserved"; this indicates that that DMA resource is not included in the pool of resources that can be assigned to a device.

Plug and Play Core Components

In order for a PC to be fully Plug and Play, it must have the four core components:

- Plug and Play system BIOS
- Plug and Play device drivers
- Plug and Play operating system
- Plug and Play-aware applications

Plug and Play System BIOS

The main responsibility of a Plug and Play BIOS is to notify the operating system of any insertions or removals of Plug and Play devices. In addition, the Plug and Play BIOS passes on configuration information about devices on the motherboard to the operating system.

The Plug and Play BIOS does not actually configure Plug and Play devices. That is the task of the Plug and Play operating system. A computer with a Plug and Play BIOS usually ships with its own Plug and Play software for configuring Plug and Play hardware devices. Any resource allocations initiated with this software should be detected by Windows 95 and are not altered. For example, a Plug and Play boot device would have to be configured with this software because Windows 95, which likely resides on the boot device, cannot load until the drive is properly configured.

Plug and Play Device Drivers

To dynamically activate a newly inserted Plug and Play device, the corresponding device drivers for that device must also be able to be dynamically loaded and unloaded from memory. Removing the driver from memory when the device is not present or not active allows Windows 95 to make more efficient use of memory.

Plug and Play Operating System

Windows 95 is fully Plug and Play-compatible and serves as the coordinator of the Plug and Play system. Windows 95 can receive messages from the Plug and Play BIOS about insertion or removal events, load and unload Plug and Play device drivers, and initiate the process of enumerating and allocating resources to Plug and Play hardware devices.

Plug and Play-Aware Applications

Plug and Play-aware applications are applications that can respond to Plug and Play messages sent out by the operating system. For example, if a laptop user's printer is connected to a docking station and is currently undocked, the printer at the docking station would show as grayed out in the Windows 95 Printers Folder until the next time the laptop is docked. Windows 95 is able to do this because the printing subsystem is a Plug and Play-aware application.

Four Scenarios Using Plug and Play

All four of the core components must be present to fully benefit from all the features of Plug and Play. However, several of the features of Plug and Play can also be used if the system and peripherals are only partially Plug and Play-compliant. One of the following scenarios will be present in a Windows 95 system, and a description of how each scenario can use Plug and Play follows:

- Plug and Play system BIOS and Plug and Play devices
- Plug and Play system BIOS and legacy devices
- Legacy system BIOS and Plug and Play devices
- Legacy system BIOS and legacy devices

Plug and Play System BIOS and Plug and Play Devices

In this scenario, all components are Plug and Play, making for the easiest configuration. As noted earlier, Plug and Play boot devices must be configured outside Windows 95. All other devices are configured dynamically after Windows 95 loads.

Plug and Play System BIOS and Legacy Devices

The Plug and Play system configures any Plug and Play-compliant devices at boot time. If the PC contains a legacy boot device, it must be properly configured before booting Windows 95. Any other legacy devices must be found and configured using the Windows 95 hardware detection routines, initiated either during installation of Windows 95 or subsequently, in the Control Panel through the Add/Remove Hardware icon.

Legacy System BIOS and Plug and Play Devices

Because the BIOS in this case is unable to provide configuration information to the operating system, Windows 95 polls the Plug and Play devices directly at boot time and configures them dynamically. Again, any legacy or Plug and Play boot devices must be configured outside Windows 95.

Legacy System BIOS and Legacy Devices

This is the scenario that existed before Plug and Play. Boot devices must be configured outside Windows 95, and all other devices are found during the hardware detection phase of installation or with Add New Hardware in the Control Panel.

The Hardware Tree

An easy way to conceptualize how a Plug and Play system sees Plug and Play devices in a PC is as a tree, which branches out from the motherboard to all installed hardware devices. Figure 11.1 shows an example of a hardware tree.

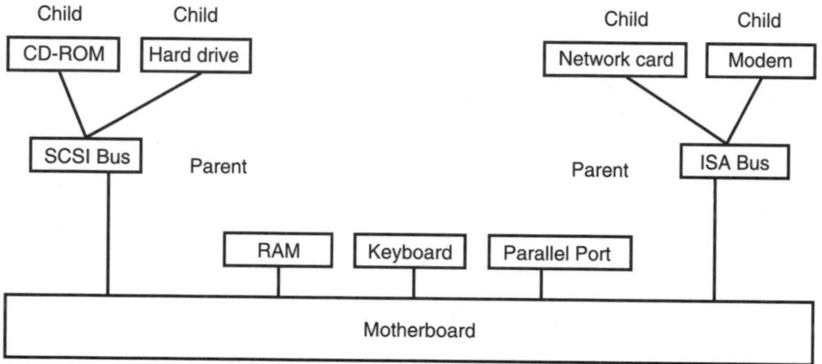

Figure 11.1

The hardware tree.

Each box on the diagram is a component that must be configured by the Plug and Play system. These components are referred to as *device nodes.* A device node can be an independent component connected directly to the motherboard (for example, the keyboard or parallel ports) or it can be connected to the motherboard through an intermediate device node. Therefore, a SCSI hard drive attached to a SCSI hard drive controller is a "child" device node to the SCSI adapter card, which acts as the "parent" device node.

To configure any device node, the Plug and Play system requires the following:

- A unique node ID.
- The type and number of resources (IRQ, DMA, I/O, memory) required by the device, known as its logical configuration.

- Any resources already assigned to this device (usually from a previous resource allocation); if this device is removed from the PC, the Plug and Play system will know which additional resources are now free for use.
- Knowing whether the node has any children attached to it.

The Plug and Play Configuration Process

When Windows 95 first boots, or when a new Plug and Play device is inserted or removed, the process of configuring all Plug and Play devices is initiated. The major steps in this process are as follows:

1. All Plug and Play devices are put into configuration mode, which effectively deactivates them.
2. Each device is examined (also known as *enumeration*) and assigned an ID that will be used to identify it.
3. The device's resource requirements are determined. If the card has multiple functions, the resource requirements of each function are examined separately (for example, a PCMCIA modem/network card).
4. After all resource requirements are determined, a working configuration that satisfies all these requirements is calculated. Each device is assigned its resources. These settings are stored in the current configuration section of its device node information.
5. All Plug and Play devices are reactivated.

Plug and Play Components in Windows 95

The configuration process described in the previous section is carried out in tandem by a number of Windows 95 components. These include the following:

- Bus enumerators
- Plug and Play BIOS

- Hardware tree and the Registry
- Device drivers
- Resource arbitrators
- Configuration Manager

Bus Enumerators

These agents are essentially a special type of software driver that knows how to search out and communicate with devices attached to a particular bus architecture. These drivers poll all devices on a particular bus for their device type and resource requirements, and assign each device a unique ID. When the Configuration Manager returns a working configuration, the bus enumerators pass on this information directly to the device.

Plug and Play BIOS

The Plug and Play BIOS is responsible for ensuring the correct configuration of various motherboard components, as well as the configuration of the boot device of the PC. Once established, this information is passed on to the Plug and Play operating system. The most important task performed by the plug and Play BIOS, however, is that of notifying the operating system of insertion or removal events. This function is crucial because it prompts the operating system to reinitiate the enumeration process in order to accommodate the newly inserted or removed device. It also allows the operating system time to notify Plug and Play-aware applications that, for example, a network card has been removed and data loss could occur if any network activity is still in progress.

Hardware Tree and the Registry

Note that the hardware tree mentioned earlier exists only in the memory of the computer. It is recreated every time the system boots from entries stored in the Windows 95 Registry, which is a hidden file called SYSTEM.DAT and has a record of all devices ever installed on the PC and their last-used settings. As Plug and Play devices are enumerated, they are added as device nodes on the in-memory hardware tree, and any settings already stored for that device in the Registry are enabled. For example, if the system detects a Plug and Play network card and finds that that card has been installed previously, it will enable the workgroup name, protocol settings, and so on that were last used for that card. If a Plug and Play device is inserted or removed, the hardware tree will reflect this change. Most of these settings can be found in the HKEY_LOCAL_MACHINE section of the Registry.

Examining Hardware Settings in the Registry

Exercise 11.2 demonstrates how the Windows 95 Registry stores information gathered by the various Plug and Play components.

> Be sure not to change any of the values in the Registry, because your computer might not function properly following these changes.

Exercise 11.2: Examining Hardware Settings in the Registry

1. From the Start menu, select **R**un. The Run dialog box appears.
2. Enter **REGEDIT.EXE** in the **O**pen box. The Registry Editor loads and displays the various keys of the Registry.
3. Click on the plus sign (+) next to HKEY LOCAL_MACHINE. A number of subkeys are displayed
4. Click on the + next to the Enum subkey. A further number of subkeys are displayed.
5. Click on the + next to the Root subkey. The subkeys of Root represent device classes.
6. Click on the + next to one of the starting subkeys beginning with "PNP." Subkeys numbered at "0000" are displayed.

7. Click the subkey numbered "0000." A description of the device and its various configuration parameters are displayed, similar to the sample shown in figure 11.2. Note that some of the values are in hexadecimal notation and therefore are not readable.

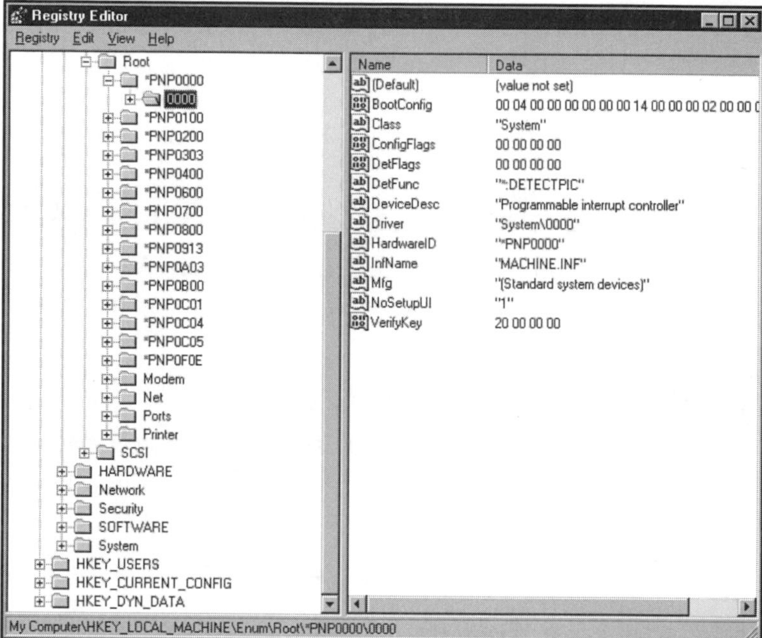

Figure 11.2

An example of detected Plug and Play device parameters.

8. Click on the other PNP device subkeys as well as the subkeys with user-friendly names such as "Ports" or "Printer." You will find configuration settings for most if not all the devices in your PC.

9. When finished, select E**x**it from the **R**egistry menu. You are returned to the desktop.

The name assigned to a device class is determined by the way it was identified. Devices enumerated by the Plug and Play system or by standard hardware detection are given a name beginning with "PNP" and ending in a four-digit hex code determined by the type of device detected. Any devices added manually through the Add New Hardware icon in Control Panel are given friendly names such as "Ports" or "Printer."

Device Drivers

Device drivers in a Plug and Play environment require functionality not typically found in a Windows 3.1 driver. Most important, they must be dynamically loadable and unloadable from memory as a Plug and Play device is inserted or removed. For example, keeping a driver in memory for a device that has been dynamically removed from the system would be inefficient. Therefore, to make more efficient use of available memory, Plug and Play device drivers unload whenever the device they support is not active. Also, to properly take part in the Plug and Play process, device drivers must have enhanced communication capabilities, namely to allow them to announce themselves to the Configuration Manager and to notify applications of Plug and Play events. Finally, Plug and Play device drivers have the capability to remain in memory but stay inactive (that is, take up no resources) until resources are assigned to the driver by the Configuration Manager.

Resource Arbitrators

Resource arbitrators are responsible for determining which device is allocated which particular resource. One resource arbitrator exists for each major resource type—IRQ, DMA, I/O address, and memory. The arbitrators must ensure, in finding a working configuration for their particular resource type, that no two devices are assigned the exact same resource because that would result in a device conflict, and both devices would likely be inoperative. The fact that the resource arbitrators are separate from the Configuration Manager allows for expandability due to the fact that any future resource types could be accommodated merely by adding a new resource arbitrator for that type, instead of redesigning the entire Plug and Play system.

Configuration Manager

The Configuration Manager is in charge of the entire Plug and Play enumeration/configuration process. It initiates the process both at system boot and when a Plug and Play device is inserted or removed after boot. It is responsible for passing parameters and commands between the other Plug and Play components in sequence. The Configuration Manager first makes a request to the bus enumerators to search their respective bus type for any devices that are Plug and Play-compatible. When the bus enumerators return with the type and resource requirements of each device, the Configuration Manager begins to build device nodes on the hardware tree for each of them. It then loads a corresponding driver for each device (if one exists), and the driver is set to await configuration parameters. The resource arbitrators are then called into play and requested to find a conflict-free configuration for all active devices. When this is complete, the resource arbitrators return the parameters to the Configuration Manager which, in turn, passes the information on to the bus enumerators to configure their enumerated devices.

Using Plug and Play with a Laptop Computer

Because laptops are one of the areas of computing most likely to benefit from Plug and Play technology, noting a few issues related to laptops and Plug and Play is worthwhile.

Windows 95 supports the creation of hardware profiles, which can be used to maintain different hardware configurations for a system. This feature is especially useful for a laptop that is used in a docking station, since different components are available to the system depending on whether or not the laptop is in the docking station.

Second, Windows 95 supports various methods of docking and undocking a laptop, such as cold docking, warm docking, or hot docking. The type of docking that can be performed with a laptop depends only on the limitations of the hardware.

Hardware Profiles

Most laptops are now available with an optional component called a *docking station.* The docking station allows users to "plug in" to additional computing power or hardware functionality with their laptop by adding a nonportable desktop station that may contain additional hardware such as a CD-ROM drive, a sound card, a network card, or additional ports, which are not available when the laptop is not docked at the station. Due to this fact, you must account for this additional hardware when configuring the laptop for its docked and undocked states. A feature of Windows 95 that addresses this issue is the capability to store multiple hardware profiles or configurations for a single PC. The hardware profile dialog box is shown in figure 11.3.

Figure 11.3

The Device Manager hardware profile selection for a network card.

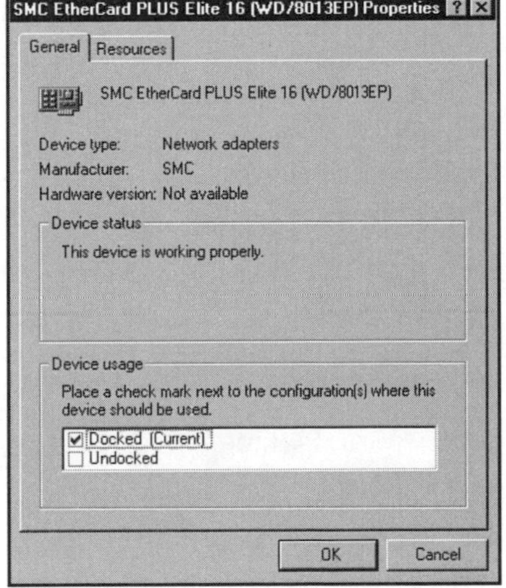

By using this feature, you can create a docked and undocked hardware profile for the laptop so that when the laptop is at the office and docked, for example, a profile would be used that has drivers for CD, network, sound, and so on, whereas the undocked profile would have these devices disabled or unchecked in the Device Manager.

If the laptop has Plug and Play functionality, the task of creating docked and undocked profiles is greatly simplified in that, when you boot for the first time in a docked state, Plug and Play enumeration occurs. You can then simply save this state as your docked hardware profile. Similarly, the next time you boot in an undocked state, enumeration will occur again, and you can then save this state as your undocked hardware profile. From this point on, the laptop should be able to automatically determine, based on the devices present in each profile, whether the laptop is docked or undocked.

If the laptop has any legacy devices, either in the system or in the docking station, the system should be booted in both the docked and undocked states before creating the respective hardware profiles. This ensures that all legacy devices have been detected and can be included in both the docked and undocked hardware profiles.

Docking Types

The three docking styles supported by Windows 95 are as follows:

- Cold docking
- Warm docking
- Hot docking

These styles are described in the following sections.

Cold Docking

Cold docking dictates that the laptop must be completely turned off in order to remove or insert it into the docking station. In this scenario, Plug and Play functionality is most often used at boot time because the hardware in the docking station cannot be removed while the laptop is on. Therefore, very few dynamic events will occur.

Warm Docking

Warm docking entails removing or inserting the laptop into the docking station while the laptop is in a suspended state. In this scenario, Plug and Play enumeration occurs after the laptop resumes full-power operation.

Hot Docking

Hot docking allows the laptop to be docked or undocked while running at full power. Any insertion or removal event immediately prompts a Plug and Play re-enumeration. Note that two types of hot docking systems exist. The first is *Auto-Eject* or "VCR style," in which a software interface is used to eject the laptop automatically from the docking station. This interactive approach allows Windows 95 the opportunity to analyze the possible consequences of ejecting the laptop, such as you having files open on the network. In this case, Windows 95 warns you that ejecting the laptop could cause data loss, and that it would be wise to close all open files before doing so.

The second type of hot docking is called *Manual* or "Surprise Style." In this type of hot docking, ejection is completely at the user's discretion, and no warnings are given regarding open files or data loss since the computer has no way of determining when the user might eject the laptop. Therefore, ensuring that all relevant files and applications have been closed before ejection occurs is the user's responsibility.

Notes on Plug and Play for Various Device Types

The following sections include technical notes regarding Plug and Play functionality on various bus architectures and device types, including the following:

- PCMCIA
- SCSI

- PCI and VESA Local Bus
- IDE
- MicroChannel Architecture (MCA) and EISA

PCMCIA

Primarily designed to enhance the portability of peripherals for laptops, the *Personal Computer Memory Card International Association* (PCMCIA) specification describes a set of standards for developing the software and hardware required to manufacture credit card-sized peripherals for laptops. Although the specification was originally intended to be used for memory cards, it has been expanded to include almost any device type imaginable, from sound cards to modems to SCSI adapter cards. This specification supports the key features of Plug and Play, including the capability to insert or remove a PCMCIA device and have the system automatically enumerate and reconfigure without rebooting the system.

In a traditional PCMCIA configuration, two software components are required: Card Services and Socket Services. These components are responsible for coordinating resource allocation for all PCMCIA cards and for enabling communication between the cards and the rest of the PC. In a Plug and Play environment, many of the functions performed by these services are handled by the Configuration Manager and a special PCMCIA bus enumerator. The Configuration Manager and PCMCIA bus enumerator ensure that PCMCIA devices are enumerated and configured in a fashion compatible with other Plug and Play devices.

SCSI

SCSI (pronounced *scuzzy*), which stands for Small Computer Standard Interface, is a bus architecture known for its capability to chain a number of devices such as CD-ROM drives and hard drives on one SCSI cable. In the past, configuring SCSI devices to work together properly has been a technical challenge, to say the least. Although most SCSI adapters do not presently support Plug and Play, a Plug and Play specification for SCSI has been developed and is slated for future implementation.

SCSI configuration must occur in two distinct phases:

1. Configuring the SCSI adapter card for appropriate IRQs, DMAs, and so on.
2. Configuring the SCSI bus and its devices—determining what SCSI ID to assign to which device, ensuring termination of the bus.

Although the current SCSI-II standard does not support automating the latter of these two phases, the emerging Plug and Play SCSI standard will allow automatic termination and ID assignment, as well as the dynamic configuration of the SCSI host adapter.

PCI and VESA Local Bus

Of the standard bus architectures, *Peripheral Component Interconnect* (PCI) is the most compatible with Plug and Play. It has the built-in capability to query PCI devices for identification and resource requirements. Most PCs that are PCI-compatible (mostly Pentiums and late-model 486s), however, have a mixture of PCI slots and ISA (standard PC) slots. Having a "PCI computer" does not mean that the Plug and Play functionality of the PCI bus is passed on to the ISA slots as well. ISA devices still must be identified and configured through the standard hardware-detection routines of Windows 95.

You need to remember that PCI devices can share IRQs, whereas ISA devices cannot. For that reason, you should configure the BIOS on PCI system IRQs that are used by ISA devices in the system. To do this, you must reserve an IRQ for the ISA devices that require them in the BIOS, usually by using a system configuration utility (SCU).

Video Electronics Standards Association (VESA) Local Bus, mostly present on older model 486s, is a high-speed bus architecture that is much less compatible with Plug and Play specifications than PCI. VESA Local Bus devices are treated like ISA devices in terms of their identification and configuration.

Windows 95 does not ship with a VESA Local Bus enumerator. However, ISA devices connected to the VESA Local Bus can still be detected by the ISA enumerator.

IDE

Integrated Drive Electronics (IDE) is primarily a standard for communication with hard drives and CD-ROM drives. Although some standard IDE hard drive controllers can sometimes auto-detect IDE hard drive parameters (heads, cylinders, sectors per track), the controller itself is not Plug and Play. It must be identified and configured using standard hardware detection routines. On systems with IDE or Enhanced IDE (EIDE) controllers, however, both the IDE drives and the controller normally are automatically detected by the Plug and Play system.

MicroChannel Architecture (MCA) and EISA

MicroChannel Architecture (MCA) is a bus architecture developed by IBM and introduced in the PS/2 line of computers. *Enhanced Industry Standard Architecture* (EISA) is a competing standard. Both of these architectures can automatically identify and configure devices attached to their bus. To integrate with Windows 95 Plug and Play functionality, an appropriate bus enumerator for the type of bus used must be present. The bus enumerator then passes configuration information on to the operating system by taking over most of the functions formerly provided by a separate proprietary configuration utility. For example, Configuration Manager would replace the EISA Configuration Utility.

Windows 95 does not ship with a MicroChannel enumerator. If necessary, it must be obtained from the OEM.

Modifying Plug and Play Device Configurations Using Device Manager

Although modifying the settings assigned to a Plug and Play device is not required under normal conditions, it might be necessary at times. These settings are stored in the registry, and can be edited manually using the Registry Editor. It is recommended, however, that the Device Manager be used instead, as incorrect parameters entered into the registry can leave the system inoperative.

In Exercise 11.3, you use the Device Manager to alter Plug and Play configuration settings.

Exercise 11.3: Modifying Plug and Play Device Settings through Device Manager

1. From the Control Panel, double-click on the System icon (alternatively, right-click on the My Computer icon and choose Properties). The System Properties sheet appears.
2. Select the Device Manager tab. A list of all hardware devices currently installed appears.
3. Click the plus sign (+) beside the Ports icon. The tree expands to show all installed ports, including serial and parallel.
4. Double-click on COM1. The Communications Port (COM1) Properties sheet appears.
5. Select the Resources tab. The resources currently assigned to the port are displayed.

6. Remove the checkmark from the Use automatic settings check box and click on the drop-down arrow in the Settings based on drop-down box. A number of alternate configurations are displayed.

7. Choose one of the alternate configurations. The resource settings change.

8. Double-click on Interrupt Request under Resource Settings. The Edit Interrupt Requests dialog appears.

9. Increase or decrease the interrupt value using the arrows. As you move through the values, the Conflict Information box notifies you of any conflicts with another device currently using that interrupt value.

10. Choose a nonconflicting new interrupt value and click on OK twice to close the Properties sheets. You are prompted to restart your PC.

11. After restarting the PC, go back to the Properties sheet of COM1 and verify the Interrupt Request setting. If no other device has requested the IRQ you chose, it should still be displayed.

12. Set the interrupt request back to 4 and click on OK twice to close the Properties sheets. You are again prompted to restart your PC.

Review Questions

The following questions will test your knowledge of the information in this chapter. For additional questions, see MCP Endeavor and the Microsoft Roadmap/Assessment Exam on the CD-ROM that accompanies this book.

1. Which three of the following are major resource types used in a standard PC?

    A. IRQs

    B. Memory regions

    C. DMA channels

    D. IDE drives

2. PCs typically come with ______ DMA channels.

    A. 2

    B. 6

    C. 8

    D. 16

3. Which three of the following are core Plug and Play components?

    A. Plug and Play device drivers

    B. Plug and Play protocols

    C. Plug and Play operating system

    D. Plug and Play system BIOS

4. All ______ must be configured outside of Windows 95 regardless of the level of Plug and Play compatibility.

    A. modems

    B. tape drive

    C. CD-ROM devices

    D. boot devices

5. The ______ is created from entries stored in the Registry every time the system boots.

   A. PNP Registry

   B. hardware tree

   C. device map

   D. device tree

6. The ______ is responsible for determining which resource is allocated to which particular device.

   A. Configuration Manager

   B. Plug and Play BIOS

   C. resource controller

   D. resource arbitrators

7. The ______ is responsible for tracking the insertion and removal of Plug and Play devices.

   A. Configuration Manager

   B. Plug and Play BIOS

   C. resource controller

   D. resource arbitrators

8. In a ______ docking environment, hardware cannot be removed while the laptop is on.

   A. hot

   B. warm

   C. cold

   D. manual

9. Which two of the following bus enumerator types do not ship with Windows 95?

   A. VESA

   B. PCMCIA

   C. SCSI

   D. MCA

10. Which of the following statements is true?

    A. PCI devices can share IRQs but ISA devices cannot.

    B. The SCSI-II standard is fully Plug and Play-compliant.

    C. The IDE standard is fully Plug and Play-compliant.

    D. PCMCIA devices should not be inserted into or removed from a system while the system is running, unless the system supports warm or hot docking.

Review Answers

1. A B C
2. C
3. A C D
4. D
5. B
6. D
7. B
8. C
9. A D
10. A

Chapter 12

Troubleshooting

In a complex operating system environment, troubleshooting technical problems or optimizing for performance is never an exact science. Although the number of possible hardware and software combinations (and resulting conflicts and configuration issues) on any given PC is virtually limitless, you can narrow the scope of any problems that may arise and, with luck, isolate the offending component(s), whether internal or external to Windows 95. More often than not, the problems are a combination of both internal and external factors. One can consider troubleshooting and optimization to be very closely related since, in a sense, poor performance is itself a serious technical problem.

This chapter looks at the following topics:

- Available technical resources
- Windows 95 tools for optimization and troubleshooting
- Using 32-bit drivers
- Optimizing the file system
- Optimizing printing
- Troubleshooting

Available Technical Resources

Countless sources of information exist to guide you in solving technical problems. They include the following:

- Online help
- Microsoft Technet

- The Internet
- The *Windows 95 Resource Kit*
- Technical support by phone
- Hardware and software compatibility lists
- Online discussion forums

Online Help

The online help facility in Windows 95 contains a great deal of technical information and also includes several interactive troubleshooting tools that can resolve many common problems.

Microsoft Technet

Microsoft Technet is a CD-ROM publication and is an invaluable tool that contains vast amounts of technical data on all Microsoft products, including electronic versions of various resource kits, driver updates, and databases of known problems.

The Internet

As more and more companies migrate their technical resources to the Internet, locating new drivers and finding technical data on software products is increasingly easy. Finding that a hardware or software manufacturer is not accessible through the Internet is rare. If new or updated drivers are required to resolve a problem, or sending a technical question through e-mail is acceptable, the Internet is the first place to go. You can also find many Windows 95 discussion groups where technical questions can be posted.

The *Windows 95 Resource Kit*

This is the A-to-Z compendium of Windows 95 technical information and, although the *Resource Kit* can be obtained electronically either from the Internet, through Microsoft's World Wide Web site, or on the Technet CD, reading large amounts of information from a book rather than from a computer screen is much easier.

Technical Support by Phone

If you are looking for help on a technical problem and you are in a situation in which intuition is more important than information, you may find contacting Microsoft Product Support directly by phone to be productive. In addition to an in-depth knowledge of the product, the technical representatives also have access to a great deal of technical data that is not available to the consumer.

Hardware and Software Compatibility Lists

These lists, which are on the Technet CD or can be downloaded from Microsoft's World Wide Web site, contain all the hardware and software that have been tested and are known to work with Windows 95 (you may find notes on how to make them work better as well). Although not seeing a product on the list does not mean that it does not work, seeing a product on the list gives you affirmation that you should continue troubleshooting, since the product is supposed to work with Windows 95.

Online Discussion Forums

If you have access to online services such as CompuServe or America Online, you can get access to a number of very useful Windows 95–related discussion groups. You also can usually directly contact Microsoft product support from these groups as well; Microsoft and other companies assign a certain number of technical support representatives to monitor the groups.

Windows 95 Tools for Optimization and Troubleshooting

Windows 95 has many built-in tools that can be used for both optimizing and troubleshooting. These tools can be accessed by clicking the Start button, selecting **P**rograms, Accessories, and then System Tools. The available utilities include the following:

- System Monitor
- Net Watcher
- System Resource Meter
- Disk utilities

If one of the preceding tools is not present in the System Tools group, it can be added using the Add/Remove Programs applet by selecting adding the tool from Accessories in the Windows Setup tab.

System Monitor

Windows 95 is equipped with a tool for monitoring various performance-related factors of the operating system environment. This tool is called the *System Monitor.* It can be used to provide real-time monitoring of system activities both locally and at remote computers, to determine the effect of configuration changes and to identify potential system performance bottlenecks.

Performance information such as how much the processor is being used, how many programs are currently running, or how many bytes are being written to a hard disk per second can be displayed in one of three formats: as a bar chart, as a line chart, or as numbers. By observing this information over time, as various operations are performed by the operating system or applications, it is possible to see how a certain operation affects a given performance parameter and tune the system to minimize any negative effects on performance.

To monitor a remote computer, the owner of that computer must have enabled remote administration and have specified you as an authorized user.

Exercise 12.1 demonstrates how to configure and use the System Monitor. The exercise assumes you have installed the System Monitor component through the Add/Remove Programs option in the Control Panel.

Exercise 12.1: Configuring and Using System Monitor

1. From the Start menu, select Programs, Accessories, System Tools, and then System Monitor. The System Monitor window appears.
2. From the Edit menu, select Remove Item. Select any listed items and choose OK. The System Monitor window should now be empty of tracked items.
3. From the View menu, verify that Line Charts is selected, and then from the Edit menu, choose Add Item. A list of system-related counter categories is displayed.
4. Select the Kernel category and the Processor Usage (%) item. Kernel: Processor Usage (%) is now displayed as a line chart.
5. From the Options menu, choose Chart, increase the Update interval to 1 second, and choose OK. The chart now updates more frequently.
6. From the View menu, choose Bar Chart. Kernel: Processor Usage (%) is now displayed as a bar chart.
7. Close the System Monitor. You are returned to the Desktop.

Tips for Using System Monitor

The following are some guidelines for using System Monitor to identify technical problems or bottlenecks:

- Run System Monitor during normal activity at first, to get a sense of how certain values change when certain actions are performed.

- Identify which items in System Monitor are applicable to the problem (for example, monitoring swap file size to determine whether more memory is needed in the system) and then set up specific tests.

Net Watcher

The Net Watcher utility can be used to create or delete shared resources on remote computers, as well as monitor access to those resources. The following factors are important when considering remote administration using Net Watcher:

- The remote PC must have File and Print Sharing enabled.
- You can access only remote systems that use the same security model you are using on your PC (share-level security PCs cannot access user-level security PCs).
- You can connect only to remote systems that use the same type of file and printer sharing (Microsoft or NetWare).

For more information on the Net Watcher utility, refer to the section "Net Watcher" in Chapter 4, "Editing User and System Profiles."

System Resource Meter

The System Resource Meter utility can be used to monitor dynamic changes in system resources. Many Windows 3.1 applications fail to release the resources allocated to them when they unload from memory, which causes the total system resource pool of the system to decrease. If you suspect an application of this behavior, it is advisable to activate the System Resource meter and observe whether subsequently closing the suspected application restores the resources to their previous levels. If this is not the case, the application may not be releasing all its allocated resources back to the operating system.

Disk Utilities

Utilities such as Scandisk and Disk Defragmenter can be used to increase performance and, especially in the case of Scandisk, to help detect potential problems with hard drives. These utilities are discussed in more detail in Chapter 6, "Managing Disk Resources and Utilities."

Using 32-Bit Drivers

One of the main ways in which performance and compatibility can be enhanced in Windows 95 is by using 32-bit protected-mode device drivers. These drivers are designed to be faster and work more efficiently in relaying data than older 16-bit drivers. As manufacturers begin updating their product lines for Windows 95 compatibility, obtaining native Windows 95 drivers for most hardware devices will become easier. A Windows 3.1 driver or MS-DOS–based driver should be used only if no 32-bit driver ships with Windows 95 and the manufacturer has not yet developed one.

A number of ways exist to maximize the use of 32-bit drivers:

- Verify that the Performance tab in the Properties sheet of My Computer shows all 32-bit components for the file system and for virtual memory.
- If you are using non-Microsoft disk compression, that compression is operating in Real mode (unless you have obtained a 32-bit compression driver since the release of Windows 95) and should be updated with a 32-bit driver from the manufacturer.
- Ensure that disk partitioning software is not being used. If a local hard drive employs nonstandard or software-based partitioning, it likely will not be able to function with the 32-bit file system drivers of Windows 95.

Optimizing the File System

A number of actions can be taken to ensure the highest file system performance, including the following:

- Remove SHARE.EXE and SMARTDRV.EXE from the AUTOEXEC.BAT because these files are not needed in Windows 95 and take up memory needlessly.
- If the Performance tab of My Computer indicates that the file system is not using 32-bit drivers, check the IOS.LOG to find the filename of the Real-mode driver that may be preventing the use of 32-bit file system drivers.
- Use Windows 95's Disk Defragmenter regularly to ensure that system performance does not degrade due to fragmentation of data on your hard drive.

Optimizing the File System for Different Roles

Because computers can be optimized for different roles, Windows 95 allows the configuration of certain performance-related file system parameters according to what role the PC is expected to play. The three possible configurations are as follows:

- Desktop computer
- Mobile computer
- Network server

The following parameters are keyed to these configurations:

- The number of most recently accessed folders that are tracked
- The number of most recently accessed files that are tracked

The settings are calculated based on each configuration's needs. For example, in the case of a network server, due to its intensive file processing needs, both the listed settings would be at their maximum to increase efficiency in retrieving files. Figure 12.1 illustrates how Windows 95 can be optimized for a particular role using the File System Properties sheet.

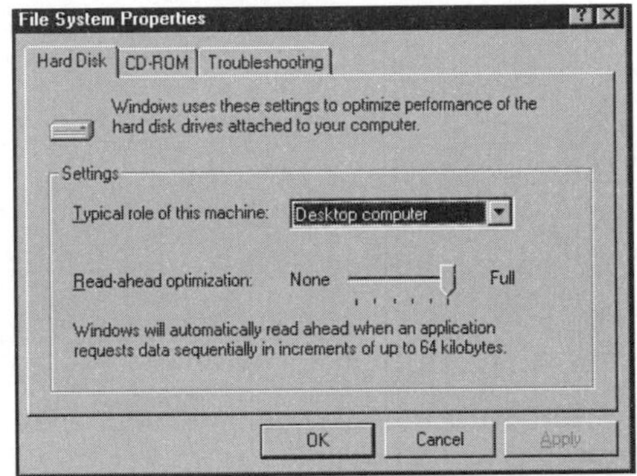

Figure 12.1

Optimizing for typical computer roles.

Optimizing Printing

The main factor in ensuring print performance is spool settings. Windows 95 spools, by default, using a proprietary internal page description format called *Enhanced Metafile* (EMF), which is discussed in more detail in Chapter 7, "Managing Printers." When printing across a network, the translation into EMF format, and ultimately into a printer-specific format called *raw,* is performed differently, depending on the operating system installed at the print server. If the print server has Windows 95 installed (which is able to interpret EMF format), then most of the rendering of the print job from EMF format into raw format is done at the server. If the print server has any other operating system installed, the EMF and raw format rendering must be done at the client, which increases the client's processing load. When printing locally, both types of rendering are done at the local computer.

A second consideration is how quickly control is returned to the user after a print job is submitted. You can configure the print subsystem of Windows 95 to return control to the user after the first page of a print job is spooled or after the last page is spooled.

This parameter can be configured from the Spool settings sheet (you must click on the Spool settings button) on the Details tab in the Properties sheet of the printer in question. Figure 12.2 illustrates the parameters available from the Spool Settings Properties sheet.

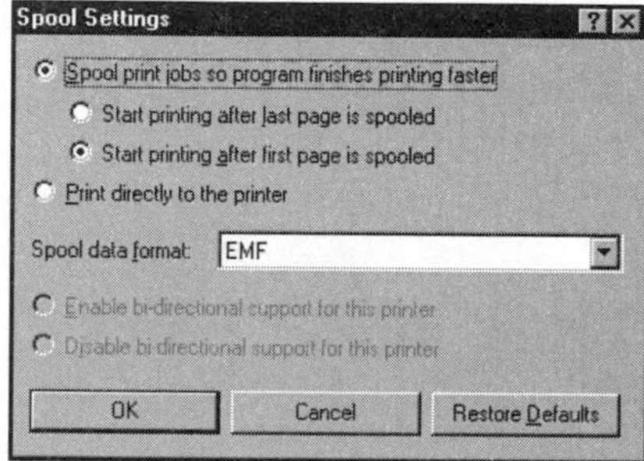

Figure 12.2

Spool settings.

Choosing to return control after the first page shortens wait time but increases printing time and consumes more disk space; the inverse is true if control is returned after the last page is spooled.

Troubleshooting

A number of steps can be followed when attempting to isolate technical problems. Some are specific to Windows 95; others are simply part of a logical approach to any problem:

1. Determine whether the problem is intermittent or occurs with regularity. If the problem is regular, your next step is to look for patterns and what factors are common to each occurrence of the problem. If the problem is intermittent, it becomes more difficult to diagnose. You should note that often, although a problem seems to occur randomly, it is in fact occurring regularly—but the factors linking each occurrence may be very obscure. It is very rare for computers to behave erratically for no apparent reason, except in the case of intermittent hardware failures, when the laws of physics are dictating system behavior.

2. Determine whether the problem began after some particular change was made to the configuration of the operating system, such as a driver update, the addition of a new modem, or a new video resolution setting. If this is the case, try to determine how the new configuration and the problem may be related.

3. Use binary logic to isolate one variable at a time in your search for the failing component. For example, if the operating system is suspect, turn off all its advanced features simultaneously. If the problem goes away, refine your search, turning the features back on one at a time until the problem reoccurs. If turning off all the features does not solve the problem, you can likely look elsewhere.

4. Determine as precisely as possible whether the problem seems to be clearly internal to Windows 95 or includes external software and/or hardware. Generally, a new install of Windows 95 to a new PC will not cause very many problems, unless these problems are related to hardware incompatibilities. The situation always becomes more complex when an existing system's software and hardware are migrated to Windows 95, since Windows 95 is then likely to inherit any existing problems with the PC as well as some potential new problems, such as Windows 3.1 applications that do not work properly under Windows 95. The best example of this methodology is booting into Safe mode, because this disables many if not all special features, drivers, and software of the operating system. If the problem goes away in Safe mode, the problem probably is limited to a few key configuration parameters.

5. Determine whether sequence is important to the problem. Is it a matter of the order in which things happen in the operating system? This can point out conflicts between different applications, for example. Does one application fail only after another particular application has loaded?

6. Is this a known or common problem? Does it occur on other PCs, or is it an isolated event? To find known problems, consult your available technical resources (discussed in more detail later) to learn potential solutions or to determine whether a known solution exists. Obviously, this is much easier to do if the problem can be reproduced on demand.

Troubleshooting Tools

A large majority of the technical problems that arise under Windows 95 can be traced back to the configuration files. Especially in upgrade situations, many settings that were necessary and that worked properly in a Windows 3.1 environment are either redundant or incompatible in a Windows 95 environment. Isolating which of these settings are redundant or incompatible with Windows 95 can be difficult. Windows 95 provides a number of tools and configuration parameters that can aid in this task:

- Safe recovery mode of Setup
- The Boot menu
- The Verify install procedure
- The Startup disk
- WIN.COM switches

Safe Recovery Mode of Setup

To avoid having to restart the entire installation procedure in the event of a system crash or other mishap during Setup, Windows 95 implements an automatic Safe Recovery mode that, when the computer is restarted following the crash, and Setup is rerun, restarts the Setup procedure at the point at which it was interrupted.

The Boot Menu

By pressing the F8 key when Windows 95 boots, you can access a boot menu that provides a number of different modes into which

Windows 95 can be booted. The menu options depend in part on what parameters are specified in the MSDOS.SYS file, but generally consist of the following:

- Normal mode
- Logged mode
- Safe mode
- Safe mode with network support
- Step-by-step confirmation
- Command-prompt-only mode
- Safe mode command prompt
- Previous version of MS-DOS

Normal Mode

This is the normal operation mode of Windows 95.

Logged Mode

When Logged mode is selected, the entire boot process is logged to a file called BOOTLOG.TXT, which catalogs VXD initializations, driver loads, and various other boot-related events.

Safe Mode

Safe mode is likely the single most important troubleshooting tool available in Windows 95. In this mode, a number of key Windows 95 components and settings are disabled, including the following:

- CONFIG.SYS and AUTOEXEC.BAT
- The [Boot] and [386Enh] sections of SYSTEM.INI
- The `Load=` and `Run=` parameters of WIN.INI
- The Startup group in Windows 95

- The Registry
- All device drivers except the keyboard, mouse, and standard VGA video driver

Disabling these items allows the separation of fundamental operating system problems from those caused by a combination of software factors. For example, in a situation in which the display is not functioning properly in Normal mode, if the problem does not appear in Safe mode, the problem probably is video driver–related and is not due to a defective video card.

Similarly, Safe mode can be used to troubleshoot scenarios such as the following:

- General Protection Faults
- Application hangs
- A hang during the boot process
- A blank screen at boot time

In some instances, you cannot use the Safe mode boot option because certain drivers in the CONFIG.SYS or AUTOEXEC.BAT are necessary for booting the system (such as partitioning software drivers). In these cases, you can boot to a Command-prompt-only mode (which processes CONFIG.SYS and AUTOEXEC.BAT) and then, using the command WIN /d:m, continue the remainder of the Safe mode boot process.

Safe Mode with Network Support

This mode is similar to Safe mode but enables Real-mode NetBEUI networking support. This mode also processes some Registry information needed to enable network support. This mode can be useful when the following problems occur:

- The computer hangs during a network operation.
- Network print operations fail.

- The computer is using a shared install of Windows 95, requires access to the shared files, and networking in Normal mode is not functioning.

Step-by-Step Confirmation

This boot mode is similar to the F8 function of previous versions of MS-DOS, permitting the user to step through the various stages of the boot process and specify whether each should or should not be completed. This mode can be very useful when you're trying to isolate boot stages to determine which may be causing a given problem. It can also be used to view system responses to various parameters in CONFIG.SYS and AUTOEXEC.BAT, which otherwise are displayed far too quickly to read.

Command-Prompt-Only Mode

Command-prompt-only boot mode is similar to a normal boot of MS-DOS. Only CONFIG.SYS, AUTOEXEC.BAT, COMMAND.COM, and the Registry are processed (along with any necessary disk compression drivers). This mode is useful in troubleshooting problems running MS-DOS applications in a virtual machine under Windows 95. If the application functions in this mode but not inside Windows 95, the problem is likely due to a compatibility issue. If the application does not function in Command-prompt-only mode, the problem is likely a configuration problem in CONFIG.SYS or AUTOEXEC.BAT, or the application may be corrupt.

Safe Mode Command Prompt

This mode functions similarly to Command-prompt-only, except that CONFIG.SYS and AUTOEXEC.BAT are not processed (disk compression drivers are still loaded). This mode can be useful in situations in which even Safe mode does not function properly.

Previous Version of MS-DOS

Although the Previous version of MS-DOS boot mode is not primarily for troubleshooting, it can be used in situations in which particular MS-DOS-related functions worked in previous versions of MS-DOS but do not seem to function properly under Windows 95. This boot mode can be used to test that functionality in both environments.

The Verify Install Procedure

If you suspect that some Windows 95 files or Registry information has become corrupted, you can have Windows 95 examine all installed components to determine whether this is the case and, if so, recopy or reconstitute the component. If Setup is rerun after installation, Windows 95 prompts the user as to whether installation should be rerun or components should be verified. If verification is chosen, the following occurs:

- A validity check is performed on all required files. If the check fails, the file is recopied from the Windows 95 installation media.
- The VMM32.VXD file is rebuilt.
- Incorrect Registry entries are overwritten.

The Startup Disk

The Startup disk can be created at installation time or later through the Add/Remove Programs option in the Control Panel. The disk serves as an Emergency Boot Disk should the operating system fail to load. The disk also contains FDISK, FORMAT, and several other MS-DOS–based file and disk utilities that may be useful in diagnosing and repairing system problems.

WIN.COM Switches

WIN.COM includes support for a number of error-isolation switches. Although some are available from within Windows 95, you may have to specify them from the command prompt in situations in which Windows 95 fails to load. These switches are specified in the format

win /d:[f] [m] [n] [s] [v] [x]

The switches function as follows:

Switch	Function
[f]	Disables 32-bit file system drivers
[m]	Starts Windows 95 in Safe mode
[n]	Starts Windows 95 in Safe mode with networking
[s]	Excludes the ROM address space between FOOO and 1 MB from use by Windows 95
[v]	Disables virtualization of hard disk interrupts
[x]	Disables use of upper memory by Windows 95

These switches can be used independently or together as part of a single command.

Troubleshooting Other Specific Scenarios

Although you cannot anticipate every potential problem that a system may encounter when Windows 95 is installed, certain courses of action are recommended for particular troubleshooting scenarios. These suggestions neither are exhaustive nor guaranteed to work in the given situation, since every technical problem is in many ways unique to its operating environment. Table 12.1 shows some possible solutions for common problems. These solutions are intended to provide examples of applicable methodologies.

Table 12.1

Troubleshooting Examples

Problem	Possible Solution
Cannot print to a local printer	Verify that the correct driver is installed, ensure that the printer's buffer is clear, try printing directly to the LPT port from a DOS prompt
Cannot print to a network printer	Ensure that File and Printer Sharing is enabled at the remote computer; verify that you have correct network protocols configured
Print jobs are not spooling properly	Disable spooling in the Properties sheet of the printer, which will indicate whether spooling is in fact the problem; verify that enough disk space is available to hold the spooled print jobs
Print jobs are garbled	Disable EMF spooling; check whether Windows 3.1 printer drivers are being used
Fatal Exception errors and General Protection Faults	Try Safe mode; try a standard VGA driver; run SCANDISK with a full surface scan to check for corrupted files
Message that communications port is already in use when attempting to use a terminal program	Verify that no fax manager software is running in the background, waiting for calls, as this ties up the communications port
A newly installed ISA device is not functioning	Check the Device Manager for conflicts with existing devices (designated by a yellow exclamation mark)
CD-ROM drive is not listed as a drive in the Explorer or the Device Manager	Most likely not a supported brand; install Real-mode driver support

Problem	Possible Solution
A device is malfunctioning, but when it is removed from Device Manager and redetected, the problem persists	Edit the Registry, delete the associated key under HKLM\Enum\Root\, restart the computer, and run hardware detection again

Review Questions

The following questions will test your knowledge of the information in this chapter. For additional questions, see MCP Endeavor and the Microsoft Roadmap/Assessment Exam on the CD-ROM that accompanies this book.

1. Microsoft Technet is ______.

   A. a CompuServe forum

   B. an Internet forum

   C. a CD-ROM publication

   D. a users group

2. Which three of the following are Windows 95 optimization and troubleshooting tools?

   A. System Resource Monitor

   B. Net Watcher

   C. System Monitor

   D. System Resource Meter

3. Which two of the following statements are true?

   A. System Monitor cannot monitor a remote PC.

   B. A share-level PC cannot monitor a user-level OC using Net Watcher.

C. System Monitor is located in System Tools in the Accessories group.

D. System Monitor is located in the System Control Panel applet.

4. The main factor in ensuring print performance is ______.

   A. spool settings

   B. driver compatibility

   C. queue management

   D. font management

5. Choosing to return control after the first page is spooled ______ wait time.

   A. increases

   B. shortens

   C. doesn't change

   D. eliminates

6. To access the boot menu, press ______ while Windows 95 boots.

   A. Ctrl+Alt+Del

   B. Alt+Tab

   C. F6

   D. F8

7. Which two of the following would be disabled in Windows 95 Safe mode?

   A. A 256-color display driver

   B. Control Panel applets

C. AUTOEXEC.BAT

D. A non-Microsoft mouse

8. ______ includes support for a number of error-isolation switches.

   A. BOOT.COM

   B. WINCHK.COM

   C. WIN.COM

   D. WIN95.COM

9. Logged Mode logs the entire boot process to a file called ______.

   A. BOOT.LOG

   B. BOOTLOG.TXT

   C. BOOT.TXT

   D. LOGBOOT.TXT

Review Answers

1. C
2. B C D
3. B C
4. A
5. B
6. D
7. A C
8. C
9. B

Part 2
Networking Essentials

Chapter 13

Network Basics

In the 1980s, the desktop computer emerged as a low-cost alternative to the high-priced mainframe. Each desktop computer was capable of integrating all peripherals and software to accomplish certain tasks, but data transfer between systems all too often required the cumbersome intervention of a human with a floppy disk.

As the computer industry grew, PC managers, marketers, users, and designers began to see the advantages of sharing data and hardware among a group of individual but cooperating PCs. The first PC network operating systems (such as Novell NetWare and Microsoft LAN Manager) were designed as add-ons to existing desktop operating systems. A new breed of PC operating systems such as Microsoft Windows 95 and Windows NT now include a fully integrated system of network services.

The integration of network services within personal desktop operating systems and the public emergence of the worldwide network—the Internet—has generated incredible momentum in the movement to "get connected." Networks have become a means of disseminating information. In order to understand the complexities of data communications and computer networking, you must have a strong foundation of network concepts and terminology. That foundation begins with this chapter, which addresses the following topics:

- Basic network concepts and components
- Primary network functions

- The differences between client/server and peer-to-peer networks
- The differences between local, metropolitan, and wide area network systems

What Is a Network?

A *network* is a group of interconnected computer systems sharing services and interacting by means of a shared communications link. The requirement of a network is, therefore, two or more individuals with something to share. One individual must be able to offer something; the other must be able to accept that something. (Network services are discussed later in this chapter.) The individual systems must be connected through a physical pathway (called the *transmission medium*). All systems on the physical pathway must follow a set of common communication rules so that data arrives at its intended destination, and so the sending and receiving systems understand each other. The rules that govern computer communication are called *protocols.*

In summary, all networks must have the following:

- Something to share (*network services*)
- A physical pathway (*transmission medium*)
- Rules of communication (*protocols*)

Merely having a transmission pathway does not produce communication. When two entities communicate, they do not merely exchange data; rather, they understand the data they receive from each other. The goal of computer networking is not merely to exchange data, but to be able to understand and use data received from other entities on the network.

Because all computers are different, are used in different ways, and can be located at different distances from each other, enabling computers to communicate is often a daunting task that draws on a wide variety of technologies.

Models of Network Computing

There are three models for network computing. The three models are as follows:

- Centralized computing
- Distributed computing
- Collaborative or cooperative computing

These three models are the basis for the various types of computer networks you'll learn about in this book. The following sections discuss the three models for network computing.

Centralized Computing

The earliest computers were large, difficult to manage, and expensive. Originally, these large *mainframe* computers were not networked in the sense you are familiar with today. Jobs were entered into the system by reading commands from card decks. The computer would execute one job at a time and generate a printout when the job was complete. Terminals, which came later, enabled users to interact with the centralized computer, but terminals were merely input/output devices that had no independent processing power. All processing still took place on the mainframe. Networks developed when it became necessary for mainframes to share services with other mainframes.

In summary, the centralized computing model involves the following:

- All processing takes place in the central, mainframe computer.
- Terminals are connected to the central computer and function only as input/output devices.
- Networks may be employed to interconnect two or more mainframe computers.

Distributed Computing

As personal computers were introduced to organizations, a new model of distributed computing emerged. Instead of concentrating computing in a central device, PCs made it possible to give each worker an individual computer. Each PC can process and store data independently. Under the distributed computing model, networking has evolved to enable the many distributed computers to exchange data and share resources and services.

In summary, distributed computing involves the following:

- Multiple computers capable of operating independently
- Tasks that are split up among the various computers
- Networks that enable the computers to exchange data and services

Collaborative Computing

Also called *cooperative computing, collaborative computing* enables computers in a distributed computing environment to share processing power in addition to data, resources, and services. In a collaborative computing environment, one computer might "borrow" processing power by running a program on other computers on the network. Or, processes might be designed so they can run on two or more computers. Obviously, collaborative computing cannot take place without a network to enable the various computers to communicate.

In summary, collaborative computing involves the following:

- Multiple computers
- Networks that enable the computers to exchange data and services
- Multiple computers that can cooperate to perform a task

Network Models

PC networks generally fall within one of two network models: client/server and peer-to-peer.

Many network environments employ both network models. For example, an organization may use Novell's client/server Netware and Microsoft's Windows for Workgroups peer-to-peer network operating systems concurrently. New desktop operating systems such as Microsoft Windows 95 employ both network models.

Client/Server Networking

In a client/server network environment, resources are located on a central server or group of servers. A *server* is a computer that is specifically designated to provide services for the other computers on the network. A network client accesses the resources available from the server but does not provide services.

Under the client/server model, hardware resources can be concentrated on network servers, and client computers can be designed with minimal hardware configurations. As an extreme example, a client computer can be completely diskless—neither hard nor floppy drive–equipped. By making requests to the servers, the needs of the client can be satisfied while the overall hardware cost expenditure of an organization is reduced.

Many network clients are mid-scale personal computers that utilize the processing power and storage capability provided by the hardware of the network server. The typical client can be an average-powered IBM 386/486 or compatible with 4 or 8 MB of RAM and a 540-MB hard disk, or a low-powered IBM XT or compatible with 640 KB RAM and a 10-MB hard disk. The client configuration is dependent on which services are required by the client.

Client/server networking is ideal in larger networks where network security is of concern. Under the client/server model, a network administrator can easily control access to network resources. Through the network operating system, the network administrator can give or withhold permission for a user to access files, printers, and other resources located on the server.

Peer-to-Peer Networking

In a peer-to-peer network environment, resources are distributed throughout the network on computer systems that may act as both service requesters and service providers. In a peer-to-peer network, the user of each PC is responsible for the administration and sharing of resources for his or her PC. (This is known as *distributed* or *workgroup administration.*)

Peer-to-peer networks are ideal for small organizations (or for home networks) with limited users where security is not of concern. Peer-to-peer networks also provide a decentralized alternative for situations in which server administration would be too large or complex a task.

Local, Metropolitan, and Wide Area Networks

Networks come in all shapes and sizes. Network administrators often classify networks according to geographical size. Networks of similar size have many similar characteristics, as you learn in later chapters. The most common size classifications are the following:

- Local area networks (LANs)
- Metropolitan area networks (MANs)
- Wide area networks (WANs)

Each of these size classifications is described in the following sections.

Local Area Networks (LANs)

A *local area network* (LAN) is a group of computers and network communication devices interconnected within a geographically limited area such as a building or campus. A LAN tends to use only one type of transmission medium (cabling).

LANs are characterized by the following:

- They transfer data at high speeds.
- They are relatively error free.
- They exist in a limited geographical area.
- Their technology is inexpensive.

Metropolitan Area Networks (MANs)

A *metropolitan area network* (MAN) is geographically limited to the area of a city. A MAN can interconnect local networks that use different hardware and transmission media.

MANs are characterized by the following:

- They transfer data at high speeds.
- They are relatively error-free.
- They exist in a limited geographical area.
- They interconnect multiple LANs.
- They are more sophisticated and complex than LANs.
- Their technology is moderately expensive.

Wide Area Networks (WANs)

A *wide area network* (WAN) interconnects LANs or MANs. A WAN may be located entirely within a state or country, or it may be interconnected around the world.

WANs are characterized by the following:

- They transfer data at high speeds.
- They exist in an unlimited geographical area.
- They are more susceptible to errors due to the distances data travels.
- They interconnect multiple LANs or MANs
- They are more sophisticated and complex than LANs and MANs.
- Their technology is expensive.

WANs can be further classified into two categories: enterprise WANs and global WANs.

An *enterprise WAN* is a WAN that connects the widely separated computer resources of a single organization. An organization with computer operations at several distant sites can employ an enterprise WAN to interconnect the sites. An enterprise WAN can use a combination of private and commercial network services, but is dedicated to the needs of a particular organization.

A *global WAN* interconnects networks of several corporations or organizations. An example of a global WAN is the Internet.

Network Services

The goals of computer networking are to provide services and to reduce equipment costs. Networks enable computers to share their resources by offering services to other computers. The most common network services are as follows:

- File services
- Print services

- Message services
- Directory services
- Application services
- Database services

The purpose of a network is to provide users with efficient access to these services. The following sections discuss each of these services in detail.

File Services

File services enable networked computers to share files. This capability was perhaps the primary reason networking personal computers became so desirable. Users need to exchange files, a problem that can be solved, if inconveniently, simply by trading files on disks. More importantly, users need to share data in common database files, something that can be done only over a network.

The working definition of file services is all network applications that store, retrieve, or move data files. A feature of file services is access control. File services enable users to read, write, and manage files and data, but they also should restrict users to authorized file operations so that files aren't accidentally overwritten or deleted.

This section examines the following file services:

- File transfer
- File storage
- Data migration
- File archiving
- File-update synchronization

File Transfer

Without a network, the options for transferring files between computers are limited. You can, of course, exchange files on floppy disks, a process that came to be called "sneaker-net" because it consisted of networking by actually running around and hand-delivering floppy disks from desk to desk. Otherwise, you can use communication software to dial another computer and transfer files via a modem or a direct serial connection.

When users are transferring files, the need for security arises. It might be necessary to limit file transfers to authorized users who are using password-controlled security systems, to assign file attributes that restrict the operations that may be performed with a file, or to encrypt files so they may be read only by authorized users.

Another important file-management task of the NOS is to regulate access to programs and data stored on the file server's hard drive. This is known as *file sharing*. File sharing is another main reason companies invest in a network. Companies save money by purchasing a single network version of an application rather than many single-user versions. Placing data files created by employees on a file server also serves several other purposes, such as security, document control, and backup.

Documents are more secure on the file server than on individual computers. Individual PCs often have limited or nonexistent security. On the file server, however, you need to know a valid login name and have appropriate security rights to access a file.

Document control is critical in a company where a document might be revised several times. In an architectural firm, for example, the design of a building might be done using a drafting program, such as AutoCAD. The architects might produce several versions of the building plan as the client comes to a decision. If the plan was stored on the individual computers of each architect, at some point the firm might not know which is the most recent version of the plans. The wrong version might have a more recent date (because of a backup, for example). If the plan was saved on a file server, however, each architect would work on the same file. The file sharing would be regulated by the operating system.

A tape backup can be installed on the server, forming the heart of a centralized backup strategy. All files located on this (or other connected servers) can be backed up regularly. This strategy is much safer than relying on individual users to back up their workstations.

File Storage

Most networks have at least some form of centralized file storage. For many years, most companies have used the online storage approach to file storage. In the *online storage* scenario, data is stored on hard disks that are accessible on demand. The files that can be accessed on a server are limited to the amount of available hard drive space. Hard drives are fast, but the cost to store a megabyte of data is fairly high. Hard drives have another disadvantage; that is, generally speaking, they cannot be removed for off-site storage or exchange, or simply to build a library of files that are seldom required but must be fairly readily available.

Almost all companies have large amounts of infrequently used data. There is no need to keep all of the financial reports available from the previous year, for example, but they had better be available in case of an audit.

Another approach to file storage is *offline storage,* which consists of removable media that is managed manually. The most popular media used are data tapes or optical disks. Once data is written to a tape or optical disk, the storage medium can be removed from the server and shelved. Users who require offline data might need to know which tape or optical disk to request. Some systems provide indexes or other aids that make requesting the proper offline storage element automatic. A system operator still has to retrieve the tape or disk and mount it on the server, however.

When the slow response of offline storage is unacceptable, a *near-line storage* approach may be selected. Near-line storage employs a machine, often called a "jukebox," to manage large numbers of tapes or optical disks automatically. The proper tape or disk is retrieved and mounted by the jukebox without human intervention. With near-line storage, huge amounts of data can be made available with only slight delays, but at a much lower cost than required to store the data on hard drives.

Storage Options

One of the most important decisions you make when designing your network is what type of hard drive and how much disk space you need. Many storage options are available.

There are three classic trade-offs in computer system designs:

- Speed versus cost
- Speed versus capacity
- Capacity versus cost

Generally speaking, the faster the access to a storage device, the more it costs. The second trade-off isn't as straightforward. In the past, faster devices almost always had less capacity (were less dense) than slower devices. This is no longer a general rule. The last trade-off, capacity versus cost, still holds true. The more capacity a device has, the greater the cost.

Speed of storage devices is measured in milliseconds (ms). A more accurate term for speed is *access time.* Access time for a hard drive, for example, is a combination of seek time and latency. *Seek time* is the time it takes the drive heads to move to the appropriate hard drive cylinder. *Latency* is the time it takes the disk to spin around to the proper sector.

Here are some common terms used in conjunction with disk drives:

- **Track.** A *track* is one of the concentric rings that logically subdivides each hard drive platter. Tracks are much like the grooves in a phonograph record. Previous recording technology physically cut grooves in a vinyl disk. The needle of the record player vibrated according to the depth and waviness of the grooves, which translated into sound waves. Unlike a record, however, a track on a disk platter doesn't spiral towards the center. Tracks remain the same distance from the center all the way around the disk platter.
- **Sector.** A *sector* is a subdivision of a track. A sector is like a slice of pie. Picture the hard drive's platter as if it were a pie. Cut rings into the pie starting at the center. Each ring is analogous to a track. Slice the pie into pieces. Each piece is analogous to a sector.
- **Cylinder.** A *cylinder* consists of all tracks that are above or below each other. A cylinder is a logical, circular-shaped division of the hard drive. Cylinders consist of concentric ring-shaped divisions of the hard drive's platters.

Figure 13.1 illustrates the concepts of tracks, sectors, and cylinders.

Figure 13.1

Tracks, sectors, and cylinders in a hard drive.

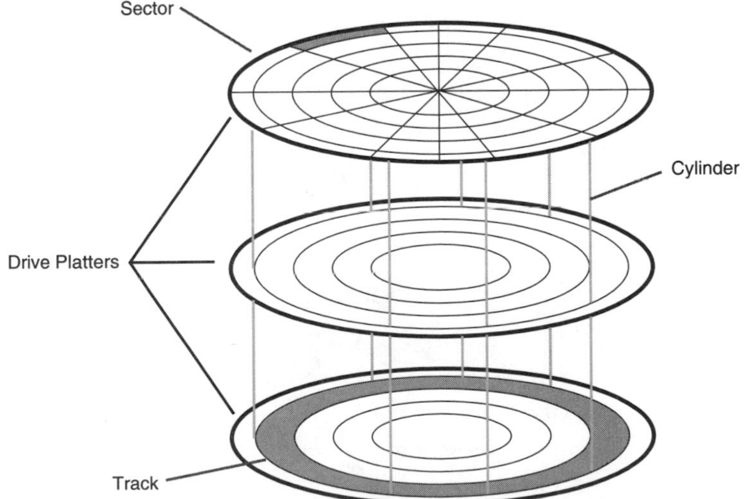

High-Speed Storage Systems

The highest speed storage is RAM (also called *DRAM*). Access time for RAM is measured in nanoseconds. The disadvantages of using RAM for storage are that it is expensive and holds information only while electricity is applied.

The next fastest device available is the hard drive. Access time ranges from 4 to 60 milliseconds. Several different types of hard drives are available. The most popular types currently available are Integrated Drive Electronics (IDE) and Small Computer Systems Interface (SCSI) drives.

IDE and EIDE Drives

IDE drives are fast and inexpensive. The electronics necessary to control the drive are integrated into the chassis of the drive itself. They aren't fully standardized, so you might have difficulty putting drives of different vendors in the same computer.

One limitation of the original IDE drive is that storage capacity is limited to 528 MB. The more recent *Enhanced IDE drive* (EIDE) avoids this limitation, providing capacities in the gigabytes. EIDE is rapidly replacing IDE. The EIDE specification was designed to make IDE drives more competitive with SCSI systems (see the following section). Another limitation of the original IDE drive is its relatively slow data transfer rate. EIDE uses the drive bandwidth more efficiently, thus allowing transfer rates closer to those possible with SCSI. The EIDE interface also includes some other features found with SCSI but not with original IDE, such as support for multiple IDE devices—IDE could support only two disk drives—and support for CD-ROMs and other non-hard drive peripherals.

SCSI Technology

SCSI technology is not limited to hard drives. A number of devices use SCSI technology to communicate with the computer. SCSI devices include hard drives, tape drives, CD-ROM drives, and a number of other more esoteric devices beyond the scope of this book.

SCSI drives do not suffer from the drive-chaining problem mentioned in the previous section. Most SCSI drives, much like IDE drives, feature an embedded SCSI controller. The *embedded controller* consists of the circuitry needed to control the drive. A separate SCSI controller that plugs into an expansion slot in the computer is necessary to control SCSI devices. You create a SCSI bus when you daisy-chain several SCSI devices together and connect them to the SCSI controller in the PC. SCSI drives can be placed inside the computer or in an external box called an *expansion chassis.* Each SCSI controller inside a PC can control up to seven SCSI devices. Most computers handle up to four SCSI controllers.

An extension to SCSI technology is known as *RAID,* which stands for *Redundant Array of Inexpensive Devices.* RAID technology chains SCSI drives together so that they function as a single unit. Various levels of protection and performance are available.

CD-ROM

CD-ROM (Compact Disk–Read Only Memory) drives do not record data. These units play back CDs programmed by the vendor. CDs are an efficient way to distribute large amounts of data. Most operating system vendors now ship their operating systems on CD. Multimedia products, which feature software, sound, and graphics (sometimes full-motion video clips), also ship on CD.

CD-ROM drives are much slower than hard drives. Capacity of a CD hovers between 500 MB and 1 GB (gigabyte, or 1 billion bytes). Many CD-ROM drives are SCSI devices. You can attach them to a SCSI controller in the file server. CD-ROM drives can be daisy-chained to other drives.

WORM

WORM (write-once, read-many) drives are gaining in popularity as archival storage devices. WORM drives are CD-ROM drives that can be written to one time only. Once written, they can be read but not rerecorded. Although this limits their use as online media, they are excellent for the purposes of archiving data and storing information such as the company's accounts for the last several years.

When writing information to the drive, the laser built into the drive head literally burns the new pattern onto the disk. Information is written to the disk one sector at a time until all sectors on the disk have been used. Information does not have to be written in one session. You can stretch the use of a single disk over several days, weeks, or months as needed.

Rewritable Optical

Some optical disk units enable you to both read and write. The most popular of such technologies is the *magneto-optical* drive. This drive has a read/write mechanism with both optical and magnetic heads. Typical access time of such devices is 100+ ms. The capacity is currently in the area of 650 MB.

Figure 13.2 illustrates the workings of the read/write mechanism. The disk is composed of a heat-sensitive magnetic material. When you want to write data to the disk, the laser heats the disk at the desired location. The magnetic head then changes the polarity of that location on the disk, thus changing it from a 1 to a 0 or the reverse.

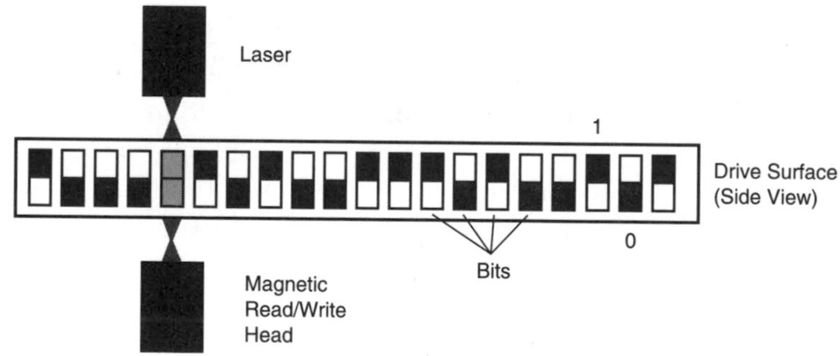

Figure 13.2

A magneto-optical drive read/write mechanism.

Other Removable Media

Several types of removable media are available. CDs, WORM disks, and magneto-optical disks fall into this category. Other sorts of removable media are variations of hard disk technology. Two types of removable hard drive systems currently are available. One technology, originally introduced as the Bernoulli hard drive system, featured a removable hard disk cartridge. The cartridges were almost twice the size of a VHS video tape. They plugged into a drive bay and originally furnished 20 MB of disk space per cartridge. This technology continues to be available, with the cartridges getting smaller and the capacity increasing.

In the other type of removable hard drive system, the cartridge is a completely self-contained hard drive. Systems typically feature IDE drive units that plug into a drive bay. The *drive bay* is little more than a connector that gains the drive access to the main bus of the computer. Access time and capacity match that of any other IDE drive.

Tape Backup Units

Tape backup units have the largest capacity of all devices discussed so far, but the slowest access speed. There are many different types of tape units, each of which is designed around a different type of tape. Most vendors also offer a tape unit that accommodates multiple tapes. These are referred to as *auto-loaders.*

Data Migration

Data migration is a technology that automatically moves less-used data from online storage to near-line or offline storage. The criteria for moving files can depend on when the files were last used, the owner of the files, file size, or a variety of other factors. An efficient data-migration facility makes it easy for users to locate migrated files.

Figure 13.3 illustrates one approach to data migration.

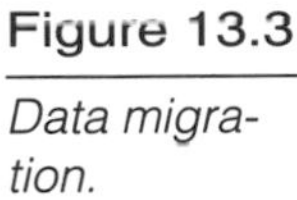

Figure 13.3

Data migration.

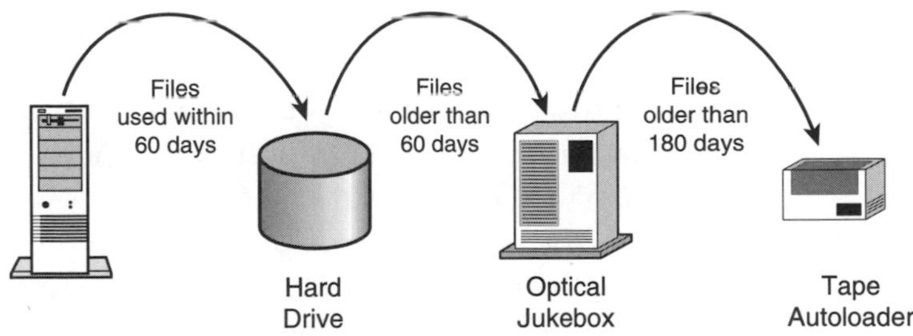

File Archiving

File archiving (also known as *backup*) is basically offline storage that is primarily geared to creating duplicate copies of online files. These backup copies serve as insurance against minor or major system failures.

Networks enable file archiving to be centralized. It's possible, for example, for a single site to back up all the servers on a network. Many current backup systems also offer the capability to back up various client workstations, making it feasible to archive all files on the network to a central facility, whether the files are located on network servers or clients.

File-Update Synchronization

In its simplest form, *file-update synchronization* is a means of ensuring that all users have the latest copy of a file. File-update synchronization services can manage files by monitoring the date and time stamps on files to determine which ones were saved most recently. By tracking the users who access the file, along with the date and time stamps, the service can update all the copies of the file with the most recent version.

File-update synchronization, however, can be considerably more involved. In a modern computing environment, it is not always feasible for all users to access all files in real time. A salesman, for example, might be carrying a notebook computer on which to enter orders. It would be impractical to dial the central LAN every time an order was to be entered, so the salesman would enter orders offline (while disconnected from the network) and store them in the laptop. That evening, he would call the central LAN, log in, and transmit all the day's orders at once.

During this process, files on the LAN must be updated to reflect new data in the salesman's portable computer. In addition, the salesman's PC might need some updating, with order confirmations or new pricing information, for example. The process of bringing the local and remote files into agreement is also known as file-update synchronization.

File-update synchronization becomes considerably more challenging when additional users are sharing data files simultaneously. Complex mechanisms must be in place to ensure that users do not accidentally overwrite each other's data. In some cases, the system simply flags files that have multiple, conflicting updates and requires a human to reconcile the differences.

Print Services

Network printing was the second big incentive for installing LANs. Here are just some of the advantages of printing on a network:

- Many users can share the same printers—a capability that is especially useful with expensive devices, such as color printers and plotters.
- Printers can be located anywhere, not just next to a user's PC.
- Queue-based network printing is more efficient than direct printing because the workstation can begin working again as soon as a job is queued to the network.
- Modern printing services can enable users to send facsimile (fax) transmissions through the network to a fax server.

In this book, *print services* are defined as network applications that control and manage access to printers, network fax, and other similar devices.

You learn more about network printing in Chapter 21.

Message Services

File services can pass data among users when the data comes in the form of a file. Today, however, many new types of data are available, including audio, video, and graphics. Text data can be simple text, or it can come in exotic forms such as hypertext (which contains electronic links to other text, documents, images, sounds, or other types of data).

Message services consist of a wide variety of services that go beyond simple file sharing to store, transfer, and access text as well as binary, graphic, video, and audio data.

In the following sections, the following four types of message services are briefly examined:

- Electronic mail
- Integrated electronic mail and voice mail
- Object-oriented applications
- Workgroup applications

Electronic Mail

Electronic mail (or e-mail) is technology for electronically transferring messages between networked computers and is the hot new reason to install a LAN. In fact, a LAN is an excellent platform for e-mail because it provides reliable, high-speed service and is low in cost.

E-mail systems can service anything from a local workgroup, to a corporation, to the world. By installing e-mail routing devices, you can transfer mail smoothly and efficiently among several LANs. Perhaps the most gargantuan e-mail system is found on the Internet, which enables users in dozens of countries throughout the world to exchange electronic messages more easily than mailing a paper letter.

Early text-based e-mail has given way to elaborate systems that support embedded sound, graphics, and even video data. Modern e-mail systems also enable traveling clients to "call in" to send and receive mail.

Integrated Electronic Mail and Voice Mail

New messaging technologies are leading to closer interoperation of e-mail and voice-mail systems. Voice mail can be more than a simple telephone answering system. Because voice-mail systems are themselves based on computers, they can be connected to networks, and voice data can be managed by messaging services. Eventually, this will enable various voice- and e-mail systems to interoperate and freely exchange data.

In the future, it may be possible for a traveling user to forward her e-mail messages to her voice mail. She then could call in and have the messages read electronically by a text-recognition system. Alternatively, speech-recognition devices might be used to read a user's voice mail and convert it to a text-based e-mail message.

Object-Oriented Applications

Objects are building blocks (consisting of abstract data types and program code) that can be combined to construct large, more complex, object-oriented applications.

Messaging services can be used as intermediaries that enable objects on the network to communicate. Messaging-service applications achieve this by acting as agents for the objects. The object simply delivers data to an agent, which is then responsible for delivering the data to the destination object. This eliminates the need for objects to have the capability of communicating with all other objects on the network.

Workgroup Applications

Workgroup applications use network services to improve communication in workgroups. Two types of workgroup applications are workflow management applications and linked-object documents.

Workflow Management Applications

Workflow management applications route electronic forms and documents among workgroup users. When reliable electronic signatures are added to the process, it becomes possible to replace numerous processes that are traditionally paper-bound.

For example, an electronic purchase-order system might function like this:

1. The requester fills in an electronic form.
2. The form is routed to the requester's supervisor for an approval signature, which is added electronically.
3. The signed form is routed to a budget manager, who ensures that funds are available. Funding verification might even take place automatically before the form is brought to the budget manager's attention.
4. The approved purchase request is used to generate a paper purchase order that can be faxed to the vendor.

You can see how users along the way can add information to the form. The pioneering example of a workflow management application is Lotus Notes.

Linked-Object Documents

Documents need no longer be regarded simply as files containing text. Modern documents can consist of many different types of objects, including text, graphics, sound, voice, spreadsheet data, and video. Various types of objects can be assembled to build documents.

Objects are more than just data. An object embedded in a document has a degree of intelligence that enables it to pass messages to the operating system and to other documents. Some sense of this operation can be seen by experimenting with OLE in Microsoft Windows.

Directory Services

A *directory service* integrates all the information about objects on the network into an overall directory structure. Network objects can consult the directory to identify and exchange messages with other network objects. The objects themselves don't need to know the address, location, or messaging formats required to communicate; all this information is provided by the directory service.

Directory services can greatly simplify network tasks. Suppose a network consists of two file servers and an e-mail server. Without directory services, the network administrator would have to manage user accounts on all three servers independently. With directory services, the network administrator can manage all three servers from a single directory structure.

The directory structure hides the physical structure of the network from applications and from users. A print server is simply a part of the network; it isn't a service being offered by a particular computer.

The actual directory, however, is stored in files that physically reside on one or more servers. When information in the directory is duplicated on several servers, a *directory synchronization* process is needed to keep all copies of the directory up-to-date.

Application Services

Application services enable applications to leverage the computing power and specialized capabilities of other computers on the network.

For example, business applications often must perform complex statistical calculations beyond the scope of most desktop PCs. Statistical software with the required capabilities might need to run on a mainframe computer or on a Unix minicomputer. The statistical package, however, can make its capabilities available to applications on users' PCs by providing an application service.

The client PC sends the request for a calculation to the statistics application server. After the results become available, they are returned to the client. In this way, only one computer in an organization requires the expensive software license and processing power required to produce the statistics, but all client PCs can benefit.

Application services enable organizations to install servers that are specialized for specific functions. The most common application servers currently are database servers, discussed in the next section. Other application services, however, are beginning to emerge.

Application servers are an effective strategy for making a network more scaleable. New application servers can be added as new types of application needs emerge. If more power is needed for the application, only the application server needs to be upgraded. A database server, for example, might grow from a PC to a multiprocessor RISC system running Unix without requiring many (or even any) changes to the client PCs.

If demand for services loads down the server and hurts performance, it's easy to move an application service to its own computer. This scalability is one of the advantages of a LAN architecture.

Database Services

Database services are the most common examples of application servers. Because database servers enable applications to be designed in separate client and server components, they are frequently called *client/server databases.*

With a client/server database, the client and server applications are designed to take advantage of specialized capabilities of the client and database systems, as follows:

- The client application manages data input from the user, generation of screen displays, some of the reporting, and generating data retrieval requests that are sent to the database server.

- The *database server* manages the database files; adds, deletes, and modifies records in the database; queries the database and generates the result required by the client; and transmits results back to the client. The database server can service requests for multiple clients more or less at the same time.

Database services relieve clients of most responsibilities for managing data. A modern database server is a sophisticated piece of software that can perform the following functions:

- Provide database security
- Optimize the performance of database operations
- Determine optimal locations for storing data without requiring clients to know where the data is located
- Service large numbers of clients by reducing the time any one client is accessing the database
- Distribute data across multiple database servers.

Distributed databases are becoming increasingly popular. They enable portions of databases to be stored on separate server computers, which may be in different geographic locations. This technique, known as *distributed data,* looks like a single logical database to users, but places the data users need in the most accessible location. East Coast sales data, for example, might be located on a database server in Boston, whereas West Coast sales data is on a server in San Diego. Special database mechanisms must be in place to keep the data in the copies of the database synchronized.

More simply, databases can be replicated; complete copies of the database can be stored in various locations. This provides a redundancy factor because disaster is unlikely to strike all copies at once. Additionally, database replication improves application response time because users can access the database locally rather than through a relatively slow WAN.

As shown in figure 13.4, the most popular strategies for replication databases are the following:

- **Master server updates.** In this scenario, a single master server receives all updates and, in turn, updates all replicas.
- **Locally driven updates.** In this scenario, any local server can receive an update and is responsible for distributing the change to other replicas.

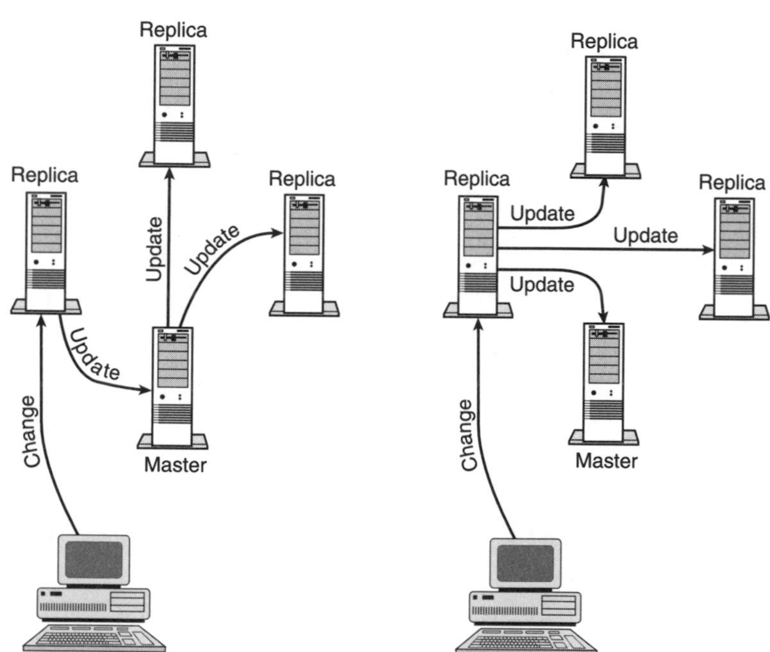

Figure 13.4

Master-driven and locally driven database replication.

Implementing Network Services in Centralized and Distributed Environments

Just as networks may be organized according to centralized or distributed models, the services offered on networks can be centralized or distributed.

A *centralized* service may be located entirely on a mainframe computer or on a LAN server that uses a server-centric NOS. On networks that employ a peer-to-peer NOS, services can be centralized or can be *distributed* on two or more computers.

A server-centric NOS does not imply a client/server relationship between workstations and the server. When a workstation is configured to function only by requesting services from the network server, network services then are centralized, but the network doesn't adhere to a client/server model.

A client/server model implies that the client is an intelligent device that cooperates with the server to manage data.

The remainder of this chapter discusses issues related to implementing network services.

Control of Resources

The centralized approach follows the adage "Put all your eggs in one basket and watch that basket very carefully." When hardware and software are concentrated, they can be maintained by experts and closely monitored with management tools. This doesn't necessarily mean that all devices are physically located in the same area, only that they are grouped for efficient and effective management.

The centralized approach also is logically simpler, and fewer disruptive events are likely to jeopardize data. When resources are distributed through a network, it can be difficult to isolate the causes of problems.

The most important resources being controlled on any network are the files that contain the organization's critical data. In most cases, organizations choose to store the most critical files on a centralized file server from which all users access and share the files. This approach is called *server-centric, client/server,* or *dedicated server file service.* It's important to understand the advantages and disadvantages of the centralized and distributed approaches.

Centralized File Services

Dedicated file servers have the following benefits:

- Files are in a specific place where they can be reliably archived.
- Central file servers can be managed more efficiently.
- Central file servers can contain expensive, high-performance hardware that expedites file services and makes the file servers more reliable.
- The cost of specialized file server technology is shared by a large number of users.

A couple of issues, however, should be considered with regard to central file services, as follows:

- When all data is stored on a single server, a single point of failure exists. If the server fails, all data becomes unavailable. This makes proper design, management, and backup of the server essential.
- Because all clients are contending for file services from a single source, average file-access times might be slower with a centralized file server than when files are stored on individual, local hard drives.

Centralized file services are generally chosen for organizations that want to achieve the highest levels of protection for their data files.

Distributed File Services

In a peer-to-peer network environment, any computer can share its files and applications with any other computer. The sharing of services must be established for each individual computer, and each user must have the skills required to manage the networking services on his or her PC. Because services are provided by many different computers, users must become aware of which computers are providing which services. Clearly, the skills and responsibility required of users is higher than for centralized file services.

Some advantages of distributed file storage include the following:

- There is no single point of failure. When a computer fails, only the files stored on that computer become unavailable.
- Individuals typically experience faster access for files located on local hard drives than for files on centralized file servers.
- No specialized server hardware is required. File services can be provided with standard PCs.

Some issues related to distributed file storage include the following:

- It's more difficult to manage the file service and to protect the integrity of files. File backup is more difficult when files are distributed across many PCs.
- Individual PCs generally don't have high-reliability hardware, including uninterruptible power supplies, disk mirroring, and so forth.
- File services provided by peers typically are not as fast as file services provided by a central file server that is specifically designed for the purpose.
- When higher performance is required, instead of upgrading one central file server, you must upgrade each computer.

Organizations tend to choose peer-to-peer networking for two primary reasons. One is a desire to network with their current stock of PCs without the expense of a centralized server. Another is that peer-to-peer is an informal networking approach that fits the working style of many organizations.

Server Specialization

Humans often specialize so that they become very good at one type of task. This approach has benefits for network servers as well. By dedicating each server computer to providing a specific set of services, it becomes possible to carefully tailor the computer to the requirements for that service. This results in optimal performance, simpler troubleshooting, and enhanced scalability. Server specialization implies that the network is being organized with a centralized approach.

Selecting Network Operating Systems (NOSs)

When vendors develop network operating systems, designers choose whether to use a centralized or a distributed model. Some network operating systems are clearly designed to implement LANs based on centralized models, including the following:

- Novell NetWare
- Banyan VINES
- OpenVMS
- IBM OS/2 LAN Server
- Microsoft Windows NT Server

On the other hand, many products are designed to implement peer-to-peer networking models, including the following:

- Novell Personal NetWare
- Microsoft Windows for Workgroups and Windows NT
- AppleTalk (the networking system for Apple Macintosh computers)
- Artisoft LANtastic

Many peer-to-peer products can be added to networks that are primarily managed by centralized servers.

Review Questions

The following questions will test your knowledge of the information in this chapter. For additional questions, see MCP Endeavor and the Microsoft Roadmap/Assessment Exam on the CD-ROM that accompanies this book.

1. Which model of network computing does not take advantage of the processing capability of a user's desktop computer?

   A. Centralized

   B. Distributed

   C. Collaborative

   D. All of the above utilize the processing capabilities of personal PCs.

2. In which model do users' personal computers process information independently from each other?

   A. Centralized

   B. Distributed

   C. Collaborative

   D. None of the above

3. In which model of network computing do computers share each other's processing capabilities?

   A. Centralized

   B. Distributed

   C. Collaborative

   D. Departmental

4. Which type of network is most likely confined to a building or a campus?

    A. Local area
    B. Metropolitan area
    C. Wide area
    D. Departmental

5. MANs typically require different ______ and ______ than LANs.

    A. file servers
    B. transmission media
    C. NOS
    D. network hardware

6. What are the size limits of a wide area network?

    A. 100 kilometers
    B. 1,000 kilometers
    C. 10,000 kilometers
    D. Worldwide

7. Which two entities can share services on a network?

    A. Servers
    B. Clients
    C. Peers
    D. Requesters

8. Which two entities can utilize services on a network?

    A. Servers
    B. Clients
    C. Peers
    D. Communicators

9. Which of the following can concurrently provide and request services?

   A. Server

   B. Client

   C. Peer

   D. None of the above

10. Which of the following is a network operating systems?

    A. OS/2

    B. NetWare

    C. Unix

    D. MS-DOS

11. The rules that govern computer communication are called ______.

    A. protocols

    B. media

    C. services

    D. network operating systems

12. Which two of the following are offline file storage media?

    A. Tape data cartridges

    B. Removable disks

    C. Hard disk drives

    D. Optical jukebox

13. Which of the following is a near-line file storage medium?

    A. Optical jukebox

    B. Hard disk drive

    C. Floppy disks

    D. Removable hard drives

14. File services are all network applications that ______, ______, or ______ data files.

    A. retrieve

    B. copy

    C. store

    D. move

15. Which file service is responsible for creating duplicate copies of files to protect against file damage?

    A. File transfer

    B. File-update synchronization

    C. File archiving

    D. Remote file access

16. When users are ______ files, the need for security arises.

    A. copying

    B. transferring

    C. printing

    D. storing

17. Which two of the following are file services?

    A. Archiving

    B. Remote file access

    C. Update synchronization

    D. Data integrity

18. Which three types of information can be processed by a message service?

    A. Text

    B. Audio

    C. Interactive

    D. Video

19. Messaging applications can enable objects on a network to communicate with each other by providing ______.

    A. transmission media

    B. protocols

    C. update synchronization

    D. agents

20. Which three statements are true regarding directory services?

    A. Directory services enable users to determine physical locations of services.

    B. Directory services manage resources on multiple servers from a central point.

    C. Directory services enable users to access network services on multiple servers.

    D. The directory may be stored on more than one server.

21. On the network, objects can consult directory services to do which two of the following?

    A. Exchange messages

    B. Find messaging formats required to communicate

    C. Identify other objects

    D. Integrate information into a directory structure

22. Which three statements are true regarding application services?

    A. Clients request services.
    B. Application services lack scalability.
    C. Application servers can be optimized to specialize in a service.
    D. Multiple services can be offered by the same server PC.

23. Which three statements are true regarding database services?

    A. A database server improves data security.
    B. All data must be located on the main database server.
    C. Database performance may be optimized.
    D. Database services enable multiple clients to share a database.

24. Which are the two most popular strategies for replication databases?

    A. Remote file access
    B. File-update synchronization
    C. Locally driven update
    D. Master server update

25. A centralized service may be located on ______.

    A. a mainframe computer
    B. a server-centric LAN
    C. a peer-to-peer LAN
    D. a stand-alone desktop LAN

26. Which three are advantages of a centralized approach to providing file services?

    A. Centralized files may be readily archived.
    B. It provides the best possible performance.
    C. Management is efficient.
    D. The cost of high-performance, high-reliability servers can be spread across many users.

27. Which two are advantages of a distributed approach to providing file services?

    A. There is no central point of failure.
    B. It's less difficult to manage than a complex, centralized server.
    C. It's easily scaled to improve performance for all users.
    D. Specialized equipment is not required.

Review Answers

1. A
2. B
3. C
4. A
5. B D
6. D
7. A D
8. B C
9. C
10. B
11. A

12. A B
13. A
14. A C D
15. C
16. B
17. A C
18. A B D
19. D
20. B C D
21. A C
22. A C D
23. A C D
24. C D
25. A B C
26. A C D
27. A D

Chapter 14

The OSI Model

Before servers can provide services to clients, communications between the two entities must be possible. Besides the cables that you see, numerous processes operate behind the scenes to keep things running smoothly. These processes are called *protocols.* As Chapter 13, "Network Basics," explains, protocols, along with services and transmission media, make up the three components of a network. This chapter explores in great detail the OSI Reference Model, which divides network protocols into seven layers.

In this chapter, you will learn about the following:

- De facto versus De jure standards
- The role of rules in the communication process
- How network protocols form protocol stacks
- The seven-layer OSI Reference Model
- The IEEE 802 standards

Standards

There are two types of standards in the network industry: *de facto* standards and *de jure* standards. In order to understand the concept of open systems architecture, you must be familiar with the concepts of de facto and de jure standards.

De facto standards arise in the industry by virtue of widespread commercial and educational use. De facto standards are often proprietary and may be unpublished and unavailable to outside vendors. Unpublished and unavailable standards are known as *closed system* standards. Published and accessible standards are known as *open system* standards. Through the introduction of the OSI model, which is discussed later in this chapter, and the growing acceptance of the concept of interoperability, many closed proprietary systems (such as IBM's Systems Network Architecture) have started to migrate toward open system standards. De facto standards are not always closed system standards; examples of proprietary open system standards include Novell's NetWare network operating system and Microsoft's Windows.

De jure standards are non-proprietary; no single company makes them or owns rights to them. They are developed with the intent of providing for greater connectivity and interoperability by making specifications public so that independent manufacturers can build to such specifications. TCP/IP is an example of a non-proprietary de jure standard.

Several permanent committees of industry representatives develop de jure standards. Although these committees are supported by manufacturer subscriptions and by major company end users, they are supposed to represent the interests of the entire community and remain independent of any particular manufacturer's interests. Subscribing to de jure standards reduces the risk and cost of developing hardware and software for manufacturers. Once a standard has been finalized, a component manufacturer subscribing to it can develop products with some confidence that the products will operate with components from other companies.

Standards Organizations

The responsibility for developing and implementing de jure standards is regulated by standards organizations. Several standards organizations, such as the International Telecommunication Union (ITU) and the Institute of Electrical and Electronic Engineers (IEEE), are responsible for several prominent network standards that support the International Organization for Standardization's objective of network interoperability.

International Standardization Organization (ISO)

The International Standardization Organization (ISO) derived from the Greek prefix *iso-* meaning *same*, is located in Geneva, Switzerland. ISO develops and publishes standards as well as coordinates the activities of all national standardization bodies. In 1977, the ISO set forth to design a communication standard based on the open systems architecture theory, from which computer networks would be designed. This model would be known as the Open System Interconnect (OSI) model.

Rules and the Communication Process

Networks rely on a great many rules to manage information interchange. Some of the issues that tend to arise at one time or another include the following:

- The procedures used to initiate and end an interaction
- The signals used to represent data on the media
- How to direct a message to the intended destination
- Procedures used to control the rate of data flow
- Methods that enable different computer types to communicate
- How to ensure that messages are received correctly

Enabling computers to communicate is an extremely complex process, often too complex to solve all at once using just one set of rules. The industry has chosen to solve parts of the problem so that the solutions can be put together like pieces of a puzzle—a puzzle that comes together differently each time to build a complete communication approach for any given situation.

The OSI Reference Model

Having a model in mind will help you understand how the pieces fit together. The most commonly used model is the *Open Systems Interconnection* (OSI) Reference Model.

The OSI model organizes communication protocols into seven layers. Each layer addresses a narrow portion of the communication process. Figure 14.1 illustrates the layers of the OSI model.

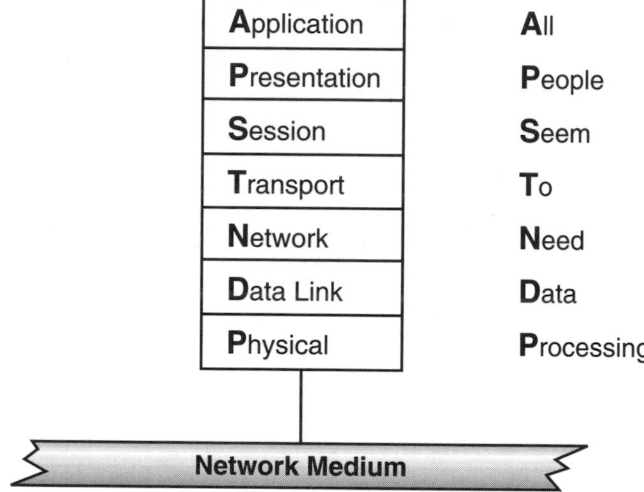

Figure 14.1

The layers of the OSI model.

Each of these layers is examined in detail later in this chapter.

Layer 1, the *physical layer,* consists of protocols that control communication on the network media. Layer 7, the *application layer,* interfaces the network services with the applications in use on the computer. Between Layers 1 and 7 are five other layers that perform intermediate communication tasks.

You need to know the names and order of the seven layers. Use the following two phrases to help you remember the first letters of the layers:

All People Seem To Need Data Processing (top down)

Please Do Not Throw Sausage Pizza Away (bottom up)

Choose one, depending on whether you are most comfortable working from the top of the model down or from the bottom up.

The network medium itself is not part of the model, which deals only with protocols. Protocols represent software constructions, whereas cabling is hardware. Networking cannot exist, however, without communication media. Sometimes, you hear the medium referred to informally as "Layer Zero" of the OSI model.

Figure 14.1 illustrates the origin of the term *protocol stack.* The OSI model breaks the communication process into layers. At each layer, different protocols are selected to solve the needs of a particular communication environment. These protocols are "stacked" one on top of the other until the communication capability is complete. A protocol stack, then, is a set of compatible, layered protocols implemented on a particular computer. Two common examples of protocol stacks are IPX/SPX, the standard NetWare protocols, and TCP/IP, the most widely implemented protocol stack in the computer industry.

A *protocol stack* is a hierarchical set of protocols that coordinate to perform a complete communication process. Each layer utilizes the services that the layer below it provides, and each layer provides services to the layer above it. Formally, layer N services layer $N+1$, and layer $N-1$ services layer N.

Two computers must be running the same protocol stacks before they can communicate; each layer in one computer's protocol stack must interact with a corresponding layer in the other computer's protocol stack (see fig. 14.2). Figure 14.2 originates the path of a message starting in the transport layer. The message travels down the protocol stack, through the network medium, and up the protocol stack of the receiving computer. If the transport layer in the receiving computer understands the protocols used in the transport layer that originated the message, the message can be delivered.

Figure 14.2

Peer communication between protocol stacks.

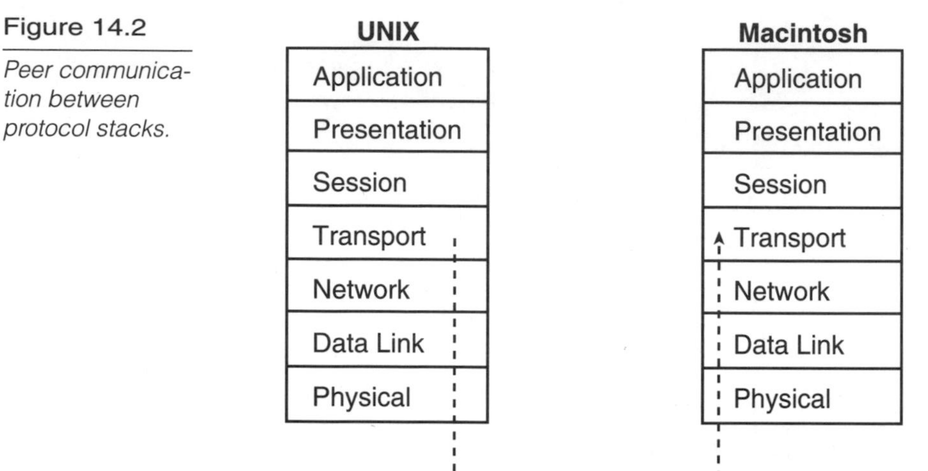

If the protocol stacks on two computers are compatible, different computer types can communicate. TCP/IP, for example, is available for almost any computer and operation system currently being made. If a Macintosh and a Unix workstation both run TCP/IP, the Mac can access files on the Unix workstation.

How Peer Layers Communicate

To communicate with its peer layer in another computer, each protocol layer adds its own information to the message being sent. This information takes the form of a header added to the beginning of the message (see fig. 14.3).

Figure 14.3

Adding headers to messages.

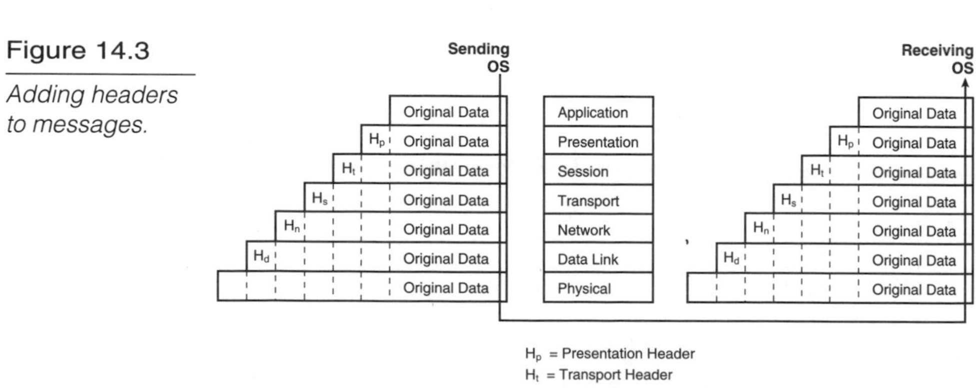

Headers are added as the message is prepared for transmission, and headers are removed (*stripped*) by the receiver after the information in the header has been utilized.

Notice that the data for each layer consists of the header and data of the next higher layer. Because the data format is different at each layer, different terms are commonly used to name the data package at each level. Table 14.1 summarizes these terms by layer.

The physical layer does not append a header because it deals with sending and receiving information on the individual bit level. The bits are assembled into longer message units in the data link layer.

Table 14.1

Data Package Names and the OSI Reference Model

Layer	Data Package Names
Application	Message (and packet)
Presentation	Packet
Session	Packet
Transport	Datagram, segment (and packet)
Network	Datagram (and packet)
Data Link	Frame (and packet)
Physical	Bit (and packet)

As table 14.1 shows, *packet* is a generic term that applies to all layers. This term, therefore, is used for non-layer-specific discussions in later sections.

OSI Physical Layer Concepts

Although the OSI physical layer does not define the media used, the physical layer is concerned with all aspects of transmitting and receiving data on the network media. Specifically, the physical layer is concerned with transmitting and receiving bits. This layer defines several key characteristics of the physical network, including the following:

- Physical structure of the network (physical topology)
- Mechanical and electrical specifications for using the medium (not the medium itself)
- Bit transmission encoding and timing

Although the physical layer does not define the physical medium, it defines clear requirements that the medium must meet, and physical layer specifications differ depending on the physical medium. Ethernet for UTP, for example, has different physical layer specifications from Ethernet for coax.

You learn more about network transmission media in Chapter 15, "Transmission Media." In Chapter 16, "Network Topologies," you learn about physical topologies, and in Chapter 17, "Data Transmission," you learn about digital and analog signaling across the physical network.

OSI Data Link Layer Concepts

As you learned in the preceding section, the OSI physical layer is concerned with moving messages at the machine level. Network communication, however, is considerably more involved than moving bits from one device to another. In fact, dozens of steps must be performed to transport a message from one device to another. Real messages consist not of single bits but of meaningful groups of bits. The data link layer receives messages called *frames* from upper layers. A primary function of the data link layer is to disassemble these frames into bits for transmission and then to reconstruct frames from bits that are received.

The data link layer has other functions as well (although all functions might not be performed by a given network protocol stack). The data link layer performs the following tasks:

- Identifies devices on the network
- Controls (and possibly corrects) errors
- Controls access to the network medium
- Defines the logical topology of the network
- Controls data flow

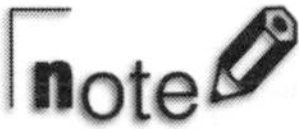

The data link layer is conventionally divided into two sublayers:

- **Media Access Layer (MAC).** Controls the means by which multiple devices share the same media channel.
- **Logical Link Control (LLC).** Establishes and maintains links between communicating devices.

Media Access Control

Any given media channel can support only one signal at a time. If two computers transmit on the channel at the same time, their signals interfere with each other, much as voices interfere when two people speak at the same time. *Media access control* is controlling access to the media so that interference cannot take place.

This section discusses three forms of media access control:

- Contention
- Token passing
- Polling

Contention

With *contention-based access control*, any computer can transmit at any time. This system breaks down when two computers attempt to transmit at the same time, in which case a collision occurs (see fig. 14.4). Eventually, when a network gets busy enough, most attempts to transmit result in collisions, and little effective communication can take place.

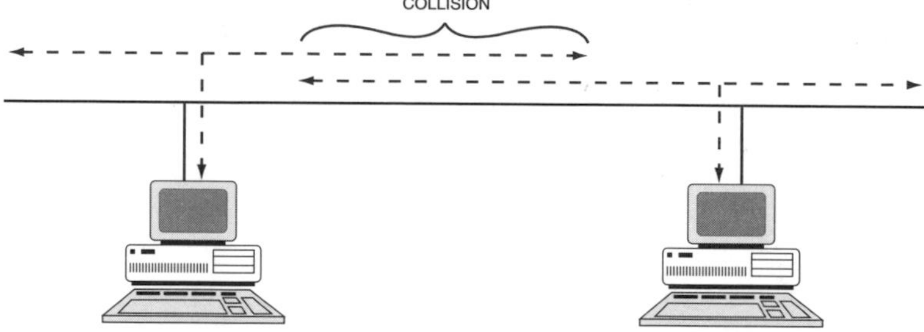

Figure 14.4

A collision on a contention-based network.

Mechanisms, therefore, usually are put into place to minimize the effects of collisions. One mechanism is *carrier sensing*, whereby each computer listens to the network before attempting to transmit. If the network is busy, the computer refrains from transmitting until the network quiets down. This simple "listen before talking" strategy can significantly reduce collisions.

Another mechanism is *carrier detection*. With this strategy, computers continue to listen to the network as they transmit. If a computer detects another signal that interferes with the signal it's sending, it stops transmitting. Both computers then wait a random amount of time and attempt to retransmit. Unless the network is extremely busy, carrier detection along with carrier sensing can manage a large volume of transmissions.

Both of these mechanisms used together form the protocol used in all types of Ethernet, which is called *Carrier Sense Multiple Access with Collision Detection* (CSMA/CD). You learn more about Ethernet networks in Chapter 19, "Network Architectures."

Apple's LocalTalk network uses the protocol *Carrier Sense Multiple Access with Collision Avoidance* (CSMA/CA). *Collision Avoidance* uses additional techniques to further reduce the likelihood of collisions.

Contention is an access-control method. CSMA/CD and CSMA/CA are protocols that incorporate contention access methods.

The following summarizes the characteristics of contention-access controls:

- Pure contention systems permit all stations to transmit whenever they want (although mechanisms are virtually always in place to limit transmission).
- Collisions always occur at some level on contention-based networks, with the number increasing geometrically as transmissions increase.
- CSMA/CD and CSMA/CA are two protocols that reduce the damage caused by collisions.

Although it sounds as if contention methods are unworkable due to the damage caused by collisions, contention (in particular CSMA/CD) is the most popular media access control method on LANs in the form of Ethernet. (In fact, no currently employed LAN standards utilize pure contention access control without adding some mechanism to reduce the incidence of collisions.)

Contention is a simple protocol that can be managed with simple software and hardware. Unless traffic levels exceed about 30 percent of bandwidth, contention works quite well. Contention-based networks offer excellent performance at low cost.

Because collisions occur at unpredictable intervals, however, no computer is guaranteed the capability to transmit at any given time. Contention-based networks are called probabilistic because a computer's chance of being permitted to transmit cannot be predicted.

Collisions increase in frequency as more computers use the network. When the number of computers on the network climbs to an unmanageable amount, collisions dominate network traffic, and few frames are transmitted without error.

All computers on a contention-based network are equal. Consequently, it's impossible to assign certain computers higher priorities and, therefore, greater access to the network.

Contention access control is well suited for networks that experience bursty traffic—that is, large intermittent file transfers—and have relatively few computers.

Token Passing

Token passing utilizes a frame called a *token,* which circulates around the network. A computer that needs to transmit must wait until it receives the token frame, at which time it is permitted to transmit. When the computer is finished transmitting, it passes the token frame to the next station on the network. Figure 14.5 shows how token passing is implemented on a Token Ring network. Token Ring networks are discussed in greater detail in Chapter 19.

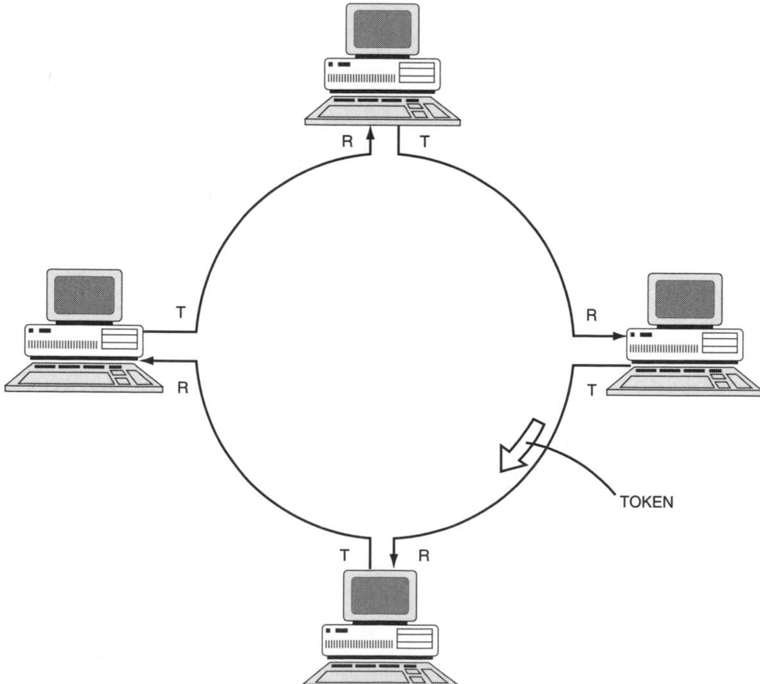

Figure 14.5

Token passing.

Several network standards employ token passing access control:

- The most common is Token Ring, defined by IEEE standard 802.5.
- IEEE standard 802.4 defines a bus network that also employs token passing. This standard is implemented only infrequently.
- FDDI is a 100 Mbps fiber-optic network standard that uses token passing and rings in much the same manner as 802.5 Token Ring.

Token-passing methods can use station priorities and other methods to prevent any one station from monopolizing the network. Because each computer has a chance to transmit each time the token travels around the network, each station is guaranteed a chance to transmit at some minimum time interval.

Token passing is more appropriate than contention under the following conditions:

- When the network is carrying time-critical data. Because token passing results in more predictable delivery, token passing is called *deterministic.*
- When the network experiences heavy utilization. Performance typically falls off more gracefully with a token-passing network than with a contention-based network. Token-passing networks cannot become gridlocked due to excessive numbers of collisions.
- When some stations should have higher priority than others. Some token-passing schemes support priority assignments.

Comparing Contention and Token Passing

As an access control mechanism, token passing appears to be clearly superior to contention. You find, however, that Ethernet, by far the dominant LAN standard, has achieved its prominence while firmly wedded to contention access control.

Token passing requires a variety of complex control mechanisms to make it work well. The necessary hardware is considerably more expensive than the hardware required to implement the much simpler contention mechanisms. The higher cost of token passing networks is difficult to justify unless the special features are required.

Because token-passing networks are designed for high reliability, building network diagnostic and troubleshooting capabilities into the network hardware is common. This further increases the costs of token passing networks. Organizations must decide whether this additional reliability is worth the extra cost.

Conversely, although token-passing networks perform better than contention-based networks when traffic levels are high, contention networks have superior performance under lighter loading conditions. Passing the token around (and other maintenance operations) eats into the available bandwidth. As a result, a 10-Mbps Ethernet and a 16-Mbps Token Ring perform comparably under light loading conditions, but the Ethernet costs considerably less.

Figure 14.6 illustrates the performance characteristics you can expect from each access control method. (This figure implies that token-passing throughput eventually reaches a zero level, which cannot, in fact, happen, regardless of the loading conditions. Although a station's access to the network might be limited, access is guaranteed with each circuit of the token.)

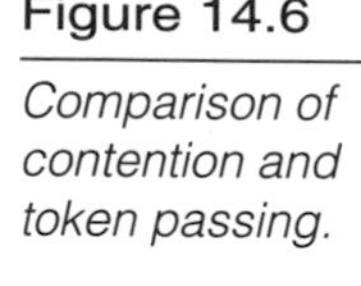

Figure 14.6

Comparison of contention and token passing.

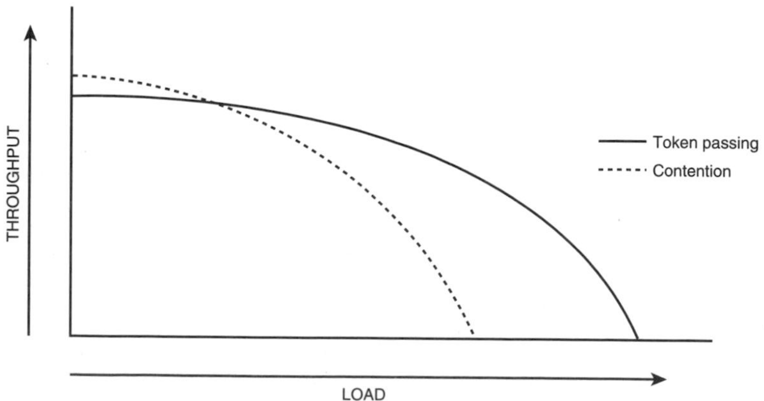

Polling

Polling is an access control method that employs a central device to regulate all access to the network. Polling is the most common access control method employed with mainframe computer networks.

The central device, called a *primary*, requests data from devices on the network, called *secondaries*. After it is *polled*, a secondary can transmit an amount of data that is determined by the protocols employed on the network. A secondary device cannot transmit unless it is polled by the primary.

Polling guarantees each device fair access to the network and is suitable for use with time-critical data. In fact, polling offers many of the advantages of token passing:

- Predictable and, therefore, deterministic access times
- Assigned priorities
- Elimination of collisions

A significant difference between polling and token passing is that polling centralizes control. This centralization can be an advantage from a management standpoint, but introduces a single point of failure. If the central control mechanism fails, the network stops functioning. Token passing uses more distributed control functions that are less subject to single points of failure.

Because polling centralizes control, secondary devices cannot communicate directly with other secondary devices. Rather, they must use the primary as an intermediary.

Further, because the primary must poll each secondary device—regardless of whether the secondary device has data to transmit—polling wastes large amounts of network bandwidth. This can result in excessive delays as some secondaries wait while others are polled.

Summary of Access Control Methods

Table 14.2 summarizes the access control methods discussed in this section.

Table 14.2

Comparison of Access Control Methods

Access Control Method	Advantages	Considerations
Contention	Simple software.	Access is probabilistic (not guaranteed).
	Once access is gained, device has complete control of the medium.	No priority mechanism.
		Collisions increase geometrically with demand.
Token passing	Each device is guaranteed media access (deterministic).	More complex software and hardware.
	Priorities might be assigned.	Might require a central control device.
	Collisions are eliminated.	
	High throughput under heavy load.	
Polling	Each device is guaranteed media access (deterministic).	Polling uses significant portion of network bandwidth.

Access Control Method	Advantages	Considerations
	Priorities might be assigned.	Polling requires bandwidth overhead, even for devices that have nothing to transmit.
	Collisions are eliminated.	

Addressing

The data link layer maintains device addresses that enable messages to be sent to a particular device. The addresses used are called *physical device addresses,* which are unique addresses associated with the networking hardware in the computer. In most cases (for example, Ethernet and Token Ring), the physical device address is burned into the network interface card at the time the card is manufactured.

The standards that apply to a particular network determine the format of the address. Because the address format is associated with the media access control method being used, physical device addresses are frequently referred to as *MAC addresses.*

The device address is not actually used to route a message to a specific device. Frames on LANs are typically transmitted so that they are available to all devices on the network. Each device reads each frame far enough to determine the device address to which the frame is addressed. If the frame's destination address matches the device's own physical address, the rest of the frame will be received. If the addresses do not match, the remainder of the frame is ignored.

Bridges can be used to divide large networks into several smaller ones. Bridges use physical device addresses to determine which frames to leave on the current network segment and which to forward to devices on other network segments. Some bridges must be programmed with the device addresses for each attached network segment, but transparent or learning bridges can learn addresses by analyzing network traffic.

Because bridges utilize physical device addresses to manage frame routing, they function at the level of the data link layer and are data link layer connectivity devices.

Transmission Synchronization

The physical layer must synchronize bit transmissions between sending and receiving devices. The data link layer, however, operates on data after the bits have been assembled to form characters, frames, or other data groups. At the data link layer, it is necessary to synchronize frame transmissions. This section discusses three mechanisms:

- Asynchronous
- Synchronous
- Isochronous

Asynchronous Transmission

Asynchronous transmission does not use a clocking mechanism to keep the sending and receiving devices synchronized. Instead, bit synchronization is used to synchronize the devices for each frame that is transmitted.

Each frame begins with a start bit that enables the receiving device to adjust to the timing of the transmitted signal. Messages are kept short so that the sending and receiving devices do not drift out of synchronization for the duration of the message. Asynchronous transmission is most frequently used to transmit character data and is ideally suited to environments where characters are transmitted at irregular intervals, such as when users enter character data.

Figure 14.7 illustrates the structure of a typical frame used to transmit character data. This frame has four components:

- **A start bit.** Signals that a frame is starting and enables the receiving device to synchronize itself with the message.
- **Data bits.** Consist of seven or eight bits when character data is being transmitted.
- **A parity bit.** Optionally used as a crude method of detecting transmission errors.
- **A stop bit or bits.** Signal the end of the data frame.

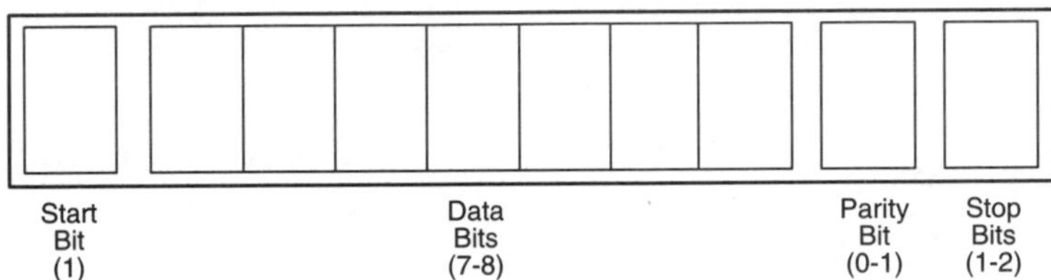

Figure 14.7
Structure of an asynchronous frame.

Error detection in asynchronous transmission uses the parity bit. Several schemes are available for using the parity bit. The most common include the following:

- **Even parity.** The parity bit is set to ensure that an even number of 1 bits are sent. If the data field has three 1s, the parity bit is set to 1 to produce a total of four 1 bits.
- **Odd parity.** The parity bit is set to ensure that an odd number of 1 bits are sent. If the data field has three 1s, the parity bit is set to 0 to produce a total of three 0 bits.

Parity techniques can detect errors that affect one bit. They might, however, be unable to detect errors that affect two or more bits.

Asynchronous transmission is a simple, inexpensive technology ideally suited for transmitting small frames at irregular intervals. Because start, stop, and parity bits must be added to each character to be transmitted, however, overhead for asynchronous transmission is high, in the neighborhood of 20 to 30 percent. This wastes bandwidth and makes asynchronous transmission undesirable for transmitting large amounts of data.

Asynchronous transmission is frequently used for PC-to-PC and terminal-to-host communication. Data in these environments is often of the bursty, character-oriented nature that is ideal for asynchronous communication. In both cases, it is also generally desirable to reduce costs of communication hardware, best achieved using asynchronous transmission.

Synchronous Transmission

Communication can be made more efficient by synchronizing the clocks on the transmitting and receiving devices. This synchronization is accomplished in two ways:

- By transmitting synchronization signals with data. Some data encoding techniques, by guaranteeing a signal transition with each bit transmitted, are inherently self-clocking.
- By using a separate communication channel to carry clock signals, a technique that can function with any signal encoding technique.

Figure 14.8 illustrates two possible structures of messages associated with synchronous transmission.

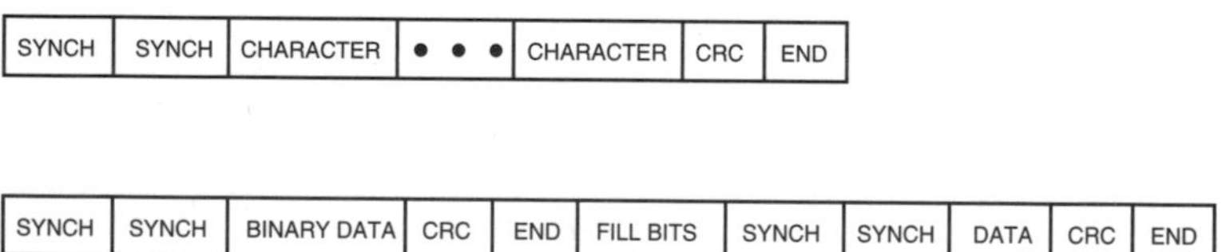

Figure 14.8
Structures of synchronous transmissions.

Both transmissions begin with a series of *synch signals*, which notify the receiver of the beginning of a frame. Synch signals generally utilize a bit pattern that cannot appear elsewhere in messages, ensuring they always are distinct and easily recognizable by the receiver.

A wide variety of data types can be transmitted. Figure 14.8 illustrates both character-oriented and bit-oriented data. Notice that multiple characters or long series of bits can be transmitted in a single data frame. Because the transmitter and receiver remain in synchronization for the duration of the transmission, frames may be very long.

When frames are longer, parity no longer is a suitable method for detecting errors. If errors occur, multiple bits are more likely to be affected, and parity techniques are less likely to report an error properly. The technique used with synchronous transmission is the *cyclic redundancy check* (CRC). The transmitter uses an algorithm to calculate a CRC value that summarizes the entire value of the data bits, which in turn is appended to the data frame. The receiver uses the same algorithm, recalculates the CRC, and compares the CRC in the frame to the value it has calculated. If the values match, the frame almost definitely was transmitted without error.

An *end bit pattern* unambiguously indicates the end of a frame. As with the synch bits, the end bit pattern frequently is a pattern that simply cannot appear in the body of the data frame, eliminating receiver confusion.

When synchronous transmission links are idle, it is common to transmit *fill bits* that keep the devices synchronized, eliminating the need to resynchronize devices when a new frame is transmitted.

Synchronous transmission offers many advantages over asynchronous transmission. Overhead bits (synch, CRC, and end) comprise a smaller portion of the overall data frame, which makes synchronous transmission's use of bandwidth far more efficient. Synchronization enables the systems to utilize higher speeds and to improve error detection.

The disadvantage of synchronous transmission revolves around higher cost, which stems from the more complex circuitry required. Consequently, synchronous transmission is employed primarily when high volumes of data absolutely must be transmitted.

Synchronous transmission frequently is used in mainframe-to-mainframe communication, as well as to achieve high efficiency levels on LANs. Both Ethernet and Token Ring, for example, utilize self-clocking signals.

Isochronous Transmission

Isochronous transmission employs a common device that supplies a clocking signal that all devices on the network share. The clocking device creates time slots. Devices that have data to transmit monitor the network and insert data into open time slots as they become available. A given time slot can be filled to capacity with multiple frames.

Isochronous transmission guarantees transmission rates, is deterministic, and has low overhead. The technique, however, introduces a single point of failure; you must ensure that the clocking device is fault-tolerant.

Connection Services

Network connection services provide a variety of functions:

- *Flow control* determines the amount of data that can be transmitted in a given time period. Flow control prevents the transmitting device from overwhelming the receiver. Flow control can take place at several protocol levels, including the LLC sublayer.

- *Error control* detects errors in received frames and requests retransmission of frames. Error control is a function of the LLC sublayer.

- *Sequence control* enables receivers to reassemble data frames into their original order. Frame size is limited, and packet fragmentation and reassembly is necessary to transmit large messages. Sequence control is a function of the network layer.

Three types of connection services provide different combinations of the above services:

- **Unacknowledged connectionless services.** Provide no flow, error, or sequence control. When required, these services must be provided by higher protocol layers. Unacknowledged connectionless service provides high performance when network communication can be safely assumed to be reliable (as on most LANs).

- **Connection-oriented services.** Provide flow, error, and sequence control through use of acknowledgments. Connection-oriented services have higher overhead, reducing performance but improving reliability when network reliability is in question (as on most WANs).
- **Acknowledged connectionless services.** Use acknowledgments to provide flow and error control on point-to-point connections.

Flow Control at the LLC Sublayer

Flow control prevents receiving devices from being overwhelmed by faster transmitting devices. Two common techniques of flow control are *guaranteed rate flow control* and *window flow control*, discussed in turn in the next two sections.

Guaranteed Rate Flow Control

In *guaranteed rate flow control*, the sending and receiving devices negotiate a mutually acceptable transmission rate. This transmission rate typically holds constant throughout an entire communication session.

To ensure that frames are received without error, some protocols require the receiver to acknowledge each frame as it is processed. If no error is detected, an acknowledgment frame is returned to the transmitter, instructing it to send the next frame. If errors are detected, the receiver does one of two things: it sends a retransmission request, or it simply waits until the transmitter times out and retransmits the frame.

Essentially, guaranteed rate flow control assumes that the receiver processes one message unit (bit or frame) for each unit transmitted. This rather inflexible approach often fails to use transmitter, receiver, and media channel capacities in the most efficient manner possible.

Window Flow Control

Buffering enables transmitters and receivers to operate with more flexibility. Buffers consist of memory that can receive data from the network and hold it until the receiver can process the data and acknowledge that it has been received.

Windowing is a technique that enables the transmitter to send several data frames prior to receiving acknowledgment from the receiver. Several frames can be buffered in the receiver as they are processed. The number of frames a transmitter can send without receiving an acknowledgment is known as its *window.*

Static window flow control limits the window size to a specific number of frames, usually defined by the number of frames that can fit in the receiver's input buffer. If the window size is 7, the transmitter can have as many as seven outstanding frames. An eighth frame cannot be transmitted, however, until one of the outstanding frames is acknowledged (see fig. 14.9).

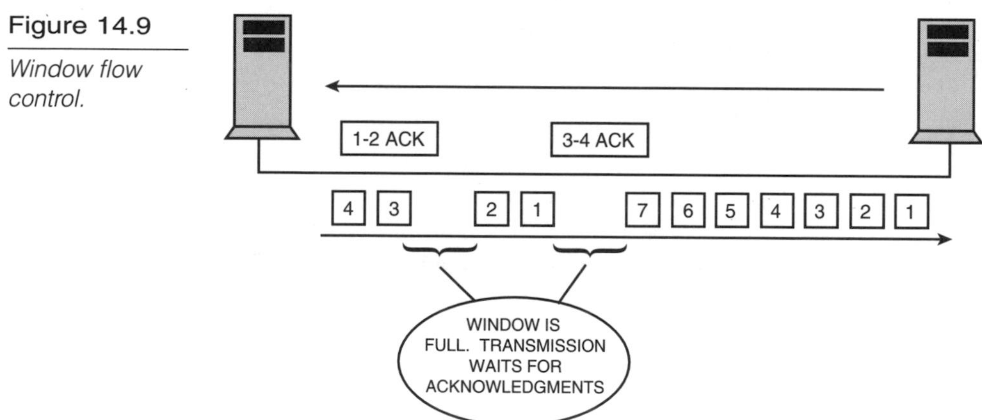

Figure 14.9

Window flow control.

Dynamic window flow control improves efficiency by enabling the communicating devices to adjust the window size. Other terms for this technique are *floating* or *sliding* windows. One dynamic window technique enables the receiver to send out a *choke frame* as its input buffer nears capacity. This choke frame signals the transmitter to slow down. After the transmitter adjusts its transmission rate downward, it slowly increases its transmission rate until it receives another choke frame. In this way, bandwidth utilization is optimized.

Error Control

Two LLC error conditions can exist:

- When CRC errors are detected
- When expected acknowledgments are not received

Recall from earlier in this chapter that synchronous data frames incorporate a cyclic redundancy check (CRC) field that can be used to detect transmission errors. When a receiving device detects a CRC error, it can transmit a *negative acknowledgment* (NAK) that requests retransmission of the frame.

When acknowledged services are employed, the transmitter expects acknowledgment (ACK) frames from the receiver for each frame (or a group of frames in a windowed protocol). When a specified interval of time expires without an acknowledgment, the transmitter assumes the frame was lost and retransmits it.

OSI Network Layer Concepts

As you learned in the preceding section, the data link layer deals with communication between devices on the same network. Physical device addresses are used to identify data frames, and each device is responsible for monitoring the network and receiving frames addressed to that device.

The network layer involves communication with devices on logically separate networks connected to form internetworks. Because internetworks can be large and can be constructed of different types of networks, the network layer utilizes routing algorithms that can be used to guide packets from their source to their destination networks.

A key element of the network layer is that each network in the internetwork is assigned a network address that can be used to route packets. The nature of those addresses and how they are used to route packets is revealed in the following topics:

- Addressing
- Switching
- Routing algorithms
- Connection services
- Gateway services

Addressing

You have already encountered the use of physical device addresses, which uniquely identify each device on a network. The network layer uses two additional address types:

- *Logical network addresses,* which route packets to specific networks on the internetwork
- *Services addresses,* which route packets to specific processes running on the destination device

Logical Network Addresses

Logical network addresses are assigned during configuration of the networks. You might be familiar with the task of assigning a logical network address to each LAN attached to the server. One of the tasks a network installer must accomplish is to make sure that each network address is unique on a given internetwork. Network addresses enable routers to forward frames through the internetwork to the appropriate networks.

Service Addresses

The operating systems on most computers can run several processes at once. When a packet arrives, you must determine which process on the computer should receive the data in the packet. You do so by assigning service addresses, which identify upper-layer processes and protocols. These service addresses are included with the physical and logical network addresses in the data frame. (Some protocols refer to service addresses as *sockets* or *ports.*)

Some service addresses, called *well-known addresses,* are universally defined for a given type of network. Other service addresses are defined by the vendors of network products.

Addressing Summary

A possible format of the address information for a packet is shown in figure 14.10. Three address components appear:

- *Physical (MAC) network addresses* identify a particular device as the source or destination of a frame.
- *Logical network addresses* identify a particular network on the internetwork as the source or destination of a packet.
- *Service addresses* identify a process or protocol on the computer that is the source or destination of a packet.

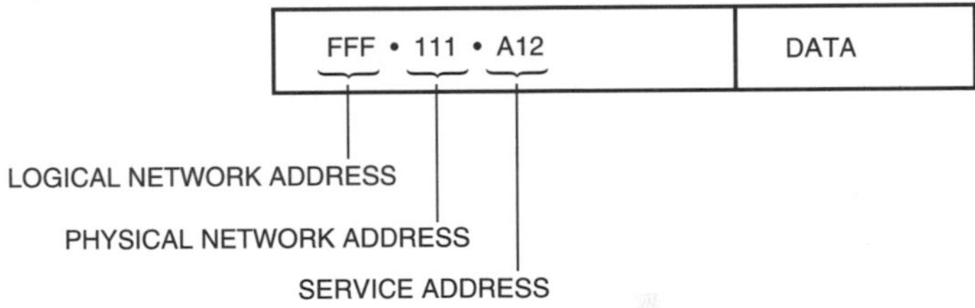

Figure 14.10
Address information showing physical and logical network addresses with a service address.

Switching

Many internetworks include redundant data paths that you can use to route messages using the following switching techniques:

- Circuit switching
- Message switching
- Packet switching

Circuit Switching

Circuit switching establishes a path that remains fixed for the duration of a connection (see fig. 14.11). Much as telephone switching equipment establishes a route between your telephone on the

East Coast and a telephone you dial on the West Coast, circuit-switching networks establish a path through the internetwork when the devices initiate a conversation.

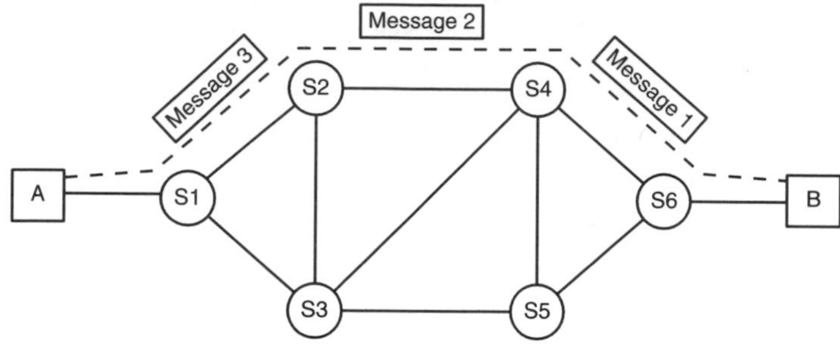

Figure 14.11
Circuit switching.

Circuit switching provides devices with a dedicated path and a well-defined bandwidth. Circuit switching is not free of disadvantages, however. Establishing a connection between devices can be time-consuming. Because other traffic cannot share the dedicated media path, bandwidth might be inefficiently utilized. Because circuit-switching networks must have a surplus of bandwidth, they tend to be expensive to construct.

Message Switching

Message switching treats each message as an independent entity. Each message carries address information that describes the message's destination. This information is used at each switch to transfer the message to the next switch in its route. Message switches are programmed with information concerning other switches in the network that can be used to forward messages to their destinations. They also may be programmed with information about the most efficient routes. Depending on network conditions, different messages may be sent through the network by different routes, as shown in figure 14.12.

Message switching transfers the complete message from one switch to the next switch, where the message is stored before being forwarded another time. Because each message is stored before being sent on to the next switch, this type of network frequently is called a *store-and-forward* network. The message switches often are general-purpose computers. They must be equipped with sufficient storage (usually hard drives) to enable them to store messages until forwarding them is possible.

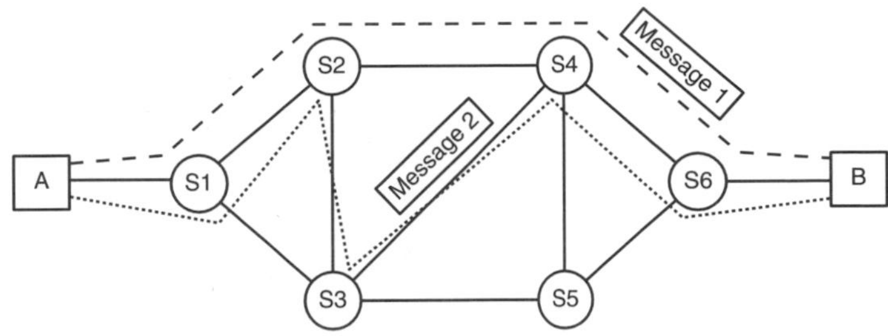

Figure 14.12
Message switching.

Electronic mail is a common application for message switching. Some delay is permissible when delivering mail, unlike the requirements when two computers are exchanging data in real time. Message switching uses relatively low-cost devices to forward messages and can function well with relatively slow communication channels. Other applications for message switching include group applications such as workflow, calendaring, and groupware.

Message switching has several advantages:

- Data channels are shared among communicating devices, improving the efficiency of using available bandwidth.
- Message switches can store messages until a channel becomes available, reducing sensitivity to network congestion.
- Message priorities may be used to manage network traffic.
- Broadcast addressing uses network bandwidth more efficiently by delivering messages to multiple destinations.

The chief disadvantage of message switching is that it is unsuitable to real-time applications, including data communication, video, and audio.

Packet Switching

In *package switching,* messages are divided into smaller packets. Each packet includes source and destination address information so that individual packets can be routed through the internetwork independently. As you can see in figure 14.13, the packets that make up a message can take very different routes through the internetwork.

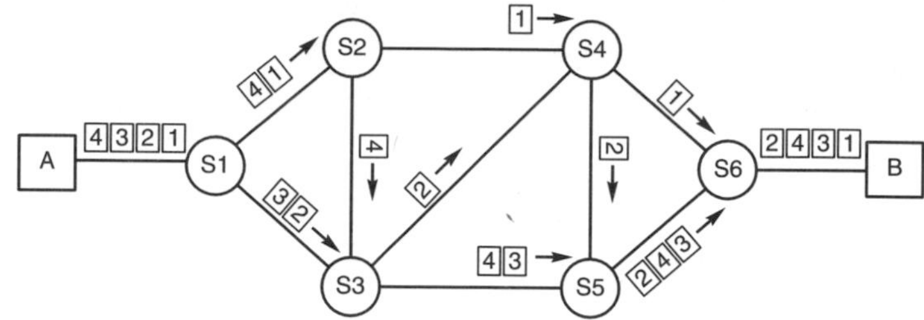

Figure 14.13

Packet switching.

So far, packet switching looks considerably like message switching. The distinguishing characteristic is that packets are restricted to a size that enables the switching devices to manage the packet data entirely in memory, without the need to store the data temporarily on disk. Packet switching, therefore, routes packets through the network much more rapidly and efficiently than is possible with message switching.

Several methods of packet switching exist. Two of those methods are discussed in the following sections:

- Datagram
- Virtual circuit

Datagram Packet Switching

Datagram services treat each packet as an independent message. Each packet is routed through the internetwork independently, and each switch node decides which network segment should be used for the next step in the packet's route. This capability enables switches to bypass busy segments and take other steps to speed packets through the internetwork. This is the specific approach shown in figure 14.13.

Datagrams are frequently used on LANs. Network layer protocols are responsible for delivering the frame to the appropriate network. Then, because each datagram includes destination address information, devices on the local network can recognize and receive datagrams they are intended to receive.

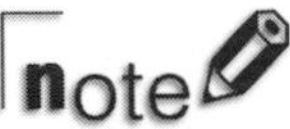

Packet switching matches the need to transmit large messages with the fairly small frame size that can be accommodated by the physical layer. The network layer is responsible for fragmenting messages from upper layers into smaller datagrams that are appropriate for the physical layer. The network layer also is responsible for reconstructing messages from datagrams as they are received.

Virtual Circuit Packet Switching

Virtual circuits operate by establishing a formal connection between two devices in communication. When devices begin a session, they negotiate communication parameters, such as maximum message size, communication windows, network paths, and so forth. This negotiation establishes a *virtual circuit,* a well-defined path through the internetwork through which the devices communicate. This virtual circuit generally remains in effect until the devices stop communicating.

Virtual circuits are distinguished by the establishment of a logical connection. *Virtual* means that the network behaves as though a dedicated physical circuit has been established between the devices that are communicating. Even though no such physical circuit exists, the network presents the appearance of a physical connection so far as the devices at the ends of the circuit are concerned.

Virtual circuits frequently are employed in conjunction with connection-oriented services, which are discussed later in this chapter.

Advantages of Packet Switching

Packet switching optimizes the use of bandwidth by enabling many devices to route packets through the same network channels. At any given time, a switch may be routing packets to several different destination devices, adjusting the routes as required to achieve the best efficiency possible at the present time.

Because entire messages are not stored at the switches prior to forwarding, transmission delays are significantly shorter than delays encountered with message switching.

Although the switching devices do not need to be equipped with large amounts of hard drive capacity, they might need a significant amount of real-time memory. Also, they must have sufficient processing power to run the more complex routing protocols required for packet switching. Among the new complexities is the need to recognize when packets have been lost so that retransmission can be requested.

Routing Algorithms

Routing refers to forwarding messages through switching networks. In some cases, routing information is programmed into switching devices. However, preprogrammed switches cannot adjust to changing network conditions. Most routing devices, therefore, have the capability of discovering routes through the internetwork and storing the route information in route tables.

Route tables do not store only path information. They also store estimates of the time taken to send a message through a given route. This time estimate is known as the *cost* of a particular path. There are several methods of estimating routing costs, as follows:

- *Hop count* describes the number of routers that a message would cross before it reaches its destination. If all hops are assumed to take the same amount of time, the optimum path is the path with the smallest hop count.
- *Tic count* is an actual time estimate, where a *tic* is a time unit as defined by the routing implementation.
- *Relative expense* is any defined measure of the cost (including the monetary cost) to use a given link.

After costs are established, routers can select routes, either statically or dynamically, as follows:

- *Static route selection* uses routes that have been programmed by the network administrator.
- *Dynamic route selection* uses routing cost information to select the most cost-effective route for a given packet. As network conditions change and are reflected in routing tables, the router can select different paths to maintain low costs.

Two methods of route discovery—distance vector routing and link-state routing—are discussed in the following sections.

Distance Vector Routing

Distance vector routers advertise their presence to other routers on the network. Periodically, each router on the network broadcasts the information in its routing table. Other routers can use this information to update their own router tables.

Figure 14.14 illustrates how the process works. In the figure, server S3 learns that server S2 can reach server S1 in three hops. Because server S3 knows that server S2 is one hop away, server S3 knows that its cost to reach server S1 through server S2 is two hops.

Figure 14.14

Distance vector routing.

Distance vector routing is an effective algorithm, but it can be fairly inefficient. Because changes must ripple through the network from router to router, it might take a while for a change to become known to all routers on the network. In addition, the frequent broadcasts of routing information produce high levels of network traffic that can hurt performance on larger networks.

Link-State Routing

Link-state routing reduces the network traffic required to update routing tables. Routers that are newly attached to the network can request routing information from a nearby router.

After routers have exchanged routing information about the network, routers broadcast messages only when something changes. These messages contain information about the state of each link the router has with other routers on the network. Because routers keep each other updated, complete network routing updates are not needed often.

Connection Services

Earlier in this chapter, you were introduced to three types of connection services:

- Unacknowledged connectionless services, which provide no flow control, error detection, or packet sequence control
- Connection-oriented services, which provide flow control and error detection with acknowledgments
- Acknowledged connectionless services, which use acknowledgments to provide flow and error control

The network layer also provides connection-oriented services, including flow control, error detection, and acknowledgments. Network acknowledgments are employed to provide flow control, error detection, and packet sequence control.

Network Layer Flow Control

The data link layer manages flow control based on the capacities of the devices that are in communication. The network layer manages flow control to avoid congestion on the network.

As you learned in the discussion about routing, the network layer determines the number of packets that are sent through a given route. By routing packets around busy links, available network bandwidth is used more effectively, and congestion is reduced. For this reason, network flow control often is referred to as *congestion control.*

Network layer flow control can permit devices to negotiate a guaranteed data rate. Static and dynamic windows also may be employed.

Receiving devices can control congestion by delaying before sending acknowledgments. Under these circumstances, the sender may assume that the packet was lost and retransmit it. To prevent unnecessary retransmission, some protocols define packets that signal congestion and enable receiving devices to explicitly request delays in transmission.

Network Layer Error Control

A variety of error conditions can be detected at the network layer. Errors in data are typically detected using CRC algorithms. Because packet header information changes at each hop (addresses change), CRC values must be recalculated by each router.

Although the network layer can implement detection of lost and duplicate packets, the transport layer typically handles these functions.

Packet Sequence Control

Recall that packet switching networks can route packets by varying routes. As a result, the packets for a message might arrive at their final destination out of order. This can be the case for both datagram and connection-oriented services.

The network layer can be configured to handle packet sequence control, although that function generally is handled at the transport layer.

Gateway Services

Routers can handle interconnection of networks whose protocols function in similar ways. When the rules differ sufficiently on the two networks, however, a more powerful device is required.

A *gateway* is a device that can reconcile the different rules used on two different networks. Gateways are commonly required to connect LANs into mainframe networks, which have completely different protocol architectures. Mainframe networks, such as IBM's SNA (see Chapter 18, "Protocol Suites") for example, do not use the same device address schemes that LANs employ (they differ in many other ways as well). You have to "fool" the mainframe network into thinking that mainframe devices are on the LAN, and make the mainframe look like a LAN, so far as devices on the LAN are concerned.

Gateways may be implemented at the network layer or at higher layers in the OSI model, depending on where the protocol translation is required.

OSI Transport Layer Concepts

The transport layer is the next layer of the OSI model. Lower-layer protocols are concerned with delivering messages between devices. The transport layer, however, is concerned with delivering messages between processes running on those devices. Whenever a device is using a multitasking operating system, and multiple processes might be running on the device, it becomes essential that messages be delivered from one process on the transmitting device to the correct process on the receiving device.

The transport layer can implement procedures to ensure the reliable delivery of those segments to their destination devices. The term "reliable" does not mean that errors cannot occur, only that if errors occur, they are detected. If errors such as lost data are detected, the transport layer either requests retransmission or notifies upper-layer protocols so that they can take corrective action.

The transport layer enables upper-layer protocols to interface with the network, but hides the complexities of network operation from them. Among its functions, the transport layer breaks large messages into segments suitable for network delivery.

Addressing

Transport layer addressing is concerned with delivering messages from a specific process on one computer to the correct process running on the destination computer. Messages can be identified in two ways: connection identifiers and transaction identifiers.

Connection Identifiers

A *connection identifier* (connection ID) might also be called a *socket* or a *port*, depending on the specific protocol implementation. The connection identifier labels each conversation and enables a process to communicate with processes running on other devices. A numeric identifier is assigned to each conversation. A service, running at higher OSI levels, identifies communications with a connection ID number that enables the transport layer to direct lower-layer addressing and deliver the messages as required.

Transaction Identifiers

Connection identifiers are used when two devices are engaged in multiple exchanges of data. *Transaction identifiers* are used when the exchange is a one-time event consisting of a request and a response. Only this simple exchange is tracked; no multiple-message conversations that might be occurring between the devices are tracked.

Address/Name Resolution

Network addresses are always binary numbers, which often are 32 bits in length. These numbers can be expressed in decimal or hexadecimal notation to make them easier for humans to identify. Long decimal and hex numbers, however, are not as recognizable as words. Some network protocols, consequently, implement a scheme of logical alphanumeric names that humans use when specifying network devices. These names are translated into numeric network addresses by a service on the network. This translation can be performed by individual network devices or by a central name server.

Service-Requester-Initiated Address/Name Resolution

With this method, a device that requires address information broadcasts a packet that requests the information for a given name, address, or service. The device that corresponds to the name, address, or service responds with the required information.

Service-Provider-Initiated Address/Name Resolution

This method employs a central directory server (also called a *name server*) that collects information that is broadcast by devices on the network. Devices that require name or address information can request it from the directory server.

Segment Development

When messages from higher-level protocols exceed the size allowed by a protocol stack for a segment, the transport layer divides outbound messages into segments of a suitable size. The transport layer also recombines incoming segments into message formats required by upper layers.

The transport layer also can combine multiple small messages into a single segment to improve network efficiency. As shown in figure 14.15, each message component is identified by a connection identifier (CID). The CID enables the transport layer of the receiving device to deliver each message to the proper process.

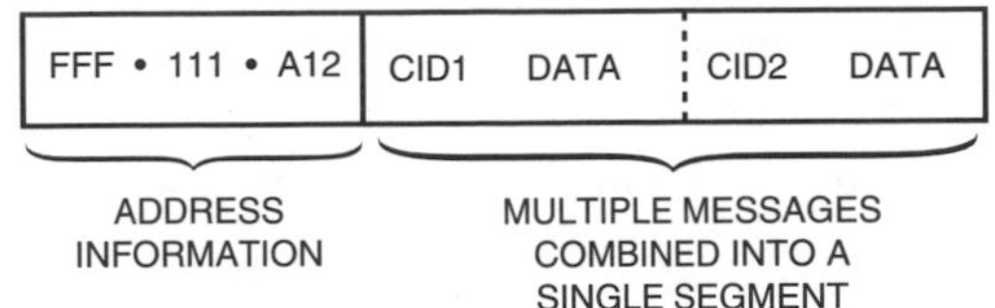

Figure 14.15
Identification of messages at the transport layer.

Connection Services

Some services can be performed at more than one layer of the OSI model. In addition to the data link and network layers, the transport layer can have some responsibility for connection services.

Segment Sequencing

One connection-oriented service provided by the transport layer is segment sequencing. When large messages are divided into segments for transport, the transport layer must resequence the segments when they are received prior to reassembling the original message.

Error Control

When segments are lost in transmission, or when segments have duplicate segment IDs, the transport layer must initiate error recovery. The following strategies for error control are available:

- Unique segment sequence numbers
- Virtual circuits, permitting only one virtual circuit per session
- Timeouts removed from the network segments that have been misrouted and have remained on the network past a specified time

The transport layer also detects corrupted segments by managing end-to-end error control using techniques such as checksums.

End-to-End Flow Control

The transport layer uses acknowledgments to manage end-to-end flow control between two connected devices.

Besides negative acknowledgments, some transport layer protocols can request the retransmission of the most recent segments. These acknowledgments are called *go back* n or *selective repeat* acknowledgments.

Go back *n* acknowledgments request retransmission of the last *n* packets. Selective repeat acknowledgments can request retransmission of specific packets. This approach is useful when the receiving device's buffers overflow before it can warn the transmitting device to cease transmission.

OSI Session Layer Concepts

The session layer manages dialogs between two computers by establishing, managing, and terminating communications.

Dialog Control

As illustrated in figure 14.16, dialogs can take three forms:

- **Simplex Dialogs.** Involve one-way data transfers. An example is a fire alarm, which sends an alarm message to the fire station, but cannot (and does not need to) receive messages from the fire station.
- **Half-duplex dialogs.** Involve two-way data transfers in which the data flows in only one direction at a time. When one device completes a transmission, it must "turn over" the medium to the other device so that that device has a turn to transmit.

  CB radio operators, for example, converse on the same communication channel. When one operator is finished transmitting, he must release his transmit key so that the other operator can send a response.
- **Full-duplex dialogs.** Permit two-way simultaneous data transfers by providing each device with a separate communication channel. Voice telephones are full-duplex devices, and either party to a conversation can talk at any time. Most computer modems can operate in full-duplex mode.

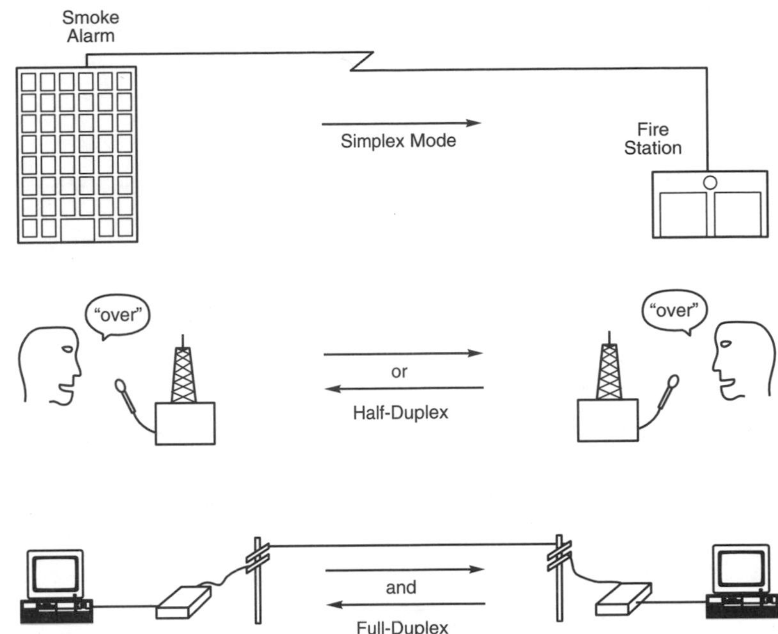

Figure 14.16

Simplex and duplex communication modes.

Costs rise for half- and full-duplex operation because the more complex the dialog technology, the more expensive. Designers of communications systems, therefore, generally use the simplest dialog mode that satisfies the communication requirements.

Half-duplex communication can result in wasted bandwidth during the intervals when communication is being turned around. On the other hand, full-duplex communication generally requires a greater bandwidth than half-duplex communication.

Session Administration

A *session* is a formal dialog between a service requester and a service provider. Sessions have at least three phases:

- **Connection establishment.** A service requester requests initiation of a service. During the setup process, communication is established, and rules are agreed upon.
- **Data transfer.** Because of the rules agreed upon during setup, each party to the dialog knows what to expect. Communication is efficient, and errors are easy to detect.

- **Connection release.** When the session is completed, the dialog is terminated in an orderly fashion.

Connection Establishment

Several tasks can be performed at the time a session is initiated:

- Specification of required services
- User login authentication and other security procedures
- Negotiation of protocols and protocol parameters
- Notification of connection IDs
- Establishment of dialog control, as well as acknowledgment of numbering, and retransmission procedures

Data Transfer

After the connection is established,the devices involved can initiate a dialog. Besides exchanging data, these devices exchange acknowledgments and other control data that manage the dialog.

The session layer can also incorporate protocols to resume dialogs that are interrupted. After a formal dialog has been established, devices recognize a lost connection whenever the connection has not been formally released. A device, therefore, realizes that a connection has been lost when it fails to receive an expected acknowledgment or data transmission.

Within a certain time period, two devices can reenter the session that was interrupted but not released.

Connection Release

This is an orderly process that shuts down communication and releases resources on the service provider.

OSI Presentation Layer Concepts

The presentation layer deals with the syntax, or grammatical rules, needed for communication between two computers.

The name "presentation layer" has caused considerable confusion in the industry because some people mistakenly believe that this layer presents data to the user. However, the name has nothing to do with displaying data, which is performed by applications running above the application layer.

The presentation layer is so named because it presents a uniform data format to the application layer. As a matter of fact, this layer is not commonly implemented because applications typically perform most presentation layer functions.

Data Translation

An important goal to strive for when designing networks is to enable different types of computers to interchange data. Although this goal seldom is met completely, effective use of data translation techniques can make it possible for many types of computers to communicate.

The following discussion covers four forms of data translation: bit order, byte order, character code, and file syntax.

Bit Order

When binary numbers are transmitted through a network, they are sent one bit at a time. Consider the binary number 11110000. The transmitting computer can start at either end of the number:

- It can start at the *most-significant digit* (MSD), which is the highest value digit, and send a 1 first.
- It can start at the *least-significant digit* (LSD), which is the lowest value digit, and send a 0 first.

Unless the sending and receiving devices agree on bit-order conventions, they change the values of the binary numbers being transmitted.

Byte Order Translation

A similar logic applies to byte orders. Complex values generally must be represented by more than one byte, but different computers use different conventions as to which byte should be transmitted first. Intel microprocessors start with the least-significant byte. Because they start at the small end, they are called *little endian.* Motorola microprocessors start with the most-significant byte and are called *big endian.* Byte order translation might be needed to reconcile these differences.

Character Code Translation

Most computers use one of the following binary numbering schemes to represent character sets:

- ASCII, the *American Standard Code for Information Interchange,* used to represent English characters on all microcomputers and most minicomputers (see fig. 14.17)

Figure 14.17

The ASCII character code.

				8	0	0	0	0	0	0	0	0
				7	0	0	0	0	1	1	1	1
				6	0	0	1	1	0	0	1	1
				5	0	1	0	1	0	1	0	1
4	3	2	1									
0	0	0	0		NUL	DLE	SP	0	@	P	`	p
0	0	0	1		SOH	DC1	!	1	A	Q	a	q
0	0	1	0		STX	DC2	"	2	B	R	b	r
0	0	1	1		ETX	DC3	#	3	C	S	c	s
0	1	0	0		EOT	DC4	$	4	D	T	d	t
0	1	0	1		ENQ	NAK	%	5	E	U	e	u
0	1	1	0		ACK	SYN	&	6	F	V	f	v
0	1	1	1		BEL	ETB	'	7	G	W	g	w
1	0	0	0		BS	CAN	(	8	H	X	h	x
1	0	0	1		HT	EM	)	9	I	Y	i	y
1	0	1	0		LF	SUB	*	:	J	Z	j	z
1	0	1	1		VT	ESC	+	;	K	[	k	{
1	1	0	0		FF	FS	,	<	L	\	l	|
1	1	0	1		CR	GS	_	=	M	]	m	}
1	1	1	0		SO	RS	.	>	N	^	n	~
1	1	1	1		SI	US	/	?	O	_	o	DEL

7-Bit ASCII Character Set

1	1	1	1	1	1	1	1
0	0	0	0	1	1	1	1
0	0	1	1	0	0	1	1
0	1	0	1	0	1	0	1
Ç	É	á		└	╨		
ü	æ	í		┴		ß	±
é	Æ	ó		┬	╥		≥
â	ô	ú	│	├	╙	▌	
ä	ö	ñ	┤	─	╘		
à	ò	Ñ	╡	┼	╒		[illegible]
å	û	ª	╢	╞	╓		
ç	ù	º	╖	╟	╫		
ê	ÿ	¿		╚	╪	♥	°
ë	Ö	⌐	╣		┘	▪	·
è	Ü		║	╩	┌		-
ï	¢	½	╗	╦	█	▪	÷
î	£	¼	a	╠	▄	•	^{n}
ì	¥	¡		═	▌	ø	^{2}
Ä	₧	«			▐		■
Å	ƒ	»	┐		▀		

8-Bit IBM Extended ASCII

- EBCDIC, the *Extended Binary Coded Decimal Interchange Code,* used to represent English characters on IBM mainframes (see fig. 14.18)

Figure 14.18

The EBCDIC character code.

				8	0	0	0	0	0	0	0	0	1	1	1	1	1	1	1	1
				7	0	0	0	0	1	1	1	1	0	0	0	0	1	1	1	1
				6	0	0	1	1	0	0	1	1	0	0	1	1	0	0	1	1
				5	0	1	0	1	0	1	0	1	0	1	0	1	0	1	0	1
4	3	2	1																	
0	0	0	0		NUL	DLE	DS		SP	&	—									0
0	0	0	1		SOH	DC1	SOS				/		a	j			A	J		1
0	0	1	0		STX	DC2	FS	SYN					b	k	s		B	K	S	2
0	0	1	1		ETX	DC3							c	l	t		C	L	T	3
0	1	0	0		PF	RES	BYP	PN					d	m	u		D	M	U	4
0	1	0	1		HT	NL	LF	RS					e	n	v		E	N	V	5
0	1	1	0		LC	BS	EOB	UC					f	o	w		F	O	W	6
0	1	1	1		DEL	IL	PRE	EOT					g	p	x		G	P	X	7
1	0	0	0			CAN							h	q	y		H	Q	Y	8
1	0	0	1			EM							i	r	z		I	R	Z	9
1	0	1	0		SMM	CC	SM				!		:							
1	0	1	1		VT					.	$	,	#							
1	1	0	0		FF	IFS		DC4		<	*	%	@							
1	1	0	1		CR	IGS	ENQ	NAK		(	)	-	'							
1	1	1	0		SO	IRS	ACK			+	;	>	=							
1	1	1	1		SI	IUS	BEL	SUB		|		?	"							

- Shift-JIS, used to represent Japanese characters

Many vendors are beginning to incorporate Unicode in their products. *Unicode,* a 16-bit code that can represent 65,536 characters in English and other languages, is organized into code pages devoted to the characters required for a given language, improving portability of products between different language environments.

File Syntax Translation

When file formats differ between computers, the formats require translation. Some situations that might require file format translation include the following:

- Copying files between a Macintosh and a DOS PC. Macintosh files actually consist of two related files called a *data fork* and a *resource fork.* PC files, on the other hand, consist of a single file.

- Copying files between DOS PCs and Unix workstations.

Properly done, these translations can be completely transparent. NetWare, for example, enables DOS, Macintosh, and Unix users to share the same files on a NetWare server by using a feature called *name space support.*

Encryption

You often want to ensure that data on a LAN is absolutely secure. Even if an eavesdropper were successful in listening in, sensitive data can be encrypted to be unusable.

Encryption techniques employ a form of reversible data scrambling that renders data unreadable without a key. A *key* is a code word or number that allows the encryption/decryption software to scramble and unscramble the data.

Given time, every encryption can be broken. High-speed computers make it feasible to crack many codes by simply trying different key values until the right one is found. A great deal of effort, therefore, has gone into creating powerful encryption algorithms boasting a low probability of failure. Two common techniques are private keys and public keys.

Private Keys

Private keys use the same key to encrypt and decrypt the message. This method has several disadvantages. The sender and receiver must be sure to inform each other of the key. If the key is intercepted, the message becomes vulnerable. Each time the key is changed—and private keys are changed often in case they are compromised—the new key must be communicated and is vulnerable to discovery.

Public Keys

With the *public key* technique, a public key is used to encrypt messages, and a private key is then used for decryption. The public key is created by a user by applying an algorithm to a private key, which is known only to the intended receiver of the message.

The sender of the message uses the public key to encrypt a message and does not know or need to know the private key. In fact, anyone who has a person's public key can encrypt a message for that person. The receiver decrypts the message by combining the public key with the private key, the latter known only to him- or herself.

The algorithms used for public-key encryption are extremely complex and make it unlikely for even a supercomputer to stumble on the correct key within a reasonable period of time (your lifetime, for example). Nevertheless, the code makers are never far ahead of the code breakers, and more sophisticated encryption techniques are always under development.

OSI Application Layer Concepts

The application layer is concerned with providing services on the network. These services include file services, print services, database services, and the other services discussed earlier in the section on network services.

A common misunderstanding is that the application layer is responsible for running user applications such as word processors. This is not the case. The application layer, however, does provide an interface whereby applications can communicate with the network.

The application layer performs two functions related to the utilization of services on the network. One function involves the advertisement of available services. Another function involves the use of the services.

Advertising Services

To inform clients of available services, the application layer advertises these services to the network. You encountered the use of service addresses in the discussion of the network layer. These service addresses provide the mechanism that enables clients to communicate with services.

The application layer can employ *active* and *passive* methods of advertising services.

Active Service Advertisement

When servers actively advertise their services, they broadcast messages announcing the services they offer. Most protocols consider these service advertisements to be valid for a limited time. Unless the information is refreshed within a specified time, clients remove the information from their service tables. Clients also can transmit messages that request specific services. Servers respond with a list of services they support.

Passive Service Advertisement

Servers also can list their services and addresses with a central service registry. Clients query the directory to determine which services are available and how to access them; this is called *passive service advertisement.*

Service Use Methods

Clients can access services using three methods:

- OS call interruption
- Remote operation
- Collaboration

OS Call Interruption

Applications on client systems request services by placing service calls to their local operating systems. A *service call* is a formal procedure set up by the designers of an operating system which provides an interface with the programs the operating system supports. Normally, these service calls invoke services on the local client PC.

When a client is configured for network operation, OS call interruption intercepts service requests. Service calls that request local resources are forwarded to the client's OS. Service calls that request network resources are transferred to the network, where they are forwarded to the appropriate server. The process is shown in figure 14.19.

Figure 14.19

OS call interruption.

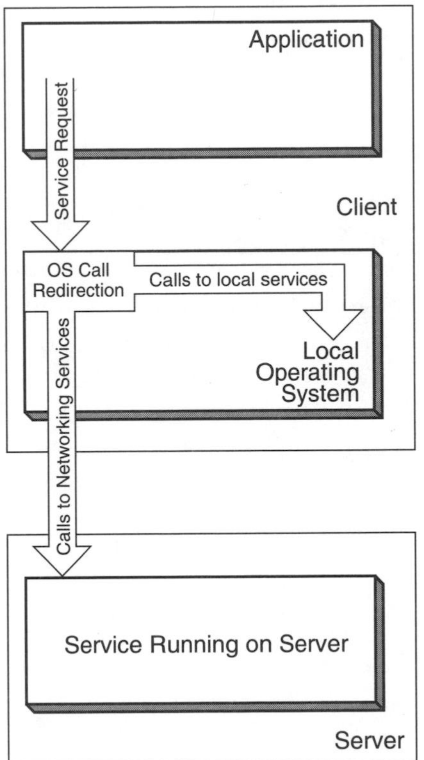

OS call interruption enables a client to utilize network services even when the OS has no inherent networking capability.

Remote Operation

When the client OS has network capability built-in, it can access the server by remote operation. The client OS interfaces directly with the network. Requests from the client OS appear to the server to be the same as requests from the server's own systems. In other words, the server isn't directly aware of the separate existence of client systems.

Collaborative Computing

Some server and client operating systems are so advanced that the border between them blurs. The operating systems work together to coordinate the use of resources on the two respective computers. Recall from Chapter 13 the discussion of collaborative computing, which consists of far more than computers simply accessing each other's services. Indeed, computers participating in collaborative computing pool all of their resources. One computer can start a process on another, for example, to take advantage of some free processing cycles. This requires the participating operating systems to be capable of a high level of cooperation.

Review Questions

The following questions test your knowledge of the information in this chapter. For additional questions, see MCP Endeavor and the Microsoft Roadmap/Assessment Exam on the CD-ROM that accompanies this book.

1. The OSI model organizes communication protocols into how many layers?

   A. 3

   B. 7

   C. 17

   D. 56

2. The layers of the OSI model (in order) are included in which of the following choices?

   A. Physical, data link, network, transport, system, presentation, application

   B. Physical, data link, network, transport, session, presentation, application

   C. Physical, data link, network, transform, session, presentation, application

   D. Presentation, data link, network, transport, session, physical, application

3. In the OSI model, what is the relationship of a layer (*N*) to the layer above it (layer *N*+1)?

   A. Layer *N* provides services for layer *N*+1.

   B. Layer *N*+1 adds a header to information received from layer *N*.

   C. Layer *N* utilizes services provided by layer *N*+1.

   D. Layer *N* has no effect on layer *N*+1.

4. Two different computer types can communicate if ______.

   A. they conform to the OSI model

   B. they are both using TCP/IP

   C. they are using compatible protocol stacks

   D. they are a Macintosh and a Unix workstation

5. Which three of the following statements regarding protocol stacks are true?

   A. A given protocol stack can run on only one computer type.

   B. Layers add headers to packets received from higher layers in the protocol stack.

   C. A protocol stack is a hierarchical set of protocols.

   D. Each layer provides services for the next highest layer.

6. Message data for any layer consists of which two of the following?

   A. Datagram

   B. A protocol

   C. A header

   D. The data of the next higher layer

7. Which two of the following terms are used to describe data units at the network layer?

   A. Datagram

   B. Message

   C. Frame

   D. Packet

8. Which two of the following terms are used to describe data units at the data link layer?

   A. Datagram

   B. Message

   C. Frame

   D. Packet

9. Which three of the following are functions of the OSI physical layer?

   A. Mechanical and electrical specifications for using the medium

   B. Generating electrical signals on the medium

   C. Network topology

   D. Bit transmission encoding and timing

10. Which protocol layer enables multiple devices to share the transmission medium?

   A. Physical

   B. MAC

   C. LLC

   D. Network

11. Which of the following is a media access control mechanism?

    A. LLC

    B. Parity

    C. Polling

    D. Synchronous transmission

12. Which of the following is an error-control mechanism?

    A. Contention

    B. Synchronous transmission

    C. CRC

    D. LLC

13. Which of the following layers establishes and maintains a link between communicating devices?

    A. Physical

    B. MAC

    C. LLC

    D. Network

14. Which two of the following statements are true?

    A. Token-passing networks perform better than contention-based networks in all traffic levels.

    B. To work well, token passing requires a variety of control mechanisms.

    C. Certain computers cannot be given greater network access in a contention-based network.

    D. Polling is the most efficient method of access control because it introduces no overhead.

15. Which of the following techniques uses network bandwidth most efficiently?

    A. Static window flow control

    B. Guaranteed rate flow control

    C. Dynamic rate flow control

    D. Dynamic window flow control

16. Which of the following access methods is centrally managed?

    A. Contention

    B. Token passing

    C. Polling

    D. Collision detection

17. Which two of the following services provides flow control?

    A. Acknowledged connectionless

    B. Unacknowledged connectionless

    C. Unacknowledged connection-oriented

    D. Connection-oriented

18. Which of the following access control methods is probabilistic?

    A. Polling

    B. Contention

    C. Token passing

    D. Sliding window

19. Which switching method employs virtual circuits?

    A. Message

    B. Circuit

    C. Packet

    D. All of the above

20. Which network layer is concerned with data encryption?

    A. Network
    B. Transport
    C. Session
    D. Presentation

21. Which network layer is concerned with delivering messages between processes on devices?

    A. Network
    B. Transport
    C. Session
    D. Presentation

22. Which network layer is concerned with address/name resolution?

    A. Network
    B. Transport
    C. Session
    D. Presentation

23. Which switching method makes the most efficient use of network bandwidth?

    A. Message
    B. Circuit
    C. Packet
    D. Methods are about equal

24. What is another name for a message switching network?

    A. Connectionless
    B. Datagram
    C. Store-and-forward
    D. Virtual circuit

25. Which is the most common network switching method?

    A. Message

    B. Packet

    C. Circuit

    D. Virtual

26. Which two statements about virtual circuits are true?

    A. They usually are associated with connection-oriented services.

    B. A virtual circuit represents a specific path through the network.

    C. A virtual circuit appears to the connected devices as a dedicated network path.

    D. Virtual circuits dedicate a communication channel to a single conversation.

27. Which of the following statements is true?

    A. Hop count is a measure of routing cost.

    B. Distance vector routing methods are technically simple and make efficient use of network bandwidth.

    C. Link-state routing protocols rely on tick counts to make routing determinations.

    D. Link-state routing protocols transmit routing information at regular intervals.

28. Which three of the following terms are related?

    A. Port

    B. Connection ID

    C. Socket

    D. Service address

29. Which switching method fragments messages into small units that are routed through independent paths?

    A. Message
    B. Packet
    C. Circuit
    D. Virtual

30. Which activity involves the use of connection IDs?

    A. Packet switching
    B. Routing
    C. Segment development
    D. End-to-end flow control

31. Which two of the following are transport layer error-control strategies?

    A. Using datagram packet switching
    B. Utilizing unique segment sequencing numbers
    C. Using time-outs to drop packets that have remained on the network too long
    D. Using parity checking to detect errors

32. Which two of the following statements are true?

    A. The data link layer deals with device-to-device traffic.
    B. The network layer deals with traffic between upper-layer processes.
    C. The transport layer deals with traffic between end nodes.
    D. All of the above are true.

33. Which two of the following methods of dialog control provides two-way communication?

    A. Simple duplex

    B. Simplex

    C. Half-duplex

    D. Full-duplex

34. Dialog control is a function of which layer of the OSI Reference Model?

    A. Network

    B. Transport

    C. Session

    D. Presentation

35. Which three of the following are functions of session administration?

    A. Connection establishment

    B. Checksum error detection

    C. Data transfer

    D. Connection release

36. Which two of the following are functions of connection establishment?

    A. Resumption of interrupted communication

    B. Login name and password verification

    C. Determining required services

    D. Acknowledgment of data receipt

37. Which two of the following are possible functions of the presentation layer?

    A. Data encryption

    B. Presentation of data on display devices

C. Data translation

D. Display format conversion

38. Which two statements are true about public-key data encryption?

    A. Encoded data is vulnerable should the public key become known.

    B. A public key is generated from a secret key.

    C. Public-key encryption is less secure than private-key encryption.

    D. The public key is used to encrypt messages, and a separate key is used to decrypt messages.

39. Which three of the following are possible functions of the application layer?

    A. Network printing service

    B. End-user applications

    C. Client access to network services

    D. Service advertisement

Review Answers

1. B
2. B
3. A
4. C
5. B C D
6. C D
7. A D
8. C D
9. A C D
10. B

11. C
12. C
13. C
14. B C
15. D
16. C
17. A D
18. B
19. C
20. D
21. B
22. B
23. C
24. C
25. C
26. A C
27. A
28. A C D
29. B
30. C
31. B C
32. A C
33. C D
34. C
35. A C D
36. B C
37. A C
38. B D
39. A C D

Chapter 15
Transmission Media

On any network, the entities must communicate through some form of *media.* Humans can communicate through telephone wires or sound waves in the air. Computers can communicate through cables, light, and radio waves. Transmission media enable computers to send and receive messages, but do not guarantee that the messages will be understood.

The most common type of media is copper cable of some sort. Common types of copper cabling include twisted pair and coaxial. *Twisted-pair cabling* used in a LAN is similar to that used to connect your telephone to the wall outlet. Network *coaxial cabling* is similar to the cable used to connect your television set to the cable TV outlet.

Many other types of media are used to connect computer systems together in a LAN. A type of media quickly gaining popularity is fiber-optic cable. Fiber-optic cable consists of a number of glass or high-grade plastic optical strands in a tough cloth and plastic wrap. Fiber-optic cables resemble coaxial cables from the outside.

You might have seen fiber-optic lamps in novelty stores, in which colored lights are fed into optical strands, giving these lamps the appearance of having dozens of pinpoints of light. The same type of fiber-optic strand is used in fiber-optic cabling.

Another media that is gaining popularity is wireless media, which is, in a sense, no media at all. Wireless transmissions use radio waves or infrared light to transmit data. Many major network vendors now offer wireless network adapters.

Some large networks use combinations of media, which is one criterion of a *complex network.* When a network uses only one type of media, troubleshooting and maintaining the network is easier. When you mix and match different types of media, difficulties arise. Mixed media require a greater level of expertise and training on the part of the network support staff. When a problem arises on the LAN, the number of areas you must investigate increases dramatically when mixed transmission media are involved.

This chapter describes the most common network transmission media. You will learn about the following:

- Common transmission media and their characteristics
- Wireless network components and support
- Public network services that provide wide-area networking support
- Connecting hardware used in computer networking

Transmission Frequencies

Transmission media make possible the transmission of the electronic signals in one computer to another computer. These electronic signals express data values in the form of binary (on/off) impulses. The signals are transmitted through the network using a combination of electronic devices (network boards, hubs, and so on) and transmission media (cables, radio, and so on) until they reach the desired destination computer, where they again are converted into data signals inside the receiving computer.

All signals transmitted between computers consist of some form of *electromagnetic* (EM) waveform, ranging from radio frequencies, up through microwave, and infrared light. Different media are used to transmit the signals, depending on the frequency of the EM waveform. Figure 15.1 illustrates the range of electromagnetic waveforms, known as the *electromagnetic spectrum,* along with their associated frequencies.

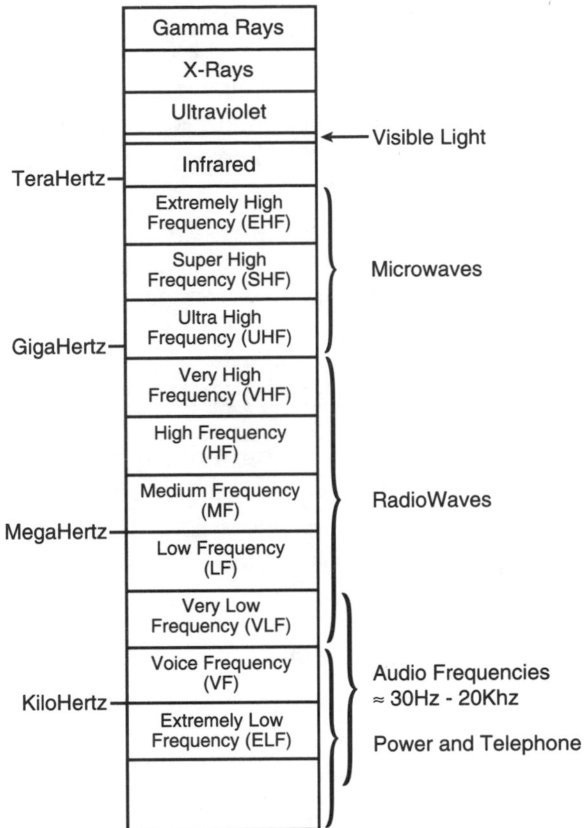

Figure 15.1

The electromagnetic spectrum.

Radio frequency waves are often used for LAN signaling. Radio frequencies can be transmitted across electrical cables (twisted pair or coaxial) or by using radio broadcast transmission.

Microwave transmissions can be used for tightly focused transmissions between two points. Microwaves are used to communicate between Earth stations and satellites. They also are used for line-of-sight transmissions on the Earth's surface. Microwaves also can be used in low-power forms to broadcast signals from a transmitter to many receivers. Cellular phone networks are examples of systems that use low-power microwave signals to broadcast signals.

Infrared light is ideal for many types of network communications. Infrared light can be transmitted across relatively short distances and can either be beamed between two points or broadcast from one point to many receivers. Infrared and higher frequencies of light also can be transmitted through fiber-optic cables.

The next sections examine examples of network transmission media, and describe the advantages and disadvantages of each media type.

Characteristics of Transmission Media

Each type of transmission media has special characteristics that suit it to a specific type of service. You should be familiar with these characteristics:

- Cost
- Installation requirements
- Bandwidth
- Attenuation
- Immunity from electromagnetic interference

The last three characteristics require some explanation.

Bandwidth

In computer networking, the term *bandwidth* has come to mean the measure of the capacity of a medium to transmit data. A medium that has a high capacity has a high bandwidth. A medium that has limited capacity has a low bandwidth.

Bandwidth can be understood through an analogy to water hoses. If a half-inch garden hose can carry waterflow from a trickle up to two gallons per minute, then that hose might be said to have a bandwidth of two gallons per minute. A four-inch fire hose, however, might have a bandwidth that exceeds 100 gallons per minute.

Data transmission rates frequently are stated in terms of the bits that can be transmitted per second. An Ethernet LAN theoretically can transmit 10 million bits per second and has a bandwidth of 10 megabits per second (Mbps).

The bandwidth that a cable can accommodate is determined in part by the cable's length. A short cable can generally accommodate greater bandwidth than a longer cable, which is one reason all cable designs specify maximum lengths for cable runs. Beyond those limits, the highest frequency signals can deteriorate and errors can begin to occur in data signals.

The term *bandwidth* also has another meaning. In the communications industry, bandwidth refers to the range of available frequencies between the lower frequency limit and the upper frequency limit. Frequencies are measured in *Hertz* (Hz), or cycles per second. The bandwidth of a voice telephone line is 400–4,000 Hz, meaning the line can transmit signals with frequencies ranging from 400 to 4,000 cycles per second.

Attenuation

Attenuation is a measure of how much a signal weakens as it travels through a medium. This book doesn't discuss attenuation in formal terms, but with regard to the impact of attenuation on performance.

Attenuation is a second reason cable designs must specify limits in the lengths of cable runs. When signal strength falls below certain limits, it can be difficult for the electronic equipment that receives the signal to isolate the original signal from the noise present in all electronic transmissions. The effect is exactly like trying to tune in distant radio signals. Even if you can lock on to the signal on your radio, the sound generally still contains more noise than the sound for a local radio station.

Electromagnetic Interference

Electromagnetic interference (EMI) consists of outside electromagnetic noise that distorts the signal in a medium. When you listen to an AM radio, you often hear noise caused by nearby motors or lightning. This is an example of EMI. Some network media are more susceptible to EMI than others.

Cable Media

Three types of cable media are discussed in this section:

- Coaxial cable
- Twisted-pair cable
- Fiber-optic cable

Coaxial Cable

Coaxial cables were the first cable types used in LANs. As shown in figure 15.2, coaxial cable gets its name because two conductors share a common axis; the cable is most frequently referred to as *coax.*

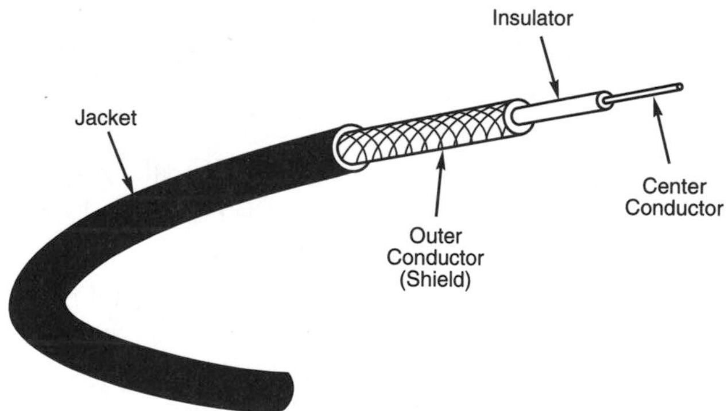

Figure 15.2

The structure of coaxial cable.

The components of a coaxial cable are as follows:

- A center conductor, usually solid copper wire (although you can use stranded wire).
- An outer conductor that forms a tube surrounding the center conductor. This conductor can consist of braided wires, metallic foil, or both. Because this conductor also protects the inner conductor from EMI, it is most frequently called the *shield.*
- An insulation layer that also keeps the outer conductor spaced evenly from the inner conductor.
- A plastic encasement (jacket) that protects the cable from damage.

Types of Coaxial Cable

All coax cables have a characteristic measurement, called *impedance,* measured in *ohms.* You need to use a cable that has the proper impedance in any given situation. The following list contains some types of coaxial cable frequently used on LANs:

- RG-8 and RG-11, 50-ohm cables used with Thick Ethernet
- RG-58, a 50-ohm cable used with Thin Ethernet
- RG-59, a 75-ohm cable used for cable TV
- RG-62, a 93-ohm cable used with ARCnet

Characteristics

You should be familiar with a number of important characteristics of coaxial cable. Those characteristics are briefly described in the following sections.

Installation

Coaxial cable typically is installed in two configurations: daisy-chained from device to device (Ethernet) and stars (ARCnet). Both are shown in figure 15.3.

Figure 15.3

Coaxial cable wiring configurations.

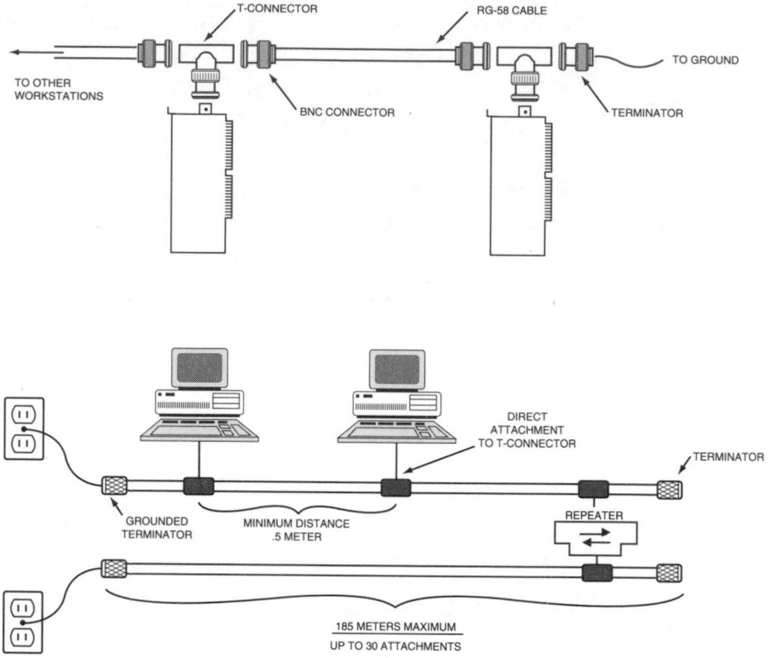

The Ethernet cabling shown in the figure is an example of Thin Ethernet, which uses RG-58 type cable. Devices connect to the cable by means of T-connectors. Cables are used to provide connections between T-connectors. One characteristic of this type of cabling is that the ends of the cable run must be terminated by a special connector called a terminator. The *terminator* contains a resistor that is matched to the characteristics of the cable. The resistor prevents signals that reach the end of the cable from bouncing back and causing interference.

Coaxial cable is reasonably easy to install. The cable is robust and difficult to damage, and connectors can be installed with inexpensive tools and a bit of practice. The device-to-device cabling approach can be difficult to reconfigure, however, when new devices cannot be installed near an existing cabling path.

Cost

The coaxial cable used for Thin Ethernet falls at the low end of the cost spectrum, whereas Thick Ethernet is among the more costly options. Detailed cost comparisons are made after the remaining cable types have been introduced.

Bandwidth

LANs that employ coaxial cable typically have a bandwidth between 2.5 Mbps (ARCnet) to 10 Mbps (Ethernet). Thicker coaxial cables offer higher bandwidth, and the potential bandwidth of coax is much higher than 10 Mbps. Current LAN technologies, however, don't take advantage of this potential.

Attenuation

All media suffer from attenuation, but coax has better attenuation characteristics than other copper cables, such as twisted pair. LANs that employ coaxial cable are limited to a few thousand meters in length.

EMI Characteristics

All copper media are sensitive to EMI, although the shield in coax makes the cable fairly resistant to EMI. Coaxial cables, however, do radiate a portion of their signal, and electronic eavesdropping equipment can detect this radiated signal.

Twisted-Pair Cable

Twisted-pair cable has become the dominant cable type for all new network designs that employ copper cable. Several reasons account for the popularity of twisted-pair cable, the most significant being low cost. Twisted-pair cable is inexpensive to install and offers the lowest cost-per-foot of any cable type.

A basic twisted-pair cable consists of two strands of copper wire twisted together (see fig. 15.4). The twists are an important part of the characteristics of twisted-pair cable. Twisting reduces the sensitivity of the cable to EMI and also reduces the tendency of the cable to radiate radio frequency noise that interferes with nearby cables and electronic components. The radiated signals from the twisted wires tend to cancel each other out. (Antennas, which are purposely designed to radiate radio-frequency signals, consist of parallel, not twisted, wires.)

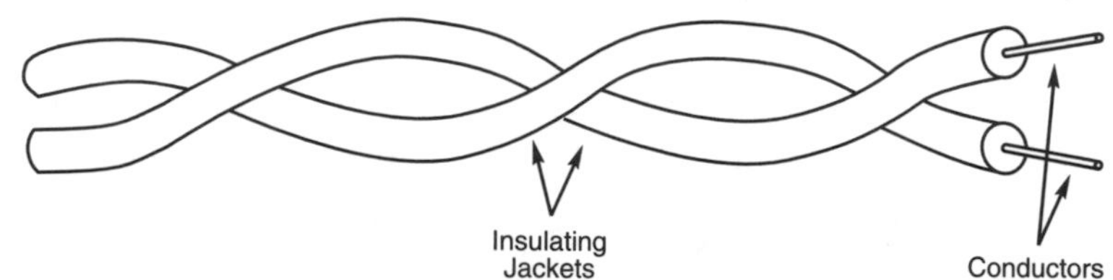

Figure 15.4

A twisted-pair cable.

Twisting also controls the tendency of the wires in the pair to cause EMI in each other. Whenever two wires are in close proximity, the signals in each wire tend to produce noise, called *crosstalk,* in the other. Twisting the wires in the pair reduces crosstalk in much the same way that twisting reduces the tendency of the wires to radiate EMI.

Two types of twisted-pair cable are used in LANs: shielded and unshielded.

Shielded Twisted-Pair (STP) Cable

The first twisted-pair cables used in LANs were *shielded twisted pair,* similar to the cable shown in figure 15.5, which shows IBM Type 1 cable, the first cable type used with IBM Token-Ring. Early LAN designers employed shielded twisted-pair cable because the shield further reduces the tendency of the cable to radiate EMI and reduces the cable's sensitivity to outside interference.

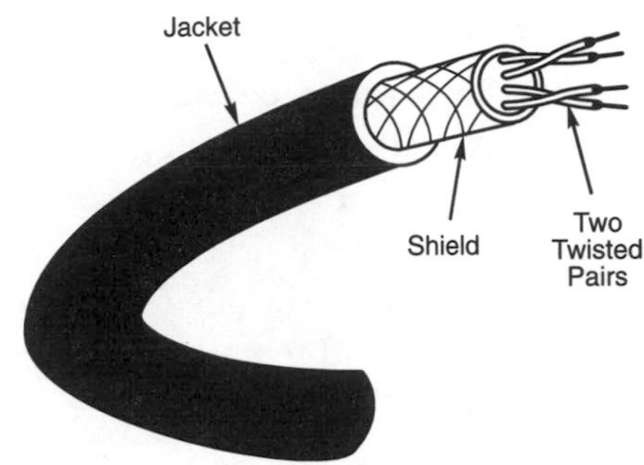

Figure 15.5

A shielded twisted-pair cable.

Coaxial and STP cables use shields for the same purpose. The *shield* is connected to the ground portion of the electronic device to which the cable is connected. A *ground* is a portion of the device that serves as an electrical reference point, and usually is literally connected to a metal stake driven into the ground. A properly grounded shield tends to prevent signals from getting into or out of the cable.

The IBM Type 1 cable shown in figure 15.5 includes two twisted pairs of wire within a single shield. Various types of STP cable exist, some that shield each pair individually and others that shield several pairs. The engineers who design the cabling system choose the exact configuration. IBM designates several twisted-pair cable types to use with their Token-Ring network design, and each cable type is appropriate for a given kind of installation. A completely different type of STP is the standard cable for Apple's AppleTalk network.

Because so many different types of STP cable exist, stating precise characteristics is difficult. The following sections, however, offer some general guidelines.

Cost

STP cable costs more than thin coaxial or unshielded twisted-pair cables. STP is less costly, however, than thick coax or fiber-optic cable.

Installation

Different network types have different installation requirements. One major difference is the connector used. Apple LocalTalk connectors generally must be soldered during installation, requiring some practice and skill on the part of the installer. IBM Token-Ring uses a so-called *unisex* data connector (the connectors are both male and female), which can be installed with common tools such as a knife, wire stripper, and a large pliers.

In many cases, installation can be greatly simplified by using prewired cables. You need to learn to install the required connectors, however, whenever your installation requires use of bulk cable.

Most connectors require two connector types to complete a connection. The traditional designation for connector types is male and female. The male connector is the connector with pins, and the female connector has receptacles into which the pins insert. In a standard AC wall outlet, the outlet itself is female and the plug on the line cord is male.

These designations originated when electrical installation was a male province, and the terms male and female gradually are being replaced. A commonly used alternative is "pins and sockets."

The IBM data connector is called a unisex connector because the connector has both pins and sockets. Any IBM data connector can connect to any other IBM data connector.

STP cable tends to be rather bulky. IBM Type 1 cable is approximately 1/2 inch in diameter. Therefore, it can take little time to fill up cable paths with STP cables.

Capacity

STP cable has a theoretical capacity of 500 Mbps, although few implementations exceed 155 Mbps with 100-meter cable runs. The most common data rate for STP cable is 16 Mbps, the top data rate for Token Ring networks.

Attenuation

All varieties of twisted-pair cable have attenuation characteristics that limit the length of cable runs to a few hundred meters, although a 100-meter limit is most common.

EMI Characteristics

The shield in STP cable results in good EMI characteristics for copper cable, comparable to the EMI characteristics of coaxial cable. This is one reason STP might be preferred to unshielded twisted-pair cable in some situations. Like all copper cables, STP is sensitive to interference and vulnerable to electronic eavesdropping.

Unshielded Twisted-Pair (UTP) Cable

Unshielded twisted-pair (UTP) cable doesn't incorporate a braided shield. The characteristics of UTP are similar in many ways to STP, differing primarily in attenuation and EMI characteristics. As shown in figure 15.6, several twisted pairs can be bundled together in a single cable. These pairs typically are color coded to distinguish the pairs.

Figure 15.6

A multipair UTP cable.

UTP cable is a latecomer to high-performance LANs because engineers only recently solved the problems of managing radiated noise and susceptibility to EMI. Now, however, a clear trend toward UTP is in operation, and all new copper-based cabling schemes are based on use of UTP.

UTP cable is available in the following five grades or categories:

- Categories 1 and 2 are voice-grade cables, suitable only for voice and for low data rates (below 4 Mbps). At one time, Category 1 was the standard voice-grade cable for telephone systems. The growing need for data-ready cabling systems, however, has caused Category 1 and 2 cable to be supplanted by Category 3 for new installations.

- Category 3 is the lowest data-grade cable and is generally suited for data rates up to 16 Mbps. Some innovative schemes, however, make possible supporting data rates up to 100 Mbps with Category 3 cable. Category 3 is now the standard cable used for most telephone installations.
- Category 4 is a data-grade cable suitable for data rates up to 20 Mbps.
- Category 5 is a data-grade cable suitable for data rates up to 100 Mbps. Most new cabling systems for 100-Mbps data rates are designed around Category 5 cable.

In a UTP cabling system, the cable is only one component. All connecting devices also are graded, and the overall cabling system only supports the data rates permitted by the lowest grade of component in the system. In other words, if you require a Category 5 cabling system, all connectors and connecting devices must be designed for Category 5 operation.

Category 5 cable also requires more stringent installation procedures than the lower cable categories. Installers of Category 5 cable require special training and skills to understand these more rigorous requirements.

UTP cable offers an excellent balance of cost and performance characteristics.

Cost

UTP cable has the lowest cost of any cable type, although properly installed Category 5 tends to be fairly high in cost. In some cases, existing cable in buildings can be used for LANs, although you should verify the category of the cable and know the length of the cable in the walls. Distance limits for voice cabling are much less stringent than for data-grade cabling.

Installation

UTP cable is easy to install. Some specialized equipment might be required, but the equipment is low in cost and can be mastered with a bit of practice. Properly designed UTP cabling systems easily can be reconfigured to meet changing requirements.

As noted earlier, however, Category 5 cable has stricter installation requirements than lower categories of UTP. Special training is recommended for dealing with Category 5 UTP.

Capacity

The data rates possible with UTP have pushed up from 1 Mbps, past 4 and 16 Mbps, to the point where 100-Mbps data rates are now common.

Attenuation

UTP cable shares similar attenuation characteristics with other copper cables. UTP cable runs are limited to a few hundred meters, with 100 meters the most frequent limit.

EMI Characteristics

Lacking a shield, UTP cable is more sensitive to EMI than coaxial or STP cables. The latest technologies make possible using UTP in the vast majority of situations, provided reasonable care is taken to avoid electrically noisy devices such as motors and fluorescent lights. Nevertheless, UTP might not be suitable for noisy environments such as factories. Crosstalk between nearby unshielded pairs limits the maximum length of cable runs.

Fiber-Optic Cable

In almost every way, fiber-optic cable is the ideal cable for data transmission: extremely high bandwidths, no problems with EMI, durable cables, and cable runs as long as several kilometers. The two disadvantages of fiber optic are cost and installation difficulty.

Figure 15.7 shows a fiber-optic cable. The center conductor is a fiber that consists of highly refined glass or plastic designed to transmit light signals with little loss. The fiber is coated with a cladding that reflects signals back into the fiber to reduce signal loss. A plastic sheath protects the fiber.

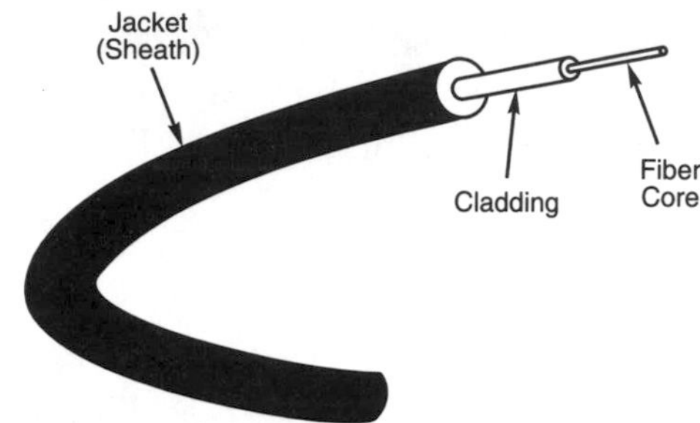

Figure 15.7

A fiber-optic cable.

Loose and tight cable configurations are available. Loose configurations incorporate a space between the fiber sheath and the outer plastic encasement; this space is filled with a gel or other material. Tight configurations include strength wires between the conductor and the outer plastic encasement. In both cases, the plastic encasement must supply the strength of the cable. The gel layer or strength wires protect the delicate fiber from mechanical damage.

Although the figure shows cables with single fibers, it's common to bundle multiple fibers into cables. A small-diameter cable can incorporate an astonishing number of optical fibers, making fiber-optic cable ideal for cabling when cable paths are clogged.

Optical fiber cables don't transmit electrical signals. Instead, the data signals must be converted into light signals. Light sources include lasers and *light-emitting diodes* (LEDs). LEDs are inexpensive, but produce a fairly poor quality of light suitable for less-stringent applications.

A *laser* is a light source that produces an especially pure light that is monochromatic (one color) and coherent (all waves are parallel). The most commonly used source of laser light in LAN devices is called an *injection laser diode* (ILD). The purity of laser light makes lasers ideally suited to data transmissions because long distances and high bandwidths are possible. Lasers, however, are expensive light sources, used only when their special characteristics are required.

The end of the cable that receives the light signal must convert the signal back to an electrical form. Several types of solid-state components can perform this service. The most common are types of photodiodes.

Optical fibers have several characteristics:

- **Mode.** Single-mode cables support a single light path and are commonly used with lasers. Multimode cables support multiple light paths and are best suited to lower-quality light sources, such as LEDs. At a much higher cost, single-mode cables with laser light sources support the longest cable runs and the greatest bandwidth. Figure 15.8 illustrates the difference between single- and multimode cables.

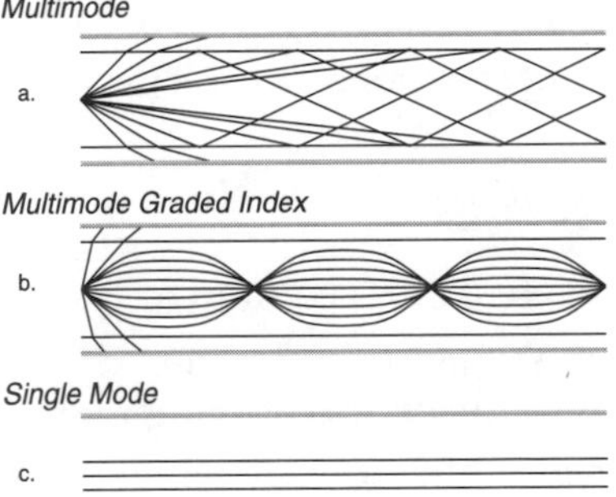

Figure 15.8

Modes of fiber-optic cables.

- **Core diameter.** The cores of fiber-optic cables are small enough to be measured in microns (millionths of a meter). The symbol for micron is μ.
- **Cladding diameter.** This dimension also is given in microns.

The following are common types of fiber-optic cables:

- 8.3 micron core/125 micron cladding/single-mode
- 62.5 micron core/125 micron cladding/multimode

- 50 micron core/125 micron cladding/multimode
- 100 micron core/140 micron cladding/multimode

Note the small core diameters of these cables. One of the significant difficulties of installing fiber-optic cable arises when two cables must be joined. The small cores of the two cables must be lined up with extreme precision to prevent excessive signal loss.

Fiber-Optic Characteristics

Like all cable types, fiber-optic cables constitute a blend of advantages and disadvantages. These are discussed in the following sections.

Cost

The cost of the cable and connectors has fallen significantly in recent years. The electronic devices required are significantly more expensive than comparable devices for copper cable. An Ethernet network board for UTP cable now can cost less than $100. Network boards for use with fiber-optic cables, however, frequently cost in excess of $1,000 each. Fiber-optic cable is also the most expensive cable type to install.

Installation

Greater skill is required to install fiber-optic cable than to install most copper cables. Improved tools and techniques, however, have reduced the training required. Still, greater care is required because fiber-optic cables must be treated fairly gently during installation. Every cable has a minimum bend radius, for example, and fibers are damaged if the cables are bent too sharply. It also is important not to stretch the cable during installation.

Capacity

Bandwidths for fiber-optic cables can range as high as 2 Gbps (billion bps). Fiber-optic cable can support high data rates even with long cable runs. UTP cable runs are limited to less than 100 meters with 100-Mbps data rates. Fiber-optic cables can transmit 100-Mbps signals for several kilometers.

Attenuation

Attenuation in fiber-optic cables is much lower than in copper cables. Fiber-optic cables are capable of carrying signals for several kilometers.

EMI Characteristics

Because fiber-optic cables don't use electrical signals to transmit data, they are totally immune to electromagnetic interference. They also are immune to a variety of electrical effects that must be taken into account when designing copper cabling systems.

When electrical cables are connected between two buildings, a common problem to be dealt with is differences between the ground potentials (voltages) between the two buildings. When a difference exists (as frequently it does), current flows through the grounding conductor of the cable, even though the ground is supposed to be electrically neutral and no current should flow. When current flows through the ground conductor of a cable, the condition is called a *ground loop*. The results of ground loops are electrical instability and various types of anomalies.

Because fiber-optic cable is immune to electrical effects, the best way to connect networks in different buildings is by putting in a fiber-optic link segment.

Because they are not electrical in nature, the signals in fiber-optic cables cannot be detected by electronic eavesdropping equipment that detects electromagnetic radiation. Fiber-optic cable is, therefore, the perfect choice for high-security networks.

Summary of Cable Characteristics

Table 15.1 summarizes the characteristics of the four cable types discussed in this section.

Table 15.1

Comparison of Cable Media

Cable Type	Cost	Installation	Capacity	Attenuation	EMI
Coaxial	Medium < Cat 5 UTP > Cat 3 UTP Thin<STP Thick>STP <Fiber	Inexpensive/ easy; may be difficult to reconfigure	10 Mbps typical	Less than STP or UTP; limited to range of few kilometers	Less sensitive than UTP, but still subject to EMI and eavesdropping
Shielded Twisted pair	Medium >UTP =Thin coax <Thick coax <Fiber	Moderate cost/ fairly easy; more difficult than UTP and coax	16 Mbps typical; up to 500 Mbps	Limits range to several hundred meters	Less sensitive than UTP, but still subject to EMI and eavesdropping
Unshielded Twisted pair	Lowest	Inexpensive/ easy	1-100 Mbps with 100-meter runs	Limits range to several hundred meters	Most sensitive to EMI and eavesdropping
Fiber optic	Highest	Expensive/ difficult	10 Mbps to 2 Gbps; 100 Mbps typical	Lowest. Range of 10s of kilometers	Insensitive to EMI and eavesdropping

When comparing cabling types, remember that the characteristics you observe depend highly on the implementations. At one time, it was argued that UTP cable would never reliably support data rates above 4 Mbps, but 100-Mbps data rates now are common.

Some comparisons are fairly involved. Although fiber-optic cable is costly on a per-foot basis, you can construct a fiber-optic cable that is many kilometers in length. To build a copper cable that length, you would need to install repeaters at several points along the cable to amplify the signal. These repeaters could easily exceed the cost of a fiber-optic cable run.

Wireless Media

Cable lends itself to fixed installations and moderate distances. When end points are widely separated or when they're moving, you might want to investigate wireless media. Several wireless media are available, of which the following are considered:

- Radio
- Microwave
- Infrared

Radio

The radio portion of the electromagnetic spectrum extends from 10 KHz to 1 GHz. Within this range are numerous bands, or ranges of frequencies that are designated for specific purposes. The following are frequency bands with which you are probably familiar:

- Shortwave
- VHF (Very High Frequency): television and FM radio
- UHF (Ultra High Frequency): television

Within the United States, the Federal Communications Commission (FCC) controls the use of radio frequencies. The majority of frequency allocations are licensed; an organization is granted an exclusive license to use a particular range of frequencies within a certain limited geographic area. Thus, you can have only one television Channel 5 within a given area. Channel 5 allocations are spread out so that they don't interfere with each other. A licensed frequency allocation guarantees the license owner a clear, low-interference communication channel.

A few frequency ranges are unlicensed, meaning, they can be used freely for the purpose specified for those frequencies. The FCC has designated three unlicensed frequency bands: 902–928 MHz, 2.4 GHz, and 5.72–5.85 GHz. The 902 MHz range has been available the longest and has been used for everything from cordless telephones to model airplane remote control. Because the 902 MHz range is quite crowded, many vendors are pushing development of devices for the less crowded 2.4 GHz band. Equipment for the 5.72 GHz remains expensive and is used infrequently.

Use of an unlicensed frequency is done at the user's risk, and a clear communication channel is not guaranteed. Equipment used in these frequency bands, however, must operate at a regulated power level to limit range and reduce the potential for interference.

Radio transmissions can be omnidirectional or directional. A radio station typically transmits an *omnidirectional* (all-directional) signal that all radios within the broadcast area can receive. Sometimes, a directional transmission might be used to direct all of the transmission power toward a specific reception point.

Various types of antennas are used, depending on the desired transmission and reception characteristics. Several antenna types are shown in figure 15.9.

Figure 15.9

Representative antenna types.

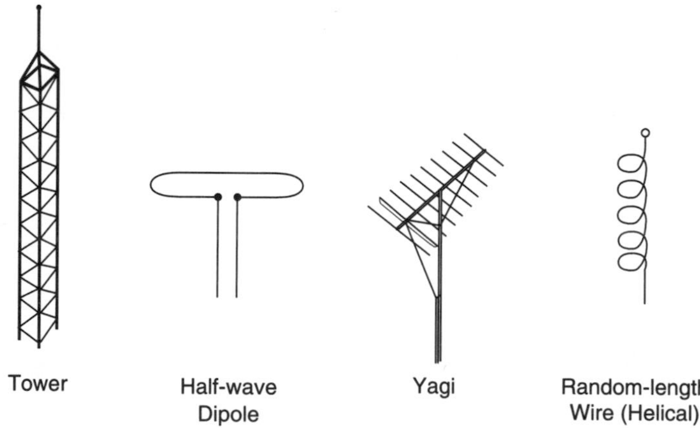

- *Broadcast towers* generally are omnidirectional, although the specific radiation pattern can be adjusted to match the FCC restrictions for a particular licensee.
- *Dipole antennas* receive a fairly broad range of frequencies and are moderately directional.
- A *random-length wire* can be used for transmission or reception. *Random-length* means that the antenna length is not specifically chosen for the frequency being transmitted or received. The antenna on a typical AM/FM radio is a random-length wire.
- A *beam antenna* uses multiple elements to tune the antenna for a specific frequency range and directiveness. A common antenna design is called the *Yagi*. A beam antenna is used to produce a fairly focused beam that can be aimed at a specific reception point (although the effect is not completely directional, and signal leaks occur in all directions).

Characteristics of Radio Transmission

The characteristics of radio transmissions change dramatically with frequency. Low-frequency radio supports limited data rates, but has a significant advantage in that it can frequently communicate past the horizon. Shortwave operators are familiar with this phenomenon, and they commonly can monitor transmissions from the other side of the Earth.

As frequency increases, transmissions become increasingly line-of-site. AM radio broadcast frequencies range from the KHz to the low MHz range. You might have had the experience of picking up an AM radio station from several states away, particularly late at night. This can occur because AM radio transmissions can bounce off the atmosphere's ozone layer. Some of the lowest-frequency AM radio transmissions can actually travel along the ground, in a phenomenon called *ground waves*. Some transmissions can bounce a considerable distance.

FM transmissions, however, seldom can be received past the horizon. You seldom clearly receive an FM broadcast beyond a range of 100 miles. This is partly a function of power, but the primary cause of the range limitation is the inability of FM frequencies to go beyond the horizon.

On a line-of-sight basis, however, high-frequency transmissions attenuate less rapidly than low-frequency transmissions.

Lower-frequency radio waves can penetrate solid materials to a greater degree than higher frequencies. Very low radio frequencies can be used to communicate with submerged submarines, although the data rates are extremely slow. Penetration capability also is a function of power. Higher-power transmissions penetrate building walls more effectively than lower-power transmissions.

As you can see, designing a radio system to have the ideal characteristics for an application requires plenty of design tradeoffs.

This section discusses three classes of radio frequency transmission:

- Low-power, single-frequency
- High-power, single-frequency
- Spread spectrum

Low-Power, Single-Frequency Radio

Low-power systems are chosen to limit the interference between nearby radio systems. Transmission ranges might be as short as 20 to 30 meters. This approach resembles cellular telephone technology, which divides geographic areas into isolated, low-power cells, enabling frequencies to be reused in nearby cells.

Although low-frequency radio can penetrate building walls, the low power used with this radio class typically requires transmitters and receivers to have a line-of-sight path. The data rates possible with low-frequency radio do not support the data rates required for LANs.

Theoretically, you could implement mobile stations with this radio class, although walls and low power limit the possible mobility.

Frequency Range

Any radio frequency can be used, but higher frequencies, typically in the GHz, generally are chosen to support higher data rates.

Cost

Cost depends on design, but can be low compared to other wireless media. As with most media, higher data rates cost more.

Ease of Installation

This characteristic also depends on design. Some single-frequency systems use licensed frequencies, and a license application must be filed with the FCC. In at least one case, however, a prominent vendor has obtained licenses in many major markets and handles the FCC paperwork for the customer.

Some single-frequency systems use unlicensed frequencies. Some troubleshooting might be needed to prevent interference from other nearby devices that use the same frequencies.

Capacity

Although the theoretical bandwidth of radio LANs is high, currently available products range from 1 to 10 Mbps.

Attenuation

Attenuation is high due to the low power levels used, but proper design turns this into an advantage by creating large numbers of independent areas that don't interfere with each other.

EMI Characteristics

EMI resistance is low, particularly in the 902-MHz band shared with other unlicensed devices. All radio LANs are vulnerable to electronic eavesdropping, although the low powers used typically reduce the range at which eavesdropping can occur to the confines of the building in which the LAN is housed.

High-Power, Single-Frequency Radio

High-power radio has data capacity similar to low-power radio, but can cover much larger areas. Transmissions can be line-of-sight or can be extended by bouncing signals off the atmosphere. Because power can be higher, this approach can result in practical mobile networking and can service stations on motor or marine vehicles.

Frequency Range

As with low-power radio, any part of the radio spectrum can be used. Frequencies in the GHz range are generally chosen to achieve high data rates.

Cost

High-power transmission equipment is considerably more expensive. Signal repeaters might be needed to extend the coverage area. Costs for high-power radio can be moderate to high.

Ease of Installation

High-power radio equipment must be operated under an FCC license by licensed personnel. Equipment must be maintained in proper order to remain within the terms of the license. Improperly installed and maintained equipment might function poorly and interfere with nearby radio services.

Bandwidth

Capacity can be high but typically falls between 1 and 10 Mbps.

Attenuation

Attenuation rates for high-power radio are fairly low. Signal repeaters can be employed to extend transmission range.

EMI Characteristics

Immunity to EMI is low, and the potential for eavesdropping is high. Signals can be easily intercepted anywhere within the broadcast area.

Spread Spectrum Radio

Spread spectrum is a technique originally developed by the military to solve several communication problems. Spread spectrum improves reliability, reduces sensitivity to interference and jamming, and is less vulnerable to eavesdropping than single-frequency radio.

Spread spectrum transmission uses multiple frequencies to transmit messages. Two techniques employed are direct sequence modulation and frequency hopping.

Direct sequence modulation breaks original messages into parts called *chips* (see fig. 15.10), which are transmitted on separate frequencies. To confuse eavesdroppers, decoy data also can be transmitted on other frequencies. The intended receiver knows which frequencies are valid, and can isolate the chips and reassemble the message. Eavesdropping is difficult because the correct frequencies are not known, and the eavesdropper cannot isolate the frequencies carrying true data. This technique can operate in environments with other transmission activity since different sets of frequencies can be selected. Direct sequence modulation systems operating at 900 MHz support bandwidths of 2–6 Mbps.

Frequency hopping switches transmissions among several available frequencies (see fig. 15.11). Transmitter and receiver must remain synchronized for this technique to work. Some systems transmit on multiple frequencies simultaneously to increase bandwidth.

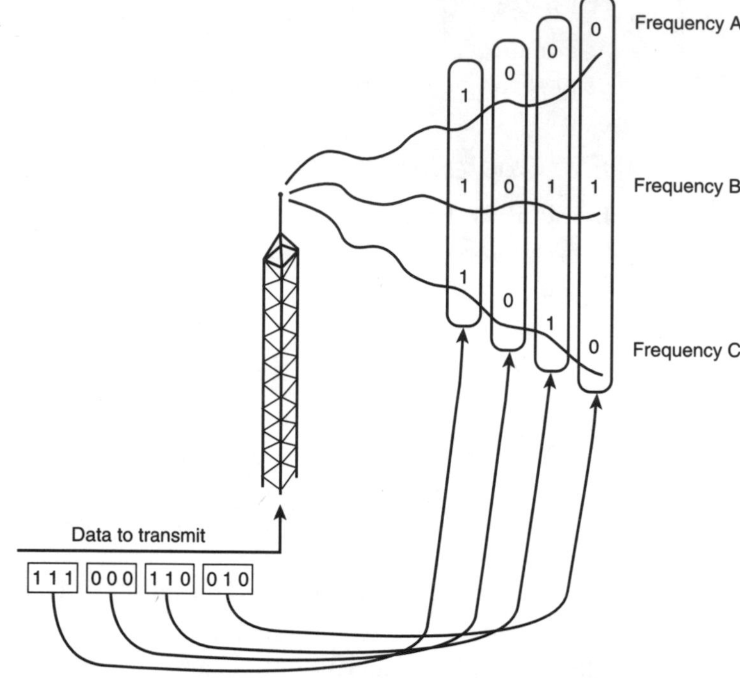

Figure 15.10

Direct sequence modulation.

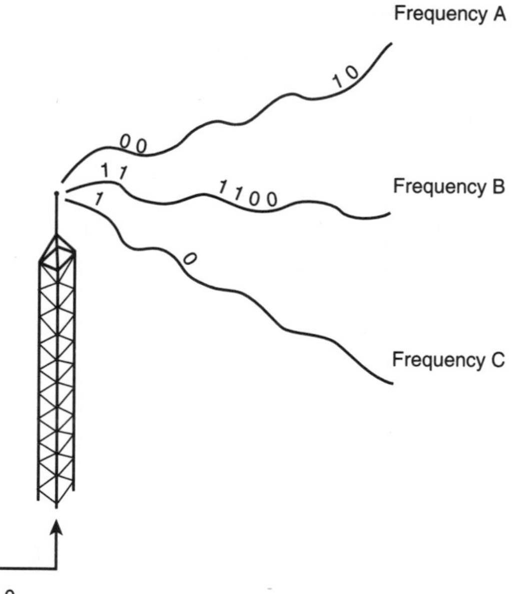

Figure 15.11

Frequency hopping.

Frequency Range

Spread spectrum systems typically operate in unlicensed frequency ranges. 900 MHz devices are common, but 2.4-GHz devices are becoming available.

Costs

Costs are moderate compared to other wireless media.

Ease of Installation

This depends on the system design and the frequencies used. Installation complexity ranges from simple to somewhat complex.

Capacity

All 900 MHz systems support bandwidth capacities of 2-6 MHz. Newer systems operating in GHz frequencies can be expected to offer higher data rates.

Attenuation

This is determined by the frequency and power of the transmitted signals. Spread spectrum LANs typically operate at low power and exhibit high attenuation characteristics.

EMI Characteristics

Although individual frequencies are susceptible to EMI, the system can seek out clear frequencies on which to transmit. Overall resistance to EMI, therefore, is fairly high. Resistance to eavesdropping is high for the reasons cited earlier.

Microwave

As shown in figure 15.12, microwave communication can take two forms: terrestrial (ground links) and satellite links. The frequencies and technologies employed by these two forms are similar, but distinct differences exist between them.

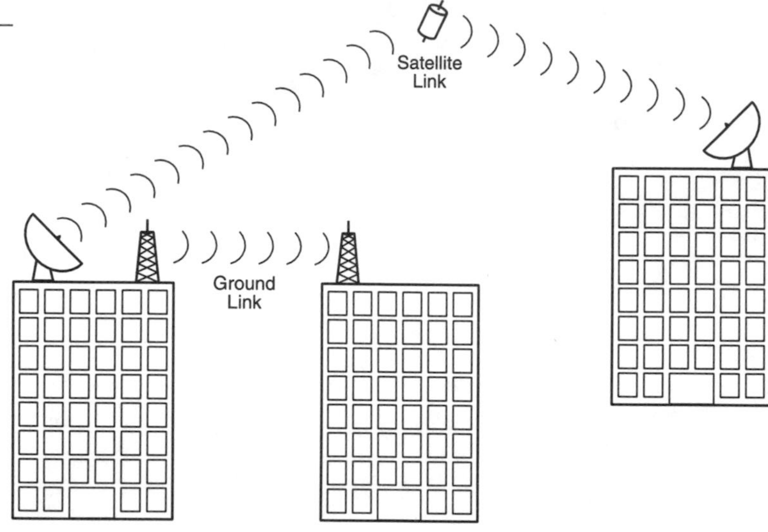

Figure 15.12

Terrestrial and satellite microwave links.

Terrestrial Microwave

Terrestrial microwave communication employs Earth-based transmitters and receivers. The frequencies used are in the low-gigahertz range, limiting all communications to line-of-sight. You have probably seen terrestrial microwave equipment in the form of telephone relay towers, placed every few miles to relay telephone signals cross country.

Microwave transmissions typically are made using a parabolic antenna that produces a narrow, highly directional signal. A similar antenna at the receiving site is sensitive to signals only within a narrow focus. Because the transmitter and receiver are highly focused, they must be adjusted carefully so that the transmitted signal is aligned with the receiver.

Microwave frequently is used as a way to transmit signals where it would be impractical to run cables. If you need to connect two networks separated by a public road, you might find that you may not run cables above or below the road. In such a case, a microwave link is an ideal solution.

Some LANs operate at microwave frequencies, operate at low power, and use nondirectional transmitters and receivers. Network hubs can be placed strategically throughout an organization, and workstations can be mobile or fixed. This approach is one way to enable workstations to be mobile in an office setting.

In many cases, terrestrial microwave uses licensed frequencies. A license must be obtained from the FCC, and equipment must be installed and maintained by licensed technicians.

Frequency Range

Terrestrial microwave systems operate in the low-gigahertz range, typically at 4–6 GHz and 21–23 GHz.

Cost

Costs are highly variable depending on requirements.

Long-distance microwave systems can be quite expensive, but might be less costly than alternatives. A leased telephone circuit represents a costly monthly expense. When line-of-sight transmission is possible, a microwave link is a one-time expense that can offer greater bandwidth than a leased circuit.

Costs are on the way down for low-power microwave systems for the office. Although these systems don't compete directly in cost with cabled networks, when equipment frequently must be moved, microwave can be a cost-effective technology.

Installation

Licensing usually is required. Many equipment providers take care of licensing along with installation. Installation is a skilled operation that generally requires licensed technicians. Setting up transmitter and receiver sites can be difficult because antennas must be precisely aligned.

A line-of-sight communication path might require the purchase of access to suitable transmitter sites.

Bandwidth

Capacity can be extremely high, but most data communication systems operate at data rates between 1 and 10 Mbps.

Attenuation

Attenuation characteristics are determined by transmitter power, frequency, and antenna size. Properly designed systems are not affected by attenuation under normal operational conditions. Rain and fog, however, can cause attenuation of higher frequencies.

EMI Characteristics

Microwave systems are highly susceptible to atmospheric interference. They also might be vulnerable to electronic eavesdropping, and signals transmitted through microwave are frequently encrypted.

Satellite Microwave

Satellite microwave systems relay transmissions through communication satellites that operate in geosynchronous orbits 22,300 miles above the Earth. Satellites orbiting at this distance remain located above a fixed point on the Earth.

Earth stations use parabolic antennas (satellite dishes) to communicate with the satellites. Satellites can retransmit signals in broad or in narrow beams depending on which locations are to receive the signals. When the destination is on the opposite side of the Earth, the first satellite cannot transmit directly to the receiver and must relay the signal through another satellite.

Because no cables are required, satellite microwave communication is possible with most remote sites and with mobile devices, including ships at sea and motor vehicles.

The distances involved in satellite communication result in an interesting phenomenon: Because all signals must travel 22,300 miles to the satellite and 22,300 miles when returning to a receiver, the time required to transmit a signal is independent of distance. It takes as long to transmit a signal to a receiver in the same state as it does to a receiver a third of the way around the world. The time required for a signal to arrive at its destination is called *propagation delay.* The delays encountered with satellite transmissions range from 0.5 to 5 seconds.

Unfortunately, satellite communication is extremely expensive. Building and launching a satellite easily can cost in excess of a billion dollars. In most cases, organizations share these costs, or they purchase services from a commercial provider. AT&T, Hughes Network Services, and Scientific-Atlanta are among the firms that sell satellite-based communication services.

Frequency Range

Satellite links operate in thelow-gigahertz range, typically at 11–14 MHz.

Cost

Costs are extremely high and are usually amortized across many users by selling communication services.

Ease of Installation

Earth stations can be installed by numerous commercial providers. Transmitters operate on licensed frequencies and require an FCC license.

Bandwidth

Bandwidth is related to cost, and firms can purchase almost any required bandwidth. Typical data rates are 1–10 Mbps.

Attenuation

Attenuation characteristics depend on frequency, power, and atmospheric conditions. Properly designed systems take attenuation into account. Rain and atmospheric conditions might attenuate higher frequencies.

EMI Characteristics

Microwave signals are sensitive to EMI and electronic eavesdropping. Signals transmitted through microwave frequently are encrypted.

Infrared Systems

You use an *infrared* communication system every time you control your television with a remote control. The remote control transmits pulses of infrared light that carry coded instructions to a receiver on the TV. This technology can be adapted to network communication.

Two methods of infrared networking are in use: point-to-point and broadcast.

Point-to-Point Infrared

Point-to-point networks operate by relaying infrared signals from one device to the next. An example of an infrared LAN is shown in figure 15.13. Transmissions are focused in a narrow beam, and the transmitter and receiver must be aligned carefully. Because the devices must be carefully placed and set up, point-to-point infrared is not suitable for use with devices that move frequently.

High-powered laser transmitters can be used to transmit data for several thousand yards when line-of-sight communication is possible. Lasers can be used in many of the same situations as microwave links, without requiring an FCC license. Consider infrared lasers for connections between buildings, particularly when they're separated by public rights of way.

Figure 15.13

Point-to-point infrared networking.

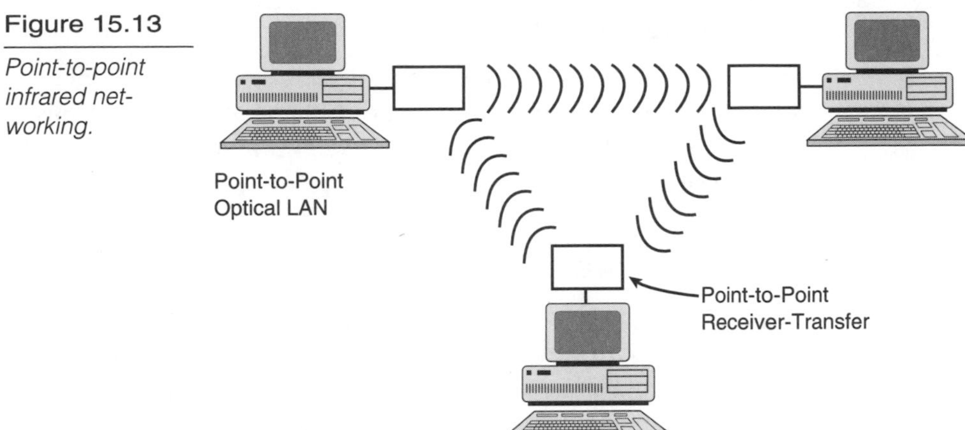

Frequency Range

Infrared light falls in a range below visible light and has a frequency range of approximately 100 GHz to 1,000 THz.

Cost

Point-to-point infrared equipment costs more than a comparable cabled network. Most systems use transmitters based on LED technology, and the hardware cost is moderate. Long-distance systems use high-powered laser transmitters, which can be quite costly.

Ease of Installation

Installation requires careful alignment of the transmitters and receivers. Lasers used in high-powered transmitters can be hazardous and can burn or damage eyes.

Bandwidth

Point-to-point infrared bandwidth ranges from about 100 Kbps to 16 Mbps.

Attenuation

In point-to-point infrared transmission, attenuation characteristics are determined by the quality of the transmission, by presence of obstructions, and by atmospheric conditions.

EMI Characteristics

Infrared devices are insensitive to radio-frequency interference, but reception can be degraded by bright light. Because transmissions are tightly focused, they are fairly immune to electronic eavesdropping.

Broadcast Infrared

Instead of focusing transmissions in tight beams, *broadcast infrared* disperses transmissions so that they're visible to several receivers. At least two approaches are possible, as shown in figure 15.14. One approach is to locate an active transmitter at a high point so that it can transmit to all devices. Another approach calls for placing a reflective material on the ceiling; devices transmit toward the ceiling where the light signals are dispersed to other devices in the room.

Frequency Range

Infrared light falls in a range below visible light and has a frequency range of approximately 100 GHz to 1000 THz.

Cost

The cost of point-to-point infrared equipment is higher than the cost for a comparable cabled network. Because lasers produce a tightly focused beam, they aren't very suitable to broadcast-type networks.

Ease of Installation

Installation is fairly simple because device alignment isn't critical. Each device must have clear transmission and reception pathways. Because these devices are sensitive to light interference, the control of ambient light is a significant installation concern.

Capacity

Typical bandwidths are less than 1 Mbps, although higher bandwidths theoretically are possible.

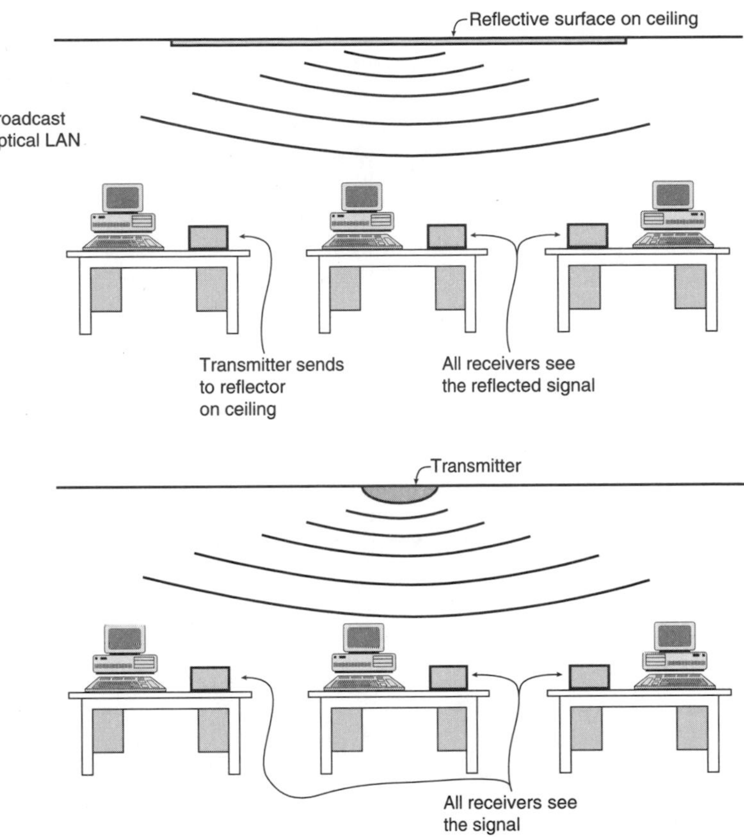

Figure 15.14

Two approaches to broadcast infrared networking.

Attenuation

Attenuation characteristics are determined by the quality of the transmission, by presence of obstructions, and by atmospheric conditions. Typical ranges are limited to tens of meters.

EMI Characteristics

Infrared devices are insensitive to radio-frequency interference, but reception can be degraded by bright light. Because transmissions are tightly focused, they are fairly immune to electronic eavesdropping.

Summary of Wireless Media

Table 15.2 summarizes the characteristics of the wireless media discussed in this section.

Table 15.2

Comparison of Wireless Media

Media Type	Frequency Range	Cost	Installation	Capacity	Attenuation	EMI Sensitivity
Low-power single frequency	All radio frequencies. Frequencies in the low GHz range are most common.	Moderate for wireless, but higher than cabled devices	Low difficulty	Below 1 Mbps to 10 Mbps	High	High EMI sensitivity. Vulnerable to eavesdropping.
High-power single frequency	All radio frequencies. Frequencies in the low GHz range are most common.	More expensive than low-power	High difficulty	Below 1 Mbps to 10 Mbps	Low	High EMI sensitivity. Vulnerable to eavesdropping.
Spread spectrum	All radio frequencies. 902-928 MHz common in the US. 2.4 GHz most common worldwide.	Moderate	Moderately difficult	2 to 6 Mbps	High	Some EMI sensitivity. Low eavesdropping vulnerability.
Terrestrial microwave	Usually low GHz, with 6 or 21-23 GHz most common.	Moderate to high, but cost-effective in many situations	Difficult	Below 1 Mbps to 10 Mbps with higher rates possible	Depends on strength and atmospheric conditions.	Low EMI sensitivity. Some eavesdropping vulnerability.

Media Type	Frequency Range	Cost	Installation	Capacity	Attenuation	EMI Sensitivity
Satellite microwave	Low GHz. 11-14 GHz most common.	High	Very difficult	Below 1 Mbps to 10 Mbps with higher rates possible	Depends on frequency, signal strength, and atmospheric conditions	Low EMI sensitivity. Moderate eavesdropping vulnerability.
Point-to-point infrared	100 GHz to 1000 THz	Low to moderate	Moderately difficult	Below 1 Mbps to 16 Mbps	Depends on light purity and intensity, as well as environmental conditions	Sensitive to intense light. Low eavesdropping vulnerability.
Broadcast infrared	100 GHz to 1000 THz	Low for wireless; higher than cables systems	Low difficulty	Up to 1 Mbps	High	Sensitive to intense light. Low eavesdropping vulnerability.

Public and Private Network Services

Communication must occur between distant points, but few organizations can justify the costs required to construct a private wide area network. Fortunately, a variety of commercial options are available that enable organizations to pay only for the level of service that they require. One option is the public telephone network. Another is to utilize a public network service, of which the Internet is an example.

The Public Telephone Network

Public telephone networks offer two general types of service:

- Switched services, which the customer pays for on a per-use basis
- Leased dedicated services, to which the customer is granted exclusive access

Switched services operate on the *Public Switched Telephone Network* (PSTN), which we know as the telephone system. Voice-grade services have evolved to high levels of sophistication and can be adapted to providing many data services by using devices such as modems. Newer switched options are providing higher levels of service while retaining the advantages of switched access.

On a switched network, subscribers don't have exclusive access to a particular data path. The PSTN maintains large numbers of paths, but not nearly enough to service all customers simultaneously. When a customer requests service, a path is switched in to service the customer's needs. When the customer hangs up, the path is reused for other customers. In situations when the customer doesn't need full-time network access, switched service is extremely cost-effective.

In the United States, the following terms are used to describe components of the PSTN (see fig. 15.15):

- The *demarcation point*, or *demarc*, is the point at which outside wiring enters the customer's premises. The demarc is a specific point in the building at which customer wiring connects to the wiring of the local loop.

- *Subscriber wiring and equipment* consists of all wiring and equipment on the customer side of the demarc. The customer owns these items and is responsible for their operation and maintenance.

- *Local loops* connect the demarc to a central office. The local loop can consist of unshielded twisted-pair wiring, fiber-optic cable, or a combination of the two.

- The *central office* (CO) switches connections between customer sites. It also supplies reliable, filtered power for the local loop.

  Central offices are interconnected by high-capacity trunk lines.

  Central offices rely on long-distance carriers to communicate with COs that are outside of the local service area. Long-distance carriers use various combinations of fiber-optic, copper, and microwave media to provide high-capacity long-distance service.

When customers require full-time access to a communication path, one option is a dedicated, leased line. Several levels of service are available. Common options are T-1 (1.544 Mbps) and T-3 (44.736 Mbps). Leased lines enable a customer to lease a specified bandwidth between two specified points.

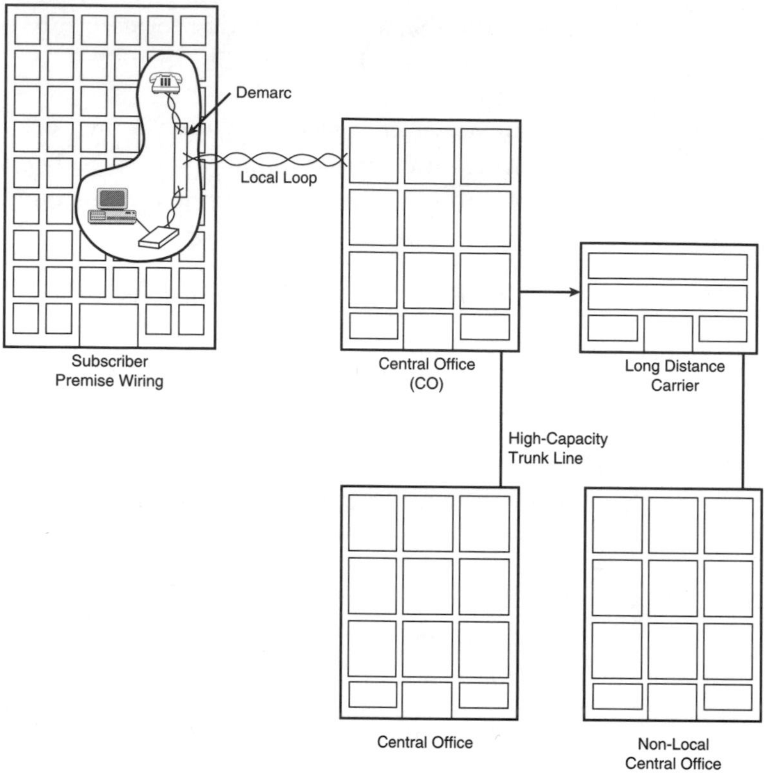

Figure 15.15

Elements of the Public Switched Telephone Service.

Many organizations need to communicate among several points. Leasing a line between each pair of points can prove too costly. Many services now are available that route packets between different sites. Among the services available are the following:

- X.25
- Frame Relay
- SONET (Synchronous Optical Network)
- ATM

Each of these services has characteristics that suit it to particular uses, and all are available on a leased basis from service providers. An organization that needs to communicate among many sites simply pays to connect each site to the service, and the service takes on the responsibility of routing packets. The expense of operating the network is shared among all of the network subscribers. Because the exact switching process is concealed from the subscriber, these networks are frequently depicted as a communication cloud, as shown in figure 15.16.

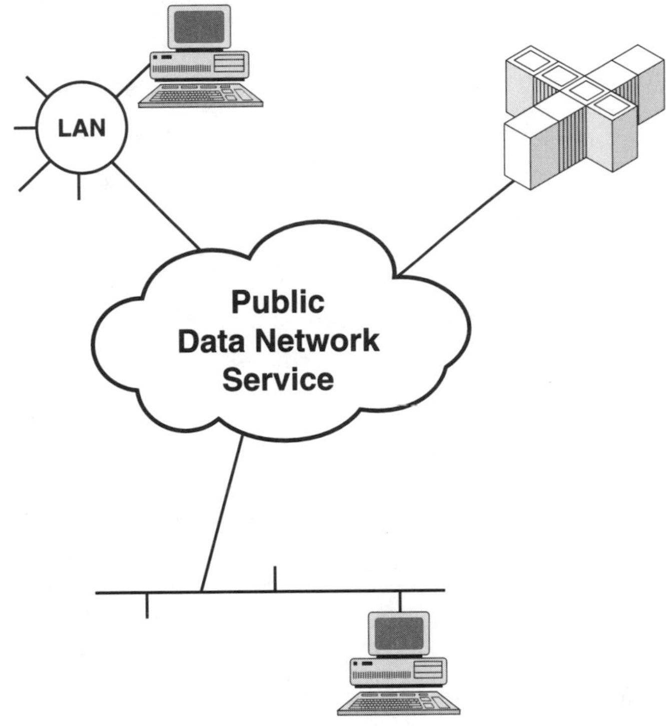

Figure 15.16

An example of a public network service.

Table 15.3 lists common network services and their associated bandwidths.

Table 15.3

Bandwidths of Network Services

Service	Bandwidth
Dedicated 56 KB (DDS)	56 Kbps
Switched 56	56 Kbps
X.25	56 Kbps

continues

Table 15.3 Continued

Service	Bandwidth
T1	1.544 Mbps
Switched T1	1.544 Mbps
Frame Relay	1.544 Mbps
SMDS	1.544 Mbps
ISDN	1.544 Mbps
E1 (Europe)	2.048 Mbps
T3	44.736 Mbps
ATM	44.736 Mbps

These data rates can be compared to common LAN services such as Ethernet (10 Mbps) and Token Ring (4–16 Mbps).

The Internet

The Internet is a cooperative venture in which huge numbers of government agencies, educational institutions, and businesses have agreed to provide shared network services. Each organization on the Internet provides some amount of communication and computing capability that is freely shared with other network users. As a result of this cooperation, the Internet has grown to encompass computers in more than 100 countries on all continents.

The United States has begun to encourage development of a national information infrastructure, popularly called the "Information Superhighway." Research is underway to develop practical methods of establishing high-capacity media (greater than 3 Gbps) with the capability of interconnecting large numbers of public and private networks.

Connecting Hardware

Each cable type has its own connectors. In the following sections you learn about some typical connectors. Many networks also require special connectivity devices, such as hubs, bridges, routers, and repeaters. Network connectivity devices are discussed in Chapter 20, "Network Connectivity."

Connectors for Multiwire Cable

A variety of physical layer standards require cables with large numbers of wires. The RS-232 serial interface commonly used for modems can utilize as many as 25 wires (although seldom are all wires actually implemented).

Several types of connectors are used for these multiwire connections, three of which are shown in figure 15.17. A wide variety of D-type connectors are available, of which the DB-25 and the DB-9 are shown. The number reflects the number of pins or sockets that the connector can accommodate. You encounter DB-9 connectors in several places. Token Ring network cards are frequently equipped with DB-9 connectors.

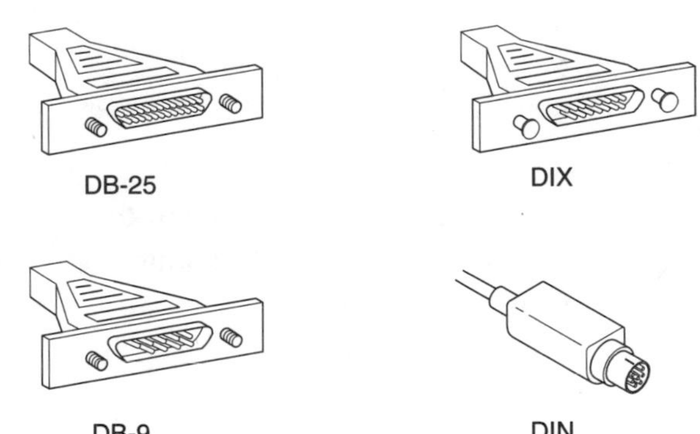

Figure 15.17

Examples of multiwire connectors.

The DIX connector resembles a DB-15 connector and is used to connect devices with Thick-wire Ethernet. The DIX connector differs from a standard DB-15 in that the DIX is secured to the mating connector with a sliding clip rather than screws. The sliding clip is installed on the connector that has sockets, which isn't shown in the figure. The connector shown in figure 14.20 is equipped with pins and with studs that mate with the sliding clip.

The fourth connector shown in figure 15.17 is a DIN connector. DIN connectors are available in various configurations, with different pin counts and pin arrangements. In networking, you are most likely to encounter DIN connectors when cabling Macintoshes into AppleTalk networks.

Connectors for Twisted-Pair Cables

The most common connector used with UTP cables is the RJ-45 connector, shown in figure 15.18. These connectors are easy to install on cables and are extremely easy to connect and disconnect. The RJ-45 connector has eight pins. You also occasionally encounter the RJ-11 connector, which resembles the RJ-45 but has only four pins.

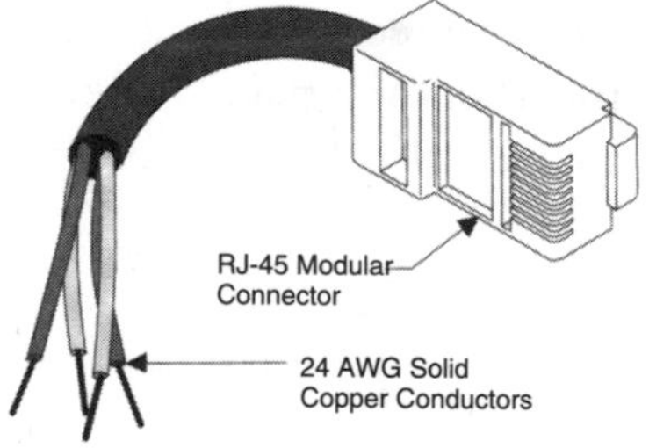

Figure 15.18

An RJ-45 connector.

Although AppleTalk and Token Ring networks can be cabled using UTP cable and RJ-45 connectors, both originated as STP cabling systems. For STP cable, AppleTalk employs a DIN-type connector, shown in figure 15.19. IBM uses the IBM Data Connector, also shown in the figure.

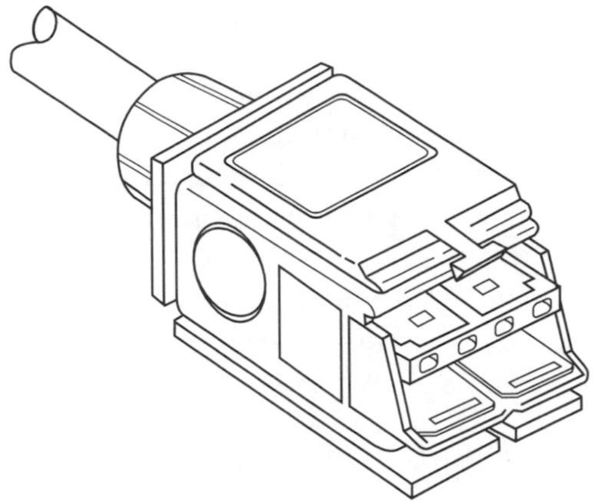

Figure 15.19

Connectors used with STP cable.

The IBM Data Connector is unusual because it doesn't come in two gender configurations. Any IBM Data Connector may be snapped to any other IBM Data Connector.

Most networking connections for STP Token Ring are made using IBM Data Connectors. The connection to the workstation, however, is made with a DB-15 connector. Figure 15.20 shows a PC set up to connect to a Token Ring network.

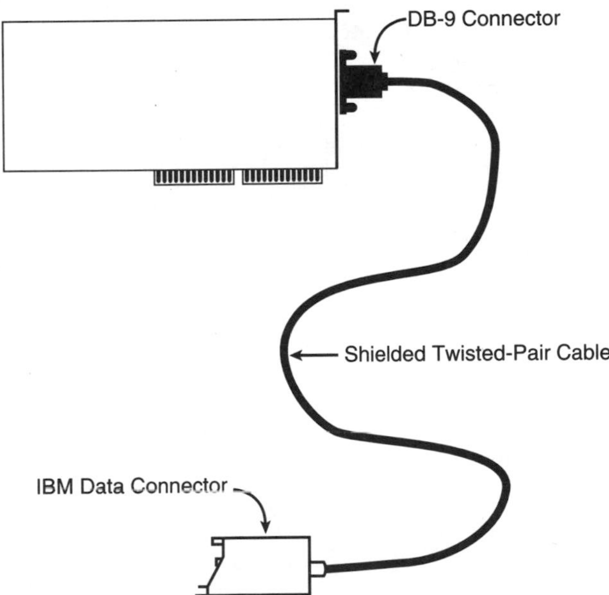

Figure 15.20

A PC ready to connect to a Token Ring network.

Connectors for Coaxial Cable

Two types of connectors are commonly used with coaxial cable. The most common connector is the *BayoNette Connector (BNC)* connector, shown in figure 15.21. This figure shows several characteristics of Thin Ethernet cabling, as follows:

- A T-connector is used to connect the network board in the PC to the network. The T-connector attaches directly to the network board, and a cable is never used at this point.
- BNC connectors attach cable segments to the T-connectors.
- Both ends of the cable must be terminated. A *terminator* is a special connector that includes a resistor that's carefully matched to the characteristics of the cable system.
- One of the terminators must be grounded. A wire from the connector is attached to a grounded point, such as the center screw of a grounded electrical outlet.

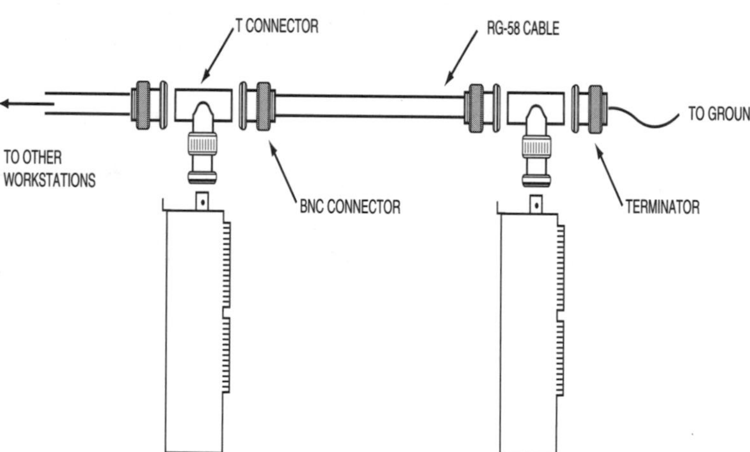

Figure 15.21

Connectors and cabling for Thin Ethernet.

Thick Ethernet uses N-connectors, which screw on instead of using a twist-lock (bayonette) fitting (see fig. 15.22). As with Thin Ethernet, both ends of the cable must be terminated and one end must be grounded.

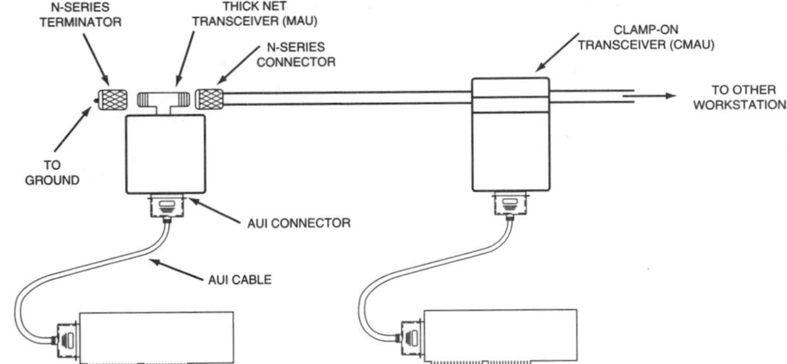

Figure 15.22

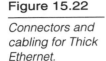

Connectors and cabling for Thick Ethernet.

Workstations don't connect directly to the cable with Thick Ethernet. The cable attachment is made using a *transceiver* (also called a *medium attachment unit* or *MAU*), which connects to the workstation using a cable called an *AUI cable.* Transceivers can connect to cables in the following two ways:

- They can connect by cutting the cable and using N-connectors and a T-connector on the transceiver. This, the original method, now is used rather infrequently.
- The more common approach is to use a clamp-on transceiver, which has pins that penetrate the cable without the need for cutting it. Because clamp-on transceivers force sharp teeth into the cable, they frequently are referred to as *vampire taps.*

Connectors for Fiber-Optic Cable

A variety of connectors are used with fiber-optic cable. The most common is the ST-connector, shown in figure 15.23. Before two devices can engage in two-way data exchange, you must have two fibers, and you frequently encounter fiber-optic cables that have connectors in pairs.

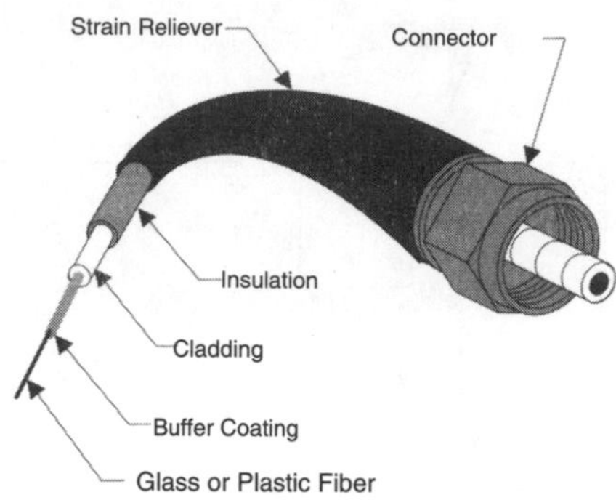

Figure 15.23

An ST connector used for fiber optic cable.

When fiber-optic cable bundles must be interfaced to individual cables, a connection center is used. Within the splice center, the individual fibers in the cable bundle can be connected to individual connectors used to connect to devices. Figure 15.24 illustrates a cabling system based on a splice center.

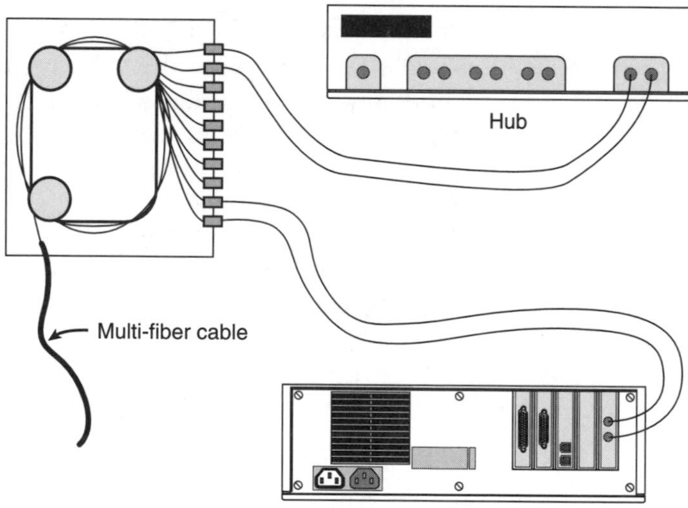

Figure 15.24

Fiber-optic cabling with a splice center.

Review Questions

The following questions will test your knowledge of the information in this chapter. For additional questions, see MCP Endeavor and the Microsoft Roadmap / Assessment Exam on the CD-ROM that accompanies this book.

1. Which of the following cable types supports the greatest cable lengths?

   A. Unshielded twisted pair

   B. Shielded twisted pair

   C. Large coaxial cable

   D. Small coaxial cable

2. Which two are advantages of UTP cable?

   A. Low cost

   B. Easy installation

   C. High resistance to EMI due to twists in cable

   D. Cables up to 500 meters

3. Which three are advantages of coaxial cable?

   A. Low cost

   B. Easy installation

   C. Good resistance to EMI

   D. Easy to reconfigure

4. Which two are benefits of shielding in a cable?

   A. Reduction in signal attenuation

   B. Reduction in EMI radiation

   C. Reduction in sensitivity to outside interference

   D. None of the above

5. Which two are disadvantages of fiber-optic cable?

   A. Sensitive to EMI

   B. Expensive hardware

   C. High installation cost

   D. Low bandwidth

6. Which of the following three cable types should be regarded as mature, well-proven technologies?

   A. Level 3 UTP

   B. STP

   C. Fiber-optic

   D. Level 5 UTP

7. Which of the following is a true statement?

   A. Telephone wiring can be reliably used for most UTP networks.

   B. Thin coaxial networks are easy to install and reconfigure.

   C. Fiber-optic cable supports cable runs of tens of kilometers.

   D. STP cable is insensitive to EMI.

8. Which cable type should be used to connect between two buildings?

   A. UTP

   B. STP

   C. Coax

   D. Fiber-optic

9. Which of the following cable types has the greatest data capacity?

   A. Category 5 UTP

   B. Thick coax

   C. Single-mode fiber optic

   D. Multimode fiber optic

10. Which three of the following are antenna types?

    A. Beam
    B. Duplex
    C. Dipole
    D. Random-length wire

11. As frequency increases, radio transmission becomes increasingly ______.

    A. attenuated
    B. rapid
    C. line-of-sight
    D. sensitive to electromagnetic interference

12. Which two statements are true of low-power, single-frequency radio systems?

    A. Transmission ranges may be as short as 20 to 30 meters.
    B. Such systems are ideal for mobile stations because low-frequency radio can penetrate walls.
    C. Transmitters and receivers must have a line-of-sight path.
    D. The data rates possible with low-frequency radio are optimal for LANs.

13. Which three of the following statements are true?

    A. Attenuation of radio waves is less with high-power signals.
    B. High-frequency radio LANs can penetrate office walls.
    C. Radio-frequency LANs have high bandwidth.
    D. Spread-spectrum technology reduces sensitivity to EMI.

14. Which two statements are true of microwave systems?

    A. Microwave transmissions do not attenuate under any conditions.

    B. All microwave systems operate in the low-gigahertz range.

    C. Microwave signals are sensitive to EMI and electronic eavesdropping.

    D. Unlike most other types of radio transmitters, microwave transmitters don't need to be licensed.

15. Which two wireless technologies are good choices for connecting two buildings on opposite sides of a highway?

    A. Satellite microwave

    B. High-power single-frequency

    C. Terrestrial microwave

    D. Broadcast infrared

16. Which two statements are true of infrared systems?

    A. Point-to-point infrared is not suitable for mobile stations.

    B. Infrared has a frequency range between 100 Ghz and 1,000 THz.

    C. Because infrared signals can be reflected, neither point-to-point nor broadcast systems need to be aligned very precisely.

    D. None of the above.

17. Which two wireless technologies are sensitive to radio-frequency interference?

    A. Microwave
    B. Spread-spectrum
    C. Infrared
    D. High-power, single frequency

18. Which of the following is not an option for leased-line service?

    A. T-1 or T-3
    B. X.14
    C. Frame relay
    D. ATM

19. Which two statements are true of the public telephone network?

    A. Switched services enable customers to pay on a per-use basis.
    B. The demarc is the place at the Central Office where a user's connection attaches to the network.
    C. Local loops connect subscriber wiring to the demarc.
    D. Central offices switch calls between customer sites.

20. DIN Connectors are primarily used for ______.

    A. connecting UTP cables
    B. cabling Macintosh computers to AppleTalk networks
    C. connecting devices with Thick-wire Ethernet
    D. none of the above

21. Which two connectors are frequently used with STP cable?

    A. T-connectors

    B. RJ-45 connectors

    C. IBM unisex connectors

    D. AppleTalk DIN connectors

22. Which two connectors are commonly used with coaxial cable?

    A. DB-25 connectors

    B. N-connectors

    C. ST-connectors

    D. BNC connectors

23. Which two statements are true of Thin Ethernet cabling?

    A. A T-connector must be used to connect the PC's network board to the network.

    B. Either end of the cable can be terminated, but not both ends.

    C. BNC connectors cannot be used.

    D. One terminator must be grounded.

Review Answers

1. C
2. A B
3. A B C
4. B C
5. B C
6. A B C
7. C

8. D
9. C
10. A C D
11. C
12. A C
13. A C D
14. B C
15. B C
16. A B
17. B C
18. B
19. A D
20. B
21. C D
22. B D
23. A D

Chapter 16

Network Topologies

A *topology* is a map of a network. The two types of network topologies are as follows:

- **Physical topology.** Describes the actual layout of the network transmission media.
- **Logical topology.** Describes the logical pathway a signal follows as it passes among the network nodes.

This chapter discusses physical and logical topologies. In this chapter, you will learn about the following:

- Standard physical topologies
- Considerations for choosing a physical topology, including ease of installation, reconfiguration, troubleshooting, and how a failure will affect the network
- Logical topologies, and the differences between logical and physical topologies

Connection Types

All network connections consist of two types of building blocks:

- Multipoint connections
- Point-to-point connections

A *multipoint connection* enables one device to communicate with two or more devices (see fig. 16.1). All the devices attached using a multipoint connection share the same network transmission medium.

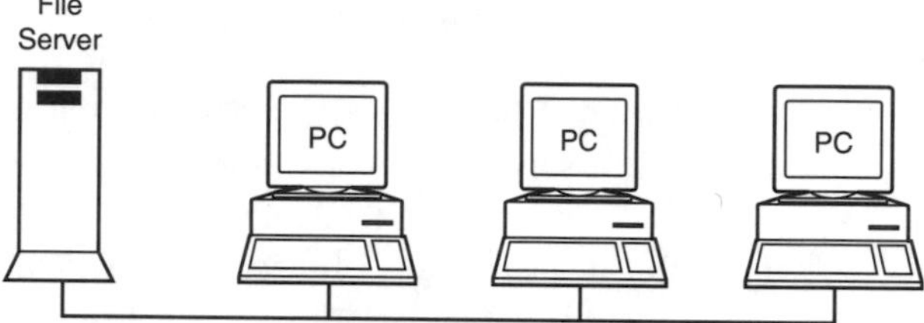

Figure 16.1

Examples of multipoint connections.

A *point-to-point connection* enables one device to communicate with one other device (see fig. 16.2). When two devices are connected through a point-to-point link, they have exclusive use of the data capacity of the link.

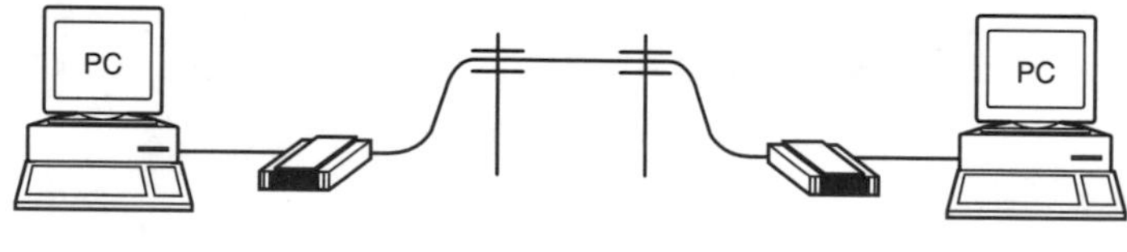

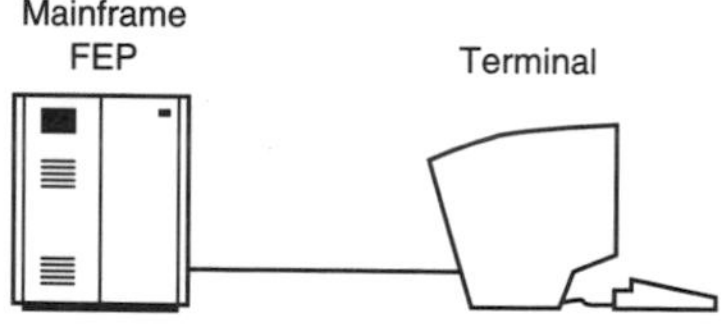

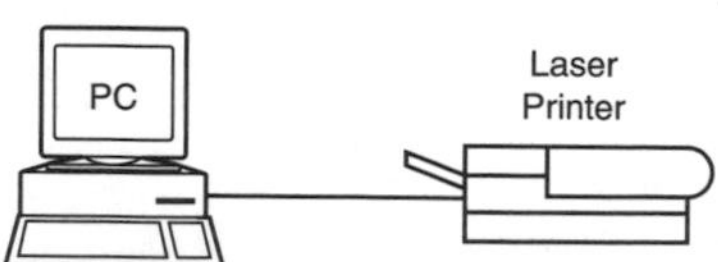

Figure 16.2

Point-to-point connections.

Larger networks can be constructed by adding point-to-point links. In this case, devices rely on other devices to relay their messages. Point-to-point links can even come full circle to form a ring, enabling messages to be passed from any device to any other device on the ring.

Physical Topologies

The *physical topology* of a network describes the layout of the network media. Different physical topologies have different characteristics in terms of performance, ease of installation, troubleshooting, and reconfiguration.

Physical Topologies Based on Multipoint Connections

In fact, only one topology is based on multipoint connections—the bus, shown in figure 16.3. Notice that all devices are connected to a common transmission medium. In some cases, the common medium is referred to as a *backbone network.*

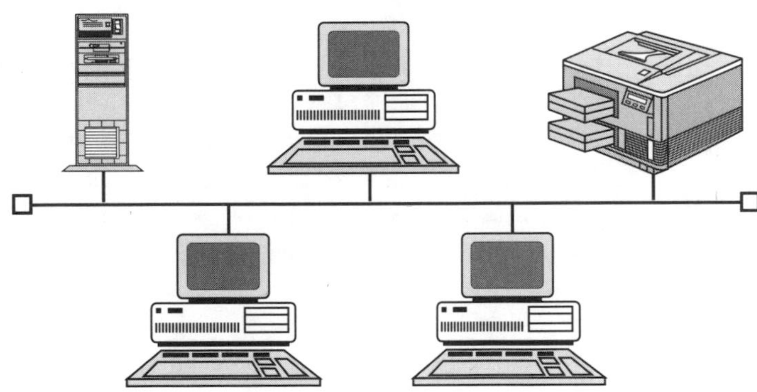

Figure 16.3

A bus physical topology.

Bus Characteristics

You've already read about the cabling and connectors used for bus topologies. Recall that the ends of the cable must be terminated and that devices may be connected along the length of the cable. Connections are performed with T-connectors or with taps (transceivers) that attach directly to the cable and use a drop cable to connect to the workstation.

Typically, signals on a bus network are broadcast in both directions on the backbone cable, enabling all devices to directly receive the signal. With some unidirectional buses, however, signals travel in only one direction and can reach only downstream devices. In this case, the cable must be terminated in such a way that signals are reflected back on the cable and can reach other devices.

Installation

Bus installation is relatively simple and requires only basic tools and skill. Cable runs generally are fairly short because running a separate cable to a central hub for each device on the network isn't necessary.

Bus networks, such as Ethernet, have carefully defined rules you must follow to achieve optimum network performance. Stations on a thick Ethernet cable, for example, should be attached at intervals that are multiples of 2 1/2 meters. All network media have attenuation characteristics that limit the lengths of cables and the number of devices that can be attached.

Reconfiguration

Bus networks can be difficult to reconfigure. If the main cable doesn't run close to the new device, it might need to be rerouted. Adding new devices often involves cutting the main cable to add a T-connector, which requires the network to be shut down. And you should adhere to rules regarding the maximum number of devices and distances at which taps are to be spaced.

Troubleshooting

Bus networks can be difficult to troubleshoot because a single fault can render the entire bus inoperative. A broken cable, for example, is the same as having two unterminated cables. Without termination, signals can reflect back into both cable segments interfering with transmissions and making the system inoperable. (In addition, of course, devices cannot communicate with devices that are on the opposite side of the break.) Because all devices are affected by a cable break, it can be difficult to isolate a break to the cable that falls between two devices.

Physical Topologies Based on Point-to-Point Connections

As shown in figure 16.4, several different topologies can be based on point-to-point connections, as follow:

- *Ring networks* utilize point-to-point links to connect devices together in a ring. Messages are forwarded around the ring and can reach any station in this way.
- *Star topologies* utilize a point-to-point link (a "drop cable") to connect each device to a central hub.
- *Mesh networks* establish a point-to-point link between each pair of computers on the network. Because the number of required links rises rapidly as the number of computers increases, large mesh networks aren't used frequently.
- *Hybrid mesh networks* are commonly used in wide area networks. No attempt is made to provide a link between each possible pair of computers. Extra links, however, are installed to provide more direct paths, extra bandwidth, and some redundancy in case links fail.
- *Cellular topologies* divide geographic areas into overlapping cells that are serviced by transmitters/receivers. Point-to-point radio links are established between a cellular data device and the transmitter in a cell. These point-to-point links are constantly reconfigured as the data device moves through the cellular network. (Multipoint links also may be established under appropriate circumstances.)

The next sections examine each of these topologies in greater detail.

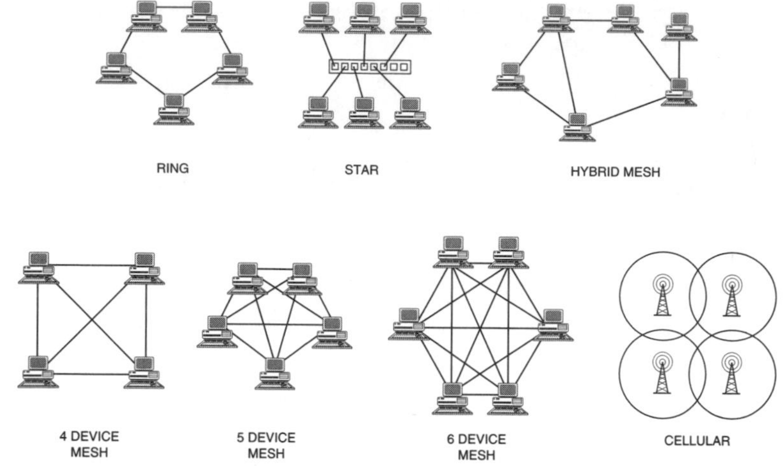

Figure 16.4

Physical topologies based on point-to-point connections.

The Ring Topology

The ring topology is circular, and signals typically travel around the ring in one direction only. Each device incorporates a receiver and a transmitter and serves as a repeater that passes the signal on to the next device in the ring. Because the signal is regenerated at each device, signal degeneration is low.

Installation

Installation is fairly simple, but the amount of cable required can go higher than with a bus. As with all networks, staying within network design restrictions, regarding cable lengths between devices, total ring length, and number of devices, is essential.

Reconfiguration

Rings can be difficult to reconfigure, particularly when devices are located at large distances.

Troubleshooting

The repeating function makes isolating cabling faults fairly easy. When a break is present in the cable, devices still can transmit to downstream devices on the near side of the break. Fault isolation becomes a matter of determining which device is not receiving signals from its immediate upstream neighbor.

Some rings incorporate redundant paths that can be switched in when a cable break occurs. The redundant path takes the form of a second ring that transmits signals in opposite directions from the main ring. When a break occurs in the main ring, the counter-rotating ring can be used to route signals around the break.

The Star Topology

A star topology networks each device with a cable that connects it to a central hub. The hub receives signals from network devices and routes the signals to the proper destination. Star hubs can be interconnected to form tree or hierarchical network topologies.

Installation

The major installation difficulty is that a separate cable must be run to connect each device to a hub. Cabling requirements are generally considerably higher than for bus or ring physical topologies.

A significant concern with star topologies is that cable lengths between hubs and devices are limited, typically to 100 meters. Therefore, you must ensure that a hub is located within 100 meters of every potential device location

Reconfiguration

The payoff for cabling to a central hub is that networks are easy to reconfigure. Most adds and moves can be accomplished by simply moving a plug to a new hub port.

Troubleshooting

Troubleshooting stars is easier than troubleshooting buses and, generally speaking, rings. Building troubleshooting features into hubs that can be monitored centrally is easy.

When the cable to a device fails, it generally affects that device only. In cases where a device cable causes problems for the entire network, it is simple to disconnect the cable from the hub. Many managed hubs automatically disconnect devices that produce network errors.

Star topologies are subject to a single point of failure. Hub failure affects all devices.

Mesh Topologies

Mesh networks consist of a point-to-point link between each pair of devices on the network. In most cases, the number of connections required limits the use of true mesh networks to a few stations. A five-device mesh network requires 24 (4×3×2) connections, but a six-device mesh requires 120 (5×4×3×2)!

Two advantages can be stated for a mesh topology. The first is that every device has a guaranteed communication channel capacity with every other device. The other is a high level of fault tolerance. Even multiple media failures are likely to the network capable of delivering messages to all devices.

More common is the hybrid network, which contains some redundant links, particularly to the most important devices or where the greatest capacity is needed. When it's essential that the network never go down, redundant links are a good form of insurance.

Installation

Mesh networks are difficult to install, and the difficulty increases rapidly as the number of devices increases.

Hybrid mesh networks are most common in wide area networks, where the links consist primarily of leased communication services. Installation is primarily a matter of setting up routers, CSU/DSUs, and so on. WAN connections of this sort can get involved to install and manage.

Reconfiguration

Mesh networks can be extremely difficult to reconfigure.

Troubleshooting

Mesh networks are easy to troubleshoot because each device keeps track of every other device.

Hybrid mesh networks introduce concerns about how signals are routed through the network. This is a skilled task that calls for sophisticated diagnostic and management systems to ensure that the network operates smoothly.

Mesh networks are extremely robust because redundant links abound. They are, therefore, seldom subject to single points of failure. Performance can degrade, however, if failure of one link causes traffic on other links to rise to unacceptable levels.

Cellular Topology

Cellular networks divide the area being serviced into cells, each of which is serviced by a central station. Devices use radio signals to communicate with the central station, and the central station routes messages to other devices. Cellular data networks can be implemented on an office level or in large geographic areas.

Installation

Installation of office-based cellular LANs differs considerably from installation of cable-based LANs. Much depends on the degree to which the office building supports the requirements of the cellular system that has been chosen. Transmitters are of limited power and cannot penetrate walls, so some building types are unsuitable. If hubs can be located so they can communicate clearly with devices, installation is relatively simple.

Reconfiguration

Within the area serviced by a hub, devices can be located and relocated easily. Hubs are often connected to other hubs using cable, however, and relocation of hubs can be more involved.

Troubleshooting

Troubleshooting depends on the network design. If hubs maintain a point-to-point link with devices, troubleshooting is simplified.

When a hub fails, all devices serviced by the hub lose service. Because devices are mobile, they can be relocated to a working area to restore service.

Logical Topologies

The preceding section introduced physical topologies, which describe how the media are physically arranged to build a network.

Besides having a physical topology, a network has a logical topology that describes the path that a signal follows on a network. The data link layer of the OSI model handles logical topologies. Logical and physical topologies of a network may be the same or different.

Token Ring (see Chapter 19, "Network Architectures") is the most dramatic example of a network having different physical and logical topologies. Figure 16.5 illustrates how computers are connected on a Token Ring network. Each computer transmits signals to the receiver on the next computer. In this way, signals travel through each station on the cabling system, eventually completing a trip back to the station that originated them. Recall that a logical topology describes the manner in which signals travel on the network. You can see why Token Ring networks have a *ring* logical topology.

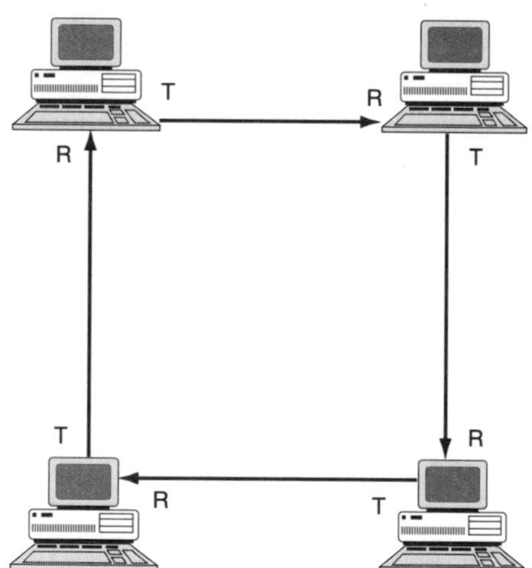

Figure 16.5

Logical topology of a Token Ring network.

Token Ring networks, however, never are physically wired in rings. Hubs are used instead, and each computer is cabled to the hub by a drop cable. Figure 16.6 shows how the computers and cables are arranged. Notice the way the cables are connected within the hub so that the transmitter side of one computer connects to the receiver of the next computer. This is exactly the same logical relationship in figure 16.5, and the logical topology is still a ring.

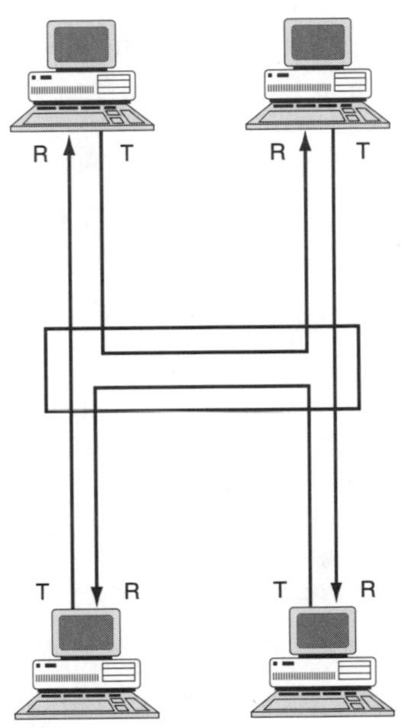

Figure 16.6

A logical ring is configured as a physical star.

Due to the manner in which each computer is cabled individually to a hub, however, the physical topology of a Token Ring is a star.

Coax Ethernet is an example of a bus network where every station is connected to every other station in a multipoint physical topology. Also, every Ethernet station broadcasts signals to every other station, resulting in a bus logical topology as well. Ethernet, therefore, has a physical bus topology and a logical bus topology (see fig. 16.7).

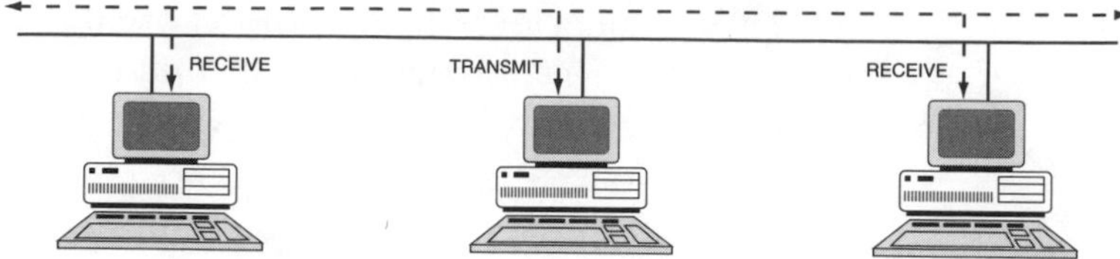

Figure 16.7

Ethernet is both a physical and a logical bus.

A 10BASE-T Ethernet network uses UTP cable and hub-based wiring, but it remains a logical bus because devices continue to communicate using multipoint communication. A 10BASE-T Ethernet, therefore, is a physical star but also a logical bus.

The following are some rules of thumb for distinguishing between physical and logical:

- If you can see it or touch it, it's physical.
- If you can't see it or touch it, it's logical.

The following are rules of thumb for distinguishing between bus and ring networks:

- If signals from each computer are received by every other computer, the network is a bus.
- If each computer receives signals from only one other computer, the network is a ring.

Review Questions

The following questions will test your knowledge of the information in this chapter. For additional questions, see MCP Endeavor and the Microsoft Roadmap/Assessment Exam on the CD-ROM that accompanies this book.

1. Which three of these network topologies consist of point-to-point links?

   A. Bus

   B. Ring

   C. Star

   D. Mesh

2. Which network topologies are subject to a single point of failure (that is, one failure can stop all network communication)?

   A. Mesh

   B. Bus

   C. Star

   D. Ring

3. Which three are true of ring topologies?

   A. Signal degeneration is low.

   B. They usually require less cable than bus topologies.

   C. Each device incorporates a receiver and a trans-mitter.

   D. Reconfiguration can be difficult.

4. Which three are advantages of star topologies?

   A. Reconfiguration is simplified.

   B. Cable costs are minimized.

   C. Active hubs can regenerate signals.

   D. They are easy to troubleshoot.

5. What is the primary feature of a star topology?

   A. The capability of forming tree or hierarchical networks

   B. Limited cable lengths

   C. Ease of configuration

   D. A central hub

6. Which two are advantages of bus topologies?
   - A. Long cable runs are possible without signal regeneration.
   - B. They often require the least amount of cable.
   - C. They are well-proven technology.
   - D. They are easy to troubleshoot.

7. Which of the following statements is true?
   - A. Logical topologies are determined by the cabling system.
   - B. A physical bus network may be a logical ring.
   - C. A physical star network can be a logical ring.
   - D. Contention can be used as an access control medium on a physical ring.

8. Which two of the following statements are true?
   - A. Coax Ethernet is a physical bus and a logical bus.
   - B. 10BASE-T Ethernet is a physical bus and a logical bus.
   - C. Coax Ethernet is a physical star and a logical bus.
   - D. 10BASE-T Ethernet is a physical star and a logical bus.

Review Answers

1. B C D
2. C
3. A C D
4. A C D
5. D
6. B C
7. C
8. A D

Chapter 17
Data Transmission

In order for network communication to take place, bits of data (1s and 0s) must somehow pass through the transmission media from the sending to the receiving node. In this chapter, you will learn some of the concepts of data transmission, including the following:

- Digital and analog signaling
- Bit synchronization
- Baseband and broadband transmissions
- Multiplexing

Digital and Analog Signaling

Signaling amounts to communicating information. The information being communicated can take one of two forms—analog or digital:

- *Analog information* is information that changes continuously and can take on many different values. An analog clock's hands move constantly, displaying time on a continuous scale.
- *Digital information* is characterized by discrete states. A light bulb is on or off, for example. A digital clock represents the time in one-minute intervals and doesn't change its numbers again until the next minute. A digital clock can represent exact minutes, but not the seconds that pass in between.

Frequently, information in one form must be converted to the other. This often involves the use of some encoding scheme that enables the original information to be recovered from a signal after the signal has been received.

When an analog or digital signal is altered so that it contains information to be communicated, the process is called *modulation* or *encoding*. AM radio transmits information by modulating the radio signal, increasing or decreasing the amplitude (signal strength) depending on the information content. Many similar schemes are used to communicate information through different types of signals.

Figure 17.1 illustrates the difference between analog and digital signals. The analog signal is constantly changing and takes on values throughout the range of possible values. The digital signal takes on only two (or a few) specific states.

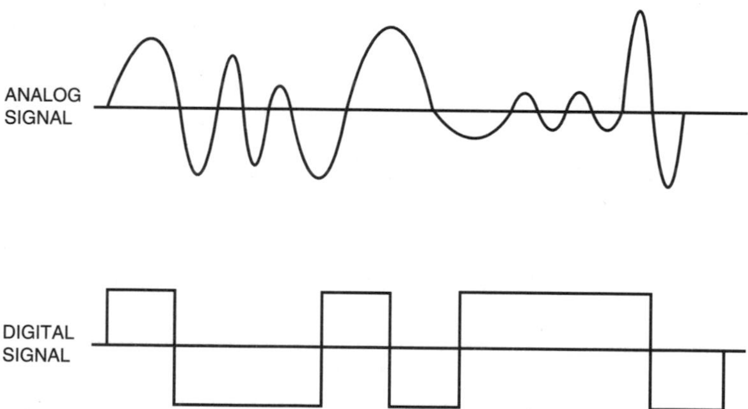

Figure 17.1

Analog and digital signals.

Digital Signaling Techniques

Computer data is inherently digital, and most networks use digital signaling. The following sections examine two methods of modulating a digital signal to encode digital data: current state and state transition.

Current State Encoding

The current state encoding technique assigns specific signal states to represent each possible data value. The signal is monitored periodically to determine its current state, from which a data value may be determined. A voltage of +5 might represent a binary 1, for example, and a voltage of –5 might represent a binary 0. Many different signal variations can be used. The important characteristic is that a given state represents one and only one data value. In figure 17.2, a high voltage represents a binary 0, whereas a low voltage represents a binary 1.

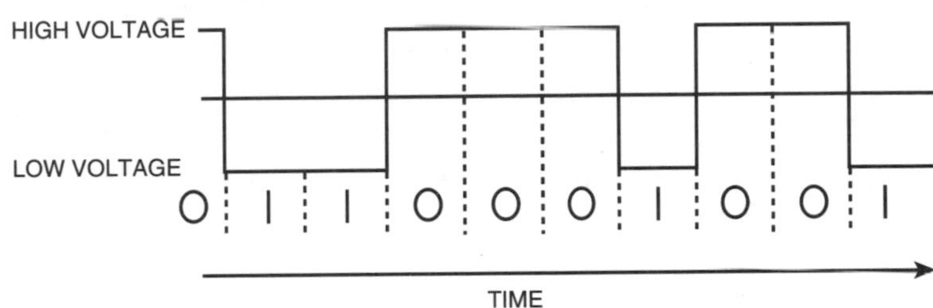

Figure 17.2

Current state encoding.

The following encoding schemes use current state encoding, although discussion of their specific characteristics is beyond the scope of this chapter:

- Unipolar
- Bipolar
- Return-to-Zero (NRZ)
- Biphase

State Transition Encoding

The state transition encoding technique uses transitions in the digital signal to represent data. This can be done in the following ways:

- A transition from high to low voltage always represents a 1, and a transition from low to high voltage always represents a 0.

- Any transition always represents a 1, and the absence of an expected transition represents a 0. This scheme is depicted in figure 17.3.

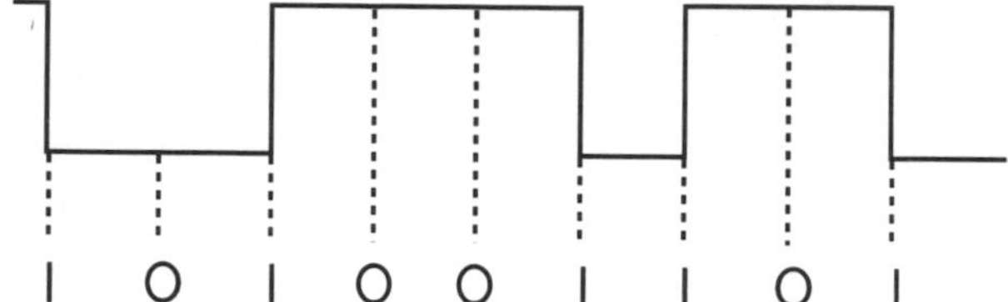

Figure 17.3

State transition encoding.

The following encoding schemes use state transition encoding, although discussion of their specific characteristics is beyond the scope of this chapter:

- Bipolar-Alternate Mark Inversion (AMI)
- Non-Return-to-Zero (NRZ)
- Manchester
- Differential Manchester
- Biphase Space (FM-O)

The terms *current state* and *state transition* are not standard terms in the industry.

The common industry term for current state is *level triggered* because recognition of a given state is triggered (initiated) by a specific signal level.

The common industry term for state transition *is edge triggered*, since either the leading or trailing edge of a signal transition (the edge of the signal transition) is used to signal that a state change has taken place.

Analog Signaling

Analog signals are constantly varying in one or more values. These changes in values can be used to represent data.

Analog wave forms frequently take the form of sine waves. The two characteristics that define an analog wave form are as follows:

- **Frequency**. Indicates the rate at which the waveform is changing. Frequency is associated with the wavelength of the waveform, which is a measure of the distance between two similar peaks on adjacent waves. Frequency is generally measured in Hertz (Hz), which indicates the frequency in cycles per second. Frequency is illustrated in figure 17.4.

Figure 17.4

Two analog waveforms differing in frequency.

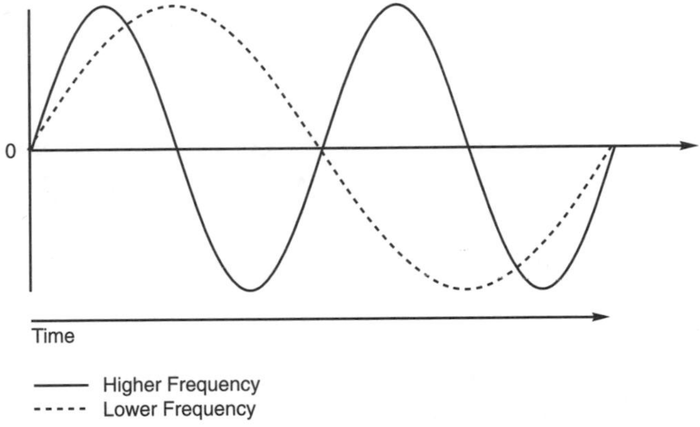

- **Amplitude**. The measure of the strength of the waveform. Amplitude is illustrated in figure 17.5.

Figure 17.5

Two analog waveforms differing in amplitude.

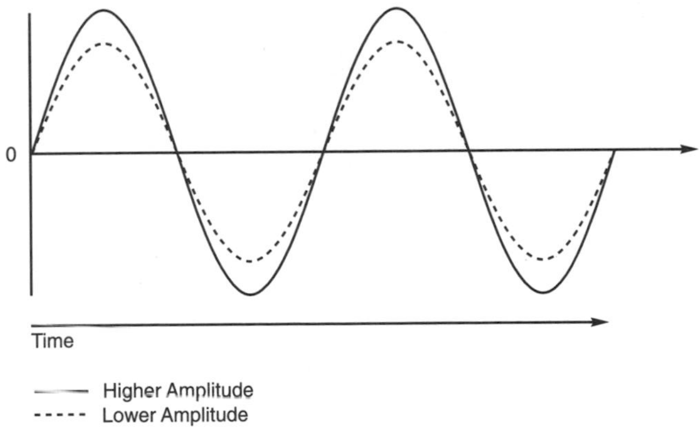

A third characteristic, *phase*, can also be defined. Figure 17.6 illustrates waveforms that differ in phase. These waveforms have identical frequency and amplitude, but they do not begin their transitions at the same time.

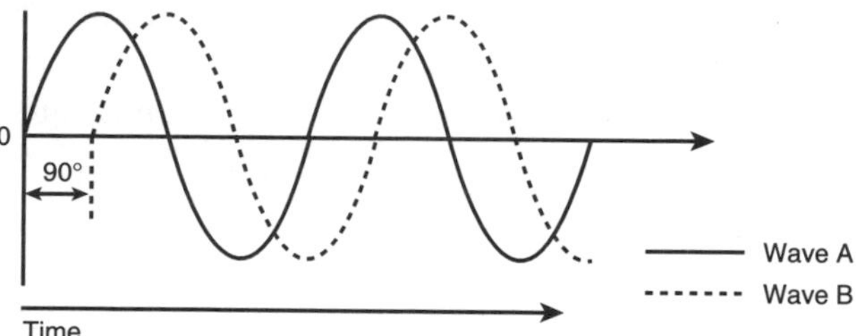

Figure 17.6

Two analog waveforms differing in phase.

In figure 17.6, WAVE B begins to rise from the reference line at the same time that Wave A is peaking. Therefore, Wave B is $^1/4$ of a wave behind Wave A. If a complete wave is represented as having 360 degrees, Wave B lags behind Wave A by 90 degrees.

In figure 17.7, notice that Wave B is a mirror image of Wave A. Because Wave B is $^1/2$ of a wave behind Wave A, Wave B lags behind Wave A by 180 degrees. Wave C is $^1/3$ of a wave behind A and lags behind Wave A by 120 degrees.

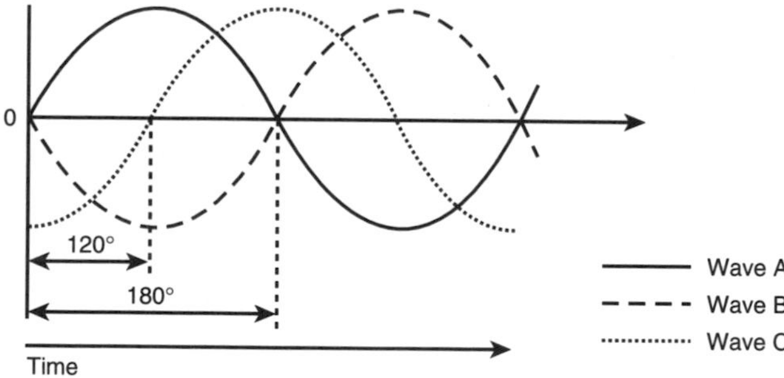

Figure 17.7

Three analog waveforms differing in phase by different amounts.

Each of these characteristics—frequency, amplitude, and phase—can be used to encode data.

Amplitude Shift Keying

Amplitude shift keying is a current state method of modulation in that specific signal amplitudes are assigned specific data values. A high-amplitude signal, for example, might be assigned a value of 1, whereas a low-amplitude signal is assigned a value of 0. The first example in figure 17.8 illustrates amplitude shift keying.

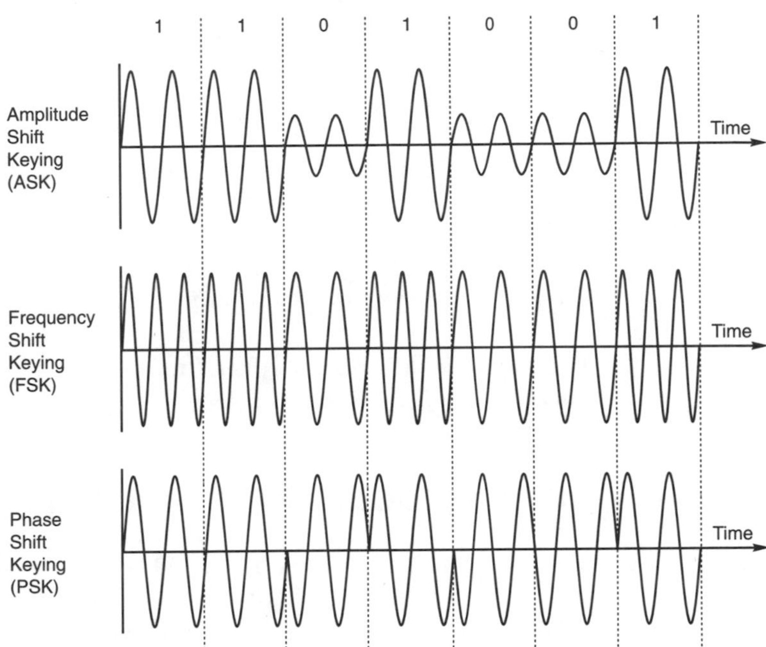

Figure 17.8

Keying methods for amplitude waveforms.

Frequency Shift Keying

Frequency shift keying is also a current state modulation method. Specific frequency values are assigned specific data values. A high frequency, for example, might represent 0, whereas a lower frequency might represent 1. The second example in figure 17.8 illustrates frequency shift keying.

Phase Shift Keying

Phase shift keying is a transition state modulation method. For example, a reference phase might represent 0, whereas a 180-degree phase shift would represent a 1 value. The process is illustrated in the third example of figure 17.8.

Bit Synchronization

With both current state and transition state modulation methods, the receiving device monitors the signal, looking for an expected characteristic. Timing is important because the receiver needs to know when it should check the incoming signal. If the check is made at the wrong time, erroneous data might be extracted.

Two methods of coordinating signal timing follow:

- Asynchronous communication
- Synchronous communication

The methods differ primarily in the way they adjust the clocks of the sending and receiving devices.

Asynchronous Communication

Although the sender and receiver have internal clocks, these clocks are not directly synchronized. Each message begins with a *start bit* that enables the receiver to synchronize its internal clock with the timing of the message. Messages are kept short so the receiver's clock will not drift out of synchronization for the duration of the message. A *stop bit* signals that the message is complete. Asynchronous techniques are primarily used to transmit character data, and the message part of the transmission is limited to seven or eight bits.

To make the system work, the sender and receiver must reach a general agreement on the speed at which data is to be transmitted. You are probably familiar with setting the data rate for modems. Even though the sending and receiving clocks are not directly synchronized, if they agree to transmit at, say, 9,600 bits per second, their clocks can remain sufficiently synchronized to enable a single short transmission to be completed.

One characteristic to note is that the signals are intermittent and the transmission media is idle except when a transmission is actually taking place. No clock signals are transmitted to keep the receiver's clock synchronized with the sender's clock.

Synchronous Communication

Synchronous communication employs a clocking mechanism to ensure that the sending and receiving devices remain synchronized. Three techniques are discussed, as follows:

- Guaranteed state change
- Separate clock signals
- Oversampling

Guaranteed State Change

Some encoding techniques are designed to ensure that state changes occur at regular intervals. The receiving device adjusts its internal clock to match the frequencies of the state changes.

Signals of this type are called *self-clocking* because the clocking information is embedded in the signal itself, and no other clocking mechanism is required.

Separate Clock Signals

The separate clock signal approach utilizes a separate communication channel to carry clocking information. The common RS-232 serial interface uses this approach. One of the wires in the cable carries clocking signals that enable the sending device to tell the receiver when it should monitor the incoming data.

This approach is useful over short distances, but becomes problematic with longer cables. Signals can travel through different wires in the cable at different rates, and at some point the clocking signal will no longer be synchronized with the signals on the data wires. RS-232 connections, for example, are typically limited to a maximum length of 50 feet for this reason.

Oversampling

With this technique, the receiver samples incoming data at a higher rate than the rate at which the data is being transmitted. If the receiver monitors at ten times the rate at which signal transitions are occurring, it is easy to determine when transitions have taken place. The extra samples also enable the receiver to determine when its clock is drifting and needs to be resynchronized.

Baseband and Broadband Transmissions

The two ways to allocate the capacity of transmission media are with baseband and broadband transmissions. Baseband devotes the entire capacity of the medium to one communication channel. Broadband enables two or more communication channels to share the bandwidth of the communications medium.

Baseband is the most common mode of operation. Most LANs function in baseband mode, for example. Baseband signaling can be accomplished with both analog and digital signals.

You have a great deal of experience with broadband transmissions, however, although you might not realize why. The TV cable coming into your house from an antenna or a cable provider is a broadband medium. Many television signals can share the bandwidth of the cable because each signal is modulated using a separately assigned frequency. You can use the television tuner to choose the channel you want to watch by selecting its frequency. This technique of dividing bandwidth into frequency bands is called *frequency-division multiplexing* (FDM) and works only with analog signals. Another technique, called *time-division multiplexing* (TDM), supports digital signals, and is described in the next sections.

Figure 17.9 contrasts the difference between baseband and broadband modes of operation.

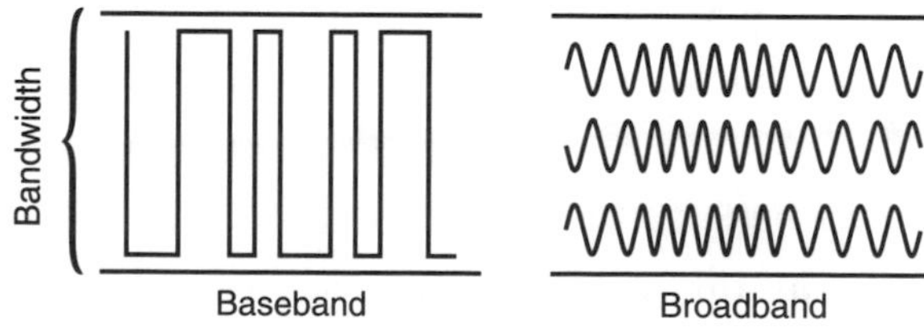

Figure 17.9

Baseband and broadband transmission modes.

Multiplexing

Multiplexing is the technique that enables broadband media to support multiple data channels. Multiplexing makes sense under a number of circumstances:

- **When media bandwidth is costly.** A high-speed leased line, such as a T-1 or T-3, is expensive to lease. Providing the leased line has sufficient bandwidth, multiplexing can enable the same line to carry mainframe, LAN, voice, video conferencing, and various other data types.
- **When bandwidth is idle.** Many organizations have installed fiber-optic cable that is used only to partial capacity. With the proper equipment, a single fiber can support hundreds of megabits or even a gigabit or more of data capacity.
- **When large amounts of data need to be transmitted through low-capacity channels.** Multiplexing techniques can divide the original data stream into several lower-bandwidth channels, each of which can be transmitted through a lower-capacity medium. The signals can be recombined at the receiving end.

Multiplexing refers to combining multiple data channels for transmission on a common medium. *Demultiplexing* refers to recovering the original separate channels from a multiplexed signal.

Multiplexing and demultiplexing are performed by a *multiplexor,* which usually has both capabilities. A multiplexor sometimes is called a *mux.*

The following two techniques are used to multiplex signals:

- Frequency-division multiplexing
- Timc-division multiplexing

Frequency-Division Multiplexing

Figure 17.10 illustrates *frequency-division multiplexing* (FDM). The technique works by converting all data channels to analog form. Each of these analog signals can be modulated by a separate frequency (called a *carrier frequency*) that makes possible recovering that signal during the demultiplexing process. At the receiving end, the demultiplexor can select the desired carrier signal and use it to extract the data signal for that channel.

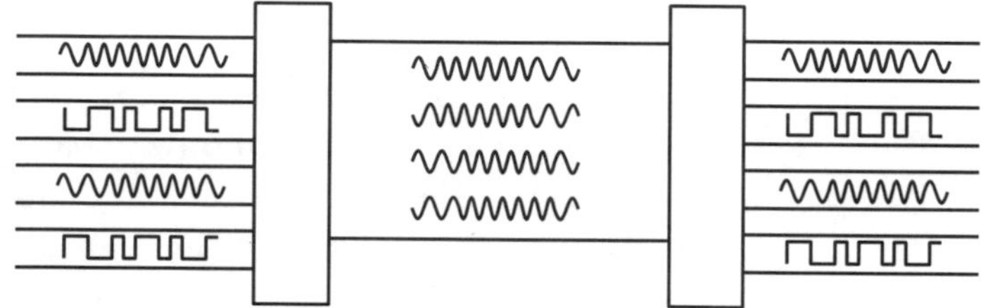

Figure 17.10

Frequency-division multiplexing.

FDM can be used in broadband LANs (a standard for Ethernet exists). One advantage of FDM is that it supports bidirectional signaling on the same cable.

Time-Division Multiplexing

Time-division multiplexing (TDM) divides a channel into time slots that are allocated to the data streams to be transmitted. Figure 17.11 illustrates the process. Provided that the sender and receiver agree on the time slot assignments, the receiver can easily recover and reconstruct the original data streams.

Figure 17.11

Time-division multiplexing.

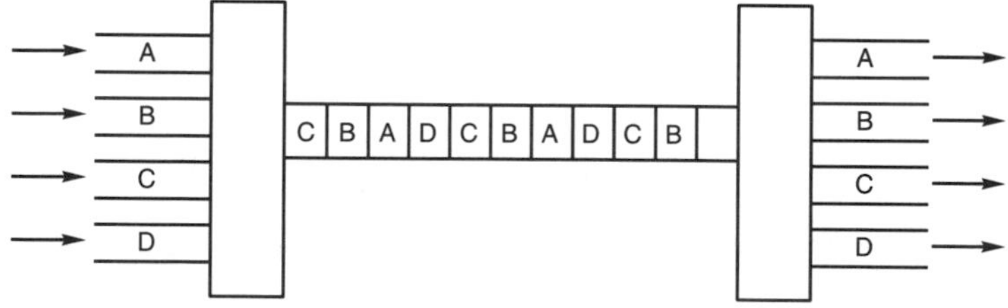

TDM transmits the multiplexed signal in baseband mode. Interestingly, this makes possible multiplexing a TDM multiplexed signal as one of the data channels on an FDM system.

Conventional TDM equipment utilizes fixed time divisions and allocates time to a channel, regardless of that channel's level of activity. If a channel isn't busy, its time slot isn't being fully utilized. Because the time divisions are programmed into the configurations of the multiplexors, this technique often is referred to as *synchronous TDM.*

If using the capacity of the data medium more efficiently is important, a more sophisticated technique, called *statistical time-division multiplexing* (StatTDM), can be used. A stat-mux uses the time-slot technique, but allocates time slots based on the traffic demand on the individual channels. Figure 17.12 illustrates the process. Notice that Channel B is allocated more time slots than Channel A, whereas Channel C is allocated the fewest time slots. Channel D is idle and no slots are allocated to it. To make this procedure work, the data transmitted for each time slot includes a control field that identifies to which channel the data in the time slot should be assigned.

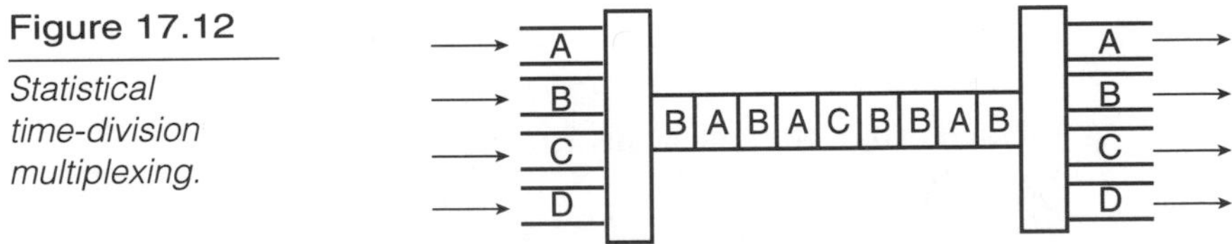

Figure 17.12

Statistical time-division multiplexing.

Review Questions

The following questions will test your knowledge of the information in this chapter. For additional questions, see MCP Endeavor and the Microsoft Roadmap/Assessment Exam on the CD-ROM that accompanies this book.

1. All signals transmitted between computers consist of some form of what?

   A. Infrared light
   B. Radio frequency
   C. Microwave
   D. Electromagnetic waveform

2. Data transmission rates often are stated in terms of ______.

   A. bits per second
   B. cycles per second
   C. attenuation
   D. none of the above

3. Which two are examples of analog data?

   A. Light from a switched electric light
   B. Sound from a radio
   C. Morse code
   D. A sine wave

4. Which two of the following are analog modulation techniques?

   A. Phase shift keying
   B. Binary modulation
   C. State transition encoding
   D. ASK

5. Which two statements are true about state transition encoding?
   A. A transition from low to high voltage always represents a 1.
   B. Any transition always represents a 0.
   C. A transition from high to low voltage always represents a 1.
   D. The absence of an expected transition always represents a 0.

6. Which two of the following characteristics of an analog waveform are directly related?
   A. Amplitude
   B. Wavelength
   C. Frequency
   D. Phase

7. Which three bit-synchronization techniques can operate without a single-channel medium, such as a single pair of wires?
   A. Guaranteed state change
   B. Asynchronous
   C. Oversampling
   D. Separate clock signals

8. Which two techniques encode data in digital form for transmission on the media?
   A. Time-division multiplexing
   B. Frequency-division multiplexing
   C. Phase shift keying
   D. Current state encoding

9. What are two ways of allocating the capacity of transmission media?

   A. Multiplexing
   B. Baseband
   C. Oversampling
   D. Broadband

10. Which of the following methods relies on the internal clocks of transmitting and receiving devices?

    A. Synchronous
    B. Isochronous
    C. Asynchronous
    D. Nonsynchronous

Review Answers

1. D
2. A
3. B D
4. A D
5. C D
6. B C
7. A B C
8. A D
9. B D
10. C

Chapter 18

Protocol Suites

In the preceding chapters, you saw how designing network protocols usually is done in pieces, with each piece solving a small part of the overall problem. By convention, these protocols are regarded as layers of an overall set of protocols, called a *protocol suite* or a *protocol stack.*

You've seen one approach to defining the layers of a protocol stack. The OSI reference model is useful as a conceptual tool for understanding protocol layering. Although protocols have been designed in strict conformance with the OSI reference model, the OSI protocol suite hasn't become popular. The main influence of the Reference Model is as a conceptual framework for understanding network communication and comparing various types of protocols.

Protocols are real implementations, in program code and hardware, of the conceptual rules defined in the Reference Model. The tasks described in the Reference Model can be performed in various ways, depending on the network designers' goals and the various protocol suites in common use. Some protocols and protocol suites existed before the OSI reference model was published and can be matched only loosely to the seven-layer model.

In this chapter, you get down to the task of examining a variety of actual protocols. You apply what you've learned about the OSI reference model to several of the most popular protocol stacks.

This chapter discusses a variety of different protocol stacks and network protocols you're likely to encounter, including the following:

- NetWare IPX/SPX
- Internet protocols (TCP/IP)
- AppleTalk
- Digital Network Architecture (DNA)
- Systems Network Architecture (SNA)
- The IEEE 802 family
- Fiber Distributed Data Interface (FDDI)
- Serial Line Internet Protocol (SLIP) and Point-to-Point Protocol (PPP)
- CCITT/ITU X.25
- Frame relay
- Integrated Service Digital Network (ISDN)and Broadband ISDN (B-ISDN)
- Asynchronous Transfer Mode (ATM)
- Synchronous Optical Network (SONET) and the Synchronous Digital Hierarchy (SDH)
- Switched Multimegabit Digital Service (SMDS)

You can find more information about many of these protocols in New Riders' *NetWare Professional Reference, Fourth Edition.*

Models and Protocols

Three stages take place before a protocol goes to work:

1. A model describes the general function of the protocol.

2. The protocol itself is defined in complete detail.

3. The protocol must be realized by software and hardware designers in real products.

Consider designing a building. The architect first produces sketches that describe the general nature of the building. Then the architect, possibly working with a specialist in particular building trades, develops blueprints that describe every detail of the building. Finally, an actual building is constructed.

Protocols are the blueprints of networking—highly detailed descriptions of all the functions at a given communication layer. Until the protocol is expressed in hardware and software, however, it cannot go to work.

Translating a protocol into hardware and software can be difficult, and different designers often have difficulty getting their equipment to interact without some tweaking, particularly in the early stages of a protocol's life. Eventually, implementation of a protocol becomes fairly routine, but you always should inquire into any compatibility testing that has been performed on a new piece of equipment.

Because designers and administrators have encountered many problems when attempting to interconnect devices that run different protocols, many organizations have pushed for open systems. *Open systems* are sets of hardware and software standards that can be generally applied throughout the industry to ease communication difficulties.

The OSI reference model has been used as one strategy for developing open systems, and some vendors have redesigned existing protocol suites to make them more compliant with the OSI model. Others—a good example is the TCP/IP community—have argued that they already have a highly functional set of protocols that are, in fact, open—in that they're freely available to everyone in the industry. As a result, the impact of the OSI model has been limited to the products of some manufacturers.

Figure 18.1 illustrates how the protocol suites discussed in this chapter relate to the layers of the OSI reference model.

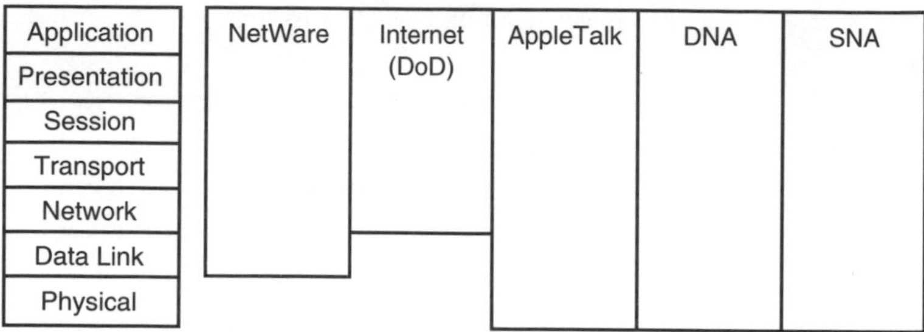

Figure 18.1

A comparison of various protocol suites to the OSI reference model.

NetWare IPX/SPX

The protocols utilized with NetWare are summarized in figure 18.2. The NetWare protocols have been designed with a high degree of modularity, making adapting to different hardware and incorporating other protocols into the configuration both easy. The discussion of NetWare protocols in this course is fairly brief, considering the importance of these protocols to NetWare engineers. For a more detailed description, consult *NetWare Professional Reference, Fourth Edition* from New Riders.

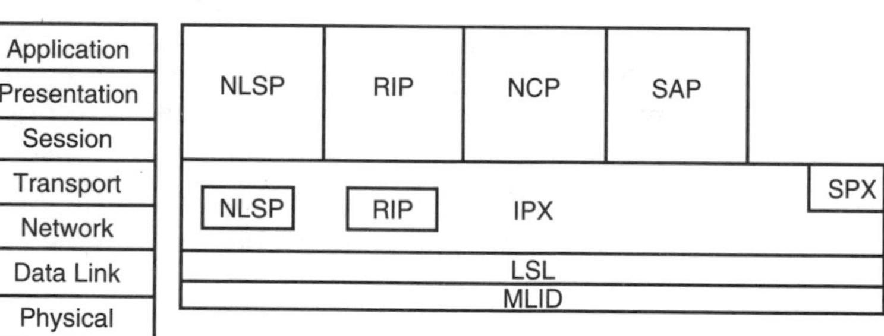

Figure 18.2

The NetWare protocol suite.

The following sections discuss the protocols in figure 18.2.

Multiple Link Interface Driver (MLID)

Multiple Link Interface Drivers (MLIDs) implement the medium access control (MAC) sublayer of the OSI data link layer. Practically speaking, *MLID* is Novell's name for the software that drives a network interface board. The specifications for writing MLIDs are defined by Novell's *Open DataLink Interface* (ODI) specification, which describes Novell's overall architecture for network protocols. An MLID must be written for each board design.

As such, the specific methods incorporated into a specific MLID depend on the underlying physical layer architecture. An MLID written for an Ethernet card uses contention access control, whereas an MLID written for a Token Ring card uses token access.

The MLID is implemented in a software driver that usually takes its name from the model number of the network board being supported. An MLID for the Novell/Eagle NE2000 card, for example, is packaged in a file named NE2000.COM.

MLIDs don't depend on any specific upper-layer protocols. One feature of the ODI specification is that multiple protocols can access the same network interface board by linking to the same MLID.

Link Support Layer (LSL)

The *Link Support Layer (LSL)* implements the logical link support *(LLC)* sublayer of the OSI data link layer and functions as the interface between the MLID and the upper-layer protocols.

When multiple upper-layer protocol stacks are being used, the LSL software is responsible for passing packets to the appropriate protocol stack.

On NetWare DOS clients, the LSL sublayer is implemented in a file named LSL.COM.

Internetwork Packet Exchange Protocol (IPX)

The *Internetwork Packet Exchange Protocol* (IPX) is a network-layer protocol that provides connectionless (datagram) service. (IPX was developed from the XNS protocol originated by Xerox.) As a network-layer protocol, IPX is responsible for internetwork routing and maintaining network logical addresses. Routing uses the RIP protocol (described later) to make route selections.

IPX relies on hardware physical addresses found at lower layers to provide network device addressing. It also uses *sockets,* or upper-layer service addresses, to deliver packets to their ultimate destinations. On the client, IPX support is provided as a component of the older DOS shell and the current DOS NetWare requester.

Router Information Protocol (RIP)

The *Router Information Protocol* (RIP) uses the distance-vector route discover method to determine hop counts to other devices. Like IPX, RIP was developed from a similar protocol in the XNS protocol suite. RIP is implemented as an upper-layer service and is assigned a socket (service address). RIP is based directly on IPX and performs network layer-functions.

Network Link Services Protocol (NLSP)

The *Network Link Services Protocol* (NLSP) is a link-state routing protocol derived from an ISO protocol named *IS-IS* (intermediate system-to-intermediate system). NLSP supports fault-tolerant mesh and hybrid mesh networks with a high level of fault tolerance.

NLSP is a new protocol with NetWare 4.1, and offers backward compatibility with IPX routers using RIP. NLSP has superior routing algorithms that route packets across an internetwork with greater efficiency. A NetWare 4.1 file server using NLSP maintains a map of the entire internetwork in RAM, and only broadcasts changes to the network. This enables the server to perform precise calculations in order to find the best route. By broadcasting only changes to the network, NLSP minimizes the excessive network traffic caused by IPX RIP. NetWare 4.1 gives you the choice of using either NLSP or the more traditional IPX RIP.

Sequenced Packet Exchange (SPX)

Sequenced Packet Exchange (SPX) is a transport-layer protocol that extends IPX to provide connection-oriented service with reliable delivery. Reliable delivery is ensured by retransmitting packets in the event of an error. SPX is derived from a similar SPX protocol in the XNS network protocol suite.

SPX establishes virtual circuits called *connections.* The connection ID for each connection appears in the SPX header. A given upper-layer process can be associated with multiple connection IDs.

SPX is used in situations where reliable transmission of data is needed. SPX sequences the packets of data. Missing packets or packets that don't arrive in the order in which they were sent are detected immediately. In addition, SPX offers connection multiplexing, which is used in the printing environment. Many accounting programs, for example, call upon the services of SPX to ensure that data is sent accurately.

Connection multiplexing is a term used to indicate where many source logical devices are attempting to communicate with many destination logical devices. A print server, for example, takes jobs from several print queues. Jobs are then routed to printers. One print queue can send a job to many printers. One printer can be programmed to handle many print queues. To avoid sending a job—or worse, part of a job—to the wrong printer, each separate logical association between a print queue and a printer is assigned a connection identifier. The print server handles many (multiple) connections.

On the client, SPX support is provided as a component of the older DOS shell and of the current NetWare requester.

NetWare Core Protocol (NCP)

The *NetWare Core Protocol* (NCP) provides numerous function calls that support network services, such as file service, printing, name management, file locking, and synchronization. NetWare client software interfaces with NCP to access NetWare services.

NCP is a high-level protocol built into the NetWare operating system kernel. This protocol covers aspects of the session, presentation, and application layers of the OSI reference model. NCP has its own miniature language that programmers make use of when writing applications for the NetWare environment. The commands that NCP understands have to do primarily with access to files and directories on a file server. NCP commands are categorized as either a request or a response. An NCP *request* is sent from a client to a server. An NCP *response* is sent from the server back to the client.

The following is an example of an NCP request/response sequence:

Request	Workstation X requests a file from file server Z.
Response	File server Z grants the request.
Request	Workstation X sends the file specification Y to file server Z.
Response	File server Z sends back directory search information regarding filespec Y.
Request	Workstation X identifies the exact file Y.1.
Response	File server Z checks security access to file Y.1.
...	
Response	File server Z sends file Y.1 to workstation X in a group of 20 packets.

Every request and every response requires an acknowledgment. This is often called the *ping-pong effect.* Just as in a game of ping-pong, for every ball you hit over the net, your opponent is supposed to hit it back. In some cases, the request/response sequence depends on an answer from the client or server. In the preceding example, the first six requests depend on a response before continuing. When the file server actually sends the data, however, the workstation doesn't need to make any response other than to acknowledge receipt of the data.

Most NetWare services don't rely on a transport-layer protocol such as SPX. In almost all cases, NCP provides the upper-layer protocol structure that provides services, connection management, and reliable delivery. In most cases, SPX isn't required and can even be left out of the client configuration.

Service Advertising Protocol (SAP)

The *Service Advertising Protocol* (SAP) is used by NetWare servers to advertise their services to the network. Each server identifies itself once a minute by transmitting a SAP packet. SAP users also can request service information by transmitting a service query packet. SAP implementations obtain service address information from IPX header information.

Internet Protocols

The Internet protocol suite (also commonly called the TCP/IP protocol suite) was originally developed by the United States Department of Defense (DoD) to provide robust service on large internetworks that incorporate a variety of computer types. In recent years, the Internet protocols have become increasingly popular and constitute the most popular network protocols now in use.

One reason for this popularity is that no one vendor owns the Internet protocols, unlike the NetWare, DNA, SNA, AppleTalk, and various other protocols. The protocol suite evolves in response to input from a wide variety of industry sources. The Internet protocol suite is the most open of the protocol suites and is supported by the widest variety of vendors. Virtually every brand of computing equipment now supports the Internet protocols.

Much of the popularity of the TCP/IP protocols comes from their early availability on Unix. The protocols were built into the

Berkeley Standard Distribution (BSD) Unix implementation. Since then, TCP/IP has achieved universal acceptance in the Unix community and is a standard feature on all versions of Unix.

Figure 18.3 illustrates the relationship of the protocols in the Internet suite to the layers of the OSI reference model. Notice that the suite doesn't include protocols for the data link or physical layers. TCP/IP was designed to work over established standards such as Ethernet. Over time, TCP/IP has been interfaced to the majority of data link and physical layer technologies.

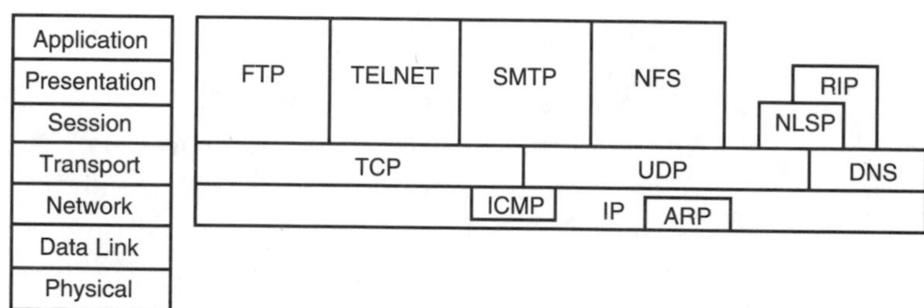

Figure 18.3

The Internet protocol suite.

It should be noted that the Internet protocols do not map cleanly to the OSI reference model. The DoD model was, after all, developed long before the OSI model was defined. The model for the Internet protocol suite has four layers (also shown in fig. 18.3). From this, you can see the approximate relationships of the layers of the two models.

The DoD model's layers function as follows:

- The network access layer corresponds to the bottom two layers of the OSI model. This was deliberately done to enable the DoD protocols to coexist with existing data link-layer and physical-layer standards.
- The internet layer corresponds roughly to the OSI network layer. Protocols at this layer are concerned with moving data between devices on networks.
- The host-to-host layer can be compared to the OSI transport layer. Host-to-host protocols enable peer communication between hosts on the internetwork. (At the time these protocols were designed, personal computers and workstations

didn't exist, and all network computers were host computers. As a result, devices on TCP/IP networks are typically referred to as *hosts.* The concept of a client/server relationship didn't exist, and all communicating hosts were assumed to be peers.)

- The process/application layer embraces functions of the OSI session, presentation, and application layers. Protocols at this layer provide network services.

A large number of protocols are associated with the Internet protocol suite. Several of these are discussed briefly in the following sections

Internet Protocol (IP)

The *Internet Protocol* (IP) is a connectionless protocol that provides datagram service, and IP packets are most commonly referred to as *IP datagrams.* IP is a packet-switching protocol that performs addressing and route selection. An IP header is appended to packets, which are transmitted as frames by lower level protocols. IP routes packets through internetworks by utilizing dynamic routing tables that are referenced at each hop. Routing determinations are made by consulting logical and physical network device information, as provided by the Address Resolution Protocol (ARP).

IP performs packet disassembly and reassembly as required by packet size limitations defined for the data link and physical layers being implemented. IP also performs error checking on the header data using a checksum, although data from upper layers is not error-checked.

Internet Control Message Protocol (ICMP)

The *Internet Control Message Protocol* (ICMP) enhances the error control provided by IP. Connectionless protocols, such as IP, cannot detect internetwork errors, such as congestion or path failures. ICMP can detect such errors and notify IP and upper-layer protocols.

Routing Information Protocol (RIP)

The *Routing Information Protocol* (RIP)in the Internet protocol suite is not the same protocol as RIP in the NetWare suite, although the two serve similar functions. Internet RIP performs route discovery by using a distance-vector method, calculating the number of hops that must be crossed to route a packet by a particular path. (See Chapter 14, "The OSI Model," for more information about distance vector routing.)

Although it works well in localized networks, RIP presents many weaknesses that limit its utility on wide-area internetworks. These weaknesses are similar to those of NetWare RIP and are causing RIP to be replaced gradually by the OSPF link-state protocol.

Open Shortest Path First (OSPF)

The *Open Shortest Path First* (OSPF) protocol is a link-state route-discovery protocol that is designed to overcome the limitations of RIP. On large internetworks, OSPF can identify the internetwork topology and improve performance by implementing load balancing and class-of-service routing.

Transmission Control Protocol (TCP)

The *Transmission Control Protocol* (TCP) is an internetwork protocol that corresponds to the OSI transport layer. TCP provides full-duplex, connection-oriented transport. When the overhead of a connection-oriented transport isn't required, the User Datagram Protocol (UDP) can be substituted for TCP at the transport (host-to-host) level. TCP and UDP operate at the same layer.

TCP corresponds to SPX in the NetWare environment. TCP maintains a logical connection between the sending and receiving computer systems. In this way, the integrity of the transmission is maintained. TCP detects any problems in the transmission quickly and takes action to correct the problem. The trade-off is that TCP isn't as fast as UDP.

TCP also provides message fragmentation and reassembly, and can accept messages of any length from upper-layer protocols. TCP fragments message streams into segments that can be handled by IP. When used with IP, TCP adds connection-oriented service and performs segment synchronization, adding sequence numbers at the byte level.

In addition to message fragmentation, TCP can maintain multiple conversations with upper-layer protocols and can improve use of network bandwidth by combining multiple messages into the same segment. Each virtual-circuit connection is assigned a connection identifier called a *port*, which identifies the datagrams associated with that connection.

User Datagram Protocol (UDP)

The *User Datagram Protocol* (UDP) is a connectionless transport (host-to-host) layer protocol. UDP does not provide message acknowledgments; rather, it simply transports datagrams.

Like TCP, UDP utilizes port addresses to deliver datagrams. These port addresses, however, aren't associated with virtual circuits and merely identify local host processes. UDP is preferred over TCP when high performance or low network overhead is more critical than reliable delivery. Because UDP doesn't need to establish, maintain, and close connections, or control data flow, it generally outperforms TCP.

UDP is the transport layer protocol used with the Simple Network Management Protocol (SNMP), the standard network management protocol used with TCP/IP networks. UDP enables SNMP to provide network management with a minimum of network overhead.

Address Resolution Protocol (ARP)

The following three types of address information are used on TCP/IP internetworks:

- **Physical addresses.** Used by the data link and physical layers.
- **IP addresses.** Provide logical network and host IDs. IP addresses consist of four numbers typically expressed in dotted-decimal form. An example of an IP address is 134.135.100.13.
- **Logical node names.** Identify specific hosts with alphanumeric identifiers. These are easier for humans to recall than the numeric IP addresses. An example of a logical node name is MYHOST.COM.

Given a logical node name, the *Address Resolution Protocol* (ARP) can determine the IP address associated with that name. ARP maintains tables of address resolution data and can broadcast packets to discover addresses on the internetwork. The IP addresses discovered by ARP can be provided to data link layer protocols.

Domain Name System (DNS)

The *Domain Name System* (DNS) protocol provides name/address resolution as a service to client applications. DNS servers enable humans to use logical node names to access network resources.

File Transfer Protocol (FTP)

The *File Transfer Protocol* (FTP) is a protocol for sharing files between networked hosts. FTP enables users to log on to remote hosts. Logged-on users can inspect directories, manipulate files, execute commands, and perform other commands on the host. FTP also has the capability of transferring files between dissimilar hosts by supporting a file request structure that is independent of specific operating systems.

Simple Mail Transfer Protocol (SMTP)

The *Simple Mail Transfer Protocol* (SMTP) is a protocol for routing mail through internetworks. It uses the TCP and IP protocols.

SNMP doesn't provide a mail interface for the user. Creation, management, and delivery of messages to end users must be performed by an e-mail application. (The most popular e-mail application on the Internet is named Eudora.)

Remote Terminal Emulation (TELNET)

TELNET is a terminal emulation protocol. TELNET enables PCs and workstations to function as dumb terminals in session with hosts on internetworks. TELNET implementations are available for most end-user platforms including Unix (of course), DOS, Windows, and Macintosh OS.

Network File System (NFS)

Network File System (NFS), developed by Sun Microsystems, is a family of file access protocols that are a considerable advancement over FTP and TELNET. Since Sun made the NFS specifications available for public use, NFS has achieved a high level of popularity.

NFS consists of the following protocols:

- **eXternal Data Representation (XDR).** Supports encoding of data in a machine-independent format. C programmers use XDR library routines to describe data structures that are portable between machine environments.

- **Remote Procedure Calls (RPC).** Function as a service request redirector that determines whether function calls can be satisfied locally or must be redirected to a remote host. Calls to remote hosts are packaged for network delivery and transmitted to RPC servers, which generally have the capability of servicing many remote service requests. RPC servers process the service requests and generate response packets that are returned to the service requester.

AppleTalk

AppleTalk is the computing architecture developed by Apple Computer for the Macintosh family of personal computers. Although AppleTalk originally supported only Apple's proprietary LocalTalk cabling system, the suite has been expanded to incorporate both Ethernet and Token Ring physical layers.

AppleTalk originally supported networks of limited scope. The AppleTalk Phase 2 specification issued in 1989, however, extended the scope of AppleTalk to enterprise networks. The Phase 2 specification also enabled AppleTalk to coexist on networks with other protocol suites.

Table 18.1 summarizes the differences between AppleTalk Phases 1 and 2.

Table 18.1

Comparison of AppleTalk Phases 1 and 2

Characteristic	Phase 1	Phase 2
Maximum zones on a network segment	1	255
Maximum nodes per network	254	About 16 million
Dynamic addressing based on supported link access protocols	Node ID	Network+ Node ID
	LocalTalk	LocalTalk
	Ethernet	IEEE 802.2 IEEE 802.5
Split-horizon routing	No	Yes

AppleTalk Phase 1 protocols don't support internetworks because addressing is limited to a unique node ID. This approach is called a *nonextended network* under Phase 2 terminology. Phase 2 also supports extended networks in which addressing is determined by a combination of a network and a node ID, and can make use of the hardware-based device IDs that are coded into Ethernet and Token Ring cards.

Figure 18.4 presents a layered perspective of the AppleTalk protocols. Each of these protocols is described in this chapter. Each AppleTalk protocol is briefly discussed below.

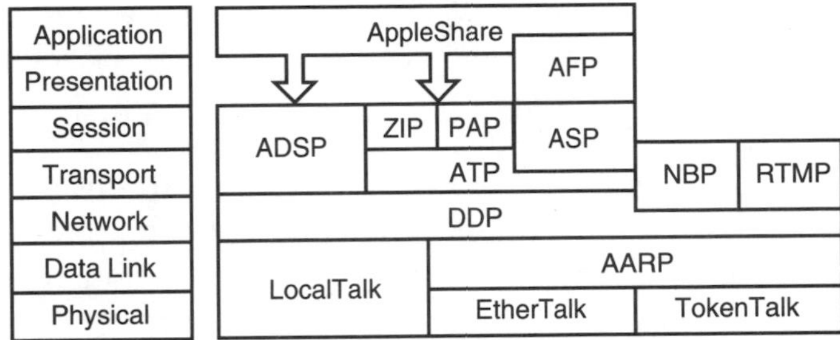

Figure 18.4

The AppleTalk protocol suite.

LocalTalk, EtherTalk, and TokenTalk Link Access Protocols (LLAP, ELAP, and TLAP)

These link access protocols integrate AppleTalk upper-layer protocols with the LocalTalk, Ethernet, and Token Ring environments.

LLAP is a protocol developed by Apple for operation with the LocalTalk cabling system, a system based on shielded twisted-pair cabling. LocalTalk is suitable primarily for small, low-performance networks. The maximum data rate is 230.4 Kbps (compared to 10 Mbps for Ethernet), and cable segments are limited to 300 meters in length and a maximum of 32 devices.

LLAP uses addresses called AppleTalk addresses that are developed dynamically on the network. LLAP is ideally suited to Macintosh's plug and play philosophy because a Macintosh can discover a unique physical address when it connects to the network without the need for any configuration.

AppleTalk Address Resolution (AARP)

Both Ethernet and Token Ring use physical device addresses that are built into the interfaces when they are manufactured. The *AppleTalk Address Resolution Protocol* (AARP) maps AppleTalk addresses to Ethernet and Token Ring physical addresses, enabling upper AppleTalk protocols to interface with the Ethernet and Token Ring physical layers.

Datagram Delivery Protocol (DDP)

Apple's *Datagram Deliver Protocol* (DDP) is a network-layer protocol that provides connectionless service between two sockets. A *socket* is the AppleTalk term for a service address. A combination of a device address, network address, and socket uniquely identifies each process.

DDP performs network routing and consults routing tables maintained by RTMP to determine routing. Packet delivery is performed by the data link protocol operating on a given destination network.

Routing Table Maintenance Protocol (RTMP)

The *Routing Table Maintenance Protocol* (RTMP) provides DDP with routing information based on a distance-vector method similar to RIP.

Zone Information Protocol (ZIP)

The *Zone Information Protocol* (ZIP) organizes devices into zones, which organize service providers into logically named groups. Zones reduce the complexity of a network by limiting users' network views to the devices they need.

ZIP functions with routers to organize service providers into zones and to resolve zone and network names.

Name Binding Protocol (NBP)

AppleTalk enables devices to have logical names in addition to their addresses. These names hide lower-layer addresses from users and from upper-layer processes.

Apple's *Name Binding Protocol* (NBP) enables an application to match a logical name with its associated address. Recall that

AppleTalk addresses are dynamic and can change from session to session. NBP obtains up-to-date information that enables devices to use a logical name to determine address information even though the address varies.

AppleTalk Transaction Protocol (ATP)

The *AppleTalk Transaction Protocol* (ATP) is a connectionless transport-layer protocol. Reliable service is provided through a system of acknowledgments and retransmissions. Retransmissions automatically are initiated if an acknowledgment is not received within a specified time interval.

ATP reliability is based on transactions. A *transaction* consists of a request followed by a reply.

ATP is responsible for segment development and performs fragmentation and reassembly of packets that exceed the specifications for lower-layer protocols. Packets include sequence numbers that enable message reassembly and retransmission of lost packets. Only damaged or lost packets are retransmitted.

AppleTalk Session Protocol (ASP)

The *AppleTalk Session Protocol* (ASP) is a session-layer protocol that establishes, maintains, and releases sessions between service requesters and service providers. The focus of ASP is on providing file services. ASP works with ATP to provide a complete transport service.

ATP messages are limited to eight packets, each with a maximum size of 578 bytes. ASP can generate multiple ATP transactions as required to control message overhead on large data transfers.

Multiple sessions can be maintained between service requesters and providers. Sessions can be requested by service requesters, but not by service providers.

Printer Access Protocol (PAP)

The *Printer Access Protocol* (PAP) is a session-layer protocol similar to ASP. As the name implies, the protocol provides printing services, but it also supports other types of connections between service requesters and providers.

PAP permits sessions to be initiated by both service requesters and service providers.

AppleTalk Data Stream Protocol (ADSP)

If you refer back to figure 18.4, you'll notice that the *AppleTalk Data Stream Protocol* (ADSP) provides a protocol stack that is an alternative to protocols that are layered onto ATP.

ADSP performs services associated with several network layers. It is considered a transport-layer protocol in that it establishes, maintains, and releases sessions between sockets. At the session layer, ADSP substitutes for ASP and PAP.

ADSP replaces ATP at the transport layer and incorporates segment sequencing and sliding window flow-control. The service provided is full-duplex.

ADSP is not transaction-based, as is ATP. Instead, ADSP uses a connection identifier and byte streams. ADSP provides better performance on lower-bandwidth channels than does ATP working with ASP or PAP.

AppleTalk Filing Protocol (AFP)

The *AppleTalk File Protocol* (AFP) provides file services and is responsible for translating local file service requests into formats required for network file services. AFP directly translates command syntax and enables applications to perform file format translations.

AFP is responsible for file system security and verifies and encrypts login names and passwords during connection setup.

AppleShare (ASP)

AppleShare is a client/server system for Macintosh. AppleShare provides the following three primary application services:

- The *AppleShare File Server* uses AFP to enable users to store and access files on the network. It logs in users and associates them with network volumes and directories.
- The *AppleShare Print Server* uses NBP and PAP to support network printing. NBP provides name/address information that enables PAP to connect to printers. The AppleShare Print Server performs print spooling and manages printing on networked printers.
- The *AppleShare PC* enables PCs running MS-DOS to access AppleShare services by running an AppleShare PC program.

Digital Network Architecture

Since its introduction in 1974, the Digital Network Architecture (DNA) has evolved several times. Its current generation is called *Phase V*. DECnet is Digital Equipment Corporation's family of products that implement the DNA architecture.

As DNA has evolved, Digital has placed a strong emphasis on use of standards-based protocols and on achieving close conformance with the OSI reference model. A variety of ISO standards are incorporated into the DNA protocol suite.

Prior to DNA Phase V, DNA relied heavily on Digital's proprietary protocols above the network layer. This stack—which includes Digital's NSP, Naming Service, Session Control, and other protocols—is still supported for the purpose of backward compatibility. Other pre-Phase V protocols also are supported at the lower network levels.

DNA Phase V introduced an alternative protocol stack based on ISO standards.

Figure 18.5 illustrates the layers of the DNA protocol suite. DNA is based on several physical and data link standards that are discussed later in this chapter, including IEEE 802.X, FDDI, and X.25/LAPB.

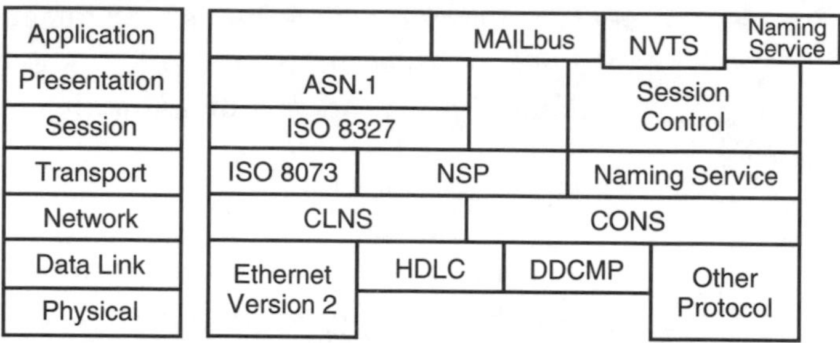

Figure 18.5

Protocols in the Digital Network Architecture.

Ethernet Version 2

Digital was joined by Intel and Xerox to develop the first version of Ethernet, a physical and data link protocol. Since that time, the standard has been updated, and the current version is Ethernet version 2.

Ethernet has the following characteristics:

- 10-Mbps signaling over coaxial cable.
- Media access control method is Carrier Sense Multiple Access with Collision Detection (CSMA/CD).
- Signaling uses Manchester encoding.

The IEEE 802.3 Ethernet standard was developed with slight modifications from Ethernet version 2. Among those changes was a modification to the frame format, which makes 802.3 frames incompatible with Ethernet version 2.

Digital Data Communications Message Protocol (DDCMP)

The *Digital Data Communications Message Protocol* (DDCMP) is a data link protocol that dates from the earliest DNA implementations and remains as an optional Phase V protocol. DDCMP has the following capabilities:

- Asynchronous or synchronous service
- Half- or full-duplex modes
- Point-to-point or multipoint operation
- Connection-oriented error control using commands and acknowledgments along with CRC-based error detection
- LLC flow control and message sequencing (Digital uses the term *message* to describe data-link-level frames.)

At the time the DNA protocols were being defined, all users interacted with central computers by means of computer terminals. Terminal support was provided by the Local Area Transport protocol (LAT), which enables terminal server devices to support multiple terminals and multiplex their traffic over a single channel. LAT doesn't conform to the OSI network layer in that packets don't incorporate routing information and cannot be routed on wide area networks.

High-Level Data Link Control (HDLC)

High-Level Data Link Control (HDLC) is a data link protocol that supports transmissions over physical layer modem communication protocols. HDLC offers the following features:

- Determines the data-frame format and the frame-transfer command syntax
- Supports asynchronous and synchronous communication
- Pcrforms LLC flow control

Connectionless-Mode Network Service (CLNS)

Connectionless-Mode Network Service (CLNS) is a connectionless network layer service that incorporates the following three ISO protocols:

- **ISO 8473.** A connectionless-mode network service that manages communication between end systems.
- **ISO 9542.** A routing protocol that operates between *end systems* (devices) and *intermediate systems* (routers). This protocol, most frequently referred to as ES-IS, can be relatively simple because it doesn't need to perform internetwork routing.
- **ISO 10589.** A routing protocol that operates between intermediate systems. IS-IS is a more complex protocol than ES-IS because it has to be able to determine routes through complex internetworks. Figure 18.6 illustrates the relationships of the two routing protocols.

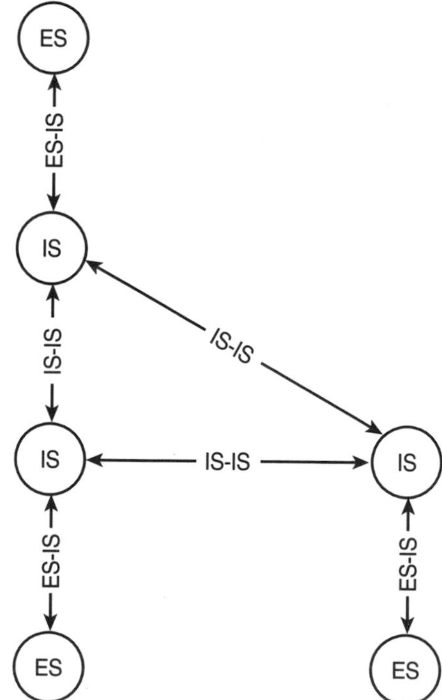

Figure 18.6

ES-IS and IS-IS routing protocols.

These connectionless protocols are used to perform route discovery and selection, addressing, and switching.

Connection-Mode Network Service (CONS)

Connection-Mode Network Service (CONS) is a connection-oriented network-layer service based on the following protocols:

- **ISO 8208.** An ISO version of the X.25 packet-switching protocol, which is discussed later in this chapter.
- **ISO 8878.** An additional protocol that enables X.25 networks to provide connection-oriented services.

CLNS is employed more commonly than CONS to provide network-layer services.

Connection-Oriented Transport Protocol Specification (ISO 8073)

ISO 8073 is a transport layer protocol that provides five service classes, tailored to different requirements. Network implementations can select a service level based on required levels of flow, error control, and packet sequencing.

Network Services Protocol (NSP)

The *Network Services Protocol* (NSP) was incorporated into the original DNA protocol suite. NSP is a connection-oriented transport protocol that manages normal or expedited full-duplex subchannels. End-to-end flow control is performed in response to congestion messages from network-layer protocols. Either windowing or guaranteed flow rates can be used to control data flow.

Session Control

Session Control is a DNA protocol that performs session and presentation layer functions. Functions performed by Session Control include the following:

- Address/name resolution.
- Transport-connection management.
- Connection identifier management.
- Selection of protocol stacks. When devices initiate a session, Session Control negotiates a protocol stack that is supported on both systems.

Session Protocol Specification (ISO 8327)

ISO 8327 is a session-layer protocol that implements the specification ISO 8326, Session Service Definition. OSI 8327 provides the following services:

- Connection establishment, half-duplex data transfer, and connection release.
- Support for multiple transport-layer connections for each session.
- Packet synchronization. The method uses tokens that can be used to request retransmission from any point.

Abstract Syntax Notation One with Basic Encoding Rules (ASN.1 with BER)

ASN.1 (ISO 8824) is a set of extensible syntax rules that establish data types and structures. The rules themselves are described in the Basic Encoding Rules. These protocols operate at the presentation DNA layer.

These standards are designed to facilitate data exchange between different systems by establishing a common set of data formats.

These translations might include conversion between character sets, number representation systems, or other data types. The rules can be extended as required to embrace new data types.

File Transfer, Access, and Management (FTAM) and Data Access Protocol (DAP)

FTAM (ISO 8571) is an application-layer file service protocol. The specification requires a certain set of document types and services, but permits vendors to create customized implementations of the protocol. Standard document types include binary, text, and hierarchical files. Standard services include file transfer and management.

Data Access Protocol (DAP)

The *Data Access Protocol* (DAP) performs file services including file creation, deletion, storage, retrieval, and transfer.

Network Virtual Terminal Service (NVTS)

The *Network Virtual Terminal Service* (NVTS) enables multiple terminal types to access computer services. A *virtual terminal* is a conceptual representation of a computer display. Both the host and the terminal-emulating device maintain a copy of this model, which serves as a common intermediate data representation that enables the host and device to exchange terminal data.

MAILbus and X.400 Message-Handling System

The MAILbus and X.400 message-handling systems provide DNA electronic messaging services. The MAILbus family of products provides proprietary mail services and use the X.400 messaging specification to interface with other X.400-based systems.

Naming Service and X.500 Directory

Naming Service is an application-level naming service that provides address/name resolution. *X.500* is a standard for a naming service. Digital has stated that the DNA Naming Service will migrate toward conformance with X.500.

A *name service* enables humans to describe network services with logical, alphanumeric identifiers. These identifiers are translated to network addresses by the naming service.

Systems Network Architecture (SNA)

Like DNA, IBM's *Systems Network Architecture* (SNA) evolved when terminals were the normal devices used to interact with centralized computers. SNA terminal networks are organized hierarchically, and when it was introduced in 1974, SNA supported only hierarchical networks. An example of an SNA network is shown in figure 18.7. The network hierarchy consists of a central control point (the host computer), controllers (communication controllers and cluster controllers), and terminals.

In 1984, SNA was updated to support distributed processing environments with a feature called *Advanced Peer-to-Peer Networking* (APPN). APPN can implement a distributed processing environment that can leverage the processing capabilities of mainframe hosts, minicomputers, and personal computers.

The next refinement of SNA, the Systems Application Architecture (SAA), was announced in 1987 and represents IBM's strategic direction.

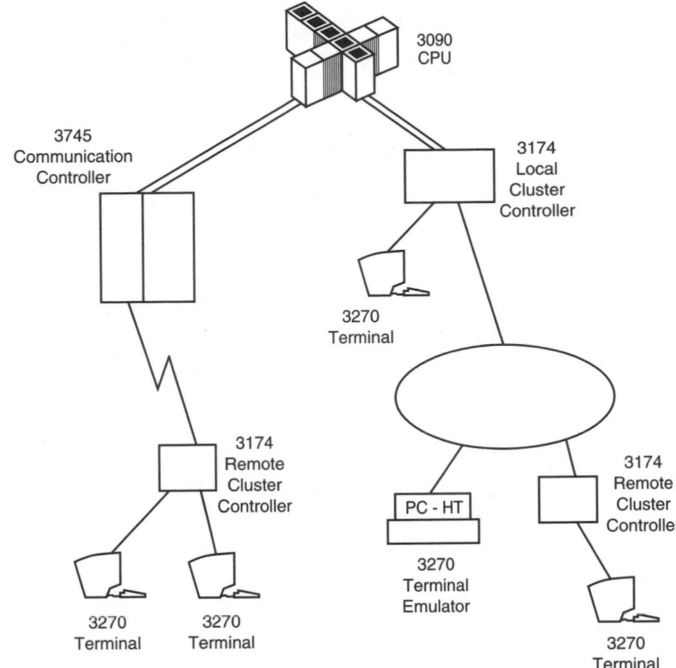

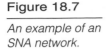

Figure 18.7

An example of an SNA network.

SNA and the OSI Reference Model

SNA wasn't developed from a preconceived, carefully thought-out model from which protocols were developed. IBM literally was pioneering the development of computer networking, and new protocols were added to meet new needs and design criteria. One result of this is that multiple protocols can be present at any given layer. Each protocol serves a somewhat different purpose in the overall scheme of SNA. As such, SNA doesn't consist of a protocol stack so much as it consists of multiple protocols that work together in different combinations to meet different needs.

SNA was a mature model by the time formulation of the OSI reference model was undertaken, and the SNA architecture had a significant influence on the definition of the OSI model. For that reason, making a comparison of the two models is important.

In addition to showing the organization of the SNA protocols, figure 18.8 compares the layers of the OSI reference model to the layers of the SNA model.

SNA layers
Transaction Services
Presentation Services
Data Flow Control
Transmission Control
Path Control
Data Link Control
Physical Control

OSI layers
Application
Presentation
Session
Transport
Network
Data Link
Physical

DIA	SNADS	DPM	User Applications	
APPC	CICS	IMS	TSO	DB2
APPN	VTAM			
NCP				
Token Ring	SDLC		X.25	
	V.35	RS-232C		

Figure 18.8

SNA protocols and the OSI reference model.

The following is a brief description of the SNA model's layers and their features:

- *Physical control* covers the same functions as the OSI physical layer. Both are concerned with the electrical, mechanical, interface, and control characteristics of the physical medium. IBM developed the Token-Ring physical layer standard for this layer, but market forces have pushed IBM to extend SNA to embrace other popular physical layer standards such as Ethernet (IEEE 802.3).

- *Data link control* includes many functions of the OSI data link layer. The *Synchronous Data Link Control* (SDLC) protocol is the SNA data link protocol and is responsible for communication between master/primary nodes and slave/secondary nodes.

- *Path control* incorporates functions from two OSI layers. Path control is responsible for flow control, a data-link-layer function. Path control also is responsible for the routing and packet disassembly/assembly functions of the network layer.

- *Transmission control* is analogous to the OSI transport layer and provides end-to-end connection services. This layer also performs encryption/decryption, services OSI provides at the presentation layer.

- *Data flow control,* like the OSI session layer, controls dialogs.

- *Presentation services* perform data translation services similar to the OSI presentation layer, but also are responsible for sharing resources and synchronizing operations.
- *Transaction services* provide application services, supporting distributed processing and management services. *SNA Distributed Services* (SNADS) is an example of a distributed service.

Network Addressable Units

SNA networks are organized hierarchically and consist of *network addressable units* (NAUs). An NAU is a hardware device or a program (or a combination of hardware and software) that can be addressed on the network. Two types of NAUs can be found: physical units and logical units.

A *physical unit* (PU) is a device consisting of the hardware, firmware, and software required to manage node communication. Communication controllers and cluster controllers are examples of physical units.

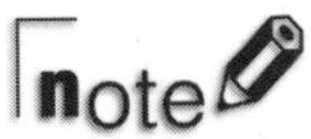

By definition under SNA terminology, a node is a physical unit (PU). Terminals, printers, and other peripherals are not regarded as nodes.

Logical units (LUs) are the end points of network communication. Examples of LUs are peripherals such as terminals, printers, and programs that communicate by means of SNA.

SNA defines several types of PUs and LUs, some of which are illustrated in figure 18.9. The types of each are discussed next.

Until the 1980s, virtually all devices on SNA networks operated in a master/slave relationship under which a master device, the control point, controls all network communication. Terminals, printers, and other peripheral devices function as slaves controlled by the master device, which uses polling to manage communication.

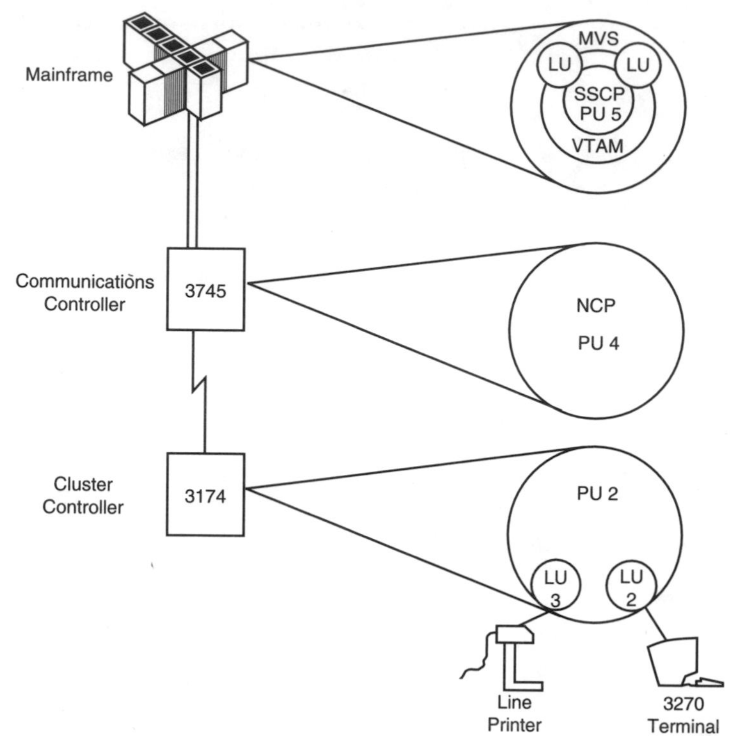

Figure 18.9

PUs and LUs in an SNA network.

During the 1980s, IBM introduced Advanced Program-to-Program Networking (APPN), which enabled LUs to communicate in a peer-to-peer fashion. LU Type 6.2 and PU Type 2.1 were introduced to support APPN.

Physical Units

SNA defines the following three types of physical units:

- **PU Type 5 nodes are host nodes.** A *host node* is the control point that manages networking in a domain. A *domain* consists of all the PUs, LUs, and other network resources that a given host can control. Domains can be divided into subareas. On SNA networks consisting of multiple hosts, terminals can be configured to access applications on more than one host.

  The host node runs a program called *Virtual Terminal Access Method* (VTAM), which provides the *System Services Control Point* (SSCP) service that controls all connection requests and network flow. All SNA network hierarchies are organized around an SSCP.

- **PU Type 4 nodes are communication controllers.** A *communication controller* is a device that runs a *Network Control Program* (NCP) and serves as a communication front-end for the host node. (For this reason, this device typically is called a *front-end processor.*) A communication controller relieves the host node of the responsibility for directly supervising remote communication resources. The IBM 3745 is a type of communication controller.
- **PU Type 2 nodes are peripheral nodes.** Typically, *peripheral nodes* are *cluster controllers,* devices that enable printers, terminals, and other devices to connect to the network. The IBM 3174 is a type of communication controller.

Some documentation states that terminals and printers also are examples of PU Type 2 devices. Terminals and printers, however, are more typically defined as logical units, discussed in the next section.

Logical units are the network end-points between which communication occurs. Quite often an LU consists of a software process that is running on a Type 2 node (a cluster controller). This process in turn services data input and output for a particular terminal, printer, or other peripheral.

The most important thing about PUs and LUs is the function, not the hardware in which the function is performed. A terminal, for example, must be serviced by a PU Type 2 function as well as an LU Type 2 function. These two functions typically are performed by the hardware and software operating in a cluster controller.

Some SNA printers might be equipped with hardware that enables them to network as PU Type 2 devices, which in turn enables them to network without a cluster controller. These printers, however, still must include the LU function as well as the PU function.

PU Type 1, a type of terminal node, is no longer in use.

All communication of PU Type 2 nodes is managed by the central control point, the SSCP. Two Type 2 devices, therefore, cannot directly communicate.

PU Type 2.1 is a new subclass of PU Type 2 that enables the device to provide a control point. This control point enables Type 2.1 PUs to engage in peer-to-peer communication.

In summary, control points manage data communication on the network. Control points are found on PU Type 5s and PU Type 2.1s only.

Logical Units

Logical units are the endpoints of SNA communication and consist of physical devices (terminals, printers, and so on) and programs. The various LU types are summarized in table 18.2.

Table 18.2

Logical Unit Types

LU	Communication Endpoints	Description
0	Program-to-program	An older LU type supporting program-to-program communication. Replaced by LU Type 6.2.
1	Program-to-device	Master/slave. SNA character-stream data on printers, card readers, and hard copy terminals.
2	Program-to-device	Master/slave. Supports terminals using the 3270 protocol.
3	Program-to-device	Master/slave. Supports printers using the 3270 protocol.
4	Program-to-program	Master/slave, peer-to-peer, or program-to-device SNA character stream to printers.

LU	Communication Endpoints	Description
6 & 6.1	Program-to-program	Peer-to-peer interprogram communication (such as CICS-CICS, IMS-IMS, CICS-IMS).
6.2	Program-to-program	Peer-to-peer Advanced Program-to-Program Communication (APPC).
7	Program-to-device	Communication using 5250 data streams, such as terminals on AS/400, System 36, and System 38.

Key SNA Protocols

Figure 18.8 shows the key SNA protocols and how they interrelate. The following sections describe some of the common SNA protocols.

Token Ring

Token-Ring is IBM's specification for a token-access LAN based on a ring logical topology. This specification was used as the basis for developing the IEEE 802.5 Token Ring standard. IBM Token-Ring originally operated at 4 Mbps but has been extended to function at 16 Mbps data rates. The Token-Ring specification describes various cable types, connectors, hubs, and wiring specifications.

Synchronous Data Link Control (SDLC)

Synchronous Data Link Control (SDLC) is a high-performance data link protocol developed to support communication between computers and to function with dedicated or dial-up lines. SDLC supports point-to-point and multipoint communication in half- and full-duplex modes. SDLC frame types can be used to communicate data or to perform control functions.

Network Control Program (NCP)

Network Control Program (NCP) is the protocol that manages network communication on front-end processors. NCP functions at the data link and network layers and supports routing and gateway functions.

Virtual Telecommunications Access Method (VTAM)

Virtual Telecommunications Access Method (VTAM) operates on the host control node and provides the *System Services Control Point* (SSCP) function for the network. The SSCP controls the network hierarchy and works in conjunction with NCPs running on front-end processors. VTAM can manage single or multiple domains and supports interconnections between networks.

Advanced Peer-to-Peer Networking (APPN)

Advanced Peer-to-Peer Networking (APPN) is the SNA architecture for network peer-to-peer communication. Any PU Type 2.1 can communicate with other PU Type 2.1 devices directly, without the need for an SSCP control node. Thus APPN supports networking without the requirement for a mainframe computer. APPN provides directory services, route discovery, and window-based flow control.

Customer Information Control System (CICS)

Customer Information Control System (CICS) is a transaction-processing environment used to build applications. Transaction processing is intended for critical applications, and CICS provides the security, transaction tracking, error recovery, transaction backout, and restart capabilities required in such demanding environments as banking and stocks trading.

Information Management System (IMS)

Information Management System (IMS) is another application-processing environment, and it supports both database and transaction management. The IMS Database Manager is a powerful hierarchical database that can operate under CICS or under the IMS Transaction Manager. IMS databases can be shared among various applications, with IMS scheduling activities and switching messages.

Advanced Program-to-Program Communication (APPC)

Advanced Program-to-Program Communication (APPC) is the IBM specification that defines LU Type 6.2.

Distributed Data Management (DDM)

Distributed Data Management (DDM) uses an OS call redirection approach to provide remote file access to SNA applications. DDM receives service requests and executes them locally or directs them to a DDM server elsewhere on the network, as appropriate.

SNA Distributed Services (SNADS)

SNA Distributed Services (SNADS) provides asynchronous distribution by implementing a store-and-forward distribution service. This service complements the synchronous delivery supported by SNA session capabilities and is useful for distributing messages and documents. Among its functions, SNADS provides an infrastructure for distribution of e-mail.

Document Interchange Architecture (DIA)

Document Interchange Architecture (DIA) defines standards for data interchange between dissimilar computer systems, and coordinates storage, transfer, and retrieval of files.

The IEEE 802 Family

The *Institute of Electrical and Electronic Engineers* (IEEE) is the largest professional organization in the world and is extremely influential with regard to setting standards. The 802 committee of the IEEE has developed a series of standards for LANs, MANs, and WANs. These standards have been recognized and reissued by the ISO as the ISO 802 standards.

Twelve subcommittees oversee the 802 standards. (A thirteenth committee has been proposed for the developing 100-BASE-X standard.) Figure 18.10 illustrates the position each standard occupies in the OSI reference model.

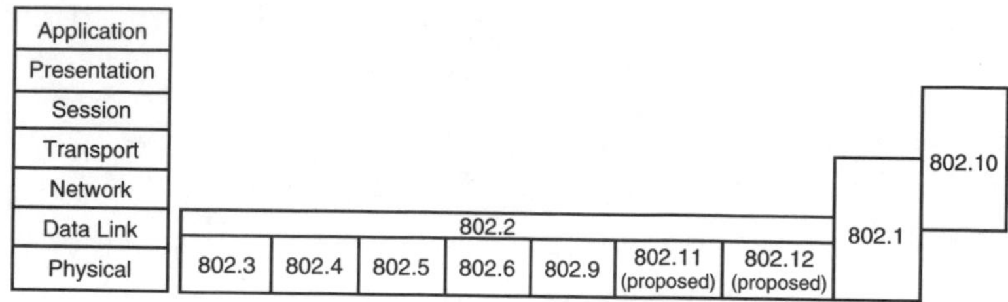

Figure 18.10

The relationship between the IEEE 802 standards and the OSI reference model.

Each of the 802 standards is briefly discussed in the following sections.

IEEE 802.2

The *IEEE 802.2* standard defines an LLC sublayer that is utilized by other lower-layer protocols. Because a single LLC protocol layer is used by lower-layer protocols, network-layer protocols can be designed independently of the network's physical layer and MAC sublayer implementations.

The LLC appends to packets a header that identifies the upper-layer protocols associated with the frame. The header also declares which processes are the source and destination of each packet.

IEEE 802.3

The *IEEE 802.3* standard defines a network derived from the Ethernet network originally developed by Digital, Intel, and Xerox. This standard defines characteristics related to the MAC sublayer of the data link layer and to the OSI physical layer. With one minor distinction—frame type—IEEE 802.3 Ethernet functions identically to DIX Ethernet v.2. The two standards can even coexist on the same cabling system, although devices using one standard cannot communicate directly with devices using the other.

The MAC sublayer uses a variety of contention access called *Carrier Sense Multiple Access with Collision Detection* (CSMA/CD). This technique reduces the incidence of collision by having each device listen to the network to determine whether it's quiet ("carrier sensing"); a device attempts to transmit only when the network is quiescent. This reduces but does not eliminate collisions because signals take some time to propagate through the network. As devices transmit, they continue to listen so they can detect a collision should it occur. When a collision occurs, all devices cease transmitting and send a "jamming" signal that notifies all stations of the collision. Then, each device waits a random amount of time before again attempting to transmit. This combination of safeguards significantly reduces collisions on all but the busiest networks.

The physical-layer definition describes signaling methods (both baseband and broadband are available), data rates, media, and topologies. Several physical layer variants have been defined. Each is named following a convention that states the signaling rate (1 or 10) in Mbps, baseband (BASE) or broadband (BROAD) mode, and a designation of the media characteristics.

The following is a list of the 802.3 variants:

- **1BASE5.** A 1-Mbps network that utilizes UTP cable with a signal range up to 500 meters (250 meters per segment). A star physical topology is use (Refer to Chapter 16, "Network Topologies.")
- **10BASE5.** Uses a large diameter (10-mm) "thick" coaxial cable with a 50-ohm impedance. A data rate of 10 Mbps is supported with a signaling range of 500 meters per cable segment on a physical bus topology. This variant is typically called *Thick Ethernet* or *Thicknet.*
- **10BASE2.** Similar to Thicknet, but uses a thinner coaxial cable that can support cable runs of 185 meters. (In this case, the "2" only approximately indicates the cable range.) The transmission rate remains 10 Mbps and the physical topology is a bus. This variant is typically called *Thin Ethernet* or *Thinnet.*
- **10BASE-F.** Uses fiber-optic cables to support 10-Mbps signaling with a range of 4 kilometers. Three subcategories include 10BASE-FL (fiber link), 10BASE-FB (fiber backbone), and 10BASE-FP (fiber passive).

- **10BROAD36.** A broadband standard that supports channel signal rates of 10 Mbps. 75-ohm coaxial cable supports cable runs of 1,800 meters (up to 3,600 meters in a dual-cable configuration) using a physical bus topology.
- **10BASE-T.** Uses UTP cable in a star physical topology. The signaling rate remains 10 Mbps. Devices might be up to 100 meters from a wiring hub.
- **100BASE-X.** A proposed standard that is similar to 10BASE-T but supports 100-Mbps data rates.

The industry is not in accord regarding the proper use of the name Ethernet. Xerox has placed the name Ethernet in the public domain, which means no one can claim authority over it. Purists often claim that Ethernet refers only to the original Digital-Intel-Xerox standard. More frequently, however, the term designates any network based on CSMA/CD access-control methods.

It is usually necessary to be specific about the standard that applies to a given network configuration. The original standard is called Ethernet version 2 (the older version 1 is still in occasional use) or Ethernet-II. The IEEE standard is distinguished by its committee title as 802.3.

The distinction is important because Ethernet version 2 and 802.3 Ethernet use incompatible frame types. Devices using one frame type cannot communicate with devices using the other frame type.

IEEE 802.4

The *802.4* standard describes a network that has a bus physical topology that controls media access with a token mechanism. The standard was designed to meet the needs of industrial automation systems but has gained little popularity. Both baseband and broadband (using 75-ohm coaxial cable) configurations are available.

IEEE 802.5

The *IEEE 802.5* standard was derived from IBM's Token-Ring network, which employs a ring logical topology and token-based media access control. Data rates of 1, 4, and 16 Mbps have been defined. The IEEE 802.5 standard does not describe a cabling system. Most implementations are based on the IBM cabling system, which uses twisted-pair cable wired in a physical star.

IEEE 802.6

The *IEEE 802.6* standard describes a MAN standard called *Distributed Queue Dual Bus* (DQDB). Much more than a data network technology, DQDB is suited to data, voice, and video transmissions. The network is based on fiber-optic cable in a dual-bus topology. Traffic on each bus is unidirectional. When operated in pairs, the two buses provide a fault-tolerant configuration. Bandwidth is allocated using time slots, and both synchronous and asynchronous modes are supported.

IEEE 802.9

The *IEEE 802.9* standard supports a 10-Mbps asynchronous channel along with 96 64-Kbps (6 Mbps total bandwidth) channels that can be dedicated to specific data streams. The total bandwidth is 16 Mbps. This standard is called *Isochronous Ethernet* (IsoEnet) and is designed for settings that have a mix of bursty and time-critical traffic.

IEEE 802.11

IEEE 802.11 is a standard for wireless LANs, currently under development. A CSMA/CD method has been approved, but the final standard is pending.

IEEE 802.12

The *IEEE 802.12* standard is based on a 100-Mbps proposal promoted by AT&T, IBM, and Hewlett-Packard. Called

100VG-AnyLAN, the network is based on a star wiring topology and a contention-based access method whereby devices signal the wiring hub of a need to transmit data. Devices can transmit only when granted permission by the hub. This standard is intended to provide a high-speed network that can operate in mixed Ethernet and Token Ring environments by supporting both frame types.

Fiber Distributed Data Interface

Fiber Distributed Data Interface (FDDI) is a standard for fiber-based networks that was developed by the X3T9.5 committee of the American National Standards Institute (ANSI). The ISO has adopted FDDI as standard 9314. FDDI was developed for WANs but has been used in MANs and LANs as well.

As shown in figure 18.11, FDDI covers the physical layer and the MAC sublayer of the OSI reference model. Most frequently, the IEEE 802.2 standard is employed for the LLC sublayer.

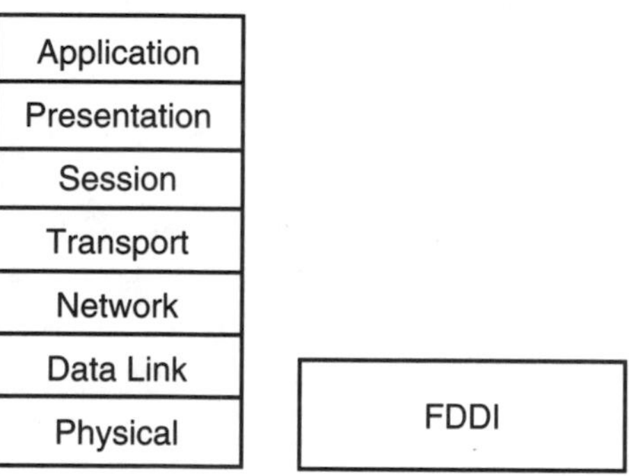

Figure 18.11

The relationship of FDDI to the OSI reference model.

FDDI is a 100-Mbps network that functions similarly to 802.5 Token Ring, and is based on token-passing access control and a ring topology. Originally developed for optical fiber cable, the standard has been extended so that it can be supported using copper UTP. Using optical fiber cable enables FDDI to support physically large networks.

Although FDDI networks can be cabled as physical stars, stars might be impractical with larger networks, and FDDI networks then are typically cabled in physical rings. Stations can be attached in two ways, as shown in figures 18.12 and 18.13. Stations on a single ring configuration are called *single-attached stations.* On a single ring, failure of the medium at any point causes the network to fail.

To provide greater fault tolerance, FDDI is typically cabled with *dual-attached stations* (DASs) using two counter-rotating rings. As figure 18.13 shows, if the cable fails at any one point, the two rings are automatically reconfigured to maintain a complete ring transmission path. (Note that a failed link between single-attached stations cannot be corrected in this manner.) Under normal operation, both rings can be used for data, and traffic can be balanced between rings. It is desirable, however, to design the network to half its dual-ring capacity and to half its size limit. If a ring failure occurs under these conditions, the total length of the two rings falls within specifications, and the traffic becomes manageable with only a single active ring.

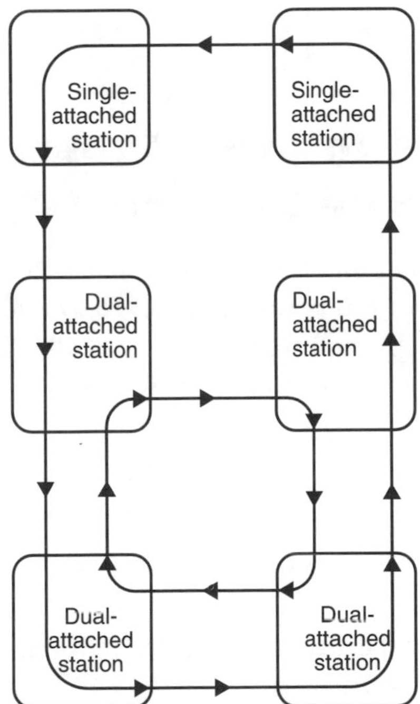

Figure 18.12

Normal operation of an FDDI network with single- and dual-attached stations.

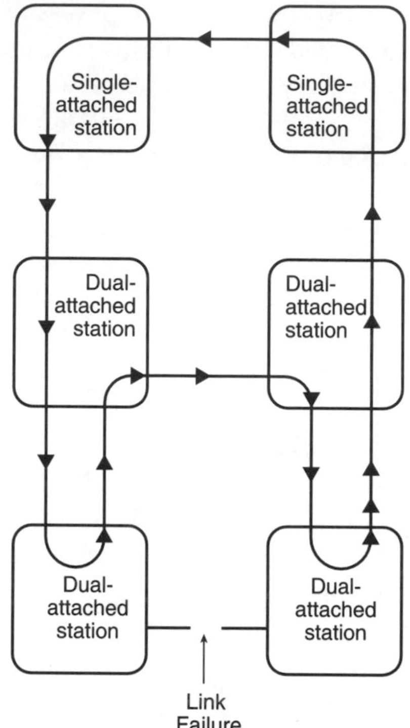

Figure 18.13

Dual-attached FDDI stations correcting for a failed link.

Serial Line Internet Protocol (SLIP) and Point-to-Point Protocol (PPP)

The *Serial Line Internet Protocol* (SLIP) and *Point-to-Point Protocol* (PPP) were designed to support dial-up access to networks based on the Internet protocols. SLIP is a simple protocol that functions at the physical layer, whereas PPP is a considerably enhanced protocol that provides physical-layer and data-link-layer functionality. The relationship of both to the OSI model is shown in figure 18.14.

SLIP was developed to provide dial-up IP connections. It is an extremely rudimentary protocol that suffers from a lack of rigid standardization such that different implementations might not interoperate.

Figure 18.14

The relationship of SLIP and PPP to the OSI reference model.

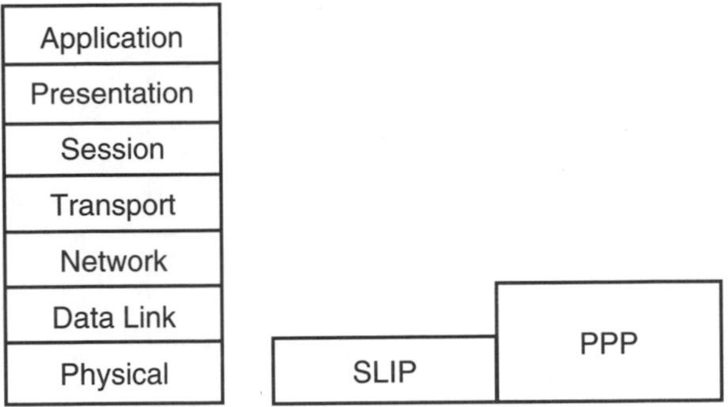

PPP was defined by the Internet Engineering Task Force (IETF) to improve on SLIP by providing the following features:

- Security using password login
- Simultaneous support for multiple protocols on the same link
- Dynamic IP addressing
- Error control

Different PPP implementations might offer different levels of service and can negotiate service levels when connections are made.

CCITT/ITU X.25

X.25 is a packet-switching network standard developed by the International Telegraph and Telephone Consultative Committee (CCITT), which has been renamed the International Telecommunications Union (ITU). The standard, referred to as Recommendation X.25, was introduced in 1974, and is implemented most commonly in WANs.

As shown in figure 18.15, X.25 is one level of a three-level stack that spans the network, data link, and physical layers.

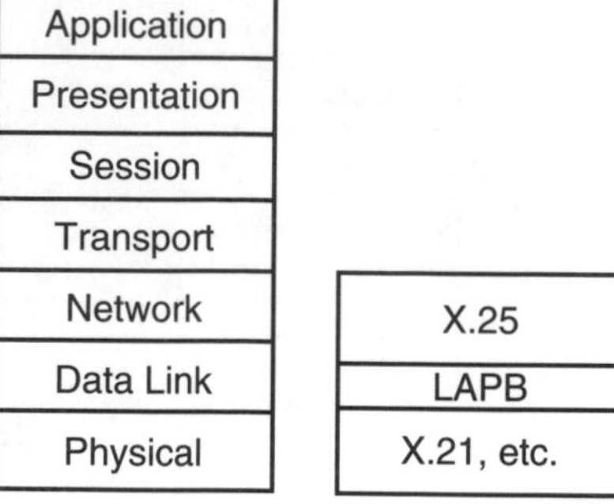

Figure 18.15

The relationship of X.25 to the OSI reference model.

Physical layer connectivity is provided by a variety of standards including X.21, X.21bis, and V.32.

Link Access Procedures-Balanced (LAPB) is a bit-oriented, full-duplex, synchronous data-link-layer LLC protocol.

X.25 packet-switching networks provide the options of permanent or switched virtual circuits. Although a datagram (unreliable) protocol was supported until 1984, X.25 now is required to provide reliable service and end-to-end flow control. Because each device on a network can operate more than one virtual circuit, X.25 must provide error and flow control for each virtual circuit.

X.25 networks are typically implemented with line speeds up to 64 Kbps. These speeds are suitable for the file transfer and terminal activity that comprised the bulk of network traffic when X.25 was defined. Such speeds, however, are inadequate to provide LAN-speed services, which generally require speeds of 1 Mbps or better. X.25 networks are, therefore, poor choices for providing LAN application services in a WAN environment.

Frame Relay

Frame relay was designed to support the Broadband Integrated Services Digital Network (B-ISDN), which is discussed in the following section, "ISDN and B-ISDN." The specifications for frame relay address some of the limitations of X.25. Like X.25, frame relay is a packet-switching network service. Frame relay is standardized by ANSI and ITU (CCITT).

Unlike X.25, frame relay assumes a more reliable network. This enables frame relay to eliminate much of the X.25 overhead required to provide reliable service on less reliable networks. Frame relay relies on higher-level protocol layers to provide flow and error control.

Frame relay typically is implemented as a public data network and is, therefore, regarded as a WAN protocol. The relationship of frame relay to the OSI model is shown in figure 18.16. Notice that the scope of frame relay is limited to the physical and data link layers.

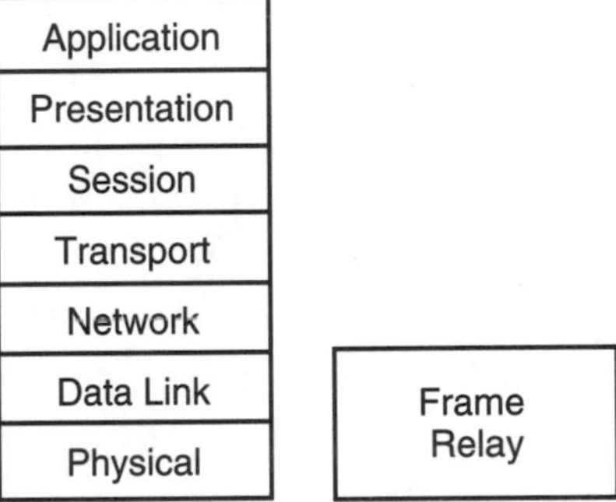

Figure 18.16

The relationship of frame relay to the OSI reference model.

Frame relay provides switched and permanent virtual circuits. Frame relay services typically are implemented at line speeds of 56 Kbps up to 1.544 Mbps (T1).

Customers typically purchase access to a specific amount of bandwidth on a frame-relay service. This bandwidth is called the *committed information rate* (CIR), a data rate for which the customer is guaranteed access. Customers may be permitted to access higher data rates on a pay-per-use, temporary basis. This arrangement enables customers to tailor their network access costs based on their bandwidth requirements.

ISDN and B-ISDN

Integrated Services Digital Network (ISDN) is a group of ITU (CCITT) standards designed to provide voice, video, and data transmission services on digital telephone networks. ISDN uses multiplexing to support multiple channels on high-bandwidth circuits. The relationship of the ISDN protocols to the OSI reference model is shown in figure 18.17.

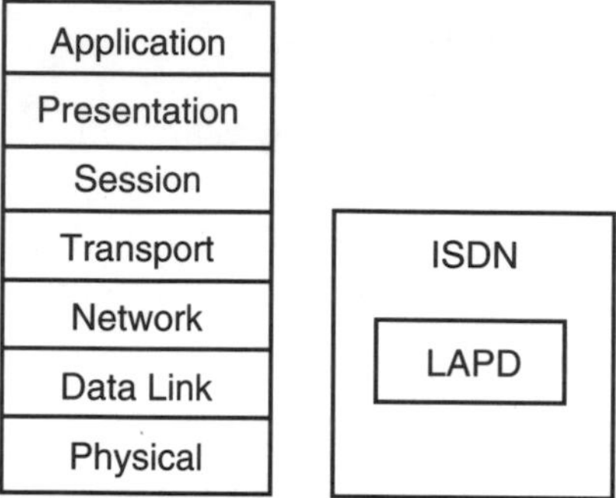

Figure 18.17

The relationship of ISDN protocols to the OSI reference model.

A variety of ISDN channel types are defined. These channel types, often called *bit pipes*, provide different types and levels of service. The various channels are described in the following list:

- A channel provides 4-kHz analog telephone service.
- D channels support 64-Kbps digital data.
- C channels support 8- or 16-Kbps digital data, generally for out-of-band signaling.
- D channels support 16- or 64-Kbps digital data, also for out-of-band signaling. D channels support the following subchannels:
    - p subchannels support low-bandwidth packet data.
    - s subchannels are used for signaling (such as call setup).
    - t subchannels support telemetry data (such as utility meters).
- E channels provide 64-Kbps service used for internal ISDN signaling.
- H channels provide 384, 1,536, or 1,920 digital service.

The following three standard channel combinations have been defined:

- *Basic rate* includes two B channels and one D channel.
- *Primary rate* includes one D channel, 23 B channels (in the U.S. and Japan), or 30 B channels (in Europe and Australia).
- *Hybrid* provides one A channel and one C channel.

ISDN functions as a data transmission service only. Acknowledged, connectionless, full-duplex service is provided at the data link layer by the LAPD protocol, which operates on the D channel.

Broadband ISDN is a refinement of ISDN that is defined to support higher bandwidth applications such as video, imaging, and multimedia. Physical-layer support for B-ISDN is provided by Asynchronous Transfer Mode (ATM) and the Synchronous Optical Network (SONET). SONET is discussed further in the following section. Typical B-ISDN data rates are 51 Mbps, 155 Mbps, and 622 Mbps over fiber-optic media.

Synchronous Optical Network (SONET) and the Synchronous Digital Hierarchy (SDH)

Bell Communications Research developed the *Synchronous Optical Network* (SONET), which has been accepted as an ANSI standard. SONET is regarded as a WAN standard.

A similar set of standards, published by the ITU (CCITT), is called the *Synchronous Digital Hierarchy* (SDH). Regional variations of SDH, including SDH-Europe, SDH-SONET (North America), and SDH-Japan, have been defined to accommodate local differences. Figure 18.18 illustrates the relationship of the SONET/SDH standards to the OSI reference model.

Figure 18.18

The relationship of SONET/SD to the OSI reference model.

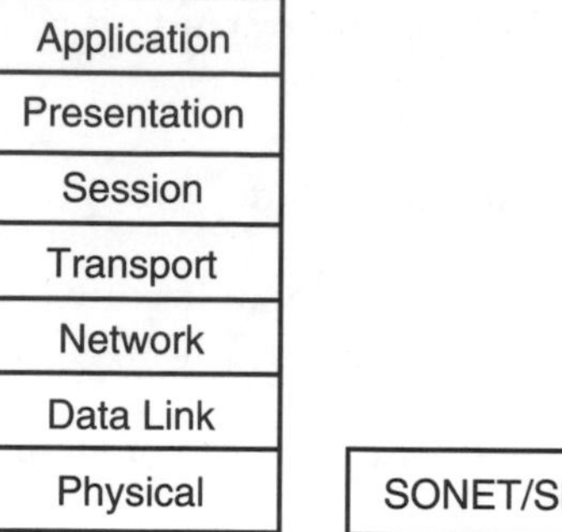

Data rates for SONET are organized in a hierarchy based on the Optical Carrier (OC) speed and the corresponding Synchronous Transport Signals (STS) employed. The basic OC and STS data rate is 51.84 Mbps. Higher data rates are provided in multiples of the basic rate. Thus OC-48 is 48×51.84 Mbps = 2488.32 Mbps.

SDH data rates begin at 155.52 Mbps, and are calculated in multiples of that rate. Thus an SDH-16 has a data rate of 2488.32 Mbps, equivalent to the SONET STS-48 data rate.

Asynchronous Transfer Mode (ATM)

Asynchronous Transfer Mode (ATM) is a high-bandwidth switching technology developed by the ITU Telecommunications Standards Sector (ITU-TSS). An organization called the *ATM Forum* is responsible for defining ATM implementation characteristics. ATM can be layered on other physical-layer technologies, such as FDDI and SONET. The relationships of these protocols to the OSI model are shown in figure 18.19.

Figure 18.19

The relationship of ATM to the OSI reference model.

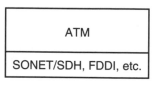

Application
Presentation
Session
Transport
Network
Data Link
Physical

ATM
SONET/SDH, FDDI, etc.

Several characteristics distinguish ATM from other switching technologies. ATM is based on fixed-length, 53-byte cells, whereas other technologies employ frames that vary in length to accommodate different amounts of data. Because ATM cells are uniform in length, switching mechanisms can operate with a high level of efficiency.

The unit of transmission for ATM is called a *cell*. All cells are 53 bytes in length and consist of a 5-byte header and 48 bytes of data. The 48-byte data size was arrived at by the standards committee as a compromise between the needs of audio and data transmission. Audio information must be delivered with little latency (delay) to maintain a smooth flow of sound. Audio engineers preferred a small cell so that cells would be more readily available when needed. For data, however, large cells reduce the overhead required to deliver a byte of information.

Asynchronous delivery is another distinguishing feature of ATM. *Asynchronous* refers to the characteristic of ATM whereby transmission time slots don't occur periodically, but are granted at irregular intervals. ATM uses a technique called *label multiplexing*, which allocates time slots on demand. Traffic that is time critical, such as voice or video, can be given priority over data traffic that can be delayed slightly with no ill effect. Channels are identified by cell labels, not by specific time slots. A high-priority transmission need not be held until its next time slot allocation. It might only be required to wait until the current 53-byte cell has been transmitted.

Other multichannel technologies utilize time-division techniques to allocate bandwidth to channels. A T1 (1.544-Mbps) line, for example, might be time-division multiplexed to provide 24 voice channels. With this technique, each channel is assigned a specific time slot in the transmission schedule. The disadvantage of this technique is that an idle channel doesn't yield its bandwidth for the creation of other channels.

Devices communicate on ATM networks by establishing a virtual path, which is identified by a virtual path identifier (VPI). Within this virtual path, virtual circuits can be established, which are in turn associated with virtual circuit identifiers (VCIs). The VPI and VCI together make up a three-byte field included in the cell header.

Other networks, such as a routed Ethernet, require a six-byte physical address as well as a network address to uniquely identify each device on an internetwork. ATM can switch cells with three-byte identifiers because VPIs and VCIs apply only to a given device-to-device link. Each ATM switch can assign different VPIs and VCIs for each link. Up to 16 million circuits can be configured for any given device-to-device link.

The following three characteristics define the classes of ATM service:

- **Time relation between source and destination.** Some data types require a precise time relationship between transmission and reception of cells.
- **Bit rate.** Constant and variable bit rates are available. Many audio and video signaling techniques require constant bit rates. Newer techniques based on data compression might have the capability to function on variable-rate services.
- **Connection mode.** Connection-oriented and connectionless services are available.

Using these characteristics, the following service classes have been defined:

- **Class A.** Timing required, constant bit rate, connection oriented.
- **Class B.** Timing required, variable bit rate, connection oriented. Data for this class must be delivered with a constant delay.
- **Class C.** No timing, variable bit rate, connection oriented.
- **Class D.** No timing, variable bit rate, connectionless.
- **Class X.** Unrestricted, variable bit rate, connection oriented or connectionless.

Although ATM was developed primarily as a WAN technology, it has many characteristics of value for high-performance LANs. An interesting advantage is that ATM makes it possible to use the same technology for both LANs and WANs.

Switched Multimegabit Digital Service (SMDS)

Switched Multimegabit Digital Service (SMDS) is a technology developed by Bell Communications Research in 1991. SMDS is related to ATM in that it transports data in 53-byte cells. SMDS supports cell switching at data rates of 1.544 to 45 Mbps.

SMDS is a connectionless data-link-layer service. IEEE 802.6 (DQDB metropolitan area network) is the primary physical-layer standard employed with SMDS, although other physical layer standards are supported as well. Figure 18.20 illustrates the relationships of these protocols in the context of the OSI model.

Figure 18.20

The relationship of SMDS to the OSI reference model.

OSI	SMDS
Application	
Presentation	
Session	
Transport	
Network	SMDS
Data Link	SMDS
Physical	DQDB, SONET/SDH, etc.

Review Questions

The following questions will test your knowledge of the information in this chapter. For additional questions, see MCP Endeavor and the Microsoft/Roadmap Assessment Exam on the CD-ROM that accompanies this book.

1. Which two protocols are designed to provide reliable delivery?

    A. IPX

    B. TCP

    C. UDP

    D. SPX

2. Which protocol enables clients to identify available NetWare servers?

    A. IPX

    B. NLSP

    C. SAP

    D. RIP

3. Which three protocols translate logical device names into device addresses?

    A. DNS

    B. NBP

    C. SAP

    D. X.500

4. If your network includes large numbers of NetWare servers, connected via a WAN, which protocol should you evaluate as a means of reducing network traffic overhead?

    A. SPX

    B. SAP

    C. NLSP

    D. RIP

5. Which NetWare protocol provides connection multiplexing?

   A. NCP

   B. IPX

   C. SPX

   D. LSL

6. Which NetWare protocol maintains a map of the internetwork, and broadcasts only changes to the network?

   A. NCP

   B. NLSP

   C. LSL

   D. SAP

7. Which of the following protocols are most similar?

   A. NetWare IPX and Internet TCP

   B. NetWare NLSP and AppleTalk RTMP

   C. NetWare NLSP and DNA CLNS

   D. NetWare RIP and Internet OSPF

8. In an NCP exchange, every request and every response requires a ______.

   A. sender

   B. receiver

   C. acknowledgment

   D. packet

9. TCP operates at the same layer as ______.

   A. NCP

   B. SAP

   C. SPX

   D. UDP

10. TCP is concerned with maintaining which two of the following?

    A. Load balancing

    B. Logical connections

    C. Transmission integrity

    D. Hop calculations

11. Which Novell protocol usually provides transport-layer functions?

    A. SPX

    B. IPX

    C. NLSP

    D. NCP

12. Which protocol suite provides the standards with the broadest industry support?

    A. AppleTalk

    B. Internet

    C. NetWare

    D. SNA

13. Which types of addresses are used on LocalTalk networks?

    A. Physical node numbers

    B. Static logical IDs

    C. Dynamic logical IDs

    D. Logical device names

14. Which protocol enables Ethernet and Token Ring networks to interface with AppleTalk protocols?

    A. RTMP

    B. AARP

C. LLAP

D. ZIP

15. Which protocol is responsible for matching users' logical device names with AppleTalk addresses?

    A. AARP

    B. ZIP

    C. NBP

    D. ATP

16. Which three AppleTalk protocols provide session-level services?

    A. ASP

    B. PAP

    C. ADSP

    D. AFP

17. Which two components are required to enable a NetWare LAN to communicate with a Digital computer?

    A. Ethernet v.2 support

    B. IEEE 802.3 Ethernet support

    C. TCP/IP

    D. NetWare for LAT

18. Which two of the following DNA protocols are regarded as presentation-layer protocols?

    A. ASN.1

    B. NVTS

    C. FTAM

    D. MAILbus

19. Which three of the following statements are true regarding SNA network addressable units?

    A. A PU Type 2 is a communication controller.
    B. An LU Type 6.2 device is capable of program-to-program communication.
    C. A PU consists of the hardware and software required to manage the resources of nodes.
    D. Control points are found on Type 5 and Type 2.1 PUs.

20. Which SNA protocols are required to implement peer-to-peer communication?

    A. DDM
    B. SNADS
    C. APPN and APPC
    D. NCP

21. Which two of the following are regarded as WAN protocols?

    A. Frame relay
    B. SLIP
    C. IEEE 802.6
    D. X.25

22. Which protocols are commonly used with IEEE 802.2?

    A. IEEE 802.3
    B. IEEE 802.5
    C. IEEE 802.6
    D. All of the above

23. What is the primary characteristic that distinguishes a cell from a packet?

    A. Cells are generally smaller than packets.
    B. Cells don't incorporate physical addresses.
    C. All cells have the same fixed length.
    D. Packets cannot be switched.

24. What are the primary differences between Ethernet version 2 and IEEE 802.3 Ethernet?

    A. They require different network hardware.
    B. IEEE 802.3 Ethernet functions at a higher data rate.
    C. They use different frame formats.
    D. Ethernet version 2 doesn't use CSMA/CD media access control.

25. Which two of the following protocols are intended primarily for use on fiber-optic cable?

    A. Frame relay
    B. FDDI
    C. SONET
    D. X.25

26. Which two of the following ATM service classes require no timing?

    A. Class A
    B. Class B
    C. Class C
    D. Class D

27. Which two of the following standards use token passing for media access control?

    A. IEEE 802.4

    B. IEEE 802.6

    C. Frame relay

    D. FDDI

28. Which two of the following standards are designed to support audio data?

    A. IEEE 802.10

    B. ISDN

    C. ATM

    D. Frame relay

29. Over fiber-optic media, typical B-ISDN data rates are ______.

    A. 51 Mbps

    B. 155 Mbps

    C. 312 Mbps

    D. 622 Mbps

30. Which two of the following network standards are well suited to delivering time-critical data?

    A. X.25

    B. IEEE 802.5

    C. Frame relay

    D. ATM

Review Answers

1. B D
2. C
3. A B D
4. C
5. C
6. B
7. C
8. C
9. D
10. B C
11. D
12. B
13. C
14. B
15. C
16. A B D
17. A D
18. A B
19. B C D
20. C
21. A D
22. D
23. C
24. C
25. B C

26. C D
27. A D
28. B C
29. A B D
30. B D

Chapter 19

Network Architectures

Chapter 16, "Network Topologies," described the following physical topologies:

- Bus topology
- Ring topology
- Star topology
- Mesh topology
- Cellular topology

The physical topologies in Chapter 16 represent general concepts. An actual implementation of one of these network topologies is vastly more complicated. In addition to worrying about the arrangements of cables, you must decide what types of cables to use, and you must use network protocols and network interface cards that are adapted to your topology.

The network industry has developed standards for some basic LAN architectures. Each of these architectures is really a package of specifications that includes descriptions of the topology, the transmission media, and the accompanying protocols. In this chapter, you will learn about the following network architectures:

- ARCnet
- Ethernet
- Token Ring
- Fiber Distributed Data Interface (FDDI)

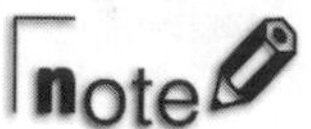

In everyday life, these network architectures are sometimes called *network topologies* because the topology is the most visible characteristic of the standard. For instance, you may hear a network administrator use the term "Token Ring topology," though (as you learn in this chapter) there is much more to Token Ring than a topology as defined in Chapter 16.

Exploring ARCnet Specifications

ARCnet is an acronym for Attached Resource Computer NETwork, founded by the Datapoint Corporation. Novell uses the term *RX-Net* to denote its form of the ARCnet architecture, and TRX-Net for the Turbo version. ARCnet uses a token-bus packet passing scheme.

ARCnet operates at 2.5-Mbps throughput and can be connected using RG-62/U coax cable or unshielded twisted-pair (UTP) wiring. Although ARCnet can support up to 255 node numbers on a single network, systems of this size aren't practical.

Figure 19.1 shows the components of a typical ARCnet card. This card is configured for use with twisted-pair wiring. ARCnet cards for use with coax cable have a Bayonet Navy Connector (BNC) twist-on connector. You will find jumpers or Dual In-line Package (DIP) switches for setting the following characteristics:

- Node number
- Base I/O address
- Memory address
- Interrupt
- Network timeout

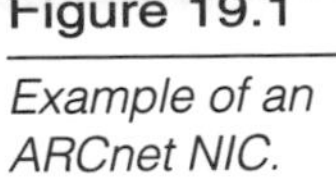

Figure 19.1

Example of an ARCnet NIC.

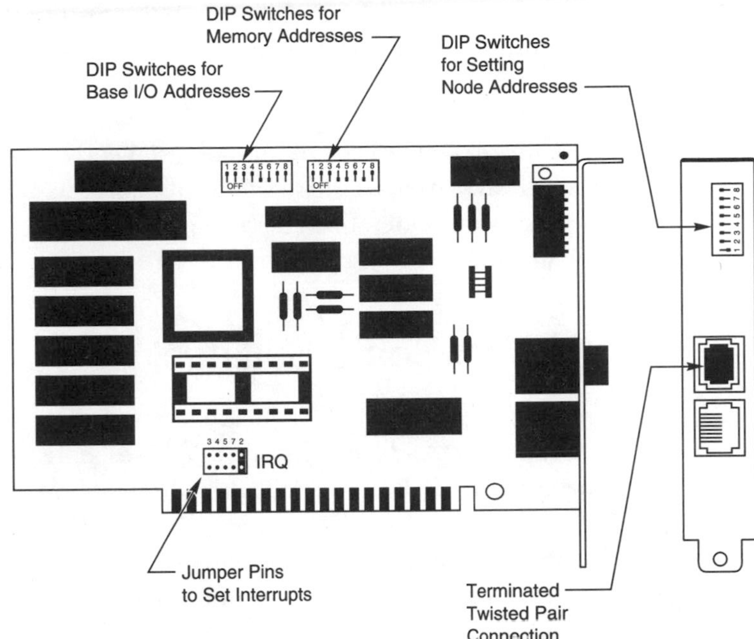

The node number and network timeout are unique to ARCnet and are described later in this chapter.

Each network interface card (NIC) on an ARCnet network receives a node number, which must be a unique number (in the range of 1 to 255) on each network.

ARCnet manages network access using a token mechanism. The token passes from the lowest number node to higher number nodes in ascending order. Lower numbered addresses get the token before the higher numbered addresses.

Traffic is controlled by assigning sequential numbers to nodes using the same order in which they're cabled. Choosing random numbers can create a situation in which a node numbered 23 can be a whole building away from the next number, 46, but in the same room as numbers 112 and 142. The token then must travel in a haphazard manner that isn't as effective as using three clients in the same office numbered sequentially, 46, 47, and 48, and numbering the client in the other building 112. Using this configuration, the packet stays within the office before it ventures on to other stations.

ARCnet was one of the topologies used early on in networking and rarely is used as the topology of choice in current LAN environments. ARCnet, however, still is a functional and cost-effective means of networking.

ARCnet Board Settings

Depending on your ARCnet card's vendor design specifications, most base I/O addresses, node addresses, and memory addresses are set using DIP switches. These addresses are set using a binary mode calculation with an on or off setting in the required switch block. Interrupt settings are made by jumper combinations at marked locations on the network interface card. Many types and brands of ARCnet cards are on the market today. Refer to the Micro House Technical Library, the documentation for the NIC, or, as a last resort, call the technical support group for the specific vendor of the component.

Most ARCnet cards require a shared memory address. Many manufacturers use the area of D000:0 to DFFF:0 as the default. Standard DOS memory is limited to the first 640 KB of a PC's memory. You can use extended or expanded memory managers, however, to make memory above 640 KB available for use by DOS programs. If you use memory above the 640-KB line (above hex address A000:0) for network boards, however, the memory becomes unavailable for use by a memory manager, which makes optimizing a PC's upper memory area difficult. If a network card requires a memory area, such as D000:0-DFFF:0, the memory available for use by DOS memory managers diminishes by 64 KB.

ARCnet Cabling

The ARCnet topology uses coax, twisted-pair, or fiber-optic cabling to connect network devices. An ARCnet network is used primarily with either coax or twisted-pair cable. *Coax* is an

RG-62/U type cable, terminated with 93-ohm terminators. *Twisted pair* uses stranded 24- or 26-gauge wire or solid core 22-, 24-, or 26-gauge type cable, terminated with 100-ohm terminators. Many ARCnet networks use a mix of both coax and UTP cabling. UTP cable is simple to install and provides a reliable connection to the clients, whereas coax provides a means to span longer distances.

ARCnet can run off a linear bus topology using coax or twisted pair. The most popular installations of ARCnet run off two types of hubs:

- **Active hubs.** Contain active electronic signals that amplify signals and split them to multiple ports. The number of ports on an active hub varies with the manufacturer, but eight is typical. A port on an active hub can be connected to a port on another active device (such as another active hub or an NIC) or to a passive hub.

- **Passive hubs.** Cannot amplify signals. Each hub has four connectors. Because of the characteristics of passive hubs, unused ports must be equipped with a *terminator*, a connector that contains a resistor that matches the ARCnet cabling characteristics. A port on a passive hub can connect only to an active device (an active hub or an NIC). Passive hubs can never be connected to passive hubs.

One of the greatest flexibilities of ARCnet is that you can integrate connections from active hubs to a linear bus connection as long as you terminate at the last connection point.

A maximum time limit of 31 microseconds is allotted for an ARCnet signal, also called a *timeout* setting. Signals on an ARCnet can travel up to 20,000 feet during the 31-microsecond default timeout period. You sometimes can extend the range of an ARCnet by increasing the timeout value. However, 20,000 feet is the distance at which ARCnet signals begin to seriously degrade. Extending the network beyond that distancc can rcsult in unreliable or failed communication. Therefore, you should increase the timeout parameter and cabling distance recommendations only with great caution.

The maximum cable distances between individual components in an ARCnet network are dependent on how the components are connected (see table 19.1).

Table 19.1

Maximum ARCnet Cable Distances

Maximum Distance	From	To
2,000 feet	Network node	Active hub
2,000 feet	Active hub	Active hub
100 feet	Active hub	Passive hub
Not supported	Passive hub	Passive hub
100 feet	Network node	Passive hub
2,000 feet	Network node	Network node
20,000 feet	Farthest node	Farthest node

In cabling ARCnet networks with coax cable, you must follow several rules:

- Never connect a passive hub to another passive hub directly.
- Passive hubs should never be used to connect two active hubs.
- Passive hubs are only used to connect an active hub and a node.
- Unused connectors on active hubs don't need to be terminated.
- Unused connectors on passive hubs must be terminated using a 93-ohm terminator.

Figure 19.2 shows an ARCnet configuration using active and passive hubs. Active hubs are required to extend the network for long distances and to configure networks that have more than four nodes. Passive hubs are used as an economical means of splitting a port on an active hub to support three devices.

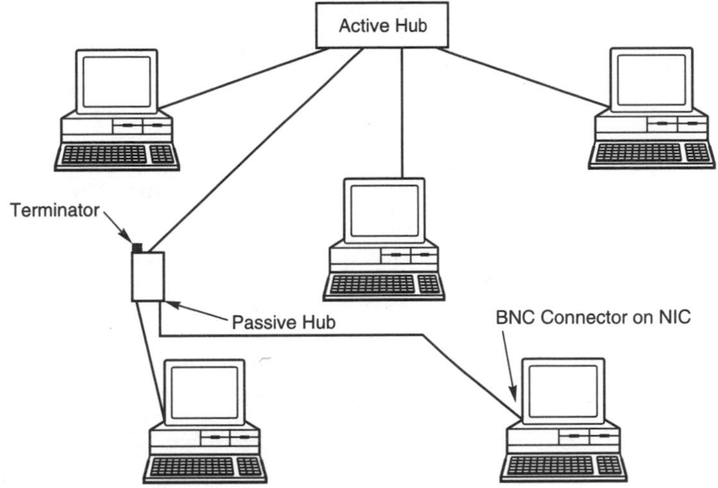

Figure 19.2

An example of an ARCnet topology using active and passive hubs and coax cable.

ARCnet Troubleshooting

Common sources of problems on ARCnet networks are as follows:

- No more than one node can have a given node address on the same network. If two or more nodes share an address, one of the two clients will lose its network connection or be unable to find a network.
- Missing terminators might not present visible problems on a small network. Missing terminators cause data retransmits on smaller systems, eventually appearing as transmit timeout errors or network errors.
- Using a terminator with an incorrect ohm rating. Coax uses 93 ohm; twisted pair uses 100 ohm. A terminator's ohm value depends on the impedance of the cable. The cable's impedance and the terminator's value should always match.
- The ARCnet bus using NICs that don't use the same impedance level. Signals become attenuated or reflected, causing interference with other signals on the wire.
- Failed NICs.
- Failed active hubs (or a port on that hub).

- Cable lengths that exceed specifications (refer to table 19.1). Twisted pair, cabled in a bus rather than a star, cannot have more than ten NICs per segment. This number varies with different manufacturers. ARCnet UTP installed in a bus configuration is generally used only in very small networks of six nodes or less. This configuration presents the major drawback of halting the network if a single cable is disconnected. In an ARCnet bus configuration, the network must be brought down to make any changes to the ARCnet cards.

- Coax connectors built or crimped incorrectly. Twist-on connectors are responsible for more intermittent errors on a network than most other failures because of their design.

Twist-on coax connectors became popular in the IBM 3XXX systems. These systems used RG-62 coax cable and operated at 1.5-Mbps throughput. The twist-on connectors aren't recommended for use on any modern LAN cable system because of the higher data rates employed.

Keep the following limitations in mind as you troubleshoot your ARCnet network:

- The maximum time it takes for the ARCnet signal to travel the length of the network is 31 microseconds.

- The maximum distance an ARCnet signal can travel between the two nodes farthest away from each other is 20,000 feet.

- The absolute maximum number of ARCnet nodes that can occupy a given network segment is 255. An ARCnet segment consists of all cabling and nodes that share a given network address.

Understanding Ethernet Specifications

Ethernet was originally developed by the Xerox Corporation, Digital Corporation, and the Intel Corporation in the early 1970s. Ethernet is also known as a *spanning tree topology* because the networks expand by branching in tree structures that don't allow redundant paths between nodes. Ethernet uses the *Carrier Sense Multiple Access/Collision Detection* (CSMA/CD) media contention access method and supports a maximum throughput of 10 Mbps. The Ethernet and 802.3 protocols are described in this chapter in the section "Ethernet Frame Types."

The origins of Ethernet are commemorated in the initials DIX, a 15-pin connector used to interface Ethernet components. The acronym DIX derives from the combination of leading letters of the founding Ethernet vendors: Digital, Intel, and Xerox.

The term *Ethernet* commonly refers to original Ethernet (which has been updated to Ethernet II) as well as the IEEE 802.3 standards. However, Ethernet and the 802.3 standards differ in ways significant enough to make standards incompatible in terms of packet formats. At the physical layer, Ethernet and 802.3 are generally compatible in terms of cables, connectors, and electronic devices.

Ethernet generally is used on light-to-medium traffic networks and performs best when a network's data traffic transmits in short bursts. Ethernet is the most commonly used network standard. It has become especially popular in many university and government installations.

Ethernet Board Settings

Most older versions of Ethernet NICs are configured using jumpers to set addresses and interrupts. Current models of NICs can be configured using a diagnostic program that enables changing of interrupt and memory address settings stored in a special memory chip on the NIC.

Figure 19.3 illustrates an example of an Ethernet NIC.

Figure 19.3

Features of an Ethernet NIC.

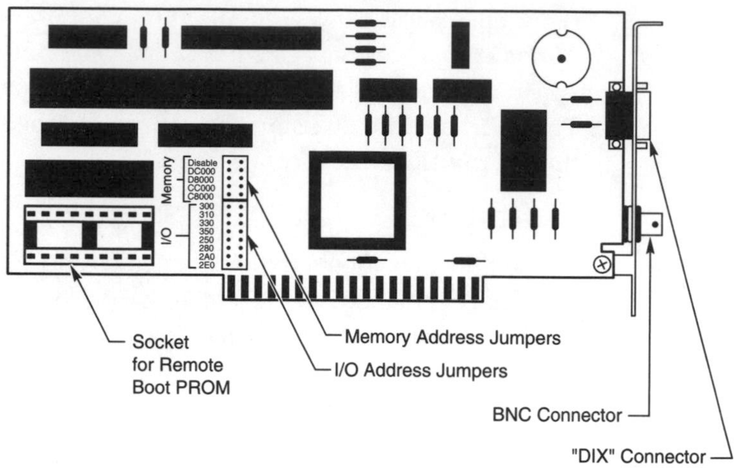

The following list mentions some of the features of the cards shown in figure 19.3:

- Shared memory selection; most Ethernet cards don't require the use of shared memory
- I/O address
- Interrupt
- Connectors
- Active connector selection jumpers
- Socket for a remote boot PROM

Ethernet cards can have one, two, or possibly all three of the following connectors:

- BNC connectors that support coax cabling
- RJ-45 connectors that support 10BASE-T (UTP) cabling
- DIX connectors used to connect to external transceivers

With some cards, DIP switches or blocks of jumpers are used to select the active connector. In many cases, however, the active connector can be selected with configuration software.

A limitation of 1,024 nodes (physical addresses) per network address exists on an Ethernet network. Addresses are assigned by IEEE to the vendor for the first three bytes of a six-byte address. The vendor is responsible for assigning the rest of the address and ensuring unique IDs.

As with the Token Ring cards, the card's manufacturer "burns" a unique node address into ROM on each NIC. Unless you override the burned-in address, address conflicts cannot occur on an Ethernet. Vendors sometimes label their cards with the node address. If the address is not visible, use the diagnostic disk supplied by the vendor.

Ethernet Cabling

A variety of cables can be used to implement Ethernet networks. Ethernet networks traditionally have been cabled with coaxial cables of several different types. Fiber-optic cables now frequently are employed to extend the geographic range of Ethernet networks.

The contemporary interest in using twisted-pair wiring has resulted in a scheme for cabling using unshielded twisted-pair: the 10BASE-T cabling standard, which uses UTP in a star topology, discussed at length later in this chapter.

Ethernet remains closely associated with coaxial cable. Two types of coaxial cable still used in small and large environments are *Thinnet* (10BASE2, also known as Cheapernet) and *Thicknet* (10BASE5). The Ethernet networks have different limitations, based on Thinnet and Thicknet cable specifications. The best way to remember the requirements is to use the 5-4-3 rule of thumb for each cable type.

The 5-4-3 rule states that the following can appear between any two nodes in the Ethernet network:

- Up to five segments in a series
- Up to four concentrators or repeaters
- Three segments of (coax only) cable that contain nodes

10BASE2

The 10BASE2 cabling topology (Thinnet), generally uses the on-board transceiver of the network interface card to translate the signals to and from the rest of the network. Thinnet cabling can use RG-58A/U or RG-58C/U coaxial type cable, 50 ohm terminators, and T-connectors that directly attach to the BNC connector on the NIC. A grounded terminator must be used on one end of the network segment.

A *transceiver* is a device that takes the digital signal from the node and translates it to communicate on a baseband cabling system. NICs that support Thinnet or 10BASE-T cable generally have built-in transceivers. External transceivers are used for Thick Ethernet although they may be used for Thinnet and UTP as well.

Use RG-58A/U cable for Ethernet topology, not RG-58U, which is for use with cable TV setups.

Advantages of 10BASE2

The main advantage of using 10BASE2 in your network is cost. When any given cable segment on the network doesn't have to be run further than 185 meters, 10BASE2 often is the cheapest network cabling option.

10BASE2 also is relatively simple to connect. Each network node connects directly to the network cable using a T-connector attached to the NIC.

Troubleshooting 10BASE2

The first step in troubleshooting a 10BASE2 network is to be sure you meet the rules for using 10BASE2. Several additional rules must be adhered to in 10BASE2 Ethernet environments, including the following:

- The minimum cable distance between clients must be 1.5 feet, or 0.5 meters.
- Pig tails, also known as drop cables, from T-connectors shouldn't be used to connect to the BNC connector on the NIC. The T-connector must be connected directly to the NIC.
- You may not exceed the maximum network segment limitation of 607 feet, or 185 meters.
- The entire network cabling scheme cannot exceed 3,035 feet, or 925 meters.
- The maximum number of nodes per network segment is 30 (this includes clients and repeaters).
- A 50-ohm terminator must be used on each end of the bus with only one of the terminators having either a grounding strap or a grounding wire that attaches it to the screw holding an electrical outlet cover in place.
- You may not have more than five segments on a network. These segments may be connected with a maximum of four repeaters, and only three of the five segments may have network nodes.

Additional troubleshooting tips are presented in the section "Ethernet Troubleshooting" later in this chapter.

The IEEE 802.3 standard for Thinnet is 10BASE2. This standard describes a 10-Mbps baseband network with a maximum segment length of approximately 200 meters (the actual limit, as stated previously, is 185 meters). Figure 19.4 shows two segments using 10BASE2 cabling.

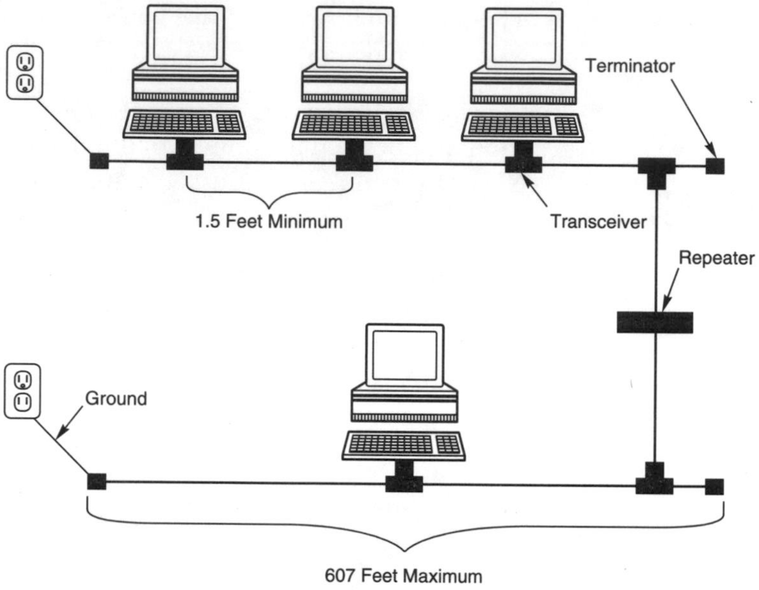

Figure 19.4

Two segments using 10BASE2 cabling.

10BASE5

The 10BASE5 cabling topology (Thicknet) uses an external transceiver to attach to the network interface card (see fig. 19.5). The NIC attaches to the external transceiver by an Attachment Universal Interface (AUI) cable to the DIX connector on the back of the card. The external transceiver clamps to the Thicknet cable. As with Thinnet, each network segment must be terminated at both ends, with one end using a grounded terminator. The components of a Thicknet network are shown in figure 19.6.

RG-11 is a 75-ohm cable. 10BASE5 requires 50 ohms.

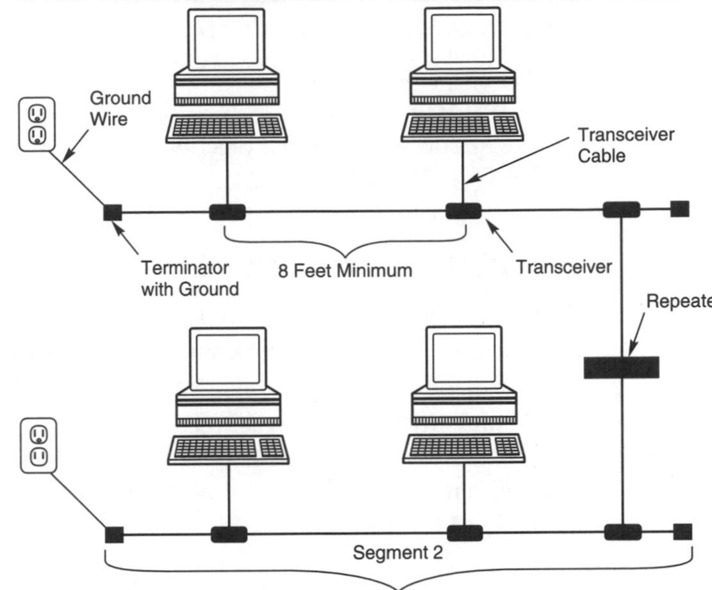

Figure 19.5

Two segments using 10BASE5 cabling.

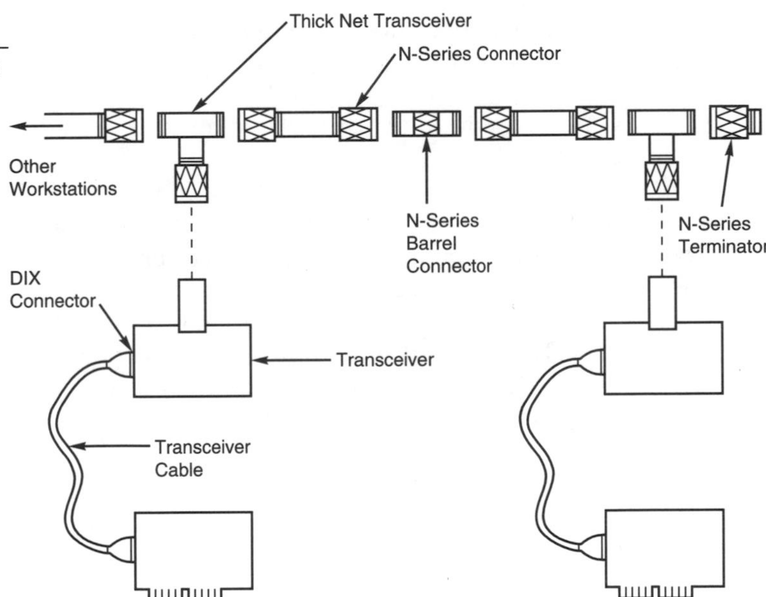

Figure 19.6

Components of a Thick Ethernet.

Advantages of 10BASE5

The primary advantage of 10BASE5 is its capability to exceed the cable restrictions that apply to 10BASE2. It does pose restrictions of its own, however, to be considered when installing or troubleshooting a 10BASE5 network.

Troubleshooting a 10BASE5 Network

As with 10BASE2networks, the first consideration when troubleshooting a 10BASE5 network should be the established cabling rules and guidelines. Several additional guidelines, along with the 5-4-3 rule, must be followed in Thick Ethernet networks:

- The minimum cable distance between transceivers is 8 feet, or 2.5 meters.
- You may not go beyond the maximum network segment length of 1,640 feet, or 500 meters.
- The entire network cabling scheme cannot exceed 8,200 feet, or 2,500 meters.
- One end of the terminated network segment must be grounded.
- Drop cables can be as short as required, but cannot be longer than 50 meters from transceiver to NIC.
- Cable segments that are cut and connected using a "Vampire Tap" should come from the same cable spool to ensure that each connected piece carries the identical electrical cabling to the other.
- The maximum number of nodes per network segment is 100. (This includes all repeaters.)

Additional troubleshooting tips are presented in the section "Ethernet Troubleshooting" later in this chapter.

The IEEE 802.3 standard that describes Thicknet is 10BASE5, which describes a 10-Mbps baseband network that can have segments up to 500 meters long. Figure 19.7 shows two segments using Thicknet and the appropriate hardware.

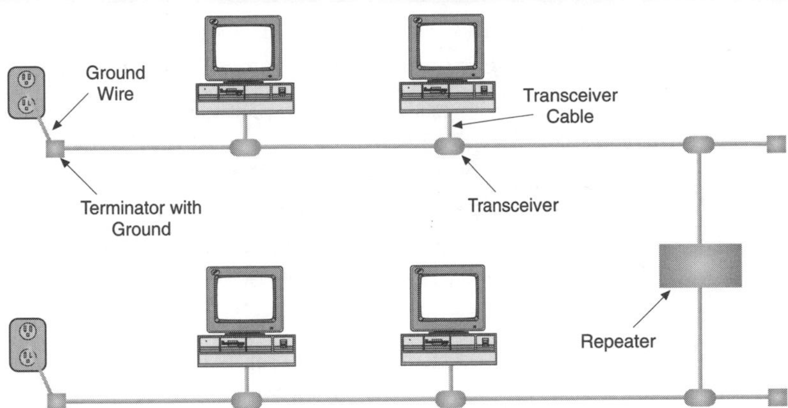

Figure 19.7

Example of Thicknet Ethernet cabling.

Thinnet and Thicknet cable can be combined to extend the distance of an Ethernet network topology. The following formula can be used to define the maximum amount of Thinnet cable that can be used in one network segment combination:

Maximum length of Thinnet that can be used = 1,640 feet	(Length of new network segment to be added)

A linear bus topology is more economical than wire because it isn't necessary to have a separate cable run for each client. On the other hand, some local problems on a linear bus can bring down the entire network.

If a break is in the cable or a streaming NIC is in the channel, the entire network can go down. *Streaming* is more frequently referred to as a *broadcast storm*, and occurs when a network card fails and the transmitter floods the cable with traffic, just like a faucet stuck open. At this point, the network becomes unusable.

10BASE-T

The trend in wiring Ethernet networks is to use *unshielded twisted-pair* (UTP) cable. UTP or 10BASE-T cable is one of the three most popular implementations for Ethernet. It is based on the IEEE 802.3 standard.

10BASE-T cabling is wired in a star topology. It functions logically, like a linear bus. The cable uses RJ-45 connectors and the network interface card can have RJ-45 jacks built into the back of the cards. External transceivers attached to a DIX connector found in combination with RJ-45 or BNC connectors on the NIC can be used to connect standard Ethernet cards into a twisted-pair topology. Figure 19.8 shows Ethernet cabling using twisted-pair cabling and a hub, also called a *concentrator.*

Figure 19.8

Example of twisted-pair Ethernet cabling.

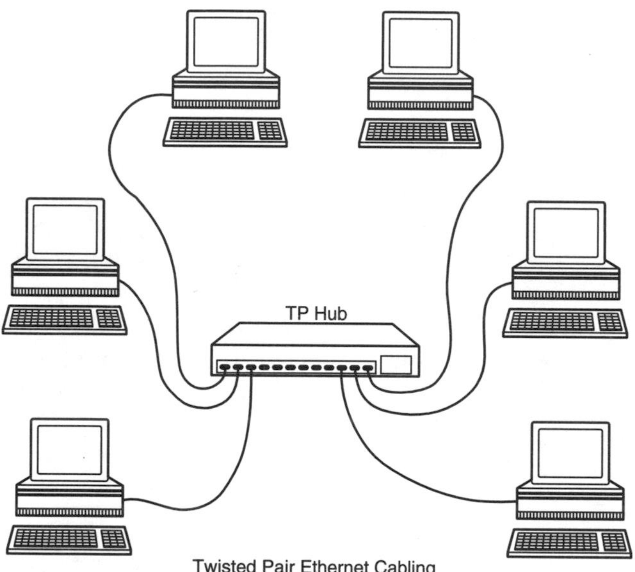

Advantages of 10BASE-T

The star wiring of 10BASE-T provides several advantages, particularly in larger networks. First, the network is more reliable and easier to manage because 10BASE-T networks use a *concentrator* (a centralized wiring hub). These hubs are "intelligent," in that they can route network traffic around a bad cable segment and can detect defective cable segments. This makes locating and repairing bad cable segments easier.

10BASE-T enables you to design and build your LAN one segment at a time, growing as your network needs to grow. This makes 10BASE-T more flexible than other LAN cabling options.

10BASE-T also is relatively inexpensive to use compared to other cabling options. In some cases in which a data-grade phone system already has been used in an existing building, this cabling can be used for the LAN.

Networks with star wiring topologies can be significantly easier to troubleshoot and repair than bus wired networks. With a star network, a problem node can be isolated from the rest of the network simply by disconnecting the cable and directly connecting it to the cable hub. If the hub is considered intelligent, management software developed for that hub type, as well as the hub itself, can disconnect the suspect port.

Troubleshooting 10BASE-T

The first step in troubleshooting a 10BASE-T network is to ensure that your network meets the rules for using 10BASE-T. The rules for a 10BASE-T network are as follows:

- The maximum number of network segments is 1,024.
- The cabling used should be 22, 24, or 26 American Wire Gauge (AWG), and be rated for an impedance of 85 to 115 ohms at 10 MHz.

Unshielded twisted-pair uses a terminator resistance level of 100–200 ohms; shielded twisted-pair uses 150 ohms.

- The maximum number of nodes is 512, and they may be connected on any three segments, with five being the maximum number of available line segments.
- The maximum unshielded cable segment length is 328 feet, or 100 meters.

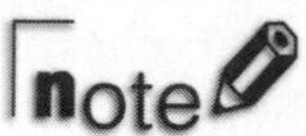

You should be able to translate cable segment lengths from feet to meters, or from meters to feet. A meter is equivalent to 39.37 inches.

Additional troubleshooting tips are furnished in the section "Ethernet Troubleshooting" later in this chapter.

10BASE-T requires that the UTP cable system be compliant with the Level IV standard. Level IV is cable-certified to operate at 10-Mbps throughput.

Ethernet Frame Types

Before information can be transmitted successfully across an Ethernet network, the sending and receiving network nodes must agree in advance on the structure of the information being transmitted. The sending node must organize the information in an orderly and predictable manner so that the receiving node can find and interpret the transmitted information. This orderly arrangement of information traveling across an Ethernet network is known as an *Ethernet frame.* Different Ethernet frame types describe different standards that specify the protocol structure (configuration of the media).

Four Ethernet frame types are available. The same Ethernet frame type must be loaded at both the server and accessing clients before proper communication can take place. The four available frame types are ETHERNET 802.3 (also known as raw ETHERNET), ETHERNET 802.2, ETHERNET SNAP, and ETHERNET II.

Raw ETHERNET (802.3) was developed before the IEEE 802.3 standard was completed and released. ETHERNET 802.3, therefore, isn't in complete compliance with the IEEE standard. ETHERNET 802.3 is used only on IPX/SPX Novell networks. ETHERNET 802.3 doesn't contain a field to specify which protocols might be contained within the packet. The lack of this field is one feature of ETHERNET 802.3 that makes it almost exclusively unique to Novell's NetWare 2.2 and NetWare 3.*x* operating systems.

Common features of the ETHERNET 802.3 standard include the following:

- A frame size between 64 and 1,518 bytes
- A preamble in the first line of the header (it contains alternating 1s and 0s to synchronize the communicating stations)
- A one-byte Start Frame Delimiter (SFD) field that follows the preamble and designates the beginning of the frame
- A six-byte field that specifies the address of the station to which the packet is being sent
- An originating address indicating the client, server, or router from which the packet was last sent
- A two-byte field that specifies the length of the data portion of the packet, and that must not have a length greater than 1,500 bytes
- A data field that must be no shorter than 46 bytes and no longer than 1,500 bytes
- A four-byte Cyclical Redundancy Check (CRC) or Frame Check Sequence that helps to ensure that the transmitted data is valid

ETHERNET 802.2 complies fully with the IEEE 802.3 standard. ETHERNET 802.2 is the default frame type used in NetWare 3.12 and NetWare 4.*x* networks. Common features of the ETHERNET 802.2 standard include the following:

- All of the same fields as the 802.3 specification
- Three additional Logical Link Control (LLC) fields, one byte long, that act much like an 802.3 header
- A frame size between 64 and 1,518 bytes

ETHERNET SNAP (SubNetwork Address Protocol) complies fully with ETHERNET 802.2 and actually is considered an enhancement to the 802.2 specification. Common features of the ETHERNET SNAP standard include the following:

- Two of the LLC fields, which contain fixed data indicating a SNAP packet
- A type field as the third of the LLC fields, which enables the packet to carry other high-level protocols within the frame structure, thus ensuring compatibility and making it possible for network operating systems to carry protocols over other types of media, such as Token Ring

ETHERNET II frame types support TCP/IP for NetWare 3.11. Common features of the ETHERNET II frame type include the following:

- A packet type field located immediately after the source address field, which is the location of the packet length field in other ETHERNET frame types
- A combined preamble and Start Frame Delimiter field that are referred to jointly as the *preamble*

Although four ETHERNET frame types are available, load only the frame type that you need to use on your network server. If it is necessary to support multiple upper-layer protocols, you can load more than one frame type on a server.

Each LAN NIC in the server must have at least one protocol bound to it. To bind a protocol to a NIC, first LOAD the NIC drivers, then bind the protocol to the NIC as in the following:

```
LOAD NE2000 port=320 int=5 frame=ETHERNET--802.3     NAME=ENE5
BIND IPX TO ENE5 NET=BAC1234
```

Ethernet Troubleshooting

Trend measurement and analysis can be applied to all network types. The use of a sophisticated protocol analyzer, such as LANalyzer for Windows and simpler tools, along with your own experience and knowledge, are two other effective troubleshooting techniques for Ethernet networks. This section covers the latter option.

When troubleshooting an Ethernet network, begin with the more obvious physical problems. For example, check to make certain that all connectors are tight and properly connected. Make certain that ground wires and terminators are used when required. Also, be certain that manufacturer's specifications are met, and that cable lengths, maximum number of nodes, and so on, are correct.

Consider the following when troubleshooting Ethernet networks:

- ▶ With 10BASE-T, make sure the cable used has the correct number of twists to meet the data grade specifications.
- ▶ Check for electrical interference. Electrical interference can be caused by tying the network cable together with monitor and power cords. Outside, fluorescent lights, electric motors, and other electrical devices also can cause interference.
- ▶ Make sure that connectors are pinned properly and crimped tightly.
- ▶ Check the cable lengths to make sure that distance specifications are not exceeded.
- ▶ If excess shielding on coax cable is exposed, make sure it isn't grounding out the connector.
- ▶ Make sure that coax cables are not coiled tightly together.
- ▶ Check the grade of the cable being used. For 10BASE2, RG-58/U is required. All 10BASE5 cable must meet Ethernet specifications.
- ▶ If using a linear bus setup, make sure the topology rules are followcd.
- ▶ Check for missing terminator or terminators with improper impedance ratings.

- Check for malfunctioning hardware, such as a bad NIC, transceiver, concentrator, T-connector, or terminator. Check to make certain that connectors have not been mixed up, such as ARCnet connectors being used on an Ethernet network.
- Test the continuity of the cable, using various physical testing devices, such as an Optical Time Domain Reflectometer, or software, such as Novell's COMCHECK utility.
- If the `Fileserver not found` error message appears, check for a mismatch in the Ethernet frame type between the server and the client.
- Verify that the LAN card is working properly. Clean the connector fingers (don't use an eraser because it leaves grit on the card); pull the card and replace it with one that you know is in working order; or run the NIC's diagnostics software.
- If NIC resource conflicts seem to be a potential cause of network problems, remove all cards except the file server NICs, then replace them one at a time until you find the conflicting card. Then correct the NIC settings and continue checking NICs one at a time. If you install new NICs, avoid using the common COM port interrupts of 3 and 4 to prevent potential Ethernet card conflicts.
- Make sure all the component cables in a segment are connected. A user who moves his client and removes the T-connector incorrectly can cause a broken segment.

Understanding Token Ring Specifications

Token Ring uses a token-passing architecture that adheres to the IEEE 802.5 standard. The topology is physically a star, but logically uses a ring to pass the token from station to station. Each node must be attached to a concentrator called a *multistation access unit* (MSAU or MAU).

Token Ring network interface cards can run at 4 Mbps or 16 Mbps. Four-Mbps cards can run only at that data rate. However, 16-Mbps cards can be configured to run at 4 or 16 Mbps. All cards on a given network ring must be running at the same rate.

As shown in figure 19.9, each node acts as a repeater that receives token and data frames from its nearest active upstream neighbor (NAUN). After the node processes a frame, the frame transmits downstream to the next attached node. Each token makes at least one trip around the entire ring. It then returns to the originating node. Workstations that indicate problems send a "beacon" to identify an address of the potential failure.

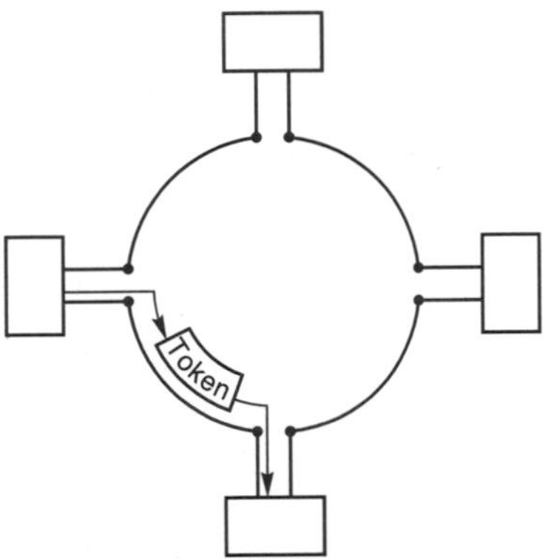

Figure 19.9

Operation of a Token Ring.

> To find out if any beacon messages have been sent on your Token Ring network, review your System Error Log, found in SYSCON by using Supervisor Options.

Token Ring Board Settings

As with the Ethernet cards, the node address on each NIC is burned in at the manufacturer and is unique to each card. The node address in some cases can be overridden by vendor-specified software instructions. (Check with the vendor of the component.) A maximum of two Token Ring cards can be installed in any node, with each card being defined as the primary or alternate Token Ring card in the machine. A typical Token Ring card is shown in figure 19.10.

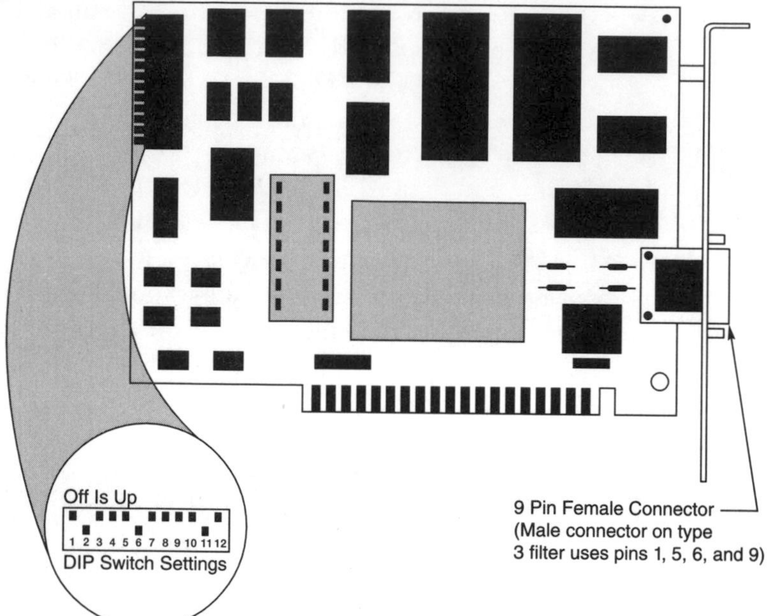

Figure 19.10

Features of a Token Ring NIC.

The following are features of a Token Ring NIC:

- DIP switches (see table 19.2)
- Nine-pin female connector
- Remote boot PROM socket

Table 19.2

IBM 16/4 Token-Ring Switch Settings

Switch Blk (Off is Up, On is Down)	1	2	3	4	5	6	7	8	9	10	11	12
ADDRESS												
CC000	Off	On	On	Off	Off	On						
DC000	Off	On	Off	Off	Off	On						
INTERRUPT												
2							Off	Off				
3							On	Off				

Switch Blk (Off is Up, On is Down)	1	2	3	4	5	6	7	8	9	10	11	12
6							Off	On				
7							Off	Off				
PRIMARY										Off		
ALTERNATE									On			
SHARED RAM												
8 KB										On	On	
16 KB										Off	On	
32 KB										On	Off	
64 KB										Off	Off	
DATA RATE												
16 Mbps												Off
4 Mbps											On	

When you load two Token Ring NICs in a NetWare file server, make sure that you configure the primary card at port address A20. The alternate card must be set at A24. For NetWare 3.1*x* or 4.*x*, in the AUTOEXEC.NCF file or at the file server console, use the following example commands:

```
LOAD TOKEN PORT=A20 INT=2 MEM=CC000 NAME=CARD1

LOAD TOKEN PORT=A24 INT=3 MEM=DC000 NAME=CARD2
```

The interrupt and base memory address on each Token Ring NIC must be set to avoid conflicts with all other components. Table 19.2 defines the proper DIP switch settings for an IBM 16/4 Token Ring card.

Each Token Ring card comes with a diagnostic disk that provides testing for the adapter. Refer to the appropriate documentation for your card for more detailed instructions.

Token Ring Cabling

Traditional Token Ring networks used shielded twisted-pair cable. The following are standard IBM cable types for Token-Ring:

- **Type 1.** A braided shield surrounds two twisted pairs of solid copper wire. Type 1 is used to connect terminals and distribution panels, or to connect between different wiring closets that are located in the same building. Type 1 uses two STPs of solid-core 22 AWG wire for long, high data-grade transmissions within the building's walls.
- **Type 2.** Type 2 uses a total of six twisted pairs: two are STPs (for networking), four are UTPs (for telephone systems). Additionally, this cable type incorporates two unshielded twisted-pairs that can be used for voice circuits. This cable is used for the same purposes as Type 1, but enables both voice and data cables to be included in a single cable run.
- **Type 3.** Type 3 has unshielded twisted-pair copper with a minimum of two twists per inch, used as an alternative to Type 1 and Type 2 cable because of its reduced cost. It has four UTPs of 24 AWG solid-core wire for networks or telephone systems. Type 3 cannot be used for 16-Mbps Token-Ring networks. It is used primarily for long, low data-grade transmissions within walls. Signals don't travel as fast as with Type 1 cable because Type 3 doesn't have the shielding Type 1 uses.
- **Type 5.** With Type 5, fiber-optic cable is used only on the main ring. Type 5 can use two 100-um or 140-um optical fibers in one fiber jacket.
- **Type 6.** A braided shield surrounds two twisted pairs of stranded copper wire. It is made up of two 26 AWG stranded-core STPs. This cable supports shorter cable runs than Type 1, but is more flexible because of the stranded conductors. Type 6 is the IBM standard for patch cables and extension cables, used also in wiring closets.

- **Type 8.** Type 8 uses a single 26 AWG stranded-core STP and is especially designed for use under carpet.
- **Type 9.** Type 9 is the same as Type 6 cable except that it is designed to be fire-resistant for use in plenum installations. It uses two STPs of solid-core 26 AWG wire and is used for long runs within the walls of a building.

Token Ring cabling is used to connect clients to the MSAU, or to connect one MSAU to another. Cables that connect between MSAUs are called *patch cables.* Patch cables also might be made of IBM Type 6 cable.

Novell defines Token Ring cabling in terms of two types of systems:

- Small movable
- Large nonmovable

The *small movable system* supports up to 96 clients and file servers and 12 MSAUs. It uses Type 6 cable to attach clients and servers to IBM Model 8228 MSAUs. Type 6 cable is a shielded twisted-pair cable with stranded conductors. This cable is flexible, but has limited distance capabilities. The characteristics of this cable make it suitable for small networks and for patch cords.

The *large nonmovable system* supports up to 260 clients and file servers, with up to 33 MSAUs. This network configuration uses IBM Type 1 or Type 2 cable. These are shielded twisted-pair cables with solid-wire conductors suitable for carrying signals greater distances than are possible with Type 6. The large nonmovable system also involves other wiring needs, such as punch panels or distribution panels, equipment racks for MSAUs, and wiring closets to contain the previously listed components.

The MSAU is the central cabling component for IBM Token-Ring networks. The 8228 MSAU was the original wiring hub developed by IBM for Token-Ring networks. Figure 19.11 shows 8228

MSAUs. Each 8228 has 10 connectors, eight of which accept cables to clients or servers. The other connectors are labeled RI (ring in) and RO (ring out). The RI and RO connectors are used to connect multiple 8228s to form larger networks.

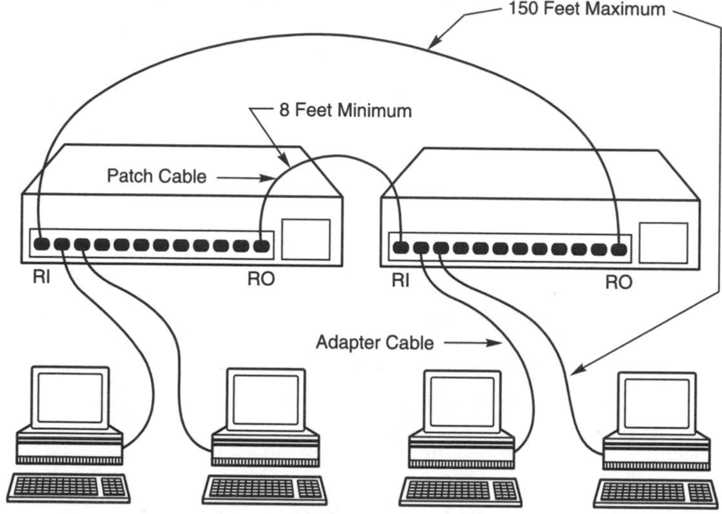

Figure 19.11

An example of Token-Ring cabling using MSAUs.

8228s are mechanical devices that consist of relays and connectors. Their purpose is to switch clients in and out of the network. Each port is controlled by a relay powered by a voltage sent to the MSAU from the client. When an 8228 is first set up, each of these relays must be initialized with a setup tool shipped with the unit. The setup tool is inserted into each port and held there until a light indicates that the port is properly initialized.

IBM Token-Ring networks use two types of connectors. NICs are equipped with a nine-pin D-connector. MSAUs, repeaters, and most other equipment use a special IBM data connector. The following two types of cables are employed:

- **Patch cables.** These cables have IBM data connectors at both ends, and they interconnect MSAUs, repeaters, and most other Token-Ring components.

- **Token-Ring adapter cables.** Adapter cables have an IBM data connector at one end and a nine-pin connector at the other and connect client and server NICs to other network components that use IBM data connectors.

Figure 19.11 shows an example of a network cabling several clients and MSAUs. The distances noted in the figure are based on the rules for the small movable cabling system.

When you connect a Token Ring network, make sure you do the following:

1. Initialize each port in the 8228 MSAU by using the setup tool shipped with the MSAU (wait for the click) before connecting a cable.
2. If using more than one MSAU, connect the RO port of each MSAU with the RI port of the next MSAU in the loop. This must physically complete a circle or ring.

A variety of rules must be observed when configuring Token Rings. The following rules apply to small, movable Token Ring networks:

- The minimum patch cable distance between two MSAUs is eight feet.
- The maximum patch cable distance between two MSAUs is 150 feet. Patch cables come in standard lengths of 8, 30, 75, and 150 feet for Type 6.
- The maximum patch cable distance connecting all MSAUs is 400 feet.
- The maximum adapter cable distance between an MSAU and a node is 150 feet.

A small movable IBM cable system consists of the following:

- Maximum of 96 nodes
- Maximum of 12 MSAUs
- Type 6 cable

A large nonmovable IBM cable system consists of the following:

- Maximum of 260 nodes
- Maximum of 33 MSAUs
- Type 1 or Type 2 cable

Token Ring networks also can be cabled using UTP cabling, which IBM calls Type 3 cable. The IEEE 802.5 standard describes 4-Mbps Token Ring using UTP cable. However, level 5 UTP is currently used for 16-Mbps Token Ring.

When using UTP wiring, a media filter must be installed between the NIC and the UTP cable. Some newer Token Ring NICs have built-in media filters and RJ-45 jacks ready to interface with UTP wiring.

Token Ring Troubleshooting

When troubleshooting a Token Ring network, as with troubleshooting other types of networks, begin with the more obvious physical problems, checking such things as connectors to see if they are tight and properly connected. You also should check to see that manufacturer's specifications are met, and that cable lengths, maximum number of nodes, and so on, are correct.

When troubleshooting Token Ring networks, you also should look for the following:

- **Any base I/O, DMA shared memory, or interrupt conflicts with other boards.**
- **The version of the client or server software driver.** Make sure that its revision level is compatible with your NIC (drivers are different for file servers and clients).
- **Proper connections of MSAUs, with ring out ports connecting to ring in ports throughout the ring.** In troubleshooting problems that you first isolate to a particular area

of the network, if you suspect the MSAU, isolate it by changing the ring in and ring out cables to bypass the MSAU. If the ring is now functional again, consider replacing the MSAU. You may also find that if your network has MSAUs from more than one manufacturer, they are not wholly compatible. Impedance and other electrical characteristics can show slight differences between manufacturers, causing intermittent network problems.

- **Other MSAU problems.** Some MSAUs other than the 8228 are active and require a power supply. These MSAUs fail if they have a blown fuse or a bad power source.
- **Correct attachments of patch cables and the adapter cable.** Remember, patch cables connect MSAUs, and the adapter cable connects the NIC to the MSAU. Patch cables, adapter cables, and MSAUs are common sources of problems. Isolating the problem is easier to do if you have a current log of your network's physical design. After you narrow down the problem, you can isolate potential problem areas on the network from the rest of the network and then use a cable tester to find the actual problem.
- **A failed NIC.** Try substituting another one known to work properly. NICs that have failure rates that exceed a preset tolerance level may actually remove themselves from the network.
- **A bad MSAU or MSAU port.** Ports may need to be reinitialized with the setup tool. Removing drop cables and reinitializing each MSAU port is a "quick fix" that is useful on relatively small Token Ring networks.
- **Incorrect card speeds.** A 16-Mbps card is inserted into a 4-Mbps ring or vice versa, for example. Neither situation is correct. The speed of the NIC is displayed when the Token Ring driver is loaded at the client.
- **The wrong type of cable for the speed of the network.**
- **Bent or broken pins on the adapter cable.**

- **Duplicate node addresses.** If you override the burned-in network addresses, you might unintentionally set duplicate node addresses.
- **The Type 3 media filter.** Check this if you connect to a 4-Mbps twisted-pair network.

One of the advantages of a Token Ring network is its built-in capability to monitor itself. This process provides electronic troubleshooting and, when possible, repair processes. When the Token Ring network can't make its own repairs, a process called *beaconing* helps. Beaconing narrows down the portion of the ring in which the problem is most likely to exist. This potential problem area is referred to as the *fault domain.*

The Beaconing Process

The design of the Token Ring network itself contributes greatly to the ability of the beaconing process to troubleshoot its own network. The design includes two types of network stations known as *Active Monitors* and *Standby Monitors.* Only one Active Monitor can exist on a network at a time. All other stations are Standby Monitors.

Generally, the first station that is powered-up and becomes part of the network is automatically the Active Monitor station. The responsibility of the Active Monitor station is to announce itself to the next active downstream station as the Active Monitor station, and request that station to announce itself to its next active downstream station. The Active Monitor station sends out this beacon announcement every seven seconds.

After each station announces itself to its next active downstream neighbor, the announcing station becomes the nearest active upstream neighbor (NAUN) to the downstream station. Each station on a Token Ring network has an upstream neighbor as well as a downstream neighbor.

After each station becomes aware of its NAUN, the beaconing process continues every seven seconds. If, for some reason, a station doesn't receive one of its expected seven-second beaconed announcements from its upstream neighbor, it attempts to notify the network of its lack of contact from the upstream neighbor. It sends a message out onto the network ring, which includes the following:

- The sending station's network address
- The receiving NAUN's network address
- The beacon type

The ring can determine which station might be having a problem from this information and then attempt to fix the problem without disrupting the entire network. This problem fix is known as *autoreconfiguration.* If autoreconfiguration proves unsuccessful, manual correction becomes necessary. Figure 19.12 shows a Token Ring network utilizing the beaconing process.

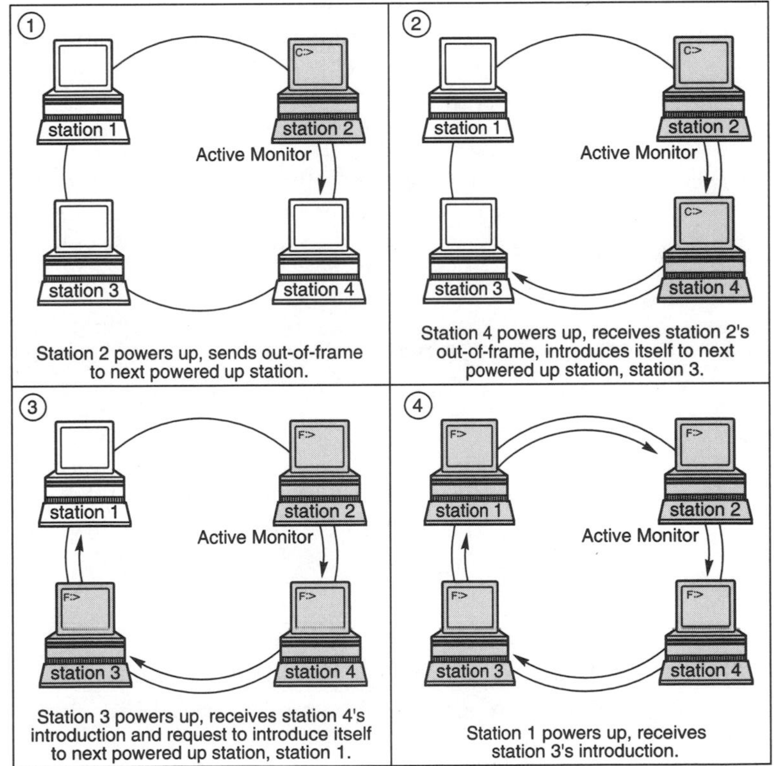

Figure 19.12

Token Ring beaconing.

Understanding FDDI

Fiber Distributed Data Interface is a LAN standard that, like Token Ring, follows the IEEE 802.5 standard for accessing the network. FDDI carries both LED and laser-generated LAN communications through fiber-optic cables.

Fiber-optic cable primarily consists of pure glass pulled into very thin wires or fibers. Many of these fibers are bundled together to form a core, which is surrounded by another layer of glass called *cladding*. The LED sends the signals through the core of this cable, and the cladding contains these signals to the core. The signal on each fiber can go in only one direction at a time. The bundle of fibers enables the LED to send multiples of signals at a time.

Unlike Token Ring and its related network interface cards that transfer data across the network at speeds of 4 or 16 Mbps, FDDI transfers information at a rate of 100 Mbps. In addition, FDDI is structured to take advantage of two rings rather than one. This Dual Counter Rotating Rings structure enables FDDI to transfer data across one ring while it performs backup and other services on the second ring.

In addition, FDDI uses multiple tokens and possesses the capability to bypass network stations designated as low priority, so it can provide faster service to high-priority network stations.

Like a Token Ring LAN, FDDI uses a token to transfer data frames around the network. After the data frame is processed by the correct network station, the token is passed on to the next attached network node.

The second ring in the FDDI network rotates in the opposite direction of the first ring. This counter-rotation enables the network to compensate for a break in the fiber. If one ring in the network becomes broken owing to a problem at one of the network stations, those stations located on either side of the break can isolate the break in the fiber by forming a single ring (wrapping) from their own ports, as shown in figure 19.13.

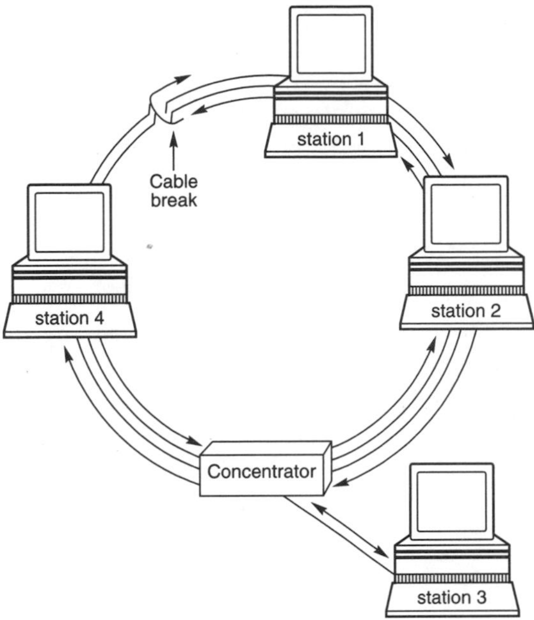

Figure 19.13

An isolated cable break in an FDDI network.

Each network station can be attached to either one ring or to both rings, depending on the class of the connected station. The two types of station classes are Class A and Class B.

Class A stations, also called *Single Attached Stations* (SAS), can be attached to only one ring at a time. Only Class B stations, or *Dual Attached Stations* (DAS), can be connected to both rings simultaneously. This designation of station classes helps to keep unstable network devices from breaking both network rings.

Another method of isolating faulty nodes in the network uses wiring concentrators. Wiring concentrators function in theory much like the Token Ring MSAU. They act as centralized cabling connection devices for network stations. Unlike MSAUs, however, wiring concentrators can communicate with stations and verify the integrity of the station-to-concentrator connection.

Advantages of Using FDDI

The capability to isolate a break in the cable and continue network communication makes FDDI an extremely reliable cabling option. FDDI offers several other advantages.

FDDI overcomes some of the performance problems experienced by traditional Token Ring networks by implementing a standard that provides fair and timely access to the network.

Increased reliability is another advantage of using FDDI. That reliability comes in several forms, including the following:

- **Information security.** Fiber-optic cable is difficult to wiretap.
- **Physical security.** Fiber-optic cable is more resistant to cable breakage than are other types of cabling.
- **Electrical security.** Fiber-optic cable isn't susceptible to electrical interference and doesn't conduct electricity.

FDDI also can transmit network packets over its cable for distances that are significantly longer than other types of cabling. On a fiber-optic cable with no cable bends or breaks that would otherwise reduce the integrity of the transmission, for example, information theoretically can travel hundreds of miles.

FDDI also has built-in management of three aspects of the network, including the following:

- **Ring Management (RMT).** Responsible for finding and resolving faults in the network ring.
- **Connection Management (CMT).** Responsible for controlling stations that insert themselves into the network or remove themselves from the network.
- **Station Management (SMT).** Makes it possible for special high-level programs to monitor the ring.

As noted earlier, FDDI networks are substantially faster than Token Ring networks, capable of communicating at a rate of 100 Mbps. They accomplish this speed not only owing to the type of cable (fiber optic) they use, but also because they use multiple tokens and can service only the high-priority network stations, bypassing the low-priority stations whenever necessary.

A fiber-optic cable also is significantly lighter in weight than, for example, twisted-pair cabling with an equivalent bandwidth.

Don't look directly at fiber-optic cable without eye protection. To check to see whether a fiber-optic port is transmitting, darken the room and place a piece of paper in front of the port. If it is transmitting, a light reflects onto the paper.

Disadvantages of Using FDDI

The two primary disadvantages of using FDDI in your network are one, because of the complexity and newness of FDDI technology, you need a great deal of expertise to install and subsequently maintain an FDDI network; and two, although the cost of the cable itself is comparable to that of UTP cabling, the concentrators and LAN adapters are relatively expensive. Therefore, the overall cost of an FDDI network for a LAN of any size can quickly become quite high.

FDDI Cabling

Various types and wavelengths of fiber-optic cables are available. A typical fiber-optic cable consists of a core made from silica, surrounded by a primary and secondary buffer, and then enclosed in a jacket. Kevlar can be added to provide strength.

The important thing to remember about choosing a fiber-optic cable is to select one based on its intended use, and to match the cable to its appropriate connectors. Figure 19.14 shows a typical duplex fiber-optic cable.

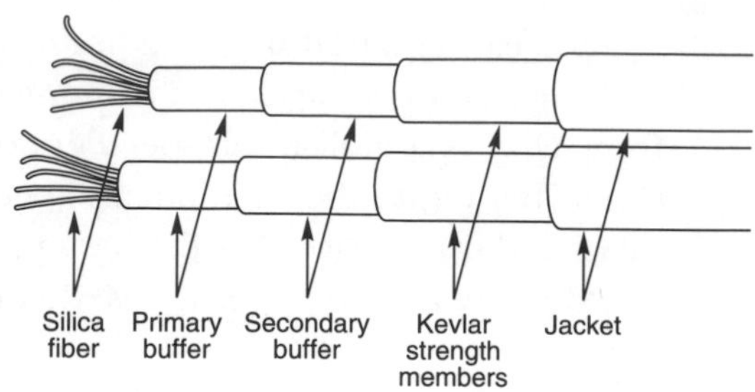

Figure 19.14

A fiber-optic duplex cable assembly.

FDDI Troubleshooting

As with troubleshooting all types of networks, begin by looking for the obvious problems, such as loose connectors, damaged cables, and so on. After ruling out these types of problems, consider other possible causes. Look first at those problems considered typical of FDDI networks:

- **Incorrect cable type for actual distance between nodes.** On an FDDI network where network information must travel thousands of feet, Multimode Fiber should be used. When distances between nodes begin to reach tens of thousands of feet, or exceed distances of two kilometers, Single-Mode Fiber is necessary.
- **Problems with communicating between network nodes.** Even small breaks in a fiber-optic cable can result in network communication problems. There are several ways to detect cable problems, except for one that requires special equipment. If a break in a segment of the cable is a complete break, you can detect the break using a flashlight. Otherwise, you can use an optical power meter and a source of light energy to test the cable. If either of these methods is insufficient, you can use the most expensive method, an Optical Time Domain Reflectometer (OTDR).
- **Dirt on connectors is another cause of communication problems between network nodes.** Data transmits through fiber-optic cables using light. You need, therefore, to keep connectors free from dust and dirt. You can clean connectors using any type of lint-free cloth dampened with alcohol. Don't use water or any type of cleaning fluid other than alcohol.

- **Communication problems also can be caused by bad connectors or by a segment of the cable that is open (incorrectly terminated).** A loss of optical power that exceeds 13.0 decibels is an indication that cable problems of this nature might exist. To correct these problems, replace faulty connectors and properly close any open cable segment.

- **A delay of up to four milliseconds in communication.** This isn't unusual for fiber-optic cable. If communication delays are a problem, consider using NetWare's Packet Burst Protocol to send multiple rather than single frames across the network, thus reducing transmission delay.

- **The network doesn't efficiently handle transmissions across cable that exceeds 50 meters, or which requires 10-Mbps or more throughput.** This problem might be directly related to the type of fiber-optic cable. If you are using plastic fiber-optic cable in your network, consider replacing all or at least some of this cable with glass cable. Speed can be affected by the type of fiber-optic cable used.

- **The path that network information must travel should be the most efficient.** If you use bridges rather than routers in your network, consider switching to network routers. NetWare network routers, or routers such as CI500 and Wellfleet certified by Novell, can choose the best path for any given packet. They are somewhat slower than bridges, however, because of the increased processing they perform. The design of FDDI translation bridges makes routers the preferred choice for FDDI networks running NetWare.

Which Architecture Should I Use?

As a network administrator or support engineer, you have to make some tough decisions on the best architecture to use for your network environment. Choosing the type of vehicle and size of engine you need to drive your loads on local streets, freeways, or highways might be a good analogy. You need to consider using Token Ring (4 Mbps or 16 Mbps) or Ethernet (10 Mbps). You also need to consider which type of cabling system you need for your network.

The factors involved in your choice include the following:

- Type of applications and their percentage of overall use
- Flexibility of setup
- Cost
- Knowledge level of your support or vendor source
- Availability of replacement or add-on components

No one architecture is better than another. Your choice is dependent on how the factors affect your network environment.

Choose the Ethernet topology for those types of networks with a light-to-medium workload. If you use standard applications, such as word processing, spreadsheets, gateway host sessions, electronic mail, and calendaring packages, Ethernet works efficiently.

Ethernet has a maximum throughput of 10 Mbps. (Standard loads usually are working around 8–9.1 Mbps.) The cost is nominal, and interchangeable components are readily available. Clients can attempt to transmit more quickly rather than waiting their turn, as is done with the Token Ring topology.

The disadvantage of Ethernet is that the size of the data frames in the packets might require more traffic to pass along the data files on the media. Also, the collision-oriented system can be degraded with the heavy use of database, imaging, multimedia, or CAD/CAM applications.

Token Ring topology is a choice for networks that tend toward heavy workloads. The size of the data frame in the packet is larger than in Ethernet. Token Ring can handle large file transfers, such as database, CAD/CAM, and multiple accesses to imaging files, more easily. Token Ring runs at 4 Mbps or 16 Mbps on many types of media. Some applications of 16-Mbps Token Ring speed aren't always as efficient as using the 4 Mbps or the Ethernet 10 Mbps.

Token Ring is more reliable because no collisions occur with the token passing scheme. The disadvantages of Token Ring are cost, station transmission capabilities, and the overhead for management of the token scheme. Also, the more clients you add to a ring, the more that performance can be degraded. Consider splitting the ring into smaller rings with fewer clients attached.

Use your best judgment on your network setup. Where your applications reside, the location of your workloads, and the availability of your network components determine whether you should use one topology or perhaps mix them.

Review Questions

The following questions will test your knowledge of the information in this chapter. For additional questions, see MCP Endeavor and the Microsoft/Roadmap Assessment Exam on the CD-ROM that accompanies this book.

1. Which statement about ARCnet is false?

   A. ARCnet can be cabled in star or bus.

   B. ARCnet uses RG-62/U for coax.

   C. ARCnet has the unique feature timeout setting of 31 microseconds.

   D. ARCnet can span a distance of 25,000 feet.

2. Which ARCnet combination isn't supported?

   A. Passive hub to passive hub

   B. Active hub to passive hub to active hub

   C. Active hub to passive hub

   D. Network node to passive hub

3. Which isn't a feature of an Ethernet board?

   A. Ethernet boards usually have DIX connectors.

   B. Ethernet boards can have thick (DIX), thin (BNC), or twisted-pair (RJ-45) connectors.

   C. Ethernet boards have internal transceivers for Thinnet.

   D. Ethernet boards have a timeout setting.

4. Which level cable is correct for 10BASE-T?

   A. Level I

   B. Level II

   C. Level IV

   D. Level VI

5. Which two of the following statements regarding FDDI are true?

   A. It follows the IEEE 802.5 standard.

   B. Like Token Ring, it uses only a single token.

   C. FDDI can transfer data at speeds of 100 Mbps.

   D. Stations must attach to the cable by a concentrator.

6. FDDI stands for ______.

   A. Fiber-based Data Distribution Interface

   B. Fiber Distributed Data Interface

   C. Fiber-optic Data Distributed Interface

   D. Fiber Data Distribution Interface

7. Which of the following is one advantage that FDDI has over Token Ring?

   A. Fiber-optic cable is difficult to wiretap.

   B. FDDI is capable of isolating cable breaks.

   C. FDDI provides fair and timely access to the network.

   D. FDDI has built-in ring management.

8. What is the main advantage of using 10BASE2 when network segments don't have to exceed 185 meters?

   A. It is relatively simple to connect.

   B. Drop cables can be used, making it easier to troubleshoot.

   C. Each node connects directly to the cable.

   D. It is the least expensive of the cabling options.

9. Which two of the Ethernet cabling options require that each end of the bus be terminated?

   A. 10BASE2

   B. 10BASE5

   C. 10BASE-T

   D. Thinnet

10. Which of the cabling options is considered the trend for wiring Ethernet networks?

    A. 10BASE2

    B. 10BASE5

    C. 10BASE-T

    D. Thicknet

11. Which of the following isn't an advantage of using 10BASE-T for cabling a network?

    A. It is easier and more reliable to manage.

    B. Centralized hubs make it easier to detect bad cable segments.

    C. Beaconing helps to isolate cable breaks.

    D. It is relatively inexpensive to use.

12. Which of the following Ethernet frame types is designated as raw Ethernet?

    A. ETHERNET_802.2

    B. ETHERNET_802.3

    C. ETHERNET_SNAP

    D. ETHERNET_II

Review Answers

1. D
2. A
3. D
4. C
5. A C
6. B
7. A
8. D
9. B A
10. C
11. C
12. B

Chapter 20

Network Connectivity

People sometimes think of a network as a single, local cabling system. Any device on the network can directly communicate with any other device on the same network. A network by this definition, however, doesn't have any connections to other, remote networks.

An *internetwork* consists of multiple independent networks that are connected and can share remote resources. It is said that internetworks consist of "logically separate but physically connected networks" that can be dissimilar in type. The device that connects the independent networks together must have a degree of "intelligence" because it must determine when packets will stay on the local network or when they will be forwarded to a remote network.

Connectivity devices perform the following functions:

- Connect media segments
- Utilize media capacity effectively
- Connect remote (logically separate) networks

The following devices are examined in this chapter devices:

- Network connectivity:
  - Network interface boards
  - Hubs
  - Repeaters

    - Bridges
    - Multiplexors
    - Modems
- Internetwork connectivity devices:
    - Routers
    - Brouters
    - CSU/DSUs
    - Gateways

Network Connectivity Devices

This section defines a variety of devices as "network connectivity devices." This definition focuses on the roles of these devices in local networks as opposed to internetworks.

Network Interface Boards

Each workstation must be equipped with hardware that enables the workstation to connect to the network. This book calls all such devices *network interface boards*, although they might not be boards at all:

- A *network interface card* (NIC) might be installed in one of the computer's expansion slots.
- The network interface circuitry might be built into the computer's main board. In this case, the connector is built into the computer's case.
- A transmission media adapter might be used.

Several types of transmission media adapters are in common use, including the following:

- Ethernet LANs use transceivers to connect DIX connectors on devices to network media. Transceivers are always used with thick coaxial cable and may be used with thin coax or UTP. NICs for thin and UTP Ethernet usually have the transceivers built in so that an external transceiver is not required.
- When UTP cable is used with Token Ring networks, a media filter might be required when operating at 16 Mbps. The media filter prevents noise from getting out onto the LAN. Many Token Ring NICs designed for 16-Mbps operation incorporate the media filter on the card.

Transceivers

Regardless of the form of the device, it includes a transceiver of some kind. A transceiver functions as both a *trans*mitter and a re*ceiver.*

The transmitter component translates the computer's internal signals to the signals required for the network. If the network uses UTP cable, the transceiver supplies the proper electrical signals to the proper type of connector. If the network uses fiber-optic cable, the transceiver translates the computer's electrical signals into the light signals required for the network.

The receiver component performs the opposite service when signals are received from the network, translating them back to a form that matches the computer's internal requirements.

Network Interface Cards (NIC)

Also called an NIC, a *network interface card* is a network board that you can install in a computer's expansion slot. NICs are the devices most commonly used to connect computers to networks.

NICs incorporate a transceiver, which can service several types of connectors. With the exception of Thick Ethernet, NICs are available to connect directly to all types of networks.

Ethernet NICs are equipped with one, two, or possibly all three of the following:

- RJ-45 connector for UTP Ethernet
- BNC connector for Thin Ethernet
- AUI connector for Thick Ethernet

Token Ring NICs are equipped with one or both of the following:

- DB-15 connector for STP
- RJ-45 connector for UTP

Transmission Media Adapters

Some vendors use the term *transmission media adapter* to describe a device that adapts one type of connector on the computer to a different type of connector that is required for the network. Several types of devices can be classified as transmission media adapters, including the following:

- **Transceivers (or MAUs).** Used to connect computers to thick coax Ethernet networks.
- **Media filters.** Adapt a DB-15 Token Ring connector to connect to a UTP network with an RJ-45 connector.
- **Parallel port adapters.** Enable laptop computers to network by communicating through their parallel ports.
- **SCSI port adapters.** Enable computers to connect to networks through a SCSI interface.

Hubs

Coaxial cable Ethernet is the only LAN standard that doesn't use hubs to bring wiring together in a central location, as shown in figure 20.1. Hubs also are called *wiring concentrators.* You encounter three types of hubs, as follows:

- Passive
- Active
- Intelligent

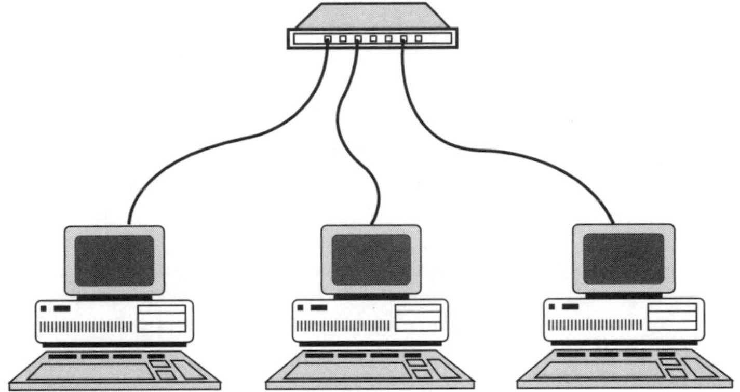

Figure 20.1

Network wiring with a hub.

Passive Hubs

This type of hub is called *passive* because it doesn't contain any electronic components and doesn't process the data signal in any way. The only purpose of a passive hub is to combine the signals from several network cable segments. All devices attached to a passive hub see all the packets that pass through the hub.

Because the hub doesn't clean up or amplify the signals (in fact, the hub absorbs a small part of the signal), the distance between a computer and the hub can be no more than half of the maximum permissible distance between two computers on the network. If the network design limits the distance between two computers to 200 meters, the maximum distance between a computer and the hub is 100 meters.

ARCnet networks commonly use passive hubs. Token Ring networks also can use passive hubs, although the industry trend is to utilize active hubs to obtain the advantages cited in the following section.

Active Hubs

Active hubs incorporate electronic components that can amplify and clean up the electronic signals that flow between devices on the network. Cleaning up the signals is called *signal regeneration.* There are two benefits of signal regeneration: the network is more robust and less sensitive to errors, and distances between devices can be increased. These advantages generally outweigh the fact that active hubs cost considerably more than passive hubs.

Later in the chapter, you learn about *repeaters,* devices that amplify and regenerate network signals. Because active hubs function in part as repeaters, they occasionally are called *multiport repeaters.*

Intelligent Hubs

Intelligent hubs are active hubs plus. Several functions can add intelligence to a hub, as follows:

- **Hub management.** Many hubs now support network management protocols that enable the hub to send packets to a central network console. They also enable the console to control the hub, ordering, for example, a hub to shut down a connection that is generating network errors.
- **Switching hubs.** The latest development in hubs is the *switching hub,* which includes circuitry that very quickly routes signals between ports on the hub. Instead of repeating a packet to all ports on the hub, a switching hub repeats it only to the port that connects to the destination computer for the packet. Many switching hubs have the capability of switching packets to the fastest of several alternative paths. Switching hubs are replacing bridges and routers on many networks.

Repeaters

As you learned in Chapter 15, "Transmission Media," all media attenuate the signals they carry. Each media type, therefore, has a maximum range that it can reliably carry data. Figure 20.2 shows the use of a repeater to connect two Ethernet cable segments. The result of adding the repeater is that the potential length of the overall network is doubled.

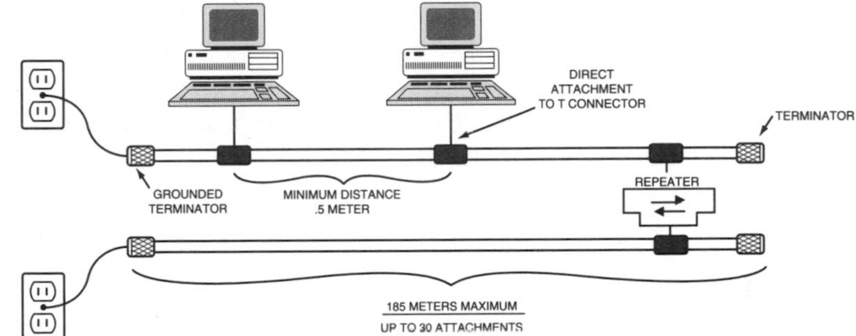

Figure 20.2

Using a repeater to extend an Ethernet LAN.

Some repeaters simply amplify signals. Although this increases the strength of the data signal, it also amplifies any noise on the network. Also, if the original signal has been distorted in any way, an amplifying repeater cannot clean up the distortion.

More advanced repeaters can extend the range of network media by amplifying *and* regenerating the signals. Signal regenerating repeaters, for example, identify the data by the signal they receive and use the data to regenerate the original signal, which amplifies the strength of the desired signal, reduces noise, and clears up any distortion. The output of a regenerating repeater duplicates the original data signal.

It would be nice if repeaters could be used to extend networks indefinitely, but all network designs limit the size of the network. The most important reason for this limit is signal propagation. Networks need to work with reasonable expectations about the maximum time a signal might be in transit. This is known as *propagation delay*—the time it takes for a signal to reach the furthest point on the network. If this maximum propagation delay interval expires and no signals are encountered, a network error condition is assumed. Given the maximum allowed propagation delay, calculating the maximum permissible cable length for the network is possible. Even though repeaters enable signals to travel farther, the maximum propagation delay still sets a limit to the maximum size of the network.

Bridges

Bridges, on the other hand, can extend the maximum size of a network. Although the bridged network in figure 20.3 looks much like the earlier example of a network with a repeater, the bridge is a much more flexible device.

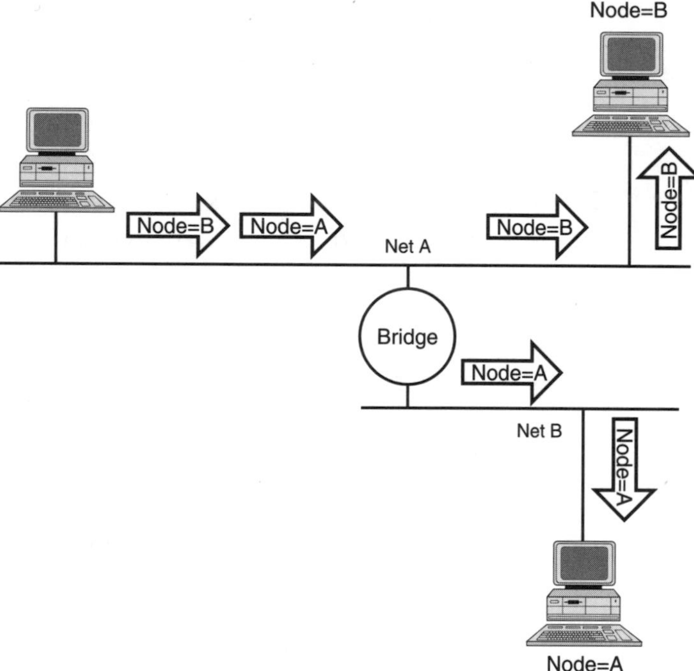

Figure 20.3

Extending a network with a bridge.

A repeater passes on all signals that it receives. A bridge, on the other hand, is more selective, and passes on only those signals targeted for a computer on the other side. A bridge can make this determination because each device on the network is identified by a unique address, and each packet that is transmitted bears the address of the device to which it should be delivered. The process works as follows:

1. The bridge receives every packet on LAN A and LAN B.
2. The bridge learns from the packets which device addresses are located on LAN A and which are on LAN B. A table is built with this information.
3. Packets on LAN A that are addressed to devices on LAN A are discarded. Packets on LAN B that are addressed to devices on LAN B are also discarded. These packets can be delivered without the help of the bridge.
4. Packets on LAN A addressed to devices on LAN B are retransmitted to LAN B for delivery. Similarly, the appropriate packets on LAN B are retransmitted to LAN A.

On older bridges, the network administrator needed to manually configure the address tables. Newer bridges are called learning bridges—they function as described in step 2. *Learning bridges* automatically update their address tables as devices are added to or removed from the network.

Bridges accomplish several things. First, they divide busy networks into smaller segments. If the network is designed so that most packets can be delivered without crossing a bridge, traffic on the individual network segments can be reduced. If the Accounting and Sales departments are overloading the LAN, for example, you might divide the network so that Accounting is on one segment and Sales on another. Only when Accounting and Sales need to exchange packets does a packet need to cross the bridge between the segments.

Bridges also can extend the physical size of a network. Although the individual segments still are restricted by the maximum size imposed by the network design limits, bridges enable network designers to stretch the distances between segments and extend the overall size of the network.

Bridges, however, cannot join dissimilar types of LANs. Bridges depend on the physical addresses of devices. Physical device addresses are functions of the data link layer, and different data link layer protocols are used for each type of network. A bridge, therefore, cannot be used to join an Ethernet segment to a Token Ring segment.

Device addresses are functions of the OSI data link layer, discussed in greater detail in Chapter 14, "The OSI Model." Bridges, therefore, are said to function at the data link layer.

Multiplexors

Multiplexors solve a different type of connectivity problem. What if you have several signals to transmit, but only one path that the signals must share? A *multiplexor* is a device that combines several signals so they can be transmitted together, and then enables the original signals to be extracted at the other end of the transmission. (Recovering the original signals is called *demultiplexing*.) Figure 20.4 shows how the process works.

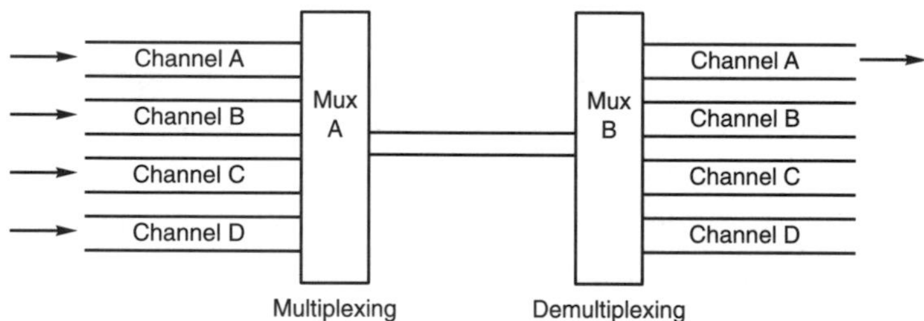

Figure 20.4

Multiplexing and demultiplexing a signal.

Modems

Standard telephone lines can transmit only analog signals. Computers, however, store and transmit data digitally. *Modems* can transmit digital computer signals over telephone lines by converting them to analog form.

Converting one signal form to another (digital to analog in this case) is called *modulation.* Recovering the original signal is called *demodulation.* The term "modem" derives from this *mo*dulation/*dem*odulation.

Modems can be used to connect computer devices or entire networks that are at distant locations. (Before digital telephone lines came around, modems were about the only way to link distant devices.) Some modems operate constantly over dedicated phone lines. Others use standard *public switched-telephone network* (PSTN) dial-up lines and make a connection only when one is required.

Common uses for modems on LANs include the following:

- Enabling users to call in and access the LAN
- Exchanging electronic mail between mail servers
- Transmitting and receiving faxes with a fax server
- Enabling LANs to exchange data on demand

Modems enable networks to exchange e-mail and to perform limited data transfers, but the connectivity made possible is extremely limited. By themselves, modems don't enable remote networks to connect to each other and directly exchange data. In other words, a modem is not an internetwork device. Nevertheless, modems can be used in conjunction with an internetwork device, such as a router, to connect remote networks through the PSTN or through an analog service, such as a 56-KB line.

The point is that a modem cannot enable remote networks to internetwork freely without the assistance of routers or bridges to manage the connection between the networks.

Modems don't necessarily need to connect through the PSTN. Short-haul modems frequently are used to connect devices in the same building. A standard serial connection is limited to 50 feet, but short-haul modems can be used to extend the range of a serial connection to any required distance.

continues

Many devices are designed to assume that modems are used. When you want to connect such devices without using modems, you can use a null modem cable, which connects the transmitter of one device to the receiver of the other device.

A modem translates digital signals for transmission on analog phone lines. A *codec* (*coder/decoder*) provides a similar service when analog signals are to be transmitted over digital phone lines, translating analog signals into digital form.

Internetwork Connectivity Devices

An internetwork consists of two or more physically connected independent networks that are able to communicate. The networks that make up an internetwork can be of quite different types. An internetwork can include Ethernet and Token Ring networks, for example.

Because each network in an internetwork is assigned an address, each network can be considered *logically separate*; that is, each network functions independently of other networks on the internetwork. Internetwork connectivity devices can use network address information to assist in the efficient delivery of messages. Using network address information to deliver messages is called *routing*. The common feature that unites internetwork connectivity devices (routers and brouters) is that they can perform routing. Some common internetwork connectivity devices are as follows:

- Routers
- Brouters
- CSU/DSUs
- Gateways

These devices are discussed in the following sections.

Routers

Bridges are suitable for relatively simple networks, but bridges have certain limitations that become more significant in complex network situations. One limitation of bridges is that a network with bridges generally cannot include redundant paths. (Redundant paths are desirable because they enable the network to continue functioning when one path goes down.)

Consider the network in figure 20.5. Both bridges are aware of the existence of Node B, and both can pick up the packet from Net A and forward it. At the very least, the same packet can arrive twice at Node B.

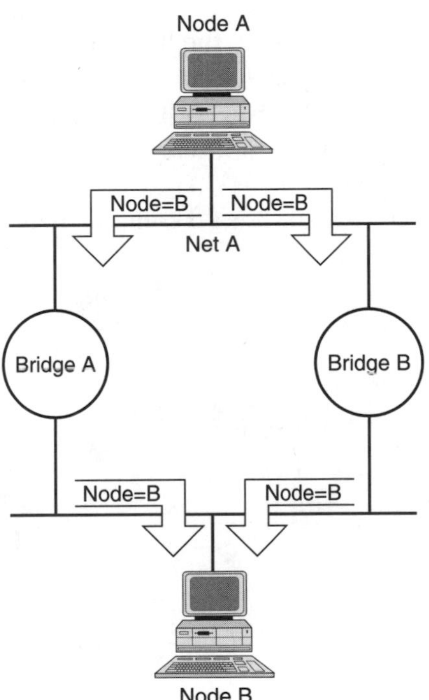

Figure 20.5

A complex network with bridges.

A worse case, however, is that these relatively unintellignet bridges can start passing packets around in loops, which results in an ever-increasing number of packets circulating on the network and never reaching their destinations. Ultimately, such activity can (and will) saturate the network.

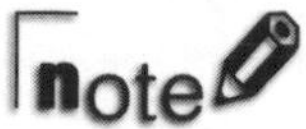

An algorithm, called the *spanning tree algorithm*, enables complex Ethernet networks to use bridges while redundant routes exist. The algorithm enables the bridges to communicate and to construct a logical network that doesn't contain redundant paths. The logical network is reconfigured if one of the paths fails.

Another problem is that the bridges cannot analyze the network and determine the fastest route over which to forward a packet. When multiple routes exist, this is a desirable capability, particularly in wide area networks where some routes can be considerably slower than others.

Routers organize the large network in terms of logical network segments. Each network segment is assigned an address so that every packet has both a destination network address and a destination device address.

Figure 20.6 shows a complex network based on routers.

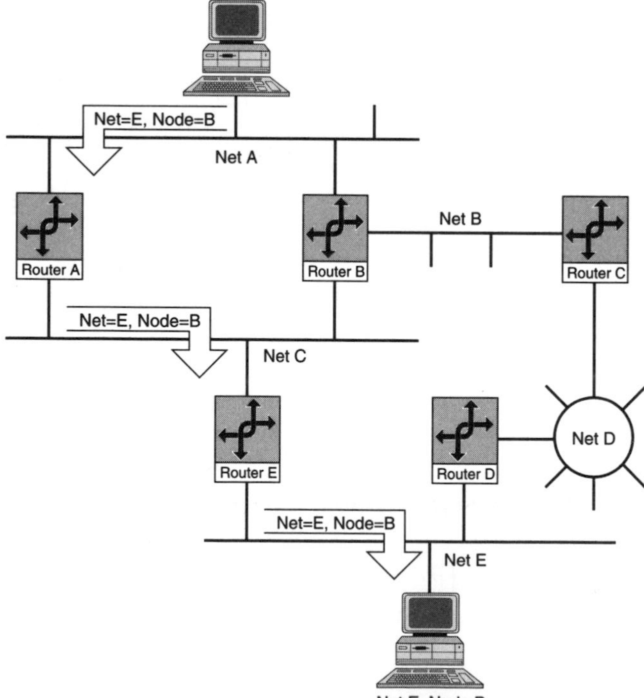

Figure 20.6

An internetwork with routers.

Recall that an internetwork consists of two or more logically separate, but physically connected, networks. By this definition, any network segmented with routers is an internetwork.

Routers are more "intelligent" than bridges. Not only do they build tables of networks' locations, but they also use algorithms to determine the most efficient path for sending a packet to any given network. Even if a particular network segment isn't directly attached to the router, the router knows the best way to send a packet to a device on that network. Router A knows, therefore, that the most efficient step is to send the packet to Router C, not Router B.

Notice that Router B presents a redundant path to the path Router A provides. Routers can cope with this situation because they exchange routing information that ensures that packet loops don't occur. In figure 20.6, if Router A fails, Router B provides a backup message path, making this network more robust.

You can use routers to divide large, busy LANs into smaller segments, much as you can use bridges. But that's not the only reason to select a router. Routers also can connect different network types. Notice that the network in figure 20.6 includes a Token Ring segment with the Ethernet segments. On such networks, a router is the device of choice.

Because they can determine route efficiencies, routers usually are employed to connect a LAN to a wide area network. WANs frequently are designed with multiple paths, and routers can ensure that the various paths are used most efficiently.

Device addresses are functions of the OSI network layer (see Chapter 14). Routers, therefore, are said to function at the network layer.

The network layer functions independently of the physical cabling system and the cabling system protocols independently, that is, of the physical and data link layers. This is the

continues

reason that routers can easily translate packets between different cabling systems. Bridges cannot because they function at the data link layer, which is closely tied to a given set of physical layer specifications.

Brouters

A *brouter* is a router that also can bridge. A brouter attempts to deliver packets based on network protocol information. If a particular network layer protocol isn't supported, the brouter bridges the packet using device addresses.

CSU/DSUs

When LANs are connected into wide area networks, the connection is frequently by means of the public telephone network. Connecting to some telephone media requires the use of a channel service network/digital service unit (CSU/DSU).

Network service providers design their media for a particular type of signal, and may require use of a CSU/DSU to translate the LAN signals to the required signal format. A CSU/DSU also isolates the local network from the public network to protect each network from noise and voltage fluctuations of the other.

For the purposes of this section, CSU/DSUs are considered internetwork devices, but this isn't strictly correct. The primary purpose of a CSU/DSU is to interface the network to a public data network. A given device might perform routing or might depend on a separate router, depending on the vendor's hardware design.

Gateways

The term *gateway* was originally used in the Internet protocol suite to refer to a router. Today, a gateway more commonly refers to a system functioning at the top (Session, Presentation, Application) levels of the OSI model, which enables communication between dissimilar upper-layer protocol systems.

Gateways can be implemented as software, hardware, or a combination of both.

Review Questions

The following questions will test your knowledge of the information in this chapter. For additional questions, see MCP Endeavor and the Microsoft Roadmap/Assessment Exam that accompanies this book.

1. Which two of the following are functions of internetwork connectivity devices?

   A. Connecting remote networks

   B. Enabling networks with different protocols to communicate

   C. Attaching devices to media

   D. Extending the range of network segments

2. Which three of the following are advantages of active hubs?

   A. They can regenerate network signals.

   B. LANs ranges can be extended.

   C. They are inexpensive.

   D. They function as repeaters.

3. A Token Ring NIC can be equipped with which two of the following?

   A. BNC connector

   B. RJ-45 connector

   C. DB-15 connector

   D. AUI connector

4. Which two networks can use passive hubs?

   A. Ethernet

   B. ARCnet

   C. Token ring

   D. All of the above

5. Which two of the following features can add intelligence to a hub?

   A. Signal regeneration

   B. Network management protocols

   C. Multiport repeaters

   D. Switching circuitry

6. Which two statements are true of repeaters?

   A. Repeaters amplify signals.

   B. Repeaters extend network distances.

   C. Repeaters regenerate signals.

   D. Repeaters can be used to extend the range of a network indefinitely.

7. Which three statements are true of bridges?

   A. Bridges amplify and regenerate signals.

   B. Bridges can connect logically separate networks.

   C. Bridges use device address tables to route messages.

   D. Bridges divide networks into smaller segments.

8. Modems can be used for which three of the following purposes?

    A. To connect remote networks

    B. To enable users to call in and access a LAN

    C. To transmit and receive faxes

    D. To extend the range of a serial interface

9. Which two of the following are functions of CSU/DSUs?

    A. Connecting networks with different protocols

    B. Connecting a network to some types of public telephone networks

    C. Routing signals between logical networks

    D. Isolating the local network from the public network

10. Why can the networks in an internetwork be considered logically separate?

    A. Each network has its own address.

    B. The networks are separated by a bridge.

    C. The networks are separated by a router.

    D. None of the above.

11. Which of the following connectivity devices functions at the data link layer?

    A. Repeater

    B. Router

    C. Hub

    D. Bridge

Review Answers

1. A B
2. A B D
3. B C
4. B C
5. B D
6. A B
7. A C D
8. B C D
9. B D
10. A
11. D

Chapter 21

Network Printing

The primary network print service functions are as follows:

- Providing multiple access to printers
- Servicing simultaneous print requests
- Printing without distance limitations
- Managing specialized equipment types
- Providing facsimile (fax) service

In this chapter, you will learn about each of these network printer service functions. You will also learn some basic facts about printers and how network printing works.

Print Services

The following sections describe the network print service functions listed in the preceding section.

Providing Multiple Access

A typical printer has a limited number of available connecting points, such as parallel or serial interface ports. In fact, many printers can have only a single active port, which means that a limited number of users' PCs can be connected to ports on a given printer. Without a network, this might mean that a printer is required for each PC.

Networks break the printer/port/PC relationship. Any user on the network can print to any network printer simply by printing through the network print service. In most organizations, this means that the number of printers can be reduced—in some cases, down to a single printer for an entire department.

Servicing Simultaneous Print Requests

When each printer is servicing several users, print services must have an organized means of achieving two goals:

- Enabling any user to print at any time
- Printing all of the users' jobs in an orderly fashion

Print services manage these complex tasks by employing a technique known as *queuing*. A *queue* is a line where items wait to be serviced; for example, theater patrons wait in a queue until a ticket clerk can service their ticket requests.

Network print queuing works as shown in figure 21.1. In the figure, you can see how print jobs from several users are collected in the queue. While printing to a queue, the users' PCs are fooled into thinking they are printing to a directly attached printer. Network printing services reroute printed data to the queue rather than to the PC's printer port.

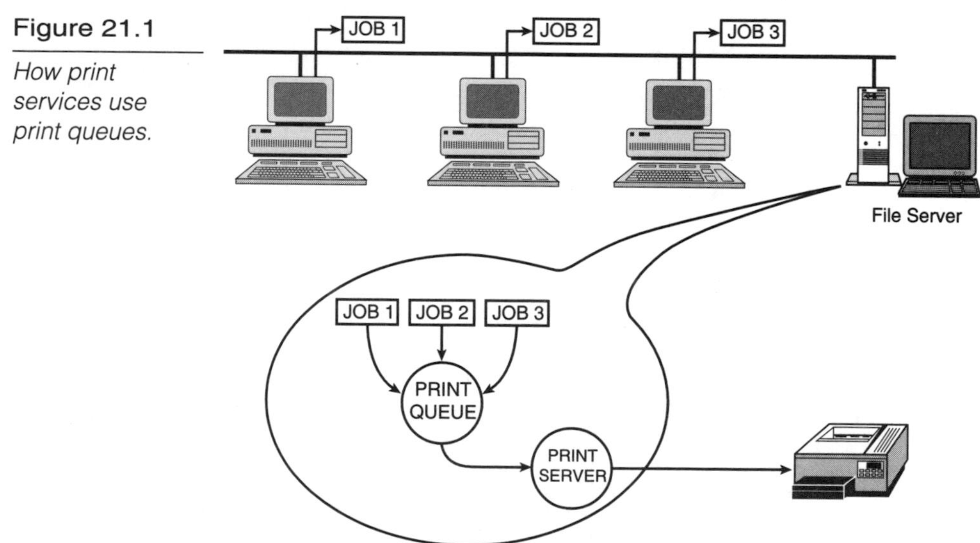

Figure 21.1
How print services use print queues.

After the jobs are in queues, the print jobs are sent one by one to a printer. Even though a printer can print only one job at a time, the appearance to the users is that they can print freely, even when the printer is busy.

Interestingly, print queuing usually services print requests more rapidly than printers that are connected directly to users' PCs. A network queue can collect print data at network speeds, which are generally much faster than printers can actually put the data on paper. After the print data is safely stored in a queue, the user can go on about his or her work knowing that the job will be printed as soon as the printer becomes available.

Printing without Distance Limitations

When a printer is connected directly to a PC, it can never be very far from the PC itself. Fifteen to 50 feet is the extreme limit of most printer cables.

Printers on a network, however, can be located anywhere. Any user can use any printer, whether the printer is nearby, in the next building, or across the country. This enables organizations to place printers where they are needed, not just where a user's PC is found.

Managing Specialized Equipment Types

Although many types of printers have decreased in cost considerably, some types of printers remain so expensive that they must be shared if owning them is to make sense. Some examples are the following:

- **High-speed printers.** Do you really want to print that 1,000-page report to your personal four-page-per-minute laser?
- **Quality color.** The best color printers, such as thermal transfer printers, cost many thousands of dollars.
- **Large-format printers and plotters.** When 8 1/2x11-inch paper isn't large enough, it might be nice to have an 11-by-17-inch printer or a plotter available.

Providing Facsimile (Fax) Service

A standard fax machine uses a scanner to read the image on a printed form, render that image as electronic signals, and transmit the signals to another fax machine, which reconstructs the original image back onto paper. Fax machines have become so popular that long lines are often encountered by users and much paper is wasted.

A new class of print service directs printed images to a device that can transmit the images as facsimiles. A network fax service enables any user to send a fax directly from a network application, such as a word processor, without needing to print the document and hand-carry it to the public fax machine. The fax service uses queuing so that many users can generate faxes simultaneously. Then the fax service takes care of transmitting the images in an orderly manner.

Moreover, a network fax server can receive faxes and route them electronically to users without generating a printout. Users can view faxes on their PCs, print them if desired, or store them as data files for future use.

Printers

In one sense, the printed output from a network printer is the only tangible product of the network. Users want to log into the network, do their work, and produce some sort of document, chart, graph, or other printed output. The printed page is generally what upper management sees, not the day-to-day workings of the network. As a result, an easy-to-use, fail-safe printing environment is essential to the existence of the network (and possibly the job of the network administrator).

Several types of printers are available, and these printers can be attached to the network in several ways. This section focuses on some of the different types of printers and where they might be used in your company.

Printers vary in speed, how the printed image is produced, the quality of the image, what type of paper is used, and, of course, cost. A printer's speed is measured in either characters per second (cps) or pages per minute (ppm). The image quality is measured in points or dots per square inch (dpi). A *point* is a term used in typesetting graphics to indicate the smallest dot of ink the printer can produce. The more dots per square inch the machine can produce, the higher the quality or resolution of the image.

Another measurement often used to categorize printer speed is *lines per minute.* This is a measurement often used with dot-matrix or line printers. This measurement has fallen into disuse with the rise in popularity of graphically oriented applications. A document produced in a Windows-based word processing application, for example, is actually printed as a graphical image rather than as a stream of words and letters. Most Windows-based programs use bitmapped graphics rather than a computer's built-in character set. Bitmapped graphics refer to the way in which characters are defined as tiny images consisting of a varying number of bits. The size and printing density of a bitmapped image can vary widely depending on its size, the type of font, whether or not it's boldfaced or in italics, and so forth. Lines per minute was used for measuring the speed of older style printers where print jobs used evenly spaced characters.

Some of the devices used to physically produce the printed image include the following:

- Daisywheel printers
- Dot-matrix printers
- Thermal printers
- Laser printers
- Inkjet printers
- Line (or band) printers
- Bubble-jet printers
- Plotters

Daisywheel printers were introduced in the early 1970s as an extension of electric typewriter technology. The *daisywheel* was named because if you look at it straight on, it has "spokes" somewhat like the petals of a daisy. The daisywheel is mounted on a print head that rotates the wheel to the proper letter under computer control. A pin inside the head pushes against the spoke that contains the proper letter. The spoke presses against a ribbon that creates an image on the page. Daisywheel printers are slow and noisy compared to other technologies. The image quality is that of a typewriter, however, which caused daisywheel printers to be popular until laser printer technology matured.

Dot-matrix printers fire a row of pins in patterns against a ribbon that in turn produces an image on paper. Dot-matrix printers are the workhorses of the computer industry. The quality of the image rivals that of low-end laser printers, as does their speed. Relatively inexpensive, dot-matrix printers are typically equipped to handle tractor-feed paper that comes in boxes of several thousand sheets. Tractor-feed paper has holes at regular intervals on either side of the paper. Modern tractor-feed paper features laser perforations that enable you to detach the strips on either side of the page, leaving paper that looks almost as good as standard typing paper. The disadvantages of dot-matrix printers are the noise produced by the print head, limits on speed, and limitations on print quality based on the physical size and arrangement of the pins.

Thermal printers, in contrast to dot-matrix printers, are whisper silent. Thermal printers produce an image by applying heat to heat-sensitive paper. The technology first appeared in tiny printers that were attached to early calculators. Later this technology reappeared in fax machines. The main disadvantage to thermal printers is that you need special heat-sensitive paper, which doesn't age well and is expensive. A recent entry into this type of technology is a printer that places tiny multicolored dots of wax onto the paper. The wax dots melt into each other, forming a continuous image whose quality rivals that of a painting.

Laser printers use plain paper copier technology. The laser printer features a paper tray that holds standard typing or copier paper. A feeder mechanism pulls the paper out of the tray one sheet at a time. A laser inside a large cylinder, known as a *drum,* etches an image on the outside of the drum. Toner, a powdery substance, is attracted to the sheet of paper resting against the drum. The toner temporarily adheres to the paper according to the patterns etched by the laser. The paper, with toner, moves by a fusing area that heats the toner, causing it to melt onto the paper.

Laser printer technology has caught the purse strings of the computer industry. The speed of the printer is limited by how fast paper can be fed through the system. The main disadvantage to laser printers is that they aren't capable of printing on multiple part forms. To get around this disadvantage, software publishers have created software that prints the entire form.

Inkjet printers spray a fine jet of ink in patterns onto the paper. Typical inkjet printers have a special cartridge that contains both the ink and the print head. Inkjet printers are quiet, fast, and inexpensive, with quality rivaling that of laser printers. As you can see in table 21.1, however, these printers are neither as fast as laser printers, nor is the quality quite as good. As with laser printers, inkjet printers cannot print on multiple part forms. Inkjet printers are excellent choices for the office workhorse, however, and are slowly replacing dot-matrix printers.

Line (or *band*) *printers* feature variations on dot-matrix technology. These are ultra-high-speed printers whose speed is measured in lines per minute. Line printers typically feature some combination of multiple tractor mechanisms to pull the paper through faster, multiple print heads, or a large array of print heads (a "band").

Bubble-jet printers feature print heads with tiny tubes arranged in patterns much like the pins in a dot-matrix print head. Initially, the tubes are filled with ink. The tubes are selectively heated, which causes a bubble to form. Eventually the bubble bursts, causing a tiny drop of hot ink to spray onto the paper. The vacuum created by the departing ink refills the tube. Because the ink is hot, it dries quickly, minimizing the tendency of ink to bleed on the paper. Bubble-jet technology has advantages and disadvantages compared to the other technologies. The image produced is better than that produced by an inkjet printer, but not quite as good as a laser printer. Bubble-jet printers are quiet, but are slower than inkjet printers. Like inkjet printers, bubble-jet printers can print on plain paper but cannot print multiple part forms.

Plotters feature a rack of different colored pens that a mechanical arm moves horizontally back and forth across the paper. Another mechanism moves the paper vertically. Between the two mechanisms, any type of line can be drawn, from straight lines to smooth circles. Plotters are typically large scale and are designed to work with blueprint-sized paper. The images produced are of excellent quality. Plotters suffer from slow speed compared to other technologies, however.

Table 21.1 lists the different printer technologies along with their features. The figures listed in this table are averages based on a sample of printers of each type.

How Network Printing Works

Network printing differs from local printing in the following two respects:

- A print job is first sent to a network print queue.
- A print server redirects the job from the queue to a network printer.

The *print queue* is a subdirectory on one of the file server's hard drives that holds print jobs in the form of a file. When the job has been collected, or the signal to "time out" has occurred, the job is released to the print server.

The *print server* acts as a kind of printing traffic cop. The print server polls the print queue to see if any jobs are ready for service. Ready jobs are received from the queue and redirected to a network printer.

While the job is in the print queue, the user who originated the job, or a network administrator designated as a print queue

Table 21.1

Printing Technology: Features and Costs

Method	Speed	Image Quality	Type of Paper	Vendors
Dot-matrix	311 cps	300 dpi	Single sheets, tractor feed, multiple-part forms	Epson, Star Micronics, Panasonic
Laser	12 ppm	300-1200 dpi	Single sheets	Hewlett Packard, Canon, Panasonic, Alps, Epson
Inkjet	180 cps	330 dpi	Single sheets	Hewlett Packard, Epson
Line/Band	372 lpm	N/A	Tractor feed	Alps, Output Technologies, CIE America
Bubble-jet	110 cps	360 dpi	Single sheets	Canon
Plotter	N/A	N/A	Blueprint paper	Calcomp, Houston Instruments, Hewlett Packard

lpm = Lines per minute

cps = Characters per second

ppm = Pages per minute

dpi = Dots per square inch

operator, can put a hold on the job, change its priority in the queue, cause it to print at a later time, or remove the job from the queue. A network administrator designated as a print server operator can similarly manage the print server. This person can start or stop printers, cancel jobs that the printer is servicing, redirect the printer to another queue, or "rewind" the printer so that information that did not print properly for some reason can be reprinted.

Figures 21.2, 21.3, and 21.4 illustrate the various ways a print job can be sent from the application program running at the user's workstation to a network printer. Note that the network printer could be attached directly to the network, attached to another user's workstation, or attached to a file server.

In figure 21.2, a print job originates at a workstation and is sent to a print queue on the file server (1). The print server redirects the job from the queue (2) to a printer on the file server (3).

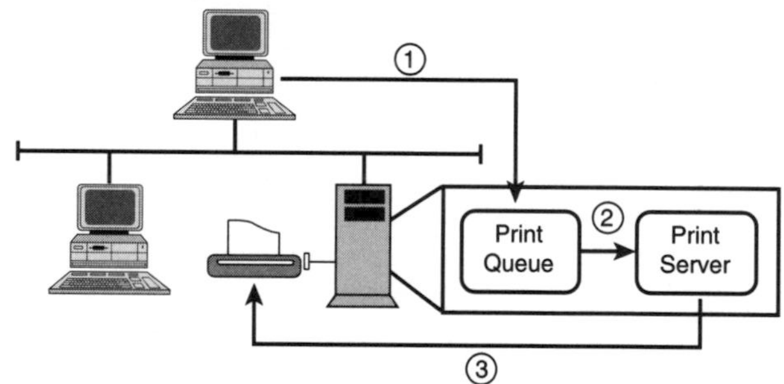

Figure 21.2

Sending a print job to a printer on a file server.

In figure 21.3, a print job originates at a workstation and is sent to a print queue on the file server (1). The print server redirects the job from the queue (2) to a workstation on the network (3). This workstation is running special software that makes its printer available to the LAN. The job is then sent, through the workstation, to its printer (4).

Figure 21.3

Sending a print job to a printer on a workstation.

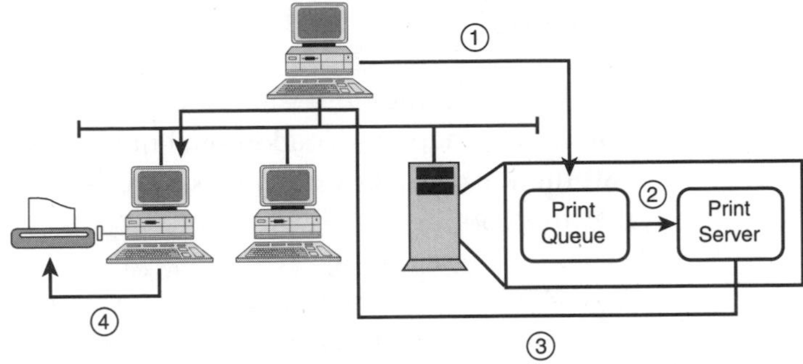

In figure 21.4, a print job originates at a workstation and is sent to a print queue on the file server (1). The print server redirects the job from the queue (2) to a printer directly attached to the network (3).

Figure 21.4

Sending a print job to a printer on the network.

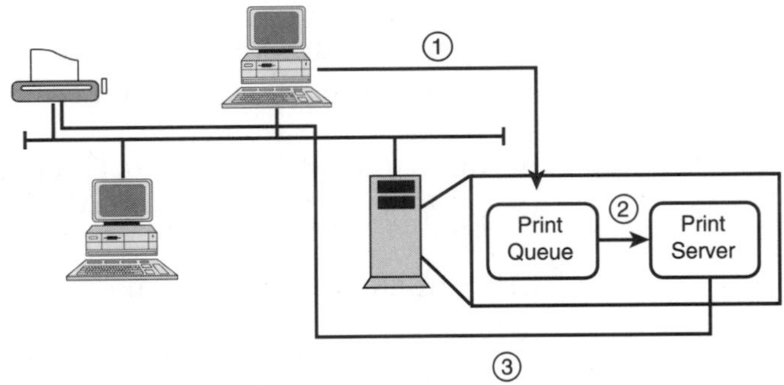

Another important element of network printing is the software that redirects the printing from the local printer port on a workstation to the network print queue. This process is often referred to as *print capture.* Workstation software can be configured to "capture" print requests that are normally routed to a workstation's local printer port.

Review Questions

The following questions will test your knowledge of the information in this chapter. For additional questions, see MCP Endeavor and the Roadmap assessment tests on the CD-ROM that accompanies this book.

1. What is the most important feature that enables networks to support printing from many users?

   A. Bubble-jet technology

   B. Printer priorities

   C. Queuing

   D. Print servers

2. When a printer is servicing multiple users, print services must achieve which two of the following goals?

   A. Break the printer/port/PC relationship

   B. Enable any user to print at any time

   C. Print all users' jobs in an orderly fashion

   D. Provide printing services for an entire department

3. Which three of the following are primary network service functions?

   A. Servicing simultaneous print requests

   B. Letting all users delete or change the priority of a print job

   C. Printing without distance limitations

   D. Providing fax service

4. A printer attached directly to a PC must generally stay within an extreme limit of ______ from the PC to function properly.

   A. 5 feet

   B. 50 feet

C. 100 feet

D. No limit

5. A network printer must generally stay within an extreme limit of ______ from a network PC to function properly.

    A. 5 feet

    B. 50 feet

    C. 100 feet

    D. No limit

6. Which printer type is well-suited for printing large, blue-print-sized paper?

    A. Daisywheel printer

    B. Laser printer

    C. Plotter

    D. Inkjet printer

7. Which printer uses plain-paper copier technology?

    A. Daisywheel printer

    B. Laser printer

    C. Plotter

    D. Inkjet printer

8. The ______ polls the print queue to see if any print jobs are ready for service.

    A. workstation

    B. printer

    C. file server

    D. print server

Review Answers

1. C
2. B C
3. A C D
4. B
5. D
6. C
7. B
8. D

Chapter 22

Network Administration

The network administrator's job involves a variety of responsibilities. Those responsibilities include the following:

- Keeping records
- Protecting data
- Managing performance
- Managing security
- Managing user accounts

This chapter describes some of the terms and concepts that define the various responsibilities of the network administrator.

Keeping Records

A detailed history of changes to the network is a tremendous aid in troubleshooting. When a problem occurs, the first thing you want to know is what has changed. A configuration management database can tell you.

Here are a few of the things your configuration records should include:

- Descriptions of all hardware: installation dates; repair histories; and configuration details such as interrupts, addresses, and so forth; backup records for each server.
- A map of the network showing locations of hardware and cabling details.

- Current copies of workstation configuration files, such as CONFIG.SYS and AUTOEXEC.BAT.
- Service agreements and important telephone numbers, such as the numbers of vendors, contractors, and software support lines.
- Software licenses, to ensure that your network operates within the bounds of the license terms.
- A history of past problems and related solutions. History tends to repeat itself, so the solutions to many problems might already be known and recorded.

Protecting Data

Natural disasters, equipment failures, power surges, and deliberate vandalism all can cause the catastrophic loss of precious network data. Protecting the data is a primary responsibility of the network administrator. Microsoft highlights these important strategies for preventing data loss:

- Backup
- Uninterruptible Power Supply (UPS)
- Fault-tolerant design

Backup

A systematic backup schedule is an essential part of any data-protection strategy. You should design a backup system that is right for your situation and the data on your network.

One way to back up a file is simply to copy it to another drive. Operating systems, however, typically have special backup commands that help you with some of the bookkeeping required for maintaining a systematic backup schedule. Most backup commands mark the file with the date and time of the backup so you (and the backup utility) will know when a copy of the file was last saved.

In addition to the various types of copy commands, Microsoft identifies the following backup types:

- **Full backup.** Backs up all specified files.
- **Incremental backup.** Backs up only those specified files that have changed since the last backup.
- **Differential backup.** Backs up the specified files if the files have changed since the last backup and doesn't mark the files as having been backed up. (A differential backup is a little like a copy command. Because the file is not marked as having been backed up, a later differential or incremental backup will back up the file again, whether or not it has changed again.)

A typical backup includes some combination of these backup types performed at regular intervals. One common practice is to perform an incremental backup each day and a full backup every week or month.

It is important to keep a log of all backups. Most backup utilities can generate a backup log. Microsoft recommends you make two copies of the backup log: store one with the backup tapes, and keep one at the computer site.

Most backups are performed with some form of tape drive. Another important step in your backup plan is deciding where to store the backup tapes. Many companies choose to make two copies of each backup tape and store one of the copies offsite.

Always test your backup system before you trust it. Perform a sample backup, restore the data, and check the data to be sure it is identical to the original.

You can attach a tape drive directly to a single server, or you can back up several servers at once across the network. Backups over the network are convenient for the administrator, but they can produce considerable network traffic. You can reduce the effects of this extra traffic if you place the computer attached to the tape drive on an isolated network segment and connect it directly to secondary network interface cards on each of the servers.

Uninterruptible Power Supply

An *Uninterruptible Power Supply* (UPS) is a special battery (or sometimes a generator) that supplies power to an electronic device in the event of a power failure. UPSs are commonly used with network servers to prevent a disorderly shutdown. The accompanying UPS software will warn users to log out. After a predetermined waiting period, the UPS software performs an orderly shutdown of the server.

Fault-Tolerant Design

You can connect network components into a fault-tolerant configuration so that one hardware failure doesn't halt the network. You can achieve network fault-tolerance by providing redundant data paths, fault-tolerant hubs, uninterruptible power supplies, and other such features.

RAID

Another way to achieve fault tolerance is through the use of a *Redundant Array of Inexpensive Drives* (RAID) system. The use of RAID enables you to set up the best disk array design to protect your system. A RAID system combines two or more disks to create a large virtual disk structure. This virtual structure enables you to store redundant copies of the data. In a disk array, the drives are coordinated into different levels of RAID, to which the controller card distributes the data.

RAID uses a format of splitting data among drives at the bit, byte, or block level. The term *data striping* refers to the capability of arranging data in different sequences across drives. Demonstrations of data splitting are shown in figure 22.1.

Your input in designing the most reliable drive setup for your network is an important responsibility. You must choose the best RAID implementation level that will meet your users' requirements in data integrity and cost. Seven levels of RAID are available on the market today: 0, 1, 2, 3, 4, 5, and 10. A higher number isn't necessarily indicative of a better choice. You must select the best level for your environment. The following paragraphs present a brief discussion of each of the seven available levels.

Figure 22.1

Examples of data striping.

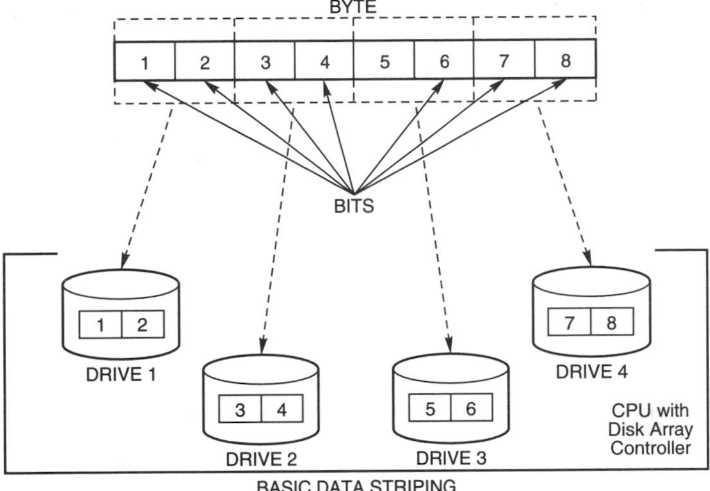

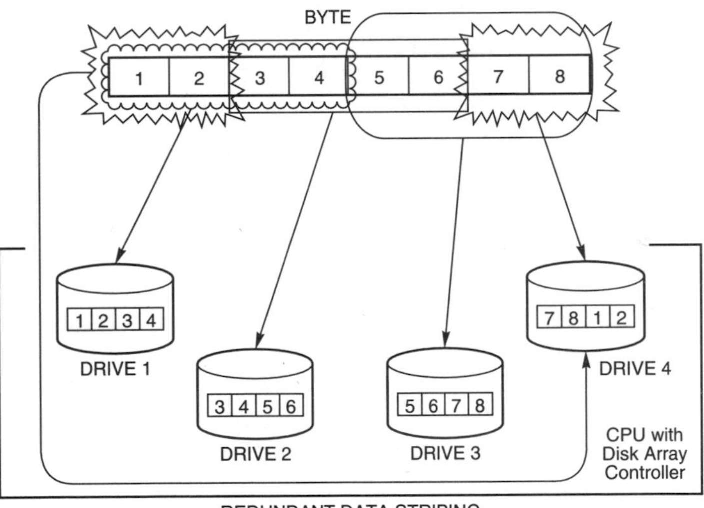

RAID 0

Level 0 uses data striping and block interleaving. This level distributes the data block by block across the disk array in the same location across each drive. Data can be read or written to these same sectors from either drive, improving performance. The failure of a single drive can bring down the system. Redundancy of data isn't provided.

RAID 1

In level 1, drives are paired or mirrored with each byte of information being written to each identical drive. You can duplex these devices by adding a separate host adapter for each drive. Mirroring provides a better performance benefit than that of RAID 0. If one drive in the pair fails, the other drive can continue to operate. This level can get expensive with the cost of drives to meet your needs for capacity. You need to make sure your power source has enough wattage to handle the additional devices.

RAID 2

This level uses data striping with bit interleave. This means that data is written across each drive in succession, one bit at a time. Faulty bits are isolated by using checksum-capable drives. This level doesn't require total data redundancy. RAID 2 drives transmit in a parallel mode, enabling a faster data-transfer rate. The write mode can be slower because each drive is working on every write attempt. The data used for checksum information is redundant. This level isn't effective or cost-efficient for use in personal computers.

RAID 3

This level uses bit interleave data striping with parity checking capabilities. Data striping is done across the drives, one byte at a time. Usually there are four or five drives at this level, with one drive dedicated for parity information to ensure the integrity of the data. RAID 3 has a very high data-transfer rate and can handle long data transfers. This level is more reliable than RAID 2. Parity maintenance can be an overhead problem and cause the write performance to slow because the parity drive must be accessed for every write. There also could be major system problems if any two drives fail. The failure of a single drive will not affect the availability of data; the array controller will use the parity drive to reconstruct the contents of the failed disk.

RAID 4

Level 4 uses block interleave data striping with parity checking. This means that this level uses a single parity drive, as does RAID 3, and uses block data striping, as does RAID 0. The drives in this RAID level function individually, with an individual drive reading a block of data. The combination of multiple drives makes multiple simultaneous reads possible. The block-level striping process is more efficient than RAID 3 byte-level striping. The downfalls of this level are the same as those of RAID 3, with the addition of the parity drive not being used to store data. If the array controller fails, the entire array cannot function.

RAID 5

This level uses block interleaved data striping with distributed check-data on all drives in the array. RAID 5 is efficient in handling small blocks and has quicker transfer rates because reads and writes can happen in parallel mode. The capability of virtual redundancy at an inexpensive cost is a benefit of RAID 5. This level isn't as fast as RAID 0 or RAID 1 because it distributes parity information across all drives. Large file transfers are done in blocks and can be slower than RAID 3, which uses parallel bytes. RAID 5 efficiency increases as the number of disks in the array increases. You can use hot spares mounted in the array cabinet. These extra drives can be picked up by the array automatically, replacing the failed drive. The data is rebuilt to the added drive to function in sequence with the rest of the array as if nothing happened. This failed drive can then be replaced on the fly.

RAID 10

This level is defined as data that is duplicated across two identical RAID 0 arrays or hard disk drives. All data that is contained on a physical drive in one array is mirrored on a drive in the second array.

Choosing a RAID Level

When you choose RAID for the customer, consider the following factors to make the best selection:

- The importance of the applications and data to the cost of downtime and lost business
- The number of users and the amount of drive capacity needed
- The size of the data blocks and whether they require direct or sequential access on the drives
- The proportion of reads to writes to the I/O activity, and the maximum transfer rate needed

Many vendors offer RAID solutions, including AST, Compaq, Dell, IBM, and Storage Dimensions. Dell Computer offers a reliable high-end file server that uses RAID 10, PCI bus architecture, a Pentium processor, and FAST SCSI-2 host adapters.

Disk Mirroring and Disk Duplexing

Disk mirroring and disk duplexing are two important system fault tolerance features that protect information in the event of hardware failure.

Disk Mirroring

Disk mirroring is defined as two hard drives—one primary and one secondary—that use the same disk channel (controller cards and cable). The process is illustrated in figure 22.2. Disk mirroring is most commonly configured using disk drives contained in the server. You soon see that duplexing enables you to configure a more robust hardware environment.

All changes to the primary disk are duplicated on the secondary so that the secondary is a mirror image of the primary. In the event that the primary drive fails, users can access data on the secondary drive as if nothing happened. Disk mirroring can be done internally in a file server if enough drive and card slots are available. A DCB can be used to provide access to an external disk subsystem. Disk drives must be the same logical size, terminated properly, and addressed correctly.

Figure 22.2

How disk mirroring works.

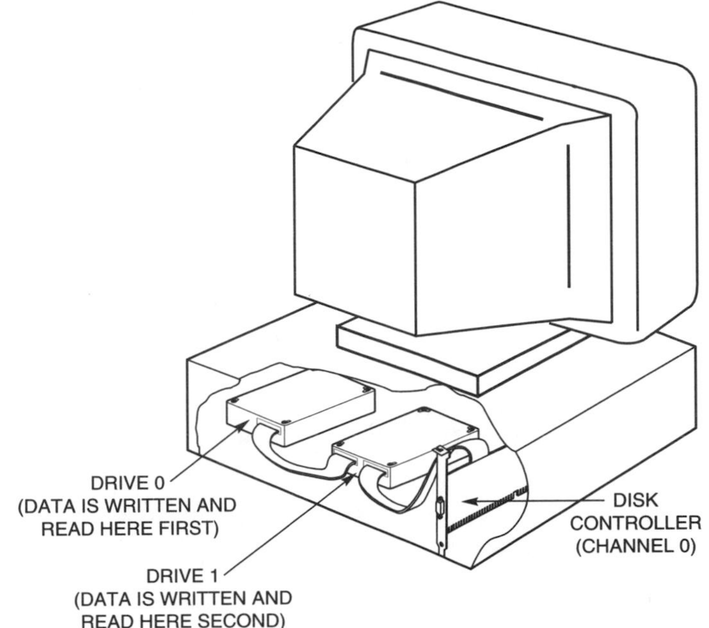

Disk Duplexing

In the event of a disk channel failure (controller card or cable), access to all data on the channel is stopped. A message appears on the file server console screen (if your users don't let you know about it first). Even though drives can be mirrored, if they're connected to the same disk controller, all disk activity on the mirrored pair ceases.

Disk duplexing performs the function of simultaneously writing data to disks located on different channels. As figure 22.3 illustrates, each hard disk in a duplexed pair is connected to a separate hard disk controller. This figure shows a configuration in which the drives are housed in separate disk subsystems. Each subsystem has a separate power supply. This is a more reliable setup than is possible with mirroring, because a failure of one disk drive power supply doesn't disable the server, which continues to work with the system that remains under power.

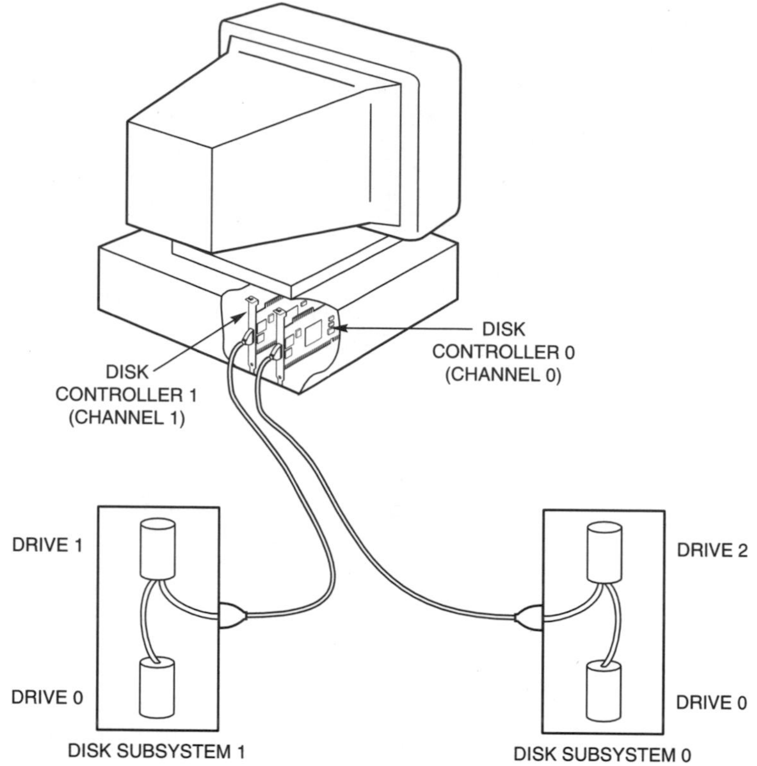

Figure 22.3

How disk duplexing works.

A duplex configuration has two disk channels. In figure 22.3, each channel has two disks.

Working on the same channel is analogous to going to a baseball game when only one gate into the stadium is open. You can enter or exit through only one gate (channel) at the stadium (file server), and the crowd (data) can get backed up on both sides. If more than one gate (another channel) is open, the crowd (data) doesn't become backed up on both sides of the fence (file server or workstation).

Duplexing protects information at the hardware level with duplicate channels (controller cards and cables) and duplicate hard drives (refer to fig. 22.3).

> Mirroring uses one controller card and two hard drives (refer to fig. 22.2). The point of failure for this setup is primarily the controller card or the cable connecting the drives to the controller card. Disk duplexing uses two controller cards and a minimum of one drive per controller card. The point of contention for failure is reduced with duplicate hardware.

Managing Performance

Performance management is the proactive companion to fault management. By monitoring the network's performance, you create "baseline" data that is a snapshot of the network performing well under normal conditions. This data is valuable for identifying deteriorating network performance and as a standard of comparison when network failures occur.

You might monitor the following parameters:

- **Response time**
- **Throughput**
- **Network load.** A measure of network traffic as a percentage of total performance capacity.
- **Errors.** All networks display some errors, but rising error levels are a clear indication of an impending problem.

Performance management enables you to plan future network enhancements, in addition to helping you anticipate problems. As network demand rises, you can add capacity before users become aware of problems.

Most network operating systems offer a network monitoring utility. Windows NT Server's Performance Monitor utility monitors and tracks hard drives, processors, memory, and network utilization.

Managing Security

Anyone who has managed a network has dealt with security management. One of your tasks is to anticipate security threats and install safeguards. You might consider selecting some of the following security provisions:

- Establishing user and group security
- Restricting internal and external access to data
- Conducting security risk assessments
- Establishing security policies
- Protecting the network from viruses
- Auditing the network to detect security breaches

The two most common models for securing network-shared resources are password-protected shares and access permissions.

Under the password-protected shares system, a user must supply a password to obtain access to a shared resource.

The access permissions system enables the network administrator to preassign a level of access to each user for each shared resource. These levels of access are called *permissions* or *privileges.* Many network operating systems have some form of access permission system. Names and exact definitions vary somewhat across the industry, but the concept is the same. Some of the Windows NT access permissions are as follows:

- **Read.** Permission to read and copy files in a shared directory.
- **Write.** Permission to create new files in a shared directory.
- **Execute.** Permission to execute files in a shared directory.
- **Delete.** Permission to delete files from a shared directory.
- **No Access.** The user is denied all access to the resource.

Many network operating systems also support group permissions. A *group* is a collection of network users. A network administrator can create a group of users with similar needs (for example, a Sales Department group or an Accounting Department group) and assign permissions to the group instead of assigning them independently to each user.

Managing User Accounts

Another major responsibility of the network administrator is creating, maintaining, and deleting user accounts. When a network administrator creates a user account, he or she must assign a number of attributes to the account, including a username, a password, and several parameters defining such things as the user's home directory and group memberships. The network administrator also must manage the access permissions (see the preceding section) associated with each user account.

Review Questions

The following questions will test your knowledge of the information in this chapter. For additional questions, see MCP Endeavor and the Microsoft Roadmap/Assessment Exam on the CD-ROM that accompanies this book.

1. An incremental backup ______.

   A. backs up parts of the specified file that have changed since the last backup

   B. backs up and marks only those files that have changed since they were last backed up

   C. backs up the files that have changed since they were last backed up, but doesn't mark them

   D. backs up the files that have changed over the course of a specified time period

2. A differential backup ______.

   A. backs up files that have changed since the last backup and doesn't mark the files as having been backed up

   B. backs up files that have changed since the last backup and marks the files as having been backed up

   C. copies all files that have been modified within a specific time period and marks them as having been backed up

   D. copies all files that have been modified within a specified time period and doesn't mark them as having been backed up

3. The best way to reduce the effects of extra traffic caused by a network backup is to ______.

   A. attach the tape drive directly to one of the servers

   B. back up each server to a nearby server

   C. place the computer attached to the tape drive on an isolated network segment

   D. back up the servers in ascending order of the size of the backup

4. UPS stands for ______.

   A. Unintentional Packet Switch

   B. Unfamiliar Password Sequence

   C. Unknown Polling Sequence

   D. Uninterrupted Power Supply

5. RAID Level 0 ______.

   A. uses bit interleave data striping

   B. uses block interleave data striping

C. doesn't use data striping

D. provides parity checking capabilities

6. RAID level 2 ______.

A. uses bit interleave data striping

B. uses block interleave data striping

C. doesn't use data striping

D. provides parity checking capabilities

7. The difference between disk mirroring and disk duplexing is ______.

A. disk mirroring is more reliable

B. mirrored disks share the same disk channels

C. duplexed disks share the same disk channels

D. no difference

8. The most common models for securing network shared resources are ______ and ______.

A. the verification interval model

B. the password-protected shares model

C. the user-group model

D. the access permissions model

Review Answers

1. B
2. A
3. C
4. D
5. B
6. A
7. B
8. B D

Chapter 23

Network Troubleshooting Techniques

Troubleshooting is an inevitable part of every network administrator's life. No matter how well you prepare for the unexpected, something is bound to erupt.

Troubleshooting is the art of seeking out the cause of a problem and eliminating it by managing or eliminating the cause. With something as complex as a computer network, the list of possible problems and causes is nearly endless. In real life, however, a large number of network problems fall into a few well-defined categories. In this chapter, you will learn about some of those categories, and you will also learn about some of the strategies and tools you can use to catch (and avoid) network problems.

Of course, no matter how effective you are at problem solving, it is almost always better to avoid problems than to solve them. Chapter 22, "Network Administration," discusses strategies for how to avoid network problems. In other chapters, you learn how to solve certain network problems once they appear. This chapter describes a general methodology for network troubleshooting and also briefly describes the following:

- Sources of support
- Network troubleshooting tools
- Common network problems

A vast number of network problems and solutions are specific to a particular network operating system. Problems that are specific to a particular operating system, and solutions that depend on a particular utility or command, are beyond the scope of this chapter.

The Troubleshooting Process

Microsoft recommends a five-step approach to network troubleshooting. The steps are as follows:

1. Set the problem's priority.
2. Collect information to identify the symptoms.
3. Develop a list of possible causes.
4. Test to isolate the cause.
5. Study the results of the test to identify a solution.

These five steps are sufficient to guide you through a myriad of network problems, and similar approaches appear in the documentation of other network vendors.

Take a closer look at each of these important steps:

1. **Set the problem's priority.** How serious is this problem? Will the network still function if you attend to other matters first? Can you quantify the loss of work time or productivity the problem is causing? Determine the severity of the problem relative to the other pressing problems you may be facing.

2. **Collect information to identify the symptoms.** Collecting information can be as simple as asking users to describe the problem in detail. One source of information is the users who are experiencing the problem. A user's description can lead to further questions, which can lead to a deeper description. If you keep a documented history of your network (see Chapter 22), you can compare the present behavior of the network with the baseline behavior. You also can look for possible past occurrences of the problem.

3. **Develop a list of possible causes.** Was the problem a result of connectivity devices? Cabling? Protocols? A faltering workstation? What do past occurrences have in common with the present occurrence? List all possibilities.

4. **Test to isolate the cause.** Develop tests that will prove or disprove each of the possible causes. The tests could be as simple as checking a setup parameter or as complicated as studying network traffic with a protocol analyzer. You learn about some of the hardware and software network testing tools in the section titled "Troubleshooting Tools," later in this chapter.

5. **Study the results of the test to identify a solution.** Your tests will (ideally) point you to the real problem, and once you know the problem you can determine a solution.

Part of the challenge of network troubleshooting is to determine how you can apply these five troubleshooting steps to your own situation.

Getting Support

You are rarely alone when you are troubleshooting network problems. An important aspect of troubleshooting is knowing where to turn for critical information on your network environment. There are many online and offline sources of troubleshooting information. Some of these sources are as follows:

- **Vendor documentation and vendor help lines.** Hardware and software vendors often provide troubleshooting tips with the owner's documentation. Vendors also often provide technical assistance by phone.

- **Bulletin Board Services (BBS).** A number of electronic bulletin boards supply networking information. You can download information on Microsoft network products from the Microsoft Download Library (MSDL). (You can reach the MSDL by dialing (206) 936-6735.) Other vendors also have active bulletin board systems, such as Novell's NetWire BBS. See vendor documentation for more information on how to reach a particular vendor's official BBS.

- **The Internet.** The major network vendors all sponsor active forums and newsgroups on the Internet, CompuServe, and other online services. See your vendor's documentation.

- **CD-ROMs.** Several vendors now market CD-ROMs with network and PC hardware information. Microsoft's TechNet contains product information, technical information, articles, and announcements. TechNet is available on a subscription basis through Microsoft (call (800) 344-2121). A Microsoft TechNet demo is included on the CD-ROM that accompanies this book. Novell's NSEPro CD-ROM is a NetWare-oriented encyclopedia of network information. The Micro House Technical Library (MHTL) is another impressive database of technical information. The MHTL addresses such items as BIOS settings for IDE drives and jumper settings for popular peripheral boards. The MHTL comes with a rich collection of informative illustrations (see fig. 23.1). The CD-ROM accompanying this book also includes a Micro House Technical Library demo.

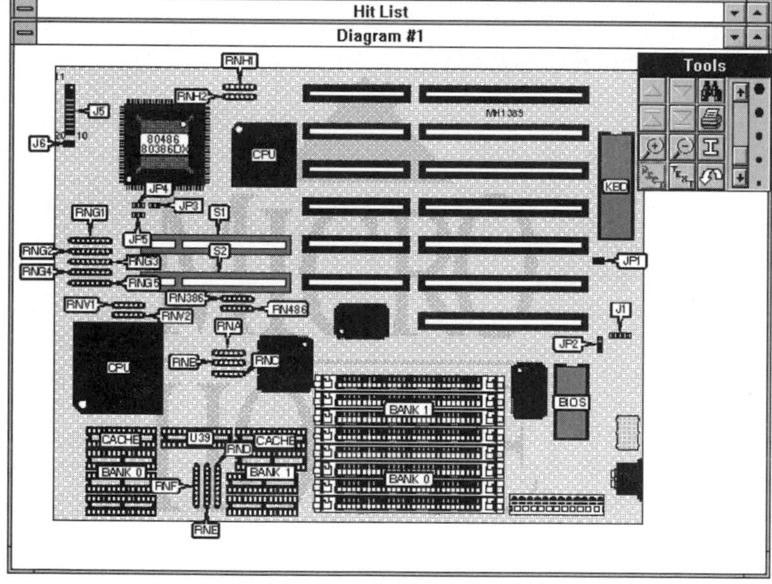

Figure 23.1

A look at a PC motherboard, from the Micro House Technical Library.

Troubleshooting Tools

Network administrators use a number of tools for searching out network problems. Some of these tools are as follows:

- **Protocol Analyzers.** *Protocol analyzers* are hardware or combined hardware and software products used to monitor network traffic, track network performance, and analyze packets. Protocol analyzers can identify bottlenecks, protocol problems, and malfunctioning network components.
- **Digital Volt Meters (DVMs).** A *DVM* is a hand-held electronic measuring tool. A DVM can check the voltage of network cables. You can use a DVM to help you find a break or a short in a network cable.
- **Time-Domain Reflectometers (TDRs).** *TDRs* send sound waves along a cable and look for imperfections that might be caused by a break or a short in the line.

There are also several diagnostic software tools that provide information on virtually any type of network hardware. A considerable number of diagnostic software packages are available at a variety of prices.

Check It Pro is one program that provides quick facts about your hardware and operating system. Check It Pro also benchmarks components and shows information about interrupts.

A variety of programs have features similar to Check It Pro's. The following shows an example of output generated at a workstation with System Information—one of the tools available in Norton's Utilities.

```
       Computer Name: IBM AT
    Operating System: DOS 6.20
  Built-in BIOS dated: Friday, January 15, 1988
      Main Processor: Intel 80386            Serial Ports: 2
        Co-Processor: Intel 80387          Parallel Ports: 3
Video Display Adapter: Video Graphics Array (VGA)
   Current Video Mode: Text, 80 x 25 Color
```

```
 Available Disk Drives: 13, A: - C:, F: - I:, P:, S:, V:, X: - Z:
DOS reports 639 K-bytes of memory:
   254 K-bytes used by DOS and resident programs
   385 K-bytes available for application programs
A search for active memory finds:
   640 K-bytes main memory     (at hex 0000-A000)
   128 K-bytes display memory  (at hex A000-C000)
   128 K-bytes extra memory    (at hex C000-E000)
 1,024 K-bytes expanded memory
ROM-BIOS Extensions are found at hex paragraphs: C000
  Computing Index (CI), relative to IBM/XT: Testing...- -- -- --
-- -- -- -- -- -- -73.0
       Disk Index (DI), relative to IBM/XT: Not computed. No
drive specified.
Performance Index (PI), relative to IBM/XT: Not computed.
```

If you are running a newer version of DOS, you can obtain much of the same workstation information using the MSD utility. Following is an excerpt from the first pages of a report run on the same machine using MSD:

```
Microsoft Diagnostics version 2.01    1/24/95    7:44pm   Page  1
   ===============================================================
    ----------- Summary Information ------------
                  Computer: Gateway/Phoenix, 486DX
                    Memory: 640K, 15104K Ext, 1024K EMS, 1024K
➥XMS
                     Video: VGA, ATI , Ultra
                   Network: Novell, Shell 4.10.00
                OS Version: MS-DOS Version 6.20, Windows 3.10
                     Mouse: Serial Mouse 7.05
            Other Adapters: Game Adapter
               Disk Drives: A: B: C: F: G: H: I: P:
                 LPT Ports: 3
                 COM Ports: 2
    --------------- Computer --------------
             Computer Name: Gateway
         BIOS Manufacturer: Phoenix
              BIOS Version: 680486 ROM BIOS PLUS Version 0.10
➥G21-2
             BIOS Category: Phoenix PC/AT Compatible BIOS
             BIOS ID Bytes: FC 81 00
                 BIOS Date: 01/15/88
                 Processor: 486DX
```

```
      Math Coprocessor: Internal
              Keyboard: Enhanced
              Bus Type: ISA/AT/Classic Bus
        DMA Controller: Yes
        Cascaded IRQ2: Yes
     BIOS Data Segment: None
-------------- Network --------------
                      Network Detected: Yes
                          Network Name: Novell
              MS-DOS Network Functions: Not Supported
                       NetBIOS Present: No
                         Shell Version: 4.10.00
                              Shell OS: MS-DOS
                      Shell OS Version: V6.20
                         Hardware Type: IBM—PC
                        Station Number: 3
               Physical Station Number: 0060:8C84:A8DD
                         IPX Installed: Yes
                         SPX Installed: Yes
                     ODI/LSL Installed: Yes
```

Regardless of the utility you use, you should run reports regularly and store them in an easily accessible place. When problems arise, immediately run the utility again and look for any discrepancies that signal readily found problems.

Network Problems

Microsoft identifies the following common causes of network problems:

- **Network cabling.** Most network problems occur at the OSI physical layer, and cabling is one of the most common causes. A cable may have a short or a break, or it may be attached to a faulty connector. The tools discussed earlier in this chapter help search out cabling problems. If a workstation cannot access the network, disconnect the network cables and attach them to a portable PC. If the portable reaches the network, cabling probably isn't your problem. Refer to Chapter 19, "Network Architectures," for more information about troubleshooting techniques for cabling in specific network architectures.

- **Workstation malfunctions.** Sometimes the problem is a local problem on a workstation. Was a new application installed on the workstation recently? Have there been any recent changes to configuration files? Sometimes a problem on a workstation can cause a network problem. For instance, occasionally a network interface card can malfunction and flood the network with traffic in what is known as a *broadcast storm.*

- **Operating system upgrades.** Operating system upgrades can sometimes cause older programs to become incompatible with the operating system. During the transition, for a period of time some servers will be running the old version, whereas others are running the new version. Microsoft recommends that you perform a test upgrade on an isolated part of the network to make sure all hardware and software systems will function properly when the upgrade is made.

- **Server crashes.** A server disk crash can be disastrous if you aren't adequately prepared for it. Devise a system of regular backups so that you will be prepared. Depending on the nature of your data, you might want to explore other safeguards, such as a RAID fault tolerant system. (Refer to Chapter 22.)

- **Power fluctuations.** A small fluctuation in the power supply can make the network misbehave. If the power goes off completely (even for a moment) the whole network could shut down, causing users to lose their work in progress. A disorderly shutdown also can cause problems with file servers. The best solution is to prepare for a power outage before it happens. Connect each server to an Uninterruptible Power Supply (UPS); encourage your users to perform occasional saves as they work.

- **Network traffic.** If your network is running slower than it used to run (or slower than it ought to run), the problem might be that the present network traffic is exceeding the level at which the network can operate efficiently. Some possible causes for increased traffic are new hardware (a new workstation) or new software (a network computer game or some other network application). A generator or another mechanical device operating near the network may be causing a degradation of network performance. A malfunctioning network device could be acting as a bottleneck. The increased traffic also could simply be the result of increased usage. If usage is exceeding the capacity of the network, it might be time to think about expanding or redesigning your network. A protocol analyzer can help you measure and monitor the traffic at various points on your network. Chapter 19 outlines the maximum transmission rates for common LAN architectures.

Review Questions

The following questions will test your knowledge of the information in this chapter. For additional questions, see MCP Endeavor and the Microsoft Roadmap/Assessment Exam on the CD-ROM that accompanies this book.

1. Which three of the following are troubleshooting steps in Microsoft's five-step troubleshooting process?

   A. Collect information to identify the symptoms.

   B. Develop a list of possible causes.

   C. Reboot the server.

   D. Set the problem's priority.

2. MSDL stands for ______.

   A. Minor Switching Delay Log

   B. Microsoft Storage Device Language

   C. Microsoft Domain License

   D. Microsoft Download Library

3. You can use a ______ to look for breaks in network cables by measuring cable voltage.

A. protocol analyzer

B. DVM

C. time-domain reflectometer

D. MSDL

4. Most network problems occur at the OSI ______ layer.

   A. physical

   B. data link

   C. network

   D. session

5. A sudden, unexpected flood of broadcast messages on the network is known as a ______.

   A. net frenzy

   B. tornado

   C. broadcast storm

   D. electric shower

Review Answers

1. A B D
2. D
3. B
4. A
5. C

Index

Symbols

A

B

C

D

E

F

G

H

I

J-L

N

O

P

Q-R

S

T

U

V

W-Z

REGISTRATION CARD

MCSE Study Guide: Windows 95 and Networking Essentials

Name ______________________________ Title ______________________

Company ______________________________ Type of business ______________________

Address ____

City/State/ZIP ____

Have you used these types of books before? ☐ yes ☐ no

If yes, which ones? ____

____

How many computer books do you purchase each year? ☐ 1–5 ☐ 6 or more

How did you learn about this book? ____

Where did you purchase this book? ____

Which applications do you currently use? ____

____

Which computer magazines do you subscribe to? ____

____

What trade shows do you attend? ____

____

Comments: ____

____

____

Would you like to be placed on our preferred mailing list? ☐ yes ☐ no

☐ **I would like to see my name in print!** You may use my name and quote me in future New Riders products and promotions. My daytime phone number is: ______________________

New Riders Publishing 201 West 103rd Street ◆ Indianapolis, Indiana 46290 USA

Fax to **317-581-4670** Orders/Customer Service **1-800-653-6156** Source Code **NRP95**

Fold Here

PLACE
STAMP
HERE

NEW RIDERS PUBLISHING
201 W 103RD ST
INDIANAPOLIS IN 46290-9058

The Disk Install Page

The companion CD-ROM contains the following:

- **MCP Endeavor**—a testing application that helps you prepare for MCSE certification exams.
- **The Microsoft Roadmap to Education and Certification**—helps you define goals for Microsoft certification or for improving your on-the-job skills. Use this program to map your route to achieving these goals.
- **The Microsoft TechNet Sampler**—Microsoft TechNet is a comprehensive information resource for technical professionals. The Sampler provides an interactive look at content delivered to Microsoft TechNet subscribers.
- **MicroHouse Technical Library demo**—The MicroHouse Technical Library includes complete configurations, diagrams, settings, component locations, and vital need-to-know information on PC hardware. The CD-ROM included with this book offers a demo version of the library.
- **Comparing Windows 95 and Windows NT Workstation (Microsoft White Paper)**—Microsoft Windows NT and Windows 95 are compared to provide general guidelines for selecting the best desktop operating system for your needs.

Windows Installation Instructions:

1. Insert the CD-ROM into your CD-ROM drive.
2. From File Manager or Program Manager, choose Run from the File menu. (If you are running Windows 95, press the Start Button, select Run, then Run again.)
3. Type **<drive>:\INSTALL** and press Enter, (where <drive> is the drive letter of your CD-ROM). For example, if your CD-ROM is drive D, type **D:\INSTALL** and press Enter.
4. When the installation program appears, it displays a readme file that provides additional information concerning the software on this CD-ROM. When you have finished reading this information, press the OK button to proceed.
5. After a few seconds, a menu window will appear. The menu window provides a button for installing each of the programs mentioned previously. To install a program, press its button and select one item from the options list that appears. (In some cases, you can choose between 16- and 32-bit versions of the same program.)
6. Press the OK button to allow installation to proceed, and follow any subsequent on-screen instructions that appear.

Continued from previous page

Of Special Note

You can restart the menu program at any time by running MENU.EXE from the root directory of the CD-ROM. To review the readme file again, open README.TXT from the File Manager or Windows Explorer. Alternately, open README.DOC using Microsoft Word. These files contain contact information for New Riders Publishing, should you wish to contact us. Your comments and suggestions are most welcome.

Technical Support

If your CD-ROM is damaged, please contact our support department.

E-mail: Send e-mail to support@mcp.com
World Wide Web: http://www.mcp.com/nrp
Telephone: (317) 381-3833
Fax: (317) 581-4773
Mail: Macmillan Computer Publishing
Attention: Support Department
201 West 103rd Street
Indianapolis, IN 46290-1093

Copyright Notices